Silbury Hill

The largest prehistoric mound in Europe

Silbury Hill

The largest prehistoric mound in Europe

Edited by Jim Leary, David Field and Gill Campbell

Principal illustrator Eddie Lyons
Other illustrations by Deborah Cunliffe, Judith Dobie,
Chris Evans and John Vallender

Contributions by Polydora Baker, Alex Bayliss, Martin Bell, Barry Bishop,
Tony Brain, Christopher Bronk Ramsey, Matthew Canti,
Amanda Chadburn, Ros Cleal, Margaret Collinson, Gordon Cook,
Tom Cromwell, Vicky Crosby, Paul Davies, Isabel Douterelo-Soler,
Mike Edmunds, Brian Edwards, Kate Fielden, Allan Hall,
Rob Harding, Nicola Hembrey, David A Hinton, Rob Ixer, Neil Linford,
Paul Linford, Malcolm Lillie, Peter Marshall, Kayt Marter Brown,
Louise Martin, Quita Mould, Andy Payne, Joshua Pollard,
Melanie Rimmer, Mark Robinson, Robert J Smith, Jane Timby,
Paul Whitehead and Fay Worley

ENGLISH HERITAGE

Published by English Heritage, The Engine House, Fire Fly Avenue, Swindon SN2 2EH
www.english-heritage.org.uk
English Heritage is the Government's lead body for the historic environment.

© English Heritage 2013

Images (except as otherwise shown) © English Heritage,
© Crown Copyright. EH, or Reproduced by permission of English Heritage

First published 2013

ISBN 978-1-84802-045-0

Product code 51527

British Library Cataloguing in Publication data
A CIP catalogue record for this book is available from the British Library.

Application for the reproduction of images should be made to English Heritage. Every effort has been made to trace the copyright holders and we apologise in advance for any unintentional omissions, which we would be pleased to correct in any subsequent edition of this book.

For more information about images from the English Heritage Archive, contact Archives Services Team, The Engine House, Fire Fly Avenue, Swindon SN2 2EH; telephone (01793) 414600.

Brought to publication by Robin Taylor, Publishing, English Heritage.

Typeset in 9.5 on 10.75 point Charter

Edited by Liz Nichols
Indexed by Alan Rutter
Page layout by Francis & Partners
Printed in the UK by Butler Tanner & Dennis Ltd.

CONTENTS

ILLUSTRATIONS

TABLES

FOREWORD

From the initial vertical shaft of Colonel Drax and the Duke of Northumberland to the horizontal tunnelling led by Blandford, Falkner and the Dean Merewether, from the likes of Merewether to Flinders Petrie, and from Petrie to the ambitious investigations of Richard Atkinson, major research on Silbury Hill had been carried out at intervals of roughly 70 years. So in writing up the excavations of Atkinson, I blithely speculated that perhaps another such gap would pass before archaeologists once again gave into the temptation to dig into the great mound. That was in a report published in 1997. How little we all knew what was about to happen in 2000!

This volume records the ensuing excavations, related investigations and remedial works. The prime aim of English Heritage, rightly, was to ensure the integrity of the mound, and the report here chronicles in detail what was done. In achieving that goal, the opportunity was also taken to re-record the archaeology available in the horizontal tunnels, with very limited new excavation, and to re-observe the situation at the top of the vertical shaft and on the top of the mound, again with limited fresh excavation. In so doing, a stunning wealth of new observations and analyses has been created, ranging from the stratigraphic and palaeoenvironmental evidence to the discovery of long sought after letters by Drax, and from many more radiocarbon dates, modelled in a Bayesian framework, to the geophysical survey of the adjacent Roman settlement.

Beyond this, the great mound has been interpreted as a continuing building project, rather than as a monument of predetermined plan or with a necessarily finished form. It has been further set into its Late Neolithic context of the later 3rd millennium cal BC, both locally and further afield, including comparison with the development of other round mounds on the one hand and of the perhaps rival construction of Stonehenge on the other. Silbury Hill thus emerges as at the heart of local, regional and for all we know wider politics and social change in the Late Neolithic. On the basis of all these features, it is hard to overstate the importance of this report.

Should archaeologists wish to go back to the interior of the mound in the future, or indeed its surrounds, here is an indispensable and invaluable guide. Long before further intervention is likely to take place, both researchers and general readers will quarry this volume repeatedly for both fact and interpretation. High on the list of my own priorities would be to refine the chronological models even further. As an alternative to the view argued here, was this the willed vision or the planned creation of a particular group, a lineage say or a dynasty, or a sect of charismatic sages, who mobilised and motivated the labour for this astonishing construction, over a very small number of generations, in the rapidly changing circumstances of their times? We shall see.

Alasdair Whittle

ACKNOWLEDGEMENTS

Amanda Chadburn, the Inspector of Ancient Monuments and one of the first on the scene when the 'hole' was discovered, saw the difficult conservation aspects of the project through from beginning to end. Rob Harding was the overall Project Manager for English Heritage, Arthur McCallum the Clerk of Works, and Niall Morrissey the Superintendant of Works.

The establishment of an English Heritage Silbury Hill Project Board by Kevin Brown, English Heritage South-West Regional Director, in 2001 made the process of disentangling a complex conservation problem easier and this drew informed opinion and data from a number of individuals, among them Professor Richard Chandler, Andrew David, Rob Harding, Debbie Holden, Fachtna McAvoy, Richard Williams and Professor Michael Worthington helped direct the course of events. Professors Chandler and Worthington, in particular, are thanked for their valuable input, ideas and enormous support during the lengthy assessment stage. Bob Bewley, English Heritage Regional Director, led the Project Board from 2005–7 and steered the project through various stages of necessary bureaucracy into what became a major conservation project for the organisation which was led by Lorraine Knowles.

A keen interest was taken from the very beginning by the Avebury Archaeological and Historical Research Group (AAHRG) and their specialist expertise and knowledge were invaluable; their views provided focus, caution and direction.

Fachtna McAvoy directed archaeological work between 2000 and 2007, including the first few weeks of work in 2007, and prepared various assessments and reports during that period. Other archaeological fieldwork, surveys, documentary research, monitoring and analyses of various kinds were carried out by Graham Brown, Matt Canti, Mick Clowes, Tom Cromwell, Brian Edwards, Kate Fielden, Damian Grady, Ian Leonard, Paul Linford, Neil Linford, Louise Martin, Andy Payne and Bernard Thomason.

Skanska, the firm of civil engineers that secured successive contracts to provide engineering solutions to the conservation measures required, took up the challenge with enthusiasm and Mark Kirkbride in particular is thanked for his engagement through several phases of the project and his enduring support on site, not least during the tunnel excavations of 2007/8.

The greater part of the recording in the tunnel and excavation on the summit in 2007 was directed by Jim Leary. The on-site digging team comprised Dan Barrett, Tony Baxter, Danielle de Carle, Liz Chambers, James Cooper, Foxy Demeanour, Dave Fellows, Susanne Geck, Jim Leary, Ellie Leary, Fachtna McAvoy, Peter Popkin, Jenny Ryder, Duncan Stirk, Maria Vinnels and Fay Worley. The Skanska mining and engineering team consisted of Barry Carlin, Terry Hilton, Mark Kirkbride, Mick McCaffery, Vernon Nightingale, Bob Tutill and Colin Wilkinson. Chris Corden undertook filming for English Heritage and for the BBC. The interpretation team were Eleanor Collier and Eloise Metson.

Many thanks also go to Sarah May, Brian Kerr, Andrew David, Mark Bowden and Peter Topping for guidance and managerial support during and after the fieldwork. We are gratful to Pre-Construct Archaeology Ltd for providing some staff.

Sampling and analysis of environmental materials was carried out by Gill Campbell, Tony Brain, Margaret Collinson, Matt Canti, Paul Davies, Isabel Douterelo-Soler, Mike Edmunds, Allan Hall, Malcolm Lillie, Mark Robinson, Robert J Smith and Paul Whitehead. Finds processing and analysis were carried out by Polydora Baker, Barry Bishop, Ros Cleal, Nicola Hembrey, David Hinton, Rob Ixer, Kayt Marter Brown, Joshua Pollard, Alan Vince and Fay Worley.

All illustrations have been prepared by the Archaeological Graphics team of English Heritage. All reconstruction paintings are by Judith Dobie, other illustrations are contributed by Eddie Lyons, Chris Evans, John Vallender and

Deborah Cunliffe. Professional photographs are by James O Davies, Ian Leonard and Mike Hesketh-Roberts of English Heritage. Photographs and illustrations have been prepared for publication by Eddie Lyons who managed the graphics programme for the monograph. Thanks also to Sheila Keyte for her technical support throughout the project.

We would like to thank Polydora Baker and Dale Serjeantson for their comments on the antler text; Neville Gardener for providing a copy of his undergraduate dissertation on the animal bone from the 1968–70 work at Silbury; Ian Riddler for advice and discussion on antler modification and tool use; Sam Jackson for the 3D light scanning of the chalk block; and Quita Mould for assisting with identification of Saxo-Norman artefacts. The pottery assemblage was initially assessed by Alan Vince and subsequently by Kayt Marter Brown with comments from Rachael Seager-Smith and Lorraine Mepham. Thanks also to Stuart Needham, Adam Gwilt and Jody Joy for their help with regard to the Late Bronze Age or Early Iron Age bracelet.

We would like to thank Chris Page for his comments and suggestions about rotting *Equisetum*. Tony Stead, Bill Chaloner and Alan Gange (Royal Holloway), Jeff Duckett (Queen Mary College) and attendees at the plant taphonomy meeting in Utrecht 2009 are thanked for discussion of Silbury green plant preservation. John Edmonds is thanked for providing the partially fermented woad. Thanks also to Andrew Scott who introduced Margaret Collinson to Gill Campbell (as a consequence of co-supervision of PhD research by Laura McParland) and suggested that TEM study might be informative for Silbury material. Thanks also to Christopher Whitehouse for permission to use his photo of *Montia fontana*.

A great number of libraries, records offices and museums were consulted at various stages and their staff were of enormous assistance but special mention must go to those at the Wiltshire History Centre, Chippenham, the Wiltshire Heritage Museum, Devizes, the Alexander Keiller Museum, Avebury, and the National Monuments Record Centre, Swindon, in particular, David Dawson, Ros Cleal, Felicity Gilmore, Paul Robinson, Lisa Webb and Matilda Webb. Brian Edwards initially transcribed the letters from Colonel Drax, the transcription of which is used here and we thank him for his help with Figure 10.21. Brian and Kate Fielden are also thanked for their work on assessing the various archives for Silbury material. Monika Lowerre is thanked for translating extracts of Halternorth and Trense (1956). Gill Swanton and Barry Bishop are thanked for their assistance with press days and John Taylor for useful discussions of the 1968–70 intervention. We are grateful to Alex Gibson for use of his photograph of Duggleby Howe in Chapter 8.

Fig 0.1
From left to right
Brian Kerr, Arthur McCallum, Duncan Stirk, Mark Kirkbride, James Cooper, Skanska mechanic, Foxy Demeanour, Jenny Ryder, Barry Carlin, Bob Tutill, Colin Wilkinson, Jim Leary, Ellie Leary, Mick McCaffery, Terry Hilton, Vernon Nightingale. (James O Davies, © English Heritage)

We would like to warmly thank Professor Alasdair Whittle and Professor Martin Bell for refereeing the monograph. A number of other people read and commented on parts or all of the text; in this respect thanks to Mark Bowden, David McOmish, Sarah May, Andrew Reynolds, Peter Topping and Pete Wilson. Colin Richards kindly made unpublished material available.

The National Trust was helpful throughout, in particular Chris Gingell who initially reported the 'hole' and took a keen interest while every assistance was made in allowing the field at the base to be used for interventions and repairs on several occasions. In this respect English Heritage is also extremely grateful to local tenants and landowners, principally the Hues family for their great patience and understanding. All of the above are warmly thanked for the role that they have played in this unique project. Finally, mention must go to Lord Avebury, owner of the site, for allowing the interventions recounted in this report and for taking a keen interest as they progressed.

PREFACE

The Silbury Project developed as a response to an unexpected and unusual occurrence in one of Europe's best known archaeological monuments: the dangerous collapse of a forgotten antiquarian excavation shaft that had not been backfilled. The approach was, of necessity, cautious and one of conservation. Only as the implications of the various options were pursued and clarified did it become clear that it would be necessary to clear out and refill more recent exploration trenches, notably the tunnels dug to the centre in 1849 and 1968–70, as part of the solution.

There are some implications for the large number of other monuments, including large mounds that have seen excavation in past centuries, for there may be other sites with similar problems. At one level it is a matter of health and safety, but at another it concerns the preservation of archaeological deposits. We are used to damage and decay to the exterior of monuments, but damage to the interiors is usually the result of burrowing animals. However, we must also recognise that many earthworks are the very way they are simply *because* the original structures have collapsed or eroded. They are the product of damage and decay. Arresting such decay is one thing, but the extent to which there should be intervention to preserve their 20th-century form may need to be argued. Here, a unique monument has been patched up. Arresting decay of the original deposits was quite rightly the primary consideration, but in doing so potentially interesting archaeology of those 18th-, 19th- and indeed 20th-century interventions may have been compromised.

Having said this, from a research perspective, the opportunity to revisit some of the deposits at the heart of the Silbury Hill, affectionately referred to below as 'the Hill' was invaluable. Since investigation was directed by the conservation imperative, research was of necessity steered in a certain direction and the oppor-

tunity to address many of the questions about the monument simply did not arise. However, it can be said that we do know significantly more about the site than a decade ago. We have a reasonable idea of its date, of the length of time it might have taken to build, greater understanding of the nature of the materials and where they came from, of the local environment and of the Roman and medieval use. A decade ago we knew nothing of the Roman town immediately adjacent to the mound.

This monograph sets out this research. A plan of the various trenches cut into the mound in the past is provided here for ease of reference (Fig. 0.2) and the following chapters have been set out in broad chronological order. An introductory chapter describes the monument and former work on it as well as documentary research and preliminary survey work that provided context prior to the decision to reopen the 1968–70 tunnel. Chapter 2 sets out the phases of the prehistoric sequence as seen in the tunnel during the 2007 and 2008 work as well as incorporating the evidence from small-scale excavations on the summit and a watching brief on the side of the mound. Chapter 3 comprises a series of specialist contributions on the prehistoric artefacts, which together support the evidence from Chapter 2. Chapter 4 discusses the chronology of the monument. Chapter 5 reports on the investigations undertaken to understand preservation and formation processes, while Chapter 6 discusses the environmental evidence, including palaeohydrology, and places it in context. Chapter 7 outlines ways of interpreting the prehistoric mound, while Chapter 8 attempts to place it within wider context by considering land-use and social implications. Chapter 9 outlines how the mound was utilised after its primary use. It sets out the evidence for the Roman small town around Silbury and evidence for use and modification through into the Anglo-Saxon and early medieval periods. Finally, Chapter 10

N

Core 11   Core 10   Core 9

Core 8   1968-70
         Cutting 5

1968-70
Cutting 4   1968-70
                 Cutting 7

                        1968-70
                        Cutting 3a

Core 1

2007 trench   1968-70
                         Cutting 3

2001 Trench A
                 1776 shaft
Core 5   Core 6
                        Core 7   Core 2

Core 4
                                2001 Trench B

1968-69 &
2007 tunnels   Core 3

                                        1867 trenches
                                        (approx. locations)

2007
hillside works

                                1922 trench

1849 tunnels

1968-70
Cutting 6   1968-70
              Cutting 2   1922 trench
                                          1922 trenches

                        1968-70
                        Cutting 1

0   50m

Scale 1:1000

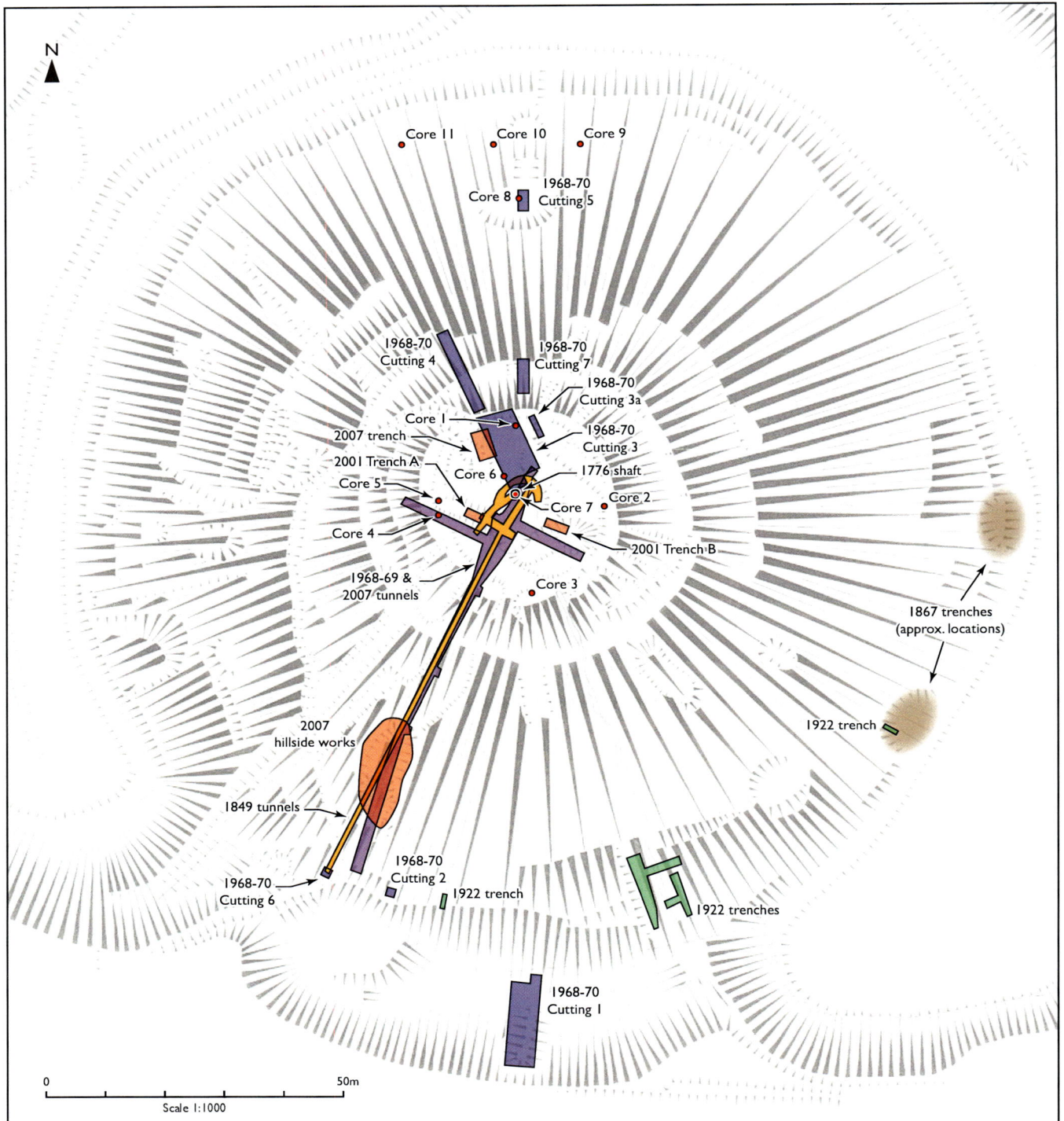

Fig 0.2
A plan of all the known
interventions into
Silbury Hill.
(Eddie Lyons and
Deborah Cunliffe,
© English Heritage)

describes the remedial works carried out to conserve the Hill and how these developed over the course of the conservation project.

It would be wrong to imagine that the work stops there. Throughout the campaign documentary research has been undertaken by Brian Edwards, Kate Fielden and others and while much of enormous interest has been revealed there is undoubtedly more to come. Somewhere no doubt, in diaries or letters, lie further details of the 1776 investigation, while more recently oral history and memories of the 20th-century activities on 'the Hill' have been recorded.

Of necessity a great number of individuals have been involved in preparation of parts of the report. We have attempted to weld them into a coherent whole, but inevitably readers will notice differences in approach between the authors of various components of the text and we are aware that contradictions may exist particularly where strongly held views conflict. Furthermore, attempting to do justice to a decade of work within a single volume has been a difficult task and it is only to be expected that much had to be left out. Where this has been the case references are made to English Heritage Research Reports that provide much supplementary material and in many cases most of the detail. These are available from the English Heritage website (http://www.english-heritage.org.uk/). The physical archive has been placed at the Alexander Keiller Museum and is available for inspection by appointment, whilst the digital archive is available from ADS and the National Monuments Record.

David Field, Jim Leary, and Gill Campbell

SUMMARY

Silbury Hill, the enormous earthen mound situated in the heart of the Marlborough Downs, and set today within the Avebury and Stonehenge World Heritage Site, is one of Europe's most remarkable archaeological sites. In 1776 Colonel Edward Drax, curious about whether the mound covered an important burial and aware of its size relative to the pyramids of Egypt, directed a group of miners to dig a vertical shaft from the summit to the centre. Later, in 1849, the Archaeological Institute of Great Britain and Ireland (later the Royal Archaeological Institute) sponsored the excavation of a horizontal tunnel into the mound in advance of their visit to Wiltshire. Smaller interventions were made in 1867, 1886 and 1922 before Professor Richard Atkinson led a third major investigation between 1968 and 1970, sponsored by the BBC and the first excavation to be televised live. Atkinson excavated a tunnel partially on the line of the 1849 one and identified four phases of construction. Neither vertical shaft nor horizontal tunnels were, as it turned out, adequately backfilled, leaving an unfortunate legacy of structural instability. This became manifest in May 2000 when the full consequence was made painfully clear as a 10-metre deep hole unexpectedly opened on the summit. This was revealed to be the remains of the 1776 shaft. Further investigation showed that the excavated tunnels were collapsing as well, and that the voids within the tunnels would eventually migrate upwards and be expressed at the surface.

After much public debate and scrutiny, the 1968–70 tunnel was re-opened in order to conserve the Hill and prevent further damage to its exceptional archaeology. This provided a unique opportunity to explore and record the body of Silbury Hill using modern archaeological methods and innovative techniques. This work has transformed our understanding of one of Britain's foremost prehistoric monuments, showing that the construction was piecemeal and organic, the mound growing incrementally rather than in major stages. The anoxic conditions within the centre of the monument have preserved delicate biological remains within the turf and topsoil used in construction. These give a unique insight into the nature of the Later Neolithic environment, attesting the managed chalk grassland habitats. Other studies undertaken include assessments of the micro preservation of environmental remains, studies of how various deposits were formed, in particular the nature of the Old Land Surface beneath the Hill, and palaeohydrological research.

The project has also revealed more about the later history of Silbury Hill and its place in the surrounding landscape. Geophysical survey has shown that it lay at the centre of a Roman settlement, which straddled the nearby A4. This discovery not only led to a small evaluation in 2010 but also provided the stimulus to revisit the Roman evidence obtained from excavation of the external ditch of the monument in 1968–70 as well as a consideration of the nature of the settlement as revealed through previous intervention.

In the medieval period the mound was once again remodelled, with evidence of significant alterations. A structure, possibly defensive and likely to be a palisade, was built on the summit in the 10th or 11th century possibly as a response to Viking raids. This process of creating a new Silbury for each new generation continues to this day.

Preparations: The Setting, Previous Research, Recent Research and Surveys

DAVID FIELD AND JIM LEARY

With contributions from Martyn Barber, Matt Canti, Amanda Chadburn, Tom Cromwell, Brian Edwards and Rob Harding

The location and landscape setting of Silbury Hill, and the topography and geology of the environs are outlined. Antiquarian and earlier archaeological work is reviewed and the circumstances leading to the intervention is summarised. The various surveys carried out to inform our understanding of the monument in advance of remedial works are described.

Introduction

The remarkable earthen mound known as Silbury Hill, the largest humanly constructed prehistoric mound in Europe, is situated among the undulating chalk hills of central southern England at the source of the River Kennet, a major tributary of the River Thames. Now known to be of Neolithic date, its purpose has long proved to be an enigma and for several centuries it presented a tantalising but difficult challenge to antiquaries who compared its massive size with the pyramids of Egypt.

In form, it is an enormous truncated cone almost 31 metres in height, though its position close to a valley floor and small stream ensures that it does not appear above the skyline of the surrounding hills and is visually inconspicuous from long distances (Fig 1.1). However, when approached close to, its sheer bulk becomes apparent. Its steep slopes contain a number of

Fig 1.1
Silbury Hill in the snow taken from the south-east. (Ian Leonard, © English Heritage)

Fig 1.2 (opposite)
Location map showing the
position of Silbury Hill
within the British Isles with
places mentioned in the text.
(Eddie Lyons, © English
Heritage; SRTM data
courtesy of the CGIAR
Consortium for Spatial
Information)

undulations and, particularly close to the summit a number of terrace-like features are present, while its base, measuring some 150 metres in diameter, is surrounded by a massive ditch that often holds water in winter.

Today the monument is turf covered, sheep-grazed, respected and managed by recent generations; the botanically rich, semi-natural chalk grassland has resulted in it being designated a Site of Special Scientific Interest (SSSI). Situated in the heart of the North Wessex Downs Area of Outstanding Natural Beauty (AONB) in Wiltshire within an area containing a high concentration of well-preserved prehistoric monuments (Fig 1.2), it remains in tune with its natural surroundings. Little over one kilometre to the north is the Wiltshire village of Avebury, the location of a massive Neolithic henge and stone settings which, along with Silbury Hill and other Neolithic and Bronze Age monuments, forms part of the UNESCO Stonehenge and Avebury World Heritage Site, while the hamlets of West Kennett and Beckhampton lie just over one kilometre to the east and west of it respectively.

The importance of the site has long been rec-ognised and it was among the earliest archaeological sites in Britain to be observed and commented upon, although it was only during the latter half of the 20th century that excavations provided any evidence of its true date. Writing in the mid-17th century, John Aubrey recorded the local tradition that King Sil or Zel was buried there on horseback and the mound raised over his grave (Fowles 1980, 680–2), a tradition not exactly frustrated when human bones along with horse riding accou-trements were discovered on the summit in about 1723 (Stukeley 1743; see below this Chapter). A shaft was sunk from the summit in 1776 (Douglas 1793, 161) and a lateral tunnel followed the old ground surface to the centre in 1849 (Tucker 1851, 297–303; Merewether 1851a, 73–81). In modern times the site achieved much attention when, during the late 1960s, it featured as the first archaeological excavation to be televised live by the British Broadcasting Corporation (BBC2) during an extensive campaign by Professor Richard Atkinson of Cardiff University, which was watched by millions of viewers enthralled by the possibility of witnessing a major discovery (Attenborough 2010; Leary and Field 2010, chapter 3). The results did not turn out as some may have hoped but nevertheless did provide an intriguing glimpse into the construction of a remarkable structure along with a series of early radiocarbon dates that importantly confirmed a prehistoric date for the site.

The mound, though not the ditch, was one of the very first monuments in the United Kingdom to be protected under the first Ancient Monuments Protection Act 1882. This Act was championed through Parliament by Sir John Lubbock, who (having persuaded local land-owners to sell it to him) then owned Silbury Hill and who agreed to place this property in state guardianship on 6 August 1883. The Hill remains in the guardianship of the Secretary of State for the Department of Culture, Media and Sport, along with land to the west now used as a visitor car park and viewing area. Today, it is managed on the Government's behalf by English Heritage, although Lord Avebury, a descendant of Sir John Lubbock, is the current owner. While the mound itself is in guardianship, the scheduled monument of Silbury Hill now includes its surrounding ditch (National Heritage List for England 1008445; Scheduled Monument 21707; formerly County Number WI 2). The site has been recorded in national inventories, National Monuments Record No SU 16 NW 21, and is located at NGR: SU 1001 6853 in the parish of Avebury. It is recorded in the Wiltshire County Historic Environment Record as No 102, 102/325. Silbury Hill has been closed to visitors since 1978 due to the ecological and archaeological damage caused by visitor erosion.

Circumstances for the project

David Field, Rob Harding and Amanda Chadburn
On 29 May 2000, a hole was unexpectedly discovered on the summit of Silbury Hill, a matter of great concern to the National Trust who at that time were managing the monument and to English Heritage who were immediately informed (Chadburn 2001; Chadburn *et al* 2005, 12; Chadburn 2008). It was apparent that a roughly square, vertical cavity some 2.25 metres across by at least 10 metres deep was present (McAvoy 2000, 1) (Figs 1.3 and 1.4). Following site inspections by English Heritage and National Trust engineers, a secure scaffolding cover was placed over the shaft on 31 May. It was very quickly realised that the cavity was likely to be the shaft dug in 1776 about which very little was known, but which it was presumed had been backfilled. The hole descended for 10.4 metres with a cavity to one

Ring of
Brodgar
Maes Howe

N
▲

Pitnacree
Tay

Courthill

Newgrange

Boyne

Duggleby
Howe

Castell
Bryn Gwyn
Ysceifiog
Llandegai A

Bull Ring

Skendleby

Gwyddelfynnyd,
Bryncrug

Grimes
Graves

Lugg
Severn

Walton
Gyrus
Avon
Wasperton

Preseli
Hills

Therfield
Heath

Silbury
Hill ●
Kennet
Thames

Priddy
Circles
Marden
Durrington Walls

Upton Lovell
Stonehenge
Wor Barrow
Avon
Thickthorn Down
Knowlton
Petersfield
Flagstones
Frome
Stour
Holdenhurst
Whitehawk
Mount Pleasant

0   250km

Scale: 1:5,000,000

Le Hoigie Bie

Fig 1.3
Aerial photograph showing
the hole on the summit as it
appeared on 30 May 2000
(SU1068/214 NMR
18745/01). (Damian Grady,
© English Heritage)

Fig 1.4
Looking down the shaft.
(Fachtna McAvoy,
© English Heritage)

side at the base, although it remained unclear whether the spoil forming the floor at this level was solid.

The mound, and particularly its summit, was monitored on a regular basis from the air (Crutchley 2005) and changes in the nature of the hole were recorded as a further series of collapses in December 2000 that had expanded into a crater with archaeological deposits exposed. As the temporary cover was evidently not preventing further collapse it was removed and the area fenced off. A remote record of the deposits was made using a reflectorless Total Station Theodolite coupled with photography, direct access being limited due to health and safety precautions. Geophysical survey of the summit in February 2001 further highlighted the unstable nature of the area around the head of the 1776 shaft (Linford and Martin 2001, 5; Linford 2001) and revealed 'anomalies associated with fissures' around the southern edge of the crater and suggested that further subsidence could occur at any time.

Two small trenches were excavated in 2001 to establish the nature of the deposits in the side of the crater (Chapter 2), but as a result of increasing concern that other cavities might exist within the mound at greater depth and beyond the reach of usual geophysical techniques, a new and untried technique (at least to archaeology), that of seismic tomography, was conducted by Cementation Skanska, a firm of engineers, and the results quality checked by two independent advisors (for full details *see* Chapter 10). In order to stabilise the crater while the work was carried out, it was temporarily lined with a geo-membrane and filled with polystyrene blocks and topped with chalk. Seven boreholes were then drilled from the summit to the base of the mound, airguns placed at the base and hydro-phones placed around the mound to receive seismic data. While the results were considered inconclusive they did point to anomalies at the site of the earlier interventions, principally those of the 1776 shaft and tunnel first dug in 1849 and reused in 1968–70, and possibly those of Wilkinson and Petrie (Fig 0.2; *see below* this chapter and Chapter 10). In addition, a further anomaly was identified rising up the northern slope where earthworks had already been noticed on the surface (*below*, this chapter) and which was subsequently referred to as the 'northern anomaly'. The latter was further investigated by coring (*see* Chapter 10) which revealed contrast in soil depth on that part of the site.

Aside from the shaft itself, the principal problem was that it was unclear the extent to which earlier interventions had been backfilled. Given this, the decision was taken to completely backfill all known and predicted voids within the Hill by re-entering the 1968–70 tunnels (rather than backfilling remotely) (Harding *et al* 2005, 18–19). This repair programme provided an ideal opportunity to revisit and record deposits within the mound to modern standards (*see* Chapters 2 and 10 for further details).

Antiquarian background and the 1776 excavation shaft

David Field

Situated close to the main London to Bristol highway, Silbury Hill was a roadside curiosity that was bound to be recorded sooner rather than later and indeed, the monument does appear to have been observed by the earliest antiquarians and travellers. Leland (Toulmin Smith 1964, 81) first noted its presence while compiling his *Itinerary* in c 1545, as did William Camden in 1607 (Gough trans 1806, 136). John Aubrey also visited the site in 1663 when he was accompanied by Charles II on his visit to Avebury (Fowles 1980; Jackson 1862, 316; Leary and Field 2010). It is William Stukeley's descriptions and illustrations made in 1723, however, that provide details of local land-use and other matters relating to the mound. In particular, he referred to Mr Halford (Holford), then Lord of the Manor, who in March 1723 'ordr'd some trees planted on this hill, in the middle of the noble plain or area at the top …' (Stukeley 1743, 41); and in another version mentioned that '… they sunk a great hole in the middle of the area and filled it with mould' as part of the planting operation (Lukis 1887, 245).

There was clearly a degree of disruption on the summit at this time and it may be that Richard Holford, the Lord of Avebury Manor, aimed to use the mound as a component in a designed landscape, an eyecatcher or mount, as there are references to both tree planting and path construction. There is some uncertainty whether the planting was of trees (plural) that would imply more than a single cutting. In one reference, planting at the centre is mentioned, but if there were others, this may help to explain traces of a shallow bank, interpreted potentially as a debased tree ring set around the lip of the summit. There is no further evidence for such a use, though the existing curving path coupled with the terraces provides a ready-made mount to surpass in size that situated just over eight kilometres to the east alongside the River Kennet at Marlborough (Field *et al* 2001; Leary *et al* forthcoming). Richard Holford left a plan of his land at Avebury, surveyed by Thomas Alexander in 1733, entitled 'Avebury Great Farm belonging to Richard Holford Esq who is lord = Royal of Avebury' (*sic*: Wiltshire Record Office 1553/71), which refers to Silbury as Zilbury and depicts it as a flat-topped conical mound, but unfortunately adds no other detail of either pathway or of trees.

Importantly, Stukeley (1743, 41) also recorded that the:

> workmen dug up the body of the great king there buried in the centre, very little below the surface. The bones extremely rotten, so that they crumbled them in pieces with their fingers … Some weeks after I came luckily to rescue a great curiosity which they took up there; an iron chain, as they called it, which I bought of John Fowler, one of the workmen: it was the bridle buried along with this monarch, being only a solid body of rust. I immerg'd it in limner's drying oil, and dry'd it out carefully, keeping it ever since very dry. It is now as fair and entire as when the workmen took it up … There were deers horns, an iron knife with a bone handle too, all excessively rotten, taken up along with it … Our bridle belonged to the harness of a British chariot …

Stukeley assumed that the skeleton was that of King Sil. The bridle has been dated to the 11th century (Chapter 9) and, assuming that the burial was associated, it may have been of that date also. He wrote to Roger Gale on 22 July 1723, the account differing in detail

> … in making a way up Silbury hill, by Mr Holford's order, they found a strange iron chain of an unusual bulk, make, and unaccountable use, on which we must summon a cabinet council of antiquaries to deliberate. In digging at the top of it to sett some trees, they took up the bones of the great king buryed there, and a Roman coin or two, which I doubt not were dropped by accident …
> (Lukis 1887, 245)

The fate of the bridle is unclear although 30 years later Stukeley wrote:

> Feb 1759 – I exhibited [to the Antiquarian Society] a drawing of the British bridle dug up with the king's body at Silbury hill, in March 1723. I exhibited the bridle itself, and many prints of

Silbury hill, the largest tumulus we know of …. I gave a large discourse upon it, and the curious contrivance in the bridle, of throwing the reins more outward than in our modern way, which gives a much greater power in governing the horse …
> (Lukis 1872, 275; for more on the bridle
> *see* Edwards 2010b, 323–4).

When a hole first appeared on the summit of the mound in May 2000 relatively little was known about the 1776 intervention other than a reference in *Nenia Britannica* (Douglas 1793) and in the later editions of *Camden's Britannia* (Gough 1806) to a shaft being dug from the summit. These referred to the Duke of Northumberland and Colonel Edward Drax who used miners to carry out the work. Unfortunately, no clear record of this episode exists but newspapers of the time clarify the date of the event and indicate that the shaft was 8 feet (2.4m) square (Whittle 1997a, 8; Field 2002; Leary and Field 2010, 28).

Other historical sources show that it was Drax who initiated the project and sought backing from the Royal Society, but his request was passed on to the Society of Antiquaries who declined to get involved. He then evidently turned to the Duke of Northumberland, a Trustee of the British Museum, for support (Leary and Field 2010, 27). Two letters, unearthed in the British Library, written by Drax to George Pitt, Lord Rivers while the former was working on the site, describe some of the activities and shed some light on these events (*see* Appendix 1.1, p 00; and Edwards 2010a for a commentary). There was no formal account or description of the intervention and it was left to the Revd James Douglas (1793, 161) to inform us that 'The only relic found at the bottom, and which Colonel Drax showed me, was a thin slip of oakwood'.

A traveller, Edward Williams, alias Iolo Morganwg, passed by in January 1777 and commented that the shaft was now 'shut up' (Cannon and Constantine 2004; Leary and Field 2010, 35) by which it could be understood to have been capped and backfilled. However, this would contrast with usual 18th-century mining practice, when shafts were normally left open, or simply capped with branches and the like as, for example, were the gunflint mine-shafts at Lingheath (Forrest 1983). Open mine-shafts still await the unwary in many moorland areas of the British Isles. Whether this approach was taken or whether the landowner of the time, Arthur

Jones, had specifically requested backfilling cannot now be easily be ascertained, although the contemporary account and the good state of the preservation of the shaft in May 2000 (*see* Fig 1.4) suggests that it was capped. Over 70 years after the event the Very Rev J Merewether lamented the lack of record about this intervention and said that mounds of spoil still survived that 'the excavators had not taken the trouble to throw in ...' (Merewether 1851a, 74).

An illustration by William Lukis made on 6 August 1849 after the visit to Silbury of the Archaeological Institute (Fig 1.5) depicts the shaft, apparently open to a depth of around one quarter of the depth of the mound (Devizes Museum DD14; original in Guernsey Museum; Edwards 2001; Sebire 2005). A later illustration published by Flinders Petrie (1924) indicates that the 1776 excavation shaft itself appears to have been poorly or only partially backfilled at best. Additionally, the shaft appears to have been open in the early 20th century as a blurred aerial photograph taken on 12 July 1925 (NMR SU 1068/8) depicts a hole or slumped area on the summit (Field 2002, 57, fig 29). Whether this was capped soon afterwards is unclear as aerial photographs taken on 13 July 1927 (NMR SU 1068/50-51) show what appears to be a mass of rank vegetation in the area of the hole. The viewpoint is too low on these to be certain whether the hole itself was still present, but the vegetation just might result from a recent

capping episode. Further photographs taken in 1933 and 1934 (NMRSU 1068/24–25: SU 1068/53–54) also depict a collapsed shaft. Remedial action seems to have taken place sometime between the summers of 1934 and 1936 as the crater was no longer visible on an aerial photograph taken on 7 June 1936 (NMR SU 1068/26), its fill or capping being surmounted by a patch of rank vegetation although it is visible again on a photograph of uncertain source reproduced by Grahame Clark in 1940 for his volume *Prehistoric England* (Clark 1940, pl 104).

Unfortunately, the recent collapse has destroyed any remaining earthworks that might relate to the 1776 shaft, although it is conceivable that part of the spoil heap survives, for a wide but irregular, almost sub-rectangular, bank of spoil around the shaft is clearly visible on a number of early aerial photographs (NMR SU 1068/24–26)and the earthwork survey (*below*, this chapter) has recorded traces of this around the northern lip of the shaft.

Archaeological excavations

David Field

Prior to the recent work, Silbury Hill has been excavated on at least six occasions (1776, 1849, 1867, 1886, 1922 and 1968–70). These have been summarised elsewhere (Whittle 1997a; Field 2002; Leary and Field 2010) and will only be described briefly here.

Fig 1.5
A drawing made by William Lukis during a visit made on 6 August 1849 with Dean Merewether. The shaft is depicted as only partly filled in and is open at the summit. The stain on the upper part of the mound is that of a paper clip (see Edwards 2001). Note that Lukis had presumed that the northern part of the ground surface had been artificially built up to create a level surface. He may have had some insight into this since Blandford and Falkner had cut some exploratory trenches in unknown locations to determine the position of the old land surface. It is now clear, however, that the land did not dip away at such an angle.
(Courtesy of Guernsey Museum)

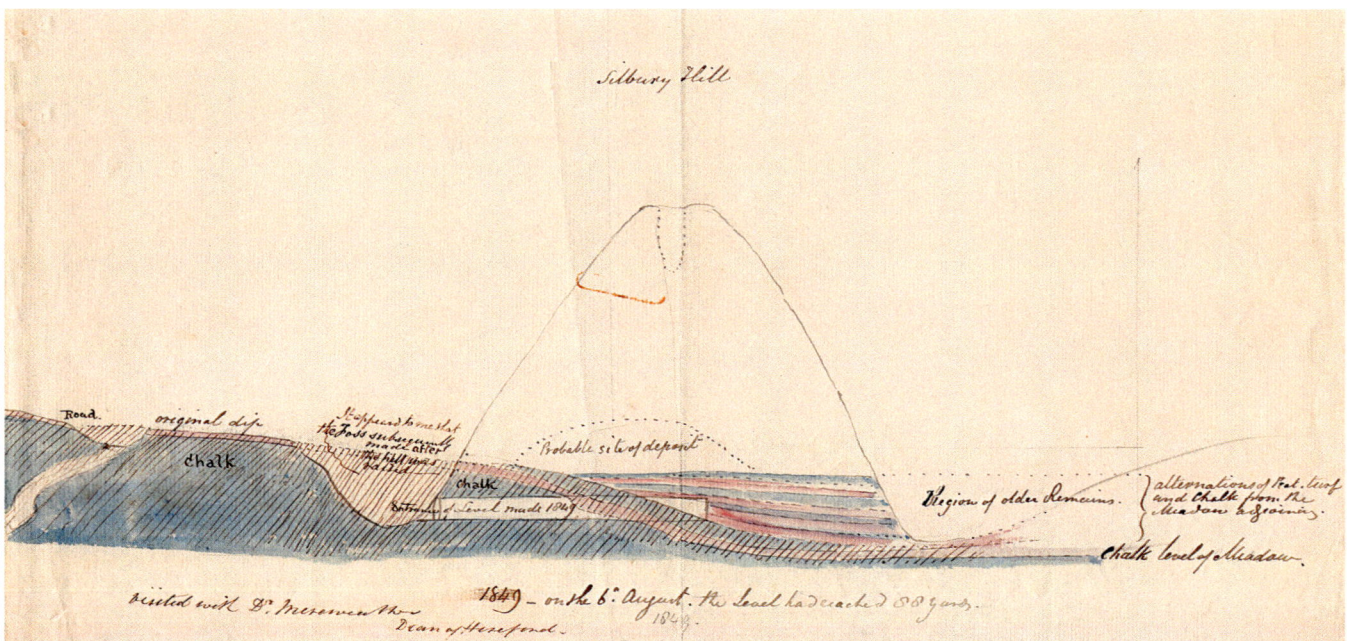

Following Drax's investigation, the mound lay undisturbed for over 70 years until increasing interest and enquiry coupled with appropriate opportunity resulted in a further bout of investigation. Having decided upon Salisbury, Wiltshire, as the venue for its annual meeting and in response to the requests of interested members, the Central Committee of the Archaeological Institute arranged for an investigation of the mound to take place during 1849. Richard Falkner, a banker from Devizes and Henry Blandford, a civil engineer from Rowde nearby, who was experienced in the construction of cuttings and embankments for railways, were employed to plan and drive a tunnel, 6ft 6ins (2m) high and 3ft (0.9m) wide along the original land surface towards the centre of the mound during the summer of 1849 (Figs 1.6 and

1.7). According to the Very Revd John Merewether, Dean of Hereford Cathedral (1851a, 75), this started from the westernmost of two causeways across the ditch situated to the south of the mound, below the original land surface. The tunnel commenced in the chalk bedrock and, inclining upwards, finally broke through into the original land surface at a distance of 33 yards (30.1m) (Merewether says 75 ft (22m)) from the tunnel entrance (Fig 1.7). From this point onwards it was necessary to use props to support the roof. Here the mound was composed of 'brownish earth chalky rubble' (Merewether 1851a, 75) and this level was subsequently followed towards the centre of the mound (Fig 1.7), where 'sods of turf and moss in layers appeared to be of the greatest thickness; … curving layers of turf lying one over the other

Fig 1.6
Plan of Blandford's 1849 tunnels (shown against plan of Silbury Hill by Ashmead & Son, of Bristol).
(Eddie Lyons,
© English Heritage)

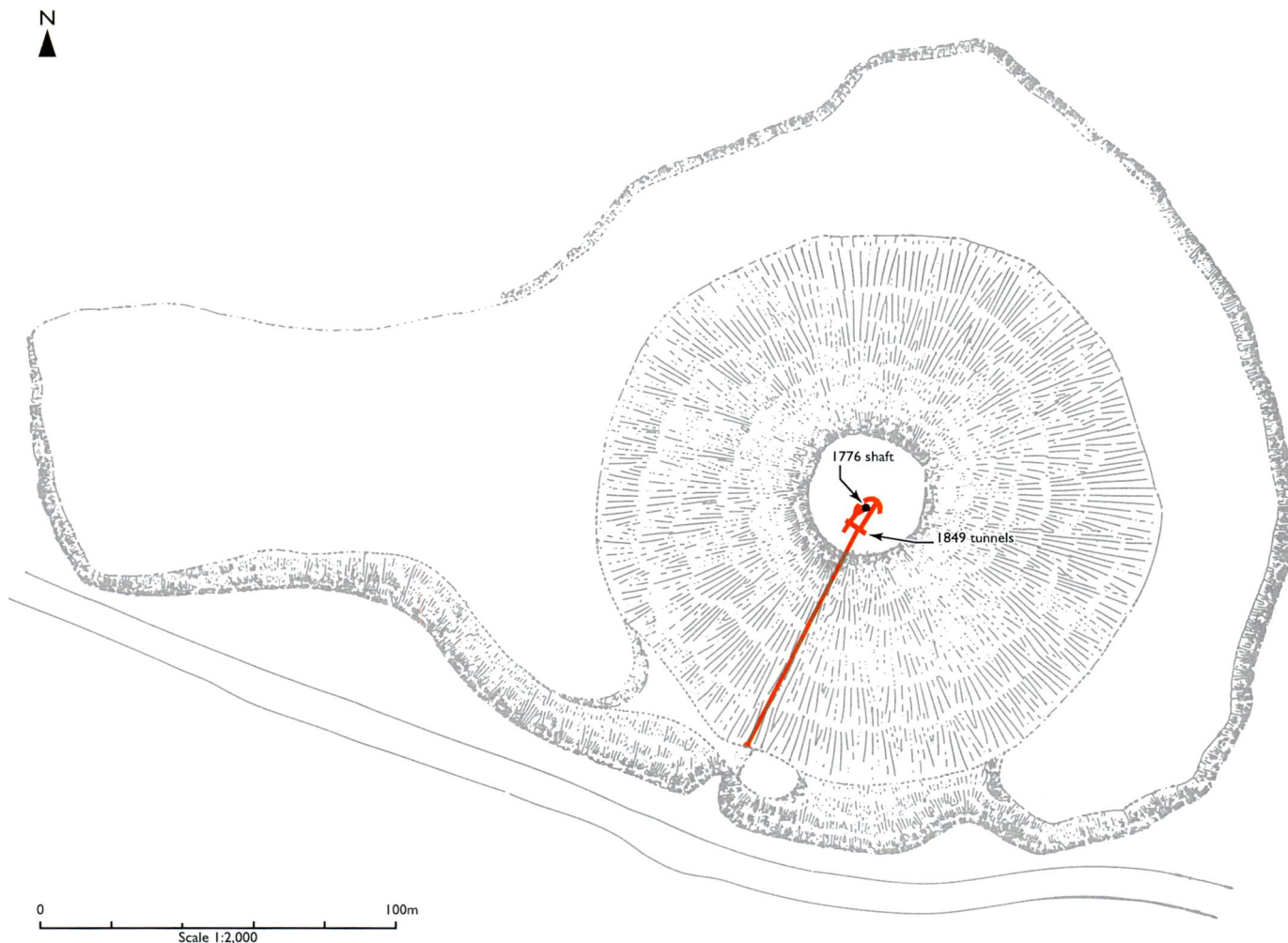

N

1776 shaft

1849 tunnels

0   100m
Scale 1:2,000

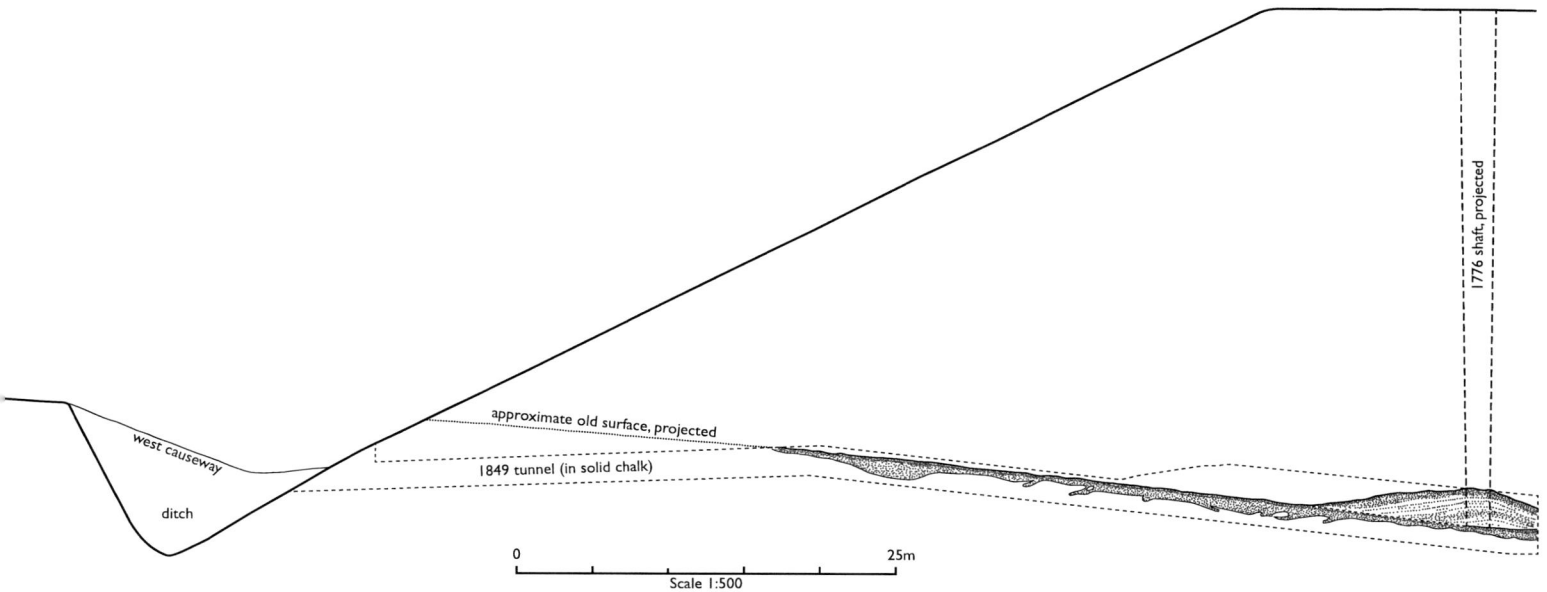

west causeway

ditch

approximate old surface, projected

1849 tunnel (in solid chalk)

1776 shaft, projected

0   25m

Scale 1:500

Fig 1.7
Section drawing of the 1849 tunnel (after Blandford) (as redrawn c 1968 for Atkinson's project). (Eddie Lyons, © English Heritage)

…' were found. 'The turf was quite black, as was also the undecayed moss and grass which formed the surface of each layer, and amongst it were the dead shells etc …' (Tucker 1851, 301).

The tunnel had been excavated beyond the centre of the mound by the beginning of August when members of the Archaeological Institute visited and the budget had been exhausted. A small group led by Merewether raised further funds and directed that side tunnels were dug. This work confirmed that the dark streak representing the old turf line was unbroken wherever investigated and there was consequently no evidence for a central grave (Tucker 1851, 301). Merewether (1851a, 80) reported that 'many sarsen stones were discovered' and suggested that they provided a kind of peristalith although it is not entirely clear whether they were within or around the turf mound (*see* Fig 1.10). Tucker simply mentioned a number of sarsens that were found in the lateral extension to the east (Tucker 1851, 300). The only finds were some fragments of antler and a few animal bones, evidently from the body of the mound. As Tucker commented, they 'may have been thrown up with the earth from the meadow below when the Hill was formed' (Tucker 1851, 301; Merewether 1851a, 75). A single deer tine was also recovered from chalk rubble.

At this point Blandford and Falkner considered that their contract with the Archaeological Institute was completed whereupon Merewether, clearly driven by a conviction that a burial lay somewhere at the centre, informed the Institute that he would take over. He arranged for a diagonal tunnel to be cut which intercepted the base of the 1776 shaft and then a curving tunnel that followed part of the line of the central mound (*see* Fig 1.6). He soon abandoned this work and, frustrated, returned to digging local barrows which he seems to have considered more productive. Excavation at the centre of the mound continued for the last two weeks of August under the direction of the Revd Bathurst Deane, when all concerned were satisfied that the old land surface had been satisfactorily explored. The tunnel was finally closed at the end of September before winter set in. It was evidently not backfilled but some of the props were withdrawn, a wall of bricks constructed close to the entrance and the mound made good (Tucker 1851, 302).

For Blandford, the excavations had disproved the idea that a burial lay at the centre. They disproved too, the idea that the mound lay over the London to Bath Roman road. Instead, as Stukeley had earlier observed (1743, 43), the road took care to avoid the mound and the mound was therefore of pre-Roman date (Tucker 1851, 303).

Details of a formerly unknown intervention were recorded in a letter from 'Archaeophilus' to the *Illustrated London News* published in June 1850 (Edwards 2010b, 324–5). This describes an excavation on the summit of the mound in which 'We had dug for, I should think, eight feet down, when the spade of one of my assistants struck against something, which returned a ringing sound'. The correspondent describes finding a piece of a blade of a dagger and a fragment of a brass horse bit.

In response to continuing controversy, in particular James Fergusson's claim that the Roman road lay beneath the mound, the Wiltshire Archaeological and Natural History Society excavated two trenches in 1867 at the estimated original ground level on the east side of the mound (Wilkinson 1867). A trench was dug either side of where the road was expected to be. The scale and precise location of each trench is now not clear (but *see below*, this chapter), but the Roman road was not encountered and the search for it was more fruitful in the field to the south (*see* Chapter 9).

Between September and November 1886 attention turned to the ditch surrounding the mound, and excavations were carried out by Alfred Pass (1887) in the meadow at the base of the Hill (Figs 1.8 and 1.17). He excavated ten test pits, described as shafts, on the ditch floor to the west and north of the mound, and the location of these was depicted on a plan prepared by Ashmead & Son of Bristol. The size of each is unknown, but workmen digging them were described in the plural so that each hole must have been large enough to take at least two individuals; in each case the shaft was taken down to the natural solid chalk bedrock. In most cases the chalk had been removed to a depth of about 4.5m, although closer to the mound this 'suddenly increased to about 21ft [6.4m], below the present surface' (Pass 1887, 248). The floor

Fig 1.8
Plan of Pass (1886) and
Petrie (1922) trenches
(shown against plan of
Silbury Hill by Ashmead
& Son, of Bristol).
(Eddie Lyons,
© English Heritage)

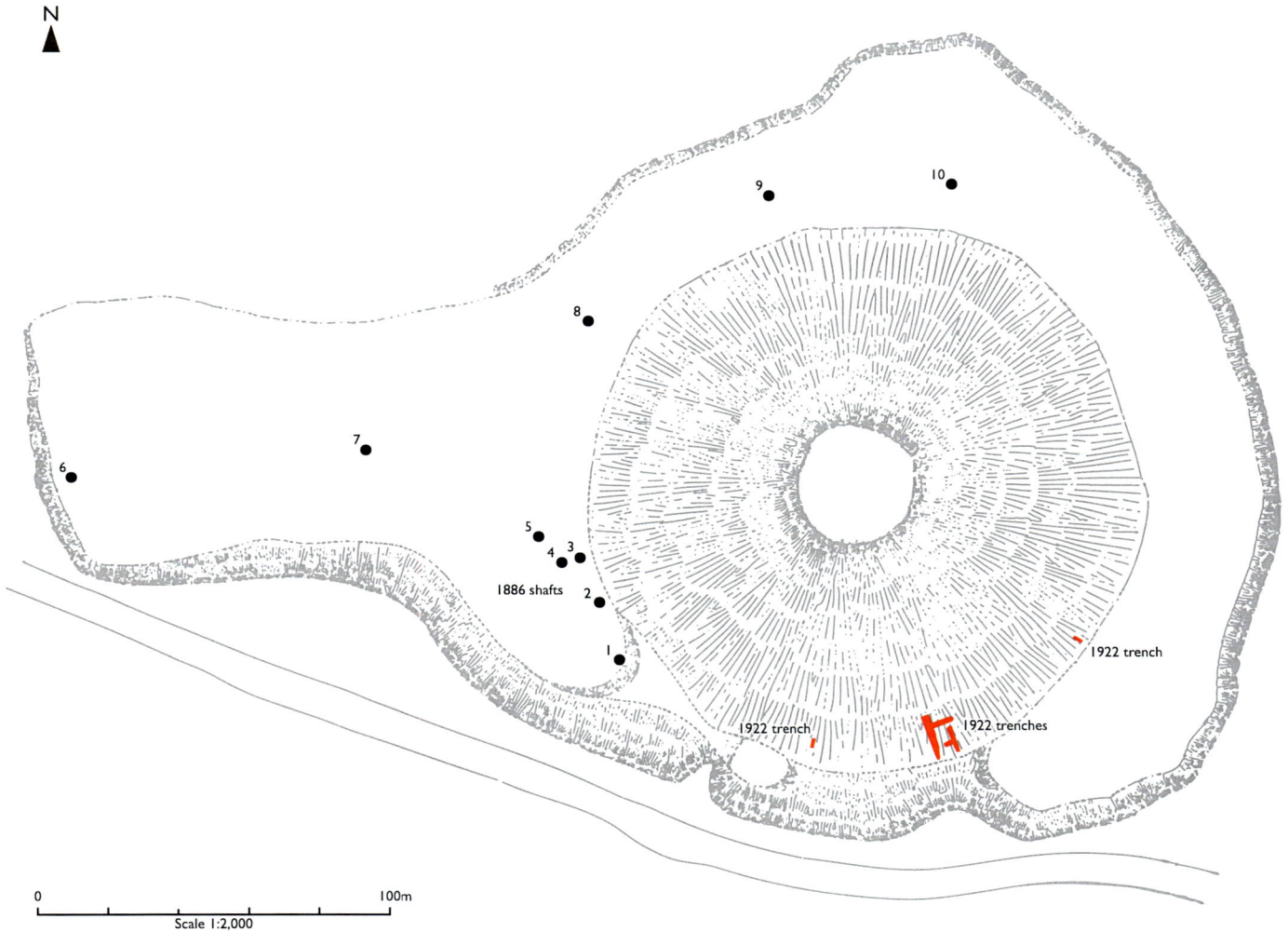

may have been uneven as Pass noted the remains of 'notches or steps' that had been cut into the chalk at the base of two of the shafts.

Some flint flakes and bones were recovered or at least noted from Shaft 6. Most of the flint retained in Devizes Museum is natural but one small flake of buff/light brown non-local material is present along with two burnt pieces and a burnt fragment of sarsen. In Shaft 5, at *c* 10ft (3m) from the surface, a layer of clay about 1ft (0.3m) thick appeared to have been stained almost black, from which level came a human femur (Devizes Museum Acc No DM2891), and this in turn lay on a further 5ft (1.5m) deposit of unstained clay. Fragments of charcoal from the black layer were collected (Devizes Museum DM2898) but not analysed. Pass retained the soil and washed it through a sieve and a number of flint flakes were recovered (Pass 1887, 250). Animal bone was of deer, ox, pig and dog, while remnants of deer and ox were also found in all the other shafts but one and sometimes small burnt sarsen stones were associated with them (Pass 1887, 251). In Shaft 2, close to the mound and ditch terminal, a coin of Marcus Aurelius was recovered at a depth of 6ft (1.8m), indicating perhaps that the upper third of the ditch deposits had accumulated since that time. Pass remarked that even in September after a long dry summer, water stood at a depth of 8ft (2.4m) in these shaft holes and believed that together with the flooded ditch extension to the west the mound would have been quite defensible.

In August 1922 Flinders Petrie turned his attention to the mound (Petrie 1924). He produced a profile drawing similar to that of Lukis (*see* Fig 1.5) that indicated that the shaft was still visible at the summit and was perhaps open at that time. He also investigated the south-eastern 'neck' or causeway across the southern ditch and determined that it consisted of solid chalk, the outer slope of which had been deposited with chalk rubble in order to 'form a smooth gradient from the road down to the neck' (Petrie 1924, 215). His plans, however, depict no excavation trench at this point and it may be that his interpretation derives from augering. He did excavate two small parallel trenches on the lower slope of the mound opposite the eastern causeway or 'neck', the westernmost for 40ft (12.1m) into the body of the mound (Fig 1.8), with an extension and tunnel at right-angles almost connecting each trench (Fig 1.9). The latter two trenches

were intended to intercept any entrance or passageway into the mound that lay along the line of the 'neck', but proved negative. Many fragments of antler, bones of red deer and pig, and flint flakes were recovered, mostly at a depth of *c* 2.4 to 3m. Some worked flints and antler fragments from this excavation are retained in Devizes Museum (Devizes Museum Catalogue, Vol 2, 86).

As the wall blocking the entrance had collapsed, the 1849 tunnel was still accessible and Petrie also investigated it in order to explore the original ground surface and provide information to link the stratigraphy with the topography beyond the mound. He determined that 'the mound was centred on a long almost level spur of down, which fell away sharply on the east' (Petrie 1924, 216), and that it chiefly consisted of deposits of chalk rubble and yellow clay usually laid in horizontal layers.

Fig 1.9
Petrie's trenches adjacent to the south-east 'causeway' (DZSWS1986.7340, Goddard Room Book CC). (Courtesy of Wiltshire Heritage Museum, Devizes)

11

An early attempt to locate a burial chamber by electrical resistivity methods was made in the late 1950s. Unlike previous investigators, McKim (1959, 176–8) considered that any burial might lie off-centre and may remain undetected by the earlier shaft or tunnels. A series of resistivity readings was taken around part of the base of the mound at 510ft (155.5m) above OD and at approximately half way up the slope at 550ft (167.5m) above OD, though the precise location of these surveys was unrecorded. The results, however, were considered unsatisfactory and did not demonstrate either the existence or absence of buried features.

This work was followed by a campaign of investigation by Richard Atkinson, funded and filmed by the BBC over three seasons in 1968, 1969 and 1970. Four films, broadcast in the BBC2 *Chronicle* series, subsequently became valuable archive material for the English Heritage project, since many of the original records had gone missing. Atkinson reinvestigated the 1849 tunnel in the Easter and summer university vacations of 1968 and summer vacation of 1969, using steel mining arches (or rings) placed at 1 yard (0.91m) intervals as a measuring device and, numbered 1–80, these became the base line for a site recording system. He took care to explore and map the central area and it became evident that Merewether's circuitous cutting had followed the line of a central gravel mound and encountered an alignment of three sarsens embedded within it (Fig 1.10). However, he chose not to re-excavate that area and instead widened the main tunnel to a maximum of 3.96m in the centre of the Hill where the 1849 works had resulted in collapsed sections (Whittle 1997a, 13). Beyond that he reduced it again, eventually taking it just past the estimated centre of the mound, a distance of 73.1m, or 80 rings, although the section was not recorded beyond Ring 73. Additionally, he drove two transverse tunnels, each 1.35m wide to the east-north-east and west-south-west, referred to as West and East Laterals respectively, to investigate the extent of the organic deposits that had been encountered as a result of the 1849 intervention (Fig 1.11). The measuring system indicates that the West Lateral was 11.8m in length and the East Lateral 15.5m.

In addition to excavating the southern part of the external ditch (Cutting 1), in 1970 Atkinson also excavated trenches Cuttings 3, 3a, 4, 5 and 7 on the summit and upper slopes in order to understand the terracing seen at the surface. In addition two small trenches (Cuttings 2 and 6) were excavated towards the base of the mound (Fig 1.11). None of these excavations were filmed. The external ditch was also investigated with a hammer source seismic survey and by coring. As part of this programme a contour survey was undertaken by the Geography Department of the University of Bristol which resulted in a plan with contours spaced at 2m intervals, clearly inadequate to depict the subtle earthworks that Atkinson knew were present. Subsequently, John Hampton of the National Monuments Record arranged for overlapping vertical photographs to be taken from the air and for Keith Atkinson of University College London to prepare a photogrammetric plot (English Heritage NMR files). This was produced as a plan with contours at 0.5m intervals, still a little too coarse to depict most of the slight earthworks. Additionally, however, a contour survey of the summit was prepared at closer resolution to provide context for the excavation trenches (Fig 1.12).

Fig 1.10
Plan prepared by John Taylor in 1968 of the centre of Silbury Hill, showing the 1849 tunnels and the position of sarsens.
(Eddie Lyons,
© English Heritage)

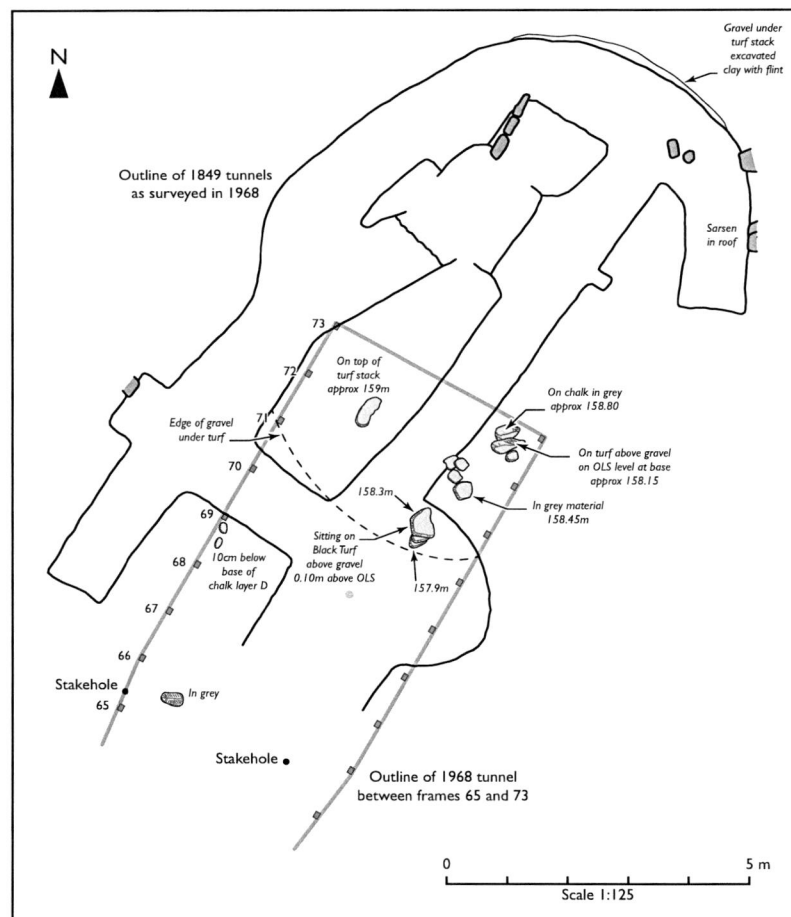

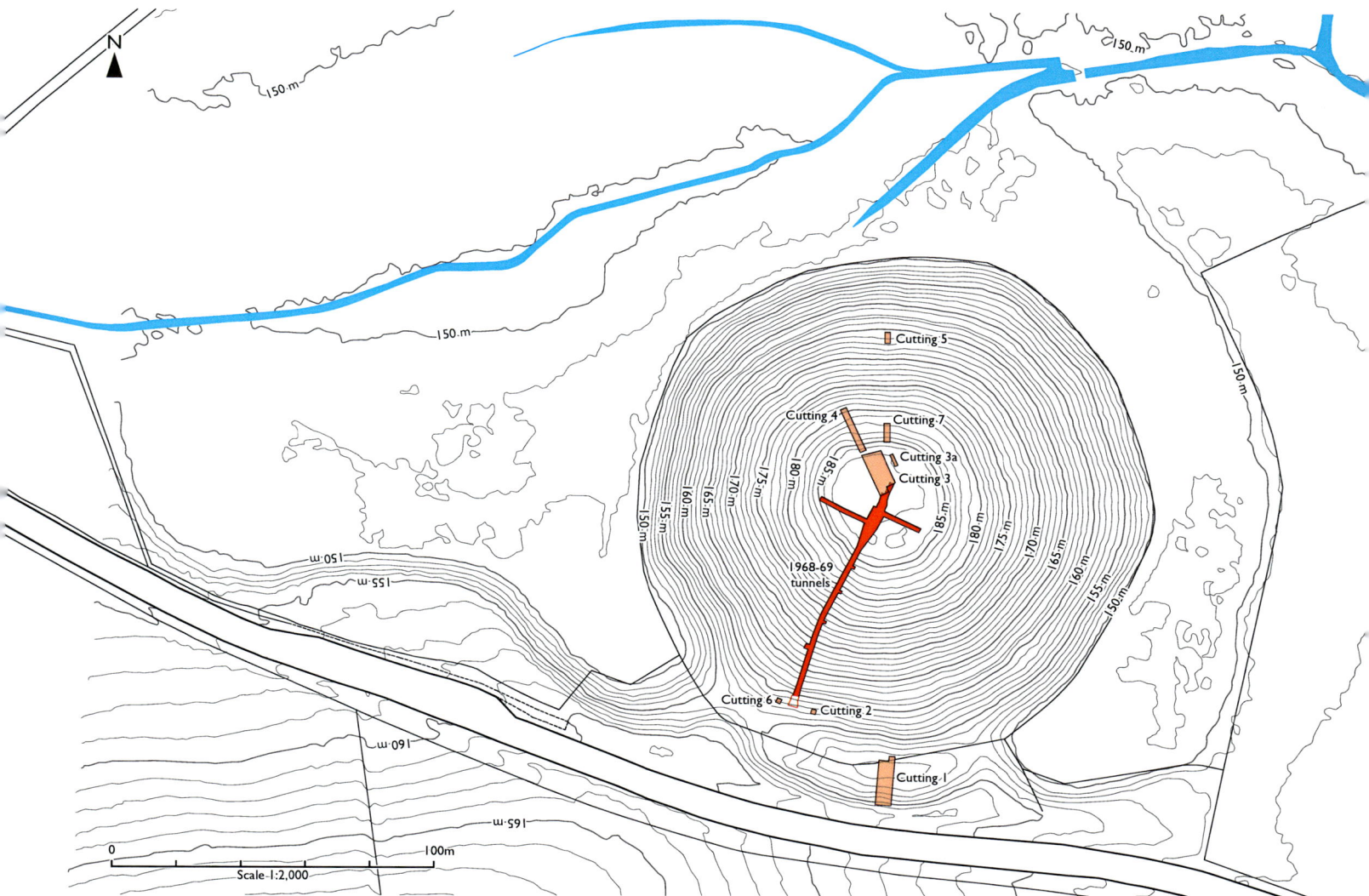

Summary of Atkinson's interpretation

Jim Leary and David Field

Richard Atkinson published five accounts of his excavations at Silbury Hill: three academic summaries, all of just a few hundred words long (1968a; 1969a; 1970), and two slightly longer popular accounts: one an article in the BBC magazine *The Listener* on the 16 January 1969 (1969b), and a chapter in an edited BBC volume from the *Chronicle* documentaries (1978). In addition, he also wrote an article prior to the start of excavations setting out the proposals (1967), as well as a BBC pamphlet to go with the documentary (1968b).

Prior to the 1968 work, radiocarbon samples on 'a mixture of antler fragments from the 1867

and 1922 excavations' were submitted and returned the 'unexpectedly late' date of 800 bc ± 100 (Atkinson 1967, 262; and *see* Chapter 4). By the end of 1968 Atkinson set out his interpretation of the construction sequence of the mound based on the first season's excavations. Noting the complexity of the deposits he simplified them into four phases: 'Silbury I' is the earliest phase comprising a primary mound 36.5m in diameter and 5.5m high: 'At its base there is a layer of gravel, capped by a heap of turf and soil revetted by a stake circle. Above this are four layers of mixed gravel, chalk and soil, each about 0.5m (20in) in thickness and each of horizontally banded construction, the result of tipping individual basket-loads of material in a controlled manner.' (Atkinson 1968a, 299). He noted well-preserved organic material within

Fig 1.11
Plan of the 1968–70 tunnels and surface excavations shown against the 1968 contour plan derived from aerial photogrammetry.
(Eddie Lyons,
© English Heritage)

Fig 1.12
The summit of Silbury Hill
in 1968, taken from
a pre-excavation field
drawing in the Atkinson
archive with the locations
of the 1970 trenches added.
(Courtesy Alexander Keiller
Museum, Avebury;
redrawn by Eddie Lyons,
© English Heritage)

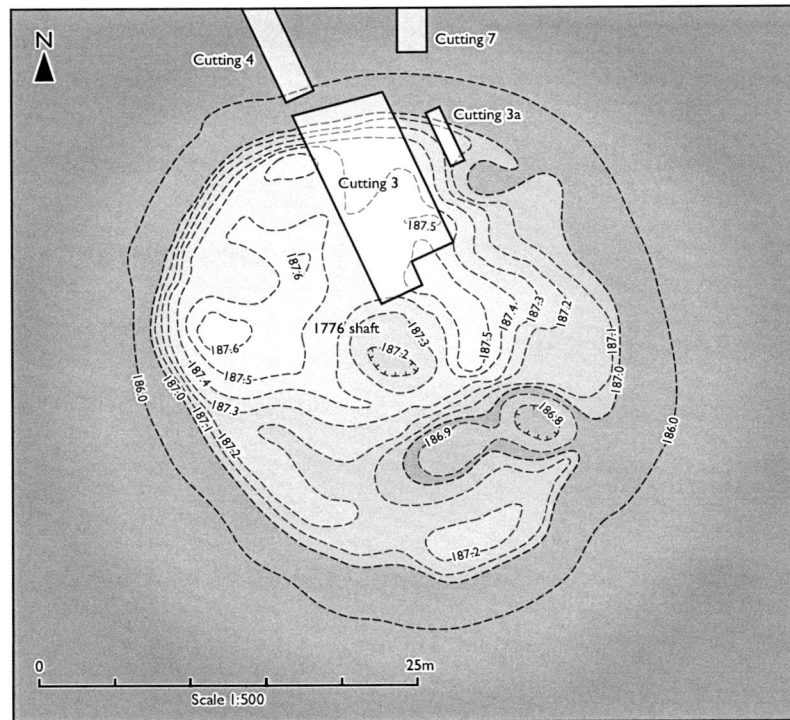

the primary mound. This was then rapidly followed by 'Silbury II', a larger mound of chalk 73 metres in diameter encompassing the earlier primary mound, and quarried from a surrounding concentric ditch. Atkinson noted that the ditch was 'deliberately re-filled before excavation was complete' (Atkinson 1968a, 299). In turn this became buried under a much larger mound of chalk 'Silbury III', the chalk for which was derived from the external ditch. This reached to the present flat summit where three concentric rubble walls hinted at internal construction methods (*see* Fig 2.30 in Chapter 2). In a final phase, 'Silbury IV', he considered that the terraces would have been filled in to provide a smooth surface in the manner of the pyramids in Egypt, and the ditch extension excavated. He presumed that the work was unfinished, particularly towards the summit, accounting for the terraces visible today. In May 1969 a radiocarbon date of 4095 ± 95BP (I-4316) was produced from 'fragments of hazel, with a small quantity of the stems and roots of other plants, all derived from the surfaces of individual turves stacked at the centre, and forming the core of the primary mound' (Atkinson 1969a, 216).

He updated the story with the results of the second and third season in 1970, in which he confirmed the previous phasing and described the trench (Cutting 1) over the external ditch. The ditch was recorded as 27 metres wide and nearly 10 metres deep with horizontal layers of chalk rubble piled against the inside edge, thought to 'have been to protect the chalk side of the ditch from weathering by frost, which would otherwise in a few years have undermined the edge of the mound and caused a series of landslides' (Atkinson 1970, 314). A hammer seismograph survey across the northern ditch provided echo soundings of its buried profile (Fig 1.13).

The report also described the two trenches (Cuttings 4 and 7) across the upper terraces on the north side of the mound, which, despite the evidence for Saxon or Norman activity, were initially interpreted as original Neolithic features. Later, however, Atkinson concluded that they had been re-cut as a response to the Danish invasions (Atkinson 1978; *see* Chapter 9), then having encountered a third terrace further down the northern slope (Cutting 5) appears to have developed a firmer view: 'This appeared to have been formed, like other similar terraces higher up the mound, in late Saxon times, possibly for defensive purposes' (Wiltshire Record Office 3293/1). Pottery of late Saxon or Norman fabric was again found (Atkinson 1970,

314; Whittle 1997a, 22), but excavation here was considered incomplete as Atkinson had evidently encountered what he described as a ditch below the terrace 'of which it was possible to excavate only the inner edge'. He wished to extend the trench to investigate this (Wiltshire Record Office 3293/1) but there is no evidence that he did so. It may be that this was the 'northern anomaly' discovered by the seismic tomography (*see* Chapter 10).

Summary of Whittle's phases

Jim Leary and David Field

In 1997 Alasdair Whittle published the material from the excavations that had survived up to Atkinson's death in 1994 (Whittle 1997a). Using the evidence from notebooks, photographs and particularly the available section drawings from the tunnel in the Alexander Keiller Museum archives, he re-interpreted the evidence, providing a somewhat more nuanced understanding of the developmental sequence. Eleven distinct phases were identified: a) central gravel mound; b) turf stack edged by stakeholes and perhaps small sarsen stones; c) four alternating capping layers over the turf stack; d) a dump of chalk and clay; e) chalk rubble dump; f) another chalk and clay dump; g) further chalk rubble dumps; h) again chalk and clay dump; j) chalk rubble; k) infilling of buried ditch; and l) outer chalk layers (Whittle 1997a, 25). Whittle was less certain of the buried ditch, suggesting that it could equally be an irregular quarry, and also suggested that the upper terraces were more likely to be later alterations than original features.

Survey of the earthworks

David Field

An analytical survey of the earthworks was carried out in 2001 by the English Heritage Archaeological Investigation team in order to record and attempt to understand the undulations visible on and around the Hill in advance of the Conservation Project. In addition to features of an archaeological nature, this confirmed that material situated above the tunnel cut in 1849/1968 was collapsing and manifested itself on the surface of the southern slope as a linear depression some 7 metres wide and up to one metre deep. A slight shadow is visible here on aerial photographs of 1933 (NMR SU 1068/53) and 1956 (NMR SU 1068/45). The surface depression is insignificantly depicted on the 1968 aerial photography or photogrammetric 0.5m interval contour plan prepared by Keith Atkinson, though when John Taylor, Richard Atkinson's mining engineer re-entered the 1849 tunnel, it was then clear that a considerable portion of the roof had collapsed and the cavity was migrating upwards (see, for example, Whittle 1997a, fig 6), and by 1997 the linear depression was visible on the slope, as noted by Whittle (*ibid*, 8).

In profile the mound appears a little lop-sided, the west and north-western slope appearing to bow out. This can readily be observed in photographs, including that on the cover of Whittle's (1997a) report. The other sides comprise a steep but steady incline and the mound tapers, achieving various angles according to position on the slopes, towards its flat summit.

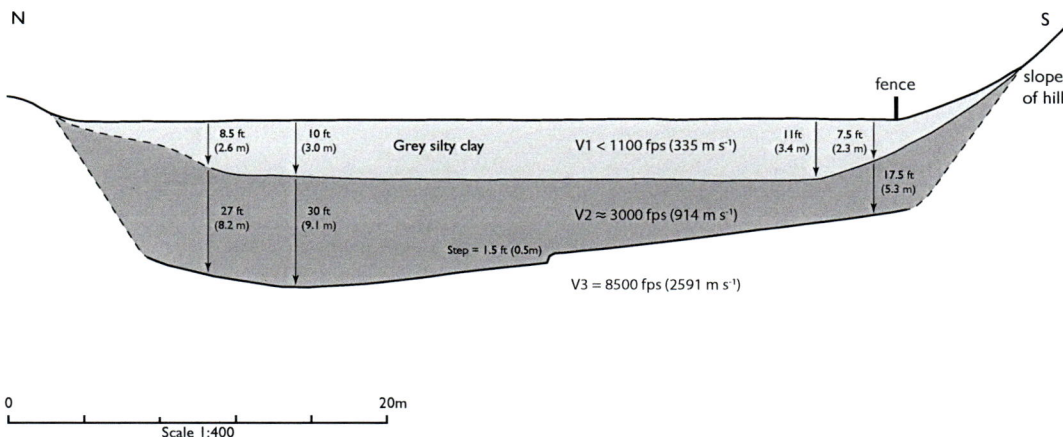

Fig 1.13
Profile of the ditch to the north of the mound taken from echo-sounding data obtained in 1968–70. (Redrawn by Eddie Lyons, © English Heritage, detail in Alexander Keiller Museum)

Fig 1.14
*Survey data obtained in
2001 plotted as 0.5m
spaced contours. Certain
irregularities can be
identified such as the
platforms on the northern,
north-eastern and south-
eastern slopes. The concave
part of the Hill in the south-
west stands out but this
forms one segment of eight
other more subtle straight
lengths that have been
highlighted in the
illustration. A west to east
profile has been added
below. Scale: 1:1250
(Eddie Lyons,
© English Heritage)*

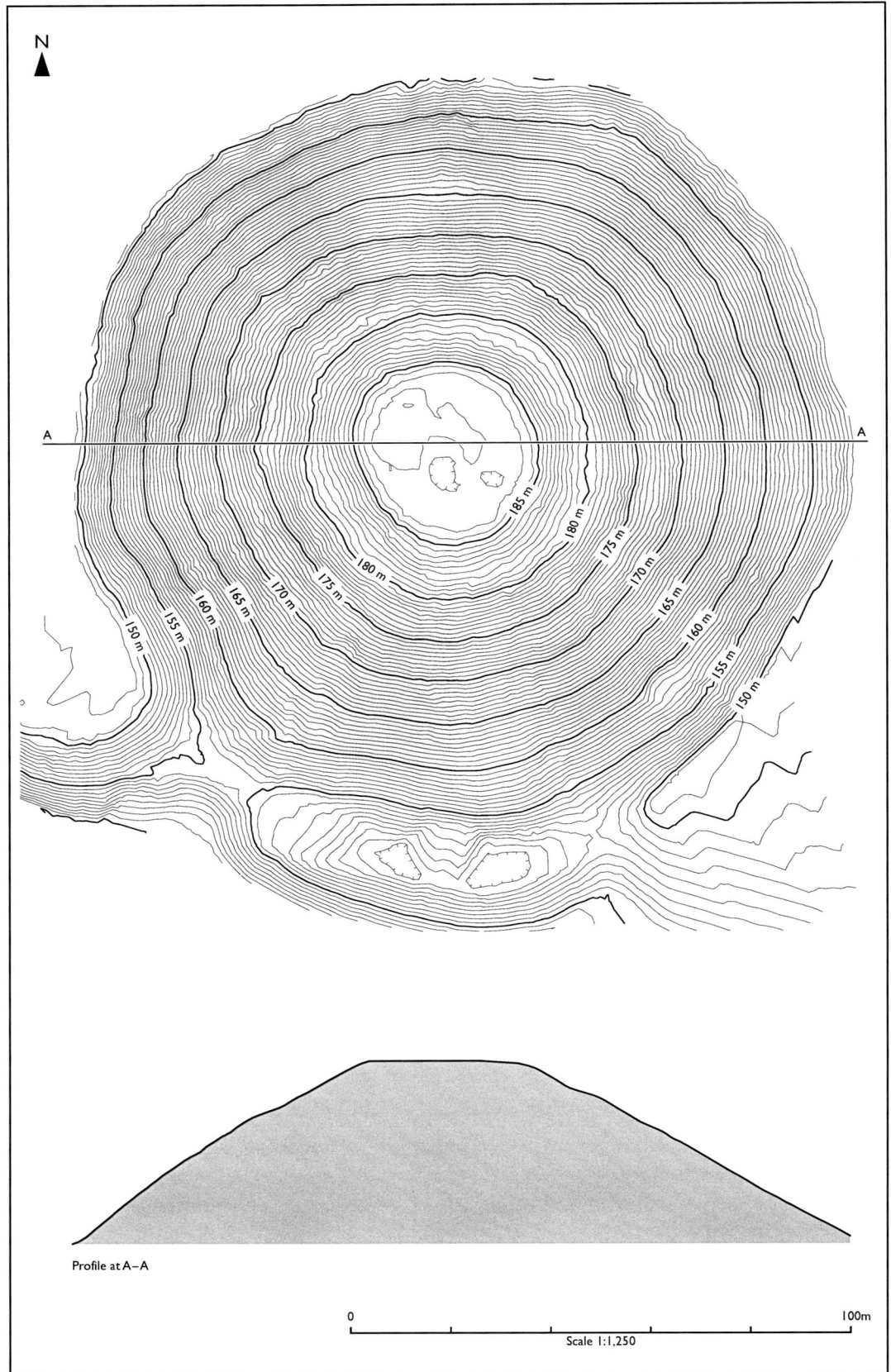

Profile at A–A

0   100m

Scale 1:1,250

Fig 1.15
Aerial photo taken at the
time of the 1968 excavations
showing the angularity of
the summit of the Hill
(NMR SU1068/20
NMR 78/51).
(© English Heritage)

Whilst not capturing subtle detail, the contour plot (Fig 1.14) helps illustrate the changing angles of slope and reveals that in plan the mound is not circular. It can be noted that the contours are spread slightly further apart in the north-east and south-west providing a kind of axis to the monument. Perhaps this related to a solar alignment, but it may simply be that it reflects the prevailing direction of the natural chalk spur. In addition, rather than forming a circle, the contours comprise a series of straight lengths or edges which, if seen on a bank or ditch, might be taken as evidence of gang working. On the steep slopes, however, it is difficult to interpret construction as taking place in this manner. It might imply some co-ordination and appears as though construction was influenced by a series of horizontal sections, braced by radial spines or spokes in a similar manner to a spider's web; some of these 'spines' can be isolated and identified at points where the contours collectively project and disrupt the general curvature. The number of straight sides is not absolutely clear, as much of the surface is now masked by weathering and erosion, but it could be as many as nine at the base, and it

is conceivable that the form changes slightly as it attains higher levels. Towards the summit it appears even more angular; on the penultimate ledge for example, an almost right-angled change in direction can be observed, while the summit itself appears to be sub-square, measuring 36m by 32m, rather than circular. This angularity can clearly be seen on an aerial photograph taken in 1968 (Fig 1.15).

There is one exception to this overall plan. In the south-west, immediately above the terminal of the external quarry ditch, the circumference appears to be concave rather than convex; the profile is more hollowed and the angle of slope steeper. This can be seen on both the 2001 survey and Atkinson's 1968 photogrammetric contour plans (Field 2002; *see also* Fig 1.11). This is difficult to explain, but perhaps the most obvious occurrence producing such a feature would be as a result of collapse of part of the mound. Today there is no further evidence revealed on the plan to support such an explanation (no rubble at the foot of the mound, for example). However, work by Pass in the ditch at this point revealed great amounts of chalk rubble together with sarsen boulders (Pass 1887,

N
▲

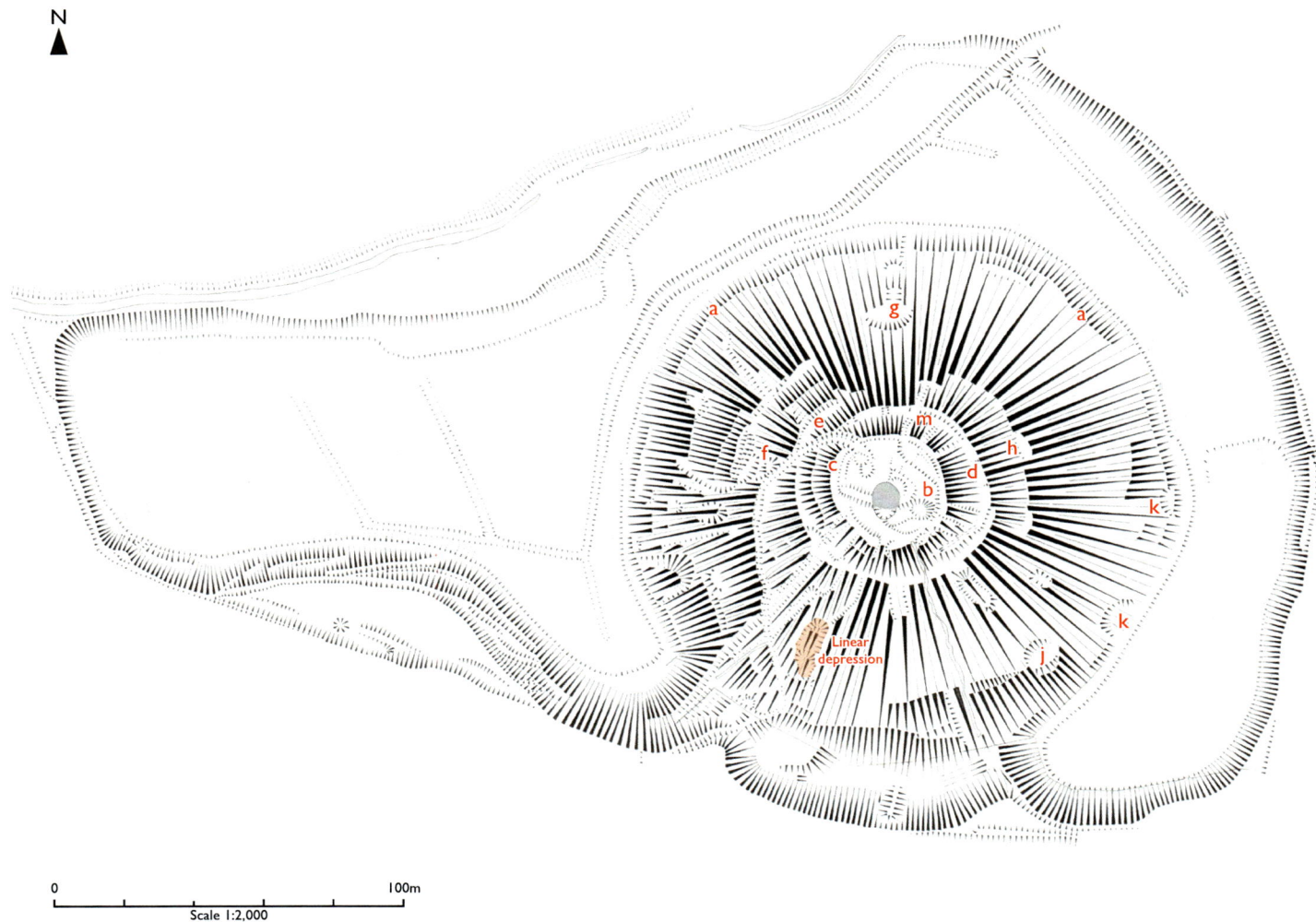

0 ├─┼─┼─┼─┼─┤ 100m
Scale 1:2,000

Fig 1.16
Survey of Silbury Hill
reduced from field drawing
at 1:500 with slopes
depicted by hachures to
illustrate relationship of
archaeological features.
See text for details.
(Deborah Cunliffe
and Eddie Lyons,
© English Heritage)

248). Merewether, Petrie and Atkinson all mention the presence of sarsen within the structure of the mound, and this is confirmed by the recent work (*see* Chapters 2 and 3), and it may be that the boulders mentioned by Pass represent the residue of a pile of collapsed material: the chalk matrix being diluted, washed and dispersed in solution before being re-deposited.

A break of slope several metres above the present ditch floor almost certainly marks the Old Land Surface (henceforth OLS) and therefore the base of the mound (a on Fig 1.16). Below this the angle of slope invariably steepens, but it marks the inner edge of the ditch rather than the lower levels of the mound. Although it is difficult to be precise, because continuity of line cannot be traced, the diameter of the mound at this level is generally about 150 metres, and even when taking weathering into account, the diameter of the original final mound must have been of this order.

The height similarly differs depending on whether it is measured from the position of the OLS where visible, and if so where, or from the present base of the ditch, *ie* the current fence line some metres below. True height at the centre of the mound, estimated as likely to be over 30 metres, was confirmed by the borehole readings from the summit as a little under 31 metres (Skanska 2001a). Taken vertically from around the perimeter it differs according to the fall of the natural ground surface and is estimated from the earthworks to be 32 metres in the north and some 34 metres in the east.

Visible archaeological features on the summit are restricted by the disturbance of the central collapsed area and the trenches cut in 1968–70. The earthworks, some quite substantial, are difficult to interpret mainly because of uncertainty over the effects of the known excavation activity and post-medieval or recent events, such as the fairs recorded in 1736 and 1747 (Field 2002), or the tree planting noted by Stukeley in 1723. Drax (*see* below) noted that there was considerable disturbance as a result of the tree planting, and tree disturbance was recorded in the 2007 excavations and during the recording of the crater deposits between December 2000 and August 2001 (McAvoy 2005a, fig A32; *see also* Chapter 9). None of these events or earthworks, however, appears to reflect the curving lines of chalk recorded in the 1968–70 excavations on the summit. Fortunately a contour plot of the summit exists among the 1968–70 archives that was plotted at intervals sufficiently close to depict earthworks (Fig 1.12). This can be compared with the modern plan. A few earthworks survive on the summit, some to over 0.5m in height. On the east side of the summit, situated between remnants of the 1776 shaft spoil heap and what may be a tree-planting ring, is a circular pit-like depression (b on Fig 1.16), some 7 metres in diameter and measuring over 0.5m in depth, of unknown function. A hollowed gully, almost an entranceway, leads into this from the west. There is no spoil bank visible around it, though such may lie beneath the other neighbouring features. It is visible on an aerial photograph taken on 8 April 1956 (SU 1068/45), so precedes the work undertaken in 1968–70, but could be the result of the tree planting episode. Certainly post-medieval disturbance and pitting was recorded during the 2007 excavation on the summit and interpreted as evidence for this episode (Chapter 2). In addition, shallow traces of an enclosing earthwork around the lip of the summit (c on Fig 1.16) were thought to potentially mark a former tree bank (Chapter 9).

At various points around the slopes are traces of horizontal terraces, platforms or breaks of slope thought by Atkinson to be remnants of his proposed ziggurat-like tiered construction. The uppermost of these ledges (d on Fig 1.16),

a maximum of 2.5m wide on the surface, lies just 4 metres below the summit. It is better seen on the north and east and barely perceptible in the south and south-west, perhaps because it had been better infilled in that quadrant or, because the prevailing wind from this direction, has resulted in greater weathering and erosion. A second ledge or terrace can be traced at c 10 metres below the summit (e on Fig 1.16), while stretches of breaks of slope that might account for others lie at 15, 19 and 27 metres below the summit (depicted by breaks in hachures). If perambulated, the upper ledge, in fact, finishes the circuit at a position below the starting point and implies a spiral arrangement. It is unclear whether this is as a result of the Neolithic construction, or of later redevelopment, but it suggests that the model of tiered construction may need to be modified and that the 'terracing' could have formed a spiral ascent of the Hill. A spiral would allow easy access and material could be relatively easily carried or dragged up to the working level; indeed the massive Belgian memorial mound at Waterloo was constructed by means of a spiral track (Rickman 1840, 403).

As a finished monument a spiral arrangement would provide the perfect processional way and of course the preoccupation with spirals in Neolithic art will not escape attention. The point equally applies if the terraces are not in fact of Neolithic date. If indeed a spiral, it is arranged clockwise from the top downwards: one would ascend anti-clockwise. Further, it is possible that, as occasionally is the case on garden mounts, other paths may take shortcuts or interrupt the flow. There is no indication that the spiral continues from the first terrace to the top of the mound, but in the south-east, a ramp, 2 metres wide, leads prominently from the upper ledge almost to the summit. Again whether this is a Neolithic feature is unclear.

Other more platform-like features are situated around the mound, both on the slopes and close to the original ground level, but remain undated. In the west are two 2m wide sub-rectangular platforms (f on Fig 1.16) that stretch for 12 metres, which are of unknown purpose but could have held structures and since they are cut by the present path, an important chronological feature as it appears to be in the same position as that depicted in a sketch by John Aubrey around 1663 (Smith 1862; Fowles 1980), they are unlikely to be of recent date. Much of the area is depicted as irregular breaks of slope on the hachured plan and while there are a number of breaks of slope that might be construction features or collapsed terraces of the mound, the area is riddled with rabbit burrows that have sometimes have disfigured archaeological features to such an extent that interpretation, other than simply as disturbed ground, is not possible.

On the northern slope a break of angle leads to a prominent crescentic platform or stance *c* 14m by 5m (g on Fig 1.16). This was the location of Cutting 5 during the 1968–70 intervention, which, like excavations on the other terraces, produced material apparently of late Saxon date (*see* Chapter 9). A trench-like scar leads downhill from this to an apron, potentially the site of the 'northern anomaly' where a further scar on the same axis appears to cut the OLS. It is conceivable that this marks the position of a trial trench cut by Blandford and Falkner prior to their work in 1849, for they evidently carried out some preliminary work at this level recording that 'some spots on different sides were opened, to ascertain the respective levels of the natural and artificial soil' (Tucker 1851, 299).

A similar crescentic platform is situated high on the north-east slope (h on Fig 1.16) and a further prominent example in the south-east (j on Fig 1.16) (Field 2002). This measures 10m by 5m and lies above a considerable apron. Some metres above it, lying just below the uppermost 'terrace' and on the same axis is a considerable scar, 13m in length by 5m wide and over 0.5m deep with the hint of a bank to one side. This may represent excavation trenching, and it is worth bearing in mind the unknown location of the trench mentioned by 'Archaeophilus' in 1850 (*above* and Edwards 2010b, 324–5).

Other similar features are situated at original ground level. In the east a small ledge 9m by 4m and little south of this a further crescentic cut some 12m by 6m (k on Fig 1.16) may represent the trench cut by the Wiltshire Archaeological Society to investigate whether the course of the Roman road extended beneath the mound, though there is some uncertainty concerning the exact location of this and it is conceivable that the platform in the south-east noted above is the location (j on Fig 1.16).

A number of linear features ascending the mound were recorded. Two of these, each 1.5m in width, are situated on the upper north and north-western slopes (m on Fig 1.16, although not visible on this hachure plan – *see* Fig 0.2 for cutting locations) between the two uppermost ledges and mark the position of Atkinson's backfilled excavation trenches formerly only known from photographs. The westernmost of these (Cutting 4), 17 metres in length, was placed from the summit, across the uppermost ledge and down to a break in slope that almost certainly marks the position of a further ledge. The second (Cutting 7), at 7 metres in length, investigated the area between the summit and the uppermost ledge.

The present pathway to the summit, eroded and hollowed in places, curves around the western slopes, starting opposite the south-western causeway and ascending to the vicinity of the tunnel entrance, then gradually ascending northwards and finally approaches the summit from the north-west. It is easy to assume that this is a feature of recent visitor wear erosion, but the route of the path is visible on early illustrations and, as mentioned above, dates from at least 1663.

Entrances

Stukeley (1743, 43) considered that the causeways across the ditch in the south provided access, leaving '... two bridges, as it were, or passages up to the hill'. The causeways themselves are misnomers, for they do not provide direct access across the ditch from original land surface to original land surface, but are themselves cut down to a depth of around 3 metres and would each need an enormous bridge were they to be used in this way. Others have suggested that the ditch in the south was unfinished and that it was subsequently intended to remove the causeways (Petrie 1924, 217).

No entrances to the interior of the monument are known. The south-east platform mentioned above is situated close to the OLS at a point where one might predict a monument of this period to have a chamber or passage. In recent times, discussion about an entrance has been ignored as it has been felt that since there is no central chamber an entrance can effectively be ruled out. Petrie was looking for an original entrance and given that it is not unknown for broadly contemporary monuments such as Bryn Celli Ddu in North Wales (Anon 2006) or Newgrange in Ireland (O'Kelly 1982) to have solar aligned entrances, it may be that an entry still remains to be discovered. At Silbury, there is disturbance in the form of crescentic platforms on the surface of the mound in both the north-east and south-east which could indicate earlier digging, although one should not rule out slumping associated with buried features or voids.

Sarsens and peristalith

No sign of a sarsen peristalith is currently visible, despite being recorded as present around the base of the mound in the past. Merewether (1851a, 74) noted stones around the base (as distinct from those that he mentioned within the mound) as did Petrie (1924, 215–16). At face value the identification of a peristalith appears a little unlikely as it is improbable that stones placed around the original land surface during the Neolithic period would remain in position on such a slope after four thousand years and particularly after remodelling in the early medieval period. The Revd A C Smith, a prominent and active member of the, then recently formed, Wiltshire Archaeological and Natural History Society wrote that there were none in 1862 (Smith 1862, 158n) as did Atkinson during the 1960s (WHC MSS RSIL930, Atkinson 1967). Several large boulders were recorded in the ditch during the 2001 earthwork survey and others were noted on the outer lip of the ditch nearby, presumably as a product of more recent agricultural activity around the mound. Small fragments of burnt sarsen were also noted along the southern edge of the site as if a process of breaking up boulders had taken place. A number of sarsen boulders were also noted to the south of the A4 where they have probably been dragged to the surface as a result of road or pipeline digging. A small standing stone situated 16 metres north of the Silbury ditch marks the canalised line of the Beckhampton Brook, while a series of split sarsens have been utilised as a sluice for the Beckhampton Brook to the north-east of the mound.

Significant numbers of boulders can still be seen in the banks of the Kennet. One might expect that the meadows around the monument once contained natural accumulations of sarsen that, as elsewhere on the Marlborough Downs, have long since been cleared for agriculture. This process of clearance may have begun early in the Neolithic, with the collecting of boulders to form the core of the West Kennet long barrow and to construct the chambers at its east end (Piggott 1962). Sarsen is quite common in local

field boundaries and the valley floor here was probably once littered with it. It is to be expected that this material might have been utilised for construction purposes although whether a circle once stood around the mound will now be almost impossible to demonstrate.

The external ditch

Situated on a declining spur, part of the mound was placed at a slight angle and camber and if horizontal construction layers were intended, more material would consequently need to be placed on the north side of the mound than the south as well as in the west and east respectively (*see* Chapter 2 for detail of the sequence). In the south and east, the sides of the ditch are steeply cut compared to the north, where the outer edge of the visible ditch is quite shallow, resulting in a broad flat bottom up to 43 metres across. Taken at the level of the original ground surface the ditch is between 38 and 53 metres in width.

The portion of the ditch adjacent to the modern highway situated between the 'causeways' is, as seen and surveyed, slightly different in character from the rest. For one thing, its width at 30 metres is considerably narrower than elsewhere. According to Atkinson's section drawing (Whittle 1997a, fig 23) its ultimate floor is more than 4.5m below the present silted level with a flat bottom 13 metres wide. Whittle pointed out, however, that during Atkinson's excavations in the south, neither the floor nor the edge of the ditch were encountered and the true lip of the ditch must therefore lie beneath the present road. In this scenario the causeways would be even more pronounced. As noted above they are not true causeways for they have been cut below the OLS by around 3 metres. Accounting for this is difficult, but the explanation preferred here is that they represent a relict trace of a former ditch cut that elsewhere has been destroyed as the ditch was deepened and widened.

In the north the ditch appears extremely broad and shallow, although Atkinson's echo sounding here hinted at the true profile and this together with data from the excavations by Pass provide an approximation of its outline (Fig 1.13).

In the west, the ditch appears to have been considerably extended and excavated into a broad rectilinear area, some 85 metres wide and 165 metres long, cut neatly in the direction of the Beckhampton Brook and marked in the

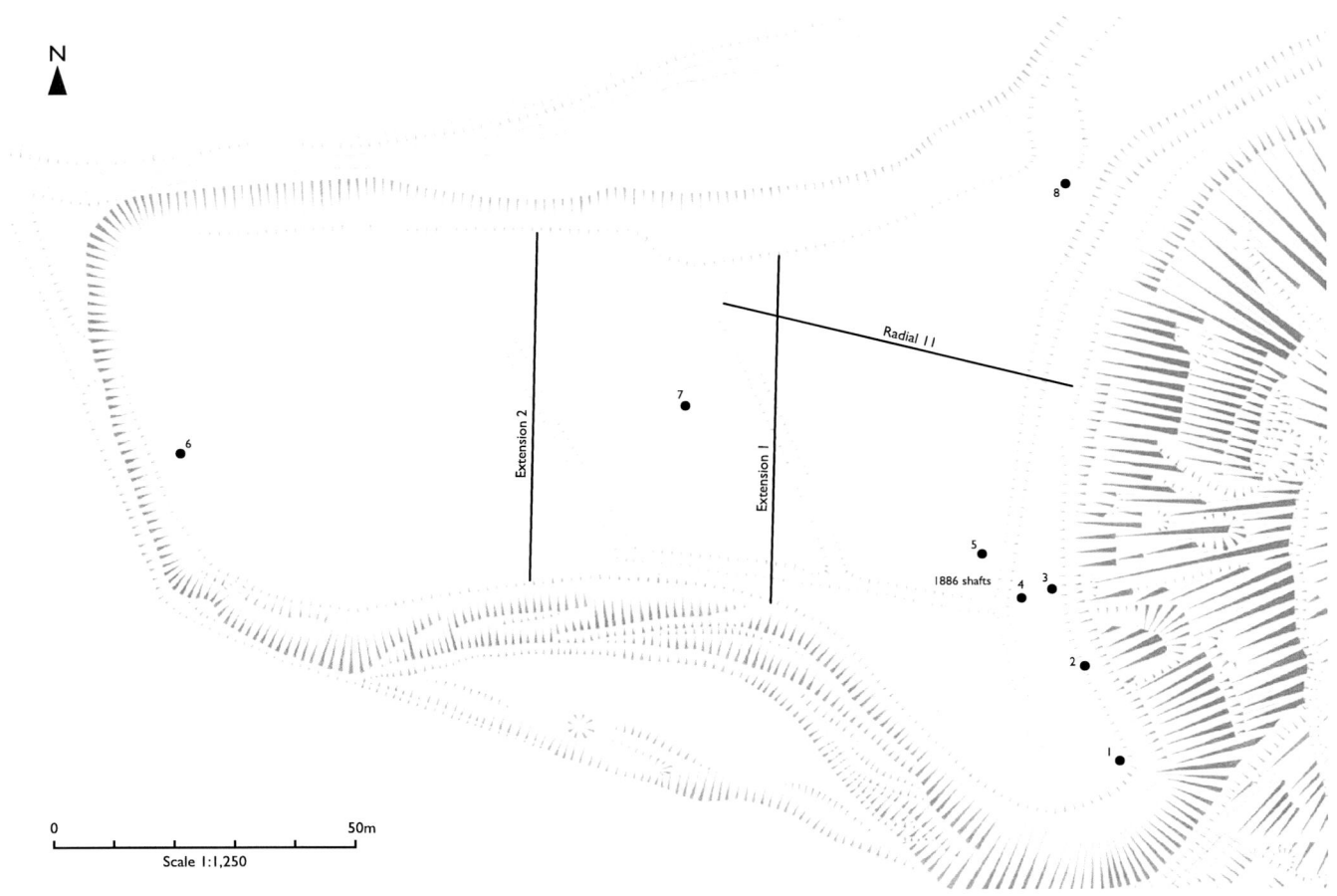

N

0 ————————— 50m
Scale 1:1,250

Radial 11

Extension 2

Extension 1

1886 shafts

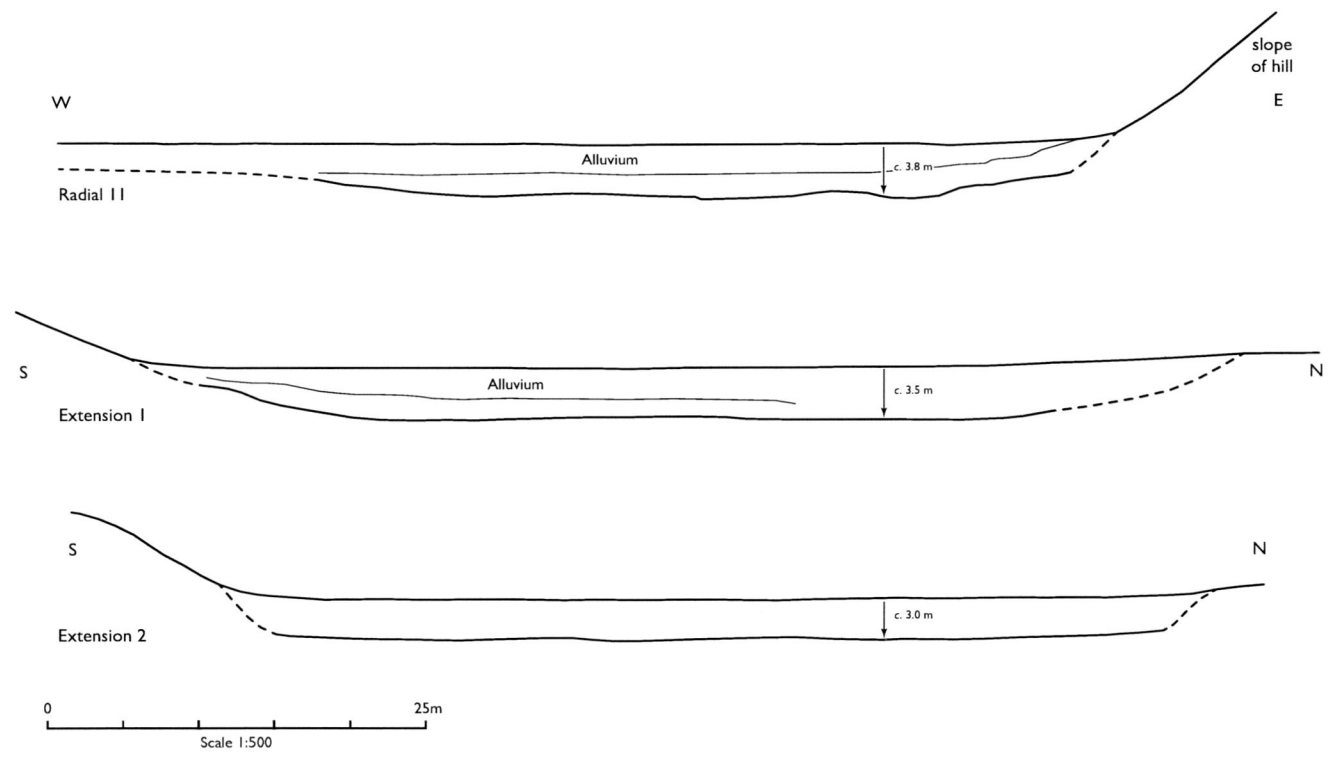

slope
of hill

W   E

Alluvium   c. 3.8 m

Radial 11

S   N

Alluvium   c. 3.5 m

Extension 1

S   N

c. 3.0 m

Extension 2

0 ————————— 25m
Scale 1:500

south by a steep quarry face 6 metres deep to its present floor, while its northern face closer to the stream is a mere one metre deep. Its true depth, however, was established by Pass (1887 above) and together with recent geophysics its profile has been modelled (Fig 1.17). The feature is usually referred to as the ditch extension but when wet it forms a reservoir and since it appears to have been designed to deliberately collect issue from the stream, additionally that the sondages sank in this area in 1887 revealed white clay that had been deposited by water, it is referred to below as a 'basin'. There is some indication from the work of both Pass and Atkinson that the ditch is deeper closer to the mound, but elsewhere, in particular towards the outer edges of the ditch and in the basin, it is assumed that the initial slope evens off to a flat floor.

There is one small hint that further cuts were made into the floor of the basin: a linear vegetation mark is difficult to account for. For just three days in early summer 2001 as the water-filled ditch dried out, a huge vegetation mark, some 10 metres wide and indicative of a substantial subsurface feature appeared to extend across the basin floor for some 50 metres towards the mound (Fig 1.18). An aerial photograph (NMR SU 1068/232) shows part of the mark and another (NMR SU 1068/158 and 161, taken on 3 January 1995) depicts the possible line of it. It is conceivable that post-

medieval ditches on the surface might have influenced the pattern of drainage here, but within this part of the ditch they are on a completely different alignment to the vegetation mark. Assuming that it marks a genuine sub-surface structure the darker vegetation suggests that a massive negative feature is present below the modern surface. Its orientation, however, is curious, running diagonally across the basin leading towards a position that is off-centre of the mound. It may be that a deeper channel, collecting from local springs, carried run off together with that of the proto-Beckhampton Brook to the deeper ditch around the mound and indeed that this provided a catalyst for the ditch extension. Additionally, such an arrangement would provide a sump to allow water-free excavation of the remainder of the basin.

Airborne remote sensing

Martyn Barber

Aerial photographs covering the Avebury World Heritage Site (WHS) and its environs were examined prior to the shaft collapse in 1997–8 as part of England's National Mapping Programme (NMP). Both before, and subsequently, several smaller-scale interpretative mapping projects were undertaken, usually focused on particular sites – for instance new discoveries recognised in the course of annual photographic reconnaissance (see, for example, Bewley *et al*

Fig 1.17 (opposite)
The ditch extension or basin to the west of the mound with the position of trenches sunk by Pass and the positions of geophysical survey transects across the ditch (above); profiles across the ditch extension based on the geophysical transects (below). Based on reduced 1:500 plan.
(Eddie Lyons,
© English Heritage)

Fig 1.18
The vegetation mark in the ditch.
(David Field,
© English Heritage)

2005; Corney 1997a; Barber *et al* 2003), or particular areas, for example to assist with the analysis of particular blocks of landscape (for example Fowler 2000a). More recently, in 2011 the NMP mapping has been enhanced by the addition of detail from post-1998 reconnaissance photographs and from the analysis of airborne lidar (light detection and ranging) data.

The mapped area comprised some 225 sq km, containing not just the village of Avebury and the WHS itself, but also extending as far as the Marlborough Downs, a small part of the Avon Vale, and the edge of the Pewsey Vale (*see* Foldout 1E). This provides some wider context although here, of course, we are concerned primarily with the immediate environs of Silbury Hill.

Probably the most important development in recent years is lidar. This differs considerably from aerial photographic survey in many key respects. It is not a photographic technology, although it is often presented as though it were – as if the results gained using lidar were directly comparable to, and an improvement on, those gained from airborne cameras (Bewley *et al* 2005).

The main features recorded with lidar around Silbury, apart from the mound itself, seem to be broadly of post-medieval or modern date, although some may have slightly earlier origins. They relate primarily to agriculture and drainage or water management. Further comments relating to aerial survey are covered in Panel 8.1 in Chapter 8, as well as Chapters 9 and 10.

Topographic difference modelling

Tom Cromwell
When the hole opened up within the 1776 shaft on the top of the Hill in May 2000 it came as some surprise to a generation which had largely forgotten about the shaft's existence. Suggestions by local residents that the mound had changed shape recently resulted in a concern that the entire mound might be unstable. To assess the possibility of movement it was considered necessary to compare a model of the Hill in its current form with a model of it from the past. A digital terrain model based on over 10,000 survey points of the mound surface was produced but finding accurate mapping with which to compare the modern survey was difficult.

The most useful data were the overlapping run of aerial photographs commissioned by the Royal Commission on the Historical Monuments of England (RCHME) in 1968 that could be used as stereo-pairs and were used to prepare a photogrammetric plan for the 1968–70 work. Accordingly, the English Heritage Photogrammetric Unit prepared a terrain model to compare with the data from the new analytical ground survey. Armed with these two models, based on data separated by 30 years, it was possible to compare the two 3D iterations, which were searched for any anomalies that had appeared or which suggested a change in the shape of the Hill. The scale of the two surveys meant that this only highlighted relatively large-scale changes, but enough to confirm that the mound was not actively slumping. Following analysis it became clear that, barring the newly revealed shaft, the Hill was not noticeably different from its appearance in 1968 and appeared to retain its structural integrity.

Topography and geology

Matt Canti and David Field
Silbury Hill lies close to the source of the River Kennet at a point where several springs augment the volume of the stream (Fig 1.19). As a winterbourne carrying a seasonal flow, the Kennet headwaters can be traced 8.5km north to Broad Hinton, or a little beyond, and the river incorporates a number of small winterbourne tributaries as it flows south through Winterbourne Bassett, Berwick Bassett and Winterbourne Monkton, ensuring almost permanent flow as it passes through Avebury. At Silbury, it gathers momentum as it is joined by a small winterbourne that rises in the Beckhampton–Devizes valley and passes immediately north of Silbury Hill flooding the ditch surrounding the monument every winter. Immediately south of the mound, a spring referred to as the Swallowhead, is located at the mouth of a narrow steep-sided, but now dry, coombe and together with the north-flowing drainage pattern on the dip slope it has influenced the dramatic change of course eastwards through West and East Kennett, Overton, Lockeridge and other villages towards Marlborough.

The course of the Winterbourne appears to have been straightened where it flows close to the base of Waden Hill, potentially as a result of water meadow construction in the 18th century. Earthwork survey (*see* Panel 9.3 in Chapter 9) indicates that former water courses can be traced on the valley floor to the east of Silbury Hill and that the stream formerly ran a little closer to the mound. South of the A4, influenced by the promontory-like spur of Waden Hill, the Kennet's course veers south-west, until it turns a sharp angle at the Swallowhead Spring to move east towards West Kennett. Similarly the course of the Beckhampton Brook may have shifted: its natural course, the lowest part of the valley, lies some 20 metres north of the Silbury ditch, after which it is channelled towards the Kennet.

Today the Swallowhead Spring, invariably bedecked with modern offerings and sacred tokens (Cannon 2005), emerges 20 metres south of the Kennet. It issues from the base of a modern plough lynchet and it may be that this had encroached on the spring and formerly the outlet lay a little further south. At the time of survey during the present project, vegetation precluded recording of any extant features but the presence of a number of sarsen boulders was noted. These may be quite natural, but appear to have been moved to provide stepping stones across the stream.

The activity of the various fluvial elements at this confluence has eroded a natural amphitheatre into the landscape, partially enclosed by Folly Hill to the north-west, the dominant Waden Hill in the east and the Beckhampton Downs in the south. This is marked by Valley Gravel that lines the Kennet Valley and some of its tributaries (BGS Sheet 266), particularly the Beckhampton Brook, and is overlain by a strip of alluvium marking the extent of fluvial deposition through into historic times. This is particularly marked around the west and north sides of the mound. The underlying rock is easily eroded Cretaceous White Chalk (Fig 1.20) and the surrounding terrain is one of typical softly undulating downland landforms. The location of the site lies at the interface of Middle Chalk with the extensive Lower Chalk and the mound appears to occupy the lower part of a Middle Chalk spur that projects north-eastwards into the Beckhampton winterbourne valley at its confluence with the Kennet. Waden Hill to the north-east, and Thornhill Field and Beckhampton Down immediately south, fall within the Middle Chalk division, and there is a small capping of flint laden Upper Chalk at the southern end of Waden Hill. To the north-west, deposits of Middle Chalk survive on the summits of Folly Hill and Windmill Hill, though the area is essentially part of the Lower Chalk that extends northwards towards Swindon. To the south and west of the site, weathering of the Upper and Middle Chalk has resulted in a pattern of broad interfluves intercut by deep coombes of asymmetrical cross-section, the result of differential thawing, spring sapping and solifluction during periglacial conditions. Sarsen boulders occur naturally across this terrain, and substantial numbers have been, and continue to be, cleared by local farmers.

Clay-with-flints caps the Upper Chalk on the higher downland further to the east and in isolated spots to the south adjacent to the chalk escarpment. This is an enigmatic deposit, found over a large part of southern England and northern Europe. It is generally composed of solutional elements from the chalk, together with remains from previously-overlying Tertiary beds (Loveday 1962; Hodgson *et al* 1967; Catt 1986; Quesnel *et al*, 2003; Barber *et al* 1999; Geddes and Walkington 2005; Scott-Jackson 2005 and references therein).

Silbury Hill itself is built on a deposit of similar material. This is somewhat anomalous, not only in being far from the interfluve where such deposits are normally found, but also *in situ* beneath the mound and visible nowhere else at the surface (Canti 2009). Evans (1968, 14) pointed out that deposits of this material could have shifted into secondary positions as a result of solifluction, and this remains a strong possibility. However, in this part of the Kennet valley, lobes of *in situ* Clay-with-flints are sometimes mapped as coming down close to the floodplain, especially at Manton (between Silbury Hill and Marlborough), where its geomorphic position matches the Silbury spur.

Since we cannot determine whether the deposit beneath Silbury Hill is *in situ* or derived from upslope, the term 'clay-with-flints' (lower case 'c') will be used informally throughout this volume to describe the material rather than to define the geological deposit.

Conclusion

A considerable amount of data has accrued as the result of past antiquarian and archaeological interventions. It has been summarised here but the reader is referred to former accounts for

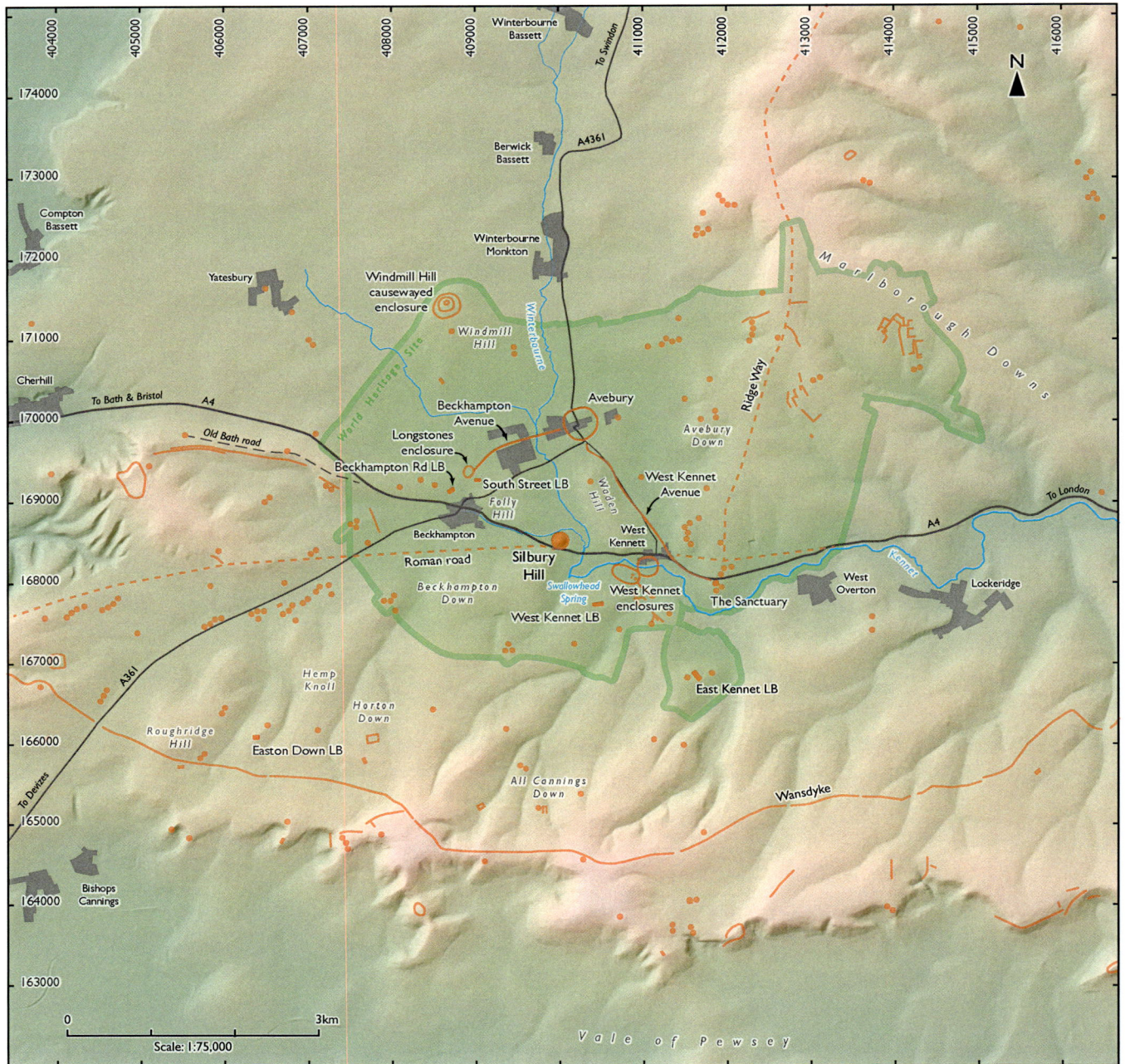

Fig 1.19
Map of local topography
showing the relationship
of local villages, the higher
downland and the World
Heritage Site boundary.
(Eddie Lyons,
© English Heritag; height
data licensed to English
Heritage for PGA, through
NextPerspectives™)

further information (Tucker 1851; Merewether 1851a; Wilkinson 1867; Petrie 1924; Atkinson 1968a; 1969a; 1969b; 1970; 1978; Whittle 1997a; Leary and Field 2010). Detail in some of the earlier accounts is supplemented by better recorded later ones and, in particular, Whittle (1997a) synthesised this and productively utilised the environmental and other data to discuss the social, regional and national role of the site. It is unfortunate that more is not known of the 1776 event, but fresh knowledge has been revealed during the course of the project as a result of intensive documentary research (Edwards 2001; 2010a and b; 2013; Field 2002; Cannon and Constantine 2004; Fielden 2013).

Historical research indicated that the 1776 shaft was unlikely to have been backfilled in its entirety, while the various surveys served to indicate that although the mound was essentially stable the possibility of hidden

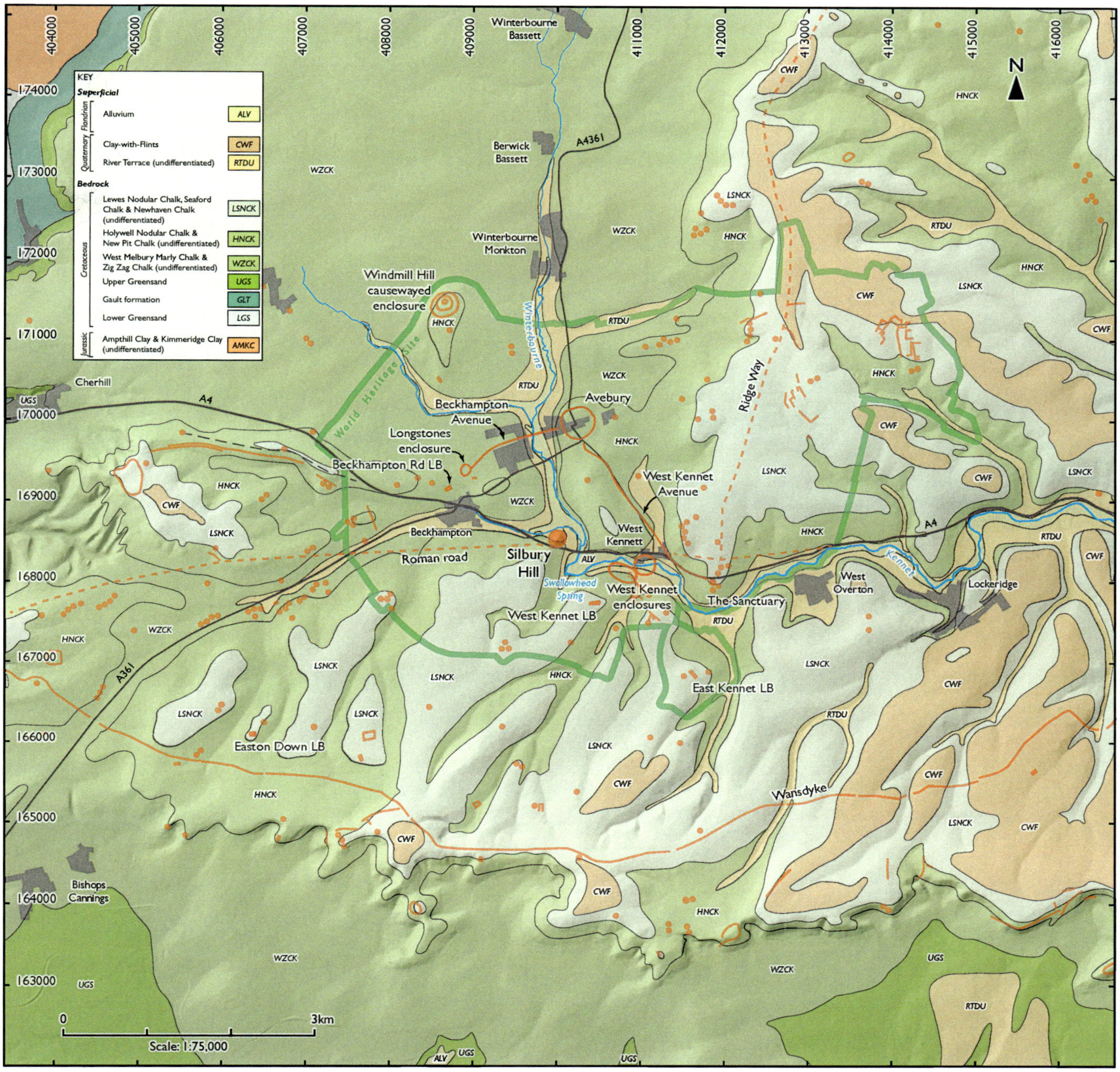

KEY

Superficial

Alluvium	ALV
Clay-with-Flints	CWF
River Terrace (undifferentiated)	RTDU

Bedrock

Lewes Nodular Chalk, Seaford Chalk & Newhaven Chalk (undifferentiated)	LSNCK
Holywell Nodular Chalk & New Pit Chalk (undifferentiated)	HNCK
West Melbury Marly Chalk & Zig Zag Chalk (undifferentiated)	WZCK
Upper Greensand	UGS
Gault formation	GLT
Lower Greensand	LGS
Ampthill Clay & Kimmeridge Clay (undifferentiated)	AMKC

Scale: 1:75,000

cavities could not be ruled out (*see* Chapter 10). A persistent anomaly remained on the northern slope and it is likely that Atkinson had encountered this in his Cutting 5. Exactly what this represents remains intriguing but one possibility is that it marks the position of one of Blandford's trenches set to establish the position of the old land surface prior to cutting the 1849 tunnel. The boreholes from the summit, initially drilled as part of the seismic tomography survey (*above* and Chapter 10), demonstrated that the tunnels cut in 1849 and 1969 had been inadequately backfilled and that voids were having a serious effect on the archaeological deposits. The effect of this could be seen on the surface and study of the earthworks revealed a surprising number of other visible features on the summit and slopes many of which are likely to represent aspects of the Hill's post-Neolithic past.

Fig 1.20
Map showing the geology of the area around Silbury Hill.
(Eddie Lyons,
© English Heritage; height data licensed to English Heritage for PGA, through NextPerspectives™)

Appendix 1.1

The Drax letters
Brian Edwards

Two letters found in the British Library from Edward Drax to George Pitt, Lord Rivers, describe part of the 1776 excavations. Further commentary can be found in Edwards (2010a). It should additionally be noted that in the second letter it appears that Drax had originally written that a cavity was reached at 82 feet, but during the course of writing he altered that figure to '95'. Drax's original estimate appears the more likely of the two, not least because the rate of excavation suggests that the greater depth would not have been reached within the timescale.

Note: To assist the reader, missing letters, punctuation and brief notes have been added in square brackets.

Bath November 4th 1776

My Dear L[or]d
On my Arrival here yesterday from Silbury Hill I found your kind favour. That my Letter Mist its way I can impute only to a gross neglect in the post office in having no one Clerk that can Decypher The Druidical Character in which mine was wrote[,] but I hope your L[or]dship['] s interest with L[or]d [le] Despencer and Mr Thynne will get that rectified, but for the future I shall direct to Hertford Street, as Hertford bridge seeming more difficult of Access then I hope Kings-Bridge will be found. Autour de [About] Silbury Hill it is my Duty to give some Account as I am at present left commandant in the absence of my Syeniors. Your liberal Hint I give your L[or]dship Credit and Thanks for; we have had 4 miners from Mendip at work there ever since Thursday sennight[.] When we had got about ten feet down, I found it was absolutely necessary to have it Timbered or the men's lives would be endangered. The first six feet I found had been moved when Trees were planted there in 1723, Some few animal Bones bits of Deers Horns &C were thrown in with the earth and a great many small snail shells[,] but they certainly came from the Surface & when the trees were planted were thrown in. As we got deeper down I found the Hill still composed of Large chalk stones as big as a man's Head thrown

in Loosely and great interstices still remained between them[.] Still as we go down we continue finding pieces of Deers Horns of a very Large size[,] in all appearance either of large Stags or else the mo[o]se Deer. At 23 foot a Large piece & at 28 feet a Large piece at 30 Feet another and nothing else as yet[.]

When I left them Saturday night we were 31 feet down and as we have by my measurement 125 feet to go before I expect to find the Deposit[,] what ever it may be[,] it will be a fortnight or perhaps 3 weeks before we get to our desired object. I have agreed with these miners at 19s p[e]r fathom for 20 fathom[,] we finding the wood[.] In digging a path to go up the Hill[,] just under the surface I found a key of a very odd and Antique make perhaps 4 or 500 years old but quite modern compared to the object of our Search. I had prepared a Barrow[,] one that I thought of the oldest make, and as it was on the Hapken [Hakpen] or Snakes Head and pointed directly to it I thought was most certainly belonging to and coeval with the Temple[,] but as I found you did not come and the men stood still for want of Timber[,] I got Through it Saturday and found it to be of the greatest antiquity made of black mold brought from the neighbouring meadow. Where the urn is usually deposited I found only a Cavity[.] The urn or vesicle in which the bones had been, being entirely consumed by the prodigious length of Time nothing remained in it but a vast heap of burnt bones[,] some Human and Some animals, many Horses Teeth entire[;] but in searching with my Hands amongst Them I found an odd im-plement of what use I cannot conceive as yet – it was Two Stones cut with exactness to fitt of an oblong square 2 Inches & a half Long[.] Another implement of Stone likewise sharpend at the End Half a foot long and Shaped with a Tool, I fancy (perhaps it is only an antiquarians Reverie) but I fancy I can make out some Characters upon it very like Hebrew or my own Handwriting; when you happen to be down I should like to open another Barrow which I think may produce some urn or other antiquity as it Lays immediately near the Sanctuary and is more perfect than the other[,] but L[or]d Pembrokes leave must be had as he is L[or]d of the mannour There. The country people wish to have it search[e]d as they say (but that is not my reason) that great lights have been seen on it in the night. Saturday I measured Silbury Hill as accurately as I could and am amazed at the ground it stands upon[,] not much less than most of the Egyptian Pyramids except the great one which I think stands on near 11 Acres. My measure agrees very well with Dr Stukelys except in the perpendicular Height Which he makes 170 feet[,] Mine but 125[,] but I believe he reckons what it was at first and allows for the Grounds settling which is visible from the west side[,] but nous verrons [we shall see] when we get down, on the whole it is vast. Dr Stukely says it contains 13,558, 809 cubic feet and would cost £20000 to raise it now but I say according to the rate of moving Earth here which they do as cheap as any where at 3^d per Cubic Yard it would cost £56495 – 0s – 9d. So much my Dear Lord for Silbury Hill till next week. I cannot take the Liberty of troubling his Grace of Northumberland with a scrawl of This kind but if your L[or]dship should happen to be sitting by him in the House [of] L[or]ds or elsewhere[,] it would be perhaps Some amusement to his Grace if you will be so kind as to Shew him the enclosed measurement and acquaint him how far we have proceeded. I believe by this time your L[or]dship will find by experience that when a man gets upon his hobby Horse it is a hard matter to get him down but I Should not shew the sincere regard I have for everything Belonging to L[or]d Rivers if I did not spare his Eyes and his Patience by concluding this unscrutinable [inscrutable] scrawl. My wife and little Sly Boats [Sarah Frances Drax] beg their kindest remembrance to Miss [Mistress] Pitt and yourself [my] L[or]d and Mr Geo[rge] Pitt

I am my Dear L[or]d
Your obliged and ever
Sincere Humble serv[an]t
Edward Drax

The second letter was written some two weeks later:

Bath Monday

Mr Dear L[or]d
On getting out of my Chaise from Silbury This morning, I found your kind favour, and as The Uncourtly Gout gives dreadful sounds of preparation I will give a short Account of my last expedition, if I can make it short; for when one's writing to those one likes writing its so like conversation it is not easy to leave of[f].

To Answer then as short as possible I have hitherto till this last expedition gone by myself and like an old Druid slept a[t] Beckhampton within the precincts of the Temple but This Time I have taken my faithfull Sarah with me/to do likewise/and glad I am That I did, as we spent yesterday one of the finest days eve that ever the sun shone on very Luminously in the Patriarchal way. We rode over and contemplated all the wonderfull remains of the old Patriarchal Religion with which the environs of Abury Abound more perhaps to those who have a Turn for enjoying and discovering those kind of works than any part of the known Globe. In our ride in a sequestered vale we met With a work which I prevailed on my fellow labourer To get of[f] and Draw It is a stupendous stone Sat up, According to the Account as your Lordship remembers in Scripture; /for I confess I don't/ and Abraham sat up a stone and call'd on the Name of the Lord. I will prevail on her to send it you. These sort of works in my opinion have more simple Grandeur, and st[r]ike with more religious admiration than the finest works of Greece and Rome; in my opinion there is the same comparison between them as between the finest Dress[e]d works of Mr ['Capability'] Brown and the Great works of nature. The Gout puts me in mind to stop and tell you that when I left Silbury Saturday night we had got down 56 feet: still made-ground, no more Horns this time. (my faithful Sarah was with me) I'm a saucy fellow to joke on such a subject, perhaps tis owing to my great security that I dare – But when we came to the depth of [82 overwritten] 95 feet we struck upon a Thing which I am sanguine enough to hope will lead to a great Discovery. It was a perpendicular Cavity That as yet appears Bottomless it is just 6 inches over[;] we have followed it already about 20 feet[;]

we can plumb it about Eleven Feet more but as a great deal of loose chalk has unfortunately fallen in, at that Depth, is a stoppage but as at present a Strong wind comes up the Hole enough almost to blow out a Candle it must have some communication with the Air or some great Cavity somewhere, at first what the miners call a Damp or foul Air come out of it into the Shaft so that they could Hardly breath[e] nor would a Candle Burn, but that is over and now a strong wind comes up; as it is in the very centre of this Great Hill and goes perpendicularly down it is matter of Astonishment The country people when we were at work at the Barrow said that on the Hill opposite on the other side the River Kennet, on a great Long Barrow set round with stones, the people at work there to get the stone had discover[e]d a Great Hole which they always had an opinion had a communication under Silbury Hill tho[ugh] on the other side of the river and a mile off. The Temple of Abury is no further. I wait with impatience the event of 2 or 3 days more as by that Time we shall have come to where the stoppage is, and then I hope shall make a further Discovery. Something that is now perished must have remained in this hole to have kept this Cavity open, as the ground is loose chalk Stones, and visibly nothing to Support it, my Dear L[or]d I must once more give you leave to put on your night Cap which I believe this long scrawl will hasten. My wife who will not think her time ill bestowed in drawing this Druid Altar for you (called in our language a Kistvaen) begs to join in kind wishes with little Sly to all yours at Stratfield Say[e]

I am my Dear Lord
With great Truth sincerely
Your very humble servant
Edward Drax

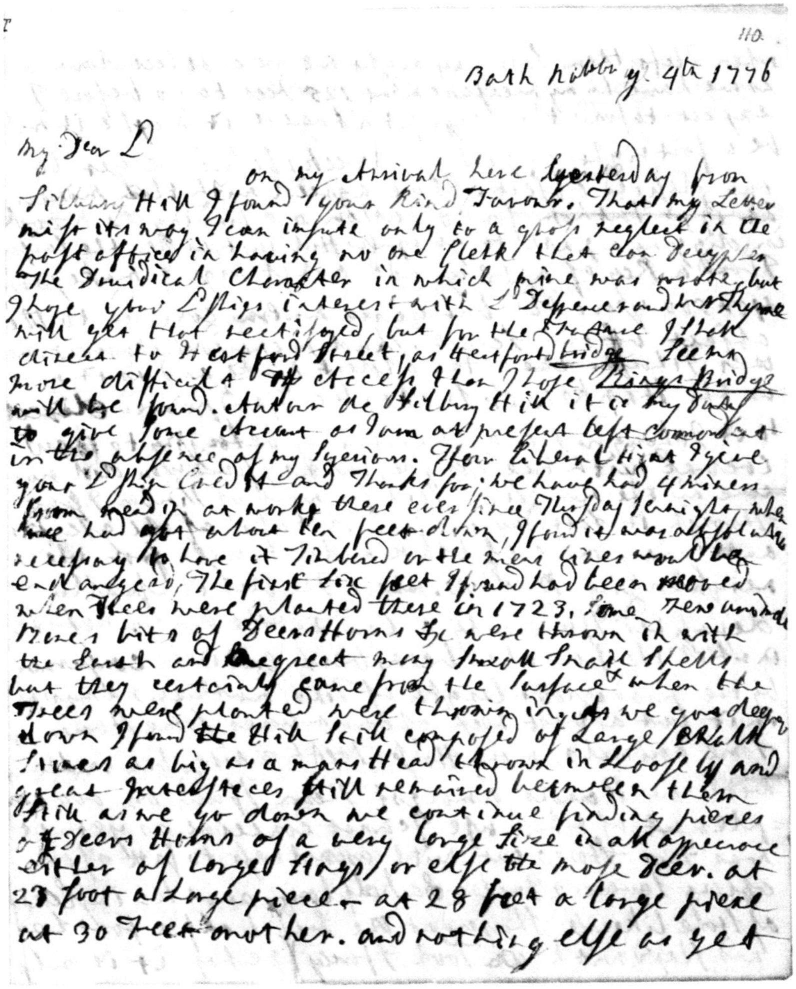

Fig 1.21
The first page from the first Drax letter

2

The Evolution of Silbury Hill: The Prehistoric Phases

JIM LEARY

With Barry Bishop, Gill Campbell, Matthew Canti, Rosamund Cleal, Tom Cromwell, Paul Davies, David Field, Rob Ixer, Peter Marshall, Joshua Pollard, Mark Robinson and Fay Worley

The prehistoric sequence recorded during the English Heritage archaeological investigations is described here, providing a fresh interpretation of the various phases of construction. The basis of this is the information obtained from the stratigraphy recorded in the sections of the tunnel, the results of a watching brief on the surface of the southern side of the mound, the excavations on the summit, and the recording in the vertical shaft. Supporting specialist contributions to this work form Chapters 3–6. The sequence is summarised at the end of this chapter. Phases relating to later periods are set out in Chapters 9 and 10.

As noted in Chapter 1, the shaft was recorded soon after the hole appeared in 2000 and following subsequent collapse the crater was recorded remotely, with excavation around the edge in 2001. The major part of the work began in May 2007 with recording and limited excavation in the tunnel, as well as further excavation on the summit and a watching brief during remedial work on the slopes (Fig 2.1). This was completed a year later in May 2008.

Methodology

Tunnel recording

The road stone infilling and collapsed chalk within the Main Tunnel was cleared by machine to Bay 57; beyond this point clay and chalk infilled the tunnel and was also removed (*see* Chapter 10). The two lateral tunnels were also cleared and all the sections were archaeologically recorded. For most of the tunnel the roof had collapsed, leaving a void above the level of the steel arches left behind by the 1968–70 excavations, but in several places there were greater voids stretching up for several metres (*see* Chapter 10). The mining arches (rings) were still in position and the same numbering system provided orientation with the 1968–70 archive; the section recorded between arches 1 and 2, for example, being referred to as Bay 1.

The tunnel sides, or sections, were recorded by photogrammetry. This involved taking stereo-photographs of each bay which could be printed on-site as scaled ortho-photos and then annotated with archaeological observations by hand within the tunnel. The stereo-photographs were geo-referenced with survey points, whilst other data were written on a magnetic board which was included in each photograph. Photographs were taken on a Kodak DCS Pro 14MPixel SLR camera and the data post-processed using Topcon PI-3000 software after the images had been white-balanced in Adobe Photoshop. The hand-drawn annotations were later digitised back on to the PI-3000 software and exported to AutoCAD as wire-frame models (*see* Bryan and Cromwell 2008 for further information). Illumination for the stereo-photography within the tunnel was a constant issue, and by the time Bay 73 was recorded the stereo-photography had become so dark that it was necessary to supplement the on-site prints with traditional hand-drawn sections of each bay. Further complications were caused by the movement of arches and thus survey points during a major tunnel collapse that began in July 2007 and which eventually led to the insertion of new arches by Skanksa (*see* Chapter 10).

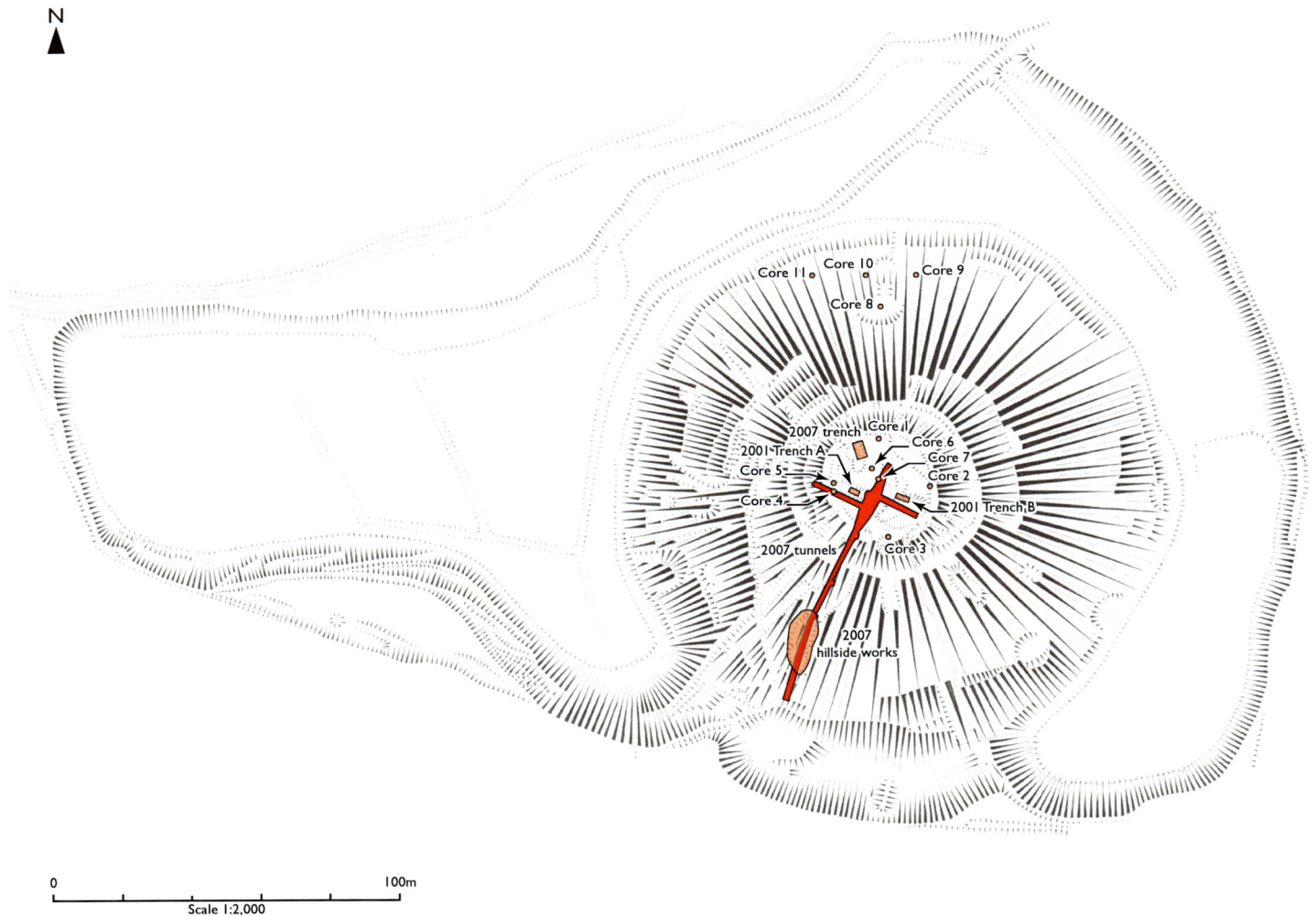

Fig 2.1
Plan of English Heritage
interventions on Silbury
Hill, 2001–7.
(Deborah Cunliffe
and Eddie Lyons,
© English Heritage)

The earliest buried ditch (Ditch 1) was the only ditch in the tunnel to be excavated. Managed by Fachtna McAvoy and using a toothless bucket, a mechanical digger cut a narrow trench through the base of the tunnel over Ditch 1 and removed the fills in four broad spits (Fig 2.2). Any finds recovered during this process were attributed to a spit. These spits were also 100 per cent sampled and either dry-sieved or floated as none of the fills proved to contain material preserved as a result of anoxic conditions. Following excavation by machine the sides were supported and the section hand recorded. This revealed numerous contexts, some of which crossed between spits. Monolith and mollusc samples were taken from the recorded sections. Other than this ditch, as

well as two pits, a stakehole and a section of a small gully, the deposits seen in the tunnel were recorded and sampled but not excavated.

The summit excavation and Hillside watching brief

The summit works involved monitoring and recording the sides of the crater following collapses and during remedial works, as well as the excavation of two small-scale trenches in 2001 either side of the crater, measuring 3m x 1.5m and 4m x 1.5m, and a further trench in 2007 measuring 5m x 3m. Excavation was in accordance with English Heritage standards and procedures as set down in the 'English Heritage Recording Manual'. The trenches were hand-excavated and deposits were removed stratigraphically. Both drawn and written records were produced, with each context recorded on a plan or section, as well as on a context sheet. The aim was to define remains rather than totally remove them, and therefore full excavation was confined to those deposits that were necessary to achieve the objectives. The position of the trenches was surveyed using Total Station EDM using Ordnance Survey grid co-ordinates. On completion of the excavation, the trenches were backfilled.

A watching brief was also conducted during remedial work to fill a hollow on the southern slope of Silbury Hill. This involved visually scanning material during the removal of the turf and topsoil by mechanical digger and hand-drawing a section of the prehistoric stratigraphy revealed.

Recovery of environmental material and finds

Over 500 environmental samples were taken during the Silbury Hill Conservation Project. Nearly all the phases identified in the tunnel sides were sampled except for a section in the main tunnel from Bay 47 (Bank 3) and the start of the West Lateral which were concealed by material from the July 2007 tunnel collapse. Samples for flotation were processed using a flotation tank based on the Siraf design with the flot being retained on a 250µm mesh and the residue on a 500µm mesh. Samples for general biological analysis (GBA) and monoliths taken for the recovery of pollen from deposits where preservation due to anoxic conditions was evident were either stored in a refrigerator at the site compound or transported to a cold store within 24 hours. GBA samples were processed in the laboratory by wet sieving down to 180 or 250µm. Details of the methodologies employed for the range of analyses undertaken are not included here but are given in the relevant research reports.

The main focus of the sampling programme was the retrieval of samples from *in situ* deposits. This principally involved taking samples from the tunnel sections following full recording but also included the 100 per cent sampling of the fills of any cut features such as stakeholes and pits that were excavated. Where GBA samples were taken from anoxic contexts or where monoliths were taken for pollen analysis, two sets of samples were taken. This was to allow the

preservation of material from within the centre of the Hill for the benefit of future research.

The stratigraphy in the tunnel was far more complex than previous work suggested, meaning more samples were required. In addition, the deposits were very unstable, making sampling difficult and meaning that there was a great deal more collapsed chalk and other material to scan on the conveyor belt (*see below*). There was also evidence of fungal growth with large cracks evident in the tunnel walls in some places. Earthworms were present throughout the tunnel backfill. The sides of the cleaned sections often came away from the walls and fell into the cleared tunnels. This meant that deposits that had collapsed away from the tunnel sides were regularly sampled and that it was not feasible to coarse sieve all the deposits derived from cleaning sections as hoped, given the sheer volumes involved.

Collapsed mound deposits recovered within the 1968–70 tunnel also provided research potential, particularly for dating. This *ex situ* material, which had either collapsed from above the tunnel or from the sides, was scanned for finds and sub-sampled as appropriate. The material was removed bay by bay and was transported by machine to the site compound where it was loaded on to a conveyor belt and visually scanned for finds (Fig 2.3).

Around 50 samples were taken from the excavations on the summit; here animal bone and molluscs were well preserved and abundant and

Fig 2.3
Archaeologists processing
material on the
conveyor belt.
(© English Heritage)

charred plant remains and charcoal were present in low concentrations. Forty-litre flotation samples were taken from all cut features, from the chalk rubble walls and from the deposits used to infill behind these walls (interwall deposits). The remaining material from these contexts was dry sieved to 10mm at the trench side to maximise the recovery of artefacts and bone. In addition, mollusc samples were taken as a series of column samples through the interwall deposits in three different locations. Some of the contexts consisted in part of loosely packed rubble with what is likely to be intrusive material, such as amphibian bone and mollusc shells, present within the loose matrix. This limited the research potential of charred plant remains and smaller vertebrate remains from these contexts, though larger remains, such as antler and bones of domestic animals, were unaffected. Three environmental samples were recovered as part of the Hillside watching brief.

Processing of finds and samples was carried out in accordance with the procedures set out in the 'English Heritage Recording Manual' and current national guidelines. Prior to the excavations, provision was made for part of the ceramic assemblage to be set aside for lipid analysis. However, in the event the assemblage was too small for this to be viable. Microwear analysis of the flint was also attempted but the results were disappointing.

Tunnels, trenches and context numbers

The numbers referred to in this volume are the unique context numbers that were assigned on site to each of the archaeological features and deposits encountered by the Silbury Hill Conservation Project, and shown within 'square' brackets, for example [3021]. Where context numbers are used that were assigned earlier by Whittle to the 1968–70 contexts, they are shown in 'curly' brackets, for example {300}. Sample numbers are shown thus: <9001>, whilst small finds numbers have the prefix SF. A Context Index of all the contexts used and a full stratigraphic matrix have been deposited with the archive. Unless otherwise stated, no context was fully excavated.

The Main Tunnel into Silbury Hill was recorded as site sub-division (SSD) 5, with the East Lateral and West Lateral recorded as SSD 8 and 9 respectively. The tunnel was recorded using unique context numbers assigned at the time of recording starting at [3001] for the west side and West Lateral, and from [4001] for the east side and East Lateral. Context numbers for the tunnel backfill started at [3801] and the below-tunnel ditch excavation from [3901]. The summit was recorded as SSD 6 and used context numbers from [4801], and the watching brief on the side of the Hill was recorded as SSD 7 and used context numbers from [4901]. Small finds were recorded using numbers from 8001, whilst environmental sample numbers started from <9001>.

Relevant section drawings of each of the recorded phases are included in this chapter, as well as plans from the summit work, and these show the location of the recorded archaeological deposits and features. The reader is also referred to the three foldout section drawings at the back of the monograph. Figure 2.4 is a schematic section showing a summary of the phases recorded in the tunnel. A section through the prehistoric deposits on the summit is given in Figure 2.29 later in the chapter.

Sequence

Phase 1: Natural deposits underlying the Old Land Surface

In the tunnel the top of the chalk bedrock ([3014]/[4012]) was seen between Bays 28 and 81; between Bays 1 and 28 the top of the chalk existed above the tunnel, and beyond Bay 81 it was concealed by the floor (see Foldout 1A and B). The top of the chalk was recorded at a maximum height of 158.7m OD in Bay 30,

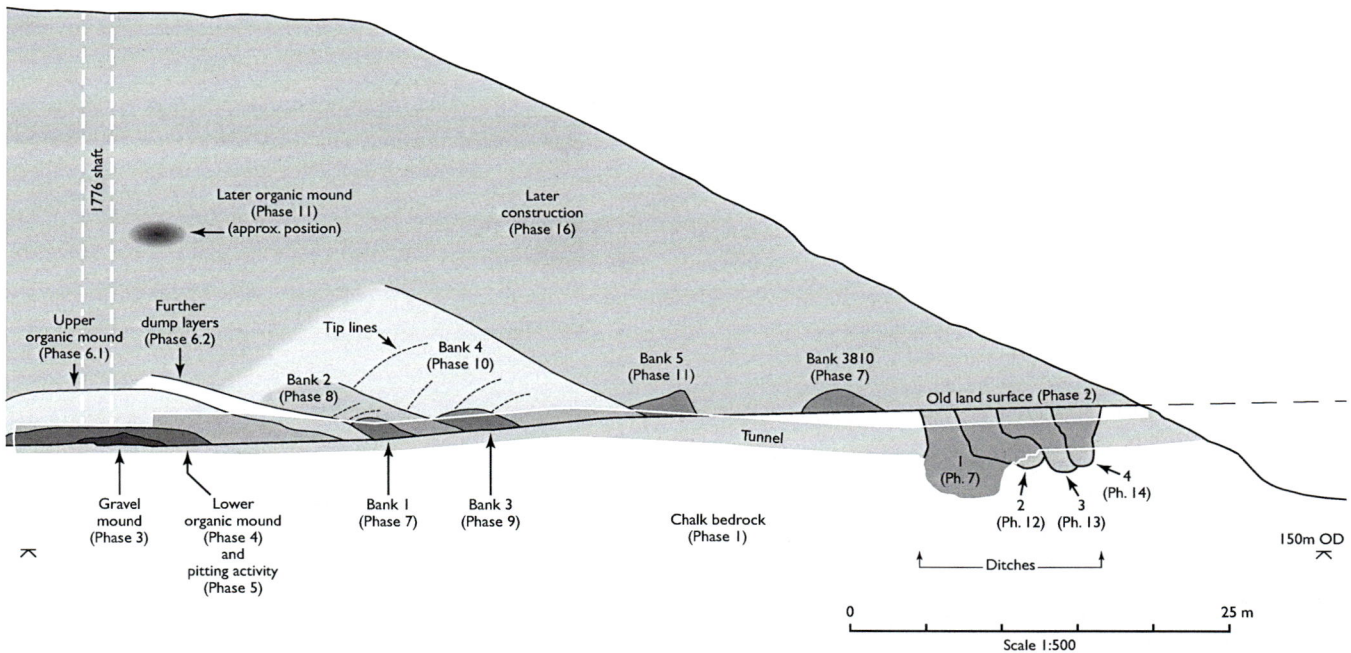

Fig 2.4
Schematic section through
the prehistoric phases
recorded within the tunnel.
(Eddie Lyons,
© English Heritage)

dropping to a level of 156.5m OD in Bay 81. This was overlain with dark yellowish-brown calcareous silty clay and flint ([3019]/[4094]) (*see* the Topography and Geology section in Chapter 1), which was generally 0.5m thick although it thinned to around 0.2m downslope to the north, sloping from 159.1m OD in Bay 36, to 157m OD right at the back of the Main Tunnel in the end face. An interface layer existed between the chalk and the clay-with-flints material. Numerous, small periglacial involutions penetrated the chalk and were filled with the overlying clay-with-flints material. Above the clay-with-flints layer was a thin band of dark, yellowish-brown very flinty clay ([3020]/[4096]), which was iron-panned in places; this was probably formed by stones having been moved down from the original soil cover (*see* Canti, Chapter 5).

Phase 2: Old Land Surface

Overlying the sequence described above was a thin, unbroken band of grey, stone-free silty clay ([3021]/[4041], referred to informally as the grey layer) varying from 0.03m to 0.1m in thickness (*see* Figs 2.4 and 2.5 and Foldout 1A–D). Described by Atkinson as the Old Land Surface (OLS) (Whittle 1997a), this deposit appears to extend under every phase of the monument, although the cores taken as part of

the seismic tomographic survey suggest that it peters out downslope to the north (Canti, Chapter 5). It was recorded at a height of 159.2m OD in Bay 34, sloping steeply down to the north to 157.48m OD in Bay 59, before levelling slightly, although still declining northwards, to be recorded in the end face at a height of 157.1m OD. It had a distinct interface with the underlying deposits, which sometimes included a marked gravelly band (*see* Canti, Chapter 5), and sometimes showed an irregular interface with the chalk mound above.

Fig 2.5
The Old Land Surface in the
tunnel, represented by
a grey band above the
clay-with-flints.
(© English Heritage)

The grey layer clearly does not represent a full soil horizon, which must have been removed at some stage prior to construction, possibly by erosion or perhaps as a deliberate act of ground preparation. This process of truncation is likely to have been an on-going event as the mound developed rather than a single episode due to the lack of vegetation growth anywhere on it. Particle size analysis shows that the OLS has originated from the underlying clay-with-flints material, the stones of which have been removed by some process, possibly by trampling or worm sorting (Canti, Chapter 5). Any evidence for earlier monuments and structures on the site is likely to have been destroyed during this process of truncation.

Even in the centre of the mound where anoxic conditions were present this deposit was relatively bare of environmental remains and contained only a very small proportion of organic material. Amongst the few remains recovered were monocot stems or leaves as well as occasional buttercup and grass seeds and fragmentary elder seeds. The occasional charred hazel nutshell fragment was recovered as well, as were fragments of moss. Insect remains were poorly preserved in this layer (see Chapter 6). Micromorphology of samples taken from the OLS shows layers, lenses and flecks of mineralised plant remains (Canti, Chapter 5).

A concentration of charcoal and charred material was recorded within a small, defined area of the upper part of the OLS on the north side of the East Lateral in Bay 7, and may well indicate the remains of human activity, such as a hearth. A small quantity of flint micro-debitage from around this area may suggest that some flint knapping accompanied the use of this feature. A slightly worn single pig maxillary 3rd premolar was also found in association with it along with several fragments of tooth enamel and 14 fragments of medium mammal-sized bone, in poor condition. The premolar may be from a domestic pig or wild boar and the fragments of enamel might derive from the same individual (see Chapter 6).

The area surrounding and including the putative hearth was 100 per cent sampled (Sample <9435>). Ninety per cent of this sample was processed as sub-sample <9821>; the rest was retained for potential future research. *Corylus* sp. (hazel) was the main component of the charcoal assemblage obtained from this sample with some Maloidae type (a group that includes hawthorn, apple, rowan and other Sorbus species) recorded along with two fragments of *Prunus* sp. (for example sloe or plum) Indeterminate root wood charcoal was also present (Campbell 2011).

The charred plant remains mirrored these findings in that a hazel nutshell fragment and a *Prunus* sp. fruit stone fragment were recovered, as well as roots or rhizomes of Poaceae (grasses), tubers of *Arrhenatherum elatius* var. *bulbosum* (onion couch) and fragments of monocotyledon stem. Single charred seeds of *Carex* sp. (sedge) and *Ranunculus acris/repens/bulbosus* (buttercup) were also noted (Campbell 2011).

The remains may reflect clearance of scrub in the vicinity to cook a meal, or they may be all that survives of a ritual event. The types of wood used here are similar to those recovered from the possible buried soil beneath the Pound Field barrow, at West Overton (Gale 1996), and from the enclosure ditch of the Longstones enclosure (Gale 2008), demonstrating that scrub or underwood species predominate, that is hazel followed by sloe were the most abundant taxa.

In the central area of the tunnel (from Bay 59 to the end face of the Main Tunnel, as well as in the East Lateral up to Bay 9 and the West Lateral up to Bay 7) the OLS has a pronounced dark brown layer between 0.01m and 0.02m thick on top of it: [3035]/[4100], which under high magnification resembles plant remains (Canti, Chapter 5), possibly imported organic material such as laid reeds.

Phase 3: Gravel Mound

The first clear evidence for construction activity recorded at the site was a low mound formed of

Table 2.1: Phase 2 contexts Old Land Surface

Context	Description	Location
3021	Old Land Surface	West face and lateral
3035	Organic layer above OLS	West face and lateral
4041	Old Land Surface	East face and lateral
4100	Organic layer above OLS	East face and lateral

dark, yellowish-brown and orange flint gravel mixed with silty loam ([3048]/[4153]), recorded between Bays 71 and 80 of the Main Tunnel overlying the Old Land Surface (Figs 2.6, 2.7 and 2.8). At its highest point, the mound was 0.8m high (a level of 158m OD) in Bay 75 and has an estimated diameter of 10 metres. A thin (0.1m thick), dark brown silty loam band ([3068]/[3069] and [4154]/[4166]) overlaid this mound on its northern and southern sides (Fig 2.7). Micromorphological investigation of this layer in conjunction with analysis of macroscopic biological remains (Canti and Campbell, Chapter 5; Chapter 6) showed that it is not a soil horizon but represents a mix of dumped topsoil and subsoil, perhaps placed to maintain the integrity and strengthen the sides of the loose Gravel Mound. Small quantities of flint micro-debitage indicate some knapping activities in the area, although the presence of a possibly Early Neolithic flint blade suggests that at least some of this activity was residual, having been already present in the material prior to use. Environmental remains suggest that this mound was constructed within an open grassland environment (Chapter 6).

A further layer was recorded within this phase, although it could just as easily relate to Phase 2. This comprised a layer of mixed light grey and orangey-brown chalk and clay ([3013]/

[3087]/[4095]), which overlay the OLS from Bay 36 (where the OLS is first apparent) until Bay 60, where it peters out (Foldout 1A and B). It may represent a trample deposit formed while the Gravel Mound was constructed. Alternatively it may represent a layer of iron panning. This phase formed part of Atkinson's Silbury I and Whittle's Phase a. Samples from this layer did not produce any environmental material.

Fig 2.6
The northern tip of the Gravel Mound and subsequent Lower Organic Mound.
(© English Heritage)

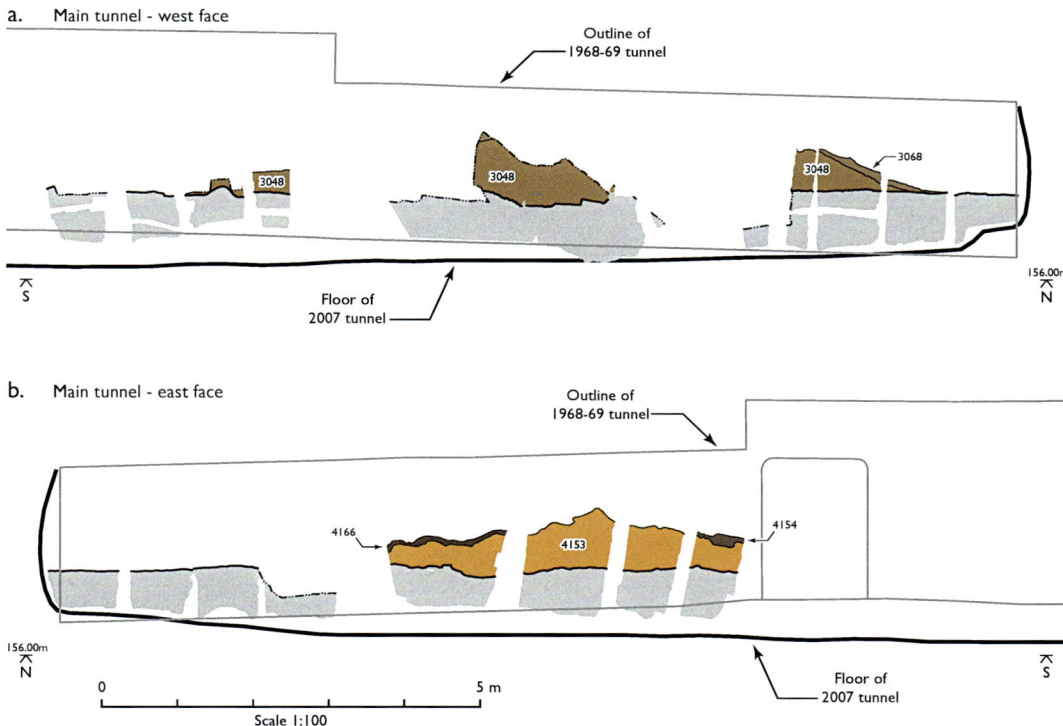

Fig 2.7
Section through the Gravel Mound in the Main Tunnel.
(Eddie Lyons, © English Heritage)

Table 2.2: Phase 3 contexts Gravel Mound

Context	Description	Location
3013	Iron Pan band or 'trample', overlying OLS	Main Tunnel west face
3048	Gravel Mound	Main Tunnel west face
3068	Dark silty layer on top Gravel Mound	Main Tunnel west face
3069	Dark silty layer on top Gravel Mound. Same as [3068]	Main Tunnel west face
3087	Poss trample layer	West Lateral north face
3089	Organic remains on top of trample layer [3087]	West Lateral north face
4095	Iron Pan band or 'trample', overlying OLS	Main Tunnel east face
4153	Gravel Mound	Main Tunnel east face
4154	Dark silty layer on top Gravel Mound	Main Tunnel east face
4166	Dark silty layer on top Gravel Mound	Main Tunnel east face

Phase 4: Lower Organic Mound and Mini-mounds

Subsequently, a series of organic layers overlay Phases 2 and 3, recorded in Bay 65 to the end face of the Main Tunnel, as well as the East and West Laterals (Figs 2.6 and 2.11 and Foldout 1A–D). Together these layers formed a coherent mound, enlarging the height of the earlier Gravel Mound to at least 1.1m high, at a level of 158.3m OD, (although the full height was not seen as it extended above the tunnel), and the diameter to an estimated 22m, (although again the full size was not seen as it extended beyond the Main Tunnel to the north) (Fig 2.8).

This mound comprised layers of dark reddish-brown silty loam with a high organic content, made up of a mix of topsoil, subsoil and turf, derived primarily from a clay-with-flint material (although topsoil and turf derived from soil developed on chalk were also present – *see* Chapter 6). In some places thin bands of gravel and chalk were also recorded, and together with the organic layers they probably represent 'basket' loads of material brought in and piled over the Phase 3 Gravel Mound.

A fragment of a flint core, waste flakes and quantities of micro-debitage may again indicate flint knapping activities associated with this phase, although it is just as likely these were present in the soil prior to being incorporated into the mound. A fragment of cattle incisor tooth enamel was also recovered, as was a portion of a cattle radius. Environmental remains from the Lower Organic Mound provide evidence for buttercups, stinging nettle, lesser stitchwort and clover, indicative of a range of grassland habitats (Chapter 6).

A stakehole was recorded on the western edge of these deposits in the northern section in the West Lateral (Bay 3); this measured 0.07m in diameter and 0.43m in depth (Figs 2.9 and 2.11d; and Foldout 1D) and was fully excavated. The lower fill of this stakehole ([3091]) comprised organic material (*see* Chapter 6), though unfortunately no remains of wood survived within the deposit (Campbell 2011), whilst the upper fill comprised slumped material from the overlying phase. Other stakeholes were recorded during the 1968–70 work, for example in the west section of the Main Tunnel at Bay 65 (Whittle's context {196}) (Foldout 2F), suggesting that this stake is part of a sequence which may demarcate the edge of the Lower Organic Mound (*see* Fig 2.8 for a plan of the stakeholes). Whether the stakes surrounding the Lower Organic Mound defined it, contained it or were a freestanding circle is not clear.

A further cut ([3092]) was also recorded on the northern side of the West Lateral (Bays 6 and 7), opposite the above discussed stakehole (Fig 2.11c and Foldout 1C). This cut was very small at only 0.18m wide and 0.19m deep and was filled with a small chalk block, the upper face of which would have been visible on the side of the Lower Organic Mound. It may represent a small edge marker, although equally it is possible that the chalk had simply been inadvertently pushed into the underlying soft deposits.

Two small and discrete deposits form what have been interpreted as separate miniature mounds. These have been placed in this phase; however, they could conceivably be earlier or slightly later (although they underlie the Phase 6 Upper Organic Mound). Context [3095] was recorded on the west side of the Main Tunnel and measured 0.95m wide and 0.2m high (157.5m OD), whilst [4181] was recorded in

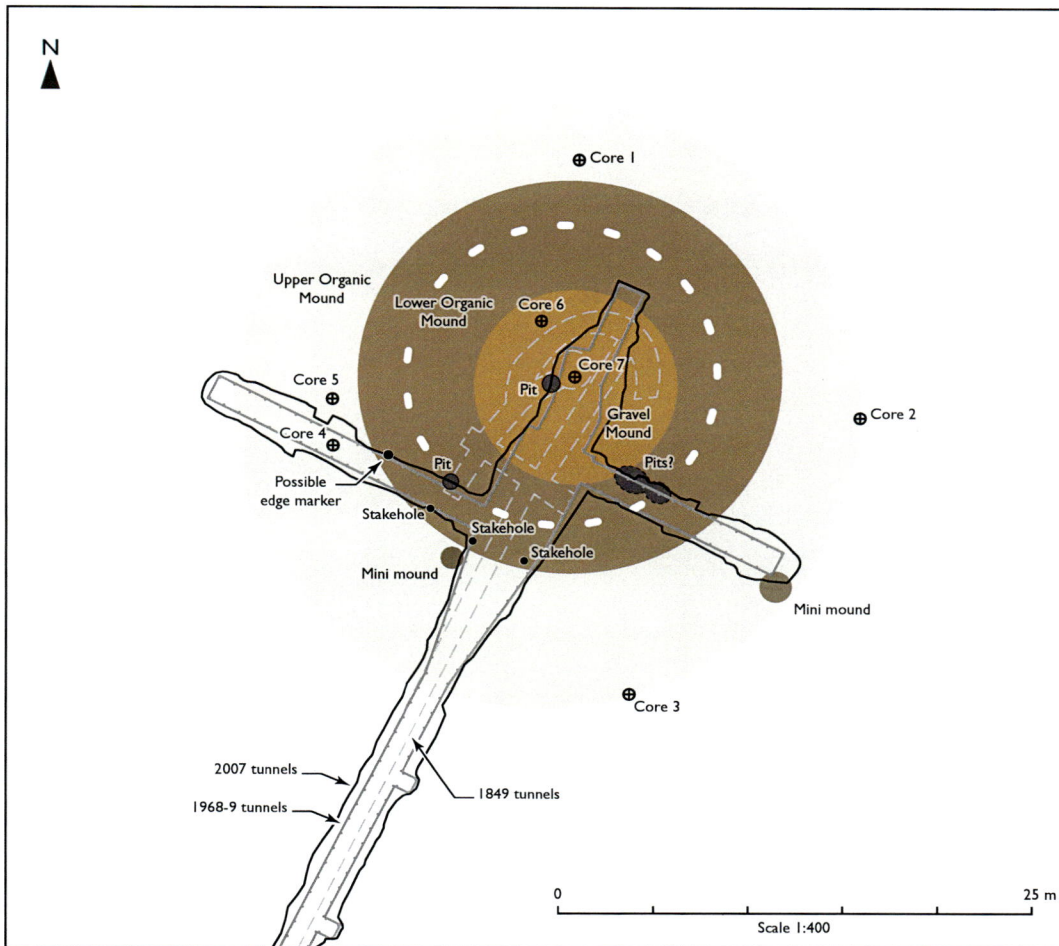

Fig 2.8
*Projected plans of the Gravel
Mound, Lower Organic
Mound, stakeholes,
Mini-mounds and Upper
Organic Mound.
(Eddie Lyons,
© English Heritage)*

both the end face of the East Lateral and the southern section (Figs 2.8, 2.10 and 2.11 and Foldout 1A and D).

Mini-mound [4181] was formed of an organic-rich greyish-brown to very dark greyish-brown silty loam intermixed with turf layers and measured 0.8m wide as seen, although it extended beyond the tunnel to the east and south, and 0.3m high (157.62m OD on the top), and was partially excavated. The biological remains from the deposit provided a wealth of evidence suggesting that they had derived from a woodland edge setting, and included yew, oak (including a fragment of an acorn cupule), hazel, bramble, sloe, crab apple, hawthorn, dog's mercury and elder. Plants such as bugle, ground ivy and wavy hair-grass also suggest such a setting. The Mini-mound also contained cereal remains such as a rachis fragment, possibly from a free-threshing wheat, as well as evidence for barley and cereal bran (Chapter 6)

and some material derived from grassland habitats. Insects were well preserved in the Mini-mound, with a high concentration compared to other contexts. Coleoptera included a water beetle and a range of ground beetles, a snail-eating beetle and dung beetles (*see* Chapter 6; Robinson 2011). It also contained a small quantity of flint micro-debitage and a decortication flake within it (Bishop, Chapter 3).

This Mini-mound appears to have had further material piled against it, which was subsequently cut through by a small gully ([4171]) on the western side (seen in Bays 12 and 13 on the south face of the East Lateral) (Fig 2.11d and Foldout 1D). It was not recorded in the end face or the northern section, and therefore is likely to be a small, interrupted gully perhaps enclosing the Mini-mound. This gully was partially excavated, and contained some flint micro-debitage, while the environmental samples from the primary fill contained charred

Fig 2.9
Stakehole recorded on
the south side of the
West Lateral. Scale 0.5m.
(© English Heritage)

Fig 2.10
Mini-mound recorded in the
corner of the end face and
south section of the
East Lateral. Scale 0.5m.
(© English Heritage)

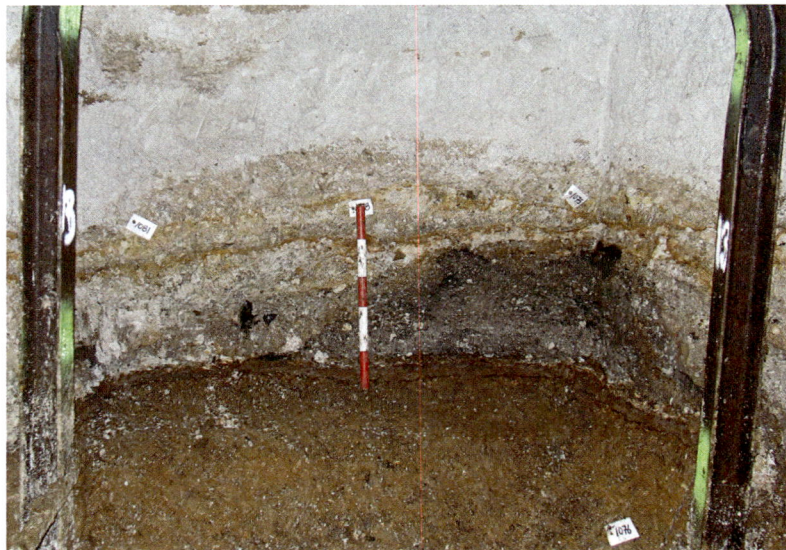

onion couch tubers, as well as moss and buttercup. Both the primary and secondary fills contained a few shade-requiring species of snail shells, although these were worn and may have derived from older material. Beetles are well preserved in these fills, with a similar range to the Mini-mound as well as a wood-boring beetle (*see* Chapter 6). Mini-mound [3095] was not sampled as part of the 2007/8 investigations due to the tunnel collapse in late July 2007 (*see* Chapters 6 and 10).

It is clear, therefore, that the earliest phases of Silbury Hill do not simply consist of one mound but a sequence of mounds which later became consolidated into a single monument. These features form part of Atkinson's Silbury

I phase and broadly correspond to Whittle's phase b.

Phase 5: Pits

Two pits were recorded in the tunnel sections and were both excavated as far as possible (Figs 2.11a and c, 2.12 and 2.13, and Foldout 1A and C). Pit [3067] was recorded on the western section of the Main Tunnel in Bays 75 and 76 and was found to cut the Gravel Mound (Fig 2.12). It measured 1m in diameter and 0.6m deep (the level of the bottom of the pit was 157.52m OD), but the full width was not seen as it was truncated to the north by an off-shoot of the 1849 tunnel, nor was the full depth, as collapsed material concealed the top of the cut, which is interpreted as cutting through the Lower Organic Mound. This pit contained two fills: the primary fill was a thin, mixed deposit of light yellowish-brown chalk and silty loam, containing flint micro-debitage, whilst the secondary fill was mid-grey to black silty loam and may well be redeposited material from the Lower Organic Mound. The primary fill contained very few remains, but environmental samples taken from the secondary fill produced a rich molluscan assemblage with both woodland and open country species present, although the former were very worn suggesting that they are likely to be residual. Plant remains were well preserved, suggesting rapid infilling. Species recorded included buttercup, thyme-leaved sandwort, common mouse-ear, salad burnet, fairy flax and grasses. Preservation of insects was also good in this pit with numerous worker ants, likely to represent an ant nest that had become incorporated in it as it was back-filled (Chapter 6; Campbell 2011; Davies 2011; Robinson 2011).

Pit [3074] was recorded on the northern section in the West Lateral in Bay 3 (Fig 2.13) and cut through the Lower Organic Mound. It measured 0.74m in width and 0.6m deep, although, again, the pit had been truncated by the 1849 tunnel. The pit was filled with a mixed deposit of mid-brown to black sandy silt, and may also represent redeposited Lower Organic Mound material. Two environmental samples were taken from it and contained low quantities of land snail shells. As with the previous pit, very worn (and therefore perhaps residual) woodland species were present, as were fresh species associated with grassland environments. The fill of this pit also produced a small number of elder

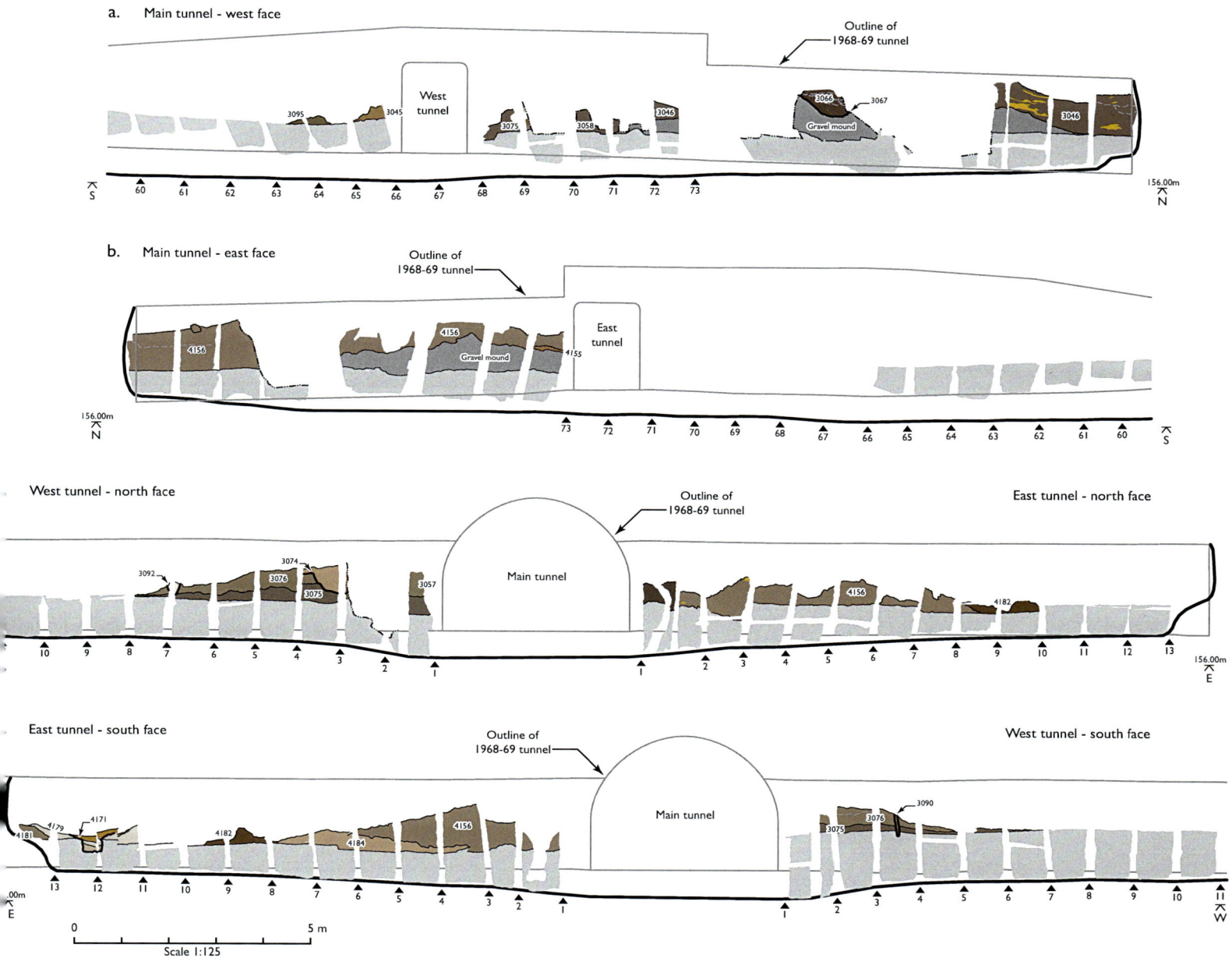

a. Main tunnel - west face

b. Main tunnel - east face

West tunnel - north face

East tunnel - north face

East tunnel - south face

West tunnel - south face

Scale 1:125

seeds, whilst moss was frequent and buttercups were fairly common (Chapter 6).

Worked flint and burnt flint was recovered from the fills of these pits. Pit [3067] produced a backed knife (Fig 3.2, no 4), a trimming flake, a blade (Fig 3.2, no 12), three small but potentially useable flakes (Fig 3.2, nos 13 and 14) and a quantity of micro-debitage. These pieces may have been deliberately discarded into the pit (see Bishop, Chapter 3). Micro-wear analysis was conducted on the flakes and

retouched implement but recortication and post-depositional damage precluded any reliable interpretations. In contrast, pit [3074] contained no large pieces of struck flint but produced a larger quantity of burnt flint (although as Bishop points out below both quantities should be regarded as small).

Pits were not recognised during the 1968–70 work. However, study of the Atkinson section drawing suggests that one may be present on the north side of the East Lateral around Bays 6 and

Fig 2.11
a and b) Sections through the Lower Organic Mound in the Main Tunnel.
c and d) Sections through the Lower Organic Mound in the East and West Laterals showing the stakehole and the Mini-mound.
(Eddie Lyons,
© English Heritage)

41

Table 2.3: Phase 4 contexts Lower Organic Mound and Mini-mounds

Context	Description	Location
3045	Part of Lower Organic Mound	Main Tunnel west face
3046	Part of Lower Organic Mound	Main Tunnel west face
3054	Part of Lower Organic Mound. Same as [3075]	Main Tunnel west face
3055	Part of Lower Organic Mound. Same as [3075]	Main Tunnel west face
3056	Part of Lower Organic Mound. Same as [3075]	Main Tunnel west face
3057	Part of Lower Organic Mound. Same as [3075]	Main Tunnel west face
3058	Part of Lower Organic Mound	Main Tunnel west face
3075	Part of Lower Organic Mound	West Lateral
3076	Part of Lower Organic Mound	West Lateral
3090	Stake hole – around Lower Organic Mound	West Lateral south face
3091	Primary fill of stake hole [3090]	West Lateral south face
3092	Possible small cut on edge of Lower Organic Mound	West Lateral north face
3093	Chalk block fill of cut [3092]	West Lateral north face
3095	Organic Mini-mound	Main Tunnel west face
3096	Secondary fill of stake hole [3090]	West Lateral south face
4101	Part of Lower Organic Mound. Same as [4156]	Main Tunnel east face
4155	Part of Lower Organic Mound	Main Tunnel east face
4156	Part of Lower Organic Mound	Main Tunnel east face and East Lateral
4170	Primary fill of linear pit or gully [4171]	East Lateral south face
4171	Gully associated with Mini-mound [4181]	East Lateral south face
4173	Secondary fill of linear pit or gully [4171]	East Lateral south face
4178	Tertiary fill of linear pit or gully [4171]	East Lateral south face
4179	Part of and modification to Mini-mound [4181]	East Lateral south face
4181	Organic Mini-mound	East Lateral south face
4184	Part of Lower Organic Mound	East Lateral south face
4185	Part of and modification to Mini-mound [4181]. Same as [4179]	East Lateral south face
4182	Part of Lower Organic Mound	East Lateral north face

7 (filled with contexts {713}–{719}) (*see* Fig 2.8 and Foldout 2H).

Phase 6: Upper Organic Mound

Phase 6.1 Upper Organic Mound

The next phase of construction sealed the pits, the Lower Organic Mound and the Mini-mounds under a series of interleaved layers. These were a very mixed series of deposits (*see* Figs 2.8, 2.14 and 2.15; and Foldout 1A–D), predominantly comprising a light to dark greyish-brown organic silty loam with lenses of gravel, orangey-brown clay and light grey chalk. Some turves were also present within these deposits. There was a mix of topsoil and subsoil, chiefly from soils that had developed over chalk, and therefore contrasting with the underlying Lower Organic Mound, the majority of which was from derived clay-with-flints material (*see* Phase 4 above, and Chapter 6). The volume of each of these deposits, which varied from as little as 0.01m to 0.15m thick, suggests that they again may represent individual 'basket' loads of material, as well as occasional individual turves.

Although the uppermost layers were not seen, these deposits are interpreted as forming a mound enlarging the earlier monument to an estimated diameter of 35 metres; it was recorded from Bay 59 to the end face of the Main Tunnel and up to Bay 14 of both the East and West Laterals. The tallest part of the mound was recorded in Bay 10 of the East Lateral at 1.66m high, but extrapolating the mound it would clearly have risen a few metres above the tunnel.

Also included within this phase were a number of naturally rounded sarsen boulders,

Fig 2.12
Pit in Main Tunnel.
Scale 0.2m.
(© English Heritage)

which clearly had been deliberately incorporated within the matrix of the mound, rather than as any sort of setting over or around it. Five sarsen stones were recorded from one of the contexts ([4157]), three of which were substantial blocks weighing between 30kg and 85kg (Pollard, Chapter 3). Further sarsens were recovered from collapsed and slumped material ([3834] and [3855]) and appear to have originated from this phase. Environmental remains from the Upper Organic Mound were generally indicative of chalk grassland (Chapter 6). A single pig phalanx in good condition was recovered from context [4172].

Context [4169] was initially thought to represent a soil horizon; however, sampling suggested that it is a random mix of topsoil and chalky subsoil representing a number of tipping events. This phase corresponds to Atkinson's Silbury I phase and Whittle's phase c.

Phase 6.2: Further dumped layers

The Upper Organic Mound was enhanced by a series of further dumped layers comprising light grey chalk with yellowish-brown silty clay lenses as well as some silty layers, and measuring a maximum of 1.1m thick. These were recorded between Bays 56 and 62 in the Main Tunnel, Bays 10 to 14 in the East Lateral, and Bays 11 to 16 in the West Lateral. The outer layer of this in the West Lateral, [3084], was considerably darker and siltier than the other layers and it was initially thought that this may represent an intact soil surface; however, micromorphogical analysis in conjunction with the evidence from the biological remains showed it consists of a random mix of topsoil and subsoil (see Canti, Chapter 5; Chapter 6).

These layers were identified by Atkinson as part of his Silbury I phase and termed 'clay capping' (Whittle's phase c) and were therefore considered as a separate phase during the recording and most of the assessment. However, it later became clear that these were further

Fig 2.13 (above)
Pit in West Lateral.
Scale 0.2m.
(© English Heritage)

Fig 2.14 (left)
The end face of the Main Tunnel showing a section through the Upper Organic Mound. Scale 1m.
(Duncan Stirk and Eddie Lyons, © English Heritage)

Table 2.4: Phase 5 contexts Pitting Activity

Context	Description	Location
3066	Secondary fill of pit [3067]	Main Tunnel west face
3067	Pit cut into top of LOM	Main Tunnel west face
3070	Primary fill of pit [3067]	Main Tunnel west face
3073	Fill of pit [3074]	West Lateral north face
3074	Pit cut into top of LOM	West Lateral north face

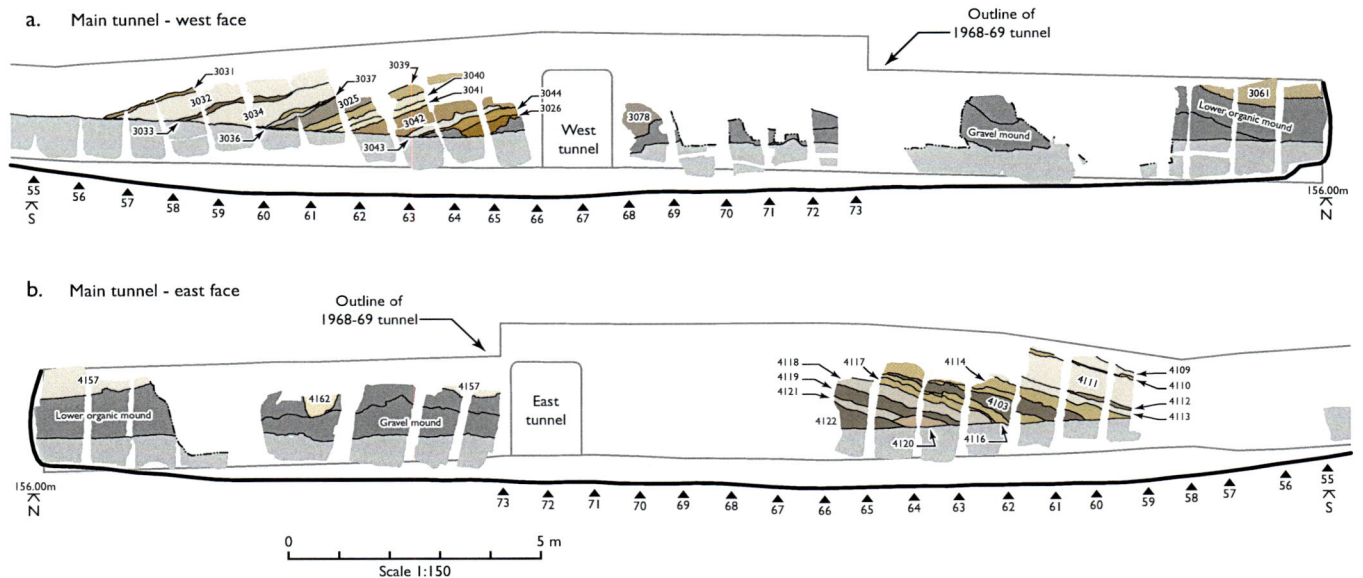

a. Main tunnel - west face

b. Main tunnel - east face

Fig 2.15 (above)
Sections through the
Upper Organic Mound in
the Main Tunnel.
(Eddie Lyons,
© English Heritage)

Fig 2.16 (below)
East section of the top of
Bank 1, as seen in a void
above the tunnel.
(© English Heritage)

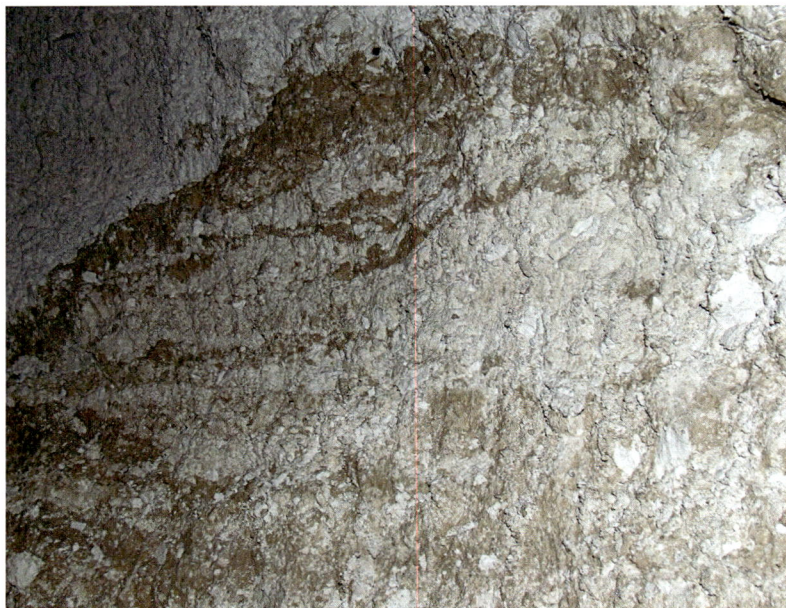

dumped layers similar to the underlying Upper Organic Mound, rather than any sort of formal 'capping', and therefore unlikely to be a separate phase of activity. These deposits must have been placed rapidly ensuring preservation of the underlying delicate biological remains.

Phase 7: Bank 1 and Ditch 1

The Upper Organic Mound was surrounded by at least five chalk and clay banks. Interestingly, some banks are remarkably consistent in their dimensions (and in some cases materials), despite being concealed by later phases,

suggesting that a memory of the earlier banks remained. This perhaps has some bearing on our interpretation of the timescale over which this activity occurred (*see* Chapter 7).

A dump of chalk and clay (termed 'Toblerone' by Atkinson – *see* in Whittle 1997a), was piled around the Upper Organic Mound to form a low bank, 3.3m wide and 1.44m high (159.00m OD, as seen) (Figs 2.16 and 2.21a and b; and Foldout 1A and B). This comprised two deposits of light yellowish-brown silty clay mixed with white chalk ([3085]/[4167] and [3088]/[3030]/ [4107]) (*see* Fig 2.18). A thin (0.1m thick) band of iron panning was recorded underlying the upper deposit but not the lower. Atkinson recorded this bank as part of the Silbury I construct, and it was part of Whittle's phase d and e.

Recorded just inside the tunnel portal were a large ditch (Ditch 1; Fig 2.2) and possibly associated internal bank (the bank was recorded as context [3810]) (Figs 2.17, 2.21b; and Foldout 1B). Although there is no direct connection between Ditch 1 and Bank 1, they have been interpreted here as being part of the same phase, the ditch possibly being the source of the raw material for the bank. However, as Whittle noted 'It is not clear to which parts of the sequence the ditch and the buried ditch or quarry should be assigned' (1997a, 25), and it may well be that the ditch and bank are some of the earliest features on the site.

The ditch cut was recorded in the eastern side of the Main Tunnel as well as in a machine-excavated slot through the tunnel floor, which

Table 2.5: Phase 6 contexts Upper Organic Mound

Context	Description	Location
3025	Part of Upper Organic Mound	Main Tunnel west face
3026	Part of Upper Organic Mound	Main Tunnel west face
3036	Part of Upper Organic Mound	Main Tunnel west face
3037	Part of Upper Organic Mound	Main Tunnel west face
3039	Part of Upper Organic Mound	Main Tunnel west face
3040	Part of Upper Organic Mound	Main Tunnel west face
3041	Part of Upper Organic Mound	Main Tunnel west face
3042	Part of Upper Organic Mound	Main Tunnel west face
3043	Part of Upper Organic Mound	Main Tunnel west face
3044	Part of Upper Organic Mound	Main Tunnel west face
3061	Part of Upper Organic Mound	Main Tunnel west face
3071	Part of Upper Organic Mound	Main Tunnel west face
3077	Part of Upper Organic Mound	West Lateral
3078	Part of Upper Organic Mound	West Lateral
3081	Part of Upper Organic Mound	West Lateral
3083	Part of Upper Organic Mound	West Lateral
4103	Part of Upper Organic Mound	Main Tunnel east face
4114	Part of Upper Organic Mound	Main Tunnel east face
4115	Part of Upper Organic Mound	Main Tunnel east face
4116	Part of Upper Organic Mound	Main Tunnel east face
4117	Part of Upper Organic Mound	Main Tunnel east face
4118	Part of Upper Organic Mound	Main Tunnel east face
4119	Part of Upper Organic Mound	Main Tunnel east face
4120	Part of Upper Organic Mound	Main Tunnel east face
4121	Part of Upper Organic Mound	Main Tunnel east face
4122	Part of Upper Organic Mound	Main Tunnel east face
4157	Part of Upper Organic Mound	Main Tunnel east face
4162	Slumped material	Main Tunnel west face
4169	Part of Upper Organic Mound	East Lateral
4172	Part of Upper Organic Mound	East Lateral
4180	Part of Upper Organic Mound	East Lateral south face
3031	Further dump layers	Main Tunnel west face
3032	Further dump layers	Main Tunnel west face
3033	Further dump layers	Main Tunnel west face
3034	Further dump layers	Main Tunnel west face
3084	Further dump layers	West Lateral
4109	Further dump layers	Main Tunnel east face
4110	Further dump layers	Main Tunnel east face
4111	Further dump layers	Main Tunnel east face
4112	Further dump layers	Main Tunnel east face
4113	Further dump layers	Main Tunnel east face
4168	Further dump layers	East Lateral

provided a clear section through to the base of the ditch (*see* Figs 2.2 and 2.21b). It was recorded as contexts [3902], [4151] and [3015] and clearly terminated in this area on the western side, a point noted by Atkinson's team and very evident on the base of the ditch in 2007. Further, as Whittle notes (1997a, 25), the ditch was not seen in the 1849 tunnel, suggesting that the position of this tunnel correlates with a genuine ditch terminus. Atkinson recorded some deposits in the west section, but these were covered with a considerable thickness of backfill in 2007/8 and it was decided not to remove this (Fig 2.21a). As noted by Atkinson, the putative ditch

terminus is aligned with the external causeway and can therefore be interpreted as an access route, or, as with other sites of this period, it may simply be a continuous ditch that had been cut in small, connected sections, this area representing one such connection.

The base of the ditch was recorded at 153.52m OD, whilst the upper profile was above the tunnel and therefore not available for recording. However, if we extrapolate the height of the Old Land Surface from the rest of the site, we can estimate that the ditch was cut at around 160m OD and therefore was nearly 6.5m deep originally. Where seen it measured 5.9m wide,

Fig 2.17
Photomosaic of bank
on inside of ditch.
(Fachtna McAvoy
and Eddie Lyons,
© English Heritage)

and if it was circular in plan we can estimate that it formed an enclosure a little over 100m in diameter. This feature has been interpreted as a ditch rather than, say, a large pit due to the associated bank and later re-cuts (*see below*), but given the small area investigated other interpretations cannot be ruled out. Whittle (1997a, 25) points to the possibility that it may have been an irregular quarry, but the section excavated in 2007 suggests that it was regular in shape, and the presence of an internal bank further highlights its somewhat more formal nature. Atkinson identified this ditch as the source of the material for his Silbury II mound.

Phase 8: Bank 2

The Phase 7 ditch may have remained open during the subsequent construction phases and is interpreted here as the source for the raw material for Banks 2, 3, 4 and 5.

Bank 2 comprised a layer of mixed chalk blocks and crushed chalk ([3029]/[3094]/ [3086] and [4106]/[4108]/[4183]) (Figs 2.18 and 2.21; and Foldout 1A and B). The top of this bank was not seen and it is possible that rather than being a bank around the previous mound, the deposit continued over it to form a larger mound. However, this is unlikely as tip lines made of lumps of clay were seen in a void above the tunnel, indicating that Bank 2 slopes back down to rest against Bank 1 (*see* Fig 2.18). If continuous, Bank 2 extended the monument outward by a further 2.5m. This formed part of Atkinson's Silbury II phase, and Whittle's phase e.

Phase 9: Bank 3

Bank 3 was another low, chalk and clay 'Toblerone' bank ([3027]/[4104]), remarkably similar in size and material to Bank 1 (Phase 7) and Bank 5 (Phase 11). The bank, which also had a small chalk rubble core, was 1.42m high and 3.6m wide, and the top was recorded as 159.6m OD (Fig 2.21a and b; Foldout 1A and B). This low mound was recorded during the 1968–70 works and formed part of Atkinson's Silbury II (Whittle's e, f and g).

Phase 10: Bank 4

Bank 4 comprised compact white chalk ([3023]/ [4098]/[4186]) (Fig 2.21a and b; Foldout 1A and B) and, as with Bank 2, was much larger and continued above the level of the tunnel and therefore the top was not recorded. Again, as with Bank 2 it feasibly could be interpreted as a mound rather than a bank. This was at least 9m wide, and formed part of Atkinson's Silbury III and Whittle's phase g.

Phase 11: Bank 5 and later organic layers

As with Bank 1 and 3, Bank 5 was a low, chalk and clay 'Toblerone' bank ([3097]/[4042]/ [4073]) (Figs 2.19 and 2.21a and b; Foldout 1A and B), measuring 3m wide and 0.78m high (as seen) and recorded at a maximum level of 160.9m OD.

The purpose of these chalk and clay banks is unclear – they certainly were more than just support for the Upper Organic Mound. Without

Table 2.6: Phase 7 contexts Bank 1 and Ditch 1

Context	Description	Location
3015	Buried ditch cut (Ditch 1)	Main Tunnel west face
3022	Iron Pan band	Main Tunnel west face
3024	Part of Bank 1 (Toblerone)	Main Tunnel west face
3030	Part of Bank 1 (Toblerone)	Main Tunnel west face
3085	Part of Bank 1 (Toblerone)	West Lateral
3088	Part of Bank 1 (chalk)	West Lateral
3810	Toblerone bank on inside of buried ditch	Main Tunnel east face
3902	Cut of buried ditch (Ditch 1)	Main Tunnel east face
4093	Bank 1 (Toblerone)	Main Tunnel east face
4097	Iron Pan band	Main Tunnel east face
4107	Part of Bank 1 (Toblerone)	Main Tunnel east face
4151	Buried ditch cut (Ditch 1)	Main Tunnel east face
4167	Bank 1 (Toblerone)	East Lateral

Table 2.7: Phase 8 contexts Bank 2

Context	Description	Location
3029	Part of Bank 2 (chalk + silt)	Main Tunnel west face
3086	Part of Bank 2 (chalk)	West Lateral
3094	Part of Bank 2 (chalk)	Main Tunnel west face
4106	Part of Bank 2 (chalk + silt)	Main Tunnel east face
4108	Part of Bank 2 (chalk + silt)	Main Tunnel east face
4183	Part of Bank 2 (chalk + silt)	East Lateral

Fig 2.18
This photomosaic of the east section shows tip lines from Bank 2 meeting the southern side of Bank 1.
(Eddie Lyons,
© English Heritage)

Table 2.8: Phase 9 contexts Bank 3

Context	Description	Location
3027	Part of Bank 3 (Toblerone)	Main Tunnel west face
3028	Part of Bank 3 (chalk rubble core of Bank 3)	Main Tunnel west face
4104	Part of Bank 3 (Toblerone)	Main Tunnel east face
4105	Part of Bank 3 (chalk rubble core of Bank 3)	Main Tunnel east face

Table 2.9: Phase 10 contexts Bank 4

Context	Description	Location
3023	Bank 4 (chalk)	Main Tunnel west face
4098	Bank 4 (chalk)	Main Tunnel east face
4186	Bank 4 (chalk)	Main Tunnel east face

doubt they increased the diameter of the mound, together extending the monument to an estimated 37.2m. Whether they also increased the height, that is, whether there was material piled on top of the banks, is unknown because it was not possible to see much of the central area above the limits of the tunnel. However, a series of organic layers interleaved with chalk, and forming what would appear to be a mound, were seen at the top of a void which had opened up high above the Main Tunnel (*see* Figs 2.4 and 2.20). These layers were not recorded archaeologically, or indeed inspected by an archaeologist, and therefore they were not given a context number. A Skanska miner, however, was able to

climb the considerable distance up the void and take a photograph as well as environmental samples from the layers. These samples produced fragments of charcoal and a charred onion couch tuber, as well as uncharred elder seeds (Campbell 2011). It is unknown how these layers, which might form a later organic mound, fit in with the deposits seen in the tunnel and what phase they should be placed in; however, their existence highlights the complexity of the monument.

Structured accrual of deposits evidently continued, however, as the tunnel dipped down through these phases of activity and below the Neolithic ground level where it was no longer

Fig 2.19
The top of Bank 5, as seen in a void above the western section of the tunnel. Vertical scale 1m; horizontal scale 2m. (© English Heritage)

Table 2.10: Phase 11 contexts Bank 5

Context	Description	Location
3097	Part of Bank 5 (Toblerone)	Main Tunnel west face
4042	Chalk rubble mound material	Main Tunnel east face
4073	Bank 5 (Toblerone)	Main Tunnel east face

possible to record them. It is likely however, based on the foregoing sequence, that the unseen overlying deposits were not formed in one single, homogenous phase, but in a series of complex phases, the mound growing in size bit by bit with each addition.

Phase 12: The infilling and backfilling of Ditch 1, and cutting of Ditch 2

The following phases (Phases 12–15) represent the infilling of Ditch 1 and its repeated re-cutting (Fig 2.22 and Foldout 1B). Although separated into different phases here, these episodes of re-cutting may well have occurred in parallel with the bank phases (Phases 7–11).

The fills of Ditch 1 were visible in the tunnel sides as well as within a machine trench cut below the floor of the tunnel. This showed that the lower fills were more silty and therefore they have been interpreted as being deposited as part of a natural infilling process. The upper fills, on the other hand, were clearly deliberately deposited. Therefore this phase has been split into two sub-phases, both of which are described below.

Phase 12.1

The primary fill of the ditch was a firm light brown chalky silt loam with a maximum thickness of 0.2m, and has been interpreted as a stabilisation layer. Three flint flakes were recovered from this layer, as well as two flake fragments, two decortication flakes, a retouched flake, a small piece of burnt flint and a quantity of micro-debitage (Fig 3.2, nos 6 and 17). Also recovered from this context was a small fragment of worn antler tine tip (Worley, Chapter 3). Overlying this were lenses of silty loam followed by a thin layer of chalk, possibly erosion from the side of the ditch (Fig 2.22), which contained a flint flake (*see* Fig 3.2, no 16). Four possible stakeholes were recorded cutting into the top of this layer; measuring between 0.17m and 0.28m in length and 0.1m to 0.16m in both width and depth, these are likely to have been cut from

higher up. A very thin dark band possibly represents another stabilisation horizon, and this was overlain by a 0.15m thick layer of chalk, followed by further thin silty chalk deposits (Fig 2.22). The above fills were all removed together in a single spit (Spit 4; group context [3920]) by the machine and separated out into individual contexts later when the section was recorded. Although 100 per cent sampled, very little charcoal or molluscs were present in any of these spits.

These fills were overlain by further deposits of silty chalk, followed by another period of stabilisation. This in turn was sealed by another chalk context: [3909] (Fig 2.22). These layers were removed as a large machine-excavated spit (Spit 3; group context [3919]) from which a fragment of antler (SF 8018) was recovered, as well as a struck flint flake, a systematic blade and a flake core (Fig 3.1, no 3), and a chunk of burnt flint weighing 35g. The flake core appears to be a variant of the Late Neolithic 'Levallois' technique, which is often associated with the manufacture of elaborate pieces such as transverse arrowheads. The contexts above this were recorded as Spit 2; group context [3918], and produced three pieces of struck flint, including a retouched piece (*see* Fig 3.2, nos 5

*Fig 2.20
Looking up to the base of organic deposits (phase 11) at the top of a void in the mound (compare Fig 2.4 for position).
(Courtesy Skanska)*

a. Main tunnel - west face

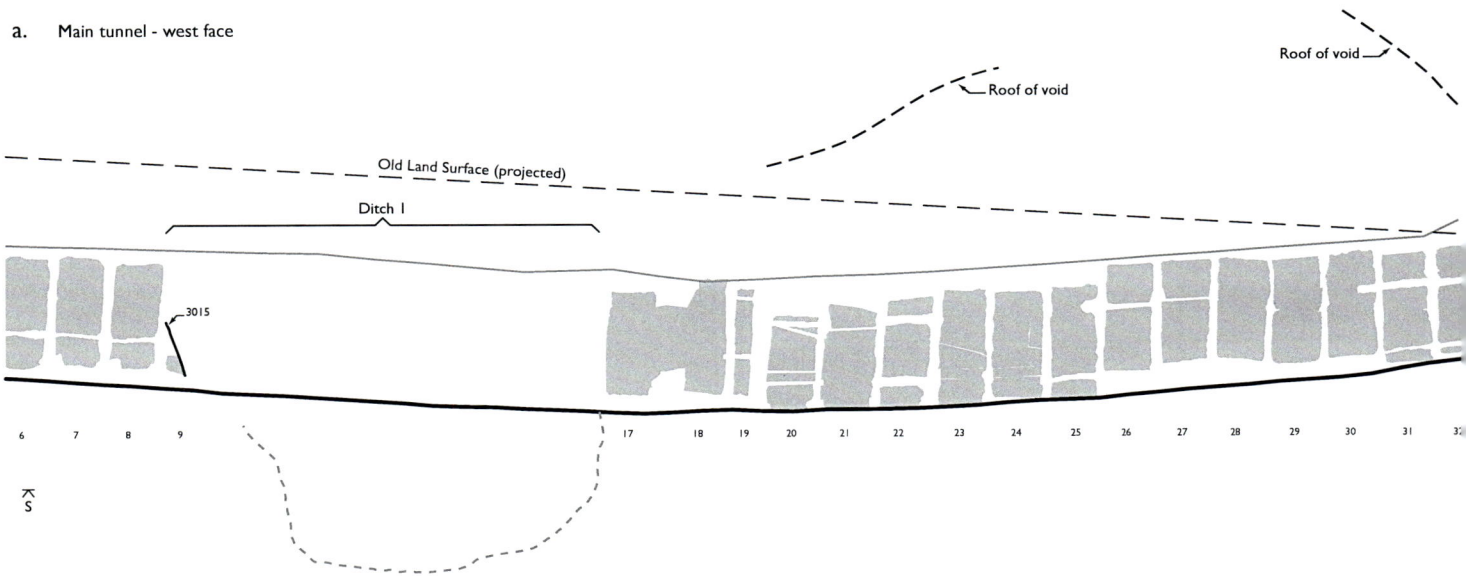

Roof of void

Roof of void

Old Land Surface (projected)

Ditch 1

3015

6   7   8   9   17   18   19   20   21   22   23   24   25   26   27   28   29   30   31   32

↖
S

b. Main tunnel - east face

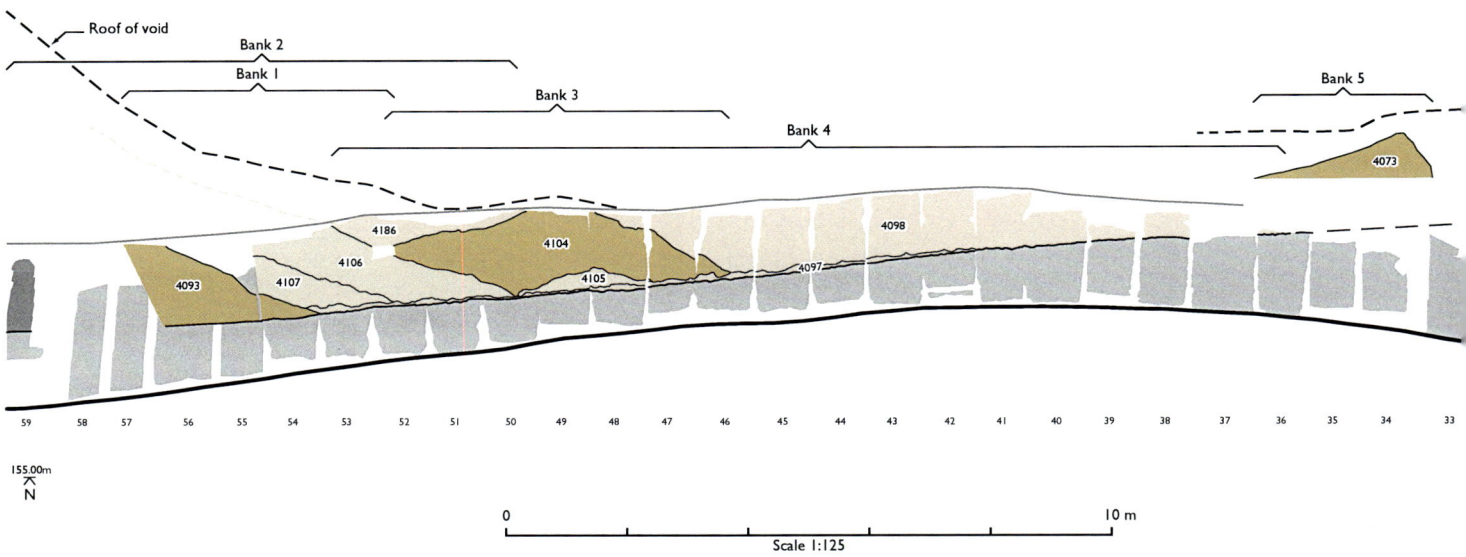

Roof of void

Bank 2

Bank 1

Bank 3

Bank 5

Bank 4

4073

4186

4098

4106

4104

4093   4107   4105   4097

59   58   57   56   55   54   53   52   51   50   49   48   47   46   45   44   43   42   41   40   39   38   37   36   35   34   33

155.00m
↖
N

0   10 m

Scale 1:125

Fig 2.21
Sections through the
banks, Phases 7–11,
in the Main Tunnel.
(Eddie Lyons,
© English Heritage)

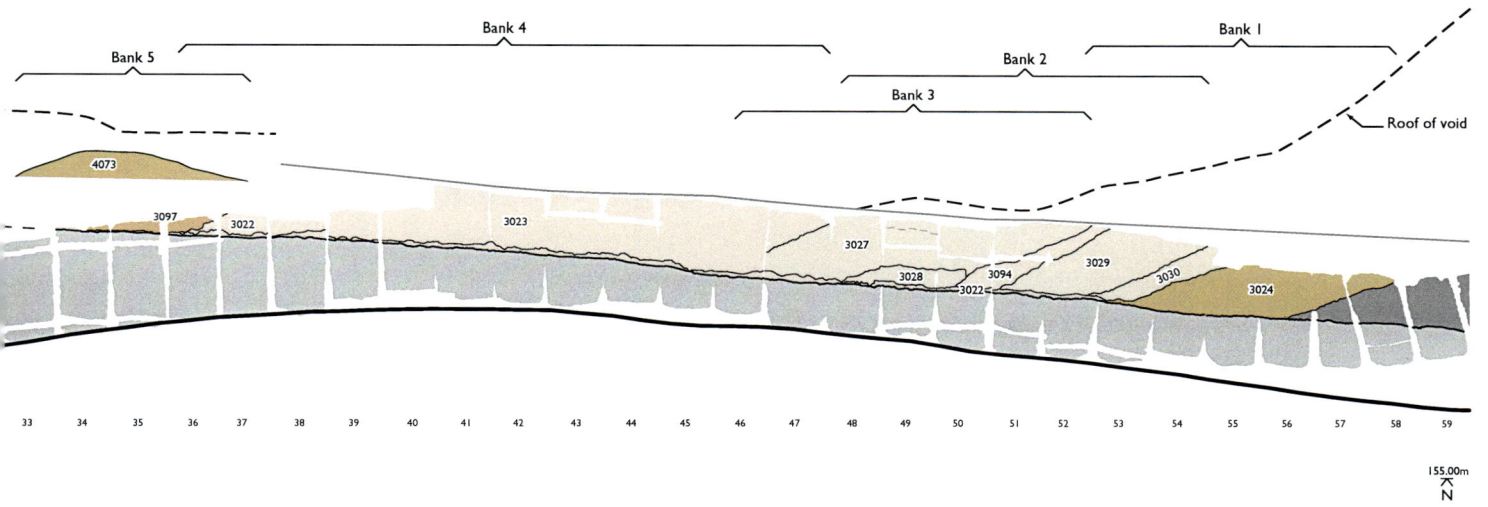

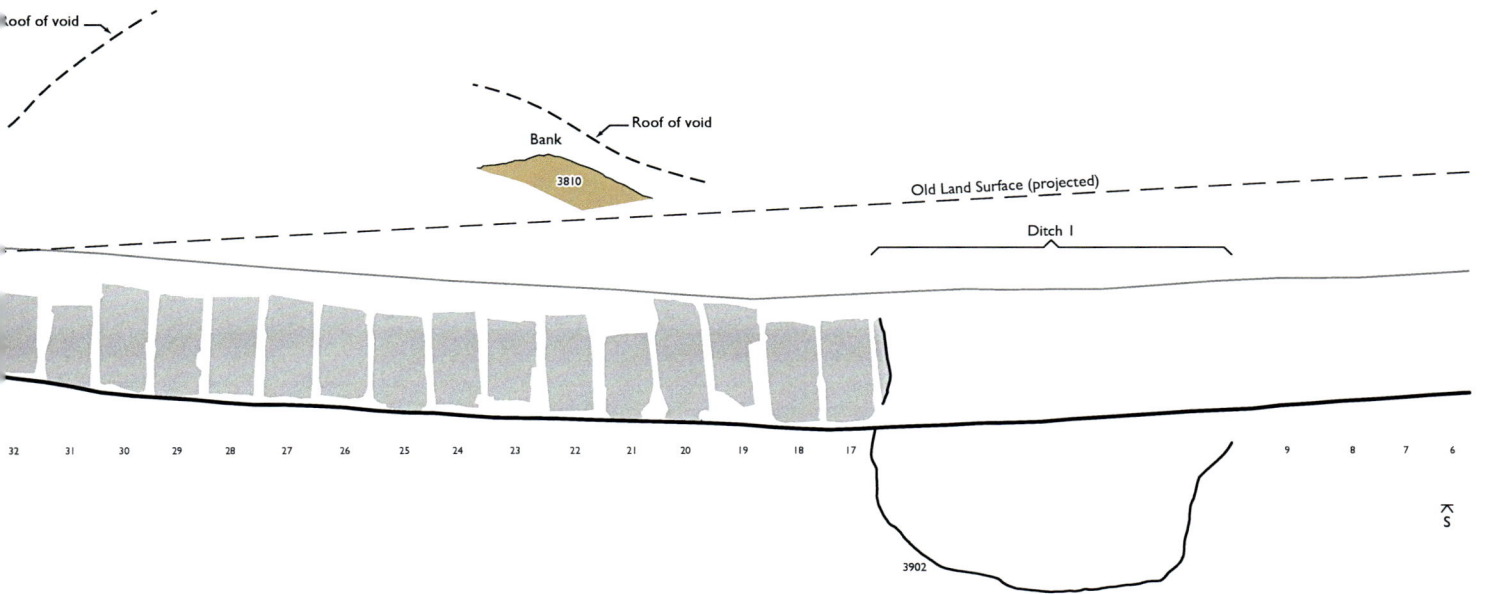

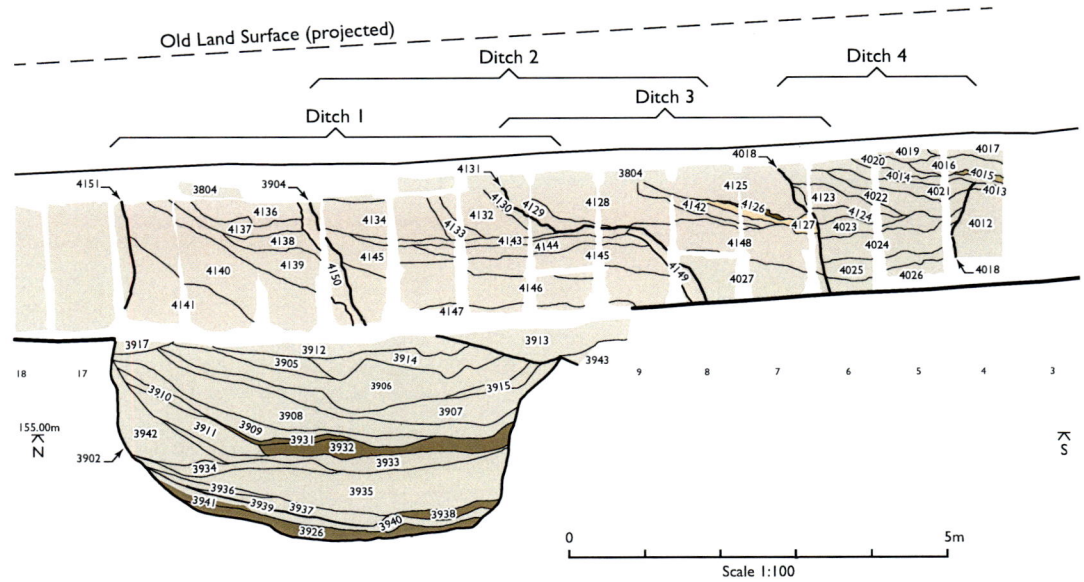

Fig 2.22
Section through the ditch
and re-cuts in the Main
Tunnel, Phases 12–15.
(Eddie Lyons,
© English Heritage)

and 15) and five antler fragments (SF 8004; SF 8015; SF 8016; SF 8017). Antler tine SF 8017 exhibited slight polish, possibly from use, towards the tip (Worley, Chapter 3). A single fossil fish tooth was also recovered from this spit. This whole process infilled the ditch by *c* 1.5m, bringing it to a level of around 155m OD. Two pieces of iron pyrites were found within these fills, although this occurs naturally in the chalk and therefore may have been incidentally incorporated.

Phase 12.2

Spit 1 (group context [3903]) represents the deposits recorded directly below the tunnel floor and link with those recorded in the tunnel sides. They largely comprised similar, homogenous white chalk deposits, some of which contained large chalk blocks, with notably fewer finds. They were considerably thicker than the underlying Phase 12.1 deposits, varying between 0.2m and 0.7m thick, and on the whole appear to have been thrown in from the northern side of the ditch (Fig 2.22). The ditch fills obviously continued above the tunnel, but they were not recorded.

Unlike the underlying deposits, these deposits were retained on the southern side by a vertical chalk rubble wall, which effectively formed a dry stone wall (Fig 2.23). This not only provides compelling evidence that this phase of the ditch had been intentionally backfilled, but also suggests that the southern side of the upper part of the ditch was left open and only the northern side of the ditch was backfilled, implying that the backfilling and re-cutting occurred at the same time. A ditch re-cut was recorded cutting the top deposits of the Phase 12.1 infilling sequence, suggesting that Ditch 1 was re-cut and partly left open (the revetting wall provided a stable side to the ditch re-cut) thus forming a second ditch (Ditch 2), which was smaller (*c* 4.5m wide) and slightly further south (Fig 2.22). The ditch, in other words, had migrated outwards, becoming smaller in the process.

Phase 13: The backfilling of Ditch 2, and cutting of Ditch 3

Ditch 2 was itself intentionally backfilled and re-cut further outwards in a similar way to Ditch

Fig 2.23
Chalk revetment wall within
backfilled Ditch 1.
(© English Heritage)

1 (Fig 2.22). The fills, which were not excavated and only recorded in the tunnel section, all comprised layers of chalk laid horizontally and held in place by a retaining wall, which was formed of large pieces of chalk blocks. Overlying the fills, including the retaining wall, was a thin band (0.1m) of compacted fine chalk, either representing washed in material, or a compacted layer of trample. The lack of molluscs at this stage suggests that it was not open for long, and therefore perhaps the latter is a more plausible interpretation. Infilling of Ditch 2 continued over this with further chalk and retaining rubble walls (Fig 2.22). The retaining wall again forms the northern face of the next ditch (Ditch 3), the second re-cut to this ditch complex, and indicates the further migration of the ditch outwards. Ditch 2 was over 4m wide (although it was truncated by Ditch 3 to the south) and at least 1.7m deep, although the top was not recorded, and had a U-shaped but slightly angular base (Fig 2.22).

Table 2.11: Phase 12 contexts Ditch 1 backfill Ditch 2 cut

Context	Description	Spit	Location
3901	Finds number over top of ditch [3902]	–	Main Tunnel east face
3903	Spit 1 – group context from ditch [3902] (Ditch 1)	–	Main Tunnel east face
3904	Cut of buried ditch (Ditch 2 – re-cut of ditch 1)	–	Main Tunnel east face
3905	Backfill of ditch [3902] (Ditch 1)	Spit 1	Main Tunnel east face
3906	Backfill of ditch [3902] (Ditch 1)	Spit 1	Main Tunnel east face
3907	Backfill of ditch [3902] (Ditch 1)	Spit 1	Main Tunnel east face
3908	Backfill of ditch [3902] (Ditch 1)	Spit 1	Main Tunnel east face
3909	Infill of ditch [3902] (Ditch 1)	Spits 1 + 2	Main Tunnel east face
3910	Infill of ditch [3902] (Ditch 1)	Spits 1, 2 + 3	Main Tunnel east face
3911	Infill of ditch [3902] (Ditch 1)	Spits 1, 2 + 3	Main Tunnel east face
3912	Backfill of ditch [3902] (Ditch 1)	Spit 1	Main Tunnel east face
3914	Backfill of ditch [3902] (Ditch 1)	Spit 1	Main Tunnel east face
3915	Backfill of ditch [3902] (Ditch 1)	Spit 1	Main Tunnel east face
3917	Backfill of ditch [3902] (Ditch 1)	Spit 1	Main Tunnel east face
3918	Spit 2 – group context from ditch [3902] (Ditch 1)	–	Main Tunnel
3919	Spit 3 – group context from ditch [3902] (Ditch 1)	–	Main Tunnel
3920	Spit 4 – group context from ditch [3902] (Ditch 1)	–	Main Tunnel
3921	Stake hole at base of ditch [3902] (Ditch 1)	Spit 4	Main Tunnel
3922	Stake hole at base of ditch [3902] (Ditch 1)	Spit 4	Main Tunnel
3923	Stake hole at base of ditch [3902] (Ditch 1)	Spit 4	Main Tunnel
3924	Stake hole at base of ditch [3902] (Ditch 1)	Spit 4	Main Tunnel
3925	Infill of ditch [3902] (Ditch 1)	Spit 4	Main Tunnel east face
3926	Organic infill of ditch [3902] (Ditch 1)	Spit 4	Main Tunnel east face
3927	Fill of stake hole [3921]	Spit 4	Main Tunnel east face
3928	Fill of stake hole [3922]	Spit 4	Main Tunnel east face
3929	Fill of stake hole [3923]	Spit 4	Main Tunnel east face
3930	Fill of stake hole [3924]	Spit 4	Main Tunnel east face
3931	Infill of ditch [3902] (Ditch 1)	Spits 1, 2 + 3	Main Tunnel east face
3932	Infill of ditch [3902] (Ditch 1)	Spits 1, 2 + 3	Main Tunnel east face
3933	Infill of ditch [3902] (Ditch 1)	Spits 2 + 3	Main Tunnel east face
3934	Infill of ditch [3902] (Ditch 1)	Spit 3	Main Tunnel east face
3935	Infill of ditch [3902] (Ditch 1)	Spit 3	Main Tunnel east face
3936	Infill of ditch [3902] (Ditch 1)	Spits 3 + 4	Main Tunnel east face
3937	Infill of ditch [3902] (Ditch 1)	Spits 3 + 4	Main Tunnel east face
3938	Infill of ditch [3902] (Ditch 1)	Spits 3 + 4	Main Tunnel east face
3939	Silty infill of ditch [3902] (Ditch 1)	Spit 4	Main Tunnel east face
3940	Infill of ditch [3902] (Ditch 1)	Spit 4	Main Tunnel east face
3941	Infill of ditch [3902] (Ditch 1)	–	Main Tunnel east face
3942	Infill of ditch [3902] (Ditch 1)	Spits 2 + 3	Main Tunnel east face
4135	Backfill of ditch cut [4151] (Ditch 1)	–	Main Tunnel east face
4136	Backfill of ditch cut [4151] (Ditch 1)	–	Main Tunnel east face
4137	Backfill of ditch cut [4151] (Ditch 1)	–	Main Tunnel east face
4138	Backfill of ditch cut [4151] (Ditch 1)	–	Main Tunnel east face
4139	Backfill of ditch cut [4151] (Ditch 1)	–	Main Tunnel east face
4140	Backfill of ditch cut [4151] (Ditch 1)	–	Main Tunnel east face
4141	Backfill of ditch cut [4151] (Ditch 1)	–	Main Tunnel east face
4150	Retaining wall - part of backfilling of Ditch 1	–	Main Tunnel east face

Table 2.12: Phase 13 contexts Ditch 2 backfill Ditch 3 cut

Context	Description	Location
3913	Fill of ditch [3904] (Ditch 2)	Main Tunnel east face
3943	Fill of ditch [3904] (Ditch 2) or poss Atkinson disturbance	Main Tunnel east face
4130	Retaining wall – part of backfilling of ditch re-cut [3904] (Ditch 2)	Main Tunnel east face
4131	Re-cut buried ditch (Ditch 2)	Main Tunnel east face
4132	Backfill of ditch re-cut [3904] (Ditch 2)	Main Tunnel east face
4133	Retaining wall – part of backfilling of ditch re-cut [3904] (Ditch 2)	Main Tunnel east face
4134	Backfill of ditch re-cut [3904] (Ditch 2)	Main Tunnel east face
4143	Compact layer in ditch re-cut [3904] (Ditch 2)	Main Tunnel east face
4144	Backfill of ditch re-cut [3904] (Ditch 2)	Main Tunnel east face
4145	Backfill of ditch re-cut [3904] (Ditch 2)	Main Tunnel east face
4146	Backfill of ditch re-cut [3904] (Ditch 2)	Main Tunnel east face
4147	Backfill of ditch re-cut [3904] (Ditch 2)	Main Tunnel east face
4149	Retaining wall – part of backfilling of ditch re-cut [3904] (Ditch 2)	Main Tunnel east face

Phase 14: The infilling of Ditch 3, and cutting of Ditch 4

In turn Ditch 3 was filled in, although the deposits were much siltier and the retaining wall technique was not used, suggesting that it had perhaps infilled naturally rather than deliberately. The fills comprised mixed chalk and silt loam, and include dark olive-brown silty clay, possibly representing a stabilisation horizon, but again were only recorded in section (Fig 2.24). This sequence no doubt continued above the evidence visible within the tunnel, but it was not recorded above this point.

These deposits were truncated by Ditch 4, a narrow feature (c 2.5m wide) with near vertical sides (Fig 2.22). As with Ditch 3 this extended below the tunnel floor and above the tunnel roof and therefore a depth of only 1.8m was recorded.

Fig 2.24
Ditch 3 infill.
(© English Heritage)

Phase 15: The backfilling of Ditch 4

Ditch 4 was backfilled with a sequence of chalk deposits between 0.1m and 0.3m thick (Fig 2.22). No finds were recorded from these fills, and they have been interpreted as representing deliberate backfill. The unweathered, vertical sides of Ditch 4 suggest that it was not open for long before this backfilling process began.

Phase 16: Final mound construction

Phase 16.1

The first few bays in the tunnel were not recorded in 2007/8 as they were concealed behind concrete supports left in place from the 1968–70 work; however, looking at the section recorded during this earlier work (Whittle 1997a; Foldout 2F and G) it is clear that Ditch 4 was re-cut again by the external ditch. The large external ditch, therefore, represents a later phase of the ditch re-cutting process, which had migrated further out. These external ditch fills were recorded in 2007/8 immediately outside the tunnel entrance in the portal area, and finds included a fragment of an eroded antler tine tip (SF 8002) (Worley, Chapter 3). Further information gleaned from earthwork survey is presented in Chapter 1.

Phase 16.2

Deposits relating to the final phases of the mound were examined in 2007 and 2008 in two areas: on the side of the monument above the tunnel portal during remediation work to fill in large hollows that had formed there, and on the summit, primarily in the trench excavated in

Table 2.13: Phase 14 contexts Ditch 3 backfill Ditch 4 cut

Context	Description	Location
4027	Infilling of ditch re-cut [4131] (Ditch 3)	Main Tunnel east face
4125	Infilling of ditch re-cut [4131] (Ditch 3)	Main Tunnel east face
4126	Infilling of ditch re-cut [4131] (Ditch 3)	Main Tunnel east face
4127	Infilling of ditch re-cut [4131] (Ditch 3)	Main Tunnel east face
4128	Infilling of ditch re-cut [4131] (Ditch 3)	Main Tunnel east face
4129	Infilling of ditch re-cut [4131] (Ditch 3)	Main Tunnel east face
4142	Infilling of ditch re-cut [4131] (Ditch 3)	Main Tunnel east face
4148	Infilling of ditch re-cut [4131] (Ditch 3)	Main Tunnel east face
4018	Re-cut buried ditch (Ditch 4)	Main Tunnel east face

Table 2.14: Phase 15 contexts Ditch 4 backfill

Context	Description	Location
4021	Backfill of ditch re-cut [4018] (Ditch 4)	Main Tunnel east face
4022	Backfill of ditch re-cut [4018] (Ditch 4)	Main Tunnel east face
4023	Backfill of ditch re-cut [4018] (Ditch 4)	Main Tunnel east face
4024	Backfill of ditch re-cut [4018] (Ditch 4)	Main Tunnel east face
4025	Backfill of ditch re-cut [4018] (Ditch 4)	Main Tunnel east face
4026	Backfill of ditch re-cut [4018] (Ditch 4)	Main Tunnel east face
4123	Backfill of ditch re-cut [4018] (Ditch 4)	Main Tunnel east face
4124	Backfill of ditch re-cut [4018] (Ditch 4)	Main Tunnel east face

2007, but also the two earlier (2001) trenches, as well as the collapsed area.

Watching brief on the southern slope

A watching brief in 2008 (*see* Chapter 10) was conducted during remediation work to fill in a hollow caused by earlier collapses on the southern slope above the portal area (Fig 2.25). The topsoil and subsoil were stripped using a mechanical digger and the area was subsequently filled with chalk. The contexts recorded in this area were formed of deposits of horizontal chalk as well as larger pieces of chalk rubble, the rubble possibly forming a retaining wall as observed for Ditches 2 and 3 revealed in the tunnel. The horizontally laid chalk is reminiscent of Petrie's description of the mound matrix encountered a little further to the east, where the deposits were separated by bands of yellow clay (1924, 217).

Fig 2.25
The Hillside works.
(© English Heritage)

The earliest deposit recorded during this watching brief was a layer of loose chalk, which contained the most complete antler pick from the excavations (reconstructed from a number of fragments) (Worley, Chapter 3; Fig 3.9). SF 8754 refits to form a fragment of beam, clearly used as a pick, retaining parts of the bez and trez tines, and has been removed below the crown. Also from this context was a chalk block retaining two separate impressions of pick working (SF 8753). The first consists of a mark visible in section with evidence for two blows, set at slightly different angles, the second blow overlying the first in part. The second mark is a hollow caused by hitting the chalk surface with a tine end (Fig 3.13). This evidence suggests that the picks were used in effect as mattocks, rather than handled wedges (Worley, Chapter 3).

Summit excavations

Three trenches were excavated on the summit – two in 2001 and one in 2007. The 2001 trenches were small-scale excavations adjacent to the crater (Trenches A and B, measuring 3m x 1.5m and 4m x 1.5m respectively) and were designed to evaluate material being eroded into the crater. The 2007 trench on the summit measured 5m x 3m and was excavated in order to better understand a series of curvilinear chalk walls that had been exposed in a large trench on the summit in 1970. For this reason one metre of the 1970 Cutting 3 was re-excavated and the trench was extended by a further two metres to the west (Figs 2.26 and 2.30).

The prehistoric deposits recorded in the 2007 trench comprised a series of layers of fine chalk dumps lain on top of one another (interwall deposits) and held in place on the northern side by large, loose pieces of chalk rubble, which effectively formed a revetment wall, one chalk lump thick (*c* 0.3m) and at an angle of between 45° and 65° (Walls 1, 2 and 3). This is a similar technique to that seen on the side of the mound during the watching brief as well as in the back-filled buried ditches within the tunnel (discussed *above*) and is clearly the construction technique used to build the outer phases of the Neolithic mound. Indeed, similar techniques have previously been recorded within the bank at Avebury by Alexander Keiller (1939, 232) and the bank at Marden henge by Geoffrey Wainwright (1971, 190).

The prehistoric deposits were recorded at a maximum level of 186.74m OD (Fig 2.29). The revetment walls recorded in the 2007 trench are

some of the same walls recorded by the 1970's team (walls {805}, {808} and {811}), although it should be noted that since they left them *in situ* (Fig 2.26) by slicing through the deposits behind them, they could not have been excavated stratigraphically, as one wall would have to be removed in order to fully see the next set of layers (*see* Fig 2.29).

Chalk Wall 1 ([4812]), the earliest recorded deposit in the 2007 trench, was only just evident in the southern part of the trench, and not excavated (Fig 2.30). From a small slot 0.6m deep on the eastern side of the trench, it could be seen that five layers of chalk had been dumped to the north of this wall. An antler tine in very good condition (SF 8523), and two other fragments in moderate condition, including a naturally shed antler burr, came from this area.

Wall 2 ([4809]) was *c* 1.7m away from Wall 1 (Figs 2.27, 2.29 and 2.30), and again revetted a number of layers of white chalk that had been dumped to the north of Wall 1. These interwall deposits (unlike the previous ones) were excavated to the full extent of the trench and contained flint flakes as well as two very small and unidentifiable sherds of pottery, which could be intrusive. On the western side of the trench and built into the revetment wall was a well-defined cluster of 11 fragments of sarsen stones (Fig 2.28). The majority of these showed signs of reduction: two had traces of negative bulbs and flake scars indicative of controlled direct percussion, whilst another had a pinkish tinge to the cortex, which is taken as evidence for burning, perhaps to assist fracture and reduction. Two stones refit and others look as if they belong to the same block (Pollard, Chapter 3). Within the same defined area were three larger fragments of antler in good condition with evidence for wear (SF 8525, SF 8526 and SF 8527). Unfortunately SF 8527 went missing from the site office soon after discovery, however photographs of it *in situ* show that it was the tip of a tine about 100mm long and in good or moderate condition, and it is thought that it would have refitted with SF 8526 to form part of the crown of an antler from a mature stag of development stage D or above (Worley, Chapter 3). These antler fragments appear to have been associated with the sarsen stone, suggesting that together they represent placed deposits. Photographs of the excavated 1970 trench (Cutting 3) also show clusters of sarsen stone built into the retaining walls, suggesting that this may have been a common feature (*see* discussion in Chapter 7; Fig 7.2).

Once again a series of layers of loose chalk, occasionally mixed with silt (interwall deposits) and containing animal bone and antler fragments, were laid on the northern side of Wall 2, and were, in turn, revetted by chalk Wall 3 ([4808]) (Figs 2.29 and 2.30), which lay *c* 1.5m away from Wall 2. A possible radial wall ([4838]) comprising pieces of chalk rubble was recorded perpendicular to Wall 3 on the western side of the trench; although very little of this was seen and it was unclear whether this was a revetment wall or a slightly more rubble-rich dump layer (Fig 2.30).

Recovered from all these deposits were a number of bones, such as badger and mole and particularly frog and toad bones, the latter being evident in abundance. However, a live common frog was also found in a void of one of the chalk walls, well within the upper levels of the prehistoric deposits, suggesting that these bones and many of the other ecofacts might be intrusive (*see* Chapter 10).

Excavated by Fachtna McAvoy in 2001, Trench A was 3m long and 1.5m wide and was located on the west side of the collapsed area (Fig 2.30). Excavation took place to a general depth of 0.4m across the trench and recorded layers of chalk and dumps of chalk blocks, which, if a larger area had been excavated, may have been revealed to form part of a revetting wall. Three flint flakes were recovered from this

context, as well as a single sherd of comb-decorated Beaker pottery with square-tooth comb impressions with a complex motif with filled or reserved triangles (Cleal, Chapter 3). A small fragment of later pottery was also recorded in this layer, suggesting that it had at some stage been disturbed, and the Beaker sherd should not be considered *in situ*.

Coeval with Trench A was Trench B, a 4m long and 1.5m wide trench that was located on the east side of the crater. A substantial chalk wall was recorded running north to south and occupying most of the trench (Fig 2.30).

Fig 2.27
Revetment Wall 2 after excavation of deposits to the north. Scale 2m.
(© English Heritage)

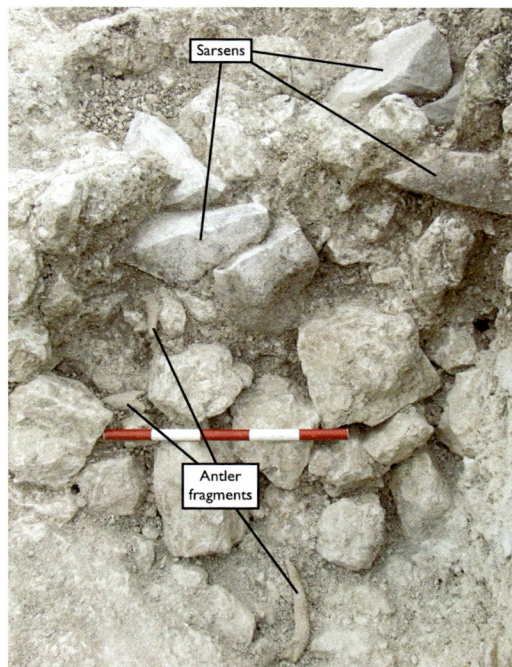

Fig 2.28
Detail of the western part of Wall 2 showing sarsen stones and antler fragments. Scale 0.5m.
(© English Heritage)

The wall was composed of a chalk rubble core, with chalk at 0.10–0.20m in size, between two chalk faces made of larger blocks *c* 0.35–0.40m in size. In hindsight this feature is perhaps likely to represent two chalk walls as well as chalk dump layers between them.

Deposits recorded in the collapsed area

Deposits were recorded in the collapsed area on the summit in January 2001, soon after it opened up and prior to temporary filling, and again in 2007 and 2008 after the temporary filling had

Fig 2.29
Section through the 2007 trench showing mound deposits and revetment walls. (Eddie Lyons, © English Heritage)

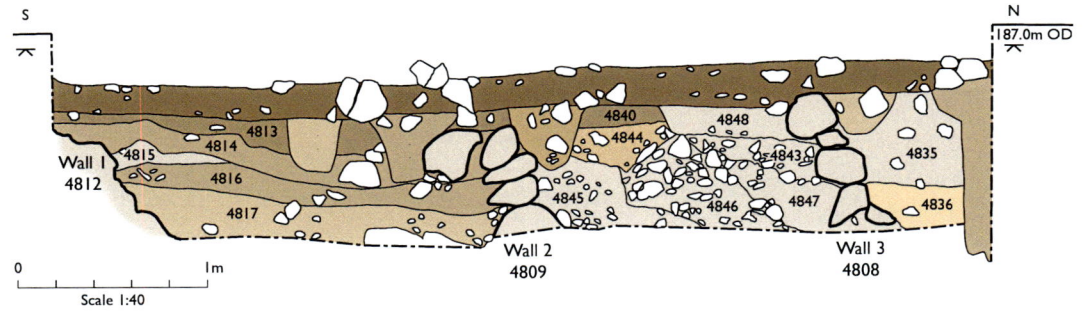

Fig 2.30
Plan of the prehistoric features on the summit. (Eddie Lyons, © English Heritage)

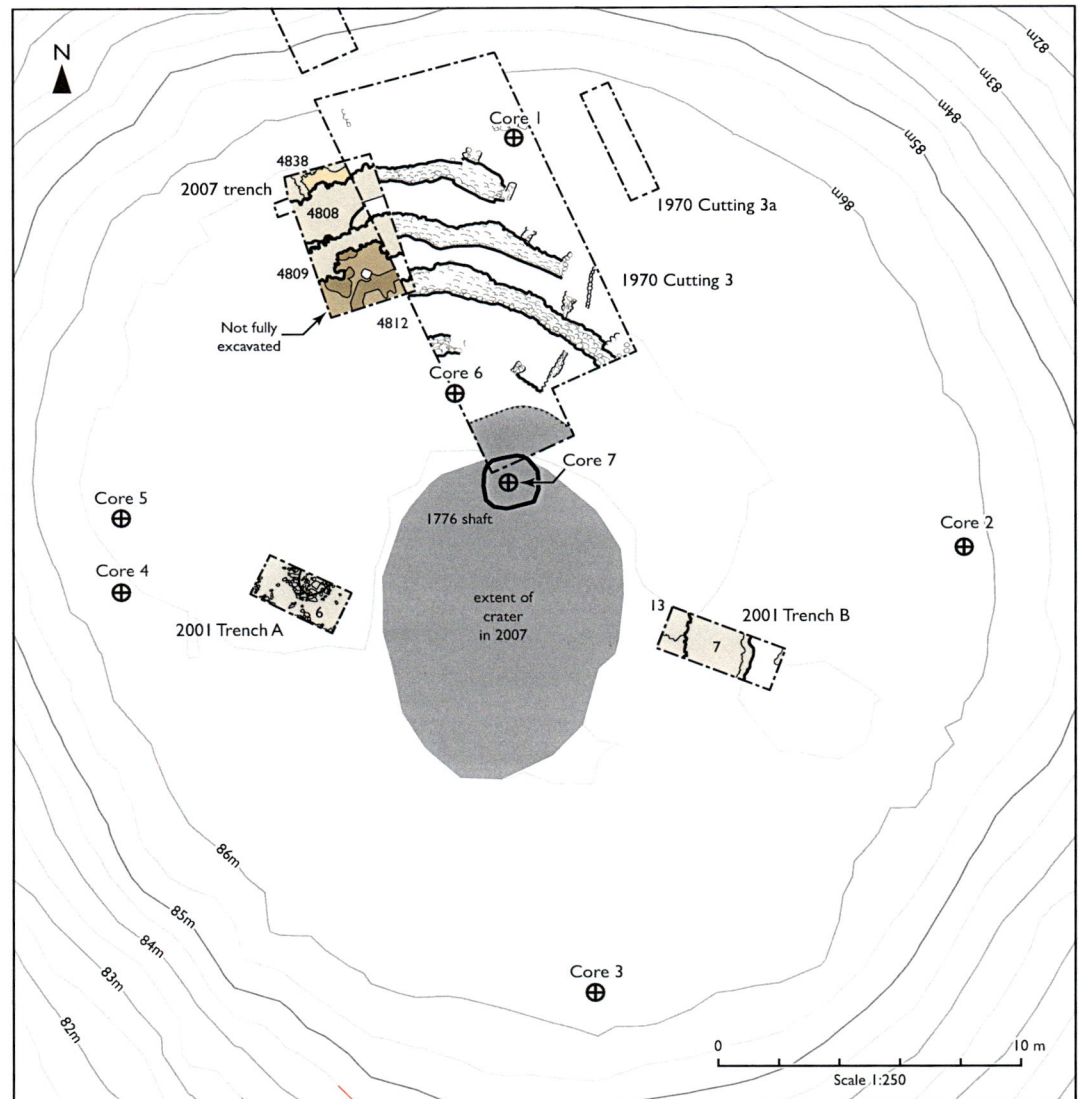

been removed (and after further collapse had occurred). The collapsed area was 11m by 8m and recorded to a maximum depth of 13.5m and therefore deposits to this depth were exposed. However, working in a crater of this depth, with loose and unstable sides, posed clear logistical and health and safety problems, and did not lend itself to accurate recording. Recording work was therefore extremely limited and the deposits were only broadly characterised. Further to this, access into the shaft to clean the sides was not possible, and therefore it was difficult to differentiate between *in situ* deposits and material that had collapsed in from the top, some of which adhered to the sides lower down often creating the erroneous appearance of features.

Generally speaking, the contexts visible in the sides of the shaft comprised a number of different contexts of loose chalk rubble, finer chalk and layers of light brown 'Toblerone' clay comprising the upper layers of the mound, some of the chalk blocks presumably represent revetting walls. Sarsen boulders were visible in one layer, seen soon after the hole opened up. The layer measured *c* 0.4m in thickness and, at around 10m from the top, coincided with the level of the first terrace upon which a sarsen boulder of similar size was observed eroding from the side during the earthwork survey. Intermittently above this was a thick pale grey layer and then reaching to the summit above this was a unit comprising chalk rubble with soil lenses and interbedded with lenses of pale grey decayed chalk.

A fragment of cattle bone (SF 8095) was recovered 3.6m from the top of the shaft in 2008, whilst a lens of mid orangey-brown chalky clay was recorded 6.8m from the top. An environmental sample of this was taken when the Clerk of Works abseiled down to the base of the shaft (Fig 2.31), and three pieces of flint micro-debitage were recovered from the sample.

Composing the mound: a summary of the phases (*see* Foldout 3K–N)

Activity on the site appears to have commenced with the ground being prepared by the removal of much of the soil horizon demarcating an area. This was evident in the tunnel sides but it is unknown how extensive this stripped area was and although the OLS was recorded as a single context, in reality the removal of the turf may

Fig 2.31
Abseiling down the side of the collapsed area to take a sample.
(© English Heritage)

well not have been a single event but a series of recurring ones – small areas prepared as the monument developed. Indeed the lack of evidence for vegetation growth supports the view that it was stripped incrementally. This on-going activity would have removed evidence for earlier features or structures. There is little evidence to suggest what activity may have occurred at this time, although a possible hearth, as evidenced by a concentration of charcoal and charred material within the OLS, may indicate some activity. The OLS in the central area had a pronounced organic layer on it which may well be imported material – and one wonders whether reeds or grasses were laid down as a mat (*see* Chapter 5). Over this a low gravel mound, no higher than 0.8m and about 10m in diameter, was constructed. The gravel was imported to the site and the sides may have been kept from collapsing by a thin layer of mixed topsoil and subsoil.

The gravel mound was enlarged by a stake-defined mound formed of organic material (Lower Organic Mound) and perhaps surrounded by smaller mounds, at least one of which appeared to have its own surrounding gully, and biological remains from it suggest a woodland edge setting, contrasting with the main mound. This enlarged the earlier mound to at least 1.1m high and perhaps as much as 22m in diameter. The material used was a mix of topsoil, subsoil and turf, derived primarily from an area of clay-with-flints material and

Table 2.15: Phase 16 contexts Final mound construction

Context	Description	Location
4014	External ditch fill	Main Tunnel east face
4015	External ditch fill	Main Tunnel east face
4016	External ditch fill	Main Tunnel east face
4017	External ditch fill	Main Tunnel east face
4019	External ditch fill	Main Tunnel east face
4020	External ditch fill	Main Tunnel east face
3007	External ditch fill	Main Tunnel west face
3008	External ditch fill	Main Tunnel
3009	External ditch fill	Main Tunnel west face
3010	External ditch fill	Main Tunnel west face
3011	External ditch fill	Main Tunnel west face
3018	Cut of external ditch	Main Tunnel west face
4006	External ditch fill	Main Tunnel east face
4007	External ditch fill	Main Tunnel east face
4008	External ditch fill	Main Tunnel east face
4009	External ditch fill	Main Tunnel east face
4010	External ditch fill	Main Tunnel east face
4011	External ditch fill	Main Tunnel east face
4	Interwall deposit	Summit (2001 trench A)
6	Interwall deposit	Summit (2001 trench A)
7	Chalk rubble wall	Summit (2001 trench B)
10	Interwall deposit	Summit (2001 trench B)
12	Interwall deposit	Summit (2001 trench B)
13	Chalk rubble wall	Summit (2001 trench B)
30	Chalk layer	Summit (2001 collapsed area)
31	Chalk layer	Summit (2001 collapsed area)
32	Chalk rubble wall	Summit (2001 shaft)
4808	Chalk rubble wall (Wall 3)	Summit (2007 excavation)
4809	Chalk rubble wall (Wall 2)	Summit (2007 excavation)
4812	Chalk rubble wall (Wall 1)	Summit (2007 excavation)
4813	Interwall deposit	Summit (2007 excavation)
4814	Interwall deposit	Summit (2007 excavation)
4815	Interwall deposit	Summit (2007 excavation)
4816	Interwall deposit	Summit (2007 excavation)
4817	Interwall deposit	Summit (2007 excavation)
4835	Interwall deposit	Summit (2007 excavation)
4836	Interwall deposit	Summit (2007 excavation)
4838	Interwall deposit	Summit (2007 excavation)
4839	Interwall deposit	Summit (2007 excavation)
4840	Interwall deposit	Summit (2007 excavation)
4843	Interwall deposit	Summit (2007 excavation)
4844	Interwall deposit	Summit (2007 excavation)
4845	Interwall deposit	Summit (2007 excavation)
4846	Interwall deposit	Summit (2007 excavation)
4847	Interwall deposit	Summit (2007 excavation)
4848	Interwall deposit	Summit (2007 excavation)
4873	Clayey deposit	Summit (2007 collapsed area)
4874	Chalk layer	Summit (2007 collapsed area)
4883	Chalk layer	Summit (2007 collapsed area)
4904	Chalk final phase of mound	Hillside Watching Brief
4907	Chalk final phase of mound	Hillside Watching Brief
4908	Chalk final phase of mound	Hillside Watching Brief
4909	Chalk final phase of mound	Hillside Watching Brief
4910	Chalk final phase of mound	Hillside Watching Brief
4911	Chalk final phase of mound	Hillside Watching Brief
4912	Chalk final phase of mound	Hillside Watching Brief

mainly from a grassland habitat, as well as bands of gravel and chalk, and, as Atkinson suggested, is interpreted as having been formed of 'basket' loads of material brought in and piled over the Gravel Mound. This material may well have been the turf, topsoil and subsoil removed during the initial site preparation, although if this was the case it would have been stored elsewhere and then returned to cover the Gravel Mound. A stakehole was recorded on the western edge of this mound and can be combined with other stakeholes recorded during the 1968–70 work to suggest that a sequence of stakes demarcated its edge.

At least two pits were then dug into the top of the central mound, both measuring at least one metre in diameter and over half a metre deep. They were rapidly infilled with turf and topsoil; worker ants preserved in one of the pits are likely to represent an ant nest that had become inadvertently incorporated during backfilling. There were a few finds consisting of low quantities of burnt and struck flint. All the above activity was completely encased by a series of mixed layers of topsoil, subsoil, turf, gravel, and chalk forming a mound about 35m in diameter and around five or six metres in height (Upper Organic Mound). The topsoil and subsoil material had derived principally from soils that had developed over chalk, rather than clay-with-flints material, contrasting with the earlier mound material and suggesting that they had been brought in from slightly further away (although not necessarily very far). A number of naturally rounded sarsen boulders, some of which were quite substantial, were incorporated within the matrix of this mound. There was no evidence that these stones formed any sort of setting over or around it, which contrasts with the 1849 descriptions (see Fig 1.10).

The central mound was then enlarged incrementally by at least five surrounding chalk and clay banks, presumably forming encircling rings around the above mound, each new ring expanding the monument outward by a few more metres. The tops of two of the banks (Bank 2 and Bank 4) were not seen and therefore could have continued over the Upper Organic Mound, covering it entirely. Banks 1, 3 and 5, however, were much smaller (c 1.5m high).

The restrictions of the tunnel meant that little could be explored above the banks, and so it is difficult to say what exactly was going on above them. Further, from Bay 34 outwards, the tunnel dipped down below the Old Land Surface. These banks may well have been a construction technique: a way of building a larger mound – bank after bank piled up over each other. Clearly further complex activity occurred above these banks since a series of interleaved organic layers was seen high up at the top of a void within the mound, perhaps forming a further organic mound higher up in the Hill. The main point to note is that activity is represented by a series of complex phases, the mound growing in size incrementally.

The material for at least the first few banks may well have been quarried from a buried ditch recorded near the tunnel entrance and buried under later phases of the mound. This ditch was over 6.5m deep and over 6m in width, and, if circular, would be about 100m in diameter. The diameter is of interest as it is directly comparable with Stonehenge and Flagstones, although they are both earlier in date (see Fig. 7.4). Although the ditch has been interpreted as contemporary with the bank phases (and this is supported by radiocarbon dates, see Marshall et al, Chapter 4), the ditch cannot be ruled out as an early feature of the monument, perhaps the earliest. The ditch cut was recorded in the tunnel side as well as in a machine-excavated slot through the tunnel floor, which provided a clear section through to the base of the ditch. It clearly terminated on the western side of the tunnel, implying a ditch terminus. This is aligned with a causeway in the external ditch and may represent an access route into the enclosure. It is not clear whether this was dug before or after the Upper Organic Mound, although presumably, if the chalk was used to build the banks, afterwards.

Ditch 1 was backfilled, the unweathered sides showing that this had been a rapid process, and then re-cut at least four times, and probably many more since it may have advanced seamlessly until manifested as the external ditch that is visible on the surface and which itself may well be the result of several phases. It is difficult to know what to make of the ditch re-cuts; perhaps causewayed enclosure ditches formed a precedent here, although they may also well represent further phases of the mound encroaching over the top, further emphasising the complex and incremental nature of activity. In other words, as the Hill expanded outwards, the buried ditch was deliberately backfilled and re-cut slightly further out. This necessity to keep the ditch open emphasises that the ditch itself may have been an important feature of the monument.

The later phases of the mound were seen in excavation trenches on the summit as well as during a watching brief on the southern side above the portal. Both these areas, but particularly the summit, showed the final phases of the mound were formed by a series of horizontal layers of fine chalk dumps, laid on top of one another and held in place by large, loose pieces of chalk rubble, which effectively formed a rough, steeply tilting, revetment wall built in concentric rings. These prevented the horizontal layers of chalk from collapsing and provided structural stability, whilst also presumably allowing rainwater to drain freely through the mound. It may be these revetment walls have surface expression in the traces of in the recent earthwork survey as a series of short straight lengths on the outer edges and in the traces of ledges. Seen on the summit and on the sides, this is clearly the construction technique used to build the outer phases of the Neolithic mound and differs from the more piecemeal organic mounds and then chalk and clay bank technique seen within the tunnel. It is impossible to tell from our work at which point the technique changed from piecemeal to a more formal approach, but it is clear that two very different styles of construction were in operation.

3

The Prehistoric Finds

BARRY BISHOP, ROSAMUND CLEAL, DAVID FIELD, ROB IXER,
JOSHUA POLLARD AND FAY WORLEY

This chapter provides individually authored summaries of the various specialist analyses of the artefacts present primarily within the prehistoric phases of Silbury Hill. It begins with a discussion of the flint recovered from the conservation project. It is suggested that the paucity of worked flint indicates that its use did not feature as part of the construction operations, and that Silbury Hill may have been kept deliberately clean of worked flint. It also notes the inclusion of large, unworked flint nodules that had been extracted directly from the parent chalk and deliberately brought to the site, although not necessarily from a great distance. Sarsen stone was also incorporated into the mound, recorded both from the Upper Organic Mound within the tunnels and from the excavations on the summit. Sarsen is locally available and therefore had not necessarily travelled far, however, it is argued that it should be considered, alongside the unworked flint nodules, the chalk, turf, gravel and soil, as a construction material, even if its incorporation did not offer any structural advantage. Examination of the stones, as discussed below, shows a difference between those recovered from the UOM and those from the summit, with nearly all sarsens from the former being unmodified, and those from the latter mostly fragmented and in some cases worked. It is argued below that the incorporation of sarsen is likely to do with its materiality. This can be contrasted with the worked flint and other domestically significant materials which appear to have been excluded. The exception being two small sherds of Beaker pottery, however these post-date the construction of the Hill.

Other types of stone incorporated into the Hill and reported on here are four struck flakes of spotted dolerite recovered from the summit, three from the 2007 excavation and one from the earlier 1968–70 work. All the fragments are from later contexts (subsoil or topsoil); however a prehistoric

origin for them remains a possibility. A worked flake of Welsh rhyolite is also discussed. This piece, recovered in the nineteenth-century from a Roman well near the base of Silbury, has characteristics with the rhyolite that defines the majority of Group VIII axes.

The fragmented sarsen on the summit appears to be associated with red deer antler fragments. The antler is a relatively small and highly fragmented assemblage probably deriving from tools used in the construction of the mound. Further evidence for the use of antler tools to construct the mound comes from a block of chalk bearing the imprint of antler strikes. It is suggested that those antlers deposited at Silbury may have been placed rather than casually discarded.

The flint

Barry Bishop

A total of 409 pieces of worked flint and 21 pieces of burnt flint were recovered during the Silbury Hill Conservation Project, the bulk of it during the 2007/8 remedial works. Also present throughout the monument are numerous flint nodules that show few signs of modification beyond occasional mechanical 'knocks'.

The majority of the worked flint, 260 pieces, consist of small flakes, flake fragments and pieces of knapping shatter that measure 10mm or less in maximum dimension (termed here micro-debitage). Virtually all of this was recovered from samples and most of the pieces are only a few millimetres in size.

Of the remaining 149 pieces, 42 (28%) were recovered from undisturbed prehistoric contexts associated with the construction of the monument. Sixty pieces (40%) came from collapsed mound contexts infilling the tunnels and are also likely to have been closely associated with the construction of the monument, whilst the remainder, 47 pieces (32%) were recovered from post-prehistoric disturbance and contexts on the mound's surface and could potentially post-date its construction. A much greater proportion of the micro-debitage, some 94%, was recovered from the prehistoric contexts, presumably at least partly reflecting the sampling methodology. The burnt flint also predominantly came from prehistoric contexts with small quantities present in the soil horizons as recorded on the summit (Table 3.1).

Burnt flint

Twenty-one pieces of burnt flint, weighing 119g, were recovered from five of the phases (*see* Table 3.1). This material was variably burnt but all to the degree that it had changed colour and become fire-crazed. The quantities present do not indicate large-scale deliberate production but rather the incidental burning of flint from hearths or other uses of fire. The largest quantities came from Ditch 1 ([3902]) and from

the Phase 5 pits, notably pit [3074], but burnt flint was also present in smaller quantities in the Gravel Mound, in the 'interwall' deposits and from residual contexts on the summit. The quantities from any of the contexts are minimal and, despite the extensive sampling, very few small burnt flint fragments were recovered, suggesting that the use of fire and activities associated with it, such as food preparation, played a very limited role at the site during the monument's construction.

Worked flint

Materials

The raw materials consist of thermally affected nodular flint that varies from a 'glassy' trans-lucent grey/black to a more opaque matt black, both having speckled and mottled grey cherty inclusions. Where present, cortex is rough and slightly weathered with frequent thermal scars and 'potlid' spalls on the surface. The cortex on

Table 3.1: Quantification of lithic material by phase

	Unretouched flakes over 10mm max diam						Blades over 10mm max diam			Cores			Retouched						Micro-debitage		Burnt flint	
	Decortication	Trimming	Core Modification	Mis-struck	Useable	Fragment	Micro-blade	Prismatic	Non-prismatic	Flake	Minimally worked	Shattered fragments	Backed Knife	Edge blunted	Denticulated	Miscellaneous	Piercer	Serrate	Flakes	Fragments	Number	Weight (g)
Total	**38**	**20**	**3**	**1**	**39**	**17**	**1**	**2**	**4**	**5**	**6**	**5**	**1**	**3**	**1**	**1**	**1**	**1**	**193**	**67**	**21**	**119**
Ph 2																			23	6		
Ph 3						1		1											31	9	1	6
Ph 4	2	1										1							39	23		
Ph 5		1			3				1				1						47	15	11	24
Ph 6																			8	2		
Ph 11		1																	16			
Ph 12	4		1		7	4	1	1	1	1				2					16	6	4	64
Ph 16	1	3			2	1						1							3		1	8
Ph 17	6	5							1			1							7	3		
Ph 18	1				1																	
Ph 20.1	8	8			8	7						1							3	3	4	17
Ph 20.2	16	1	2	1	18	4			1	4	6	1		1	1	1	1	1				

some pieces had been stained brown and these are likely to have derived from deposits of clay-with-flints as recorded beneath the monument. A single piece, from collapsed tunnel deposits, had been struck from a rounded alluvial pebble although it is not entirely certain that it was deliberately struck.

Silbury sits on the interface of the Holywell Nodular Chalk Formation (Middle Chalk) and the West Melbury Marly Chalk Formation (Lower Chalk), which, in this part of the sequence, is not known to contain quantities of large nodular flint. The nearest nodular flint-bearing chalk (Upper and upper parts of Middle Chalk) occurs to the south-west of Silbury some 300m away and at Waden Hill, c 400m to the north-east. However, colluvial deposits containing derived flint nodules similar to those used for Silbury's worked flint assemblage extend into the valley floor closer to the monument.

There is no obvious evidence for any use of mined flint within the struck assemblage but, interestingly, the unworked flint nodules found within the main chalk body of the monument are mostly unweathered and have a thick powdery cortex, indicative of being extracted directly from the chalk. They are of a broadly similar type of flint to that used for the struck assemblage but, as the latter was made from derived nodules, are not likely to be the source for the raw materials. As flint nodules are not present in the chalk in the immediate vicinity, these must have been brought to the site and deliberately incorporated into the monument.

Technology and typology

The assemblage as a whole was dominated by knapping waste and only around a third of the flakes and blades can be considered as potentially useable. The retouched pieces formed a relatively high proportion of the assemblage; although only contributing 2% of the whole, this is increased to over 5% if the micro-debitage is excluded (*see* Table 3.1).

No typologically diagnostic pieces are present but the technological characteristics of the bulk of the assemblage is typical of later 3rd and early 2nd millennium BC industries. A few pieces are, however, likely to pre-date Silbury's construction, although these cannot be certainly associated with the site as they may have been introduced within their burial matrix. Most notable are the micro- and prismatic blades characteristic of Mesolithic or Early Neolithic industries recovered from the Gravel Mound, collapse from the Organic Mound and from the fill of Ditch 1.

The bulk of the assemblage is likely to be at least broadly contemporary with the construction of the monument (Marshall *et al*, Chapter 4). Overall, reduction appears to have been rather opportunistic with little effort made to prepare cores or attempt standardised removals. Consequently, flakes are variable in shape and size but tend towards being small, broad and thick, and are comparable with flakes from other Later Neolithic or Early Bronze Age industries as aggregated by Pitts (1978, 194) (Tables 3.2 and 3.3).

Table 3.2: Metrical characteristics of flakes

All unretouched flakes measuring 10mm or more in at least one dimension

	Length	Breadth	Width
Maximum (mm)	65	58	22
Minimum (mm)	4	4	1
Average (mm)	26.8	24.3	6.7

Table 3.3: Unretouched flake shapes

Shape	Narrow blades	Blades	Narrow flakes	Flakes	Broad flakes
Breadth / Length Ratio	0.21–0.4	0.41–0.6	0.61–0.8	0.81–1.0	1.0+
All complete unretouched flakes (%)	1.2	11.8	28.2	24.7	34.1

The principal technological attributes of the unretouched flakes also demonstrate an expedient and somewhat unstructured approach to reduction (Table 3.4). Striking platforms were rarely modified and two-thirds of the flakes are plain or cortical types, with nearly all of those that were modified being only lightly edge-trimmed. The striking platforms tend to be wide, varying from 1mm to 15mm and averaging at 3.9mm. A predominant use of hard hammer percussion is indicated by the high frequency of pronounced bulbs of percussion and hinged distal terminations. The majority of dorsal surfaces have unidirectional flake removal scars and nearly a quarter are predominantly cortical, indicative of both primary working and short, simple reduction sequences. This is also supported by the high number of flakes retaining cortex; 14% have wholly cortical dorsal surfaces and nearly 65% retain some cortex.

The cores equally reflect an expedient approach to reduction; all are flake cores with 6 of the 11 recovered being minimally reduced, these having only a few flakes removed, although few of the cores could be described as extensively reduced (Table 3.5). Two of the remainder are multi-platformed, two have single platforms and one is centripetally reduced, this having been made on a large flake (Fig 3.1). In addition to the complete cores, five conchoidally fractured chunks, representing fragments of cores that shattered during reduction, are present. The centripetally worked core came from the fill of Ditch 1 ([3919]; Fig 3.1, no 3) and the remainder from collapse material infilling the tunnel.

There was little evidence for any of the cores being pre-formed prior to concerted flake removal, nor for attempts to rejuvenate the cores once they started to fail. Overall they reflect a rather opportunistic approach to obtaining

Table 3.4: Principal technological attributes of unretouched flakes

Principal technological attributes of all unretouched flakes							
Striking platform type % (n=108)		Bulb of Percussion Type % (n=109)		Distal Termination Type % (n=100)		Dorsal Scar Pattern % (n=114)	
Abraded	0.9	Diffuse	27.5	Feathered	54.0	Cortex > 75%	23.7
Cortical	16.7	Hemispherical	8.3	Hinged	40.0	Multidirectional	11.4
Dihedral	1.9	Pronounced	64.2	Overshot	3.0	Opposed	2.6
Edge trimmed	16.7			Stepped	3.0	Parallel	3.5
Facetted	0.9					Orthogonal	2.6
Plain	50.0					Unidirectional	56.2
Shattered	12.9						

Table 3.5: Descriptions of cores

Context	Phase	Type	Weight (g)	Comments
3919	12.1	Centripetal	30	Made on thick flake segment, Bifacial centripetal flaking producing small short flakes. Very simple 'Levallois' variant? (Fig 3.1 no 3)
3812	20.2	Minimal	72	Angular thermally fractured nodule with a short series of narrow flakes removed from one end
3817	20.2	Single platformed	195	Slab of tabular flint with a short series of wide flakes removed from one edge, possibly abandoned as thermal flaws started to emerge (Fig 3.1 no 1)
3830	20.2	Minimal	96	Angular thermally fractured nodule with a short series of narrow flakes removed from one end
3840	20.2	Minimal	67	Angular thermally fractured nodule with a few flakes removed from one end
3840	20.2	Minimal	121	Angular thermally fractured nodule with a short series of narrow flakes removed from one end
3841	20.2	Single platformed	49	Nodular fragment with many attempts at flake removal but generally unsuccessful due to thermal flaws
3851	20.2	Multi-platformed	37	Several flakes removed but abandoned due to thermal shattering
3851	20.2	Minimal	91	Angular chunk with a few flake attempts made at various locations
3854	20.2	Minimal	61	Angular chunk with a few flake attempts made at one end
3860	20.2	Multi-platformed	50	Produced mostly short flakes but some narrow flakes removed at an earlier stage (Fig 3.1 no 2)

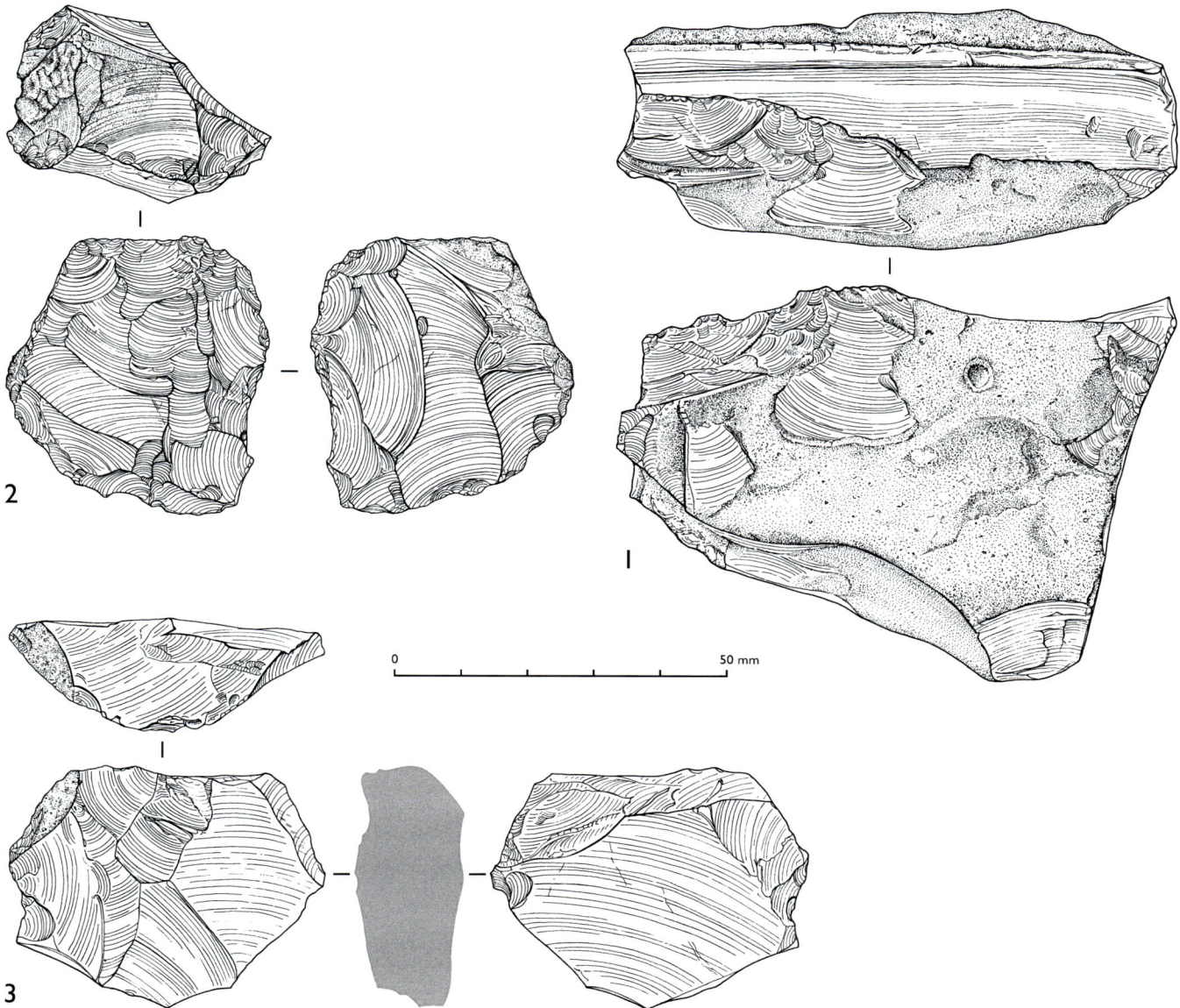

0 ——————— 50 mm

suitable flakes, although the centripetally reduced core, recovered from Ditch 1 ([3919]), is a very simple variant of the Later Neolithic 'Levallois' technique. These are often associated with the preparation of blanks used for more elaborate retouched forms, such as transverse arrowheads. No such pieces were recovered, however.

Eight retouched implements were recorded; these mostly consisted of simple edge-blunted flakes made on broad blanks that would have been suitable for simple cutting or piercing tasks (Fig 3.2, nos 4–11; Table 3.6). None of the

normally ubiquitous scrapers are present, nor are there any elaborate implements or 'prestigious' types, such as arrowheads or axes. Overall, the retouched component is restricted and demonstrates a rather expedient and functional approach to obtaining suitable edges, and probably manufactured as needed. The backed knife (Fig 3.2, no 4) was recovered from the secondary fill of pit [3067] and two of the edge-blunted flakes were recovered from the fills of Ditch 1 ([3918] and [3926]; Figs 3.2, nos 5 and 6), with the remainder coming from unstratified or tunnel fill deposits.

Fig 3.1
Flint cores from the 2007/8
Silbury excavations.
1 [3817] Single platformed
core from tunnel collapse;
2 [3860] Multi-platformed
core from tunnel backfill;
3 [3919] Centripetally
worked core from Ditch 1.
(Chris Evans,
© English Heritage)

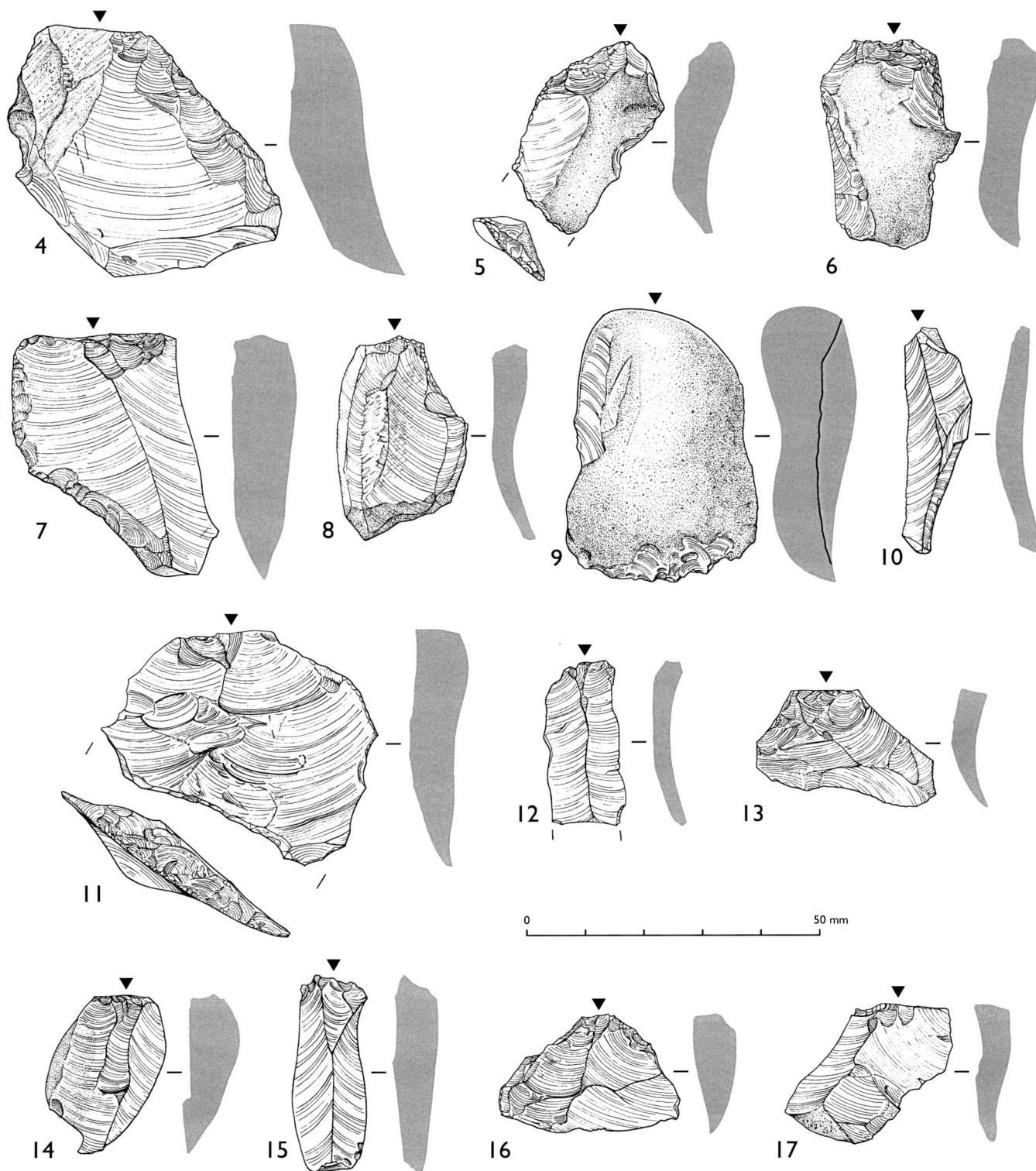

Table 3.6: Descriptions of retouched implements

Context	Phase	Sub type	Length	Breadth	Width	Comments
3066	5	Backed knife	43	49	14	Thick irregular flake with sporadic light steep scalar retouch along parts of left dorsal – backed cutting flake? (Fig 3.2 no 4)
3918	12.1	Edge blunted	30	28	9	Cortical flake with fine straight steep retouch truncating distal end, worn from use (Fig 3.2 no 5)
3926	12.1	Edge blunted	37	24	7	Short stretch of fine scalar blunting on left dorsal near bulbar end, this and cortex may have aided handling, opposed margin shows microscopic traces of wear and rounding, use as cutting implement? (Fig 3.2 no 6)
3002	20.2	Edge blunted	44	34	10	Flake with variable scalar retouch along right lateral. Represents reuse of a flake after it had recorticated (Fig 3.2 no 7)
3146	20.2	Piercer	36	22	6	Short stretch of moderate steep scalar blunting on left dorsal near bulbar end, would enable holding/hafting. Distal is pointed and cortical but is worn – possible used for piercing, despite the cortex? (Fig 3.2 no 8)
3819	20.2	Denticulated	48	40	15	Thick cortical flake with irregular semi-steep slightly denticulated retouch on distal dorsal (Fig 3.2 no 9)
3832	20.2	Serrate	40	11	4	Fine straight serrations along right lateral margin on an unsystematic blade, worn but no gloss (Fig 3.2 no 10)
4902	20.2	Miscellaneous	43	46	9	Broad flake with distal removed by oblique snap and scar modified with moderate, straight scalar retouch. Some light edge damage to opposed margin – possibly blunted for use as cutting implement? (Fig 3.2 no 11)

Micro-debitage made up the greatest proportion of the entire assemblage, contributing over 60 per cent. These pieces all show conchoidal fracture and the majority have clear striking platforms and flaking scars on their dorsal surfaces. They certainly appear to be the product of knapping and such pieces are produced in large quantities during reduction. It is, however, necessary to exercise some caution as small, conchoidally fractured pieces can be generated, particularly in relatively small quantities, from other activities involving the mechanical movement of flint, including its extraction, transport and redeposition. Their identification is largely dependent on the sampling programme, as generally they will only be found through fine sieving. During this investigation, sampling was undertaken extensively and on a range of different context types so there should be a reasonably comprehensive coverage of possible *in situ* knapping and tool production activities.

Distribution and contextual associations

Phase 2: Old Land Surface

No pieces of macro-debitage were identified from the pre-monument contexts although small quantities of micro-debitage were present within the OLS in samples taken from the possible hearth ([4041] <9821>), suggesting that limited knapping may have accompanied the use of this feature.

Phase 3: Gravel Mound

The surface deposits of the Gravel Mound also provide some evidence of knapping in the form of micro-debitage. A small systematically produced blade and a flake fragment are also present. The blade at least is unlikely to have been made much after the Early Neolithic and this suggests that it may have been already present in the material that was imported and used in this mound's construction.

Phase 4: Lower Organic Mound

Further evidence for knapping is present in the Lower Organic Mound ([3075], [3046], [4156] and [4182]). This includes a fragment from a core and two waste flakes along with 23 pieces of micro-debitage. The Mini-mound ([4181]) and linear feature ([4171] and [4173]) also produced similar evidence for knapping in the form of a decortication flake and 39 pieces of micro-debitage. As with the material from the Gravel Mound, it is uncertain whether this indicates sporadic and low-level flintworking associated with these features or that it was already present in the soil when it was imported. No diagnostic pieces were present. All the flintwork represents knapping waste but a small blade was present amongst the micro-debitage from the main mound, which may hint at pre-construction flintworking.

Fig 3.2 (opposite) Struck flints from the 2007/8 Silbury excavations. 4 [3066] Backed knife from pit [3067]; 5 [3918] Flake with blunting along distal from Ditch 1; 6 [3926] Edge blunted flake from Ditch 1; 7 [3002] Edge blunted flake from tunnel backfill; 8 [3146] Possible piercer, unstratified; 9 [3819] Denticulated flake from tunnel collapse; 10 [3832] Serrate from tunnel collapse; 11 [4902] Miscellaneous retouched flake from mound depression; 12 [3066] Blade from pit [3067]; 13 [3066] Flake from pit [3067]; 14 [3066] Flake from pit [3067]; 15 [3918] Blade from Ditch 1; 16 [3925] Flake from Ditch 1; 17 [3926] Flake from Ditch 1. (Chris Evans, © English Heritage)

Phase 5: Pits

Worked flint and burnt flint was recovered from the fills of the two pits. Pit [3067] produced a backed knife, a trimming flake, a blade, three small but potentially useable flakes and 22 pieces of micro-debitage (Fig 3.2, nos 4, 12–14). Some of these may have been struck from the same pieces of raw material, although attempts at refitting were unproductive. They appear to form a small collection of useable or retouched cutting flakes and, as a collection, they were perhaps more likely to have been deliberately discarded into the pit rather than redeposited from the mound into which it was cut. Micro-wear analysis was conducted on the flakes and retouched implement but recortication and post-depositional damage precluded any reliable interpretations. In contrast, the other pit, [3074], contained no larger pieces of struck flint but did produce 40 pieces of micro-debitage that may have been residually introduced. Pit [3074] also produced relatively larger quantities of burnt flint than pit [3067], at 23g as opposed to only 1g, although both should be regarded as small. Variations in the pits' contents may suggest, if somewhat tentatively, that some discretion was exercised in determining what was being deposited.

Phase 6: Upper Organic Mound and further dump layers

The Upper Organic Mound did produce ten pieces of micro-debitage but no other evidence of flintworking, and no worked flint was recovered from either the further dump layers or the slumped layers associated with the mound ([3834] – Phase 20.2). Again, worked pieces may also have been present within the soil before it was imported to the site.

Phases 7–11: Banks 1–5 and Ditches

The only worked flint or burnt flint recovered from any of the deposits within these phases consisted of 16 pieces of micro-debitage from Bank 5 ([4073]) and a single piece from the organic deposits recorded in the void above the main tunnel.

Phase 12: Fills of Ditch 1

Ditch 1 ([3902]) produced relatively large assemblages of macro-debitage from throughout its fills, with evidence for flintworking in the form of micro-debitage also being recovered

from its lowest, organic, fill. This assemblage principally consists of knapping waste but nine useable flakes and blades and two retouched edge-blunted flakes are also present (Fig 3.1, no 3; and Fig 3.2, nos 5, 6, 15–17). One of the blades was systematically produced, much more heavily recorticated than the rest of the assemblage and almost certainly residual. The remainder of the assemblage, although too few in number to date confidently, would certainly not be out of place in a Later Neolithic context and its condition would suggest that the production of useable and retouched pieces had occurred in the vicinity. Micro-wear analysis was conducted on the core, useable flakes and retouched implements but, again, post-depositional modification precluded any reliable interpretations. The presence of 64g of burnt flint fragments, a small amount but representing over half of all of the burnt flint recovered during the investigations, suggests the presence of hearths, or at least activities involving fire, in the vicinity.

Phases 13–15: Ditches 2, 3 and 4

No worked flint or burnt flint was recovered from any of the deposits associated with these phases. This is due to the fact that these ditches were not excavated in plan, but only recorded in section.

Phase 16: Final mound construction

The only material to certainly come from the main chalk construction of the monument is from the 'interwall' deposits excavated on the summit. This comprises knapping waste including micro-debitage, two useable flakes and a small quantity of burnt flint.

Phases 17–20.1: Medieval to recent activity

The assemblages from these phases came from post-prehistoric disturbance as recorded on the surface of the mound. They could therefore relate to either the mound's construction or to activities conducted on its surface after it had been completed. The assemblages are dominated by knapping waste with relatively few useable flakes and no retouched pieces present. The quantities are too small to provide reliable information but, technologically and metrically, they appear indistinguishable from the assemblages associated with the mound's construction. They provide no evidence for any significant post-construction use of worked flint at the monument.

Phase 20.2: Tunnel collapse/infill

The largest quantities of worked flint from the investigations came from the collapsed mound material removed from the tunnels, although no micro-debitage was recovered from these deposits. It should, however, be noted that these pieces of worked flint were recovered from the conveyor belt (*see* Chapter 2 for methodology), which is not necessarily conducive to the recovery of micro-debitage. Although technically unstratified, most of the assemblage probably originated from the main bulk of the monument and is presumably associated with its construction. It consists of both knapping debris and useable pieces and includes 10 of the 11 cores and 5 of the retouched implements recovered during the investigations (Fig 3.1, nos 1 and 2; Fig 3.2, nos 7–11). It suggests a very low-level but persistent presence of worked flint throughout the body of the monument. It most probably reflects the occasional and opportunistic production of useable flakes and tools, presumably for use during the construction works.

Table 3.7: Flint finds in the Alexander Keiller Museum recovered during the 1968–70 excavations from the tunnel. Assessed by David Field

Find no	Location	Description	Flint	Other features
7	Found '2'' below base of OGS in flint layer above clay with flints. Between rings 31 and 32 HLV'	Side and end scraper. Abrupt retouch to left edge. Distal end retouched at angle and R distal curved to form retouched nose.	Grey-olive flint.	Small patch of cortex on dorse and some small patches of ?ferrous encrustation on some scars.
10	'49–50'	Flake with some microscopic spalling on right edge at distal end.	Grey mottled flint	
11	'Tunnel-clay with flints below OLS Rings 45–6'	Multi-platform core	Grey mottled flint	Some cortex – scar adjacent to cortex is patinated and may have been exposed on surface
12	'Tunnel 45–6 flint flake'	Secondary flake	Light grey mottled flint	Some cortex left with patches of iron staining. Ferrous-like concretions on dorse. Evidence of mis-hits and platform cleaning
14	'Tunnel Rings 45–46 clay with flints below OLS'	Possibly core rejuvenation piece	Dense olive-grey flint	Small sturdy broken piece
15	'Clay with flints below OLS in area centred 49–50'	Small platform rejuvenation flake	Grey flint	
17	'Tunnel 59–60 [crossed out] 58–59 [inserted] below humus layer'	Sturdy broken flake probably natural		Some apparent retouch along one edge but this could also be natural
21	'Rings 63–64 Just above OLS in layer of unworked flints'	Single platform blade core		Probably Mesolithic. Some weathered cortex remaining. Removals patinated bluish. Fractured recently or re-knapped (3 flakes detached) at distal end
101	'Rings 67–8 above OLS'	Flake with abrupt retouch at proximal end		Retouch forms scraper-like implement. Bluish patina. Frost fractured. Some weathered cortex
240	'Extension ring 2, 0.6m above OLS in dark material (dark soil, light grey chalk and flint material)'	Flake core with 2 platforms	Light to dark grey flint with patch of very weathered crust. Not directly from chalk.	

Table 3.8: Flint finds in the Alexander Keiller Museum recovered during the 1968–70 excavations from the external ditch. Assessed by David Field

Find no	Location	Description	Flint	Other features
234	'Cutting G 234 S Bank Base of Midden 4.00m West 5.10m North 0.15m'	Knife or retouched blade	Light-grey mottled flint with no patina	Butt detached and missing. R edge on dorse retouched and two denticulations, one of which also has retouch on bulbar face. Fine retouch along L dorsal edge
336	'S4 Chalky silt'	Side scraper on large thick long or blade-like flake	Patinated white	Abrupt retouch on right edge of dorsal surface with notch towards distal end
358	'S4 Chalk silt'	Core.	Chalky cortex	Small irregular nodule of flint
385	'N7 Hard packed light buff chalk silt'	Large flake with bifacial detachments.	Patinated white	Used as core. Small part of edge at one end trimmed for ?scraping
393	'S4 Buff silt spheroidal flint RH'	Hammer stone	Flake scars patinated	Evidence of bruising and battering all over. Some large flake removals and part broken away evidently the result of fossil weakness
1224	'S2 Midden'	Sharpening flake from axe retouched to form knife-like implement	Mottled light grey flint	Some areas smoothed off as if by water

Table 3.9: Flint finds in the Alexander Keiller Museum recovered during the 1968–70 excavations from the summit and slope. Assessed by David Field

No	Location	Description	Material	Other features
431	?Summit. 'central grave (?) pit Gravelly clay filling, 0.98 below grid at 0.73E 1.60N'	End and side scraper on almost circular flake	Dark grey flint with cortex on dorse and just a hint of blue patina on bulbar face	
144	'On mole heap on slope, south side'	Barbed and tanged arrowhead	Patinated white	Tip missing and tang snapped off in antiquity. 'Found by workman'

Table 3.10: Chance flint finds from around Silbury in the Alexander Keiller Museum. Assessed by David Field

Location	Description	Material	Other features
Silbury meadow 'field adjoining Silbury Hill 1916'.	Edge-ground narrow flint chisel	Dark-grey flint with bulbar face slightly patinated. Weathered cortex	Lenticular cross-section The butt is broken and missing. Edge ground on both faces, but to greater degree on the dorse; also along one side edge.
Silbury meadow	Ripple-flaked oblique transverse arrowhead	Brown-grey flint	Tip and a portion of one face missing. Rippled flaking extends right across one face but only at edge on the other.

Discussion

The use of flint at Silbury

The worked flint from Silbury may be regarded as small in scale, opportunistically created and with a restricted tool inventory. Some evidence for *in situ* knapping is present in the turf and soils used in its earliest phases although there are good reasons to suppose that at least some of this material may have been incidentally imported along with its matrix. It does, nevertheless, suggest that the places that the turf and soils came from may have previously witnessed knapping events, and therefore have held some cultural significance. Possible evidence of deliberate deposition is suggested by the small group of useable flakes found in pit [3067], which can be contrasted with the near absence of worked flint, but higher quantities of burnt flint recovered from associated pit [3074]. Most of the assemblage, however, was scattered in very low densities throughout the bulk of the monument. It is probably associated with activities relating to the construction works but also appears to represent fortuitously abandoned or lost implements and waste. It can be favourably compared in terms of raw material use and core reduction techniques to other assemblages from the area, such as the West Kennet Palisaded Enclosures (Whittle 1997a, 88–93), the Sanctuary (Pollard 1992; 2001a), the Beckhampton Avenue and Longstones Cove (Snashall 2008). Nevertheless, the Silbury assemblage is generally smaller (see below), more opportunistically produced and with a smaller and less varied range of retouched items, it being perhaps most comparable to the assemblage from Falkner's Circle (Gillings et al 2008, 149–50).

Given the quantities of deposits removed and examined during the restoration works, the most interesting aspect of the worked flint assemblage from Silbury is its small size. Notwithstanding the very real difficulties in trying to assign flint assemblages to specific social practices (see, for example, Brück 1999), the size and the restricted composition of the Silbury assemblage contrasts noticeably with those generated through broad-based residential or domestic activities. This is also reflected by the very low quantities of burnt flint that were recovered, it being normally found in abundance where domestic activities are identified. Indeed, the paucity of usually ubiquitous flintwork, which would presumably still be required in some quantity even if only for the construction operations, almost suggests that the site was being kept deliberately clean, with a separation made between the site itself and the domestic tasks necessary to sustain the workforce (see also Chapters 6, 7 and 8).

Flint use in the Avebury area

Worked flint scatters with more convincing domestic characteristics have been identified in the Avebury area through fieldwalking and excavation, some present as great densities of lithic material up to 1 sq km in extent (Smith 1965a,

210–16; Holgate 1987; Whittle 1993; Whittle et al 2000). These are concentrated on the slightly higher ground overlooking the Avebury/ Silbury basin, particularly along the slopes of Windmill Hill, at the foot of the Downs to the east of Avebury, on the northern part of Waden Hill and on the elevated ground between Silbury and South Street long barrow. However, these densities drop off markedly in the immediate environs of Silbury as well as towards the other contemporary monuments (Holgate 1987, fig 1).

Holgate (1987) contrasts the large and extensive spreads of Later Neolithic and Bronze Age material with the small and restricted spreads of Mesolithic and Early Neolithic flintwork. The latter, he suggests, are the result of temporary camps of limited size and duration, whilst the former are argued to represent 'permanently occupied farmsteads'. These spreads do seem to represent types of activity that utilise worked flint to a much greater intensity and for a far more varied range of tasks than is seen at Silbury. There remain problems in associating these with the residencies of Silbury's builders. The dating of surface collected flint assemblages is vague and Holgate makes little differentiation between 3rd and 2nd millennium BC industries. Although portions of these scatters are undoubtedly of 3rd millennium date, much of the flintwork recorded by Holgate could relate to Middle or Late Bronze Age inhabitation. It is also unclear what scale of occupation these extensive spreads relate to. Even if of Later Neolithic date, they could have accumulated from long-term, shifting or restricted mobility settlements, perhaps of a type envisioned by Holgate (1987; see also Pollard 1999), but equally they could represent midden accumulations from periodic large-scale gatherings, such as witnessed at Durrington Walls (Chan 2009).

Despite these uncertainties, there does appear to be a separation between these intensively occupied areas and the monuments in the area, which suggests a subtle spatially organised landscape with segregation between routine and other activities. This also appears to be the case elsewhere in Wessex. Field (2008; 2009) demonstrates that the densest distributions of flint do not coincide with the distribution of Later Neolithic monuments and suggests that ceremonial activities and those concerned with settlement and everyday life were kept spatially discrete (see also Chapters 6 and 8).

Flint use at the other monuments

The assemblage from Silbury clearly contrasts markedly with the extensive scatters in the vicinity, but it is perhaps more constructive to consider how it compares to assemblages from the other broadly contemporary local monuments. One of the largest lithic assemblages excavated in the area came from the Longstones Cove and the Beckhampton Avenue (Gillings *et al* 2008). Over 4,000 worked flints were recovered but, other than its size, the assemblage is comparable to Silbury's in that it was expediently made and contains a restricted range of retouched types, dominated by cutting and piercing tools but with very few scrapers present (Snashall 2008). Its contextual distribution is also interesting. There is very little worked flint that can be associated with the earlier Longstones Enclosure or previous occupation at the site, nor within the construction levels of either the Cove or the Avenue. Both test pitting and fieldwalking in the vicinity showed the area to be virtually devoid of worked flint and other evidence of occupation (Holgate 1987; Gillings *et al* 2008). Worked flint from individual knapping episodes and deliberately chosen flint implements, however, were deposited in very large quantities around specific stones in the Cove and, to a lesser extent, the Beckhampton Avenue. This occurred after the stones had been erected and presumably as part of the ceremonies and performances conducted at the monuments. A similar scenario has been recorded at many other monuments in the Avebury area, whereby worked flint is virtually absent from construction levels but is used as placed deposits at significant locations during their use, including Avebury itself (Smith 1965a), the West Kennet Palisaded Enclosures (Whittle 1997a), the Sanctuary (Pollard 1992; 2001a), the West Kennet Avenue and Faulkner's Circle (Gillings *et al* 2008). During this latter, post-construction use and deposition of flint, other material, such as bone and pottery, was often deposited; again these are rarely found in deposits relating to the prior use of the area or the construction of monuments, including Silbury.

The role of flint at Silbury

The assemblage is remarkably consistent with other assemblages from many of the monuments in the area and indicates that the extensive use of worked flint did not feature as part of the construction operations. It may be argued that the sites were kept deliberately clean of worked flint and other domestic 'debris' (*see also* Chapters 6, 7 and 8).In seeking possible explanations for the paucity of worked flint at Silbury, it may be instructive to consider how other types of stone were employed. The numerous unworked flint nodules were mostly recovered during the emptying of the tunnels and most likely derived from the main body of the mound. They were not the source for the worked flint industry but had been extracted directly from the parent chalk and deliberately brought to the site, although not necessarily from a great distance. In this regard, the nodules might be compared to the sarsen boulders incorporated into the Upper Organic Mound, collapsed tunnel fill and within the main bulk of the monument at the summit. Interestingly, the sarsens from the lower deposits are unmodified whilst those from the summit do show evidence of various degrees of deliberate fracture (*see* Pollard, this chapter). A few worked flints were recovered from the deposits at the summit but, except for small quantities of micro-debitage that may have been already present in the deposits used to construct the mound, no worked flint was recovered from the Upper Organic Mound. In general, it seems that the unworked flint nodules and the sarsens may have been both physically and conceptually associated, with similar conventions surrounding their appropriate use, but, apparently, this did not extend to the worked flint. Instead, it would appear that worked flint, burnt flint and perhaps other domestically significant materials were being excluded deliberately. It was only during the ceremonies and performances associated with the use of the monuments in the area that worked flint was considered a suitable medium to be used and deposited but, so far, such practices have yet to be identified at Silbury.

In attempting to understand the significance and use of worked flint in the context of Silbury, it may be necessary to move beyond its simple functional and economic values and explore its perceived metaphorical qualities. For many traditional societies there is an understanding that the physical world was created by, and even from, ancestral or creation beings (*see*, for example, Burton 1984; McBryde 1984; 1997; Morphy 1989; Taçon 1991; Brumm 2004; Boivin 2004; Saunders 2004; Taçon and Ouzman 2004). As the creation or even substance of supernatural entities, stone can be perceived to have qualities and powers that go beyond its geological or mechanical properties. Similar perspectives are apparent from the prehistoric record in Britain, and these have important implications for where flint might be obtained, the manner in which it was gathered, how it was subsequently worked and the social duties different types of implements could perform as participants within an active material culture (for example Edmonds 1997; 1998; Cooney 1998; Topping 2004; 2005; Conneller 2008; McFadyen 2008). The cultural and symbolic properties embedded within stone often determine how, where and by whom it can be worked, as well as its desirability and suitability for use within particular spheres of practice.

Returning to Silbury, there seems to be a dichotomy between the symbolic or spiritual qualities of worked flint on one hand and the sarsen and unworked flint nodules on the other. This spills over into the appropriate range of contexts they were used in. Unravelling the possible metaphorical qualities given to stone during the Later Neolithic is highly speculative. Nevertheless, for Wessex, Parker Pearson (2004; see also Bender 1998; Parker Pearson and Ramilisonina 1998) suggests that unmodified stone, such as sarsen and unworked flint nodules, can be seen as signifying, and perhaps even being, the petrified remains of ancestral or creational beings, this being justified by recourse to recent material practices in Madagascar. Such beliefs may have been reinforced by the finding of fossils within stone such as chalk, the odd, 'organic' shape of flint nodules perhaps recalling bones set within a white, petrified body. The central pit of one of the barrows on Kings Barrow Ridge near Stonehenge, for example, held not human remains but a collection of oddly shaped flint nodules (Passmore 1940), which Parker Pearson (2004, 85) suggests may have represented the bones of the most ancient ancestors.

This divergence between the use of unworked flint nodules and worked flint tools suggests that their transformation through knapping also changed their metaphorical qualities. As unworked stone, nodules may have been regarded as closely related to ancestral or creational realms. Through knapping, they are brought back into, and add potency to, the technologies required in the present world. Put simply, it is possible that worked flints were associated with the living, the here and now, and as such needed to be kept apart from the ancestral or spirit world, such as embodied by the corporeal materiality of Silbury itself.

The sarsen stone

Joshua Pollard

Blocks of sarsen stone were recorded during the 1849 and 1968–70 excavations as forming part of the make-up of Silbury Hill (Merewether 1851a; Whittle 1997a). A further 46 sarsens (weighing in total 779.4kg) were recorded during the 2007/8 excavation from contexts relating to early stages of mound construction and from the summit, the latter built into the chalk block walling, the interwall deposits and deriving from Atkinson's topsoil (Table 3.11). This account is based on detailed recording of those pieces retained, and on-site records of those backfilled at the end of the 2007/8 excavation. Thirteen sarsens were retained because of signs of obvious or suspected working, and are described in detail below.

Sarsen is a highly resilient Tertiary sandstone that occurs in boulder form, ranging from fist-sized lumps of a few kilograms to blocks upwards of 100 tonnes. Ubiquitous within the Upper Kennet Valley, it was deposited in extensive spreads on the surface of valley bottoms and sides under periglacial conditions (Geddes 2000, 60–4). Antiquarian records and archaeological evidence illustrate that the current restricted distribution of sarsen on the region's downlands is largely a product of medieval and post-medieval field clearance (Long 1858; Smith 1885; King 1968; Bowen and Smith 1977; Fowler 2000a; Field 2005).

Description

Twenty sarsens, weighing 409.7kg, were recovered from tunnel (that is early phase mound): [3834], tunnel fill of collapse and 'ooze' from shaft; [3855], slumped turf stack; and [4157], part of the Upper Organic Mound. The size range was varied, but three blocks from [4157] were substantial, weighing between 30kg and 85kg. Only one stone from these lower mound contexts showed evidence of possible modification, a block from [3834] that had split. Two stones from [3834] ('k' and 'f') were retained because they displayed areas of smoothing. However, later examination failed to reveal traces of intentional surface modification such as pecking or clear striations resulting from their use for grinding or polishing, and it is considered that the localised surface smoothing was produced by natural agencies (for example water action).

Table 3.11: Sarsen from the 2007/8 excavations

Context	ID	Location	Modified	Unmodified	Weight range (kg)	Weight average (kg)
3834	a–c; e–g; i–k; m–p	Tunnel	I	12	3.2–15.7	9.4
3855	h; q	Tunnel	–	2	19.0–43.8	31.4
4157	s–t; v–x	Tunnel	–	5	12.7–85.0	44.9
Unknown	d; r	Tunnel	I	I	12.3–50.0	31.2
4801	17–21; 23–24	Summit	5	2	3.9–9.7	6.2
4805	12–13	Summit	–	2	14.7–38.5	26.6
4809	1–11	Summit	11	–	15.2–38.0	15.2
4845	14	Summit	I	–	3.3	3.3
4857	SF 8524	Summit	I	–	25.9	25.9
Crater	15–16	Summit	2	–	6.3–38.0	22.2

In contrast to the assemblage from lower mound contexts, 20 of the 24 sarsens from the summit of the Hill exhibit evidence of modification. This takes various forms, from simple splitting, the removal of one or more flakes, or localised burning, to more systematic working. Many of the fragmentary stones retain areas of cortex, covering as much as 80 per cent of the surface. Where it is possible to gauge the original size of blocks, none appears to have been above one metre in maximum dimension. Pinkish tinges to the cortex of fragments from the Crater, [4809] and [4857], along with localised spalling on Stone 16 from [4809] are taken as evidence of burning, utilised to induce thermal fracture of the stones as an initial stage in reduction. Fracture and reduction of boulders was also achieved through controlled direct percussion, as evidenced by traces of negative bulbs on Stones 1 and 3 from [4809] and flakes/flake scars themselves. Much of the reduction, however, was unsystematic, and appears to have involved smashing of the stones. Two of the stones (nos 3 and 5) from chalk wall 2 [4809] refit and others look to belong to the same block.

Three sarsen fragments from the summit might be regarded as unfinished artefacts. Stone 23 from [4801], Atkinson's topsoil, is a split fragment which has been further worked by the removal of three small flakes from the edge, producing a roughly sub-oval shaped piece (Fig 3.3). While perhaps too irregular, it has the appearance of a quern 'rough-out'. Fragments 14 and 17, from interwall deposit [4845] and [4801] respectively, refit to form a block 250 x 340 x 100mm (Fig 3.4). A large flake scar forms one side, the other being cortical. Several small flakes have been removed from the edge, giving the refitted block a roughly sub-oval shape. Where remaining, the cortical surface displays

traces of light pecking, and on one part of this surface a shallow concavity has been produced, c 120 x 80mm in extent, within which the surface is smoothed, probably by grinding. This piece starts as a complete stone or large fragment which undergoes surface modification, perhaps to turn it into a polissoir. It was then split, thinned and roughly shaped through flaking. Conchoidal features show the block was then deliberately split in two by a single blow to the upper face.

Notes on sarsens retained for the archive

'Crater'

ID 16: Split piece, 330 x 190 x 120mm. Cortex on one side, with slight pinkishness in places. 'Flake-like' with a triangular cross-section. Possibly large broken flake.

Tunnel fill of collapse and 'ooze' from shaft [3834]

ID 'k': Small, essentially unmodified piece, 240 x 210 x 90mm. This is a sub-rectangular block retained because of smooth upper and lower faces. No clear striations or pecking, so not a polissoir, the smoothing probably a product of water action. One small flake scar at one end, but likely resulting from damage rather than intentional working.

ID 'f': Complete sarsen, 270 x 240 x 180mm, with reddish-brown cortex. Unmodified, though with signs of ancient (ie geological) fracture. One face smoothed, hence retention, but this is natural.

Atkinson's 'topsoil' [4801]

ID 23: Fragment, 260 x 230 x 70mm, with irregular cortex (Fig 3.3). Fractured piece or

Fig 3.3
Worked sarsen fragment 23.
(Chris Evans,
© English Heritage)

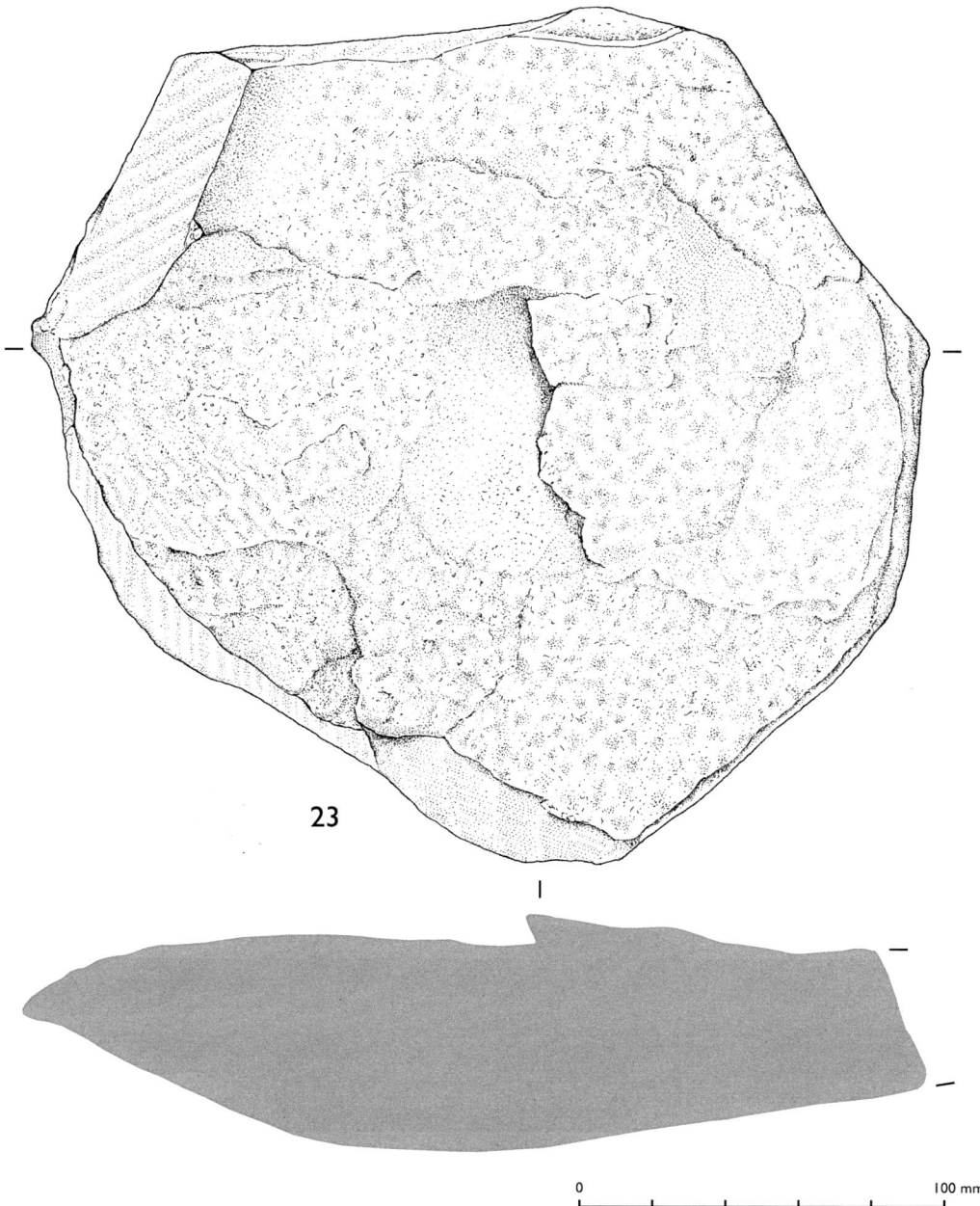

23

0   100 mm

large flake fragment, with a series of ?three small flake removals from the edge, producing a roughly sub-oval shaped piece. It has the appearance of a quern 'rough-out', but is perhaps too irregular.

Atkinson's topsoil [4801] and interwall deposit [4845]

Flaked block made up of two refitting pieces: ID 17 ([4801]), 250 x 200 x 90mm and ID 14 ([4845]), 230 x 150 x 100mm (total size 250 x 340 x 100mm) (Fig 3.4). Cortical surface, where remaining, shows traces of light pecking. On one part of this surface a shallow concavity has been produced, *c* 120 x 80mm, within which the surface is smoothed, probably by grinding. There is an incipient cone of percussion on this.

One large flake scar which creates the 'dorsal' surface has been struck from a fracture plane. Two further flakes/fragments were removed

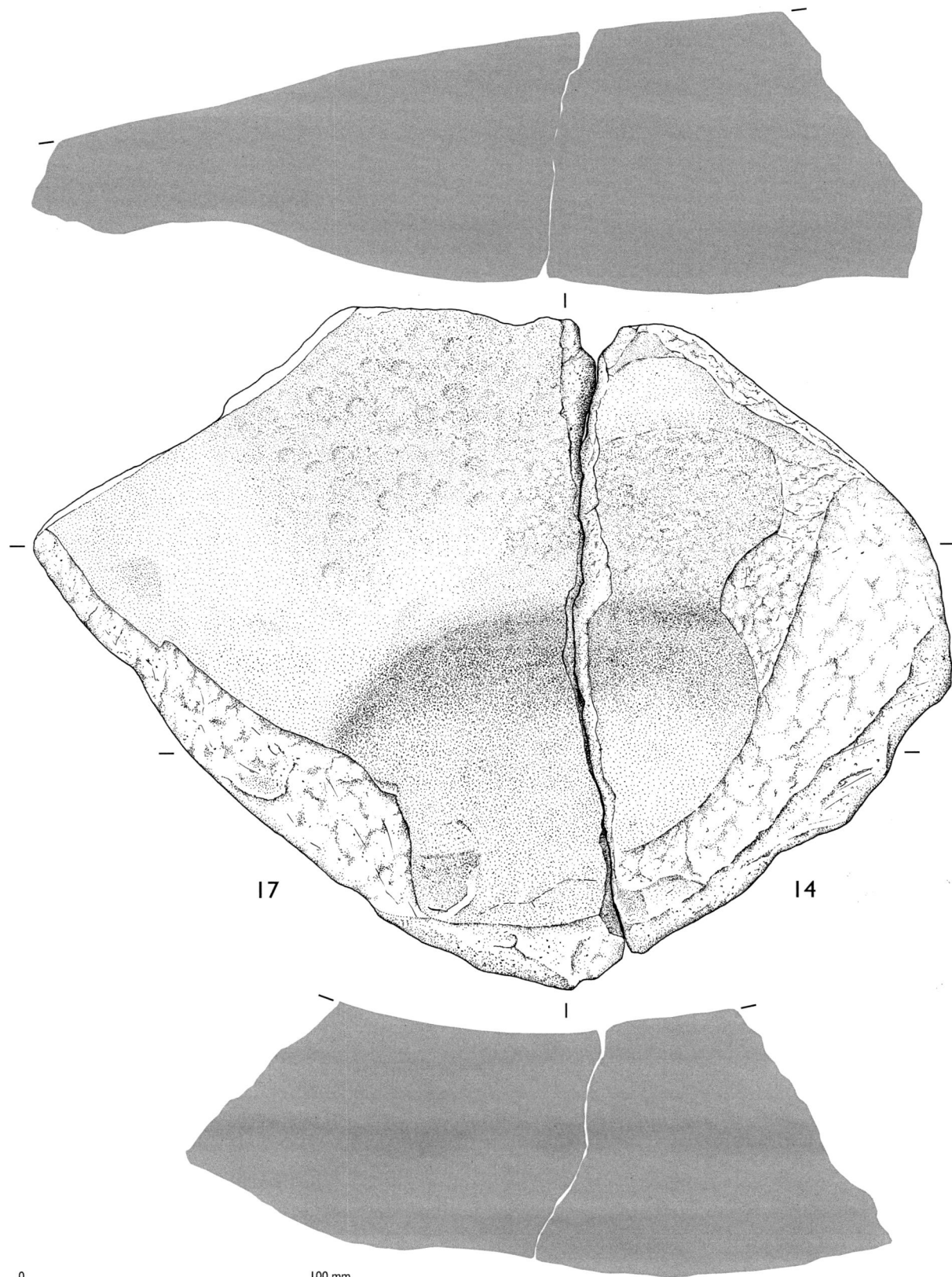

17   14

0   100 mm

using the cortical surface as a platform; another three were struck from the dorsal face. Small flakes have been removed from one end. Conchoidal features show the block was split in two by impact to its centre.

Chalk wall 2 [4809]

ID 1: Fractured piece, 370 x 160 x 120mm. 70% cortex. Piece split by a blow to the cortical surface, leaving a negative bulb of percussion. This could have occurred accidentally/ incidentally. Radial outer fracture. From a small/medium-sized sarsen.

ID2: Fractured piece, 380 x 220 x 100mm. A large flake fractured at the proximal end. One, possibly two, prior removals are visible as scars on the 'dorsal' face. Scar of small flake struck from break surface (could be accidental). One face preserves cortex, to which there is a slight pinkish tone.

ID 3: Fractured piece, 260 x 210 x 210mm. Large area of cortex remains, this with a pinkish/ reddish-brown tinge. Seemingly split by percussion, one small flake then removed. Refits with ID 5. Original stone >0.6m.

ID 4: Fractured piece, 340 x 300 x 150mm. 80% cortex. Very similar to 3 and 5, and probably from the same block.

ID 5: Fractured piece, 290 x 280 x 220mm. 50% cortex. Refits with ID 3.

ID 6: Fractured piece, 400 x 250 160mm. 20% cortex. Likely evidence of thermal fracture to cortex as indicated by a pinkish hue and localised spalling, producing a rough surface. Original block size impossible to estimate.

Fill [4857] of probable pit [4858], summit

SF 8524: Fractured piece, 370 x 280 x 240mm. 50% cortex, pinkish in places, two main fracture planes. From medium-sized block (c0.5–1.0m).

Discussion

It is clear both from the 2007/8 and earlier excavations that whole and fragmentary sarsens were deliberately incorporated in the make-up of the Hill. Those from the summit included a substantial number of large fragments built into the chalk block Wall 2 [4809]; analogous to those recorded by Atkinson as incorporated in his chalk walling {802} and {808} (Whittle 1997a, 20). The early stages of mound construction were also intimately associated with sarsen, as evidenced by the stones from

[3834], [3855] and [4157]. Describing the results of the 1849 excavation, Merewether records a sarsen capping to the primary mound, comprising 'many sarsen stones … some of them placed with their concave surfaces downwards, favouring the line of the heap … and casing, as it were, the mound' (1851a, 79–80). Note should also be taken of Merewether's claim that medium-sized sarsen boulders were set at c 5m intervals around the base of the Hill (Merewether 1851a, 74) (although see 'Sarsen and peristalith' section in Chapter 1). Based on this description, the Upper Organic Mound and final mound were 'capped' or 'contained' in various ways with stone (although it should also be noted that 2007/8 work indicated that the sarsens were contained within, and not on, the Upper Organic Mound – see Chapter 2). Either way, sarsen must be considered, alongside chalk, turf, gravel and soil, as a construction material, even if its incorporation did not offer any structural advantage.

Examination of those stones recovered in 2007/8 shows a marked qualitative difference between Upper Organic Mound and summit contexts, with nearly all sarsens from the former being unmodified, and those from the latter mostly fragmented. The presence of refits among the fragments from wall [4809], and the absence of associated fine debitage, indicate that individual stones were split elsewhere (perhaps at the base of the Hill) and probably as required for each section of walling. Where it is possible to gauge the size of the original blocks from which the summit fragments derive, none are particularly large (being less than one metre in maximum dimension). Megalithic settings were not being broken up for the purpose. Inasmuch as it was locally available, none of this stone need have been brought far, and may have been encountered in superficial periglacial/solifluction deposits during the digging of the quarry ditches. This said we should not, of course, preclude its transportation from natural spreads or artificial structures at a distance from the Hill. Associations and biographies of stone (cf Gillings and Pollard 1999) were as important as constructional expediency.

Why sarsen was incorporated in the construction of Silbury Hill is more difficult to determine, but the answer likely relates to its perceived qualities – its materiality (see discussion in Chapter 7). It certainly invoked interesting depositional responses, seen with the intimate placing of red deer antler fragments between the sarsen fragments used in summit

Fig 3.4 (opposite)
Worked sarsen fragments
14 and 17.
(Chris Evans,
© English Heritage)

walling [4809] (*see* Fig 2.28). Merewether records related depositional acts from the primary mound, where bone fragments (including large mammal ribs), small sticks and an antler tine had been placed on top of several of the stones (Merewether 1851a, 80). This explicit depositional link between sarsen and organic materials stands in stark contrast to the seemingly deliberate exclusion of bone and antler from the stone-hole fills of contemporary megalithic settings in the region (Gillings *et al* 2008, 202). Were the Silbury sarsens thought of as categorically different to megaliths, and if so did this relate to their size or origin?

Elsewhere in the region during the second half of the 3rd millennium BC we see sarsen being employed in varying circumstances. Large blocks, for example, were used to create the megalithic settings of the Beckhampton and West Kennet Avenues (Smith 1965a; Gillings *et al* 2008). By the turn of the millennium distinct traditions had developed of covering individual Beaker burials with sarsen, and of placing graves at the feet of standing megaliths (Pollard and Reynolds 2002, 128–30). Taken together with the inclusion of small sarsens in the secondary fills of the chambers and passage of the West Kennet long barrow (Piggott 1962, 26–30), there is good reason to believe a metaphoric or ontological connection was believed to exist between certain types of stone and mortuary/ancestral domains (Parker Pearson and Ramilisonina 1998).

In other contexts, like that of Silbury Hill, it is difficult to discern an explicit link between stone and mortuary or ancestor-veneration practices; this need not of course imply an absence of connection. More analogous to the Silbury circumstance may be those instances of small or fractured sarsens being worked into larger constructions, rather than megalithic settings as such. In discussing Henry Meux's 1894 excavation through the bank at Avebury, Gray refers to several pieces of 'rough sarsen' being found on top of the buried soil (Gray 1935, 104), suggesting they were used to mark out or initiate earthwork construction. Unmodified sarsen boulders up to 0.8m across were also used extensively as packing in the palisade trenches of the West Kennet Palisaded Enclosures (Whittle 1997a). Whittle notes that in Trenches F and J of enclosure 1 there were 'particularly striking concentrations of large sarsens in the middle and upper parts of the inner ditch'

(1997a, 57), locations that look to flank an entrance gap. Placing stones around boundaries, at entrances, or as 'cappings' to a mound, perhaps gives us a sense of their perceived protective or apotropaic power, whether that invoked ancestral agencies or not.

The dolerite fragments from Silbury Hill

Rob Ixer

Macroscopical and microscopical petrographical analysis of three struck flakes from the summit of Silbury Hill ([4805], subsoil) from the recent excavations, and one flake from the 1968–70 work ('396 Silbury Hill 26/7/69 396 Summit 3.90/1.60/-20 Topsoil'), now in the Alexander Keiller Museum, shows them to be typical spotted dolerites/preselites as found in the Preseli Hills of south-west Wales including Carn Menyn. These fragments, however, came from later contexts (subsoil and topsoil).

Their petrography is the same as most of the Stonehenge preselite orthostats (SH33 group) and their size and shape are consistent with the smaller preselite debitage from Stonehenge.

Introduction

Methodology and summary of samples supplied.

Three samples from the summit of Silbury Hill and a single flake from the Alexander Keiller Museum were provided for petrographical examination (Fig 3.5). They were from sub-soil and topsoil excavated material; all four appeared to have been flaked.

Initially the exposed surfaces were investigated using a x20 hand lens and the Geological Society of America rock-color chart.

A polished thin section was prepared from one of the samples (from the 2007 trench) by cutting a slice and grinding and polishing it to the correct thickness. It was investigated using transmitted light petrography in plane polarised and crossed polarised light using x6.3 and x12.5 objectives with x12.5 eye pieces giving overall magnifications of x80 and x155. By further examination in reflected light using x8 air and x16 and x40 oil immersion lenses all opaque phases greater than two microns in size were visually identified.

Background and comparative material

The spotted dolerites of the Preseli Hills have been of special interest since Thomas (1923) first recognised them as being the same lithology as the majority of the bluestone orthostats from Stonehenge. Despite this and for almost the next 70 years little systematic petrographical work was done on them until the transmitted light descriptions by Bevins *et al* (1989), later repeated and augmented by Thorpe *et al* (1991, 127). The opaque mineralogy (reflected light petrography) of the dolerites was first described by Ixer in Appendix A in Thorpe *et al* (1991, 150–2) and later expanded and compared with a number of the Stonehenge orthostats in Ixer (1996; 1997). A further set of samples from Carn Menyn have been described (macroscopically and in transmitted and reflected light) by Ixer in Darvill *et al* (2008) and two more preselite orthostats from Stonehenge in Ixer and Bevins (2011a).

These petrographical studies have all demonstrated that although there is some lithological variation, particularly in the degree of epidotisation, the majority of the Stonehenge and Preseli Hills dolerites can be regarded as characteristic and 'uniform' in thin section.

Ixer (1997, 13) suggested that most of the spotted dolerites sampled from the Stonehenge orthostats were sufficiently similar that they could be grouped together as 'group SH33' with only a few orthostats having enough petrographical difference to be excluded.

Results

The three struck flakes of preselite-spotted dolerite from the Preseli Hills vary slightly in the amount and size and density of their characteristic pale spotting. In two very similar samples (1.6g and 2.2g) pale pinkish grey spots 0.5–0.7mm in diameter are present in hand specimen and in the third, the largest sample, similar size spots are visible in polished thin section but not in hand specimen.

Petrographically the third preselite is a highly altered ophitic dolerite now comprising clinopyroxene-altered plagioclase-altered iron titanium oxide minerals with abundant secondary chlorite and epidote. It has millimetre diameter, metamorphic alteration spots that carry characteristic chrome-rich spinels.

The transmitted and reflected light

petrography of this sample is almost indistinguishable from that belonging to preselites from Carn Menyn and members of the SH33group.

The size, shape and macroscopical lithological characteristics of the 1968–70 spotted dolerite flake from the Alexander Keiller Museum suggest that it belongs with the three more recently excavated spotted dolerite flakes found on Silbury Hill. The metamorphic spots are slightly larger but this is not of significance.

Although none of the flakes could be fitted together all four could have been struck from a larger artefact. They do appear to belong together.

Spotted fine-grained dolerite. Site code 661. [4805] (1.6g)

Macroscopical description:

Abundant, pale pinkish grey (5YR 8/1 on the Geological Society of America rock-color chart), 5.0–6.0mm diameter, metamorphic spots are present within a fine-grained (0.5–1.0mm diameter) matrix comprising intergrown pale-coloured feldspar-black opaques-and dark green mafics.

Spotted fine-grained dolerite. Site code 661. [4805] (2.2g)

Macroscopical description:

Rare, pale pinkish grey (5YR 8/1 on the Geological Society of America rock-color chart) 5.0–7.0mm diameter, metamorphic spots are

Fig 3.5
The four dolerite fragments from Silbury Hill. The top three were recovered in 2007 and the bottom one in 1970. (Eddie Lyons, © English Heritage, and Rosie Ixer, Goodprovenance)

present within a fine-grained (0.5–1.0mm diameter) matrix comprising intergrown pale-coloured, altered feldspar-black opaques-and dark green mafics. Overall the mottled rock is a greenish grey (5GY 6/1) colour.

'Unspotted' fine-grained dolerite. Site code 661. [4805] (3.5g)

Macroscopical description:

Unlike the other two fragments this struck flake macroscopically appears unspotted. It comprises a uniform, fine-grained (average grain size is 0.5–1.0mm in diameter) intergrowth between pale-coloured, altered feldspar-black mafic minerals/opaques-dark green mafics and minor amounts of pistachio-green epidote. One end is covered by a thin coating of secondary minerals lining a joint plane.

Microscopical description:

In thin section 5.5mm diameter, pale spots are rare and occur together with clear pyroxenes up to 2mm across, 1mm diameter, brown-green chlorite and 1mm long, altered iron titanium oxide minerals within a cloudy matrix. Overall the rock is a light greenish-grey (5GY 8/1).

Spotted fine-grained dolerite. Silbury Hill 26/7/1969. FN 396 Summit 3.90/1.60/.20 (1.9g)

Macroscopical description

Pale pinkish-grey (5YR 8/1 on the Geological Society of America rock-color chart), up to 8.0mm diameter, metamorphic spots are present within a fine-grained (0.5–1.0mm diameter) light greenish-grey (5GY 6/1) matrix comprising intergrown pale-coloured feldspar-black opaques-and dark green mafics.

A rhyolite fragment from a Roman well south of Silbury Hill

Rob Ixer

A flaked rhyolite with strong affinities with IPG Axe Group VIII was originally identified by David Field from an archive collection of material in Wiltshire Heritage Museum, Devizes (DZSWS 572. NC, S 441 B 6351) excavated from a Roman well to the south of Silbury Hill in the 19th century, and subsequently sent to the author for analysis.

Macroscopical description

A macroscopical examination with a x20 hand lens and the Geological Society of America rock-color chart showed the flake to be a dark-coloured, (dark greenish-grey 5GY 4/1 on the Geological Society of America rock-color chart), cryptocrystalline siliceous rock. A 1.5mm thick, pale buff (yellowish-grey 5Y 7/2) weathering crust is present on the unflaked surface. The main body of the rock carries numerous, pale yellow, spherical areas, up to 0.5mm in diameter. The rock has a sub-conchoidal fracture with greasy feel and is sharp to the touch. The cut surface shows a fine-grained uniform medium bluish-grey (5B 5/1) rock with pale yellow-white spots up 0.7mm in diameter.

Comparison with Implement Petrology Committee Axe-head Group VIII

The Implement Petrology Committee Group VIII artefacts are described as manufactured from rhyolites with 'an even and finely-textured micro-crystalline mosaic of quartz and possibly feldspar with scattered irregular non-homogeneous accumulations of leucoxene' (Keiller *et al* 1941, 63) cropping out at Carnalw just north of the spotted dolerite exposures of Carn Menyn in the Preseli Hills.

The presence of 'spongy clusters of fine-grained titanite up to 1mm in diameter are the defining feature of this lithic' (Jenkins *in* David and Williams 1995, 459) and a very typical example of the group is shown in photomicrograph A, plate VI in Stone and Wallis (1951, 131). The Roman Well rhyolitic lithic conforms well with this description and is similar to photomicrograph A. Ixer and Bevins (2010) have discussed and dismissed Carnalw as a source for Group VIII axes and this is in broad agreement with Jones and Williams-Thorpe (2001) who have shown that a number of Group VIII axe-heads are chemically different from rocks cropping out at Carnalw. Those authors suggest that the axes were manufactured from 'rhyolites' from a number of unspecified localities in Wales.

Comparison with provenanced Stonehenge material

Approximately 50 fine-grained bluestones from Stonehenge were examined and directly compared with this Silbury lithic. The

Stonehenge material comes from Aubrey Hole 7, the Stonehenge Avenue, the Heel Stone area and from the April 2008 excavation of Darvill and Wainwright. The Stonehenge lithics include fine-grained rhyolites/rhyolitic tuffs informally called 'rhyolite' and 'rhyolite with fabric' (Ixer and Bevins 2010; 2011b). These lithics include the type specimens of the sub-groups 'snowflake' and 'zebra' that are characterised by pale-coloured areas within the uniform blue matrix. Comparison with the Silbury lithic show the Stonehenge bluestones to have a strong planar fabric (foliation) and that the pale areas are discoidal in shape. These Stonehenge bluestones can be matched to specific outcrops on Craig-y-felin at Pont Saeson (Ixer and Bevins 2011b).

All the required macroscopical characteristics for inclusion within rhyolite with fabric as defined by Ixer and Bevins (2011b) are missing from the Silbury lithic. Similarly comparison with argillaceous tuffs from Stonehenge (informally called 'rhyolite with sub-planar texture') and calcite-bearing tuffs ('rhyolite with sub-planar texture and voids') show the Silbury lithic to have none of the characteristics required for inclusion into those two groups, notably a lack of a foliation, voids or presence of fine-grained mica. In addition the lithic is most unlike the Altar Stone sandstone, the Palaeozoic sandstones, the spotted dolerite and types of sarsen found at Stonehenge.

Conclusion

The Silbury lithic is identified as a rhyolite and in particular has petrographical characteristics with the rhyolite that defines the majority of Group VIII axes. Despite being a Welsh rhyolite the Silbury rhyolite lithology is one that has not been recognised from either the extant orthostats or debitage from Stonehenge.

The prehistoric pottery

Rosamund Cleal

The excavations on the summit produced two prehistoric sherds: one certainly Beaker sherd with comb impressed decoration (Fig 3.6) and one plain sherd which on the evidence of its fabric may probably be assigned to the same tradition. Although retrieved from disturbed contexts and clearly post-dating the construction of the mound these sherds are discussed here.

Description

Single decorated sherd of Beaker pottery. Interwall deposit [4], <520>. (6g)

The sherd was examined under x20 magnification with a binocular microscope. The fabric is reasonably hard, with a hackly fracture, and contains grog (small, sub-angular pieces <1mm) as a reasonably frequent inclusion (fragments are difficult to distinguish from the matrix but may be in the region of 15–20 per cent by surface area) and quartz as rounded grains. Rare flint is present (angular white fragments <1mm) and there is one substantial piece of chalk (maximum dimension 3mm) and rare smaller pieces (<1mm).

The sherd is partially oxidised, with an orange-brown external surface (Munsell 7.5YR 5/4 – 5/6 Brown to Strong brown), black core with a thin (2mm) orange layer below the external surface, and a mid-brown internal surface (Munsell 7.5 YR 5/3 Brown). The condition is slightly worn, with sharp edges smoothed off but with no loss of external surface detail.

The decoration is clearly of pendant triangles around the belly of the vessel, each filled with horizontal lines, all executed in comb-impression. The scheme in the area where the slack waist rises into the upper body of the vessel is less clear. A single angled line of comb impression is likely to belong to a broader triangle rising from the belly, filled with most of the horizontal lines which are visible in that area. Alternatively, it is possible that the area above the belly was largely filled with horizontal lines and that the surviving line is the remnant of a reserved triangle or other geometric shape. Two combs seem to have been used for decoration: one with squarer teeth for the filling of the triangles, and one with rectangular teeth for the outlines.

Single undecorated sherd, probably of Beaker pottery. Found in an >8mm dry sieved sample from [2]. 4g

The fabric was hard to very hard, with a smooth fracture and contained sparse to moderate small fine pieces of grog (<1mm, 5–10 per cent by surface area), fine quartz sand, rare to sparse mica and flint (<2mm, most less). Small dark glassy grains (<1mm) were also present; these are likely to be iron oxides, but could be glauconite, and there was rare to sparse mica.

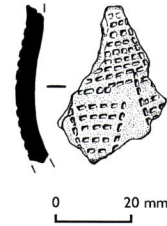

0   20 mm

Fig 3.6
Beaker sherd with comb impressed decoration. (Chris Evans, © English Heritage)

The core was bicoloured by the exterior and interior colours (7.5 YR 5/6 Strong Brown, and 5YR 5/6 Yellowish Red respectively. The sherd was in a worn condition, particularly on the interior.

Discussion

The fabrics of both sherds are reasonably typical of Beakers which are neither particularly fine nor coarse. Combinations of more than one inclusion type, particularly flint, quartz sand and grog, are characteristic of Beaker pottery (Cleal 1995a, fig 16.2, 190) and fabrics with glauconite and mica are known in the north Wiltshire area (Cleal 1992, 62).

The decorated sherd belongs to a vessel dating to the main period of Beaker use in southern Britain, that is, from around 2200 cal BC to the early 2nd millennium cal BC. It is almost certainly from a long-necked vessel, without a marked belly angle, and the sherd comes from a 'waist' area of gentle change in profile from the belly to the neck. Although the proportions of upper body to lower body cannot be calculated it seems more likely to belong to a long-necked rather than a short-necked form because of the upper body profile (there is enough present to show that the profile is not turning sharply outwards to the rim). In Stuart Needham's (2005) classification it would fall into the Long-Necked class, and in Clarke's classification (Clarke 1970) into the Late Southern (S3) group in which the change of angle at the belly is sometimes not marked by more than a few horizontal lines and in which triangles above and below the 'waist' do occur. A vessel from Little Downham, Cambridgeshire, shows how crowded this area can be and also illustrates a scheme in which there are narrower triangles below the angle and broader triangles above, where they are part of a running reserved chevron scheme (Clarke 1970, fig 959). Late Southern Beakers are not common in Wessex and there are no local close parallels, but Developed Southern Beaker (S2) are more frequent, and a Beaker of this group from Lockeridge, West Overton, 5km east of Silbury Hill, also shows some similarity, with filled triangles above a narrow reserved strip around a slack 'waist' (Clarke 1970, fig 899). Needham suggests that his Long-Necked forms are likely to have appeared from at least 2200 BC, and may have continued in use until the early 2nd millennium BC, perhaps as late as 1800 BC (Needham 2005, 195–8, fig. 13).

Occurrences of Beakers from the centuries of widespread Beaker use, when Beakers were undoubtedly the dominant ceramic type in southern Britain, are reasonably common within the landscape around Silbury Hill. Less than 1km to the south there were several vessels represented by sherds in the west chamber of West Kennet long barrow, cleared in 1859 (Cunnington 1927, pls X and XI). There are also many vessels of this time period represented at Windmill Hill, mainly excavated by Alexander Keiller (Smith 1965a, 80–2, pl XVII). Hamilton, in commenting on the pottery from the Keiller excavations in the context of the local area, noted that this 'suggests a contemporary landscape where Beaker pottery was deposited in abundance' (Hamilton 1999, 307). Given this context, it would be more surprising if Beaker pottery were not represented at Silbury Hill, than that it is.

The antler

Fay Worley

The relatively small and highly fragmented assemblage of antler recovered from 2007/8 excavations at Silbury Hill probably derives from tools used to construct the mound, although interpretation as tools can only be confirmed in a few cases. Further evidence for the use of antler tools to construct the mound comes from a block of chalk bearing the imprints of antler strikes. The construction of the mound must have required a considerable number of antler picks, a seasonal resource. The acquisition of antlers would have exerted demand on the Later Neolithic economy. Once picks were beyond their use-life they may have been recycled (further modified into other tools or artefacts) or discarded. Comparison with contemporary assemblages from sites such as Avebury and Marden Henge suggests that deliberate deposition is a feature of the period and therefore a number of picks may have been so deposited on Silbury Hill, or perhaps in the surrounding ditch (Worley 2011a).

Methods and terminology

All antler fragments were quantified (by count, refitting recent breaks where possible, and weight) and, when possible, identified to species and region of the antler. The condition of fragments from each context was graded (poor, moderate, good or very good) and any evidence of antler working, use wear or modification was noted. Suitably complete fragments were measured following established conventions (Haltenorth and Trense 1956; Ahlén 1965; von den Driesch 1976; Clutton-Brock 1984; Legge 2008) to enable comparison with contemporary assemblages from elsewhere in Britain. Additional length and diameter measurements were also noted to aid description of fragments. The stage of development of the antlers was recorded following Schmid (1972, 89).

The nomenclature used for antler tines follows that used in comparative site reports (Clutton-Brock 1984, 11; Serjeantson and Gardiner 1995; Legge 2008, 573). The terms *tip*, *body* and *base* are used to describe regions of individual tines; *ventral* and *dorsal* are used to describe the side of tines towards and away from the skull. The terms *proximal* and *distal* are used to describe areas of the beam, proximal being that closest to the burr and skull. *Lateral* and *medial* describe the sides of both tines and the beam, towards and away from the midline of the body.

The assemblage

The antler assemblage was highly fragmentary, particularly that from within the tunnel collapse deposits. Most fragments comprised only a small piece of tine or beam and many could not be identified to any particular region of the antler. The minimum number of antlers represented in the assemblage was estimated using representation of diagnostic areas and by comparison with the mean weight of antler picks from contemporary sites. The assemblage includes burr fragments from a minimum of three antlers, all naturally shed. There are 15 tine tips, also indicating a minimum of three antlers, assuming a maximum of six tines per antler (Hillson 1992, 9), or two antlers (following Serjeantson and Gardiner's (1995, 417) note that a crown can have up to ten tines). The assemblage comprises 1.9kg of antler fragments, equivalent to four picks based on the Grimes Graves mean pick weight or five picks based on the Durrington Walls mean weights (Clutton-Brock 1984, 12), although this comparison does not take into account the different taphonomic histories of the antlers from these sites, or the potential size differences in the antlers used at the sites.

Antler was recovered from collapse deposits within the tunnel, the buried ditch, the possible external ditch, works on the Hillside and summit

(Table 3.12) (*see* methodology in Chapter 2), in contexts representing Phases 12.1, 16.1, 16.2, 20.1 and 20.2. The antler assemblage proved to be important to the scientific dating programme and 13 samples were radiocarbon dated (Marshall *et al*, Chapter 4), including specimens from all locations from which antlers were recovered.

Antler from buried ditch [3902]
(Phase 12.1)

A small quantity of antler was recovered from the primary level and spits 2, 3 and 4 of the ditch fill (Table 3.12), together representing at least two tines. The primary fill of the ditch [3926] included a single small fragment of worn tine tip (from sample <9036>), from a different tine to the other fragments from this ditch. Five fragments of polished and worn tine tip were recovered from the second spit of the buried ditch [3918], four of which (SF 8004 x2, 8016 and 8017) refit. The fifth fragment (SF 8015) may also represent the same tine. The third and fourth spits of the ditch each produced poorly preserved indeterminate fragments of antler (SF 8018 and 8006).

Antler from the possible external ditch
(Phase 16.1)

A single, heavily eroded tine tip (SF 8002) was recovered from [3008].

In situ *antler from summit excavations*
(Phase 16.2)

Excavations on the summit produced a small assemblage of *in situ* antler, recovered from six interwall deposits. Deposit [4813] contained a fragment of shed burr and an indeterminate fragment, [4814] contained a tine tip, [4848] produced two refitting fragments of worn tine tip, and [4838] and [4835] indeterminate fragments. Deposit [4845] contained large fragments from two worn tines (SF 8525 and 8526; Fig 3.7). A further fragment (SF 8527) was stolen prior to analysis and is now only known from excavation photographs (Fig 3.8), which, combined with the location of modern fractures on SF 8526 and the testimony of the on-site environmental archaeologist who suggested that SF 8526 and 8527 refitted, can be used to suggest that the two fragments may have formed part of the crown of an antler, a region suggested to have been used as 'rakes' at contemporary sites (for example Legge 1981, 100). The antler would have been at development stage D or above (Schmid 1972, 89). Tine SF 8525 had an undulating shape (Fig 3.7), which may indicate that it was from a mature stag.

Table 3.12: The antler assemblage quantified by count and weight. The 'Quantity' column counts refitting fragments from recent breakage separately only if they were recorded under different small finds numbers

Location	Context	Small find(s)	Quantity	Weight (g)
Buried ditch 3902 deposits (Phase 12.1):				
Primary fill	3926	–	1	0.5
Spit 2	3918	8004, 8015–7	5	14.1
Spit 3	3919	8018	3	1.9
Spit 4	3920	8006	2	0.9
TOTAL			11	17.4
Possible external ditch deposits (Phase 16.1):				
Ditch fill	3008	8002	1	2.9
TOTAL			1	2.9
In situ Hillside and summit deposits (Phase 16.2):				
Interwall deposit	4813	–	2	11.9
Interwall deposit	4814	8523	1	5.6
Interwall deposit	4835	–	1	3.4
Interwall deposit	4838	–	1	0.3
Interwall deposit	4845	8525–6	2	113.3
Interwall deposit	4848	–	2	1.7
Final phase mound	4904	8751–2, 8754	27	377.5
Final phase mound	4910	8757	1	90.5
TOTAL			37	604.2
In situ Hillside and summit deposits (Phase 20.1):				
Topsoil	4804	8502	1	21.6
Subsoil	4805	–	5	23.8
TOTAL			6	45.4
In situ Hillside and summit deposits (Phase 20.2):				
Chalk topsoil interface	4905	8755	6	281.2
TOTAL			6	281.2
Tunnel collapse deposits (Phase 20.2):				
Bay 31–35	3830	8049	1	1.9
Bay 32	3817	8021–8	8	54.1
Bay 33	3823	8052–4	3	1.3
Bays 34–6	3829	8019–20	2	25
Bays 36, 38, 41	3826	8029, 8044, 8046–7, 8050	5	17.9
Bay 41	3843	8048	1	3.1
Bay 50	3844	8010, 8056–92	38	135.9
Bay 58	3845	8093	1	111.7
Bay 67	3848	8094	1	1.2
Bay 75–6	Unstrat	8116	1	92.9
West Lateral Bays 12–13	3857	8109	1	49.8
TOTAL			62	494.8
Unstratified deposits:				
Crater collapse	4889	–	3	427.5
Unstratified	Unstrat	8758	1	4.1
TOTAL			4	431.6

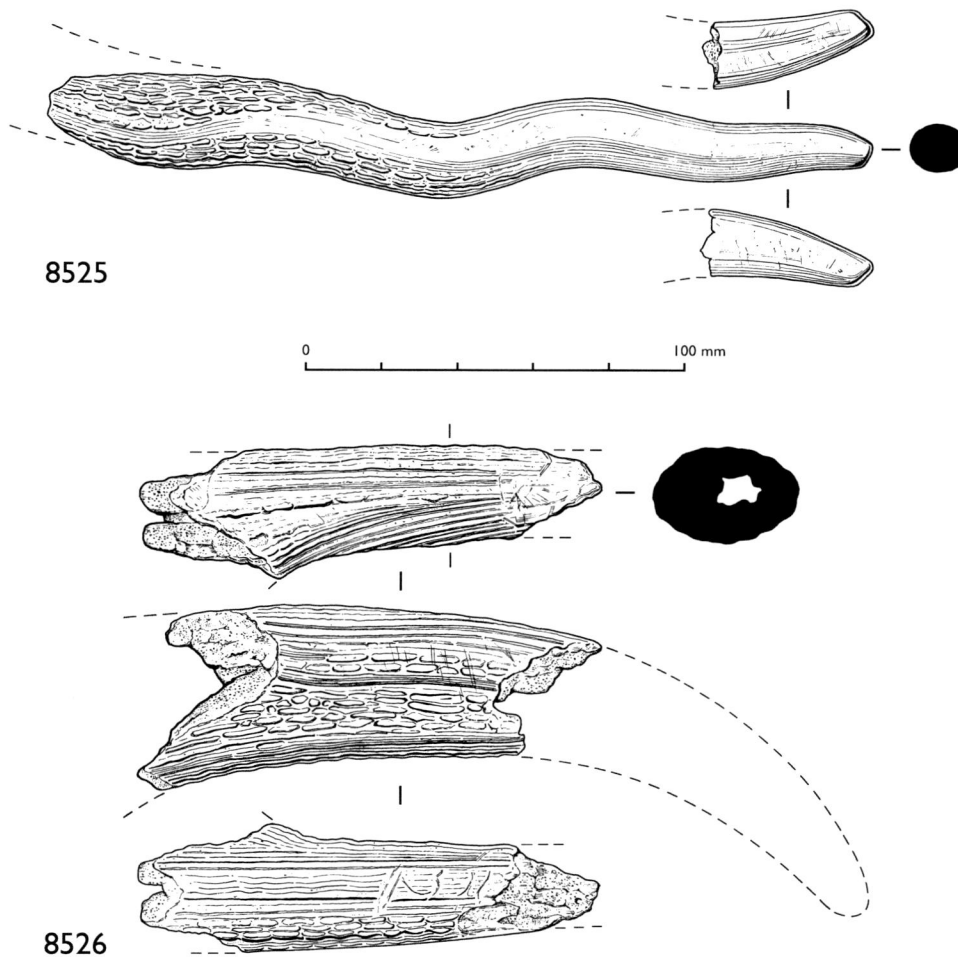

Fig 3.7
Tine SF 8525 (top) and
crown tine SF 8526
(bottom).
(Chris Evans,
© English Heritage)

In situ *antler from Hillside excavations*
(Phase 16.2)

An *in situ* assemblage was also recovered from final phase mound deposits on the Hillside ([4904] and [4910]). The most complete antler tool from the excavation was a pick recovered from [4904] (SF 8754) (Fig 3.9). This 390mm long implement was reconstructed from 12 refitting fragments. It comprised a heavily pearled and guttered beam and the origins of two tines. The antler was at development stage D or above. The tool is described further below. Context [4904] also contained 19 further tine and beam fragments. The antler from [4910] (SF 8757) comprised four refitting fragments of worn tine, which may have been gnawed by a deer (*see* discussion below).

In situ *antler from the summit excavations*
(Phase 20.1)

The subsoil on the summit of the Hill [4805] produced five fragments of antler, and the topsoil [4804] a further tine, probably from an antler crown, the tip of which had been worn.

In situ *antler from the Hillside excavations*
(Phase 20.2)

The interface between the chalk and the topsoil on the Hillside works [4905] produced one of the largest pieces of antler. Specimen SF 8755 comprised refitting fragments of the base of an antler at development stage E or above, extending *c*240mm along the beam from its shed burr, and including 44mm of the brow tine and 71mm of the bez tine (Fig 3.10).

Fig 3.8
Crown tines SF 8526 and SF
8527 in situ. Tine SF 8527
was stolen prior to analysis.
A second view of SF 8527
can be seen in the box in the
top left side of the figure.
(© English Heritage)

Fig 3.9 (opposite)
Antler pick SF 8754.
(Chris Evans,
© English Heritage)

Antler from collapse within the tunnels (Phase 20.2)

Antler fragments were found sporadically in collapse within individual tunnel bays (Table 3.12). The ubiquity of modern breaks on the fragments is likely to have been caused by their displacement from the Hill makeup through tunnel collapse events. This, together with the evidence of voids in the Hill structure, means that we cannot be certain where the antler was originally deposited in the Hill. It also means that many of the fragments may have originated from a small number of antlers. The following paragraphs review the tunnel antler assemblage in order of recovery, moving from the exterior to the centre of the mound.

The first antler fragments were found when excavation reached Bays 31 to 35, 28.3m into the Main Tunnel, shortly after the tunnel emerged into the mound from the underlying bedrock. A small assemblage (14 fragments, 82g) was recovered from the collapse in the following 5.5m of Main Tunnel (Bays 31–6), the majority of which came from Bay 32. The Bay 32 fragment group comprised eight pieces of antler, all potentially from a single naturally shed burr. Four small fragments of antler from Bay 33

(context SF 3823), and a fragment from Bays 31–5 may also have originated from this same single antler. Two refitting fragments of tine body (SF 8019) were recovered from Bays 34–6; these were in a poorer condition than the rest of the antler from the tunnels, with a distinct brown-coloured band comprising the outer *c* 2mm of the fragment, bounding white coloured inner antler, in contrast to the uniform white colour of the rest of the antler recovered from chalk in the tunnel (as seen in, for example, Fig 3.12). The brown colouration corresponded to elevated concentrations of iron (*see* Dungworth in Worley 2011a, Appendix 1), perhaps due to proximity to the iron tunnel supports introduced into the Hill in the 1960s. Five fragments (20g) of antler were recovered from Bays 38 and 41.

Over 60 per cent (38 fragments weighing 135.9g) of the antler fragments from the Main Tunnel were recovered from Bay 50, 45.7–46.6m into the tunnel. This group comprised 29 small indeterminate fragments of antler, some of which displayed prominent guttering, together with fragments from at least three tines, and three larger beam or tine body/base fragments. A large fragment of red deer beam and tine (SF 8093; Fig 3.11) was recovered from collapse [3845] in Bay 58, 53–53.9m into the Main

Tunnel. The specimen comprised a 197mm section of beam, one end of which was broken in the recent past. The beam has been split longitudinally, tapering to the external surface of the antler at the distal end of the specimen. This break might relate to its use as a tool (*see below*).

An indeterminate fragment of antler (SF 8094) was recovered from collapse in Bay 67, 61.3–62.2m into the Main Tunnel. A single, substantial fragment of tine (SF 8116, Fig 3.12) was recovered from Bay 75 or 76, 68.6–70.4m into the Main Tunnel, within the area of the Organic Mound. The tine is more robust than the antler fragments found within chalk deposits, and a much darker brown colour than any other fragment. A single fragment of beam or tine body was recovered from slumped material [3857] in West Lateral Bays 8–14. This fragment had a brown colouration to both the cortical and cancellous structure of the antler. The colouration is similar to that observed in the outer margins of fragment SF 8019 from the main tunnel.

Unstratified antler including summit collapse

Collapsed chalk [4889] in the crater on the summit of the Hill contained two relatively large pieces of antler and a smaller fragment of beam. The largest piece comprised a 285mm long beam fragment. One end of the beam had been broken off recently and the other had broken in antiquity, possibly connected to use as a tool. The second large piece of antler was from a crown and refitted from eight fragments. Both the large pieces of antler bore possible cut or chop marks (discussed further below).

Antler from previous investigations at Silbury

Previous antiquarian and archaeological excavations at Silbury Hill have also described finding antler – sometimes reported as deer-horn or stag's horn. With the exception of those from 1968–70 excavations, the antlers were not available for re-analysis and are considered here from secondary sources. There are no illustrations of the assemblages. A proportion of the antler from the 1968–70 assemblage has been re-examined as part of this research (Worley 2011b).

The earliest known investigation into Silbury Hill is the sinking of a shaft through its centre by Drax in 1776. Recently uncovered personal letters written by Drax (Appendix 1.1 *in* Chapter 1; Edwards 2010a; Leary and Field 2010) report

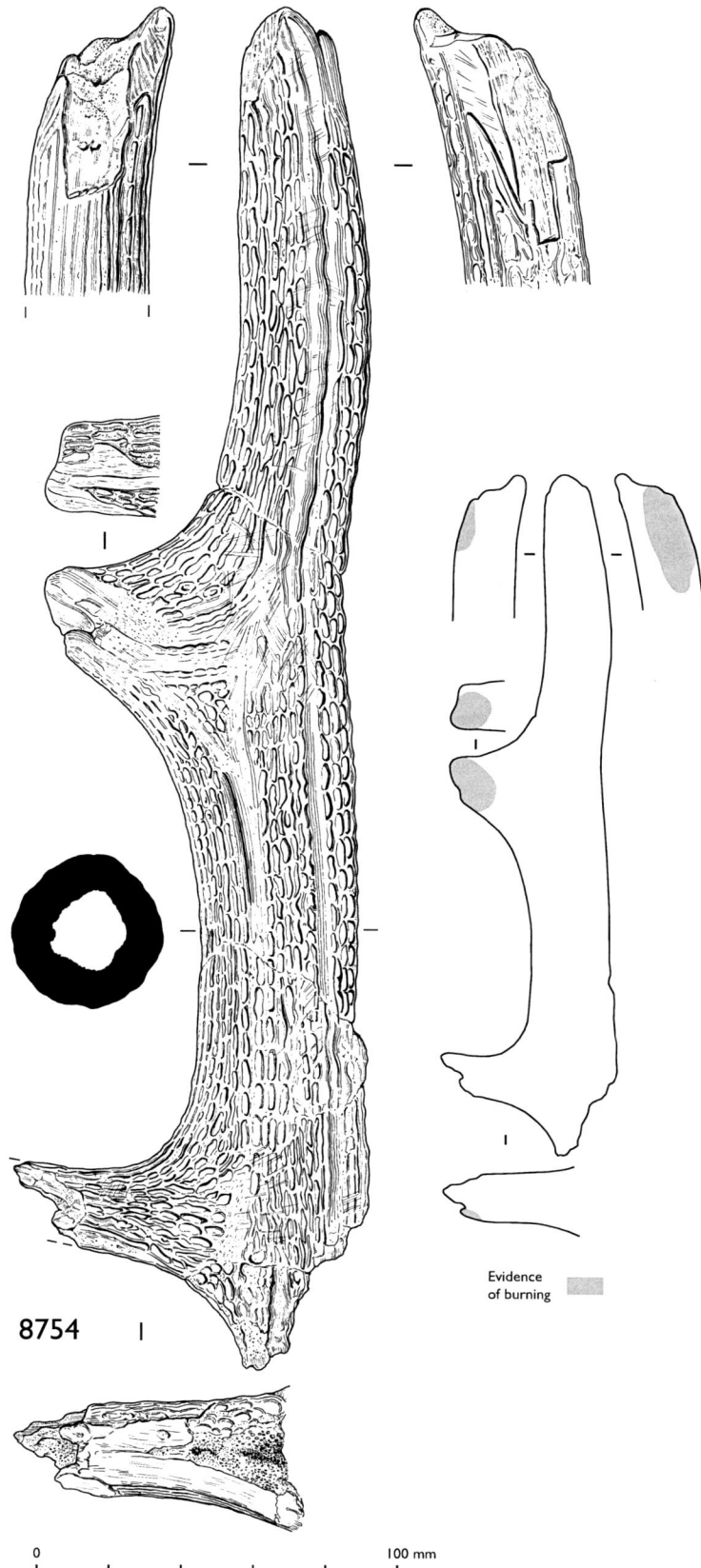

8754

Evidence of burning

0   100 mm

Fig 3.10
Shed antler SF 8755.
(Chris Evans,
© English Heritage)

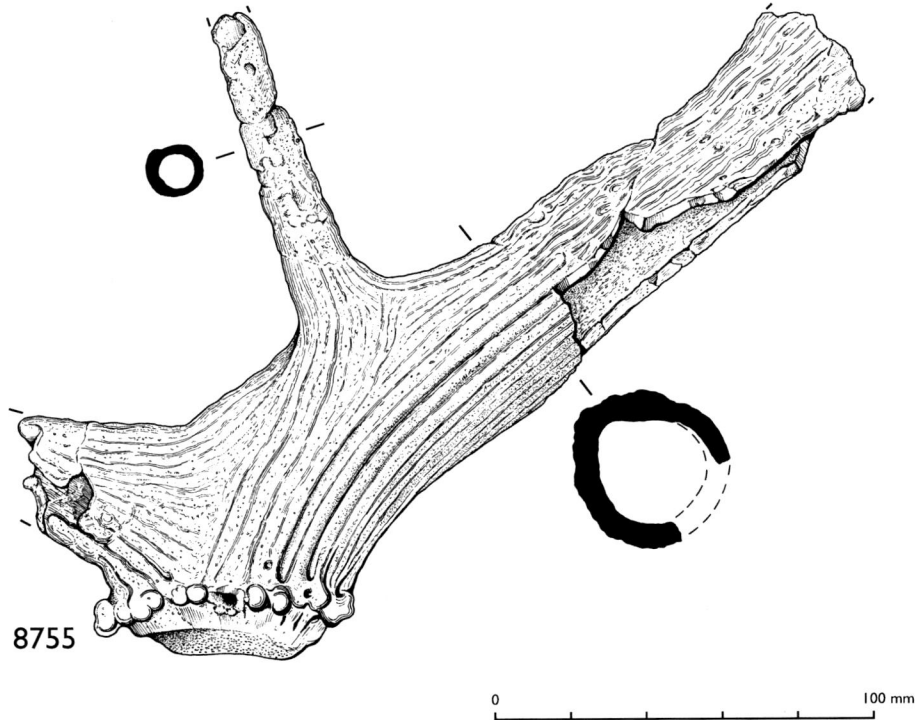

Fig 3.10
Shed antler SF 8755.
(Chris Evans,
© English Heritage)

8755

0   100 mm

that some fragments of antler were recovered within the top 6 feet (1.8m) of the shaft, which he believed to be intrusive from 18th-century tree-planting, and three further antlers were found within the Hill's structure at depths of 23 feet (7.0m), 28 feet (8.5m) and 30 feet (9.1m) below the summit of the Hill. Thereafter, no further fragments were found to a depth of 56 feet (17.1m), at which point the report concludes. The fragments from within the Hill's structure are described as large and either from a large stag (red deer) or moose, the latter identification being very unlikely.

John Merewether (1851b) reported finding two antler tines while tunnelling into the Hill in 1849. The first is described as 'a portion of the tine of a stag's antler of the red deer species' (Merewether 1851b, 11) found 30 yards (27.4m) into the tunnel, 'immediately above the ground-line'. The reported location is just one metre short of the position in the tunnel where the 2007/8 investigation began to encounter antler fragments. The second tine was found in the organic core of the mound and is described as in a 'strong and unusually compact state' (Merewether 1851b, 16), mirroring the preservation difference noted in antler from the organic and chalk deposits in the 2007/8 assemblage.

In 1867, excavations by the Wiltshire Archaeological and Natural History Society to the eastern foot of the Hill recovered 'six portions of antlers of red deer; three of these were shed horns, two of the others may have been used for implements – the bases having been rounded as if by use' (Wilkinson 1867, 115). No further information is given and there are no illustrations of these antlers. The Wiltshire Heritage Museum catalogue of 1934 does list two antlers as 'Horns of red deer, found in Silbury Hill, during the excavations there, Oct 1867. Probably used as the picks in the construction of the Hill. WAM xi, p. 114–5' (pers comm Webb 2010), referencing Wilkinson's article. However, the catalogued antlers themselves are contradictorily labelled as 'found in digging flint on Beckhampton Downs' and from 'a rabbit burrow at Kingston Deverill, 1886'.

There were two 20th-century excavations at Silbury. Petrie reportedly recovered antler fragments whilst excavating two trenches into the side of the mound in 1922 (Atkinson 1967, 260), and further fragments were recovered from the 1968–70 excavations. At least some of the antlers recovered by Petrie in 1922 and the Wiltshire Archaeological Society in 1867 were radiocarbon dated prior to the 1968–70 excavations (Atkinson 1967, 262) and it can be assumed that they were destroyed during this process.

The 1968–70 assemblage was studied by Neville Gardner as an undergraduate thesis (Gardner 1987) and later published (Gardner 1997). Gardner reports two fragments of antler from the excavations in the ditch surrounding the mound (1997, 49), that 'sporadic animal bone and pieces of red deer antler were found in the tunnelling of 1968' (1997, 47) and that from excavations on the summit '51 antler fragments were also found. 11 worn tine tips and 2 fragmentary shed burr pieces could be identified. Another piece of shed antler had had the brow and trez tines removed, as well as the beam above the trez, leaving the small bez as a working point; the back of the burr was much damaged' (1997, 49). Re-analysis of the 1969–70 antler assemblage has recently revealed that the antler tool described by Gardner had both brow and bez tines as working points when deposited and confirmed the presence of three shed, well-developed antlers (stage E–F), which may all represent tools (Worley 2011b).

Following a collapse on the summit of the mound, English Heritage evaluation trenches recovered a red deer antler tine from a deposit of chalk rubble and a second fragment of beam or tine in the collapsed area on the summit (Baker 2001a; 2001b).

Condition of the 2007/8 assemblage

The assemblage was highly fragmented, most breaks being recent. In general, the majority of the assemblage (76% by weight, 83% by fragment count, Table 3.13) was graded as in moderate or poor condition. Preservation varied in the assemblage. Fragments from chalk deposits were generally cream in colour and had a chalk-like texture, while those from the organic deposits in the centre of the mound were more robust and dark brown in colour. The condition of tine SF 8019 suggests a different taphonomic history, as discussed above.

There was little evidence for burning on the antler fragments, the only example being localised burning on SF 8754, probably related to modification into a tool. There was also little evidence for root etching or scavenger gnawing suggesting that the antlers were not accessible to rodents or carnivores, and so probably buried rapidly. The only evidence for gnawing is found on SF 8757, a tine from final phase Hillside

deposits [4910]. Parallel striations on this fragment suggest that it may have been gnawed by a deer. Deer-gnawed antlers have been recovered in other near contemporary assemblages, including Hambledon Hill (Legge 2008, 579). Deer are thought to gnaw shed antlers to supplement minerals in their diet; the infrequency of deer gnawed antlers in the Silbury assemblage may relate to the natural availability of calcium in the local chalkland environment (following Legge 2008, 574), but may also indicate that the antlers were collected soon after shedding in the spring, before they could be scavenged.

Evidence for the species, age and size of deer

Species identification and age of the deer

The guttering and pearling on many of the fragments, together with the size and tine

Fig 3.11 (above top) Antler SF 8093. (Ian Leonard and Mike Hesketh-Roberts, © English Heritage)

Fig 3.12 (above) Tines SF 8116 (bottom), SF 8010 (top) and SF 8076 (centre). Note difference in colour and condition of the fragments. (Ian Leonard and Mike Hesketh-Roberts, English Heritage, © English Heritage)

Table 3.13: Condition of the antler assemblage quantified by weight and fragment count

Condition	Buried ditch	External ditch	In situ Hillside & summit	In situ summit	In situ Hillside	Tunnel collapse deposits	Unstratified	Total
	Phase 12.1	Phase 16.1	Phase 16.2	Phase 20.1	Phase 20.2	Phase 20.2	–	–
Quantified by number of fragments								
Very good	–	–	3%	17%	–	3%	–	3%
Good	45%	–	14%	–	–	10%	50%	14%
Moderate	9%	–	81%	83%	–	68%	50%	63%
Poor	45%	100%	3%	–	100%	19%	–	20%
Total	11	1	37	6	6	62	4	127
Quantified by weight								
Very good	–	–	1%	48%	–	29%	–	9%
Good	81%	–	22%	–	–	11%	20%	15%
Moderate	3%	–	77%	52%	–	54%	80%	59%
Poor	16%	100%	–	–	100%	6%	–	17%
Total	17.4g	2.9g	604.2g	45.4g	281.2g	494.8g	431.6g	1877.5g

formation of the larger fragments indicate that many, if not all, of the antlers are red deer (*Cervus elaphus*). Only males (stags) grow antlers in this species. A new set of antlers are grown annually from the second year of life. The antlers begin to form around early April each year, first appearing as a bony growth from the pedicle, which projects from the frontal bones, and covered with skin, known as the velvet. The antlers continue to grow until around August, at which time the blood supply to the antler is disrupted, the velvet dies and detaches from the underlying bony antler, which becomes hard. The antler is naturally cast in spring (late March/early April), although the date of casting can be affected by factors such as population pressure, environment and social position of the stag (Clutton-Brock *et al* 1982, 270; Bartoš and Hyánek 1983).

Generally, each set of antlers is progressively more massive and complex than the last, until they begin to reduce in size during the stag's post-prime years (Bubenik 1983, 423–5). However, along with age of the stag, the environment, stress and social position within the herd, can be reflected in the size and conformation of antlers (Bartoš and Hyánek 1983; Suttie and Kay 1983). The conformation of antlers is therefore best attributed to an antler stage, rather than an age-at-death. Fragmentation of the Silbury assemblage has negated assigning development stages to the majority of the fragments, however, at least two are

from individuals of stage D or above, and one is at stage E or above. This suggests that more developed antlers were selected, presumably as their conformation, mass and strength would be best suited to excavating chalk.

The undulating shape of tine SF 8525 (Fig 3.7) is unusual. It is hypothesised that it may be due to nutritional deficiency or old age; the latter suggestion is supported in hunting literature. No additional pathologies were noted in the assemblage.

Biometry

Measurements, combined with stage of development, can be used to investigate the size of red deer antlers in Neolithic Britain and any standardisation in the choice of antlers deposited on archaeological sites. However, biometric data recorded from antler is subject to methodological and biological difficulties. Methodological difficulties include lack of standardisation and poor definition of measurements, reflecting the variable morphology of antlers and lack of clearly defined measurement points, and application of inappropriate measurements which were originally developed as a method of scoring hunting trophies, and not modified antler tools. Biological difficulties concern the declining size of post-prime age antlers.

Only two specimens from the Silbury assemblage could be measured following established conventions: SF 8755 from the Phase 20.2 Hillside chalk topsoil interface and SF 8754 from

Table 3.14: Antler measurements

Specimen and measurement description	Measurement ID	Data (mm)
Small Find 8754 (4904) Phase 16.2		
Circumference of lower beam	5[3]	c.141[6]
Small Find 8755 (4905) Phase 20.2		
Circumference of burr	28[1] 39[2] 4[3] 1[4]	>201[5]
Anterior-posterior diameter of burr [taken as diameter of coronet]	2[4]	64
Distal circumference of the burr	40[2]	191
Ventro-oral point of burr to upper side of basic part of brow tine	33[1]	57
Minimum distance between basic parts of brow tine and bez tine	34[1] 15[4]	109
Length from burr to thinnest point between the brow and bez tines		
[taken to distal margin of coronet at anterior point]	6[4]	86

1 (Ahlén 1965, 102–3); 2 (Von den Driesch 1976, 36); 3 (Haltenorth and Trense 1956); 4 (Clutton-Brock 1984); 5 Coronet partly abraded; 6 Beam refitted

Phase 16.2 mound deposits. Both exhibited damage at some measurement points. The measurements are presented in Table 3.14.

Comparing antler SF 8755 to other Neolithic assemblages, the circumference of the burr (>201mm, however the coronet was partially abraded) indicates that the specimen is within the lower half of the size range recovered from Stonehenge (155–299mm, 222mm mean; Serjeantson and Gardiner 1995, 419) and Grimes Graves (133–280mm, 213mm mean; Clutton-Brock 1984, 25), and very similar to the mean of those recovered from Durrington Walls (103–260mm, 199mm mean; Clutton-Brock 1984, 25). Measuring 191mm, the distal circumference of the burr is within the range of 22 measured antlers from Windmill Hill (115–228mm, 182mm mean) (Grigson 1965) and slightly smaller than three antlers from Avebury (measuring 200, 200 and 219mm) (Gray 1935, 148–55), although only the larger antlers from that site appear to have been measured.

The circumference of the lower beam measurement was taken as the smallest circumference between the brow and trez tines, following Haltenorth and Trense (1956) and is perhaps similar to (although not the same as) Legge's beam circumference measure, which is taken 'above the brow, or brow/bez, tines, at that point where the antler again becomes roughly cylindrical' (Legge 2008, 574). Antler SF 8754 measured 141mm, within the range, but larger than the mean size for Hambledon Hill antlers (Legge 2008).

Very little can be concluded from biometric data from only two antlers, however they do conform to the size range recovered from contemporary sites, reflecting both the size of Neolithic deer in Britain and the choice of antlers acquired for use as tools.

Evidence for the use of antler tools at Silbury

Intrinsic evidence that the assemblage represents antler tools

Polished, pitted or worn tine tips were noted on several fragments from the 2007/8 Silbury assemblage. Although these modifications might result from using the antler to quarry chalk, they can also be caused by the behaviour of the deer themselves, through activities such as spreading scent, rutting and sloughing antler velvet (Olsen 1989; Jin and Shipman 2010). Therefore, these characters alone cannot confirm that the antler fragments were from tools. There are, however, five specimens exhibiting more convincing evidence that they were tools: specimens SF 8754 and SF 8755 from the final phase mound, SF 8093 from tunnel Bay 58 and two unstratified specimens from the summit collapse.

Antler SF 8754 (Fig 3.9) is the most convincing tool in the Silbury assemblage. As noted previously, the distal end of the beam and the trez tine appear to have been removed in antiquity. The bez may also have been removed in antiquity. A slight darkening of the surface associated with more prevalent fine cracking, suggests that heat may have been applied to the surface of the antler at the point where the distal beam and trez tine body were removed (there is also extremely faint and inconclusive evidence for this at the distal end of the bez tine fragment). This suggests that the antler may have been modified into a pick, with the distal beam forming the handle and the proximal tine, probably the brow tine, forming the blade of the pick. The brow tine and burr appear to have been removed in antiquity, with the ventral surface of the bez tine having been 'peeled' away. It is likely that rather than being part of the modification to create the tool, this action broke the tool and led to its discard. SF 8754 is a right side antler.

While antler SF 8755 (Fig 3.10) did not exhibit any conclusive evidence for modification, such as the removal of tines or division of the beam, the posterior and medial region of the coronet does appear to have been battered, which can occur if a pick is hammered into chalk or used as a hammer itself, and is seen in assemblages from others sites (for example Marden Henge, Worley, in preparation). Antler SF 8755's brow tine was lost in antiquity, possibly ending the use life of the implement as the bez is too slender to have been used as the main blade of a pick.

Antler SF 8093 (Fig 3.11) is much less complete than SF 8754 and does not exhibit any evidence for the intentional removal of the tine body (although this may have occurred). The evidence that it may represent a tool comprises a longitudinal split to the beam. This split may have formed the blade of a pick, a wedge or have resulted from dividing the beam at this point, either intentionally, or when the tool was broken. SF 8093 is also probably a right side antler.

The two fragments from collapsed chalk [4889] in the crater on the mound's summit bore possible tool marks. The first was a section of beam, one end of which may have been intentionally broken to modify the antler into a tool, most likely the handle of a pick. The beam bore a heavy transverse chop, which may have been inflicted as the antler was modified into a tool, or may have resulted from post-depositional damage during antiquarian investigations into the mound. The second fragment was a crown, the region of antler sometimes interpreted as a rake. The crown bore a fine transverse cut across the distal face of the junction between the tines. Although this may be a cut mark, recent research has shown that similar marks may be inflicted through natural deer behaviours (Jin and Shipman 2010).

Antler tool marks on a chalk block SF 8753

While the majority of the antler fragments provide no intrinsic evidence that they were tools used in the construction of the chalk mound, there is direct evidence of this from marks left on a sub-angular block of chalk recovered from final phase layer [4904] in the Hillside excavation (Fig 3.13). The block bears imprints of strikes from antler tools in two locations. The first strike (marked 'A' in Fig 3.13) penetrated directly into the chalk and may relate to an adjacent plane of fracture of the block, the second and overlying third strikes are revealed in cross-section (marked 'B' in Fig 3.13), the chalk having fissured at the point of their impact. In both locations, the tool's imprints have a roughly circular cross-section and a curved profile; conforming in morphology and size to an antler tine. As suggested by Riddler (*in* Leary 2009), the overlying second and third strikes suggest that the antler was being used as a pick in this instance.

Discussion of the use of antler tools at Silbury

Antler assemblages from contemporary sites such as Avebury (Gray 1935) Durrington Walls (Clutton-Brock 1984), Grimes Graves (Legge 1981; Clutton-Brock 1984), Hambledon Hill

Fig 3.13
Chalk block SF 8753 bearing antler tool strike marks.
(A and B)
(Ian Leonard and Mike Hesketh-Roberts,
© English Heritage)

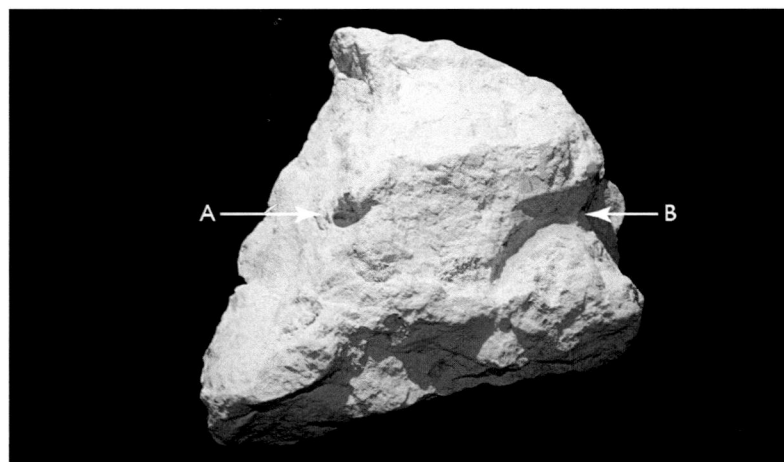

(Legge 2008), Marden Henge (Wainwright 1971, 223), Mount Pleasant (Wainwright 1979, 171–6), Stonehenge (Serjeantson and Gardiner 1995) and Woodhenge (Wainwright 1979, 171–6) generally comprise numerous largely complete antler tools, with the antlers often modified in a consistent way. In contrast, the much smaller antler assemblage from Silbury Hill is highly fragmentary with only two examples of a recognisable tool type (picks SF 8754 and SF 8755) and three further possible antler tools. The wear and polish on many other fragments cannot be distinguished from that which can occur naturally. In addition to the antlers themselves, evidence for the use of antler tools at Silbury includes a chalk block bearing the imprints of antler strikes. The Silbury example is not the first time that marks left by antler tools have been identified in chalk. Similar marks have been found at sites such as the flint mines of Blackpatch, West Sussex (Goodman *et al* 1924) both on loose blocks of chalk and *in situ* in the flint mine's gallery walls, and at Stonehenge, where the hole for sarsen stone 9 was found to contain the tip of an antler still embedded in the chalk (Cleal 1995b, 194). Marks like these and the consistent methods for modifying antlers inform our understanding of how antler tools were used to mine or quarry chalk.

Evidence for the technique used to modify the antlers into tools at Silbury is slight. Whereas other assemblages such as Marden (Worley in preparation) and Stonehenge (Serjeantson and Gardiner 1995) present clear and common evidence for the application of direct heat to aid dividing the antlers, and perhaps to help smooth fractured edges, in the Silbury assemblage only SF 8754 bears any evidence for this, and that evidence is faint. There is also no evidence for sawing or chopping antler as seen elsewhere (for example Legge 2008). These modification marks may have been masked by the depositional environment and post-depositional fragmentation of the Silbury assemblage.

There is no evidence for antler from killed deer in the Silbury assemblage, rather the burrs had all been naturally shed. This may be an intentional choice on the part of the mound's builders as shed antler has reached its maximum size and for much of the year is harder than that developing on the head of the deer. However, as contemporary sites utilise both shed and harvested antler, it may also be a product of the small sample collected.

Implications for antler acquisition and deposition

The volume of chalk used in the construction of Silbury Hill is estimated to be between 235,522 and 239,133 cubic metres; for the purposes of this report the smaller estimate will be used. Following previous assumptions that the use-life of an antler pick is a single day (Sieveking, cited in Clutton-Brock 1984, 16) and that around 3 cubic metres of solid chalk can be excavated with an antler pick in a day (Atkinson and Sorrell 1959, 59), the construction of Silbury Hill may have required around 78,500 antler picks. Bayesian radiocarbon analysis conducted as part of this project has suggested that the Hill may have taken between 55 and 155 years to be built (Marshall *et al*, Chapter 4), indicating that, on average, somewhere in the region of 500–1,400 antler picks would have been required annually for the construction of Silbury Hill. While this estimation is based on a number of variables, estimates and assumptions (use-life of an antler pick, daily volume of chalk excavated, constant rate of construction, Bayesian modelling of radiocarbon dates) and so should not be regarded as accurate, it does serve to highlight the scale of demand for antler that the construction of Silbury Hill would have placed on the Later Neolithic economy. In addition, the lack of evidence for antlers from killed deer in the assemblage suggests that this demand was seasonal, fresh shed antler only being available in the spring, and that therefore antler collection may have been a significant annual activity rather than relying on happenstance. If the local deer herds and economy were not able to meet the demand for antler, it may have been a traded commodity and brought to Silbury for the construction works (as was previously suggested by Clarke (1914, 143), referring to some of the antlers at Grimes Graves).

Sanders (1910, 112–13) suggested that worn out and broken antler tools were sometimes discarded with rubble in the backfill of redundant mine shafts and chambers at Neolithic flint mines. At Silbury Hill, although we have only examined a small proportion of the mound, it appears that relatively little antler was discarded in its makeup, and it is obvious that the minimum number of antlers represented by this and earlier excavated assemblages cannot represent all the tools used to build the monument. Perhaps the majority of worn out antler tools were taken elsewhere and recycled into other artefacts. Perhaps also it was important to keep the Hill 'clean' due to its ceremonial nature. Following this argument, those antlers which were deposited in the Hill may have been purposively placed rather than casually discarded. On recovering an antler from Silbury, Merewether (1851b, 16) noted that 'This being the second instance in which this portion of the stag's horn has been found in these operations, it is not improbable that it may have been specially regarded'. Antler implements are similarly absent from the majority of the site at other contemporary ceremonial monuments, but have been found in groups in their ditches, for example at Woodhenge (Wainwright 1979, 175–6) and Avebury (Gray 1935; Wainwright 1979). These have been interpreted as votive deposits marking the completion of the monument. Perhaps a similar cache of antler tools awaits discovery in the unexcavated ditch surrounding Silbury Hill.

4

The Silbury Chronology

P D MARSHALL, A BAYLISS, J LEARY, G CAMPBELL, F WORLEY,
C BRONK RAMSEY AND G COOK

The problem of when Silbury was built is crucial for if we can answer this, we already know enough to define, at least in outline, the culture concerned and by inference the society which it represents (Atkinson 1967, 261)

This chapter outlines a chronology for Silbury Hill, showing how the recent work has refined the existing chronological model, providing precise estimates for the constructional stages of the monument and an estimate for the length of time it took to build. Four models are put forward and discussed. The preferred chronological model places construction of the Lower Organic Mound in the second half of the 25th century cal BC, with the Upper Organic Mound completed in the late 25th or early 24th centuries cal BC. The final stages of Silbury were finished in the late 24th or early 23rd centuries cal BC, estimating that it took between 55 and 155 years to build. The next dated episode of activity on the summit took place in the 10th or 11th centuries cal AD.

Previous dating

Thirty radiocarbon measurements have previously been obtained on samples from Silbury Hill (Bayliss *et al* 2007a, table 1; Whittle 1997a, table 1; Table 4.1). Bayesian modelling placed the completion of the primary mound (Atkinson Silbury I) in the 24th or 23rd century cal BC (Bayliss *et al* 2007a, 42). Although no formal estimates for the construction of the chalk mound could be derived from the data available it was suggested that part of the chalk mound will have been completed shortly after. The final completion of the mound could have followed relatively soon after this, or not have taken place until sometime around 2000 cal BC depending on different readings of the archaeology.

Objectives

The archaeological works undertaken in 2007 and 2008 as part of the remedial work on the mound have provided the opportunity to refine the existing chronological model for the monument (cf Bayliss *et al* 2007a) and address the key question that the original work had been unable to irrefutably answer – how long did it take to build Silbury Hill?

Estimates for the length of time it may have taken to build Silbury have ranged from a quick build of little more than a decade (Atkinson 1968a; 1970), 'a rather more lengthy process' of maybe one or two generations (Whittle 1997a, 26) to *140–435 years (95% probability; build Silbury (Model 1);* Fig. 6; Bayliss *et al* 2007a) or *220–365 years (68% probability)*.

The new dating programme was designed to tackle the following objectives: to provide precise estimates for the constructional stages of the monument and to estimate the length of time it took to build.

Sampling

The programme of archaeological recording undertaken as part of the work to stabilise the monument in 2007/8 produced a large number of samples and some antler artefacts which could be sub-sampled for radiocarbon dating. The contextual integrity of these samples is variable, and includes antler fragments recovered from chalk rubble collapse within the tunnel, environmental samples taken from recorded deposits in the tunnel section and material recovered from controlled excavation on the summit of the Hill or in the buried ditch under the chalk mound (*see* Chapter 2 for recovery techniques).

In order to exploit fully the stratigraphic sequence contained within Silbury Hill for Bayesian modelling, any samples submitted for radiocarbon dating had to have excellent taphonomic integrity and on the basis of archaeological evidence indicated that the material had a clear association with the past activity to be dated. Such 'informative' prior information (*see* Bayliss *et al* 2007b) not surprisingly can seriously impact on the estimates derived from a chronological model – if they are wrong the resulting chronology will also be wrong.

Although the importance of the relationship between sample/context/archaeological event has been stressed for many years (for example, Waterbolk 1971; van Strydonck *et al* 1999; Bayliss 2009), it has yet to be routinely incorporated into decisions about sample submission. A rigorous yet pragmatic approach was therefore taken to choosing our samples.

The main categories of samples submitted for dating are listed below together with an outline of our archaeological reasoning for their reliability.

Antler tools

Broken fragments of antler tools were incorporated into chalk rubble used to build the mound and therefore must be functionally related to its construction. Such an inference was made more secure when chalk blocks retained impressions of antler tools having been used on them (Worley, Chapter 3). In addition, antler tine fragments from the primary fill of the ditch were interpreted as being functionally related to the digging of the feature. Given the fragmentary nature of the antlers recovered from the mound and in order that all potential samples were independent, that is to ensure that the same antler was not dated twice, samples were selected following the re-fitting exercise (Worley, Chapter 3).

Short-lived fragments of non-charred plant remains from turves

Turf and topsoil were clearly identifiable in the tunnel section (*see* Cornwall *et al* 1997; Evans 1972) and probably derive from de-turfing of the land surface prior to construction of the monument (Canti 2009, 308). For uncharred seeds to have survived within turf and topsoil

prior to burial they could not have been very old, especially if the grass had formed on an old plough soil that had been uncultivated for a few years (Cornwall *et al* 1997, 28). Authenticated examples of seeds surviving in soils for 80–100 years are known from a limited number of soil types, although experimental work at Overton (Carruthers and Straker 1996; Hendry *et al* 1996; Chapter 6), a calcareous grassland plant community, suggests seed decomposition would have been relatively rapid.

As turf can only come from a limited number of environments, for example heath and grassland, since turf *per se* does not form in woodland nor is it present in arable fields (van Nest *et al* 2001, 642; Chapter 6), it was possible to choose material with a reduced chance of being residual. This was undertaken by selectively avoiding plant remains associated with 'old woodland' or material that had been charred before being incorporated into turf material, and also by avoiding seeds typical of 'seed banks'.

For example sample <9200> from the Lower Organic Mound consisted of topsoil and turf with seeds. We therefore deliberately avoided stinging nettle and chickweed seeds (typical of soil seed banks); and blackberry/raspberry seeds (associated with woodland). Instead grassland taxa such as buttercup, sedges and monocotyledonous stems and leaves were selected (*see* Chapter 6) that should have only been a few years old when a turf was cut.

Due to the very small size of the identifiable material in the turf samples (*see* Chapter 6) multiple seeds/plant fragments were selected to obtain sufficient carbon for radiocarbon analysis, although if possible these were all from the same species. Finally, in order to determine the reliability of the results from turves it was attempted to date more than one 'bulk' sample from a turf to ensure the statistical consistency of the measurements (cf Ward and Wilson 1978).

Single fragments of short-lived charred plant remains

Single fragments of short-lived charred plant remains functionally related to the context from which they were recovered, in this case charcoal from the purported hearth deposit on the OLS [4041] should date the last burning event.

Short-lived non-charred plant material from the Mini-mound

The samples from the Mini-mound [4181] produced plant remains typical of a mosaic of habitats including grassland, woodland and scrub. This was interpreted as material brought from a woodland edge location, in contrast to the turves from the Lower Organic Mound, and as such could be older than the Mini-mound.

Samples from the fills of negative features

Duplicate measurements were obtained on samples from the fills of negative features in order to determine the statistical consistency of the results (Ward and Wilson 1978). If the results are consistent the latest calibrated date should provide a reliable estimate for the infilling of the feature.

Samples

Five samples (OxA-17470–17474) from antlers retrieved during conservation work in the summer of 2007 were submitted to the Oxford Radiocarbon Accelerator Unit (ORAU) (Table 4.2) to provide an improved chronology for Silbury Hill as part of a television documentary into the conservation of the monument to be aired that autumn. The samples all came from the work to record the deposits and stratigraphy visible in the sides of the tunnel opened by Atkinson and were collected from a conveyor belt after initially being machined by a dumper truck (*see* Chapter 2 for recovery techniques).

A further 29 samples were submitted for dating as part of the formal post-excavation programme of 2009–2010 (Table 4.3). Thirteen samples were submitted to ORAU, two of which failed due to very low yields following pre-treatment. The 11 samples that produced results came from four red deer antlers, one animal bone, two single entity charred macro-fossils, and four collections of 'bulked' waterlogged plant remains.

The remaining 16 samples were submitted to the Scottish Universities Environmental Research Centre (SUERC) in 2009–10. The two samples that failed both comprised multiple fragments of monocotyledonous stems and were both too small to yield enough CO_2 following pre-treatment for analysis. The other samples comprised six red deer antlers,

one pig's tooth, two charred macrofossils and six waterlogged plant fragments.

Laboratory methods

At SUERC the charred and waterlogged plant material was pre-treated by the acid-base-acid protocol (Stenhouse and Baxter 1983) and the mammal bone and antler using a modified version of the Longin method (Longin 1971). CO_2 from the pre-treated samples was obtained by combustion in pre-cleaned sealed quartz tubes (Vandeputte *et al* 1996) and the purified CO_2 was converted to graphite (Slota *et al* 1987). The samples were measured by Accelerator Mass Spectrometry (AMS), as described by Xu *et al* (2004).

At the Oxford Radiocarbon Accelerator Unit samples of charred and waterlogged plant remains were prepared using the methods outlined in Brock *et al* (2010). The mammal bone and antlers were processed using the gelatinisation and ultrafiltration protocols described by Bronk Ramsey *et al* (2004a). The samples were combusted, graphitised and dated by Accelerator Mass Spectrometry (AMS) as described by Bronk Ramsey *et al* (2004b).

Two samples processed at Oxford had low yields of carbon, and so produced small targets which gave low currents in the AMS. These results are reported as experimental measurements, distinguished by the laboratory code 'OxA-X' and thus should be interpreted with caution.

Both laboratories maintain continual programmes of quality assurance procedures, in addition to participation in international inter-comparisons (Scott 2003), which indicate no laboratory offsets and demonstrate the validity of the precision quoted.

Results

The radiocarbon results are given in Tables 4.1–4.3, and are quoted in accordance with the international standard known as the Trondheim convention (Stuiver and Kra 1986). They are conventional radiocarbon ages (Stuiver and Polach 1977).

Calibration

The calibrations of the results, relating the radiocarbon measurements directly to calendar dates, are given in Tables 4.1–4.3 and in Figure 4.1. All have been calculated using the calibration curve of Reimer *et al* (2009) and the computer program OxCal (v4.1) (Bronk Ramsey 1995; 1998; 2001; 2009). The calibrated date ranges cited in the text are those for 95% confidence. They are quoted in the form recommended by Mook (1986), with the end points rounded outwards to ten years or five years for those measurements with errors <25 BP. The ranges in plain type in Tables 4.1–4.3 have been calculated according to the maximum intercept method (Stuiver and Reimer 1986). All other ranges are derived from the probability method (Stuiver and Reimer 1993).

Methodological approach

A Bayesian approach has been adopted for the interpretation of the chronology from this site (Buck *et al* 1996; Bayliss *et al* 2007b). Although the simple calibrated dates are accurate estimates of the dates of the samples, this is usually not what archaeologists really wish to know. It is the dates of the archaeological events, which are represented by those samples, that are of interest. In the case of Silbury Hill, it is the chronology of the monument that is under consideration, not the dates of individual samples. The dates of this activity can be estimated not only using the scientific dating information from the radiocarbon measurements, but also by using the stratigraphic relationships between samples.

Fortunately, a methodology is now available which allows the combination of these different types of information explicitly, to produce realistic estimates of the dates of interest. It should be emphasised that the posterior density estimates produced by this modelling are not absolute. They are interpretative estimates, which can and will change as further data become available and as other researchers choose to model the existing data from different perspectives.

The technique used is a form of Markov Chain Monte Carlo sampling, and has been applied using the program OxCal v4.1 (<http://c14. arch.ox.ac.uk>). Details of the algorithms employed by this program are available from the on-line manual or in Bronk Ramsey (1995; 1998; 2001; 2009). The algorithm used in the model described below can be derived from the structures shown in Figs 4.2, and 4.4–4.7.

Sequence and samples

The following section concentrates on describing the archaeological evidence which has been incorporated into the chronological models, explaining the reasoning behind the interpretative choices made in producing the models presented. These archaeological decisions fundamentally underpin the choice of statistical model.

Old Land Surface

Measurements on hazelnut fragments and Maloideae branchwood (both single entity samples – Ashmore 1999) from the concentration of charred material, interpreted as a hearth, in the upper part of the OLS [4041] on the north side of the East Lateral in Bay 7, are statistically consistent (T'=0.2; v=1; T'(5%)=3.8; Ward and Wilson 1978) and could therefore be of the same actual age. These two measurements are also statistically consistent (T'=6.0; v=2; T'(5%)=6.0) with the weighted mean of the two measurements obtained from the pig radius (Sample 5; Bayliss *et al* 2007a), and once again highlights the inexplicable late measurements obtained on the mammal bone from the OLS at the base of the primary mound (OxA-13211; Bayliss *et al* 2007a). OxA-13211 has been excluded from all subsequent Bayesian modelling of the radiocarbon results as it clearly is not related to pre-mound activity.

Gravel Mound

The low mound, overlying the OLS, formed of flint gravel with silty loam (Gravel Mound) did not have any material that fulfilled our criteria for selecting samples for radiocarbon dating.

Lower Organic Mound and Mini-mound

In contrast to the Gravel Mound the subsequent Lower Organic and mini-mounds both comprised thick layers of organic-rich deposits made up of a mix of subsoil, topsoil and turf from which samples could be obtained.

Measurements on four fragments of monocotyledonous stems (OxA-22082) and five *Ranunculus* seeds (SUERC-24090) from sample <9200> context [4156] are statistically consistent (T'=0.2; v=1; T'(5%)=3.8) and could be the same actual age. Together with the one sample from <9824> context [3046] that dated (OxA-X-2352-53) all three results from the Lower Organic Mound are statistically

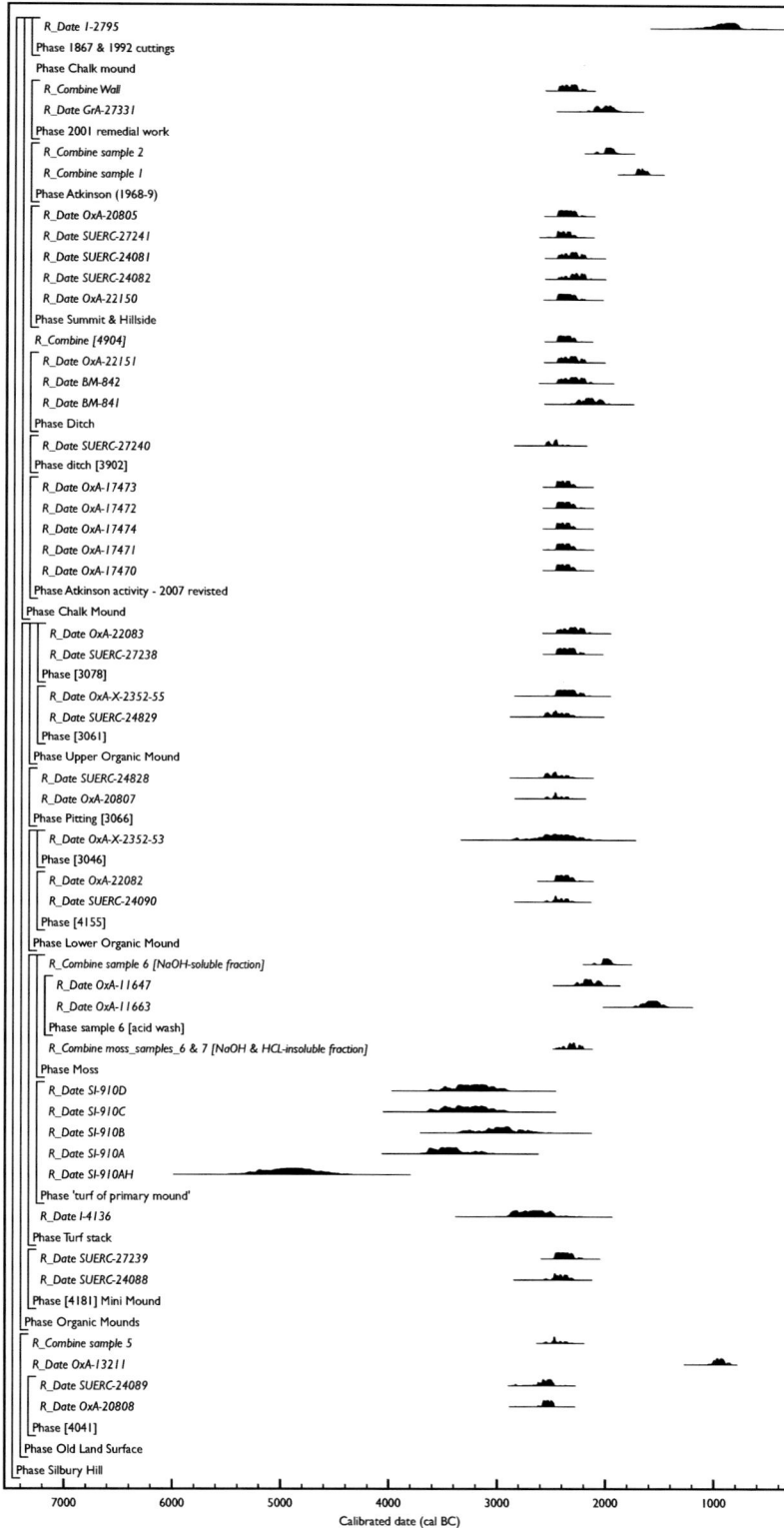

Fig 4.1
Probability distributions
of dates from Silbury Hill
(prehistoric). Each
distribution represents the
relative probability that
an event occurred at
a particular time.
These distributions are the
result of simple radiocarbon
calibration (Stuiver and
Reimer 1993).
(Peter Marshall,
© English Heritage)

consistent (T'=6.0; v=2; T'(5%)=6.0). Both samples clearly contained turf, lumps were still present following processing of <9824> (*see* Chapter 6), and thus the selection criteria for targeting non-residual 'turf' material in the samples would seem to be justified.

Two samples were dated from the Mini-mound (SUERC-24088 and SUERC-27239) and the measurements are statistically consistent (T'=0.8; v=1; T'(5%)=3.8) and could be of the same actual age.

The Mini-mound and Lower Organic Mound are stratigraphically equivalent and all five measurements are statistically consistent (T'=1.8; v=4; T'(5%)=9.5) and could therefore be the same actual age, suggesting they are contemporary.

The samples are all therefore from material/plants that were growing/incorporated on the surface of the turf and so should only be a few years old when the turves were cut to construct the Mini-mound/Lower Organic Mound.

Pit activity

Two pits cut through the top of the Lower Organic Mound, pit [3067] and pit [3074]. Measurements on a 'fresh' fragment of a large (unidentifiable) mammal bone (SF 8038) (OxA-20807) and bulked seed sample (SUERC-24828) from the secondary fill [3066] of pit [3067] are statistically consistent (T'=0.1; v=1; T'(5%)=3.8). As the secondary fill may be redeposited material from the Lower Organic Mound and there is no functional relationship between the samples and feature we have elected to treat the two measurements as only providing *termini post quos* for the infilling of the pit. These results do, however, provide a further constraint on the stratigraphically later Upper Organic Mound.

Upper Organic Mound

After the pitting activity mound building continued and the pits and Lower Organic Mound/Mini-mound became sealed by a series of interleaved layer deposits that also incorporated some turves. This enlargement of the earlier mound resulted in the formation of the Upper Organic Mound, which has an estimated diameter of *c* 35m. The organic material was chiefly from soils that had developed over chalk and therefore contrasted with those from the underlying Lower Organic Mound which predominantly derived from clay-with-flints.

Samples were dated from two contexts

[3061] and [3078] that both seem to contain a significant 'turf' element (*see* Chapter 6). Replicate measurements on monocotyedonous stems (OxA-X-2352-55) and three *Ranunculus* seeds (SUERC-24829) from <9375> context [3061] are statistically consistent (T'=0.1; v=1; T'(5%)=3.8) as are those on monocotyledonous stems (OxA-22083) and a twig (SUERC-27238) from <9335> context [3078] (T'=0.3; v=1; T'(5%)=3.8).

Once again all four samples from the Upper Organic Mound are statistical consistent (T'=2.7; v=3; T'(5%)=7.8) demonstrating that the samples do not contain significantly residual material.

Moss samples

The dried moss samples (Table 4.1) picked from the three blocks of turf collected by John Evans during the 1968–70 excavation could come from either the Lower Organic or Upper Organic Mound as both contained turves. Given that it is difficult to determine with any confidence which they are associated with, they have been modelled as being stratigraphically later than the OLS but earlier than the Banks and Ditch.

Banks 1–5 and Ditch 1

A low bank was constructed of chalk and clay (termed 'Toblerone' by Atkinson: Whittle 1997a) around the Upper Organic Mound, the raw material for which is interpreted as deriving from the large ditch [3902] recorded just inside the portal.

Ditch [3902] may have remained open after Bank 1 was completed and used as the quarry for the raw materials for constructing the subsequent banks (Banks 2–5). The primary fill [3926] of ditch [3902] contained a small fragment of antler that is interpreted as being related to its construction (SUERC-27240). The five antler samples dated in 2007 (OxA-17470–17474) derive from collapsed material that probably originated from within the banks (*see* Table 4.2 for further details). Given the circumstances under which this material was recovered it has not been possible to securely identify the precise stratigraphic relationship of the antlers to one another or Ditch 1.

Final mound construction

The fourth and final re-cutting of the ditch [3902] (Ditch 4]) may be represented by re-cut [3018], although concrete support posts left in place by Atkinson's excavations obscured the sequence. An antler (OxA-22151) from the chalk fills of the ditch/re-cut ditch was dated and should relate to the phase of final mound construction, as do the two British Museum measurements (BM-841 and BM-842) from the external ditch excavated by Atkinson.

Deposits relating to the final phase of the mound were examined in a number of areas: on the side of the monument above the portal during the 2008 watching brief; on the summit primarily in the trench excavated in 2007; and trenches excavated in 2001 in the collapsed area.

Hillside

A total of 27 antler fragments refitting to form one, two or three pieces (Worley, Chapter 3) were found in the earliest deposit recorded on the side of the mound [4904], together with a chalk block retaining impressions of being worked with antler mattocks (Worley, Chapter 3). Consequently, the antler has been interpreted as being 'functionally' related to the excavation/working of chalk for the mound's construction. Replicate measurements on antler (SF 8751) are statistically consistent (T'=0.0; v=1; T'(5%)=3.8) and so a weighted mean has been taken before calibration (4904; 3891 ±21 BP).

Summit

The earliest recorded deposit in the 2007 trench on the summit was a chalk wall [4812] (Wall 1) to the north of which five layers of chalk had been deposited. An antler tine (SF 8523) from [4814] (SUERC-24082) and a naturally shed burr from the stratigraphically later [4813] (OxA-22150) were dated from the sequence of chalk deposits.

A second wall [4809] c 1.7m away from Wall 1 revetted these chalk deposits and in the same way a number of chalk deposits had been dumped to the north of Wall 2. Three large fragments of antler were recovered from chalk deposit [4845], one of which, SF 8525, which exhibited evidence for use wear, was dated (SUERC-24081). The stratigraphically latest deposit in the sequence of chalk deposits was [4848] from which a further antler fragment (SUERC-27241) was dated.

The chalk deposits to the north of Wall 2 were, in turn, revetted by a further chalk wall [4808] (Wall 3). In a similar fashion to Walls 1 and 2 a series of chalk layers were deposited to the north of Wall 3. From the latest of these layers [4835] a further antler fragment (OxA-20805) was dated.

These walls may be associated with completion of the upper part of the mound and wall [7] excavated in Trench B in 2001 from which replicate measurements on a single antler produced a weighted mean of 3870±25 BP (Wall; Bayliss et al 2007a).

The Bayesian models

Model A

Although Atkinson proposed three major stages for the development of Silbury Hill (Silbury I – primary mound; Silbury II – chalk rubble mound; and Silbury III – final mound) he did think of it as a continuous process (Atkinson 1968a; 1969a) on the grounds that no stratigraphic or geo-archaeological evidence was found for a hiatus in activity. Recent work has also failed to find any compelling evidence for an interrupted constructional history so our first chronological model (Fig 4.2) interprets the construction of the mound as a single continuous phase of activity (Buck et al 1992). In reality this means that once building of Silbury started it continued at a fairly uniform rate until it was finished.

Following Bayliss et al (2007a, 40) OxA-13211 and I-2795 have been excluded from the model. The chronological (Fig 4.2) model shows poor agreement between the radiocarbon dates and stratigraphy (Amodel=45%).

An overall agreement index of 60% is recommended as the threshold for showing consistency between the prior information and the radiocarbon results included in a model (Bayliss et al 2007b; Bronk Ramsey 1995). Two samples have low individual index of agreement values; *sample 1* (A=11%) and *SUERC-27240* (A=19%). If the individual index of agreement for a sample falls below 60% (Bronk Ramsey 1995; 1998), the radiocarbon result is regarded as inconsistent with the sample's calendar age if the latter is consistent with the sample's age relative to the other dated samples. This can indicate that the radiocarbon result is a statistical outlier (more than two standard deviations from the sample's true radiocarbon age), but a very low index of agreement may be indicative of the sample that is residual or intrusive (that is that its calendar age is different to that implied by its stratigraphic position).

The location of *Sample 1* was not precisely recorded (Bayliss *et al* 2007a) and thus potentially it relates to a later phase of modification of the mound and not its final manifestation. It is thus excluded from the revised model shown in Figure 4.3.

SUERC-27240 would seem to be too old for its context. The antler was small, it was the only fragment that was not hand collected, and it came from the >4mm fraction of sample <9036>. The primary fill of Ditch 1, from which it was recovered, has been interpreted as a stabilisation layer and the antler fragment could therefore be residual material washed in as part of this process rather than relating to its construction. Alternatively it could be a simple statistical outlier. In either case it clearly does not provide a date for its context so we have also excluded it from the model shown in Figure 4.3.

The model (Fig 4.3) shows good agreement between the radiocarbon results and stratigraphy (Amodel=71%) and provides an estimate for the completion of the Lower Organic Mound/Mini-mound of *2460–2395 cal BC (95% probability: Lower Organic Mound_constructed, Fig 4.3)* and probably *2445–2405 cal BC (68% probability)*. The Upper Organic Mound was finished in *2420–2355 cal BC (95% probability: Upper Organic Mound_constructed, Fig 4.3)* or *2400–2365 cal BC (68% probability)*.

The banks that encircled the earlier organic mounds were completed by *2375–2320 cal BC (95% probability: Banks constructed, Fig 4.3)* and probably by *2360–2330 cal BC (68% probability)*.

In this model completion of the mound is estimated to have taken place in *2135–2055 cal BC 95% probability: end_Silbury Hill, Fig 4.3)* or *2125–2085 cal BC (68% probability)*. But it should be noted that the dated antler from the 2001 excavations on the summit (*GrA-27331*) and *Sample 2* from the Atkinson archive are significantly younger than any of the other dated antler from the summit and Hillside deposits. The effect of these two samples is to make estimates of the length of time for construction of the monument extremely long; *270–390 years (95% probability; Fig 4.4)* and probably *295–350 years (68% probability)*.

Model B

Following the alternative model proposed by Bayliss *et al* (2007a, 42) [model 2] a further model was constructed that regards the three antler samples (Samples 1 and 2; GrA-27331) as

relating to later modifications on the mound and not its initial completion. SUERC-27240 is also excluded for the reasons outlined above. Model B also interprets the construction of the mound as a single continuous phase of activity.

The model (Fig 4.5) shows good agreement between the radiocarbon results and stratigraphy (Amodel=78%) and provides an estimate for the completion of the Lower Organic Mound/Mini-mound of *2460–2395 cal BC (95% probability: Lower Organic Mound_constructed, Fig 4.5)* or *2450-2410 cal BC (68% probability)*. The Upper Organic Mound was constructed by *2435–2360 cal BC (95% probability: Upper Organic Mound_constructed, Fig 4.5)* and probably *2425–2370 cal BC (68% probability)* and banks by *2410–2330 cal BC (95% probability: Banks constructed, Fig 4.5)* or *2375–2335 cal BC (68% probability)*.

Completion of the mound in this model is estimated to have taken place in *2335–2270 cal BC 95% probability: end_Silbury Hill, Fig 4.5)* and probably *2335–2285 cal BC (68% probability)* and its construction to have taken *55–155 years (68% probability; Fig 4.4)*.

It is though exceptionally difficult to find any plausible reason why, in addition to the Sample 1 antler, the other two samples (Sample 2 and GrA-27331) should be excluded. The context of GrA-27331 could be questionable as it is recorded as 'being from a layer of large chalk blocks with voids recorded in the hole at the top of Silbury' – that is the hole that opened in 2001, so it could be intrusive. The location of Sample 2 in the outer part of the mound does not seem open to question.

Samples 1, 2 and OxA-13211 were all affected by a problem with the early implementation of the ultrafiltration method at ORAU (Bronk Ramsey *et al* 2004a); however, Bayliss *et al* (2007a, 37–8) provide conclusive evidence that the quoted ages (Table 4.1) are accurate.

It is significant though that the antler measurements from the summit and Hillside excavations in 2007/8 together with those from the antler recovered in 2001 associated with a 'wall' are statistically consistent (T'=4.7; v=8; T'(5%)=15.5), while Samples 1, 2, and GrA-27331 are considerably younger.

'... no major pauses ... a rather more lengthy process of construction'

Whittle (1997a, 26) highlighted that if a lengthier period of construction took place 'the question of intervals is left open'. The proposed phasing resulting from the new fieldwork thus allows an alternative reading of the constructional history to that of one continuous build. The phasing has been simplified (*see* Chapter 2 for a full account) as follows for the purposes of constructing a chronological model:

Phase 2   Old Land Surface
Phases 4–6   Organic Mounds
Phases 7–15   Banks and ditches
Phase 16   Final Mound construction

This means the construction of the monument can be interpreted as a number of continuous phases of archaeological activity (Buck *et al* 1992) that may have gaps between then.

Model C

The chronological model (Model C) shown in Figure 4.6, excluding Sample 1 and SUERC-27240, shows good agreement between the radiocarbon results and stratigraphy (Amodel=69%) and estimates for the completion of major phases of construction are shown in Table 4.4.

Construction of the mound is therefore estimated at *260–460 years (95% probability*; Fig 4.6) and probably *295–375 years (68% probability)*.

Model D

Finally, a revised version of Model C was consructed with Sample 2 and GrA-27331 excluded in addition to sample 1 and SUERC-27240 as in Model B (*see above*).

This model (Fig 4.7) shows good agreement between the radiocarbon results and stratigraphy (Amodel=70%) and estimates for the completion of major phases of construction are shown in Table 4.5.

The distributions for the later phase of construction of Silbury Hill (Banks and Final Mound) in Model D (Fig 4.7) are strongly bi-modal due the nature of the calibration curve in the later 25th and 24th centuries BC. Even the 'informative' prior information provided by the stratigraphic relationships between samples is not enough to overcome the 'wiggles' in the calibration curve.

Time to choose?

All four models presented for the chronology of Silbury Hill show good overall agreement (Bronk Ramsey 1995; Figs 4.3, 4.5–4.7), and

thus each of the archaeological interpretations is consistent with the radiocarbon dates. The question of model choice has been addressed by Bayliss *et al* (2007b, 7) and given the statistical criteria for all four models (indices of agreement and convergence) is such that they are all plausible, we are only left with making an archaeological selection. If purely archaeological criteria are used, then the evidence for an interrupted constructional history (that is a constructional history with significant gaps (Models C and D)) is lacking, as the monument does not contain any evidence for a hiatus in construction such as the development of soils (Canti 2009; Chapters 2 and 5).

Fairly continuous construction (Models A and B) therefore probably best reflects the archaeological evidence for the building of the mound. Both Models A and B are consistent in placing the completion of the Lower Organic Mound in the second half of the 25th century cal BC and the Upper Organic Mound by the mid-24th century cal BC. The banks were completed in the 24th century cal BC.

The obvious discordance is in estimates for when completion of the final chalk mound and in essence the monument we see today took place. This was either a relatively quick process (Model B) or drawn out over many hundreds of years (Model A). On the basis of the secure contextual location of the antler samples recovered during the 2007/8 excavations we prefer Model B that sees completion of the monument in the late 24th or early 23rd centuries cal BC, with some later modifications taking place episodically through the early Bronze Age.

Estimates for the length of time it may have taken to build Silbury Hill have ranged from a quick build of little more than a decade (Atkinson 1968; 1970), 'a rather more lengthy process' of maybe one or two generations (Whittle 1997a, 26) to *140–435 years (95% probability; build Silbury (Model 1)*; Fig 6; Bayliss *et al* 2007) or *220–365 years (68% probability)*. Our preferred model estimates that it took *1–160 years (95% probability; Model_B_construction)* or *55–155 years (68% probability; Model_B_construction)* to build Silbury (*see* Fig 4.8).

Early medieval activity on the summit

A series of features were recorded on the summit cutting the prehistoric deposits, some of these were postholes whilst others had the appearance

Fig 4.2

Probability distributions of dates from Silbury Hill [Model A]. Each distribution represents the relative probability that an event occurs at a particular time. For each radiocarbon date, two distributions have been plotted: one in outline which is the result of simple radiocarbon calibration, and a solid one based on the chronological model used. The other distributions correspond to aspects of the model. For example, the distribution 'Lower Organic Mound_constructed' is the estimate for when the Lower Organic Mound was completed. The large square brackets down the left-hand side of the diagram and the OxCal keywords define the overall model exactly. (Peter Marshall, © English Heritage)

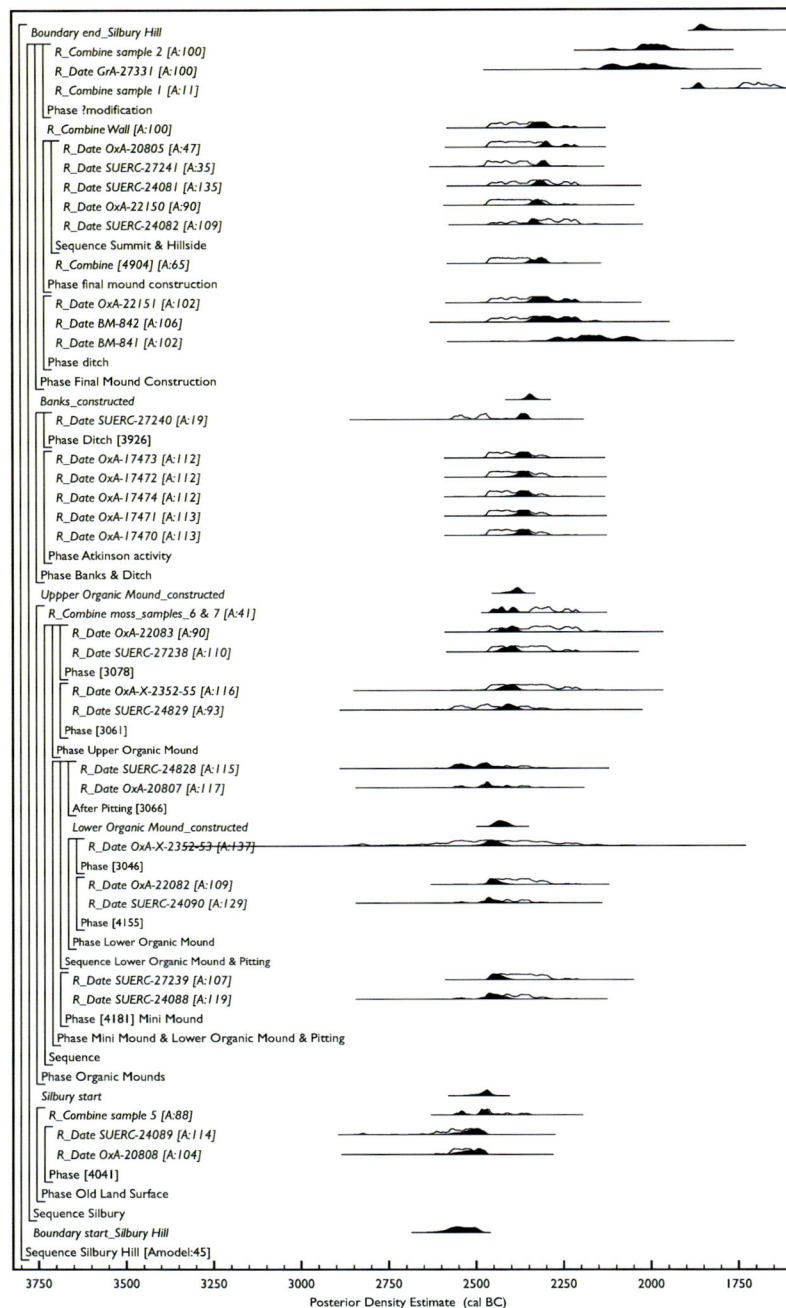

of relating to burrowing animals (*see* Chapter 9). The most substantial feature from this later phase of activity on the summit was posthole [4821] which was filled by [4820]. SUERC-24087, a sample from a pig pre-maxilla, provides a *terminus post quem* for the infilling of the posthole of cal AD 890–1030 (Fig 4.9, and Table 4.3).

Pit [15] cut layer [11] in Trench B from the 2001 excavations and was filled by [9]. Two samples were submitted from the fill [9] – a charred Pomoideae fragment (OxA-20809) and a single wheat grain (SUERC-24091). The two measurements are statistically consistent and the latest date OxA-20809 (cal AD 895–1025) provides the best

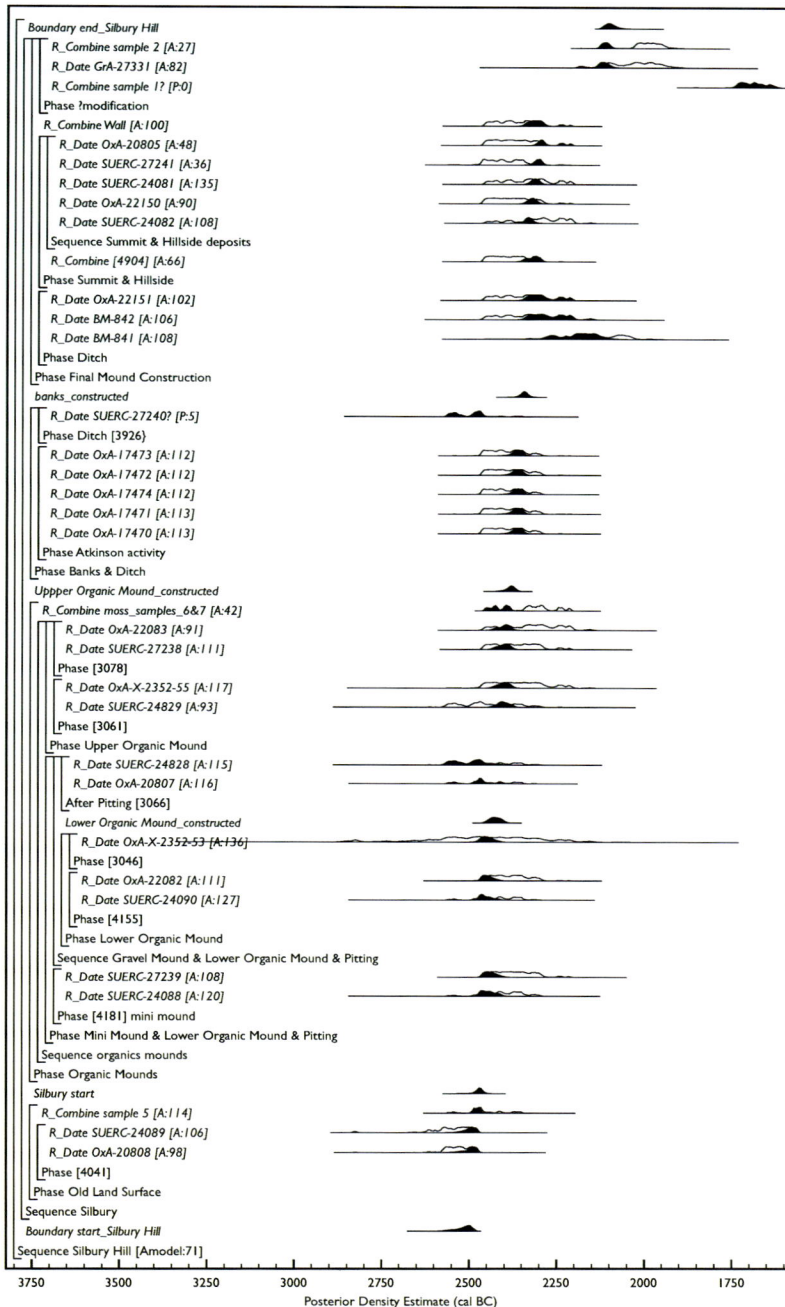

Fig 4.3 Probability
distributions of dates from
Silbury Hill [Model A].
Measurements followed by ?
have been excluded from the
model for reasons explained
in the text. The format is
identical to that
of Figure 4.2.
(Peter Marshall,
© English Heritage)

estimate for the infilling of the pit (Fig 4.9; Table 4.3).

Interpretation

All three measurements from the two features on the summit are statistically consistent (T'=2.1; v=2; T'(5%)=6.0) and would therefore suggest a short-lived episode of activity in the 10th to 11th centuries cal AD. Activity on the summit on this time may therefore be related to modification of the terraces on the northern slope identified by Atkinson (1970, 314) that produced Saxon/Norman pottery and a silver quarter penny of Ethelred II (AD 1009–16).

Fig 4.4
Probability distributions
of the number of years it
took to construct Silbury
Hill (Models A, B and C)
derived from the models
shown in Figures 4.3, 4.5
and 4.6.
(Peter Marshall,
© English Heritage)

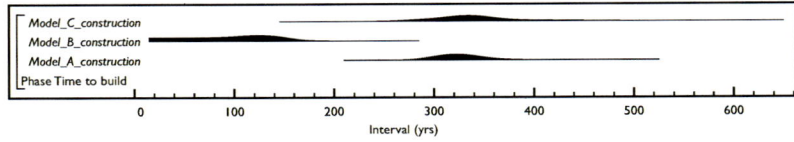

Fig 4.5
Probability distributions
of dates from Silbury Hill
[Model B]. The format
is identical to that
of Figure 4.2.
(Peter Marshall,
© English Heritage)

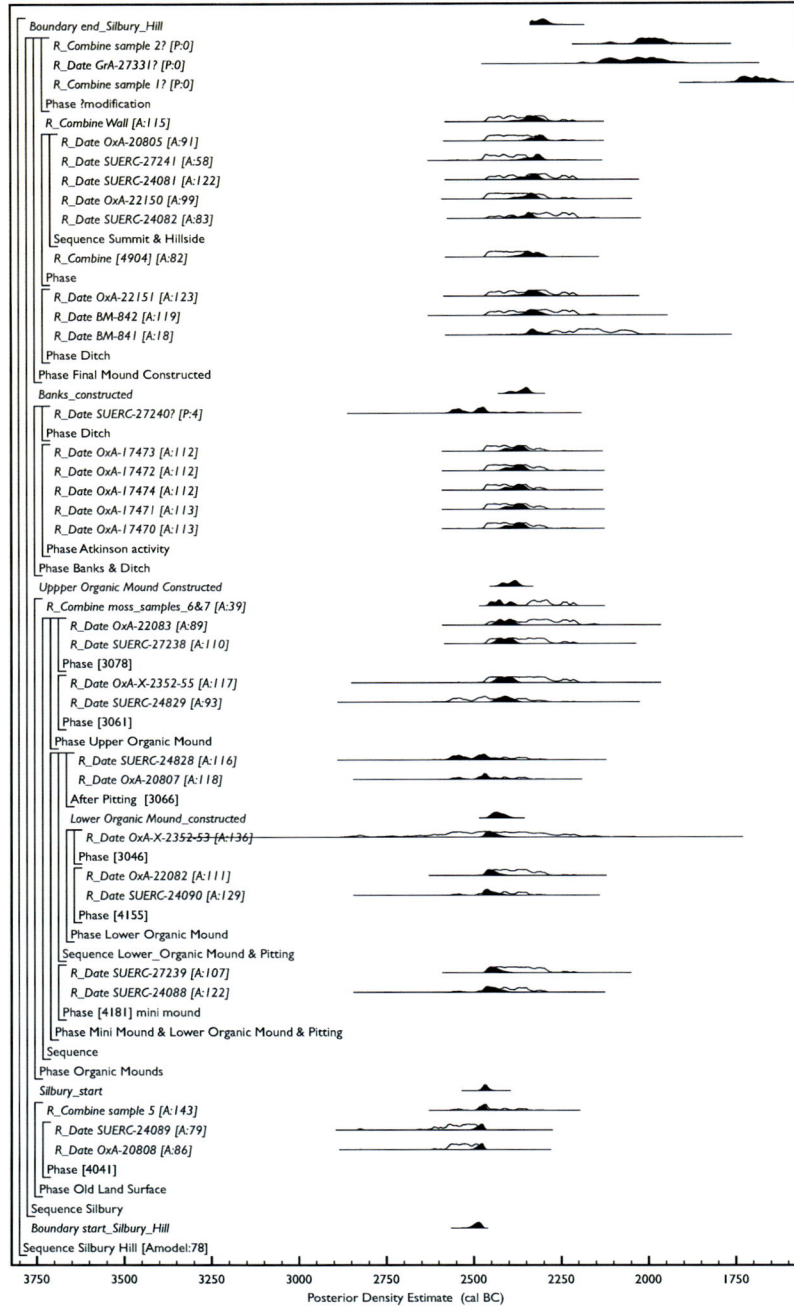

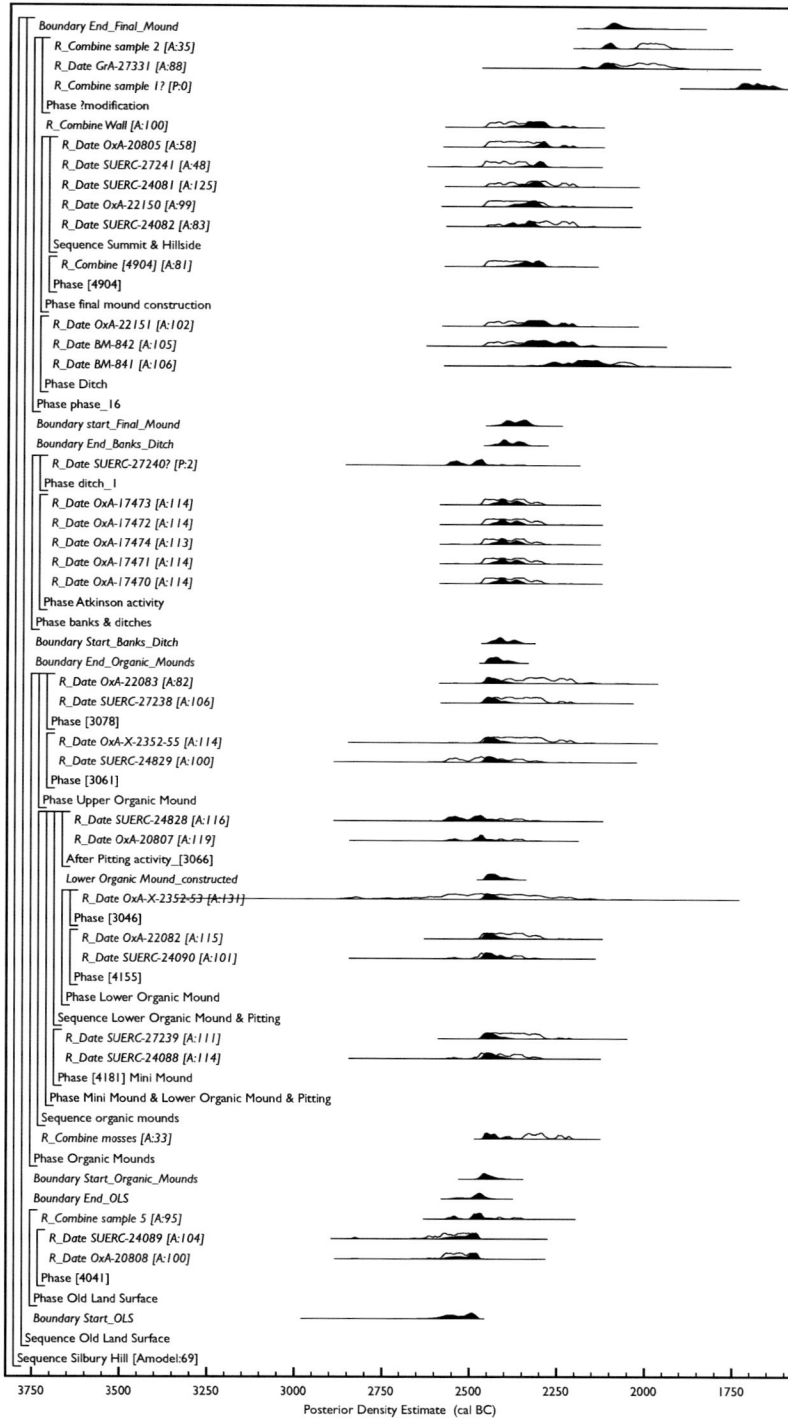

Fig 4.6
Probability distributions
of dates from Silbury Hill
[Model C]. The format
is identical to that
of Figure 4.2.
(Peter Marshall,
© English Heritage)

Fig 4.7
Probability distributions
of dates from Silbury Hill
[Model D]. The format
is identical to that
of Figure 4.2.
(Peter Marshall,
© English Heritage)

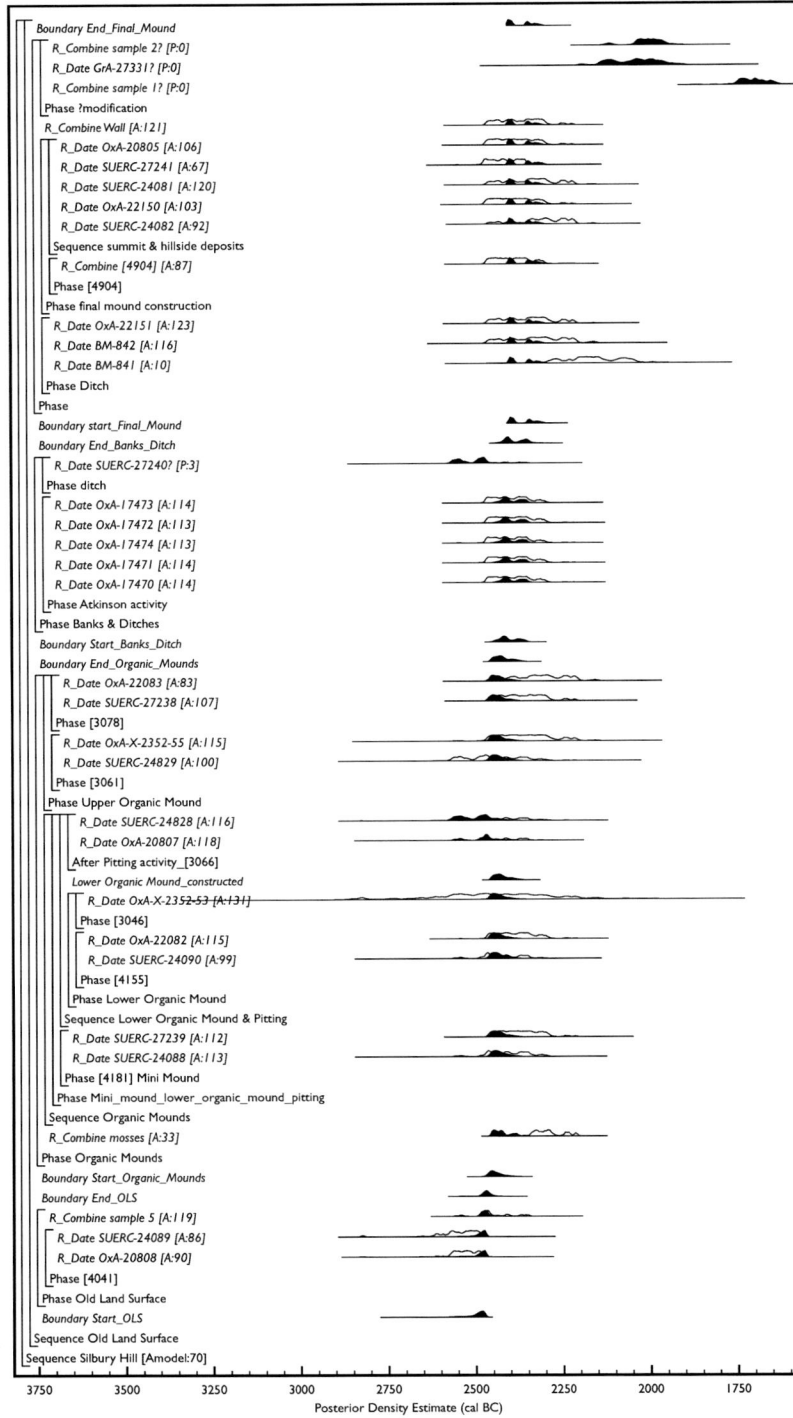

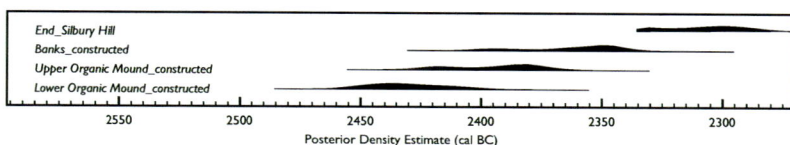

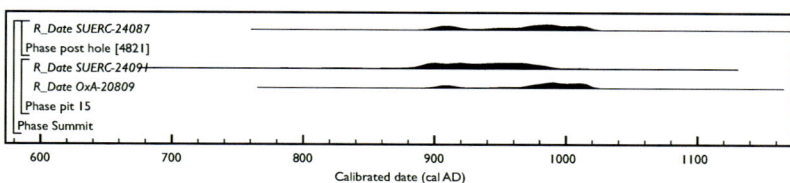

Fig 4.8
Posterior density
estimates for the date
of constructional events at
Silbury Hill derived from
Model B (Fig 4.5).
(Peter Marshall,
© English Heritage)

Fig 4.9
Probability distributions
of dates of medieval activity
on Silbury Hill. Each
distribution represents
a relative probability that
an event occurred at
a particular time.
These distributions are the
result of simple radiocarbon
calibration (Stuiver and
Reimer 1993).
(Peter Marshall,
© English Heritage)

Conclusions

Our preferred chronological model [Model B] places construction of the Lower Organic Mound in the second half of the 25th century cal BC, with the Upper Organic Mound completed in the late 25th or early 24th centuries cal BC. The banks surrounding the Upper Organic Mound were in place soon after and the addition of the chalk mound saw Silbury finished in the late 24th or early 23rd centuries cal BC.

After some sporadic activity throughout the early Bronze Age, the next dated episode of activity on the summit took place in the 10th or 11th centuries cal AD.

Table 4.1: Previously published radiocarbon measurements from Silbury Hill

Laboratory number	Material and context	Radiocarbon Age (BP)	$\partial13C$ (‰)	Weighted Mean (BP)	Calibrated date range (95% confidence)	Posterior Density Estimate (95% probability)
Old Land Surface						
OxA-13211*	Sample 4 (Bone 690 find 433), indeterminate mammal bone, sheep/goat size, from the OLS below the primary mound (0.87E, 1.31N-1.26N, at eastern edge of 'pit' or disconformity in layers at base of the primary mound: Whittle 1997a, 20)	2792±34	-20.4		1020–840 cal BC	–
OxA-13333*	Sample 5, proximal pig radius (Bone 559 find 241), from the OLS at ring 4 of western lateral tunnel, in area of primary mound (Whittle 1997a, fig 12)	3916±28	-20.8	3944±24 (T´=3.5; T´(5%)= 3.8; v=1)	2550–2345 cal BC	2495–2460 cal BC
GrA-27332	Sample 5, replicate of OxA-13333	4015±45	-21.4			
Primary mound						
I-4136	Small twigs, ?hazel from bark (excavator's identification), and plant stems and roots, from surface of turves in core of primary mound; all unburnt material	4095±95			2910–2450 cal BC	

Table 4.1: Previously published radiocarbon measurements from Silbury Hill

Laboratory number	Material and context	Radiocarbon Age (BP)	∂13C (‰)	Weighted Mean (BP)	Calibrated date range (95% confidence)	Posterior Density Estimate (95% probability)
SI-910AH	NaOH-soluble portion of SI-910A of turf from the primary mound	5995±185		SI-910AH is significantly too old (T'=75.2; T'(5%)=11.1; v=5); without this, 4515±52 (T'=5.8; T'(5%)=9.5; v=4)	5350–4450 cal BC	
SI-910A	Organic matter 2mm size from turf of primary mound	4675±110			3370–3020 cal BC	
SI-910B	Organic matter 1-2mm size from turf of primary mound	4315±110				
SI-910C	Organic matter 0.5-1mm size from turf of primary mound	4570±120				
SI-910CH	NaOH-soluble portion of SI-910C	4465±130				
SI-910D	Organic matter under 0.5mm size from turf of primary mound	4530±110				
OxA-11663	Sample 6A (SILB3), dried mosses (see Bayliss et al 2007a, table 2) from surface of a turf from the primary mound (acid wash only)	3295±60	-28.1	(T'=38.2; T'(5%)=3.8; v=1)	1740–1430 cal BC	
OxA-11647	Sample 6B (SILB5), dried mosses (see Bayliss et al 2007a, table 2) from surface of a turf from the primary mound (acid wash only)	3746±40	-30.4		2290–2030 cal BC	
OxA-14640	Sample 6 (TS1b), dried mosses (see Bayliss et al 2007a, table 2) from surface of a turf from the primary mound (NaOH-soluble fraction)	3735±50	-28.9	3634±21 (T'=6.9; T'(5%)=7.8; v=3)	2125–1935 cal BC	
GrA-28555	Sample 6 (TS1a), replicate of OxA-14640 (NaOH-soluble fraction)	3710±80	-29.9			
OxA-14642	Sample 7 (TS2b), dried mosses (see Bayliss et al 2007a, table 2), from surface of a turf from the primary mound (NaOH-soluble fraction)	3612±31	-28.8			
GrA-28467	Sample 7 (TS2a), replicate of OxA-14642 (NaOH-soluble fraction)	3585±40	-29.9			
OxA-14641	Sample 6 (TS1b), dried mosses (see Bayliss et al 2007a, table 2) from surface of a turf from the primary mound (NaOH and HCl-insoluble fraction)	3898±31	-28.1	3848±17 (T'=6.4; T'(5%)=7.8; v=3)	2460–2205 cal BC	2465–2380 cal BC
GrA-28465	Sample 6 (TS1a), replicate of OxA-14641 (NaOH and HCl-insoluble fraction)	3770±40	-28.9			
OxA-14643	Sample 7 (TS2b), dried mosses (see Bayliss et al 2007a, table 2), from surface of a turf from the primary mound (NaOH and HCl-insoluble fraction)	3848±31	-27.8			
GrA-28466	Sample 7 (TS2a), replicate of OxA-14643 (NaOH and HCl-insoluble fraction)	3840±40	-28.9			
Chalk mound						
OxA-13210*	Sample 1, antler tine, probably red deer. Not precisely located, but from early part of tunnel excavation in April 1968 and recorded as 'e.side of chalk block wall'; There are chalk block walls around rings 11–13/14 on both sides of the tunnel (Whittle 1997a, figs 10–11) about 14–18m into the mound, in the makeup of the chalk mound, and the sample should belong here	3401±36	-22.1	3396±27 (T'=0.0; T'(5%)= 3.8; v=1)	1750–1620 cal BC	
GrA-27336	Sample 1, replicate of OxA-13210	3390±40	-23.7			

Table 4.1: Previously published radiocarbon measurements from Silbury Hill

Laboratory number	Material and context	Radiocarbon Age (BP)	∂13C (‰)	Weighted Mean (BP)	Calibrated date range (95% confidence)	Posterior Density Estimate (95% probability)
OxA-11970	Sample 2, red deer antler, from clean chalk material above floor of tunnel at ring 12 on west side of tunnel, in the outer part of the mound (Whittle 1997a, figs 10–11)	3634±30	-23.3	3633±25 (T´=0.0; T´(5%)= 3.8; v=1)	2130–1920 cal BC	
GrA-27335	Sample 2, replicate of OxA-11970	3630±45	-23.7			
GrA-27331	Sample 661-200100864 (see Bayliss et al 2007a, table 1), red deer antler, from context 30, large chalk blocks, approximately 2m below the top of the mound, seen in the sides of the hole recorded in 2001	3655±45	-23.2		2200–1890 cal BC	
I-2795	A mixture of antler fragments from the 1867 and 1922 cuttings on the east mound side	2750±100	–		1200–770 cal BC	
Chalk walling at top of mound						
OxA-13328*	Sample 661-851, red deer antler, from context 7, the outer face of a very substantial chalk wall, approximately 0.7m below the top of the mound in Trench B of excavations in 2001	3856±39	-22.6	3870±25 (T´=0.2; T´(5%)= 3.8; v=1)	2470–2210 cal BC	2390–2290 cal BC
OxA-14118	Sample 661-851, replicate of OxA-13328	3878±31	-22.5			
South ditch						
BM-841	Red deer antler, from near the excavated base (not more precisely recorded) of the south ditch cutting of 1969 (Whittle 1997aa, fig 23). The cutting reached to within 1m of the base of the ditch.	3752±50			2300–2020 cal BC	2395–2275 cal BC
BM-842	Red deer antler, as BM-841	3849±43			2470–2140 cal BC	2390–2285 cal BC

Table 4.2: Radiocarbon measurements from Silbury Hill dated in 2007

Laboratory number	Material and context	Radiocarbon Age (BP)	∂13C (‰)	Calibrated date range (95% confidence)	Posterior Density Estimate (95% probability)
	Atkinson activity				
OxA-17470	Red deer antler from [3843] (S:41) (SF 2007 28048). Collapsed material over bay S:41 and derived from bank [4073].	3902±29	-21.9	2480–2290 cal BC	2420–2345 cal BC
OxA-17471	Red deer antler from [3844] (S:50) (SF 2007 28076). Collapsed material over bay 50.	3902±29	-21.9	2480–2290 cal BC	2420–2345 cal BC
OxA-17474	Red deer antler from [3845] (S:58) (SF 2007 28048). Collapsed deposit above bay 58.	3907±27	-21.0	2480–2290 cal BC	2420–2345 cal BC
OxA-17472	Red deer antler from [3829] (S:34-36) (SF 2007 28019). Collapsed material over bays 34, 35, and 36, derived from bank [4073].	3896±28	-23.0	2480–2280 cal BC	2420–2345 cal BC
OxA-17473	Red deer antler from [3817] (S:32) (SF 2007 28022). Collapse of cobbly chalk deposit over bay 32.	3907±28	-21.2	2480–2290 cal BC	2420–2345 cal BC

Table 4.3: Radiocarbon measurements from Silbury Hill dated in 2009–2010

Laboratory number	Material and context	Radiocarbon Age (BP)	∂13C (‰)	Weighted Mean (BP)	Calibrated date range (95% confidence)	Posterior Density Estimate (95% probability)
	Old Land Surface					
OxA-20808	Hazelnut fragments (from the same hazelnut) from [4041] - sample <9821>, sub sample of <9435>. [4041] is a concentration of charcoal comprising charred hazel nutshell fragments and other charred remains as well as two pig or wild boar teeth. It was recorded within a small, defined area of the upper part of the OLS (4041]) on the north side of the East Lateral in Bay 7, and is thought to indicate the remains of a hearth.	4012±29	-24.6		2620–2460 cal BC	2510–2465 cal BC
SUERC-24089	Maloideae branchwood (single entity) as OxA-20808	4030±35	-27.0		2840–2470 cal BC	2510–2465 cal BC
	Summit					
OxA-20805	Red deer antler from [4835] one of a series of layers, the others being [4839] and [4836] that were laid on the northern side of the wall (chalk wall [4808] (Wall 3)) on the summit.	3883±27	-22.1		2470–2230 cal BC	2355–2285 cal BC
OxA-20806	Red deer antler (SF 8751) from [4904] the earliest deposit recorded on the side of the monument. A layer of loose chalk [4904], which contained a number of antler fragments. The context also contained a chalk block retaining two separate impressions of working. The first consists of a mark visible in section with evidence for two blows, set at slightly different angles, the second blow overlying the first in part. This evidence suggests that the picks were used in effect as mattocks.	3892±27	-22.3	3891±21 (T´=0.0; T´(5%)= 3.8; v=1)	2470–2290 cal BC	2385–2295 cal BC
SUERC-24086	Replicate of OxA-20806	3890±30	-23.0			
SUERC-24081	Red deer antler from [4845] (SF 8525) one of a number of layers of white chalk that had been dumped to the north of Wall 2 [4809] on the summit. A sarsen stone recovered from [4845] refitted with a stone recovered from the topsoil. Three fragments of antler in good condition were recovered from a small and well-defined area of context [4845].	3855±30	-23.1		2470–2200 cal BC	2385–2300 cal BC
SUERC-24082	Red deer antler from [4814] (SF 8523), one of a series of five layers (the others being [4817], [4816], [4815] and [4813]) that had been dumped to the north side of chalk wall [4812] (Wall 1), the earliest recorded deposit in the 2007 trench on the summit.	3840±30	-23.4		2470–2200 cal BC	2400–2320 cal BC
SUERC-27241	Red deer antler from [4848] one of a number of layers of white chalk that had been dumped to the north of Wall 2	3915±30	-23.2		2480–2290 cal BC	2370–2295 cal BC
OxA-22150	Red deer antler from [4813] one of 5 layers of chalk that had been dumped to the north of wall [4812] (Wall 1). The earliest recorded deposit in the 2007 trench.	3888±32	-21.6		2480–2210	2390–2310 cal BC
	Pit cutting top of Lower Organic Mound					
OxA-20807	Large flat animal bone (SF 8038) from [3066] the secondary fill (mid-grey to black silty loam) of pit [3067] was one of two that cut through the top of the Lower Organic Mound. It was recorded on the western section of the Main Tunnel in Bays 75 and 76 and measured 1m in diameter and 0.6m deep.	3946±28	-22.8		2570–2340 cal BC	2570–2525 (21%) or 2500–2405 (74%) cal BC
SUERC-24828	*Ranunculus acris* (1)/ cf. *acris* (1) cf. *bulbosus* (2.5) as OxA-20807	3960±45			2580–2300 cal BC	2580–2410 cal BC

Table 4.3: Radiocarbon measurements from Silbury Hill dated in 2009–2010

Laboratory number	Material and context	Radiocarbon Age (BP)	∂13C (‰)	Weighted Mean (BP)	Calibrated date range (95% confidence)	Posterior Density Estimate (95% probability)
	Mini-mound part of Lower Organic Mound					
P24563	Cereal size straw fragments (waterlogged) from [4181] – sample <9808> ([4181], sub sample of <9425>). [4181] formed the Mini-mound part of the Lower Organic Mound, and was formed of an organic-rich greyis- brown to very dark greyish-brown silty loam intermixed with turf layers and measured 0.8m wide.	Failed due to very low yield				
SUERC-24088	Yew berry, as P24563	3925±35	-21.7		2550–2290 cal BC	2475–2405 cal BC
SUERC-27239	Crataegus sp. twig (4 years old) from [4181] <9827>. See SUERC-24088	3885±30	-28.1		2470–2210 cal BC	2470–2405 cal BC
	Lower Organic Mound					
OxA-X-2352-53	*Ranunculus acris/bulbosus* (1) + *Stellaria gramineae* (3) from [3046b] <9824>. [3046] together with [3045], [3054], [3055], [3056], [3057] and [3058] were a series of organic layers that formed part of a coherent mound enlarging the height of the earlier Gravel Mound to at least 1.1m, termed the Lower Organic Mound.	3950±100	-26.9		2860–2140 cal BC	2480–2415 cal BC
GU-18780-	Monocot stem (4 fragments), as OxA-X-2352-53	Failed due to very low yield				
OxA-22082	Monocotyledonous stem (4 fragments) from [4156a] <9200>. Together with [4155] [4156] on the east side of the main tunnel was a series of organic layers that formed part of a coherent mound enlarging the height of the earlier Gravel Mound to at least 1.1m, termed the Lower Organic Mound.	3902±33	-27.3		2480–2280 cal BC	2475–2415 cal BC
SUERC-24090	*Ranunculus* cf. *acris* (3)/ *cf. bulbosus* (1)/ *acris/repens/bulbosus* (1), as OxA-22082	3935±30	-25.9		2560–2340 cal BC	2480–2410 cal BC
	Upper Organic Mound					
OxA-X-2352-55	Monocotyledonous stem (4 fragments) from [3061a] <9375>, one of a series of contexts on the western side of the main tunnel that formed part of the Upper Organic Mound. The size of these deposits suggests that they represent basket loads of material.	3878±45.	-28.6		2480-2200 cal BC	2450-2380 cal BC
SUERC-24829	*Ranunculus acris/bulbosus* (3) as OxA-X-2352-55	3950±50			2580–2290 cal BC	2450–2375 cal BC
OxA-22083	Ranunculus acris/repens/bulbosus (1) cf. bulbosus (1) from [3078b] <9335>, one of a series of contexts on the western side of the main tunnel that formed part of the Upper Organic Mound that sealed the pits and Lower Organic Mound.	3848±39.	-29.4		2470–2150 cal BC	2450–2375 cal BC
GU-18783	Monocotyledonous stem (4 fragments), as OxA-22083	Failed				
SUERC-27238	Indeterminate twig from [3078c] <9335> OxA-22083	3875±30	-27.9		2470–2200 cal BC	2450–2375 cal BC
	Ditch 1 and Ditch 4					
SUERC-27240	Red deer antler from [3926] SF 9036 from the primary fill of Ditch 1. The fills of Ditch 1 were visible in the tunnel sides as well as within a machine cut trench below the tunnel.	3965±30	-22.1		2570–2400 cal BC	–

Table 4.4: Posterior density estimates for the dates of archaeological events at Silbury Hill (Model C), derived from the model described in Figure 4.6

Event	95% probability	68% probability	Parameter (Fig 4.6)
Lower Organic Mound constructed	2465–2380 cal BC	2460–2415 cal BC	Lower Organic Mound_constructed
Upper Organic Mound constructed	2460–2375 cal BC	2455–2410 cal BC	Upper Organic Mound_constructed
Bank and Ditches constructed	2435–2340 cal BC	2420–2350 cal BC	Banks_constructed
Final Mound constructed	2135–1965 cal BC	2125–2065 cal BC	End_Silbury Hill

Table 4.5: Posterior density estimates for the dates of archaeological events at Silbury Hill (Model D), derived from the model described in Figure 4.7

Event	95% probability	68% probability	Parameter (Fig 4.7)
Lower Organic Mound constructed	2460–2375 cal BC	2460–2410 cal BC	Lower Organic Mound_constructed
Upper Organic Mound constructed	2460–2370 cal BC	2450–2405 cal BC	Upper Organic Mound_constructed
Bank and Ditches constructed	2435–2330 cal BC	2420–2390 (41%) or 2370–2340 (27%) cal BC	Banks_constructed
Final Mound constructed	2450–2375 (52%) or 2355–2295 (43%) cal BC	2435–2420 (17%) or 2410–2380 (35%) or 2355–2310 (43%) cal BC	End_Silbury Hill

5

Understanding Preservation and Formation Processes

MATTHEW CANTI, MARGARET COLLINSON, GILL CAMPBELL, TONY BRAIN,
ROBERT J SMITH, MALCOLM LILLIE, AND ISABEL DOUTERELO-SOLER

... a layer of dark black stacked turves began to appear. On breaking apart lumps of this, the surface vegetation still appeared green, though much flattened. Beetles and snails are visible, the former apparently in an excellent state of preservation (Site diary, 22 July 1968; Whittle 1997a, 16)

One of the original objectives of the archaeological investigations undertaken as part of the Silbury Conservation Project was 'to sample significant deposits for understanding of the mechanisms involved in the preservation of delicate biological materials preserved in the centre of the Hill' and 'to investigate the current state of preservation within the Hill, including evidence for active and past decay' (McAvoy 2006, 7). The first part of this chapter reports on the studies carried out in order to meet these objectives: investigations into the cellular and ultrastructural preservation and the microbiological content of material obtained from the Lower Organic Mound sampled from the end face of the Main Tunnel. The investigation was partly undertaken with a view to carrying out further analyses on samples preserved ex situ in future years. It was hoped that the work would inform our understanding of the future preservation potential of the deposits.

The second part reports on the analysis undertaken to understand the formation processes and the way in which the various materials that make up the central part of the mound were modified and employed in the construction process, namely the formation process of the Old Land Surface (Phase 2), the origin of the Gravel Mound (Phase 3), the nature of possible turf lines or topsoil bands seen in the tunnel sections, and the nature of the organic layer [3035 and 4100] seen directly overlying the grey clay layer under much of the central area of the Hill.

Understanding preservation

The preservation of delicate biological remains within the centre of Silbury Hill has been heralded since the Archaeological Institute excavations in 1849, but only began to be fully appreciated following the pioneering environmental analyses undertaken during Atkinson's work. These analyses established not only that some of remains within the centre of the Hill were extremely well preserved (some of the molluscs still retained their proteinaceous coats (Evans 1972, 266); a number of individuals observed that 'the grass was green' (Susan Limbrey and Brian Durham, pers comm)), but also showed that chalk grassland was already established in the vicinity of Silbury prior to the inception of the monument, a result confirmed by the recent analyses (*see* Chapter 6).

There were a number of limitations to the analyses of environmental remains from the 1968–70 intervention, the most serious of which was the lack of documentation for the locations of the samples. This meant that it was not always possible to establish whether a particular species had been recovered from the Old Land Surface (OLS) or from within Silbury I (for example, the turf stack). Some seeds were recorded as concentrations within either the turf stack or the OLS suggesting considerable heterogeneity, for example *Urtica dioica* (stinging nettle) and *Montia fontana* (blinks) (Williams 1997), but whether this was the result of different materials or turves from different habitats being incorporated into the mound or surviving buried underneath it remained unknown.

Similarly, Mark Robinson (1997, 36 and 40) observed that the preservation of insects in the deposits varied from good to very poor with those from the turf stack generally better preserved than remains from the OLS. He speculated that at least part of this variation was because some of the remains had already partially decayed within the turves used to construct the mound, but whether this was really the case or whether it was due to differing preservation conditions in different parts of the mound, the use of different materials, or some other factor remained unresolved.

Work on the material retrieved from Core 6 taken as part of the seismic topographic survey by Skanska in March 2003 (Fig 2.1; Skanska 2003; *see also* Chapter 10) went some way towards confirming that varying preservation was related to the nature of the construction material. Remains within the humic layers of the turves were well preserved, degraded within the topsoil and fragmentary within the subsoil (Canti *et al* 2004; Robinson 2004). However, it was recognised that these results could not be extrapolated to Silbury I as a whole. It was thus felt that the 2007/8 intervention should explore this question further.

Also of interest was the mechanism (or mechanisms) by which anoxic conditions had persisted within the centre of the Hill resulting in the preservation of delicate biological remains. The existence of multiple iron pans as seen in the records of the 1968–70 excavations (*see* Canti *et al* 2004, figs 3 and 4) indicated that preservation conditions varied on a micro-scale with reduction playing a major role.

Nevertheless, there was no evidence within

the cores retrieved as part of the seismic survey for solid iron pans indicating that the preservation conditions were not analogous to those found within some early Bronze Age barrows in Scandinavia where the 'core' of the mound is almost completely encased by iron pan resulting in waterlogged and strong reducing conditions (Holst *et al* 2001; Canti *et al* 2004, 14) and where deliberate soaking of the 'core' appears to have been part of the construction process (*see* Breuning-Madsen *et al* 2002). Rather the principal mechanisms leading to anoxic conditions within Silbury Hill were thought to be constant temperature and wetness coupled with limited gaseous exchange and the extreme compression of the deposits caused by 'the enormous weight of the mound' above (Evans 1972, 267).

It was, however, recognised that the nature of the preservation conditions within Silbury Hill required further exploration and in particular the current state of anoxic preservation needed to be assessed in relation to the effect the voiding and collapse of the 1849 and 1968–70 tunnels may have had upon this important palaeoecological evidence. At the same time the project sought to use innovative techniques in the hope that the results from Silbury Hill could be compared with those from other sites in the future.

Methodology

Originally, it was envisaged that large diameter cores of the primary deposits of Silbury consisting of turves and other organic material would be taken to a depth of 0.5m into the tunnel sides from a number of locations to investigate the current state of preservation of delicate biological remains within these deposits and the mechanisms involved in that preservation. The plan was to cut large diameter cores out of the sides of the tunnel, prior to trimming or refreshment so that any decay that had taken place could be investigated. However, the unstable nature of the deposits exposed in the sides of the tunnels (*see* Methodology in Chapter 2 and Chapter 10; Campbell 2011) meant that this plan had to be adapted. Only the deposits at the end of the main tunnel were considered stable enough to core in this way. The extraction of a large core from the back wall of the main tunnel was duly attempted but had to be abandoned as the large diameter corer hit a sarsen stone about 150mm into the deposits.

Fig 5.1
Section of the end wall of the Main Tunnel showing the location of cores <9441>–<9448>. (Eddie Lyons, © English Heritage)

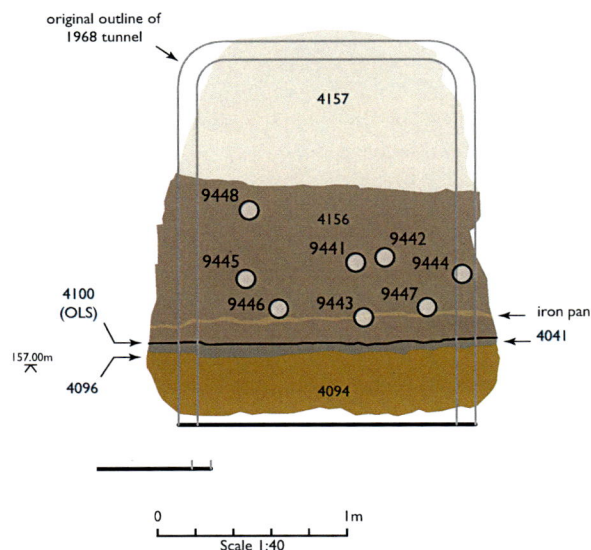

Instead, eight half-metre horizontal 100mm diameter cores (<9441>–<9448>) were taken from a number of points in the end wall of the main tunnel (Figs 2.14, 5.1 and 5.2a). This was less than ideal but was the best that was possible in the circumstances. Core <9448> disintegrated on sampling and is stored at English Heritage (Fort Cumberland) along with the intact Cores <9441>, <9442>, <9443 and <9446>. Cores <9444> and <9447> were used by Hull University for microbiology assessment. Core <9445> was taken to Royal Holloway University of London for study of preservation of organic material.

The cellular and ultrastructural preservation in material from Core <9445>

Margaret Collinson, Tony Brain, and Gill Campbell

The outer surfaces of Core <9445> were cleaned with a razor and the core was subsampled at three sampling intervals with increasing distance into the mound, namely 30–70mm, 150–190mm and 230–270mm from the tunnel wall. At each sampling interval different lithologies (up to four) were sampled separately (Fig 5.2b). Lithologies were described as follows at 190mm depth (Fig 5.2b): (a) rubble and thin band of mud to outer edge too small to separate, (b) organic mud and silt between rubble layer and fibrous layer, (c) organic rich fibrous layer, green plant material seen at sharp junction with d, (d) organic rich mud below fibrous layer. Each sub-sample was divided into two. One subset (each *c* 20 grams) was fixed for Transmission Electron Microscopy and the second subset (variable 20–80 grams) was frozen (wrapped in foil and then in polythene bags) for alternative applications in the future.

Methodology

Transmission electron microscopy (TEM)

Samples were fixed according to standard protocols for biological materials, in 2.5% glutaraldehyde in 0.1M phosphate buffer, in order to prevent any further alteration to the tissues after their extraction from the core. All fixation was completed within a maximum of 10 hours after removal of cores from their context in the end wall of the main 1968–70 tunnel at Silbury Hill. After fixation the lithology (c) samples were rinsed in distilled water, teased apart under a dissecting microscope, and organic particles were picked for detailed study. The individual pieces of picked organic material were then post fixed in 1% osmium tetroxide, dehydrated in an acetone/water series and embedded in Spurr resin. Ultrathin sections (*c* 70nm thick) were cut with a diamond knife, stained with uranyl acetate and lead citrate and studied using a Hitachi H7600 TEM fitted with an AMT digital camera system. Remaining unused material was returned to the initial fixative and stored in 25ml plastic sterilin tubes.

Scanning electron microscopy (SEM)

Samples of green and yellow plant material were mounted from a water droplet onto the emulsion side of a small piece of negative film mounted on an SEM stub. Samples were then sputter coated with gold and examined using an FEI Quanta 200F field emission SEM.

Tests to determine if mineral material could be removed without damage to tissues

Mineral material attached to organic material can cause major problems for TEM sectioning as mineral grains can be dragged across the specimen by the knife, or they can damage the knife. Replicate samples were treated with

Fig 5.2
Sampling and plant materials from the Lower Organic Mound
a) Numbered core sample locations in the Organic Mound at the end wall of the Main Tunnel;
b) Vertical section through core <9445> with lithologies marked (see sampling for explanation, scale bar in cm);
c) Green plant material on the surface and yellow plant material beneath at the junction of lithologies c and d from the right side of Fig 5.2b; scale bar 1mm;
d) Rootlet fragments in place in sediment from below Fig 5.2c; scale bar 1mm;
e) Side view of outer portion of cleaned core <9445>, tunnel end at left of image. Scale bar in cm.
(Margaret Collinson and Eddie Lyons, © English Heritage)

hydrochloric acid followed by hydrofluoric acid to remove carbonates and silicates respectively (standard technique for extracting small organic particles from siliciclastic rocks). The resulting mineral-free organic matter was then prepared for TEM observation as described above. Some replicates of this material were also prepared without osmium tetroxide post fixation to determine whether this stage was necessary. Results showed no discernible differences between osmium and non-osmium treated samples indicating that this stage could be omitted for acid-treated samples. Unfortunately, however, some tissue damage was observed in acid-treated samples by comparison with untreated samples. Therefore only gentle physical brushing in water or fixative prior to embedding could be undertaken in an attempt to remove adherent sediment or mineral grains.

Results

General observations

It had been the original aim to compare different plant organs from named species between the three samples. Unfortunately this was not possible; no dicotyledon leaves or leaf fragments were seen and only a single seed of *Ranunculus* cf. *acris* was found. Therefore broad categories of organic material were selected and each is discussed below. No obvious wood fragments or charcoal fragments were observed. Beetle elytra were very rare (only one or two specimens encountered in each sample) and these were single elytra not associated with other body parts. Rootlet material occurred as isolated fragments, not attached to other plant material.

In the samples used in this investigation green plant material was clearly present in specific layers as a surface deposit (Fig 5.2c). The strands/sheets of material were randomly orientated and overlapped one another, but did not descend into the underlying organic matrix. In the 150–190mm sample a natural split occurred at the sharp junction between the organic rich layer (lithology c) and the underlying muddy lithology (d) (Fig 5.2c) and green plant material was situated on that junction.

In contrast, yellow plant material did not form a surface coating but could be seen through gaps in green plant material (Fig 5.2c) and penetrating through some thickness of sediment or amongst sediment lacking green plant. Yellow plant material was very variable in dimension, pieces could be turned to reveal an outer surface all around the lateral margins but bases and apices were incomplete indicating the fragmentary nature of the material. Yellow plant material was not obviously attached to rootlet material.

Iron staining was present 20mm into the core and continued for a further 70mm along the organic-rich layer (Fig 5.2e).

Green plant material

Green plant material has a bottle green to bluish-green colour and occurs as overlapping thin sheet-like strands at the surface of the organic-rich fibrous layer (Fig 5.2c). It has a longitudinally banded appearance with pale strands at around 200 micron intervals and a finely longitudinally striated appearance between these bands (Fig 5.2c). This resembles the general morphology of a grass leaf blade.

However, under the SEM this material shows no stomata and no surface pattern of any kind, merely a faint undulation (Fig 5.3a, b). The material is also extremely thin and flexible, readily rolling up or folding when removed from liquid. In TEM section green plant material consists of two very thin cuticle-like membranes but there are no internal cell walls or compartments of any kind and no discrete membrane bound organelles can be recognised (Fig 5.4). The internal material consists of a matrix containing patches of stacked bilayered membranes identical to thylakoid plastid

Fig 5.3
Green plant material in SEM.
a) Single strand (sediment debris remains attached to the surface);
b) Detail of clean portion of surface, an undulating featureless thin membrane, revealing the thinness of the strand where cracked.
(Margaret Collinson, Tony Brain and Eddie Lyons, © English Heritage)

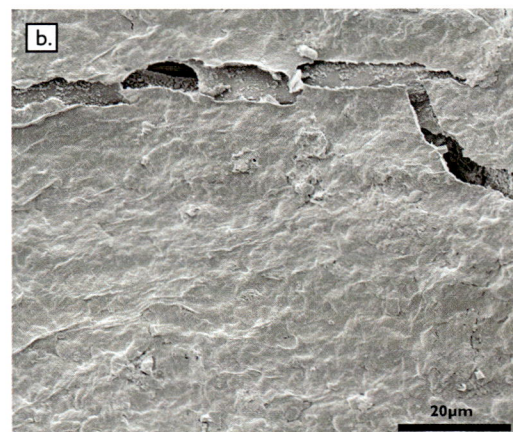

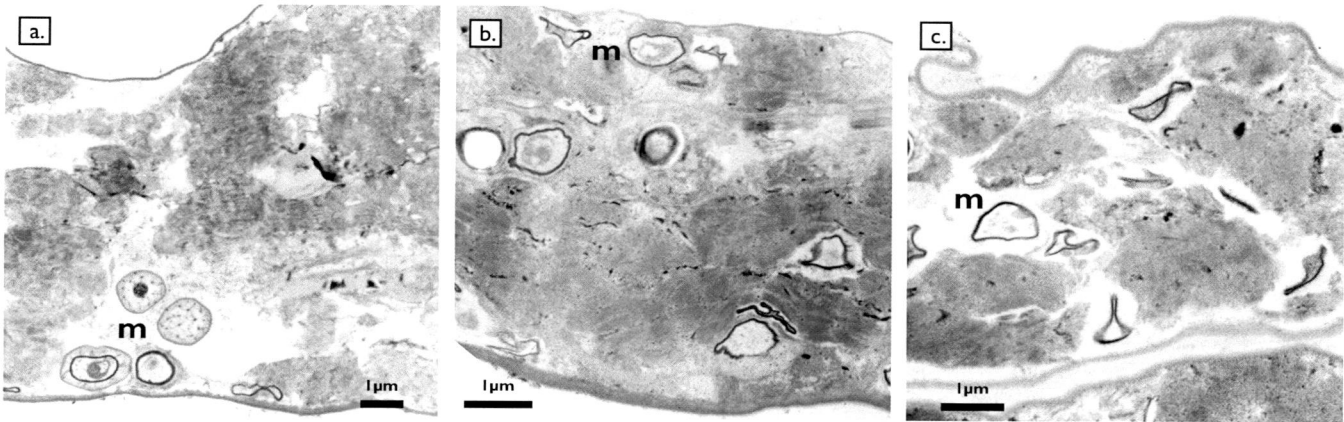

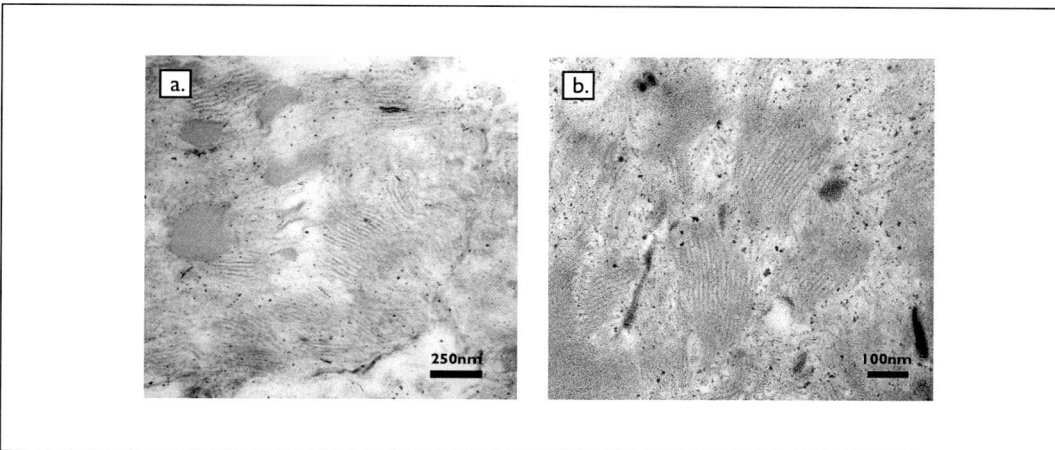

Fig 5.4 (top)
Green plant material
in TEM section.
a) Sample 30–70mm;
b) Sample 150–190mm;
c) Sample 230–270mm.
All samples show the same
preservation with two thin
cuticle-like membranes
enclosing granular material
with patchy variation in
electron lucency. Figure 5.5
shows detail from these
patches. No cellular
structure is present.
m indicates examples of
microbes which are scattered
through the specimens.
(Margaret Collinson,
Tony Brain and Eddie Lyons,
© English Heritage)

Fig 5.5
Details of green plant
material from Figure 5.4
in TEM section showing
remnants of thylakoid
membrane stacks from
chloroplasts.
a) Sample 30–70mm;
b) Sample 150–190mm.
(Margaret Collinson,
Tony Brain and Eddie Lyons,
© English Heritage)

membranes and here interpreted as membranes derived from chloroplasts (Fig 5.5). Microbes (Fig 5.6d–f) are abundant within green plant material.

Yellow plant material

Initially it was thought that yellow plant material was the same as green plant material, representing old dead and decaying material versus green plant material that was likely to have been living when incorporated into the mound. This hypothesis proved incorrect and yellow plant material is utterly different to green plant material.

Under the SEM yellow plant material reveals clear longitudinally elongated epidermal cells covered by a cuticle with hair bases (Fig 5.7a–c). No stomata were observed and outer surfaces have longitudinal striations and wrinkles. Yellow plant material is not flexible when lifted out of water and pieces observed by LM, SEM (Fig 5.7a) and TEM show continuity of epidermis around the compressed margins. This material

seems to be fragments, derived from compressed cylindrical or broadly oval plant material such as herbaceous stems or thick leaf bases. TEM thin sections (Fig 5.8) show a variable appearance in yellow plant material, some of which is strongly compressed, but all specimens preserve clear cellular structure. In some cases (Fig 5.8c, d; Fig 5.9a) the cuticle has separated from the outer epidermal cell wall and microbes have penetrated between these two layers. The epidermis may be partly detached (Fig 5.8d) from underlying tissues. In both specimens from sample 150–190mm, thin cell walls have undergone some compression whilst thick cell walls, such as xylem elements (Fig 5.9b, labelled 'x'), retain three-dimensional shape. Preservation of xylem cell wall layers is patchy, even within a single cell.

Specimens from the 30–70mm sample show a different decomposition. The cuticle has separated from the epidermal cell wall but has also begun to disintegrate, as have internal tissues (Fig 5.8a, b). Only small patches of cells are preserved.

121

Fig 5.6
Microbes from plant material in TEM section. a–c From yellow plant material; d–f From green plant material.
a, b) Specimens with very variable structure with partially detached outer layers and varying shapes of the dark (electron dense) layer;
c) shows three different morphologies in a single field of view linking the variants seen in a and b to an intact specimen;
d) Five specimens, three of which are intact and probably represent different planes of section;
e) Detail of intact specimen from d, probable equivalent of tangential section through f but not passing through the dark (electron dense) layer;
f) Detail of intact specimen from d showing all wall layers.
(Margaret Collinson, Tony Brain and Eddie Lyons, © English Heritage)

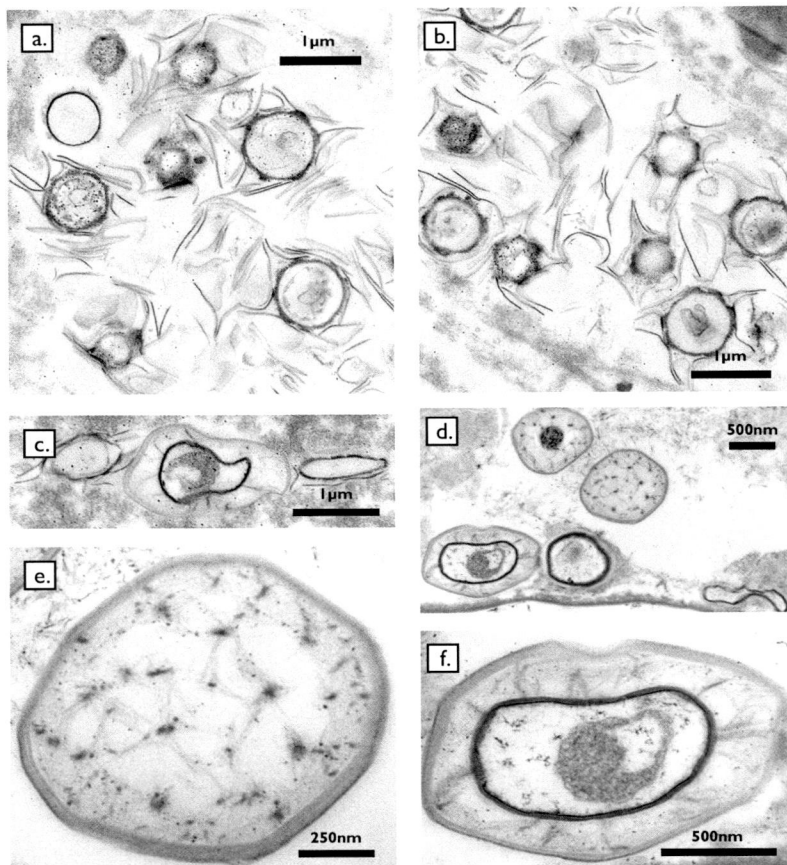

Fig 5.7 (below)
Yellow plant material in SEM.
a) Portion of specimen showing opening of a compressed former cylinder revealing inner surface;
b) Detail of inner surface from a showing upstanding anticlinal walls of rectangular epidermal cells; c) Detail of outer surface from a showing longitudinally aligned striation and wrinkling and probable hair base.
(Margaret Collinson, Tony Brain and Eddie Lyons, © English Heritage)

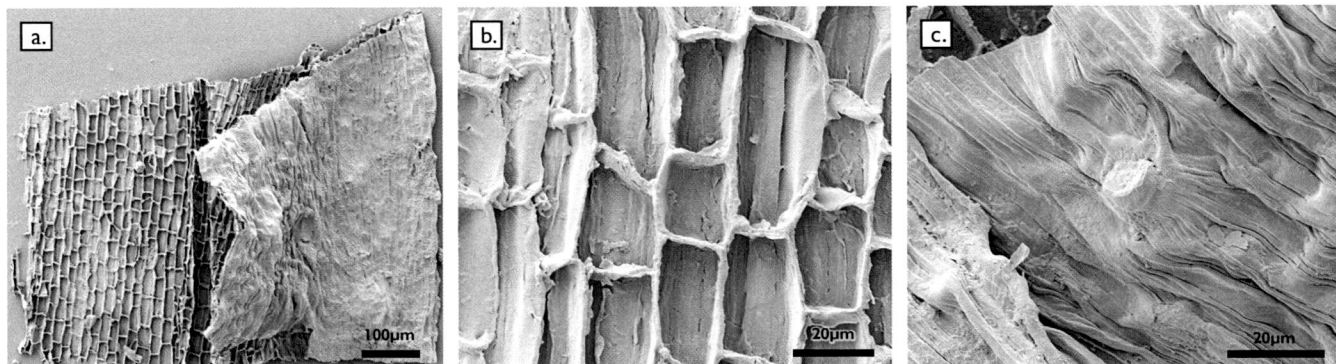

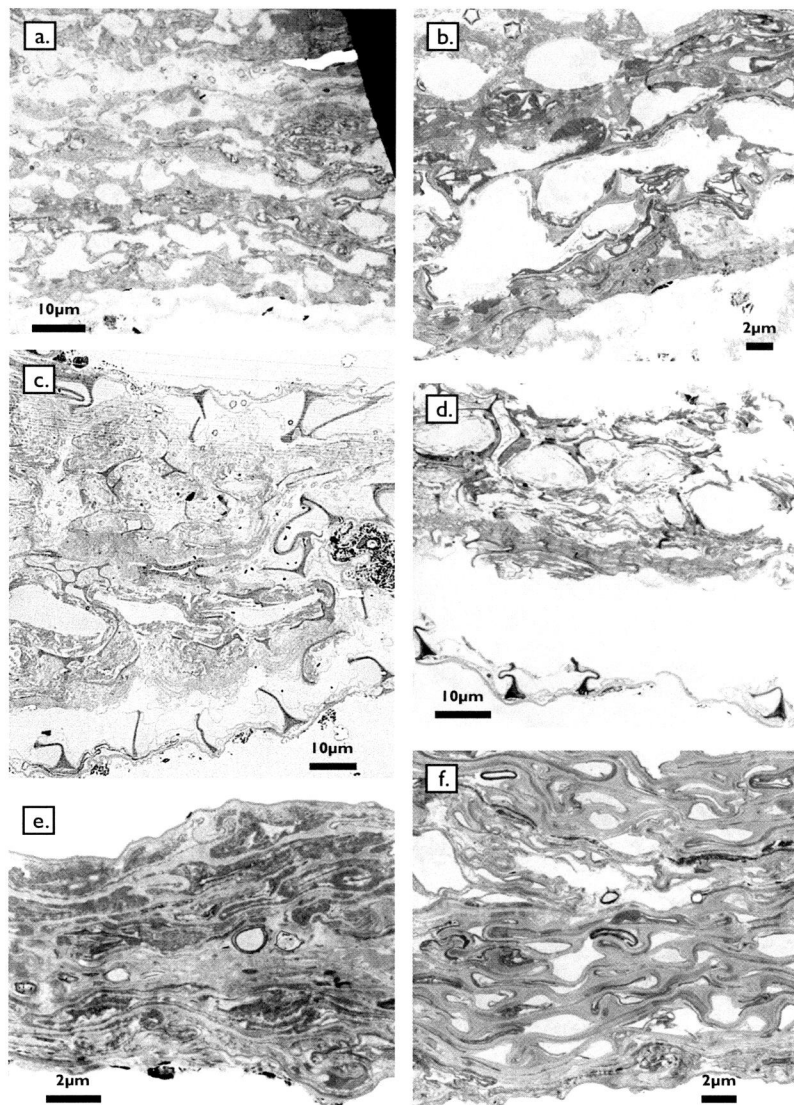

Fig 5.8
Yellow plant material in
TEM section. a, b) Sample
30–70mm;
c, d) Two specimens sample
150–190mm;
e, f) Two specimens sample
230–270mm.
a, b) Specimen with
detached degraded cuticle
(pale grey electron lucent
base of image) and areas
of cellular preservation
interspersed with degraded
material;
c, d) Specimens with
epidermis and cuticle seen as
a clear layer, partially
detatched in c and totally
detached in d (see Figure
5.9a for labelled detail of
epidermis from c), also
patches of other cells clearly
preserved and showing
varying degrees of
degradation in thick cell
walls in d;
e, f) Strongly compressed
specimens, with folded and
collapsed cell walls and
variable amounts of cellular
preservation. Cuticle not
visible due to compression.
(Margaret Collinson,
Tony Brain and Eddie Lyons,
© English Heritage)

Fig 5.9 (right)
Details of yellow plant
material in TEM section
sample 150–190mm from
Figure 5.8c.
a) Detail of epidermis with
labelled components
(c – cuticle, eaw – epidermal
anticlinal wall, oepw – outer
epidermal periclinal wall,
iepw – inner epidermal
periclinal wall). The cuticle
has detached from the outer
epidermal periclinal wall
and microbes can be seen as
small spheres between the
two layers.
b) Detail of five cells of the
primary xylem tissue (x)
showing variable
preservation of the thick cell
walls, in one case (bottom
right) the original cell shape
is barely discernible whereas
the adjacent cell to the left
has almost the entire wall
preserved.
(Margaret Collinson,
Tony Brain and Eddie Lyons,
© English Heritage)

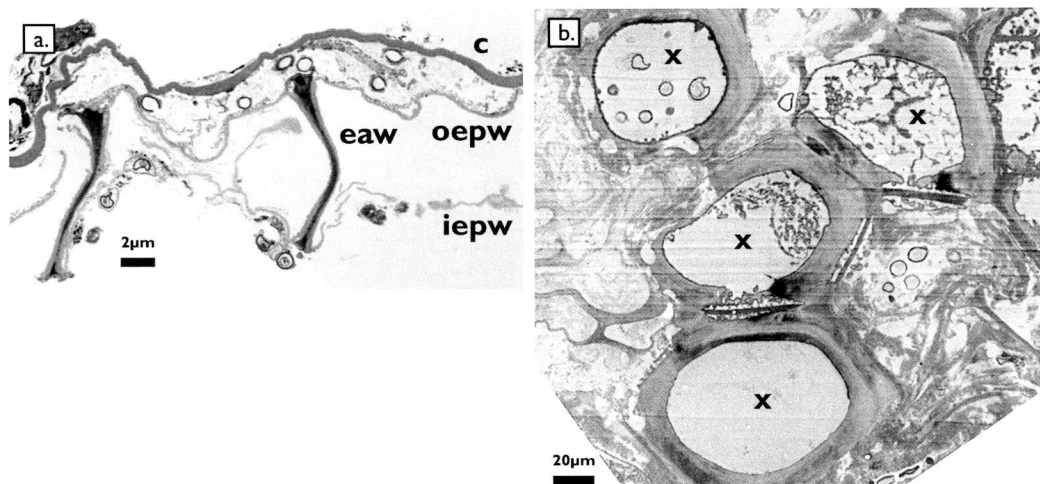

Fig 5.10
Rootlets in TEM section.
a, b) Sample 30–70mm,
c, d) Sample 150–190mm,
e, f) Sample 230–270mm.
a, c, e) Portions of rootlet
showing 3D cellular
preservation of the
endodermis (en) layer and
tissues internal to that;
b, d, f) Details of cells of the
endodermis showing
characteristic 'V–U' shape
of wall thickenings in
section; d also shows the
variation of preservation
between adjacent cells.
(Margaret Collinson,
Tony Brain and Eddie Lyons,
© English Heritage)

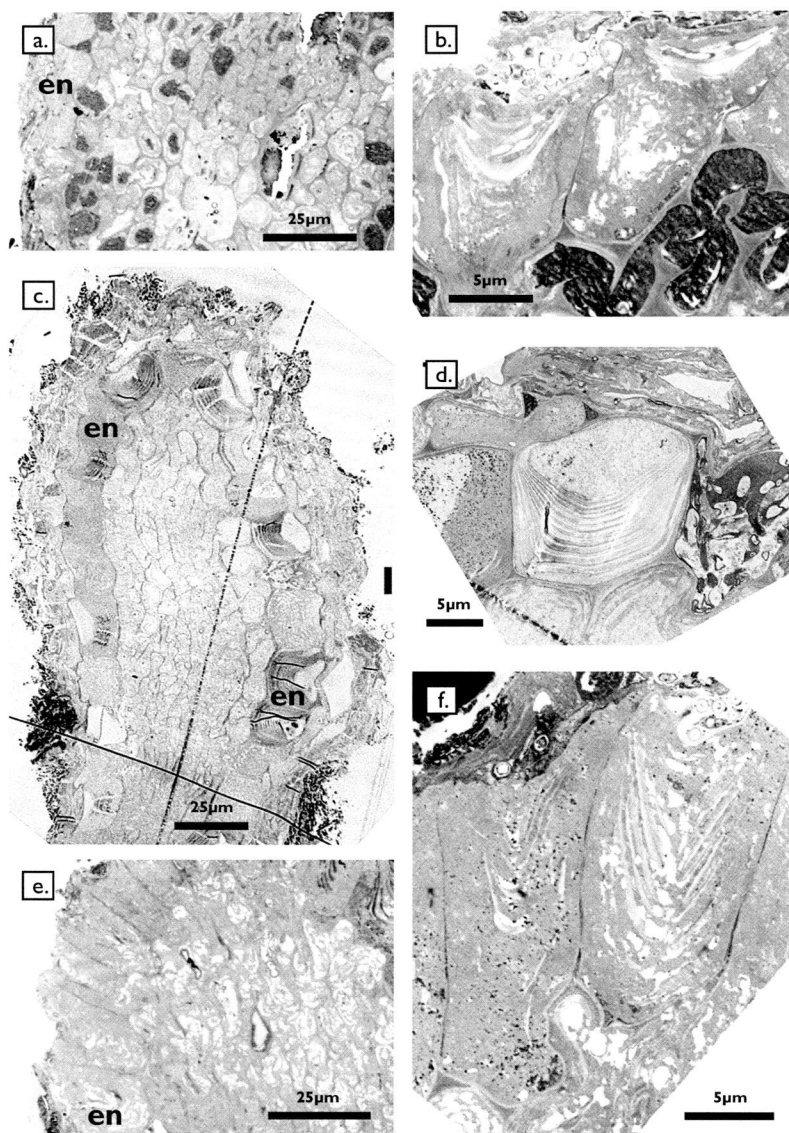

In contrast, in the 230–270mm sample, specimens are strongly compressed (Fig 5.8d, e). The cell structure is clearly preserved, although it is necessary to look carefully at the images to see the distorted cell walls. Cuticle cannot be clearly recognised, it may be compressed at the surface or it may have decayed. In spite of the cellular preservation no discrete membrane bound organelles were recognised and no thylakoid membranes were observed in any yellow plant material studied. Microbes are scattered throughout the tissues (Fig 5.6).

Rootlets

Rootlet material confers some of the 'fibrous' texture to the organic-rich layers. The rootlets are small but appear three dimensional when *in situ* (Fig 5.2d). In TEM section, at all sample levels, it is apparent that the three-dimensional preservation of cell walls and cell shape is restricted to cells internal to the endodermis (Fig 5.10 a, c, e, endodermis labelled 'en'). Outside the endodermis the cortical cells are either poorly preserved, very strongly compressed or both. No outer cuticle could be recognised. Mineral matter has remained attached to the outside of the rootlets (black electron dense material). Some endodermis cells are very well preserved, with the diagnostic differential wall thickening and thick layers of cell wall being clearly observed (Fig 5.10d). However, not all cells show the same cell wall preservation, even in a single section of a single specimen (Fig 5.10c, d) indicating either original differences in cell structure (such as transfer cells) or variable cell wall decomposition. In all sample levels some cells preserve the characteristic endodermal wall layering (Fig 5.10b, d, f).

Beetle elytra

Beetle elytra from all sample levels show ultrastructural preservation of the finely multilaminated exocuticle and the layered endocuticle (Fig 5.11). Samples from 30–70mm and 230–270mm preserve a multilayered endocuticle (Fig 5.12), whereas that from 150–190mm only preserves three endocuticle layers (Fig 5.11b). Previous TEM of beetle elytra (Margaret Collinson personal observation) suggests that typically endocuticle is at least the same thickness as exocuticle which implies loss of a number of endocuticle layers in the Silbury 150–190mm sample.

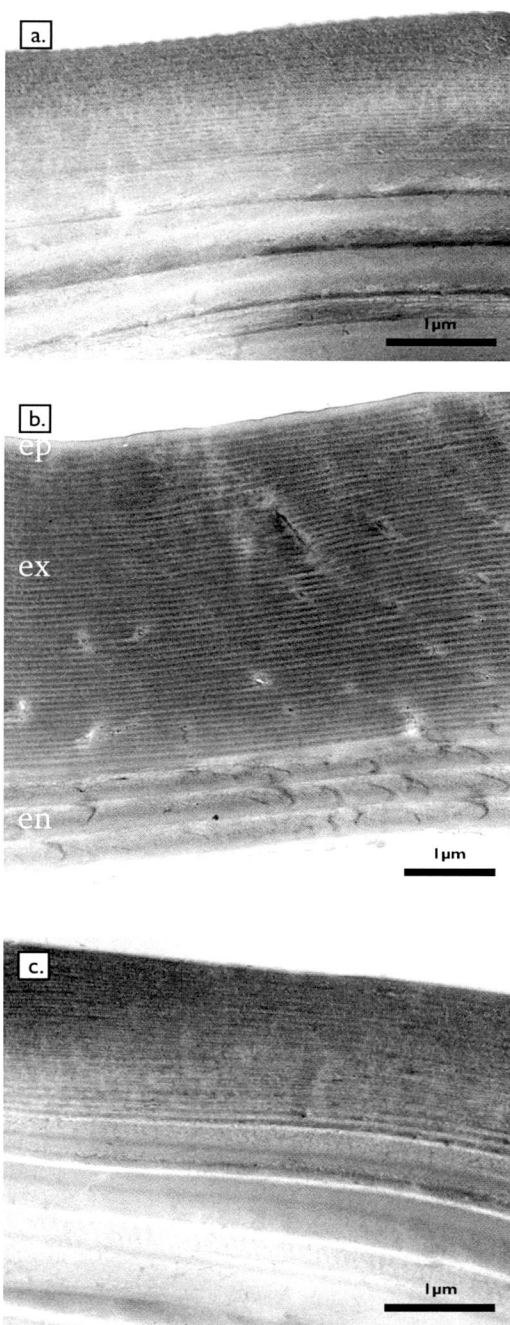

Fig 5.11
Beetle elytra in TEM section showing finely laminated exocuticle (ex, upper portion of each image) and layered endocuticle (en). a) Sample 30–70mm; b) Sample 150–190mm; c) Sample 230–270mm. Samples 30–70mm and 230–270mm are indistinguishable, sample 150–190mm has relatively thicker exocuticle with respect to endocuticle layers, has fewer endocuticle layers preserved (only three) and has a thick clearly distinguishable epicuticle (ep). Figure 5.12 shows the full thickness of a and c. (Margaret Collinson, Tony Brain and Eddie Lyons, © English Heritage)

Microbes in plant material

Small, single-celled spheres are abundant throughout the green and yellow plant material (Fig 5.6). Multiple morphologies are present such that the appearance in section may be of a single electron dense (black in image) ring through to forms with multiple 'faceting' on this ring (Fig 5.6a, b). Some specimens have an outer encircling layer of more electron lucent material (grey in image) that may be partly or fully

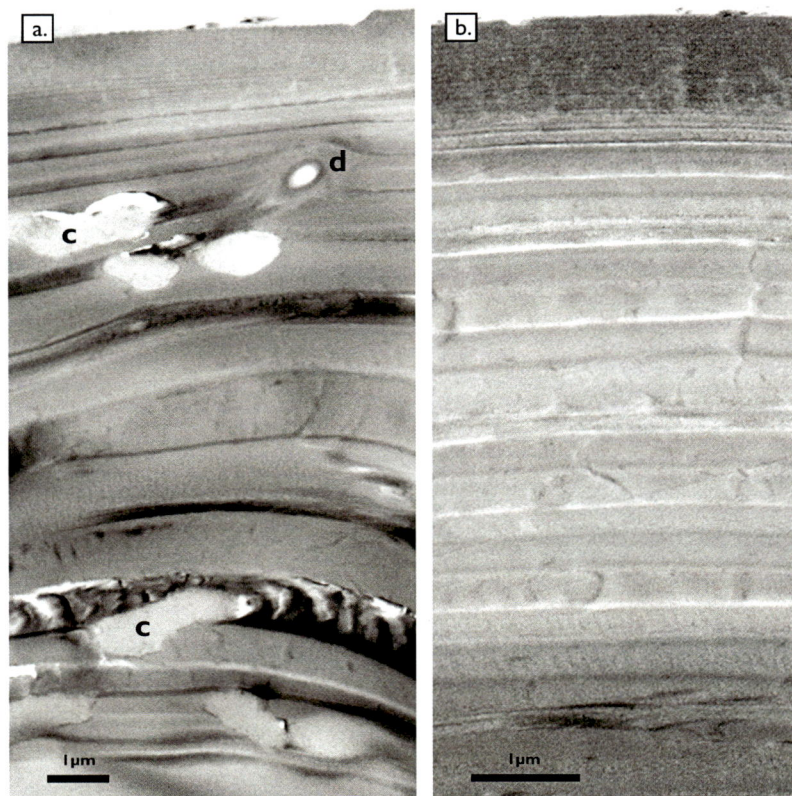

Fig 5.12
Beetle elytra in TEM section.
a) Same specimen as
Fig 5.11a, sample 30–70mm;
b) Same specimen as Fig 5.11c,
sample 230–270mm. The
finely laminated exocuticle is
at the top of the images and
multiple layers of endocuticle
are preserved beneath. The
distortion in both images,
especially in a, is due to
problems sectioning this
material. In a, the letter d
indicates a cuticle duct while
the letter c indicates cavities in
the endocuticle. These cavities
may be scattered (as in a) or
clumped and in sample b they
occurred in such concentrated
patches that endocuticle
organisation could no longer
be distinguished so they are
not illustrated.
(Margaret Collinson,
Tony Brain and Eddie Lyons,
© English Heritage)

detached into thin 'flakes' (Fig 5.6a, b). Transitional stages exist between all of these in a single field of view (Fig 5.6c). In addition, as seen in Figure 5.6d, some of the variation in appearance is likely to result from different planes of section. For example Figure 5.6e might be equivalent to a section taken perpendicular to Figure 5.6f in a tangential plane at the left or right end of the specimen, outside of the black layer.

Fine organic particles

Following tests using HF (hydrofluoric acid) treatment (see Methodology) the opportunity was taken to examine the dispersed fine organic fraction from the 150–190mm sample by TEM. This fraction (Fig 5.13) contains a variety of fragments, mostly electron lucent strands possibly derived from decomposition of cellulosic cell walls, and a few small isolated cells. Some electron dense fragments may be derived from lignified tissues. Notably, the microbes, so prevalent in yellow and green plant material (Fig 5.6), are very rare in the dispersed fine fraction.

Discussion of preservation states and variation within and between samples

Degradation and timing

All organic material studied shows some degradation. In the case of the beetle elytra this must have occurred after death of the organism. However, in the higher plant materials the organs we have studied might have senesced and degraded whilst their parent plant lived on. One or two of the beetle elytra were incomplete (but too few were recovered to make any overall assessment of their fragmentation). The higher plant material was fragmentary and fragments were intertwined as well as lying at various angles to the lithological junctions. These characteristics are more suggestive of litter accumulations (natural or human-produced) than of intact rooted surfaces. Degradation may have taken place in the litter and/or after the organic-rich sediment was incorporated into the mound.

Higher plant material

Yellow plant material and rootlets both exhibit cellular preservation including parenchyma, xylem and endodermis. These cells and tissues have different chemical compositions ranging through cellulose to lignin-cellulose-hemicellulose complexes to suberin. These molecules are more resistant than others (such as cytoplasmic constituents) and survive in plant fossils, although each has different survival potential (see Collinson 2011 for a review). Unequivocal evidence for lignin is known from the Mesozoic (>150 million years ago) (van Bergen et al 2004) whilst, although cellulose is well known to be more labile (for example, Meyers et al 1995; van Bergen et al 1994), it has been reported (as polysaccharide products and modified extracted cellulose strands) in exceptionally preserved fossils that are up to 45 million years old (Yang et al 2005; Richter et al 2008). Therefore, preservation of these cell and tissue types, with their different chemical compositions, is not unexpected in the archaeological samples from Silbury.

The essential characteristics of yellow plant material and rootlets (cell and tissue preservation in both) are the same in all three sample levels for all different cell and tissue types. However, there are some variations between specimens both within and between sample levels (for example, Fig 5.8). Differences in the degree of physical compression are the main factor which contributes to the striking difference in appearance of the thin sections of yellow plant material from sample level 230–270mm (Fig 5.8e, f) compared to other levels (Fig 5.8a–d). This could be related to numerous possible variables in the depositional setting or in mound construction and does not imply any difference in the organic preservation. Further differences are seen in the preservation states of tissues with the sample from level 30–70mm more poorly preserved (fewer recognisable cells, cells more separated) than those from 150–190mm and 230–270mm. In older plant fossils from the Miocene to Eocene (c 8 to 45 million years old) drastic variation in tissue preservation has been recorded even within the same sample level. At extremes, leaf fossils may be represented in the fossil record only by their cuticle or by fully preserved leaf anatomy comparable to a modern leaf (Collinson 2011). Some leaves have no cuticle preserved yet do have recognisable internal anatomy (Gupta *et al* 2007b), whilst in other leaves there is no remnant of tissue organisation preserved in spite of the leaf being perfectly recognisable in hand specimen as a morphologically well-preserved specimen (Gupta *et al* 2007b). Decay experiments show that even one year of decay can result in major tissue loss (Gupta *et al* 2009, fig 3).

There are also differences in preservation of cell walls within a single specimen of the higher plant material as seen by variations between cells within a single TEM section. These are especially evident in the rootlet endodermis (Fig 5.10b, d, f) and in the xylem cells of yellow plant material (Fig 5.9b). Assuming that degradation of primary xylem is similar to that of wood (secondary xylem) in archaeological materials this can be mediated by fungi or bacteria (the former in more aerobic conditions) and involves initial removal of polysaccharides followed by demethylation of lignin (van Bergen *et al* 2000 and references there cited). Kim and Singh (2000) reviewed wood degradation in archaeological materials in wet environments and illustrated numerous examples by TEM. Their images show differential loss of structure in adjacent parts of cell walls and various types of alteration of patches of cell walls by soft rot

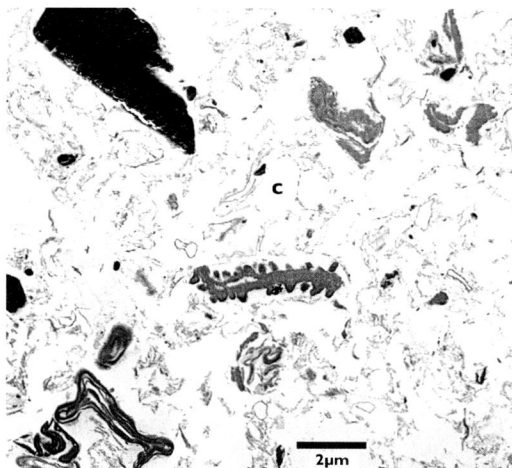

2µm

fungi, tunnelling bacteria and erosion bacteria.

In some specimens of yellow plant material cuticle is seen as a layer separated from the underlying epidermal cell wall (Fig 5.8a–d; Fig 5.9a), whilst in other specimens cuticle is not readily recognisable as a distinct layer (Fig 5.8 e, f). Following decay experiments on plant cuticles TEM observations showed that the cuticle/epidermal cell wall junction separates after only 30 weeks decay (Collinson *et al* 1998). In some samples of ancient fossil leaves from a single horizon examined by TEM some may lack cuticles whilst others have very well preserved cuticle (Gupta *et al* 2007b; Collinson 2011).

Based on variations in overall appearance and size it is likely that yellow plant material is derived from more than one species and/or from different stages in growth, both of which may also contribute to variability in preservation. The same may well be true for rootlets. The variations seen within Silbury higher plant material are to be expected as a consequence of spatial variability in degradation within a single specimen or single sample. These facts, together with the known preservational variations in higher plant material noted above, argue against assigning any significance to the slight differences in tissue or cell preservation seen between the higher plant materials from different sample levels at Silbury.

Beetle elytra

Beetle elytra from all three sample levels preserve the layered cuticle (Fig 5.11). The preservation of epicuticle and exocuticle is particularly clear in the sample from 150–190mm (Fig 5.11b), yet some endocuticle layers

Fig 5.13
Fine dispersed organic debris in TEM section. Most electron lucent (grey) particles are probably derived from cellulosic cell walls, some of which are still just recognisable as groups of cells (c) whilst others are much smaller isolated but intact cell walls. Microbes with the characteristic black electron dense ring, like those from within plant material (see Fig 5.6), are absent. The angular electron dense (dark) fragment may be a tiny wood fragment. (Margaret Collinson, Tony Brain and Eddie Lyons, © English Heritage)

have been lost from this sample. In contrast the samples from 30–70mm and 230–270mm are almost identical (Fig 5.11a, c; Fig 5.12), both having the multilayered endocuticle preserved (Fig 5.12). It is important to note that the cavities seen in Figure 5.12a are also present in the sample from 230–270mm but their concentrated occurrence makes endocuticle difficult to see and is not illustrated here. These cavities appear similar to those produced by soft rot fungi in wood cell walls (Kim and Singh 2000).

Multilayered endocuticle, comparable to that from a living relative, is preserved in the elytra of complete exceptionally preserved weevils from the Oligocene (25 million years old) (Gupta et al 2007a). Although chemically altered, these specimens also preserve a small proportion of chitin/protein moieties indicative of the original chemical composition of a chitin/protein complex. Survival of chitin/protein is very rare in arthropod fossils (Gupta and Briggs 2011), and its survival may be linked to the preservation of endocuticle in the Oligocene weevils (Gupta et al 2007a). Endocuticle is typically lost in older arthropod fossils (Gupta et al 2007a) but commonly some layers survive in Pleistocene fossils (Margaret Collinson personal observation).

The preservation of exocuticle and endocuticle in all sample levels and the essentially indistinguishable specimens from samples 30–70mm and 230–270mm, with multilayered endocuticles, indicates minimal alteration of beetle elytra and no difference between the different sample levels. The slight difference in appearance of the specimen from sample 150–190mm, including different relative thickness of exocuticle, and distinct thick epicuticle, may indicate that it is from a different species.

Microbes

The abundance of the microbes within plant material, but their rarity in the dispersed fine organic faction (Fig 5.13), suggests that they may have played a role in plant decomposition. This is supported by their presence between the separated cuticle and epidermal cell wall (Fig 5.9a) and within cavities in tissues. The microbe morphology and size bears some resemblance to both erosion bacteria and cavitation bacteria illustrated in TEM sections of degrading wood cell walls by Kim and Singh (2000). However, their specimens (for example Kim and Singh 2000, fig 3 and fig 5) all seem to resemble the intact specimens from Silbury (that is Fig 5.6f and the central specimen in Fig 5.6c). Further comparison is hindered by different magnifications of images, but it is tempting to speculate that the broken outer wall layers in Silbury microbes (Fig 5.6a, b) might indicate that they too were degrading and hence no longer active after the material was buried in the mound. Some support for this suggestion comes from the analysis by Smith et al (see below) that found minimal microbial activity in cores taken at the same time as our samples. An alternative possibility is that the Silbury microbe material includes a number of different life cycle stages. Speculation aside, it is not possible to draw any conclusions about the microbes in the plant material without an extensive comparative TEM study of various bacteria.

The unusual preservation of green plant material

Green plant material shows almost identical preservation in the different sample levels (Figs 5.4 and 5.5). The only slight difference observed is in the quality of images of the membranes (Fig 5.5). This is likely, at least in part, to result from different planes of section. Variations in preservation state within each specimen, simply as a consequence of autolysis, would also be expected for such labile constituents.

There are rare examples of ancient higher plant fossils tens of millions of years old with preservation of plastid organelles and membranes. These include those in Eocene conifer leafy shoots preserved in Baltic amber (Koller et al 2005), in Eocene conifer leaves from litter layers in the Canadian High Arctic (Schoenhut et al 2004) and in Miocene oak leaves preserved in lacustrine sediments at Clarkia (Niklas and Brown 1981; Margaret Collinson personal observation). All of these are from sites known for their exceptional preservation and all occur in leaves with cellular preservation.

The preservation of plastid membranes in Silbury green plant material in the absence of any contextual organelles or cell structure defies ready explanation. It seems impossible that such alteration could have happened after incorporation into the Silbury Hill mound given that other associated organic material is still readily recognisable. Further investigations of this material are presented in Appendix 5.1 (see also Collinson et al 2011b).

Conclusions

Preservation of cellular and ultrastructural detail is closely comparable in all samples. Small differences observed in some cases can be accounted for either by (i) variation in the state of decomposition of the material prior to incorporation in the mound or (ii) typical known variations in preservation of the organic materials in any fossil assemblage, (iii) differential compression probably after incorporation in the mound or (iv) the origin of the material from different species in different samples. Furthermore, these detailed investigations which focused on an undisturbed area of the Lower Organic Mound at the back of the Main Tunnel indicate that, away from the tunnel sides in areas not disturbed by earlier excavations, cellular and ultrastructural preservation of the organic material has not been affected.

Green plant material has no cellular structure or organelles but preserves ultrastructure of chloroplast membrane stacks in a matrix enclosed between two very thin cuticle-like layers (*see also* Appendix 5.1). Yellow plant material is derived from higher plants and preserves cellular structure, with clear cell walls but does not preserve organelles or plastid membranes. Rootlet material is derived from higher plants and preserves three-dimensional cellular structure within the endodermis and the ultrastructure of the differentially thickened endodermal cell-wall layering is always evident in spite of variable preservation of cells even within a single thin section. Beetle elytra preserve ultrastructure of cuticle layers including the less resistant endocuticle. Unidentified microbes (probably bacteria) occur throughout plant material and their rarity in the dispersed fine organic fraction suggests a specific association with plant decomposition. Their taxonomy and biology is not known.

Microbiological assessment of Cores <9444> and <9447>

Robert J Smith, Isabel Douterelo-Soler and Malcolm Lillie

Cores <9444> and <9447> were sub-sampled for microbiological assessment. Five sub-samples were extracted from the centre of both cores at 50mm, 100mm, 200mm, 300mm and 350mm intervals along their length from the tunnel face (0mm).

Two phases of microbiological assessment were carried out. The aim of Phase I was to understand microbiological community diversity and activity in the sediment samples and to identify the implications of their presence in terms of the current preservation status and preservation potential of Silbury Hill. This was achieved by using a number of conventional microbiological techniques including bacterial abundance, extracellular enzyme activity, ^{14}C-leucine assimilation and Biolog ecomicroplates.

Following on from this, Phase II took a more targeted approach seeking to identify the number and types of bacteria which might be implicated in the decay process of organic material within the sediment of Silbury Hill. This was achieved by counting all the viable (living) bacterial cells in each sample (total viable counting [TVC]), and culturing/gram staining bacterial colonies found within the sediment samples. The results of both phases of investigation are summarised below; full accounts, including detailed methodologies, are given in Lillie *et al* forthcoming and Smith forthcoming.

Bacterial abundance

The results shown in Table 5.1 indicate that abundance is greater in Core <9447> than in Core <9444>. Furthermore, the general trend for bacterial abundance in both cores is that abundance tends to increase as depth increases. There are, however, several exceptions to this trend, with decreases in bacterial abundance at 300mm and 350mm depths in Core <9447>; and a higher than anticipated increase in bacterial abundance at 50mm depth in Core <9444> (when compared to the other bacterial abundance values).

Extracellular enzyme activity

Extracellular enzyme activity using the three assays (phosphatase, glucosidase and leucine aminopeptidase) generally remains low throughout the sediment profile of both cores (Tables 5.2 and 5.3; cf Douterelo-Soler 2007; Lillie and Smith 2008). The values of glucosidase remain similar throughout the profile of both cores, whilst phosphatase tends to decrease with depth. However, the value of leucine aminopeptidase at all depths in Core <9447> is higher than the corresponding values in Core <9444>.

Table 5.1: Variation in bacterial abundance obtained at different depth intervals from Cores 9444 and 9447

Core 9444 (depth in mm)	Abundance	Core 9447 (depth in mm)	Abundance
50	0.8	50	0.9
100	0.3	100	1
200	0.4	200	1.5
300	0.4	300	1.4
350	0.5	350	0.9

Table 5.2: Individual extracellular enzyme activities of the samples obtained at different depth intervals from Core 9444

Depth (in mm)	Phosphatase	Glucosidase	Leucine aminopeptidase
50	0.353	0.305	0.134
	0.33	0.458	0.039
		0.367	
100	0.268	0.317	0.074
	0.212	0.553	0.011
	0.238	0.384	
200	0.162	0.68	0.168
	0.12	0.11	0.145
	0.141	0.11	0.169
300	0.086	0.17	
	0.105	0.183	0.212
	0.071	0.195	0.301
350	0.271	0.309	0.231
	0.266	0.335	0.19
	0.19		0.213

Table 5.3: Individual extracellular enzyme activities of the samples obtained at different depth intervals from Core 9447

Depth (in mm)	Phosphatase	Glucosidase	Leucine aminopeptidase
50	0.702	0.287	1.225
	0.71	0.382	1.623
	0.716	0.375	1.584
100	0.208	0.276	0.904
	0.159	0.205	1.038
	0.247	0.209	0.121
200	0.515	0.293	0.122
	0.315	0.273	1.154
	0.325	0.311	0.872
300	0.257	0.173	0.83
	0.357	0.124	0.948
	0.419	0.122	0.872
350	0	0.296	0.955
	0.702	0.276	1.024
	0.71	0.277	1.088

Table 5.4: Variation in ^{14}C-leucine assimilation obtained at different depth intervals from Cores 9444 and 9447

Core 9444 (depth in mm)	Mean average	Standard Deviation	Core 9447 (depth in mm)	Mean average	Standard Deviation
50	0.03	0.02	50	0.02	0.00
100	0.04	0.03	100	0.01	0.00
200	0.02	0.00	200	1.96	0.94
300	0.00	0.00	300	0.57	0.16
350	0.01	0.00	350	0.11	0.00

¹⁴C-leucine assimilation

The results are shown in Table 5.4. ¹⁴C-leucine assimilation uptake by microbes in the samples obtained from both cores remains low throughout their profiles (cf Douterelo-Soler 2007; Lillie and Smith 2008); however, beyond 200mm depth in Core <9447>, leucine assimilation rates decrease from a peak at 200mm depth of 2.00 µmol g-1 h-1, to 0.60 µmol g-1 h-1 (at 300mm depth) and 0.10 µmol g-1 h-1 (at 350mm depth).

Biolog ecomicroplates

The results obtained from both cores generally indicated that the microbial communities present at all depths (horizontally into the mound) were able to metabolise the substrates provided. Figures 5.14a and 5.14b, showing carbon source utilisation at 350mm, are included here as examples (the full data set is available in Smith forthcoming).

Total Viable Counts

Table 5.5 shows the variation in aerobic and anaerobic bacterial cell numbers at different (horizontal) depth intervals in Cores <9444> and <9447>. Comparison of Total Aerobic Viable Counts (TAeVC) and Total Anaerobic Viable Counts (TAnVC) show that there are a greater number of aerobic bacteria present through the profile of both cores than anaerobic bacteria. The results also show that there are more aerobic and anaerobic bacteria in Core <9444> than in Core <9447>. Furthermore, in general terms, the numbers of aerobic and anaerobic bacteria present in Core <9444> tend to increase as depth increases, whereas in Core <9447> this trend is not evident (particularly in respect of the higher numbers of bacteria at 20mm and 300mm depths, in relation to the remaining depths in the core).

Culturing/gram staining

Table 5.6 shows the descriptions of bacterial population types obtained from a variety of different depth intervals in Cores <9444> and <9447>. Identification of each bacterial species is determined by the colony morphological characteristics outlined in the table. Out of the 13 bacterial colonies that were cultured and gram stained, five colonies were representative of the

Table 5.5: Total Aerobic and Anaerobic Viable Counts from sediments samples obtained from Cores 9444 and 9447

Core 9444 (depth in mm)	Aerobic TVC	Anaerobic TVC
50	5.1×10⁷	1.6×10⁴
100	7.2×10⁷	1.2×10⁴
200	7.9×10⁷	6.1×10⁴
300	8.0×10⁷	5.0×10⁴
350	7.7×10⁷	5.0×10⁴

Core 9447 (depth in mm)	Aerobic TVC	Anaerobic TVC
50	2.0×10⁷	70
100	5.6×10⁷	3.0×10³
200	5.0×10⁷	3.0×10³
300	1.9×10⁷	<10
350	4.3×10⁷	<10

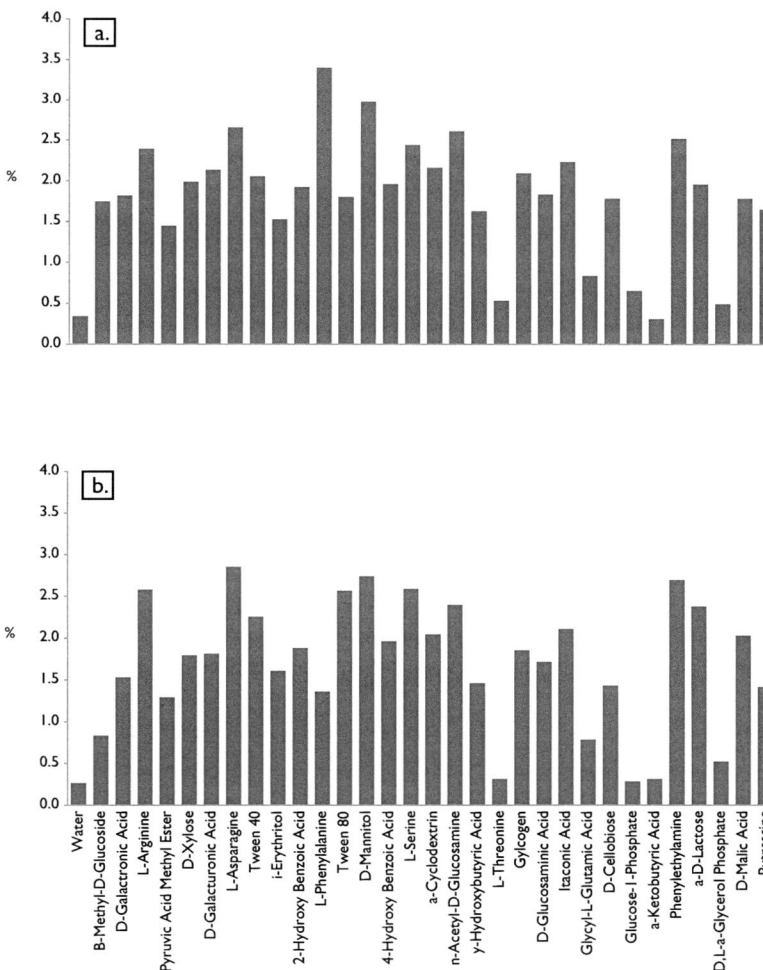

a.

b.

*Fig 5.14
Carbon source utilisation by the soil microbial community from
a) Core 9444 at 350mm depth,
b) Core 9447 at 350mm depth).
(Eddie Lyons, © English Heritage) (data from Lillie et al forthcoming)*

gram negative rod species of bacteria, five colonies represented gram positive cocci bacteria, whilst the remaining three colonies were indicative of moulds.

Table 5.6: Bacterial population types obtained from Cores 9444 and 9447

Colony Morphology	Bacterial Species
Yellow, round, entire, shiny, flat	Gram positive cocci
Cream, round, entire, mucoid, raised	Gram negative rod
Cream, umbonate, dry, raised	Mould species
Cream, round, entire, shiny, raised	Gram negative rod
Cream, round, entire, shiny, raised	Gram positive cocci
Cream, round, entire, dry, umbonate	Gram positive cocci
Pinky white, round, entire, umbonate	Gram negative rod
Cream, round, entire, dry, umbonate	Gram positive cocci
Cream, round, entire, mucoid, flat	Gram negative rod
White, umbonate, dry, raised	Mould species
Yellow, round, entire, mucoid, flat	Gram negative rod
Yellow, irregular, flat	Gram positive cocci
Pink, irregular, flat	Mould species

* Note – it was not possible to gram stain bacterial colonies present in each of the sediment samples in Cores 9444 and 9447 due to the lack of suitable species for culturing. As a consequence, the bacterial colonies displayed above can only be used as general indicators of the types of bacteria that are present within the sediment of Silbury Hill

Discussion

Although the findings highlighted above indicate that bacterial abundance increases with depth, and that this abundance differs between the locations of Cores <9444> and <9447>, not only are the abundance of bacteria in the samples obtained from both cores low (when compared to standard soils and peat where measurements of c 10 x 109 cells g-1 fresh weight are in evidence (Douterelo-Soler 2007; Lillie and Smith 2008), but there is little variation in abundance throughout the profile of both cores.

The number of aerobes present in both cores (at all depths) is greater than the number of anaerobes. Due to the very compact and highly anaerobic nature of the sediment prior to excavations at Silbury Hill, it is suggested that (over time) changes in environmental variables (such as temperature, moisture content, redox potential, pH and so on) associated with the past and current archaeological investigations may have increased the numbers of aerobic bacteria in some of the sediment samples. As a consequence, it is possible that these environmental perturbations may have also reduced the number of anaerobic bacteria present in the sediment samples in both cores.

The results of extracellular enzyme activity measurements and ^{14}C-leucine assimilation indicate that bacterial production is low throughout the profiles of both cores. The

contrasting leucine aminopeptidase values in evidence between the cores suggest that changes within the physical composition of the sediment matrix (that is clays, sands and so forth) are in evidence. It is proposed that these physical changes are related to the original anthropogenic deposition of the sediment and are not due to environmental perturbations occurring as a result of past archaeological interventions.

The observations from the Biolog analysis of the sediment samples obtained from Cores <9444> and <9447> also demonstrate that there are low levels of metabolic activity within the bacterial communities identified in all of the samples studied. The soil microbial communities utilised a number of carbohydrates (N-acetyl D glucosamine, D-cellobiose and D-mannitol), amino acids (L-asparagine, L-arginine and L-serine) and the amine, phenylethylamine, to a greater extent than other carbon sources, throughout the soil profiles. This patterning suggests that fast-growing microbes are responsible for the utilisation of the more easily available substrates (carbohydrates, amino acids and amines) and therefore play an important role in community physiological profiles.

The results of the culturing and gram staining procedure have identified that both the gram negative rod and gram positive cocci bacterial species present within the sediment samples obtained from both cores are typical of those found in a variety of standard sediment/soil types. However, the moulds that were also identified within the sediment samples are likely to exist in locations where there is moisture and humidity. The presence of these microscopic fungi therefore indicate that the moisture content in the samples obtained from both cores has increased (which is probably indicative of either the past and/or recent archaeological interventions), consequently promoting the growth of these species.

Conclusions

When compared to standard soils and peat which contain bacterial numbers of c 10 x 109 cells g-1 fresh weight (Douterelo-Soler 2007; Lillie and Smith 2008), it is considered that the numbers of bacteria present within each core (and at all depths) are relatively low. There are a greater number of aerobic bacteria present through the profile of both cores than anaerobic bacteria, and very low bacterial activity occurs throughout the profile of both cores. Differences between the cores are probably attributable differences in the physical composition of the deposits sampled (for example, the percentage of organic matter). The gram negative rod and gram positive cocci bacterial species present are typical of those found in a variety of standard sediment/soil types. The presence of moulds suggests that moisture content in the deposits has increased (which is probably indicative of water ingress caused by incomplete back-filling of past archaeological interventions and by humidity increase resulting from the intervention in 2007/8) consequently promoting the growth of these species.

The bacterial abundance and activity in all the samples studied indicate a relatively low potential for the biological degradation of organic material. However, one must be aware that despite low levels of activity, the biological decay of organics can still occur in both oxidising and reducing environments (B Jordan 2001; Smith 2005; Smith and Lillie 2007), with further biodegradation possible where environmental conditions do not remain in stasis.

Understanding formation processes

Matthew Canti and Gill Campbell

A number of analyses were undertaken to answer questions concerning the nature of the deposits encountered during recording of the

tunnel sections in 2007/8. These were:

- the formation process of the OLS
- the origin of the Gravel Mound
- the nature of possible turf lines or topsoil bands seen in the tunnel sections
- the nature of the organic layer seen directly overlying the grey clay layer.

The main focus of this research was geoarchaeological analysis but some related archaeobotanical analysis was also undertaken. The following accounts provide a summary of the investigations carried out. A full account of the geoarchaeological analysis is given in Canti (2011) while further details of the archaeobotanical investigation are given in Campbell (2011).

The formation process of the Old Land Surface

Matt Canti

Throughout the tunnels, a relatively stone-free, dense grey layer formed the OLS, at the junction between the chalk overburden and the underlying clay-with-flints material (*see* Chapter 2, Phase 2; Figs 2.5 and 2.6; Foldout 1A–D). In particle size terms, this layer was mostly silty clay loam or silt loam texture, but the more informal and descriptive term 'grey clay layer' will be used throughout this discussion. The layer was as little as 30mm thick in some places (Fig 5.15) but tended to gradually thicken

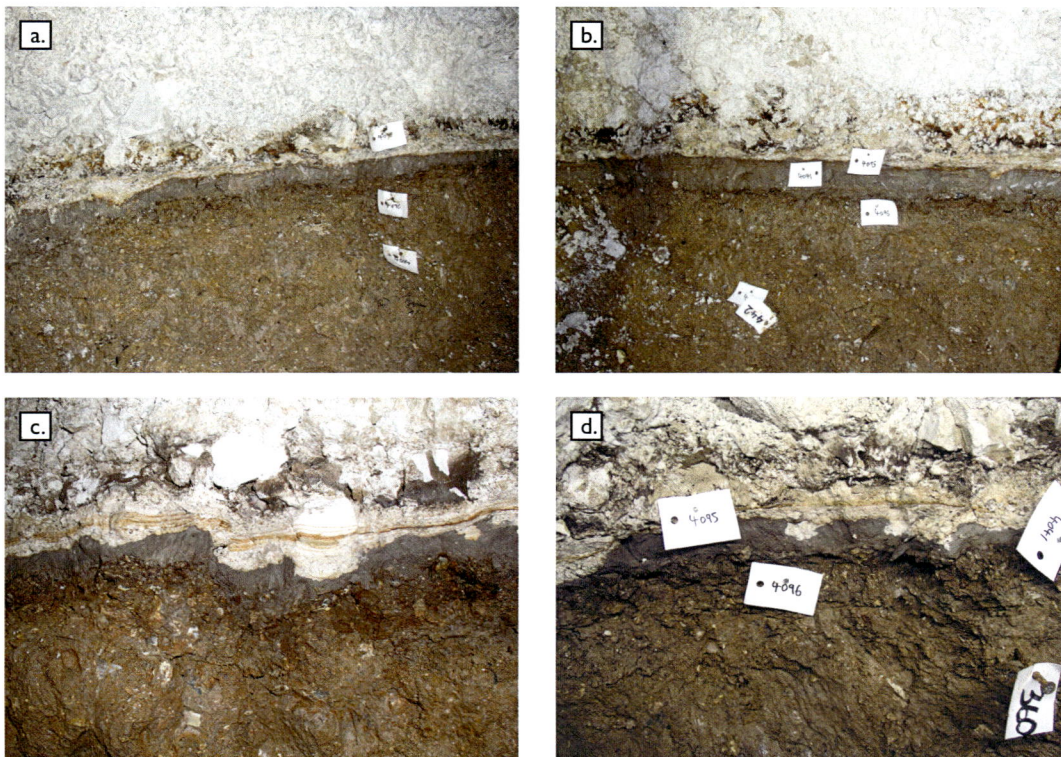

Fig 5.15
a, b) Thin examples of the grey clay layer at Bays 43 and 39;
c, d) Irregular upper surfaces of the grey clay layer around Bays 39–46.
(Photographs by Matt Canti, © English Heritage)

downhill (towards the centre of the mound) and was as much as 100mm thick in some locations. It mostly had a smooth interface with the chalk above it, but also sometimes showed irregular upper surfaces (Fig 5.15c and d).

The grey clay layer often had a sharp interface with the underlying clay-with-flints material, sometimes including a marked gravelly band. Variants on this basic morphology were found in the main tunnel exposures to the south and in the lateral tunnels. Towards the centre of the Hill, the grey layer was frequently less pronounced, and showed more gradual changes with depth.

In order to see comparative profiles, soils were examined on some low slopes of a nearby farm (North Farm, Overton), where unmapped shallow clay-with-flints material frequently forms the subsoil. The profiles (Fig 5.16) generally showed between 150 and 250mm of stone-free silty clay loams over a stony clay loam subsoil which gradually merges into orange-brown clay-with-flints material at about 500mm depth. When considering these profiles as analogues for the pre-construction soil on the Silbury spur, we must allow for 4,000 years less soil development, and for colluvial accumulations on the modern soils. These variations probably allow enough uncertainty to explain the deeper, less distinct examples of the OLS as complete or near-complete buried soils. However, even with fairly generous assumptions, it cannot be argued that the thinner layers of grey clay such as can be seen on Figure 5.15 could simply be a compressed version of these types of soils.

Hypotheses to explain these more extreme examples can be grouped into two categories:
1) The Silbury spur had soil cover similar to those in Figure 5.16. A large proportion was removed and subsequent human activity or erosion produced the stony layer and the grey silty layer by processes as yet unknown.
2) The Silbury spur had a different soil cover to the profiles in Figure 5.16. Instead, it had areas of intensely worm-sorted topsoil with a stone layer sitting almost on the subsoil interface. The worm-sorted topsoil was partially removed during construction, leaving the remainder to become the grey layer on compression (Rimmer 2007).

Sampling

Sampling for scientific tests on the OLS was carried out at 14 locations along the whole length of the tunnels (Fig 5.17). Each sample location consisted of matched Kubiena tins (for micromorphology) and bulk samples of the whole stratigraphy. The possibility of alluvium being actively placed on the clay-with-flints material (to create the grey clay layer) was also considered, and four samples of the alluvium from 200mm depth around Silbury were collected (see Canti 2011). Although the modern alluvium is thought to be post-medieval (Evans et al 1993), it is unlikely that there would be radical differences between these samples and the alluvium present when Silbury was being built, because of the similarities of source geology.

Particle size analysis

Particle size analysis was carried out on all the grey clay layer and clay-with-flints samples from each sample location and the four alluvial samples. The results are presented on Fig 5.18.

Fig 5.16
Soil profiles on derived clay-with-flints from North Farm, Overton, 3 km east of Silbury Hill. Profiles b and c were on slopes; a was on an interfluve.
(Matt Canti,
© English Heritage)

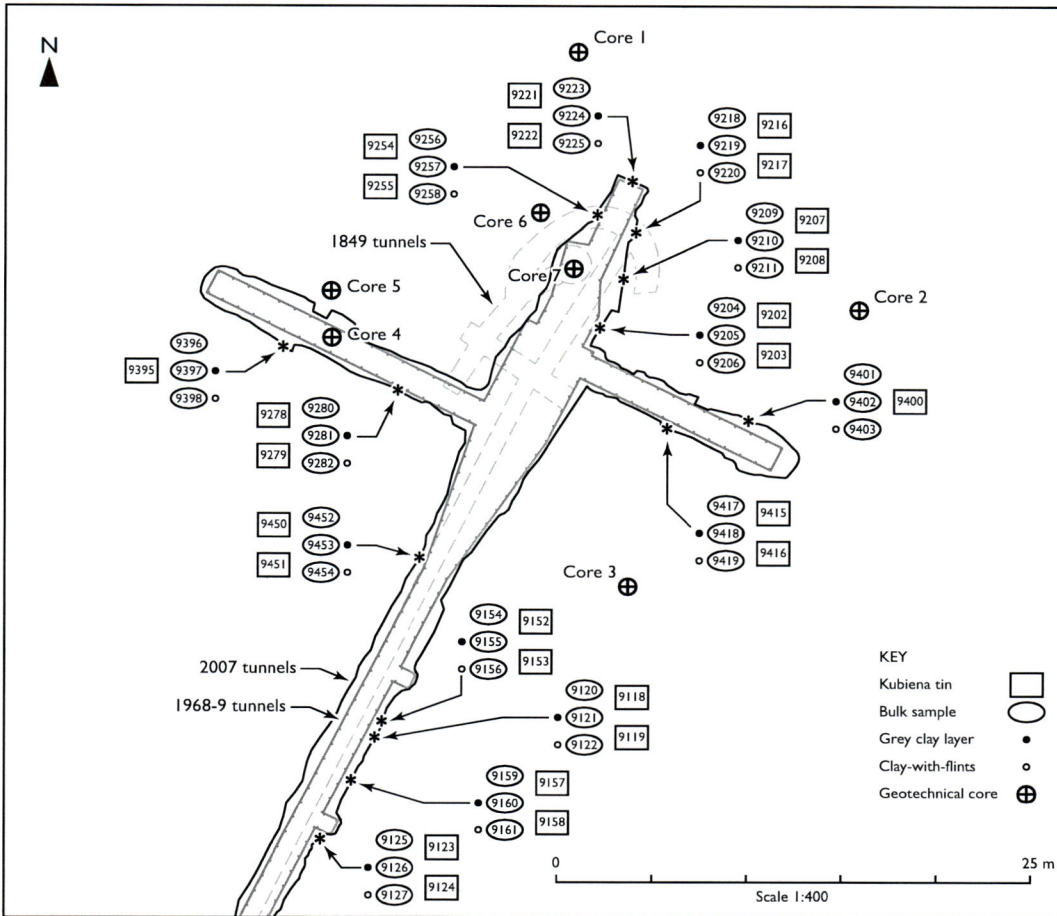

Fig 5.17
Tunnel plan showing all 14 locations where sample groups were taken of the OLS and the locations of Cores 1 to 6 taken as part of the seismic tomographic survey. (Eddie Lyons, © English Heritage)

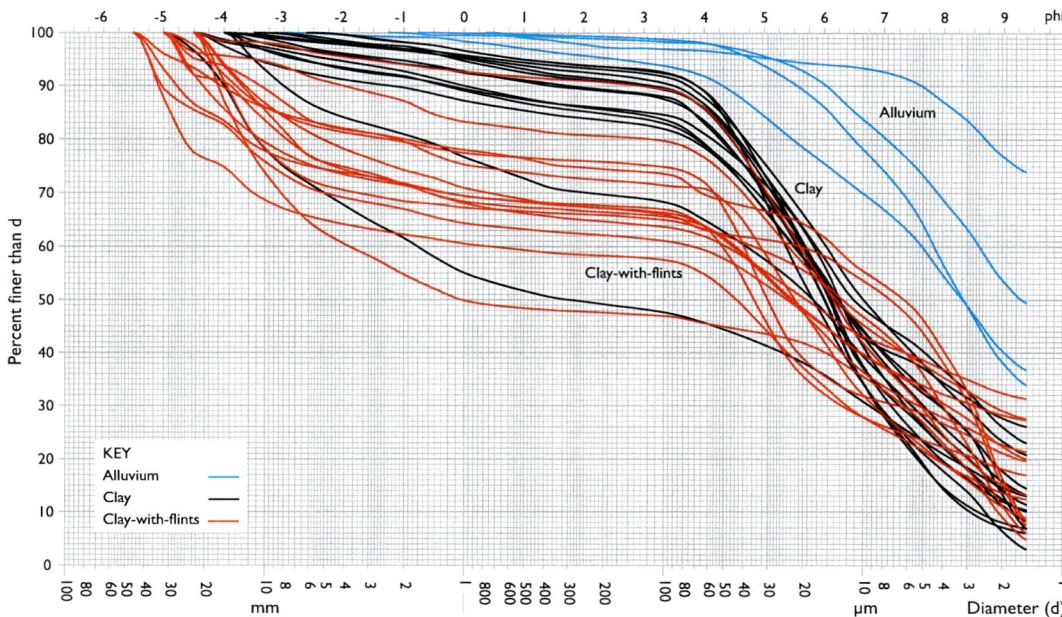

Fig 5.18
Particle size analyses of all samples of the (grey) clay layer, clay-with-flints material and alluvium. (Matt Canti and Eddie Lyons, © English Heritage)

It is immediately apparent that none of the curves are anything like the alluvium. In addition, microscopic analysis of the silt fraction showed the alluvium to consist of large amounts of calcite (in addition to the clay), whereas the grey clay layer's silt fraction is formed mostly of quartz. Alluvium is therefore discounted as an origin for the grey clay layer.

The remaining curves show high variability in the coarse end of the spectrum, especially where large flints did or did not get included in the sample. These flints are essentially random contents of the clay-with-flints deposit, and do not have any implications for Holocene processes. If we examine the <2mm curves, there is still wide variation (see Canti 2011), but the main difference is that the clay (<2µm) content of the grey layer is generally lower than the clay-with-flints material, and the silt content is higher. This can be seen clearly in Figure 5.19 where the mean particle size analysis of the two types of deposit is plotted on one diagram.

Using these mean values, we can say that, roughly speaking, the grey clay layer could be derived from the clay-with-flints material if most of the stones larger than 2mm were removed, and the clay content was reduced by 10 per cent.

Micromorphology

All of the Kubiena tins were impregnated with Crystic resin. Slides were then cut from all of the grey clay layer samples and a few of the underlying clay-with-flints samples. The clay-with-flints slides did not provide any useful information, so only the grey clay layer samples were studied. An account of all the samples analysed can be found in Canti (2011), but for the purposes of this volume, only a summary is presented below.

The micromorphology showed a range of staining, panning and layering events within the grey clay layer at Silbury. Iron and manganese pans are found both above the OLS (in the chalk overburden) and within the grey clay layer suggesting that the panning is a largely post-depositional process.

Some slides showed distinct remains of plant matter mainly near the top of the grey clay layer (see below Main Tunnel Bay 43E, <9157>), but also within more complex perhaps multiple accretion events (see below West Lateral Bay 5S, <9278>). Others show a uniform grey clay layer containing no features other than faint iron/manganese pans (see below Main Tunnel Bay 39E, <9123>).

Main Tunnel Bay 43E, <9157>

Figure 5.20 shows the sample in the tunnel wall and the whole slide produced from it. A clear example of the thin grey clay layer is present in the section and both the top and bottom of this layer are contained within the slide of <9157>.

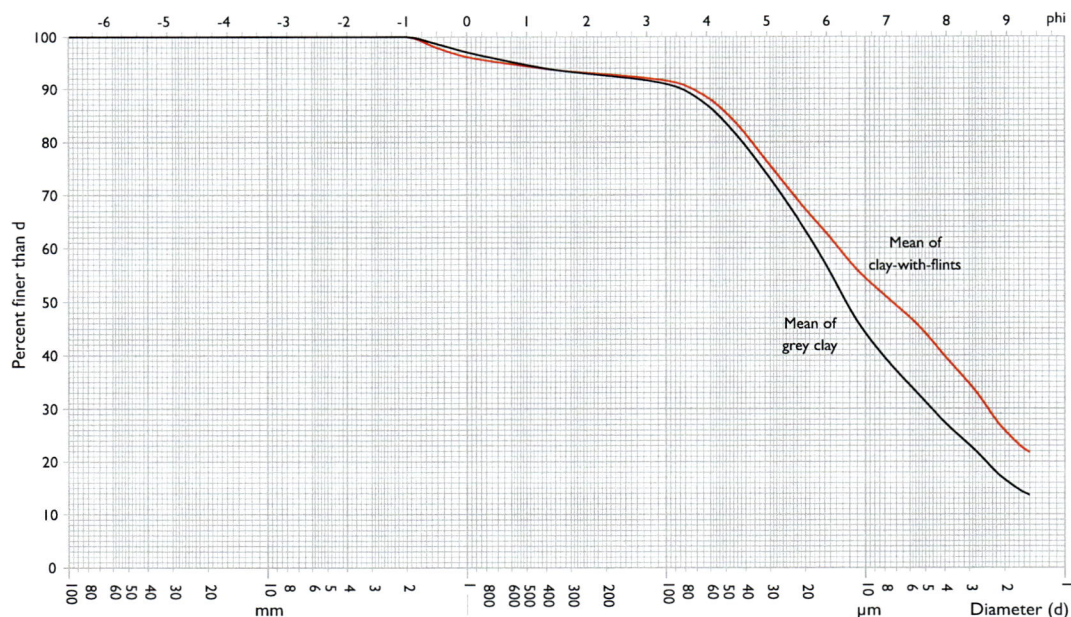

Fig 5.19
Mean particle size analyses of <2 mm fraction of the grey clay layer and the derived clay-with-flints. (Matt Canti and Eddie Lyons, © English Heritage)

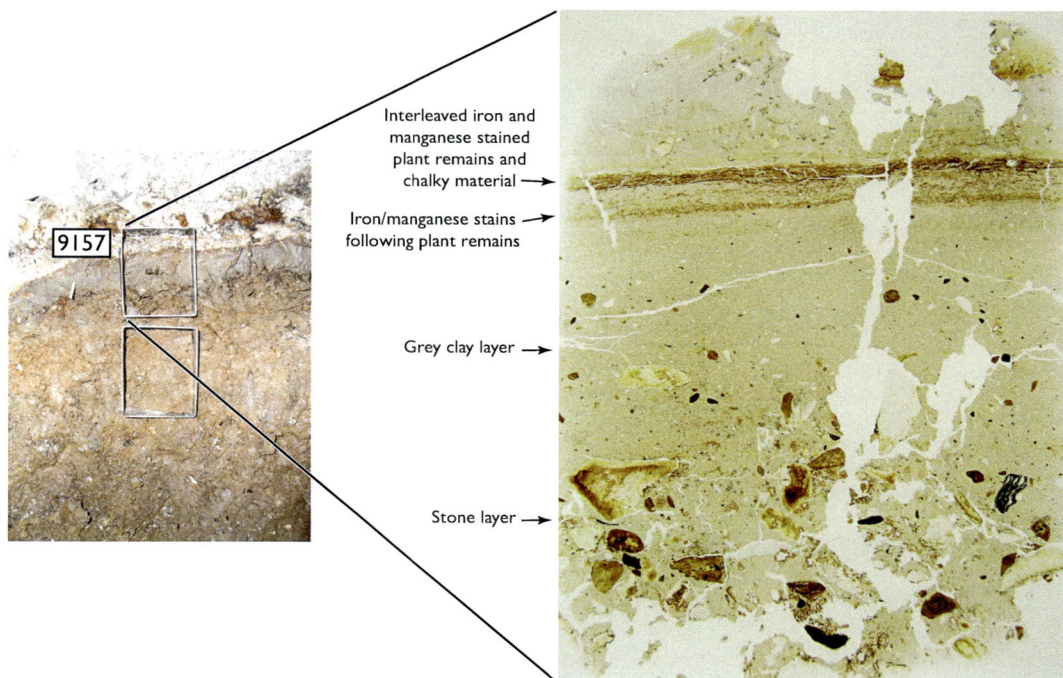

Fig 5.20
Sampling point and whole
slide of <9157>.
(Matt Canti
and Eddie Lyons,
© English Heritage)

Interleaved iron and
manganese stained
plant remains and
chalky material →

Iron/manganese stains →
following plant remains

Grey clay layer →

Stone layer →

The grey clay layer is about 35mm thick and sits on a pronounced stone band. The topmost part of the grey clay layer is characterised by a clear double line of iron staining. The upper line is about 1–2mm thick and can be seen close-up to be composed of many fine lines and lenses of iron, giving the strong impression of multiple layers of impregnated plant matter (Fig 5.21). Between these layers there are bands of chalk fines. The lower line is more diffuse and is made up of organic-stained matrix material rather than individual lines.

Fig 5.21
Close up of the top of the
OLS in <9157> showing
the thick upper line of iron
staining clearly made up
of individual iron/organic
matter lines or lenses and
the less pronounced lower
line made up of organic
matter impregnating
the matrix
(cross-polarised light).
(Matt Canti,
© English Heritage)

West Lateral Bay 5S, <9278>

This sampling point has a deep layer of mixed dark materials in the upper half of the slide, including topsoil, chalk fragments and clay-with-flints material (Fig 5.22). Bedded plant matter is evident in the lower middle of the slide corresponding to the darkest line on the field photo, and occasionally below it. This profile must, therefore, have more than one accretion event represented in the slides, and cannot simply be a compressed whole soil because of the topsoil band going through the middle (Fig 5.23). However, the lower third of <9278> and top of <9279> could be a truncated clay-with-flints profile.

Fig 5.22
Sampling point and whole slide of <9278>.
(Matt Canti and Eddie Lyons, © English Heritage)

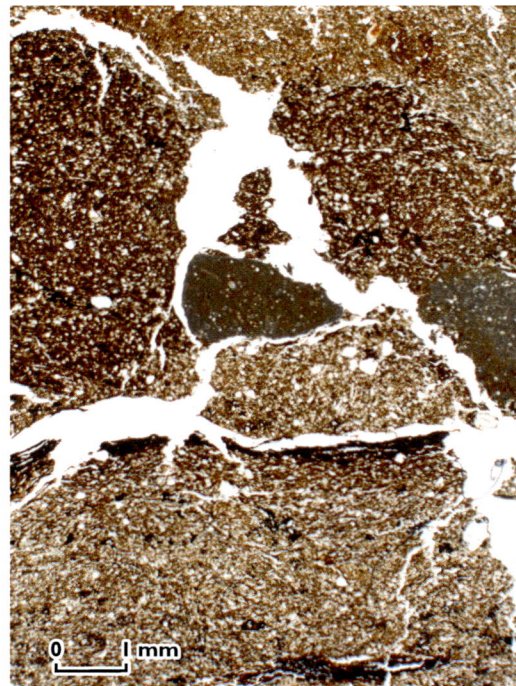

Fig 5.23
Close up of <9278> showing topsoil and chalk in the grey clay layer (plane polarised light).
(Matt Canti, © English Heritage)

Main Tunnel Bay 39E, <9123>

At this location (*see* Fig 5.17), the grey clay layer is between 20 and 35mm thick, and situated on a distinct band of large flints, all contained within the slide. The top of the OLS is marked by distinct panning in the chalk overburden (Fig 5.24), occasionally interleaved with iron and manganese stained plant remains. Otherwise, the grey clay layer is notably clean and uniform, showing no banding or iron deposition in its lower parts (Fig 5.25).

Evidence from the cores retrieved as part of the seismic topographic survey

As part of the seismic tomographic surveys carried out between 2000 and 2003, seven boreholes were drilled from the top of Silbury Hill through to the solid geology (Figs 5.17 and 2.1; Chapter 10; Skanska 2001b; 2003). The cores recovered as part of this survey work are the only information we have on the OLS outside

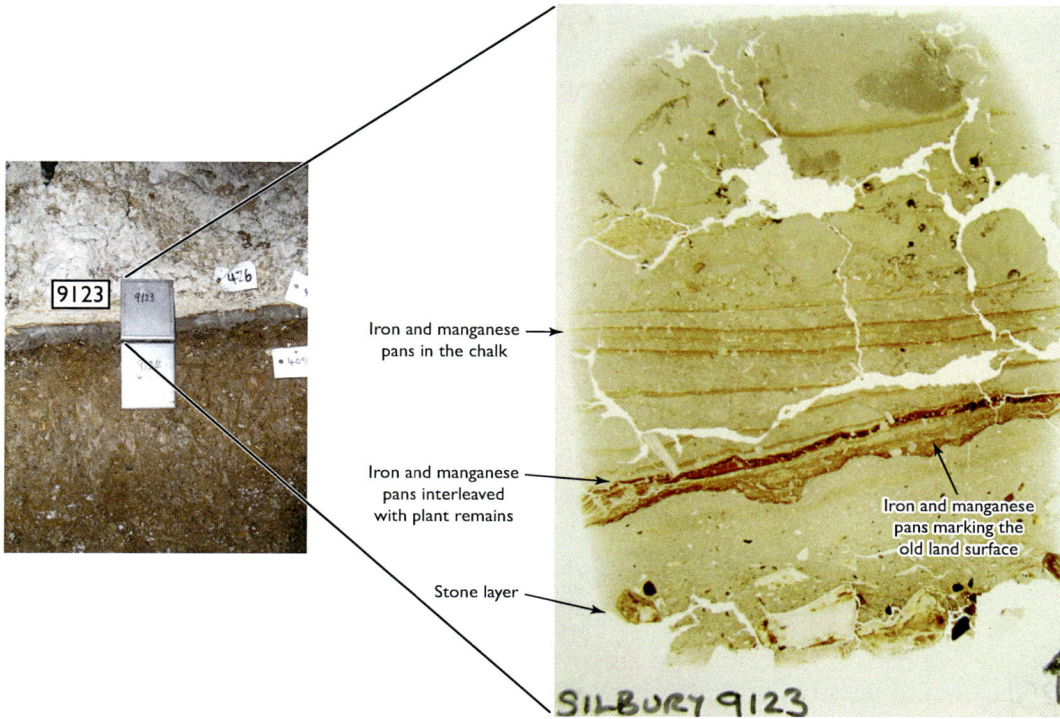

Fig 5.24
Sampling point and whole
slide of <9123>.
(Matt Canti
and Eddie Lyons,
© English Heritage)

Iron and manganese
pans in the chalk

Iron and manganese
pans interleaved
with plant remains

Iron and manganese
pans marking the
old land surface

Stone layer

SILBURY 9123

0   1 mm

Fig 5.25
Close up of <9123>
showing the clean, almost
uniform grey clay layer,
beneath iron stained chalk
(cross polarised light).
(Matt Canti,
© English Heritage)

the area sampled during the tunnel excavations.

Core 7 was drilled through the backfill of the 1776 shaft and is therefore not relevant to this study. Figure 5.26 shows the OLS portions of the remainder (Cores 1–6). Close examination reveals the following characteristics:

Core 1: An OLS is present (156.25–156.30m OD) consisting of a grey clay layer resting on clay-with-flints material, as found in the tunnels generally.

Core 2: There are no clear remnants of soil cover, but only a weakly organic top to a cut

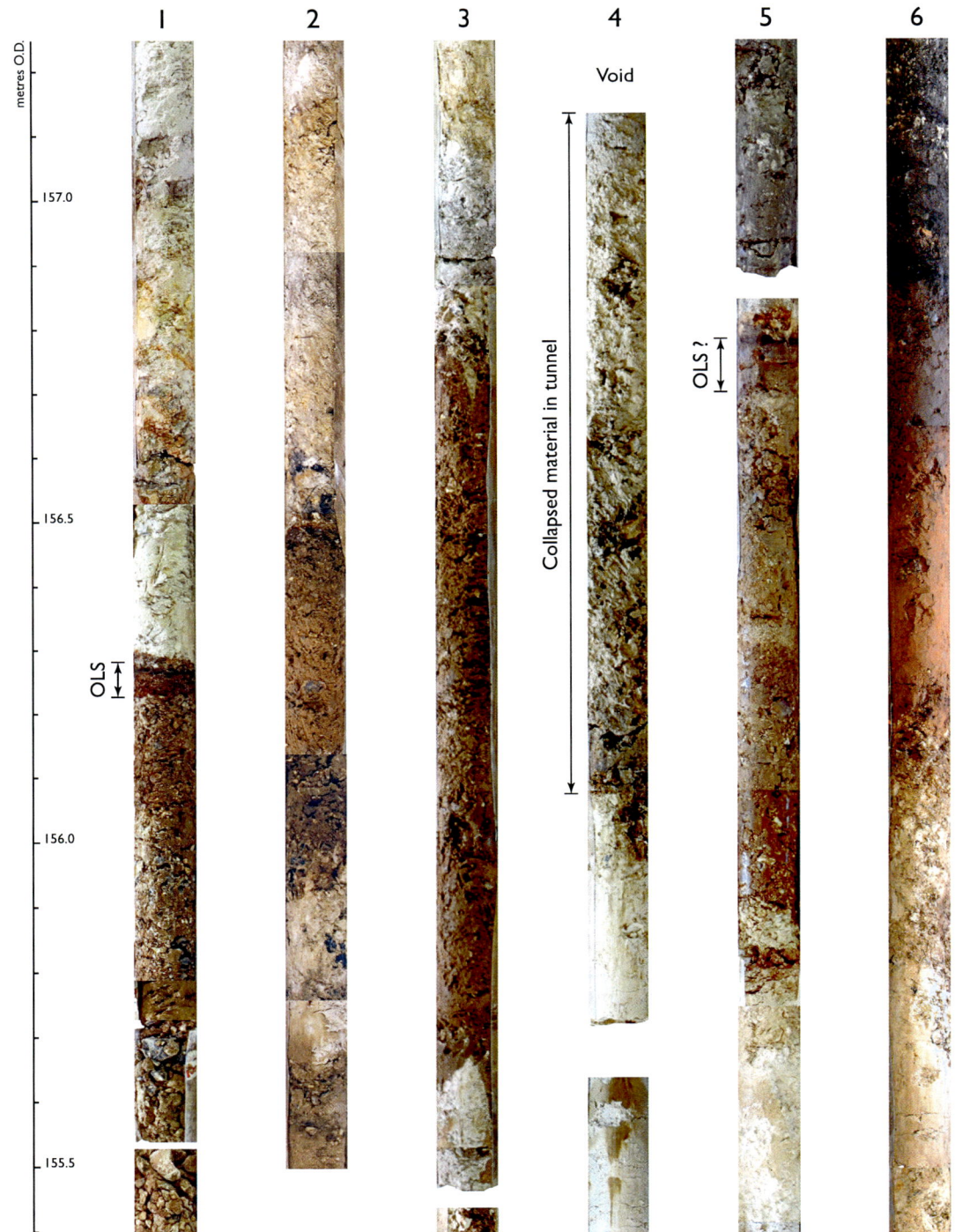

Fig 5.26
The OLS portions
of Cores 1–6.
(Eddie Lyons,
© English Heritage)

subsoil surface beneath the chalk base of the Hill at 156.45–156.50m OD.

Core 3: Core 3 contains no true OLS. There is a contaminated (probably trampled) cut subsoil surface at 156.80–156.85m OD.

Core 4: Core 4 was drilled through a void in the tunnel fills.

Core 5: Core 5 contains a grey clay layer at 156.70–156.80m OD that is broadly similar to the OLS exposures in the tunnels.

Core 6: Core 6 is atypical because the clay-with-flints type layer (156.64m downwards) is represented by unusually pure clay with very low stone content. Over that is about 200mm of brown soil that could be the topsoil of an *in situ* soil profile formed over this clay, but could also be a turf deposited on the OLS.

Summary of evidence from the cores

From the cores, we can therefore conclude that to the north of the Main Tunnel end wall, the OLS continues for at least 10 metres with the same characteristics as were found in the tunnels. However, to the east, judging by Cores 2 and 3, there was a tendency for the whole soil profile to be stripped before the main chalk Hill was thrown up.

Discussion

The two hypotheses put forward to explain the state of the OLS were first that a large proportion of a natural profile like those in Figure 5.16 had been removed and subsequent human activity or erosion had produced the stony layer and the grey silty layer; or second that the Silbury spur had areas of intensely worm-sorted topsoil with a stone layer sitting almost on the subsoil interface. The worm-sorted topsoil was partially removed during construction, leaving the remainder to become the grey layer on compression.

The first of these hypotheses would obviously require a very effective soil-removing process to have been at work on the land surface, probably before Silbury Hill was built. A significant point in its favour was the fact that Cores 2 and 3 contained no soil layer at all (*see above* 'Evidence from the cores'), suggesting that the whole soil profile (but not all the underlying clay-with-flints material) had been removed at least from parts of the eastern side prior to construction of the Hill. Of incidental interest is that this could tally well with the fact that two ceramic types (Windmill Hill and Peterborough ware) from

nearby sites (Avebury and West Overton respectively) show features consistent with being manufactured from clay-with-flints material (White and Canti 2011). Areas could have been stripped of their soil profile, which was used for ceramic manufacture. If this was the case, then the formation of the stone layer could perhaps occur relatively simply as a product of erosion removing the finer material from an exposed clay-with-flints type subsoil surface.

However, continuing with the first hypothesis, it is the creation of the grey clay layer which is the most difficult to substantiate. The idea of alluvium being emplaced or even deposited somehow was rejected on particle size and mineralogical grounds (*see above*, 'Particle size'). The particular characteristics of the thinnest examples of the grey clay layer led to the suggestion that they might represent the result of trampling. Extensive trampling could have occurred before the Hill was built, and must have occurred as part of the mound building process, but its effect on clay-with-flints material was not easy to predict.

Consequently an experiment to test the idea was set up at North Farm during 2008–9 (Project 5689). An area of Clay-with-flints on a similar slope to the Silbury OLS (3.2–4.7°) was variably stripped either close, or right down to the subsoil, and then trampled either with or without watering. Once a muddy mass was made on the surface, it was generally observed that footfalls tended to push down or suck up the whole subsoil mass including its stone content, rather than preferentially favouring a particular size grade. Although a layer with no visible stones was produced quite quickly subsequent rainfall revealed the stone content just beneath the surface. No hint of real stone sorting or production of a stoneless layer was found after around six hours trampling (around three hours each under different moisture conditions, watered and unwatered), and it was concluded that this was not a possible mechanism.

Although a number of interesting possibilities have emerged from the study, the difficulty of recreating the grey clay layer means that the second hypothesis, that is, that the stone layer and grey clay layer represent a truncated earthworm sorted profile, is currently the only feasible possibility. This was the conclusion of the excellent study by Rimmer (2007). Earthworm action is capable of deep sorting (*see*, for example, Canti 2003, fig 7), and in this instance a fairly intense example would be needed. Although the process is commonly associated with more calcareous soils than those found on clay-with-flints material, these soils may have been more calcareous in the past due to a probable loess content (*see* John Catt's analysis in Cornwall *et al* 1997). Furthermore, the unusual lowland position of the Silbury deposit and possible calcareous inputs from upslope could perhaps overcome any inhibition due to acidity.

In this scenario, the Silbury builders would, therefore, have found a strongly sorted topsoil and de-turfed it, perhaps to provide material for the organic mound. They cut well above the stone layer in many cases producing the OLS examples with a deeper grey clay layer. Towards the south, perhaps stimulated by the increasing distance from the turf stack, they tended to go deeper and arrived at just 20 or 30mm above the stone layer, producing the profiles seen in Figure 5.15c and d. The greyness of the grey clay layer would arise from reduction of the organic matter still left in the earthworm casts rendering the iron compounds soluble.

It seems likely, based on this view, that the grey clay has not generally undergone a complex depositional history, but shows horizontal bands due either to trampling at the surface which had the effect of producing layers of plant matter interleaved with grey clay or with chalk (for example, <9157>), or simply to iron/manganese panning which tends to be roughly horizontal. It also possible that some of the layers of plant material could derive from cut vegetation laid on the surface (*see below* and Appendix 5.1).

Assuming that the de-turfing exercise generally produced the material for the Lower Organic Mound, then the thinner parts of the grey layer under the Gravel Mound would have to be a product of earlier de-turfing or erosion. Whatever the source of the Gravel Mound material, there could not therefore be a simple planned concentric building exercise placing a Gravel Mound straight on to the just de-turfed OLS. Possible explanations would be that de-turfing had additional significance for the Silbury builders, or that the early phases developed slowly without a clear plan. We cannot really answer such questions without knowing the general layout of the gravel and organic mounds in the unexcavated northern sector of the Hill.

The origin of the Gravel Mound

Matt Canti

Although the Gravel Mound material could simply be one deposit found in the valley and transported to the site, the possibility exists that it was produced by human action deliberately sorting the stones from the clay-with-flints type soil then dumping them on the mound either deliberately or as discard as part of some other process.

This hypothesis was not formulated during the fieldwork, so only a single large sample of the Gravel Mound was available to work with. However, five large samples of the clay-with-flints material had been taken, and these provide a good basis for the comparison with the Gravel Mound. Both the clay-with-flints material and the Gravel Mound samples were subjected to complete particle size analysis (*see* Canti 2011), and a relatively simple sorting, settling or picking type of operation could be shown to transform the clay-with-flints material into the Gravel Mound curve by retaining the coarser components. By trial and error, the best fit realistic sorting process has been established as:

Retain 100% of clay-with-flints material > 8mm

Retain 75% of clay-with-flints material 8mm–4mm

Retain 50% of clay-with-flints material 4mm–2mm

Retain 25% of clay-with-flints material < 2mm

We should, of course, ask how practical such an operation would be for people without metal. Although a rudimentary 8mm sieve could perhaps be constructed from straight stem wood (for example withies), it would be short-lived with the friction from all the flints. Alternatively a thick clay slip could be either settled or fished by hand to produce a similar crude sorting result.

It must be reiterated that the Silbury builders could have found a natural gravel deposit in the valley (perhaps from the river bed or from seasonal streams) that had similar particle size characteristics because it was itself partially derived from eroded clay-with-flints material. However, the mollusc assemblage (*see* Chapter 6; Davies 2012) does not contain any wetland or slum species as would be the case if it had been collected from an existing stream bed, so an exposure of gravel resulting from erosion (such as severe storms) seems more likely.

The nature of possible turf lines or topsoil bands seen in the tunnel sections

Matt Canti and Gill Campbell

In the Main Tunnel, a dark layer ([3068], [3069] not shown, [4154] and [4166]) was identified overlying the top of the Gravel Mound (Fig 2.7 and Foldout 1A and B). In the field it was thought that this layer might result from a brief period of *in situ* soil development, or be made up of laid turves or other imported material. A micromorphology sample (<9249>) and a General Biological Analysis (GBA) sample (<9252> sub-sample <9280>) were taken across this layer from the east section at Bay 77 to help resolve this issue.

Both the macro-scale view of the thin section slide and also the microscopic detail (*see* Canti 2011) show that the dark line of soil material is a mix of topsoil, chalk and flints without any size grading of aggregates or other process features (for example burrows, pore-fillings) which would indicate soil *in situ*. In addition the GBA sample contained a reasonable sized assemblage of well-preserved biological remains in contrast to the gravel mound itself which produced very few remains other than molluscs (*see* Chapter 6; Campbell 2011; Davies 2012; Robinson 2011). It is therefore concluded that this is a dumped layer, consisting of a mixture of turf, topsoil and some subsoil.

In the East Lateral another dark band was recorded ([4169], Foldout 1C) which could perhaps have been an intact soil developed over the Upper Organic Mound/further dump layers or possibly a layer of inverted turves. A pair of Kubiena samples was taken across the feature, from the north section within Bay 11, to try and answer this question (*see* Canti 2011). The dark soil was entirely made of a mixture of topsoil material and lumps of chalky subsoil. These are randomly mixed and show no grading of one material into another, nor size grading as would be expected from surface processes. It is therefore concluded that the material is not an intact soil surface or turf line.

Similar lenses or layers of darker silty clay material [3084] were seen within the further dump layers in the West Lateral. A single GBA sample (<9320>, sub-sample <9822>) was analysed from a dark grey band within layer [3084] from the north section of Bay 13 (*see* Foldout 1C). A mixture of turf, topsoil and some subsoil was suggested for the few remains recorded with the molluscan assemblage indicating shaded conditions, while in contrast the insect and plant remains were typical of grassland (*see* Chapter 6; Campbell 2011).

The dark layer [4166], which overlies the slopes of the Gravel Mound but is absent from its flat top would appear to have been laid down as a means of consolidating the sides of the structure as part the construction process. The dark bands and lenses observed within the later phases of construction may well have served a similar purpose. This seems to have been carried out as and when required to help stabilise sloping ground. These layers may also mark temporary routes lost once covered by further tipping events.

The nature of the organic layer above the grey clay layer of the OLS

Gill Campbell

Within the earlier phases of the monument the OLS was an organic dark layer [3035] and [4100] overlying the grey clay layer. It was unclear, however, whether this dark band was derived from *in situ* turf, pieces of turf laid green face down on a ground surface that was stripped of vegetation or whether the layer might represent cut vegetation placed on a stripped ground surface with mound material then placed directly on this. Assessment of biological remains from the OLS suggested that vegetation or turf laid down on a stripped surface were the most likely explanations (*see* Campbell in Leary 2009). However in order to investigate this further an intact block of stratigraphy comprising part of the Upper Organic Mound, the OLS and the underlying clay-with-flints material was examined in detail.

Block Sample <9277>

<9277> was taken from material that had collapsed away from the south section of the West Lateral in Bay 12 (Foldout 1D). It contained a particularly thick dark band above the grey clay layer and there was also one recognisable turf within the mound deposits (Fig 5.27) which formed part of the block. The sample therefore seemed a good candidate with which to undertake an investigation into the nature of the

Fig 5.27
Photographs of block sample
before the removal of each
sub-sample.
(Eddie Lyons,
© English Heritage)

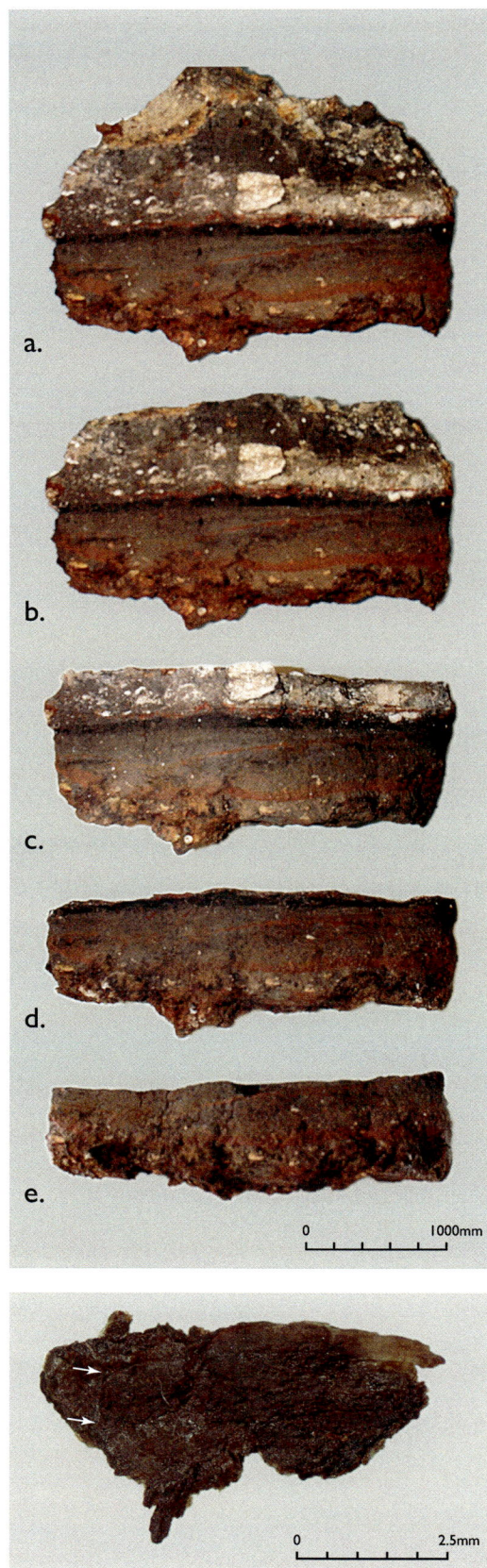

a.

b.

c.

d.

e.

0   1000mm

Fig 5.28
The cut ends of the
plant remains.
(Gill Campbell,
© English Heritage)

0   2.5mm

dark band. Sub-samples were taken from the block in turn, from every distinct deposit rather than at a given sample interval. In other words the top of the recognisable turf was sampled separately from its underlying topsoil; similarly, the dark band was sampled separately from the grey layer and the material directly above it. This resulted in a total of six sub-samples varying in size from 0.3 to 1 litre from the block (Fig 5.28). The sub-samples were processed in the same way as the other samples processed as part of the analysis phase (see Chapter 6 and Campbell 2011).

Results

The results of the archaeobotanical analysis are presented in Table 5.7. Further details are given in Campbell 2011. The first sub-sample <9829> was taken from the top part of the block following cleaning of the surface. It comprised approximately 100mm in depth (Fig 5.27a and b). Sampling stopped when a recognisable turf line was reached. This was not continuous across the whole width of the block and it is possible that more than one turf was sampled in the subsequent sub-sample <9380> (Fig 5.27b).

<9829> produced only a few plant remains, mainly grasses, a few fragments of *Sambucus nigra* (elder) comprising less than one seed, a rather degraded broken seed of *Ajuga reptans* (bugle), two fragmented seeds of *Polygonum aviculare* agg. (knotgrass), and a possible seed of the Caryophyllaceae family. Five *Cenococcum* sp. sclerotia were also recorded suggesting the presence of sods. The results are consistent with what might be expected from topsoil with a little turf included. The material was all very fragmented with the exception of the insects.

Sub-sample <9830> also produced a small assemblage. Roots and rhizomes formed the main component, but some grass remains and a single *Ranunculus* subgen *Ranunculus* (buttercup) achene were also found along with four *Cenococcum* sp. sclerotia. Fragments of elder seeds were slightly better represented in this sample. The results can be taken as indicative of turf, especially the many roots, although they do show that the number of species present, and preserved, in any one turf can be very low.

The next sub-sample from the block <9831> comprised mainly chalk rubble with some soil coming down onto the dark organic band immediately above the grey clay layer [3021], sampled as sub-sample <9832> (Fig 5.27c and d). <9831> produced slightly more in the way of

Table 5.7: Results of the analysis of block sample <9277>

		9829	9830	9831	9832	9833	9834
	Sample	9829	9830	9831	9832	9833	9834
	Sub-sample of	9277	9277	9277	9277	9277	9277
	Context number	3083/4	3083/4	3083/4	3087/9	3021	3020
	Context	UOM	UOM	UOM	OLS	OLS	Natural
	Volume in litres	0.30	0.40	0.55	0.30	1.00	0.65
	Weight in kg	0.563	0.778	0.949	0.306	1.046	0.682
	Phase	6.1/2	6.1/2	6.1/2	3	2	1
	Mesh size in microns	250	250	250	250	250	250
Taxon (element)	**Common name**						
Ranunculus cf. *acris* L.	Meadow buttercup				7		
R. cf. *repens* L.	Creeping buttercup				4		
R. cf. *bulbosus* L.	Bulbous buttercup				1		
Ranunculus acris/ repens/ bulbosus	Buttercup			2	21		
Ranunculus subgen *Ranunculus*	Buttercup			1	2		
Urtica dioica L.	Stinging nettle				2		
Corylus avellana L. (nutshell fragment)	Hazel					2c	
Stellaria graminea L.	Lesser stitchwort				5		
Caryophyllaceae indet.		(1)					
Polygonum aviculare agg.	Knotgrass	2					
Rubus sp.	Bramble, raspberry etc.			(1)			
Trifolium type (flower)	Clover type				4		
Trifolium type (calyx)	Clove type				1		
Ajuga reptans L.	Bugle	(1)					
Sambucus nigra L.	Elder	mni 1	mni 2	mni 1	mni 1[2]	mni 1[2]	mni 1
Cirsium sp.	Thistle				2		
Leontodon sp.	Hawkbit				2		
Carex sp.	Sedge			mni 1			
cf. *Poa annua* L.	Annual meadow-grass				1		
cf. *Bromus* sp.	Brome				1		
Poaceae indet.	Grass	1			4		
Poaceae indet. (culm node)		1	1		26		
Monocot stem/leaves		+	+	+	++++		
Dicot stem			+		+		
Indeterminate seed				1			
Inderminate root/rhizome		+ &1c	++++	++	+	1c	
IGNOTA					1	2	
Bone						+	+
Bud scales					1		
Cenococcum sp.		5	4	5		2	
Charcoal		+	+			++	++
Charcoal <2mm		+[1]	+	+		++	+
Earthworm egg		++	++	+			+
Earthworm granules							
Green plant		*	*	*	*		
Moss		+	+	++	+++		
Molluscs							
Chalk with lichen		2					
Insects +		+	+	++	++[3]		
frass					1		
Wood		+					
?Thyme leaves				*	*		

1 One tiny piece of conifer charcoal is present
9829 Very fragmentary material –apart from insects. Indet twig. Molluscs are notably absent
2 Only very tiny fragments
3 Lots of ?insect eggs

seeds than <9830>, with fewer grass remains although roots and rhizome fragments were frequent and *Cenococcum* sp. sclerotia were also present. The seeds recovered were generally in rather poor condition with the exception of two buttercup achenes which were somewhat better preserved.

Sub-sample <9832>, comprising the dark organic layer [3087/3089] (Fig 5.27d), produced by far the most material, as would be expected. Buttercup achenes were plentiful with three species being tentatively identified: *R. acris* (meadow buttercup), *R. repens* (creeping buttercup), and *R. bulbosus* (bulbous buttercup). Stems and leaves of monocotyledons were abundant, with grass culm nodes and caryopses well-represented along with *Trifolium* type (clover and the like) flowers and calyxes. Some of the stems appear to have been cut as they have very sharp flat ends (Fig 5.28). There were relatively few roots/ rhizomes and no *Cenococcum* sp. sclerotia. *Stellaria graminea* (lesser stitchwort), *Cirsium* sp. (thistle) and *Leontodon* sp. (hawkbit) seeds were also recorded along with very tiny fragments of elder seed. Insect eggs were frequent within the small insect assemblage and fragments of moss were common.

The results from this sub-sample indicate the presence of some turf with the possibility that this was augmented by material that was deliberately cut. This is suggested by the concentration of remains in comparison with the other recognisable turf (sub-sample <9829>) and the presence of cut stems.

Sub-sample <9833> was taken from the grey clay layer immediately beneath the dark organic band (Fig 5.27e shows the block before this was removed). This layer was approximately 100mm deep at this point. As can be seen from the results, roots and rhizomes were absent apart from one charred specimen. The other remains recovered were also charred apart from two *Cenococcum* sp. sclerotia and some very tiny elder seed fragments. These results strongly suggest that the dark band does not represent *in situ* turf developed on the truncated surface as more remains of roots and more seeds forming part of the soil seed bank would be expected. In other words the samples should be very similar to sub-samples <9829> and <9831>.

Having said this it is possible that the absence of material in this layer could be due to ingress of oxygen from below causing decay to occur. This seems unlikely, however, as one would expect this fine-grained, compacted layer to preserve material well if it was present in any quantity at the time of burial.

Sub-sample <9834> was taken from the flinty gravel and clay natural (Fig 5.27e). Remains were very sparse, as would be expected, with only elder seed fragments, charcoal and the occasional earthworm egg recovered.

Discussion

The results from the block sample <9277> show that there was no *in situ* turf developed on the OLS. This is supported by the results of the geoarchaeological analysis of the OLS (*see* Canti, this chapter) and by the results of the analysis of the GBA sample <9238> taken from underneath the Gravel Mound (*see* Chapter 6).

The presence of a dark organic band, even where no overlying turf and topsoil was present, such as below the Gravel Mound (Fig 2.6 in Chapter 2) shows that this band is not derived from turf laid face down on top of a ground surface stripped of vegetation but rather suggests that vegetation was deliberately laid on the stripped OLS prior to the gravel being placed on top of it. This is further suggested by the apparent cut ends of the grass remains seen in <9832> (*see* Fig 5.28) and as noted by Dimbleby and others (Gill Swanton, pers comm). The concentration of remains found in sub-sample <9832> is explained if a turf was placed vegetation face down on top of this laid vegetation producing an extra thick dark organic band at this point.

The laying of vegetation might be to do with the need to cut the taller vegetation from turf prior to harvesting (Ó Danachair 1957) and the production of a soft surface for construction. It might also have a ritual significance. For example, on 5 July (Old Midsummer Day) on the Isle of Man, the Tynwald (the Manx parliament) is held. The business of the day is preceded by a service in the local church of St John. The church, Tynwald Hill and the processional way linking the two are strewn with green rushes gathered from the nearby farm of Ballaleece. This resource was formerly provided by the farmer as his Lord's rent and is probably connected with a traditional tribute of rushes or green meadow grasses paid on this day to the guardian god of the island Mannanan-beg-mac-y-leir (Garrard 1984, 77; Moore 1891). The feast of St Bridget on 1 February is marked in a similar manner on the island. The floor of the house is swept clean and a symbolic carpet of rushes or straw placed on the floor before the Saint is invited in (Garrard 1984, 77).

Grass strewing and rush bearing ceremonies were commonly carried out in churches in England on the day the church was first dedicated. The old covering of rushes or grass on the floor of the church was replaced with new fresh material, usually involving some form of procession accompanied by dancing and merrymaking. Versions of the custom are still carried out in a few parishes. The strewing of hay is often carried out close to midsummer as it is associated with the hay harvest (Hole 1978, 259–61).

Conclusion

The results from the analysis of the block sample suggest that the laying down of vegetation on the OLS may have formed part of the construction process. The presence of laid vegetation and cut vegetation in addition to turves is also suggested by layers of plant matter found within the grey clay layer and from the analysis of the green plant material (*see* Appendix 5.1).

Concluding remarks

Studies undertaken on material retrieved from the end wall of the Main Tunnel showed that at this location within the tunnel preservation of delicate biological remains was good. However, it should be noted that the end section of the tunnel represented the limit of previous interventions and was far more compacted than either the end walls of the laterals or the tunnel sides as a whole. While in some of the plant materials examined cellular structure was preserved, green plant material, which was retrieved from this location, as well as that present in other contexts (*see also* Chapter 6) exhibited an unusual preservation. It lacked cellular structure with only part of the choroplasts remaining identifiable between thin cuticle-like layers. Couched woad (Appendix 5.1), out of a number of different materials examined, was found to bear the closest resemblance to this green plant material which superficially resembles grass. This suggests that the green plant material is the result of an unusual mode of preservation, although the exact mechanism remains unknown.

The preservation of cellular and ultrastructural detail was closely comparable in all samples indicating that the earlier interventions had not affected preservation at this location within the tunnels. While microbes were more abundant within the plant material than in the within the surrounding sediment, numbers were very low overall compared to standard soils and peats and there was very low bacteria activity. Aerobic bacteria were more abundant in the samples than anaerobic bacteria. This may be related to past and recent interventions, as may the presence of moulds. Variation within the different sub-samples taken from the cores retrieved from the end wall of the Main Tunnel location is likely to be attributed to varied nature of the sediments sampled rather than other factors.

There is evidence for the OLS being largely truncated under the mound as investigated in the tunnel sides and it seems that vegetation may have been placed on this stripped surface in at least some places. The most likely scenario is that prior to building the area was stripped of turf and that the stripped turf was incorporated into the mound. We cannot tell, however, from the small window that we have, whether one or more events was involved. It is probable that the material used to make up the Gravel Mound was derived from gravel exposed at the surface as a result of erosion, there remains the possibility that it results from human action. A stream bed source for the gravel is unlikely given the absence of slum or aquatic molluscs. No intact soils or turf layers were found to exist within the part of the Hill investigated. Rather these distinct organic layers consisted of a mixture of topsoil and subsoil. They appear to have been deliberately laid down as a way of consolidating the deposits beneath, for example to support the sides of the Gravel Mound.

Appendix 5.1

Further investigations of the green plant material

M Collinson, T Brain and G Campbell
There is much anecdotal evidence for the presence of 'grass that was still green' underneath Silbury Hill. The 2007/8 excavations recovered green plant material from Phases 4, 5, and 6.1 (*see* Chapter 6). No definite fragments were found in samples from the OLS but it is possible that some of the remains of vegetative matter evident in the thin sections prepared for the geoarchaeogical analysis represent this material (Canti 2011).

Fig A5.1.1 (top left)
Silbury green plant material
as it appears in situ on
surfaces as thin strands with
blue green to bottle green
colour (see also Fig 5.2c).
(Margaret Collinson ,
© English Heritage)

Fig A5.1.2 (left below)
Silbury green plant
(a) and green leaf
(b) from the Mini-mound
[4181], sample <9827>,
showing clear net venation
and margin with trichomes.
(Gill Campbell,
© English Heritage)

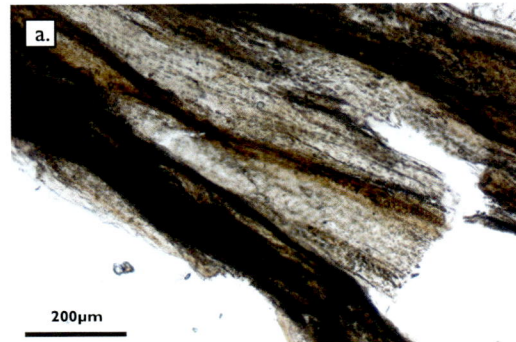

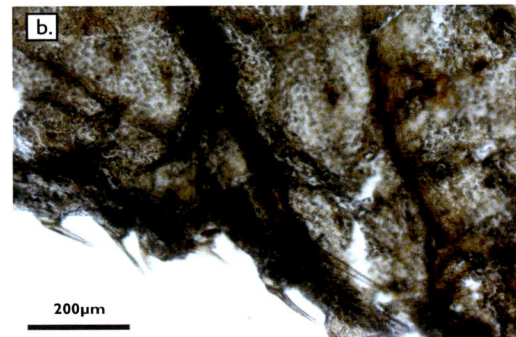

Fig A5.1.3 (far right top)
TEM showing typical
preservation of Silbury
green plant material
(see also Figs 5.3–5.5).
a) Section through a single
strand showing outer
membrane on each surface,
lack of cellular structure,
electron dense (dark)
granular bodies (degraded
plastids) and microbes (one
of which is labelled m);
b) thylakoid membranes
from chloroplasts.
(Margaret Collinson,
Tony Brain and Eddie Lyons,
© English Heritage)

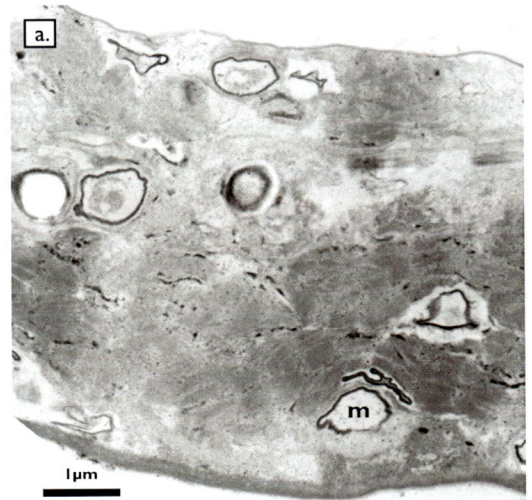

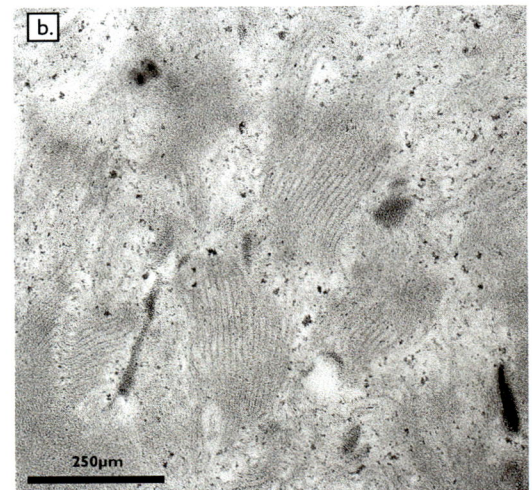

Fig A5.1.4 (far right)
A piece of Silbury yellow
plant material with
overlying green plant
material photographed after
storage in fixative. Most of
the green colour has been
lost leaving green plant
material as thin
membranous translucent
pale sheets or strands.
Brown patches are organic
rich sediment from which
the sample is derived.
(Margaret Collinson
and Eddie Lyons,
© English Heritage)

At low magnification this material resembles grass fragments (Fig A5.1.1), some with square ends as reported in Whittle (1997a, 140; see also Chapter 2). There were also rare occurrences of leaf fragments (Fig A5.1.2).

While remains of moss and leaves such as holly found in archaeological deposits can retain their colour, this is not usually the case for the vast majority of macroscopic plant remains. Furthermore ultrastructural investigation of this material by transmission electron microscopy (TEM) reveals that it totally lacks any cellular structure. Seen in TEM it consists of two thin outer membranes enclosing electron denser (darker in the image) granular bodies (Fig A5.1.3a) that contain portions of thylakoid membranes derived from chloroplasts (Fig A5.1.3b). After prolonged immersion in fixative some of the green colour is lost, indicating that it may be at least partly soluble. The material becomes semi-translucent and the thin, almost membraneous, nature is even more strikingly evident (Fig A5.1.4).

Given the unusual nature of this green plant material and that it often occurred as a thin surface layer of randomly orientated strands (500µm and up to 1mm wide and up to a few mm in length) within the deposits suggesting deposition by some agency, investigations were carried out to try and determine what it was and how the unusual preservation had come about. A number of possible sources were considered and comparative material selected to test these possibilities.

A full list of the comparative material examined is given in Table A5.1.1. Individual pieces of fresh, partially rotted, or fermented plant material were fixed and embedded for TEM as described by Collinson *et al* (main text; 2011a). Those from marine plants were briefly rinsed first to remove salt water. Fresh or dried vertebrate droppings were fixed and then teased apart so that individual plant fragments could be selected for embedding. Both opaque and translucent plant fragments were used. Slug faeces were fixed and embedded as complete entities.

Table A5.1.1: Comparative material used for investigating the green plant material

Comparative material	*Reasoning*
Rotted (composted) *Equisetum telmateia*	Dr Chris Page, an expert on pteridophytes, suggested this horsetail as a possibility as the narrow cylindrical branches break up readily into short internodal strands, ultimately becoming translucent. Horsetails would have been present in the vicinity of Silbury and could have been used as an abrasive
Zostera marina: Complete leaves, in various stages of rotting, collected from a beach strandline, Dorset.	Eelgrass becomes blue green in colour then translucent during decomposition (Collinson personal observation). A monocotyledon, it could yield elongate strands from between veins after rotting. Eelgrass has been used as a packing or stuffing material from the early Bronze Age (Gale and Cutler 2000)
Complete pieces of thallus of: a green seaweed (sea lettuce, *Ulva lactuca*), a red seaweed (*Mastocarpus*) collected in partially rotted condition from a beach strandline, Dorset.	The lack of higher plant cellular structure seen in the green plant material could be due to it being seaweed. Given the distance of Silbury from the sea and the absence of other marine evidence this was thought unlikely but worth considering.
Leaf of heterosporous water fern *Pilularia globulifera*	Included as an example of a freshwater aquatic plant. The submerged narrow cylindrical leaves (which lack lamina) are of similar breadth to Silbury green plant fragments
Lichen growing on elder tree, Queen Elizabeth Country Park, Hampshire	The absence of any typical higher plant cellular structure in Silbury green plant could potentially be explained by a lower plant derivation. Surface growing lichens were considered as a possibility.
Lichen growing on turf , parade ground, Fort Cumberland, Hampshire	
Dried droppings from Brent Geese, Langstone Harbour, Hampshire	Droppings from large birds such as geese contain a degree of part digested plant material for various types including grass.
Fresh droppings from Canada Geese, London Park	
Surface-dried cow dung, unimproved chalk grassland, Butser Hill, Hampshire	This material may have been deliberately or incidentally incorporated into the organic mounds, in a fresh or decayed and dispersed state.
Dry sheep dung from chalk pasture at Overton Down, North Farm, Wilts	
Dried and fresh droppings from the slug *Arion ater* produced following feeding on composted lettuce.	No slug pellets were found in samples examined from the excavations. It is likely that they would have been present and there are numerous land snails. Slug droppings disperse readily during rain such that plant fragments separate from the matrix.
Couched woad (*Isatis tinctoria*) that had undergone a 2nd fermentation and been dried, but not sieved or crushed (from J Edmonds, Chiltern Open Air Museum 1991; Edmonds, 2000).	This material was included as an example of partly digested/ fermented plant material from one of the author's (GC) reference collection rather than because the presence of woad was suspected.

Fig A5.1.5 (right)
TEM of modern lichens.
a) lichen 1 showing outer
(top of image) compacted
fungal hyphae in the cortex
and underlying algal layer
where algal cells (labelled
a) occur amongst fungal
hyphae;
b) lichen 2, showing loosely
arranged fungal hyphae
with algal cells (labelled a)
in the algal layer;
c) detail from b of algal cell
(labelled a) and fungal
hyphae.
(Margaret Collinson,
Tony Brain and Eddie Lyons,
© English Heritage)

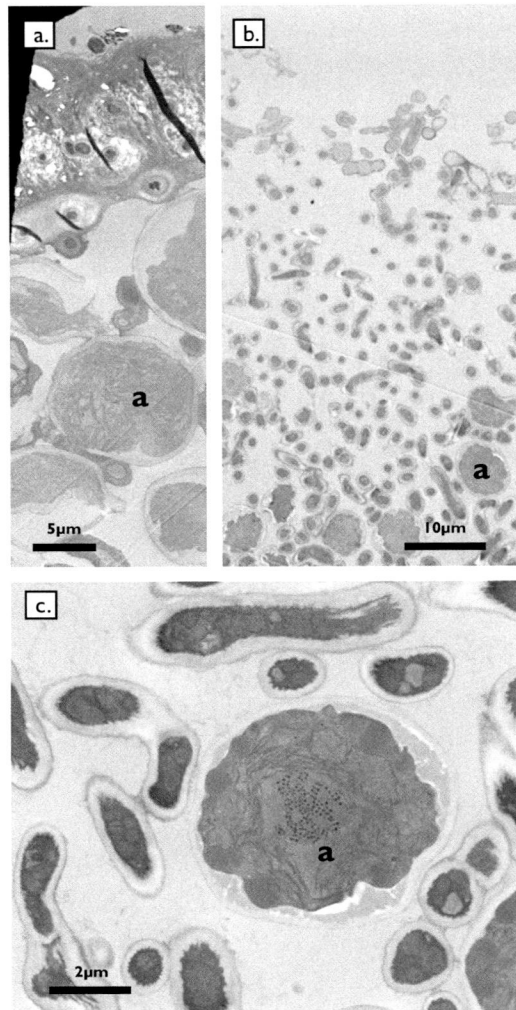

Fig A5.1.6 (right)
TEM of slug faeces.
a) area with cellular
structure;
b) area with no cellular
structure showing clusters of
microbes (m) and degraded
cell contents some of which
are clumps of electron dense
granular bodies (labelled g);
c) detail of granular body
showing thylakoid
membranes from plastids;
d) detail of microbes which
resemble one morphology
present in Silbury green
plant (see text).
(Margaret Collinson,
Tony Brain and Eddie Lyons,
© English Heritage)

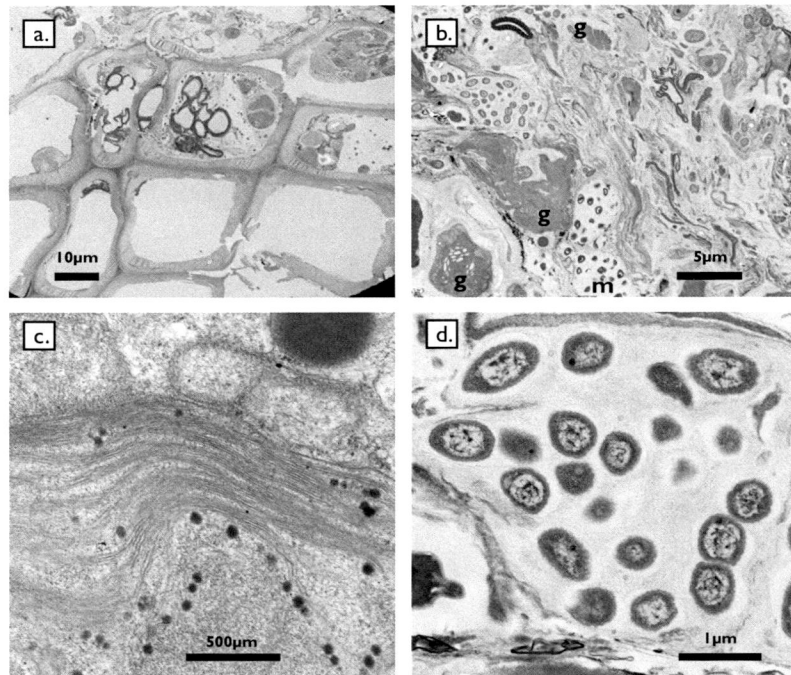

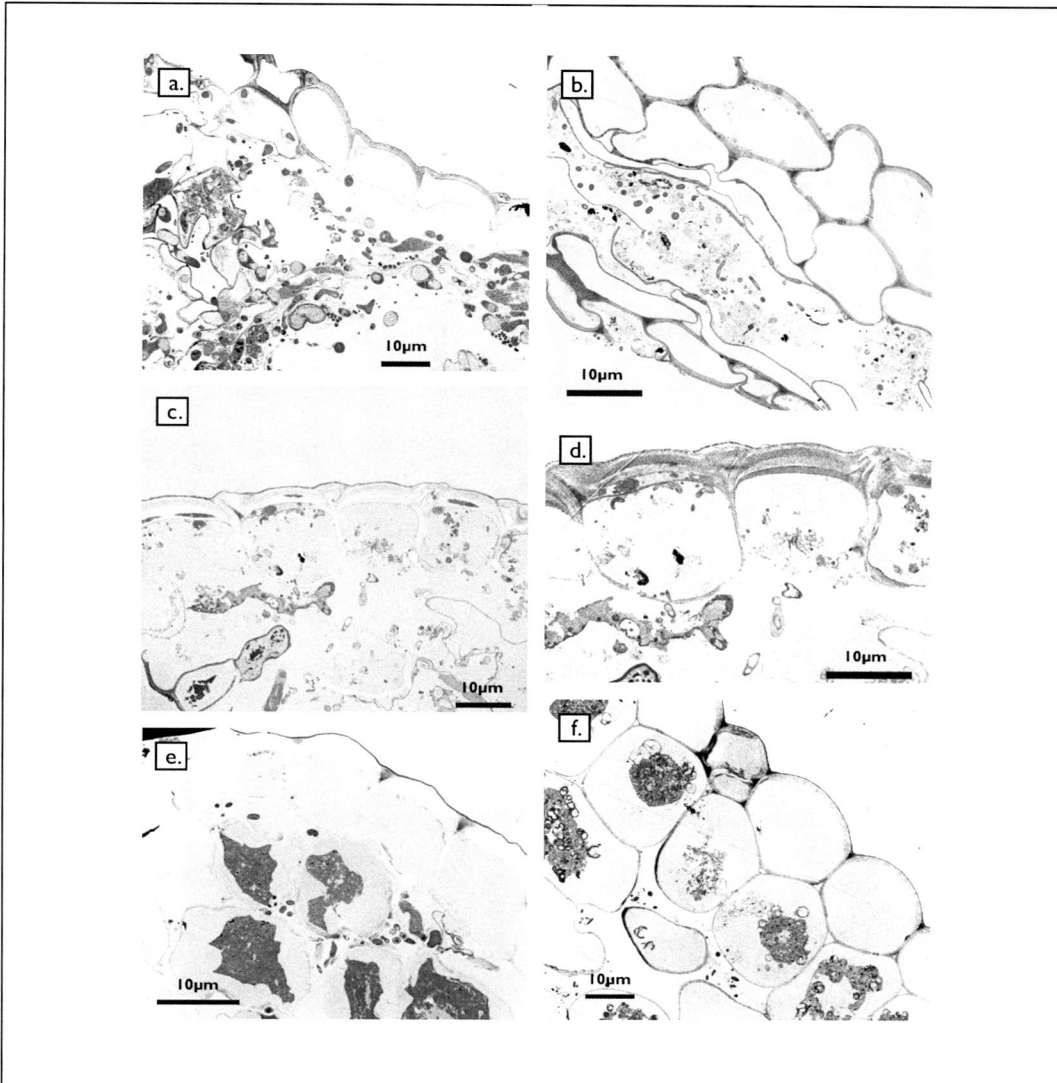

Fig A5.1.7
TEM of plant fragments picked from herbivorous vertebrate faeces, all have cellular structure and show various stages of degradation of cell walls and cell contents. a and b) from sheep,
a) an opaque plant fragment,
b) a translucent plant fragment, the latter showing far less remaining cell contents;
c and d) from cow dung, d) detail from c showing initial degradation of outer cuticle leaving a recognisable thin outer membrane (still attached at this stage);
e) from Brent goose dropping, showing clear outer cuticle membrane and electron dense clumps of degraded plastids in cells;
f) from Canada Goose dropping, degraded plastids in cells disaggregating resulting in loose membranes.
(Margaret Collinson, Tony Brain and Eddie Lyons, © English Heritage)

Results

The lichen thallus consists of compact or loosely intertwined fungal hyphae, which are intermixed with algal cells in the algal layer (Fig A5.1.5). It is quite different from all other material studied.

Slug faeces (Fig A5.1.6) are used as an example to show the range of ultrastructural organisation encountered in faeces, parts of which (Fig A5.1.6b) can resemble Silbury green plant in internal organisation. Furthermore, microbes are encountered in all the faeces (Fig A5.1.6d). Although some images are similar to microbes from Silbury green plant (compare Fig A5.1.6d with Fig 5.6e main text), the overall range of morphologies in Silbury green plant material is much greater (Fig 5.6 main text).

All unprocessed and animal processed plant material retains cellular structure (Figs A5.1.6a, A5.1.7–5.1.9). This is in stark contrast to Silbury green plant (Figs A5.1.3a, A5.1.11b; Collinson et al 2011 a and b and main text). Some epidermal cells show initial stages of alteration of the outermost cuticle layer which appears as a distinct electron dense layer though still attached (Fig A5.1.7d, e) or is in the early stages of detachment (Fig A5.1.9d). These examples indicate how the very simple outer membranes found in Silbury green plant may have originated.

Partially fermented plant material (couched woad) lacks cellular structure (Fig A5.1.10a), contains granular electron dense bodies (Fig A5.1.10a, b), preserves plastid membranes (Fig A5.1.12c) and contains microbes (Fig A5.1.10d). Fragments that may have been

Fig A5.1.8
TEM of outer surface of
partially rotted green
seaweed (sea lettuce, Ulva)
showing distinctive thick
walled cells and degrading
cell contents.
(Margaret Collinson,
Tony Brain and Eddie Lyons,
© English Heritage)

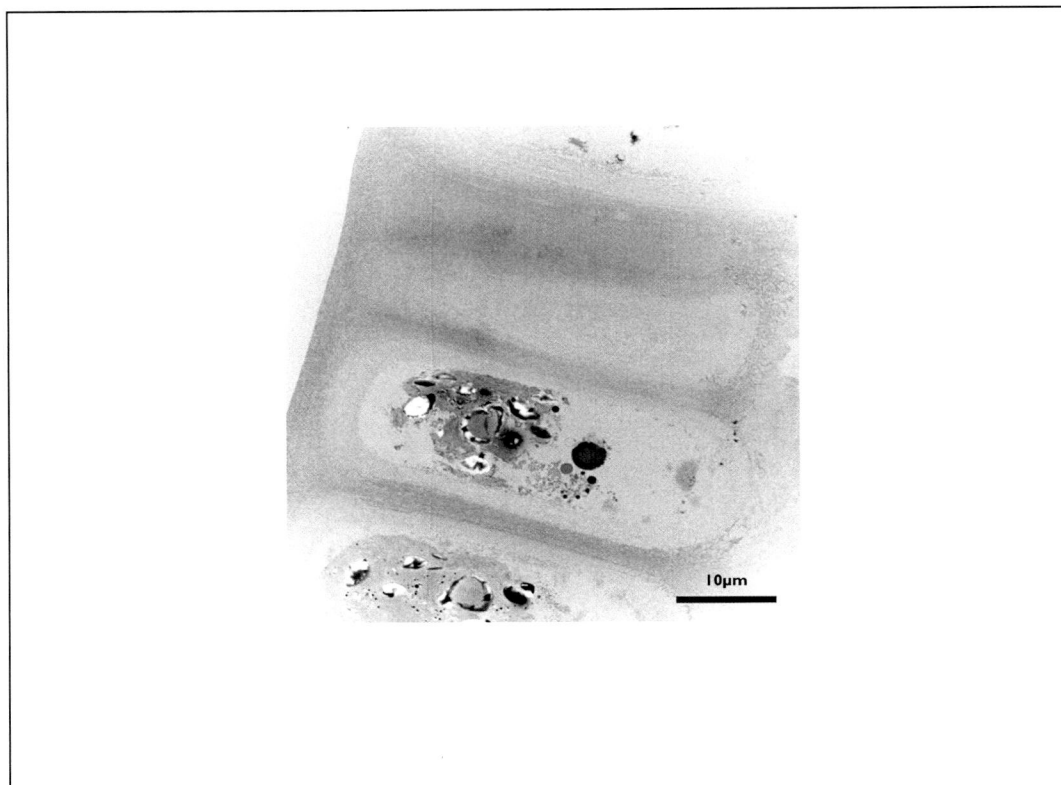

Fig A5.1.9
TEM of higher plant
material, all showing clear
cellular structure.
a) Partially rotted horsetail
(Equisetum), inner tissue
degraded resulting in loose
cell wall layers, 'speckly'
appearance of epidermis
is due to silica particles
(confirmed by X-ray
microanalysis on the
TEM block);
b) Pilularia, essentially
unaltered (large spaces are
normal air spaces in this
submerged leaf);
c and d) eelgrass (Zostera)
c green sample showing
minimal alteration, electron
dense bodies are plastid
clumps,
d translucent sample
showing disintegration
of plastids and separation
of cuticle layers.
(Margaret Collinson,
Tony Brain and Eddie Lyons,
© English Heritage)

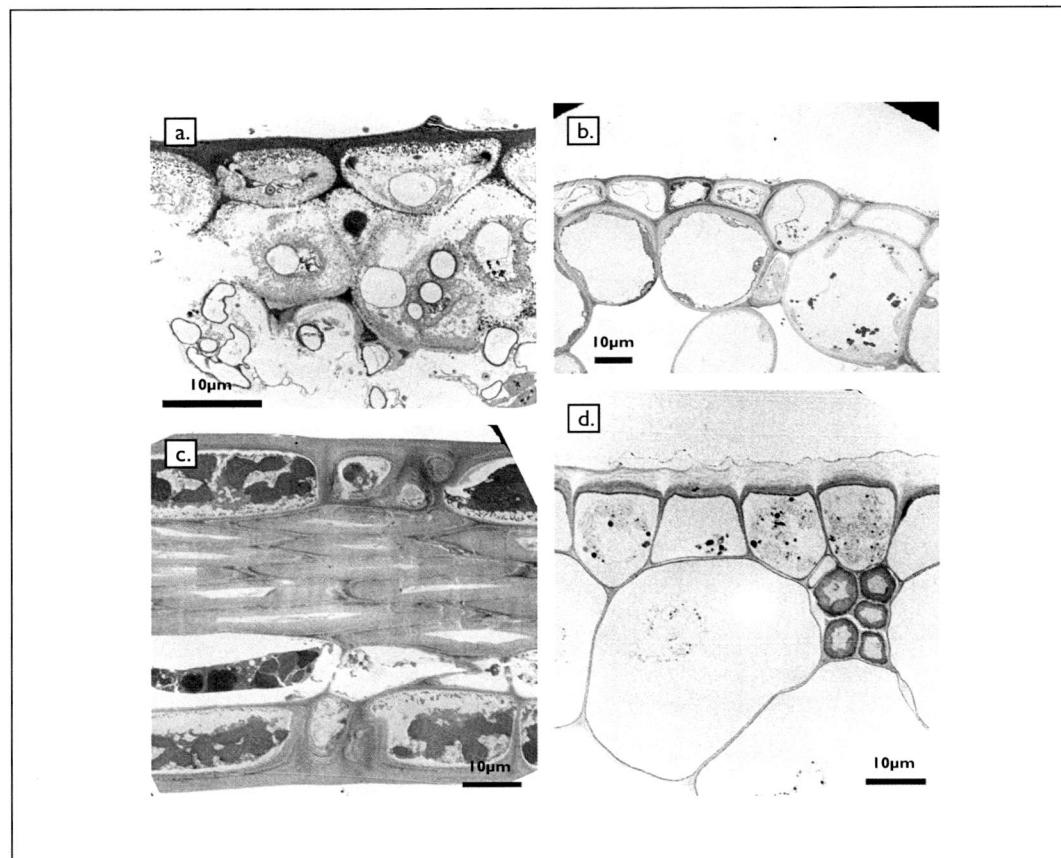

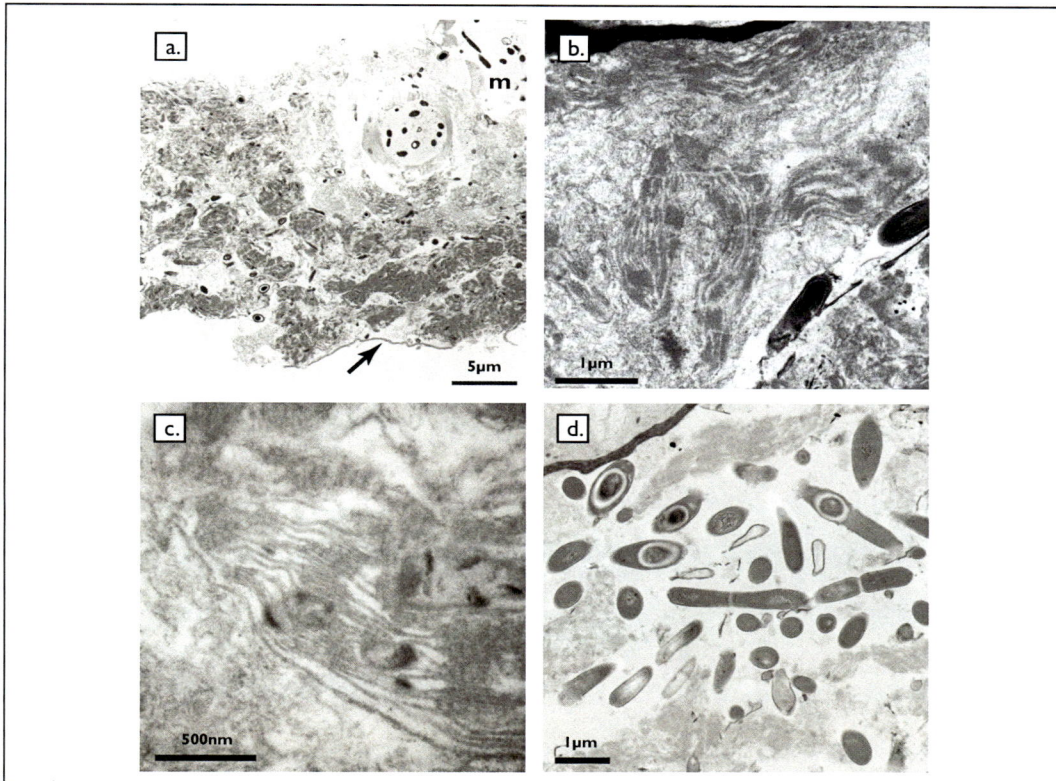

Fig A5.1.10
TEM of couched woad (Isatis tinctoria)
a) showing lack of cellular structure, electron dense (dark) granular bodies, scattered and clustered microbes
(one cluster is labelled m) and fragment of outer membrane (arrow);
b) detail of granular bodies showing stacks of thylakoid membranes indicating that granular bodies are derived from partially degraded chloroplasts,
c) detail of thylakoid membranes from chloroplasts;
d) detail of microbes.
(Margaret Collinson, Tony Brain and Eddie Lyons, © English Heritage)

part of an outer membrane are rarely present (Fig A5.1.10a, arrowed), though there are no continuous membranes enclosing the material.

Silbury green leaf

The ultrastructure of Silbury green leaf (Fig A5.1.11a) has some similarity to that of Silbury green plant from the same context (Fig A5.1.11b) and from other contexts (Fig A5.1.3a; Collinson *et al* main text, Fig 5.3) in lacking cellular structure and containing electron dense granular bodies. However, there are clear cuticle flanges (Fig A5.1.11a labelled f) representing areas where cutin of the leaf cuticle has penetrated down into the anticlinal epidermal cell walls. These are absent in Silbury green plant. In addition green leaf is much less compacted than green plant and contains features that may represent layers of degraded cell walls (arrows in Fig A5.1.11a). No distinct plastid membranes were observed in green leaf whereas they were present in green plant from the same context (Fig A5.1.11b). In the larger area of section, viewed at low resolution by light microscopy, green leaf shows a section through a vascular strand or vein, a feature (Fig A5.1.12c) not present in Silbury green plant that merely

varies in thickness depending on the amount of internal content (Fig A5.1.12d).

Interpretation of Silbury green plant material

All the unprocessed, partly rotted and animal processed plant materials studied here retain cellular structure. Cellular structure is clearly preserved in the Silbury organic mounds as shown in yellow plant material and rootlets (Collinson *et al* 2011a; and main text). Therefore, the absence of cellular structure in Silbury green leaf (Fig A5.1.11a) and Silbury green plant (Figs A5.1.3a, A5.1.11b) requires a special explanation, particularly so in view of the presence of preserved plastid thylakoid membranes in Silbury green plant (Figs A5.1.3b, A5.1.11c). Silbury green plant is interpreted here as higher plant material in which all cellulosic and lignified cell walls have been lost and only a thin outermost cuticle has survived. Internal cell contents have degraded, modified plastids, represented by electron dense granular bodies, form the bulk of the surviving material and these include identifiable fragments of plastid thylakoid membranes.

Fig A5.1.11
TEM of Silbury plant
material <9827> from the
Mini-mound [4181],
a) green leaf showing lack
of cellular structure but
probable remnants of cell
wall layers (examples
arrowed), outer membranes
with cuticle flanges (f), and
degraded cell contents
including electron dense
(dark) granular bodies
(degraded plastids);
b) Silbury green plant,
section through a single
strand showing outer
membrane on each surface,
lack of cellular structure and
electron dense (dark)
granular bodies (degraded
plastids)
c) thylakoid membranes
from chloroplasts.
(Margaret Collinson,
Tony Brain and Eddie Lyons,
© English Heritage)

Fig A5.1.12 (right)
Semi-thin sections
demonstrating major
differences in plant
materials as seen in low
magnification light
microscopy.
a) single fragment of plant
material from cow dung
with cellular preservation;
b–d) no cellular
preservation
b) bulk partially fermented
plant material;
c) single piece of Silbury
green leaf (v = vein);
d) single piece of Silbury
green plant material (note
variation in thickness along
length); c and d from [4181]
sample <9827>.
(Margaret Collinson
and Eddie Lyons,
© English Heritage)

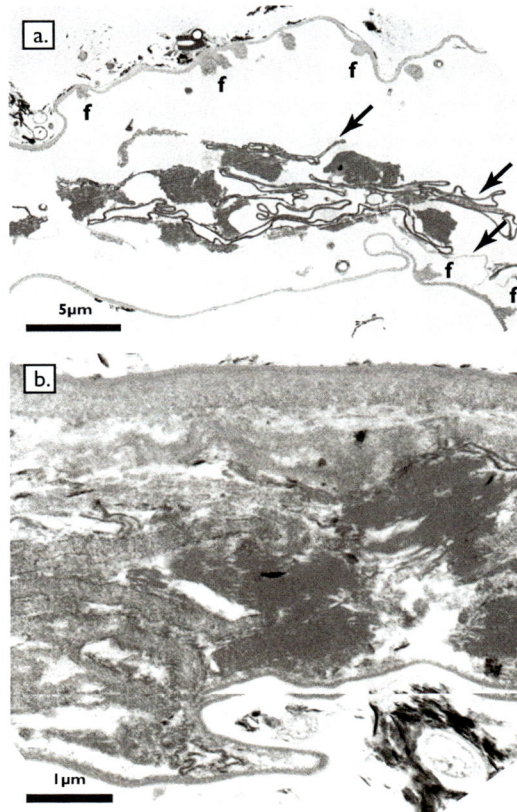

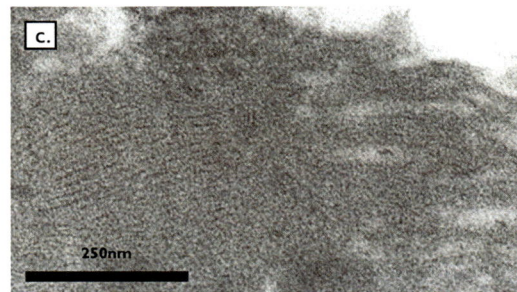

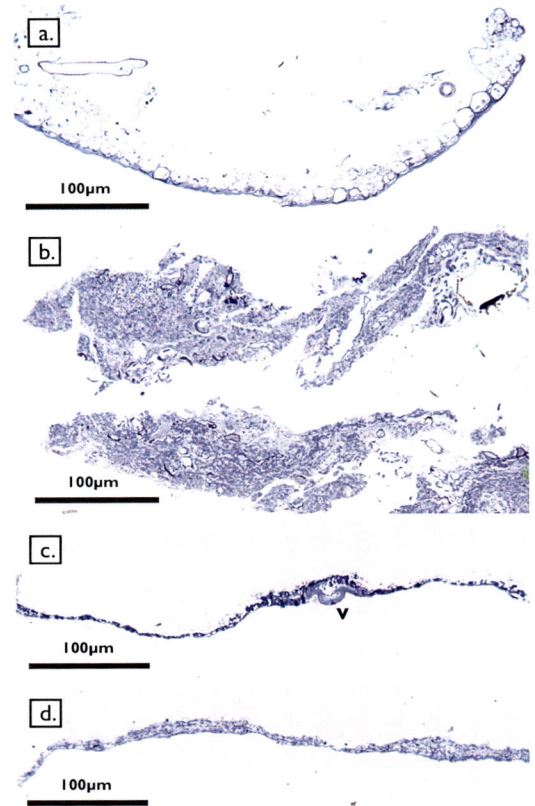

Amongst the wide range of comparative material studied here that which is most similar in ultrastructural preservation to Silbury green plant is the couched woad (Figs A5.1.10, A5.1.11b). This lacks cellular structure and contains electron dense granular bodies (Fig A5 1.10a) some of which are clearly partially degraded plastids (Fig A5.1.10b). It preserves plastid membranes (Fig A5.1.10c) and contains microbes (Fig A5.1.10d). There is no clear enclosing membrane in the sample examined although fragments, that may have been part of a membrane, are rarely present (Fig A5.1.10a arrow). Silbury green plant seen *in situ* is clearly fragmented into strands (Fig A5.1.1), indicating that it was cut, torn or shredded at some point prior to deposition.

Silbury green leaf clearly represents a different plant to Silbury green plant as it shows net venation, marginal trichomes and internal cuticle flanges. The loss of cellular structure, however, suggests that green leaf has been subjected to the same process as green plant. It is possible that few fragments of green leaf were accidentally incorporated during the process which produced green plant.

Unfortunately the identity of the higher plant from which green plant is derived is unresolved as there are no diagnostic features remaining. However, the distribution of the green plant material within the organic mounds that form part of the early phases of the Hill where the remains of turves are attested (Chapters 2 and 6; Campbell 2011) suggests that the two are connected.

Silbury green plant material may result from a process somewhat analogous to dew retting of flax and hemp where the green material was in effect over retted with loss of cellulose and lignin (Boase 1918; Henriksson *et al* 1997; Cutshall 1943). Alternatively the green plant material may represent the waste from some unknown process involving deliberate fermentation with the waste being incorporated into the mound.

Whatever the case, further comparisons of the Silbury green plant material with experimentally produced fermented plant material are required, using appropriate plant species. Ideally this should include different plant materials, deliberately fermented, as well as material cut, trampled, and then treated in a variety of different ways: left to rot on the soil surface, piled up and then buried almost immediately. Further details regarding this study are given in Collinson *et al* 2011b.

Appendix 5.2

A transect across valley sediments west of Silbury Hill

Melanie Rimmer and Martin Bell

The buried soil under Silbury Hill is arguably one of its most significant and unusual features. To understand its context and origins, a survey of the sediments in a transect across the valley west of the monument was undertaken. Coring was carried out to identify the soil and sediment materials in the surrounding area and determine any similarities to the buried soil profile. In particular, the material called 'clay-with-flints' in the buried soil was of interest, as there are a number of types of deposit given this name (Scott-Jackson and Walkington 2005; above, Chapter 1).

A transect was taken running on a north–south axis 300m west of the mound, across the Silbury Hill car park and up the slope on either side (Fig P5.2.1; Rimmer 2007). Core spots were recorded using GPS. For most an Edelmann hand auger was used; three power cores (P1, P2, and P4) were also taken, and field recording was carried out with reference to Munsell soil charts.

The topsoil is a humic silty clay with flint and chalk stones, varying in stoniness depending on the extent of recent ploughing. On both north and south slopes, the underlying horizon is silty clay colluvium, which contains flints on the north slope and is chalky on the south slope. On the north slope patches of a more clay-rich unit are found below this, which could represent either a Bt horizon or a further clay-flint colluvium. The soils on the southern slope are thinner than on the north slope, probably reflecting erosion due to more extensive cultivation of this field. At the top of the slope in Core 12, a thicker deposit of clay containing a small amount of flint is found. On the north

slope, the soil profile sits on soft Lower Chalk, while on the south slope, the bedrock is Middle and Upper Chalk (BGS 1974).

In the valley bottom, a thick deposit of pale silty stone-free alluvium was present on either side of the stream between Power Core P1 and P2. On the north side underlying the colluvial deposits, a gravelly silt extends up to the start of the slope in Core 2. This is either the valley gravel mapped in this area (BGS 1974), or a further colluvial unit which is stonier than the overlying material. Power Core P1 also has a gravel unit at its base, probably valley gravel, while the majority of the other valley cores rest on chalky Pleistocene meltwater deposits to a depth of over three metres. In the centre of the valley, there was extensive disturbance around the Silbury Hill car park, with asphalt found in the upper deposits above alluvium. South of this, the cores at the bottom of the south slope either side of the road contain a deposit of a clay material containing flints, 570mm thick in Core 1, resting on chalk meltwater muds.

The clay and flints material at the base of the southern slope is of particular interest, as it appears to be similar to the 'clay-with-flints' found under Silbury Hill, and is on the same side of the valley only 300 metres further west. Its position at the base of the slope precludes it being clay-with-flints *sensu stricto,* as this narrowly defined deposit is normally only found at the top of the chalk interfluves (Quesnel *et al* 2003). Other deposits sometimes described as 'clay-with-flints' include plateau drift and brickearth (Scott-Jackson and Walkington 2005). In this case, the position at the bottom of the south slope and its heterogeneous appearance suggests that the material was soliflucted during the Pleistocene, deriving from a clay-with-flints or similar deposit upslope to the south, the remnants of which may be present in Core 12. An analysis using clay and heavy mineralogy of the buried soil 'clay-with-flints' and the transect deposits would confirm whether they are related in this way.

This brief survey of the soil materials in the valley just west of Silbury Hill shows that a deposit of clay and flints which may be of the same origin as the 'clay-with-flints' material under the Hill exists, and that its origin can be explained as a soliflucted Pleistocene deposit derived from, but not corresponding to clay-with-flints. This may provide further opportunities to determine the extent of alteration of the buried soil by comparison with the soliflucted clay and flints in the valley.

155

*Fig A5.2.1
An aerial view of Silbury showing the position of the cores and the auger transect results.
(Eddie Lyons,
© English Heritage, Aerial photography Licensed to English Heritage for PGA, through NextPerspectives™)*

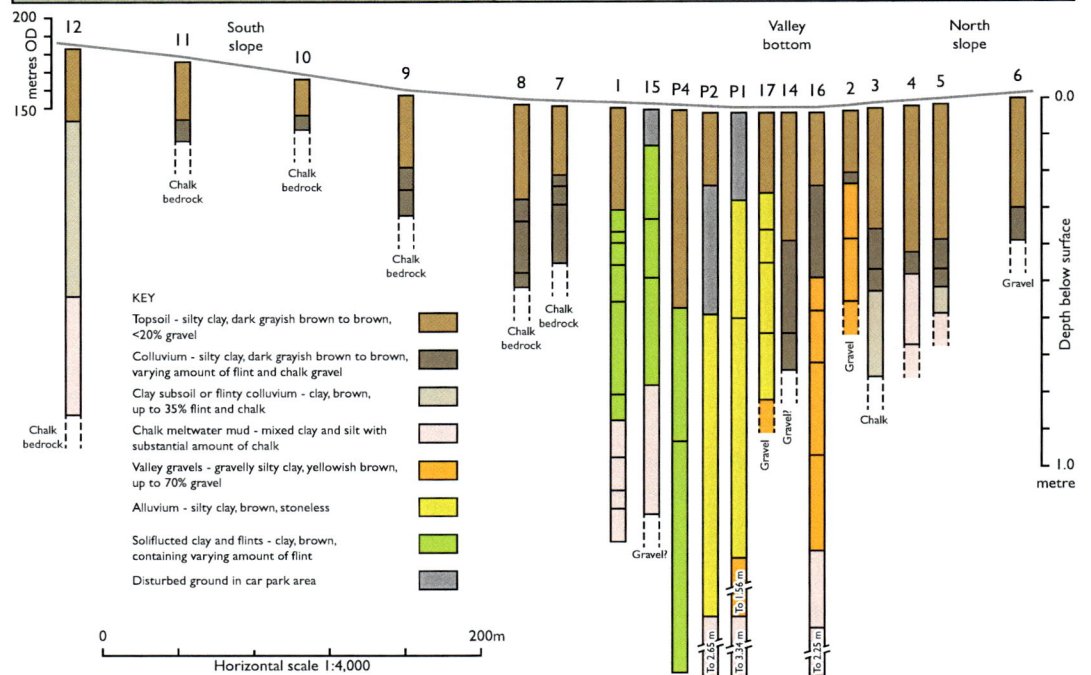

KEY

Topsoil - silty clay, dark grayish brown to brown, <20% gravel

Colluvium - silty clay, dark grayish brown to brown, varying amount of flint and chalk gravel

Clay subsoil or flinty colluvium - clay, brown, up to 35% flint and chalk

Chalk meltwater mud - mixed clay and silt with substantial amount of chalk

Valley gravels - gravelly silty clay, yellowish brown, up to 70% gravel

Alluvium - silty clay, brown, stoneless

Soliflucted clay and flints - clay, brown, containing varying amount of flint

Disturbed ground in car park area

6

Silbury Hill: Understanding the Environment

GILL CAMPBELL

*With Paul Davies, Mike Edmunds, Allan Hall, Peter Marshall, Mark Robinson
and Paul Whitehead, and Fay Worley*

This chapter summarises the results from the detailed analyses of the biological remains recovered from samples as well as the animal bone recovered from prehistoric contexts. In contrast to Chapter 5, which is cocerned with preservation studies and understanding the formation processes of particular contexts, this chapter focuses on what the material can tell us concerning the nature of the Later Neolithic environment. It also describes work undertaken to understand the palaeohydrology of the area before broadening out to discuss the evidence for cereal cultivation and the management of the landscape.

The environmental evidence from the interior of the mound and prehistoric vertebrate remains from the summit

Gill Campbell, Mark Robinson, Paul Davies, with Allan Hall and Fay Worley

There was very little in the way of charred plant remains and charcoal recovered from the deposits underlying or forming the make-up of the Hill with the exception of a single possible hearth found within the Old Land Surface (*see* Chapter 2). Some of the turf and topsoil used in the early phases of construction also produced some charcoal and the occasional charred hazel nutshell fragment. This material was only present at low concentrations, however, and could date from any time up to the incorporation of a particular piece of turf or topsoil. Although this widely dispersed charred material provides some information on the history of land use and, potentially, human activity up to the point of burial, the lack of chronological resolution

means that it is of low research potential and, with the exception of the material from the hearth, no detailed analysis was therefore undertaken.

Within the later phases of the mound and within the ditch fills very little in the way of plant remains were present. In fact, the absence of charred plant remains, whether the scattered remains of hearths, or the general rubbish that might be expected where people are living and working, could be argued to suggest that the construction process was separated from everyday activities. This paucity of material is also reflected within the animal bone and artefact assemblages (Worley 2011c; Gardner 1987, 43 and table 4.1; Gardner 1997; Bishop Chapter 3) and could be indicative of the ritual nature of the construction process whereby it was important to keep the site clean (*see* discussion in Chapter 7). Alternatively it may be that cooking and eating took place adjacent to the site or on other parts of the monument not encountered as part of the investigations.

For this reason it is only the macroscopic plant remains, pollen and insects preserved as a result of anoxic conditions, in conjunction with the molluscan remains where present, that allow us to explore the nature of the Later Neolithic environment. Thus, this discussion focuses on the biological remains preserved as a result of the anoxic conditions, as well as the molluscs, found within the deposits close to the centre of the mound and pertaining to the earlier phases of construction as we currently understand it.

Details of all the samples analysed are given in Table 6.1 (at the end of this chapter). The type of remains analysed from any given sample was partly dependent on whether the remains were present, or at least sufficiently well preserved/ numerous to merit analysis. For example, pollen was only preserved within the Lower Organic Mound in samples with a clay-with-flints type matrix, while occurrence of molluscs within the deposits was highly variable.

As well as sampling in order to recover artefacts, biological remains and for geoarchaeological investigations, sampling was undertaken for optical stimulated luminescence (OSL) dating, environmental magnetism, uranium series dating and microbiological assessment. In addition, X-ray fluorescence (XRF) readings were taken from the deposits at several locations. These readings are stored in a separate database and form part of the site archive. Details of all the samples taken are also included in the archive. A number of samples from the Old Land Surface (OLS), the Gravel Mound [4153], layer [4166] sealing part of the Gravel Mound, the Mini-mound [4181], pit [3067] and from a clay band within the Lower Organic Mound [4156] were also assessed for the presence of diatoms. Only one possible valve was found meriting no further work (Sidell 2009).

A brief summary of the results of the biological analysis of the samples for Phases 2–6 is given below. The full species lists for each sample analysed can be found in Tables 6.2 to 6.25 at the end of this chapter. Figure 6.1

shows the relative abundance of different insect species groups. The groups used follow those of Robinson (1991, 278–81) and the group to which a given species belongs is shown in the relevant tables. Details of the methodologies employed in the various analyses, further comparisons with the assemblages recovered from the 1968–70 excavations and further discussions can be found within the individual EH research reports (Campbell 2011; Davies 2012; Forster *et al* 2012; Hall 2012; Robinson 2011; Worley 2011c). Nomenclature follows Stace (1997) for wild plants, Zohary and Hopf (1994, table 3, table 5) for the cereals, Anderson (2005) for molluscs, and Kloet and Hincks (1977) for insects.

Methods for the analysis of animal bone are given in Chapter 9 and in Worley 2011c. The recovered identifiable bones and teeth from the earliest deposits, amounting to some 10 fragments, comprised cattle, suid (pig or wild boar), anuran (frog or toad) or micro-mammal, the latter taxa representing animals inhabiting the local environment of the Hill, whilst the cattle and suid remains may represent farmed or hunted species. None of this material exhibited any butchery marks or pathological lesions. No conclusions can be drawn from this small sample, beyond the occurrence of species. The 1968–70 tunnelling also produced a small assemblage of 18 fragments of animal bone

Fig 6.1
Percentage of terrestrial Coleoptera. Species groups expressed as a percentage of the total terrestrial Coleoptera (ie aquatics excluded). Not all the terrestrial Coleoptera have been classified into groups. (Mark Robinson and Eddie Lyons, © English Heritage)

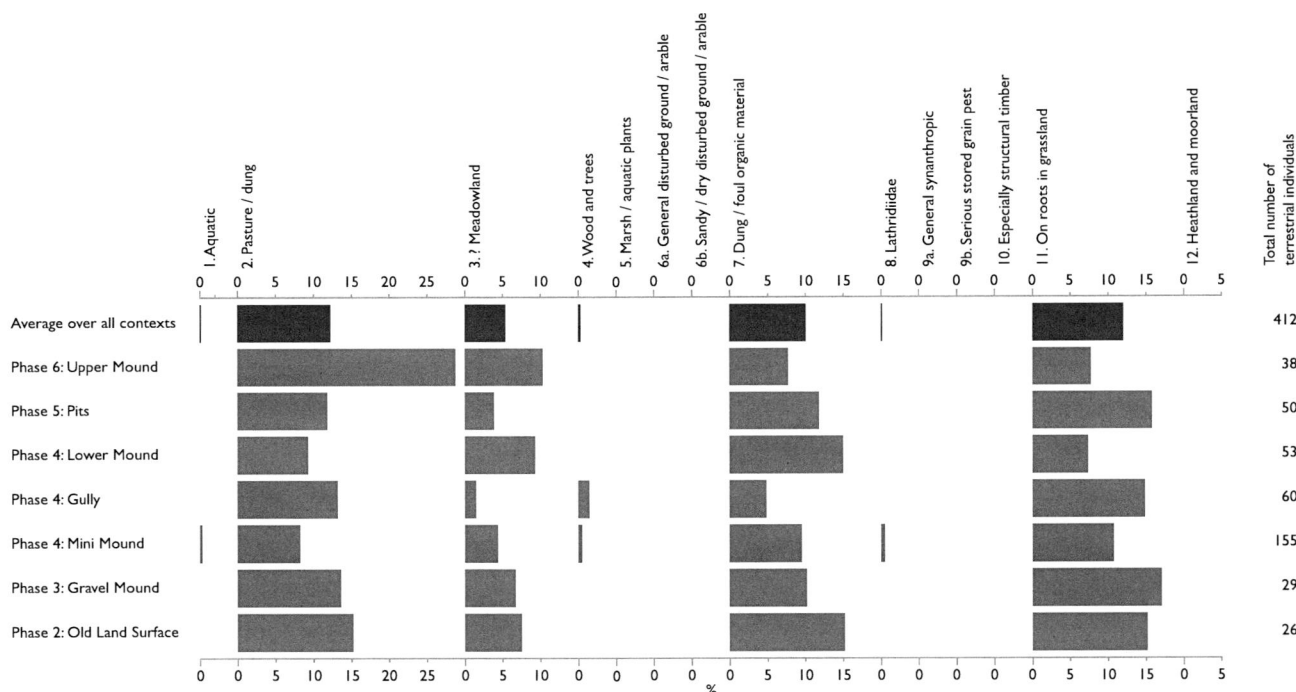

(Gardner 1987, 45–7), two of which were identifiable: a fragment of red deer antler and a fragment of pig radius.

Two fossil shark teeth were recovered from Phase 12.1 and 12.2 fills of Ditch 1 as part of the 2007/8 excavations, while a third was found in chalk trample above the OLS during the 1968–70 excavations (Silbury 26, Alexander Keiller Museum). These are of geological origin, likely to be incidental inclusions, and therefore excluded from further comment.

Biological remains from the Old Land Surface Phase 2 (Tables 6.2–6.6)

Samples from the OLS contained few insects and uncharred plant remains and these were poorly preserved. The Coleoptera were all species of grassland habitats including *Mecinus pyraster* which feeds on *Plantago lanceolata* (ribwort plantain) and *P. media* (hoary plantain), *Phyllopertha horticola* whose larvae feed on the roots of grassland plants, *Megasternum obscurum* which occurs in a range of decaying organic material including animal droppings and scarabaeoid dung beetles of the genus *Aphodius* which generally occur in animal droppings on pasture (Table 6.2). Uncharred monocotyledon stems and leaves were frequent. The seed remains included decay resistant seeds such as fragments of *Sambucus nigra* (elder), and *Ranunculus* sp. (buttercup) achenes as well as sclerotia of *Cenococcum* sp. (Table 6.3). Only the sample (<9238>) from below the Gravel Mound produced any molluscs, 12 individuals in total (Table 6.5), while pollen was very poorly preserved and only present in very low concentrations with the exception of a sample (<9264/2>) from [3035] in the west section of Bay 81 (*see* Foldout 1A, and Fig 2.6). This sample produced mainly grass pollen, hazel, fern spores and some alder (Table 6.6).

Biological remains from the Gravel Mound Phase 3 (Tables 6.3, 6.6, 6.7–6.9)

A single sample <9819> was analysed from within the main body of the Gravel Mound. It was largely devoid of uncharred plant remains, insects and pollen but molluscs were plentiful, principally *Vallonia costata* and *V. excentrica* with some *Vertigo pygmaea*, *Helicella itala itala* and *Trochulus hispidus*. Similarly, sample <9814> from [3069], a grey layer directly overlying the Gravel Mound and through which pit [3067] was cut, contained very few remains other than molluscs (Tables 6.3, 6.7, 6.9).

In contrast, the dark layer overlying the mound (sample <9820>, [4166] Foldout 1A and B, and Fig 2.7) produced considerable numbers of uncharred plant remains, a large mollusc assemblage and the insects were better preserved and present in higher concentrations (Tables 6.3, 6.7). Pollen and spores were very sparse and generally poorly preserved. The mollusc assemblage from this layer was broadly comparable with that from the body of the Gravel Mound: *Vallonia costata, Vallonia excentrica, Vertigo pygmaea* and *Helicella itala itala* predominated. Several of the *Vallonia excentrica* and *Helicella itala itala* appeared remarkably fresh, as if buried rapidly. Several of the *Clausilia bidentata* recovered were quite worn. Some shells were also blackened, indicating burning (Table 6.9). Grass remains and seeds of Caryophyllaceae were relatively abundant with buttercups, *Urtica dioica* (stinging nettle), *Montia fontana* (blinks), *Euphrasia/Odontites* sp. (eyebright/red bartsia) and *Carex* sp. (sedge) also recorded (Table 6.3). The Coleoptera included *Agrypnus murinus* which has larvae that occur on the roots of grassland plants, *Sitona lepidus* which feeds on Fabaceae particularly *Trifolium* spp. (clovers), *Xantholinus glabratus* which readily occurs in the droppings of herbivores and various scarabaeoid dung beetles such as *Geotrupes* sp. and *Onthophagus* sp. (Table 6.7). Remains of other insects were very few although there were a couple of Hemiptera (true bugs) including the grass-feeding *Aphrodes bicinctus* and a Diptera (fly) puparium (Table 6.8).

It was thought in the field that this layer might present a buried soil. The results suggest, however, that it consisted of a mixture of turf, topsoil and some subsoil, an interpretation supported by geoarchaeological analysis (*see* Canti 2011; and Chapter 5).

Biological remains from Phase 4 (Fig 2.11, Tables 6.6, 6.10–6.14)

Lower Organic Mound

The samples analysed from the Lower Organic Mound produced a wide range of macroscopic remains in varying concentrations. Pollen was also quite well preserved and three samples from this phase were analysed in full. Spheroidal

Carbonaceous Particles (SCPs) were recorded in all three samples (Table 6.6). Overall the remains are indicative of dry grassland. However, there was some variation between samples (*see below*). Woodland taxa and wetland taxa were generally absent or present in very low quantities.

A single cattle incisor enamel fragment was hand collected from the Lower Organic Mound. A further cattle bone (a fragmented left radius) was recovered from a sieved sample of the same context. The radius could not be measured, but was from quite a large, robust individual (*see* Worley 2011c).

The Mini-mound [4181] at the end of the East Lateral

This feature (Fig 2.10, Foldout 1D) produced very few molluscs, but of these a large proportion was very fresh (Table 6.13). Pollen was sparse, but reasonably preserved. As well as the usual mixture of grass, hazel and fern spores, single pollen grains of *Calluna* (heather) and indeterminate Ericaceae were recorded, as well as a number of wetland taxa. SCPs were also present (Table 6.6).

The preservation of insect remains was good and the sclerites of the Coleoptera tended to be less fragmented than from the other contexts. Carabidae (ground beetles) and Staphylinidae (rove beetles) which are often abundant in grassland were well-represented while chafer and elaterid beetles with larvae that are associated with the roots of grassland plants (Species Group 11) comprised 11 per cent of the terrestrial Coleoptera (Fig 6.1, Table 6.11). Some of the species found prefer damp grassland while one species, *Cicindela campestris* (tiger beetle), favours sunny habitats with light soil. The various Scarabaeoidea which feed on the droppings of the larger herbivores under pasture

land, as opposed to manure heap, conditions (Species Group 2) comprised 8.4 per cent of the terrestrial Coleoptera. The hydrophilid and staphylinid beetles of Species Group 7 which occur more generally in dung and also in other sorts of foul organic material comprised 9.7 per cent of the terrestrial Coleoptera (Fig 6.1). Three water beetles were present: *Colymbetes fuscus*, *Helophorus* cf. *brevipalpis* and *Hydrobius fuscipes*. They are all species of stagnant water which readily fly to colonise temporary bodies of water. There were also a few insects that are associated with woodland.

The macroscopic plant remains recovered from this context included remains indicative of grassland but also a considerable range and number of woodland or scrub taxa (Table 6.10), including yew (*Taxus baccata*) (Fig 6.2; *see also* Panel 6.1). Disturbed ground was also indicated by the occurrence of stinging nettle, blinks, common chickweed, *Capsella bursa-pastoris* (shepherd's purse), *Thlaspi arvense* (field pennycress), greater plantain and *Galium* cf. *aparine* (cleavers). Thistles were also relatively frequent in these samples in comparison with those from other contexts. These, and other members of the Asteraceae found in these samples: *Crepis* cf. *biennis* (rough hawk's beard) and *Taraxacum* sp. (dandelion) also suggest disturbed, cultivated or waste ground.

Of particular interest were some rather poorly preserved cereal remains that were recovered during assessment. These included a *Triticum* sp. (wheat) rachis node (Fig 6.3). It is closely similar in form to tetraploid free-threshing wheat rachis node but as the fragment comes from close to the base of the ear and is poorly preserved it is not possible to be certain of this identification. The fragment has been designated as *Triticum* cf. free-threshing rachis. A possible fragment of *Hordeum* sp. (barley) rachis node was also recorded as well as some possible cereal bran.

The gully [4171] associated with the Mini-mound

Molluscs and pollen were not recovered from either of the gully fills and both insects and macroscopic plant remains were present in rather low concentrations (Tables 6.10–6.12). This is probably because much of this material is re-deposited from other contexts within this area of the monument and its surroundings at the time of construction. The primary fill produced more material than the secondary

Fig 6.2
Yew (*Taxus baccata*) seed recovered from the Mini-mound [4181].
(Gill Campbell,
© English Heritage)

0   5 mm

Panel 6.1 *Prunus spinosa* L. (sloe)

Gill Campbell

Remains of *Prunus spinosa* (sloe) fruit-stones were recovered from the Mini-mound and the fills of the associated gully. A possible example was also found within one of the pits. In addition, thorn fragments, which could derive from *Prunus* sp. (sloe, bullace, plum and the like) or *Crataegus* sp. (hawthorn) were recorded from the Mini-mound and its associated gully, while two fragments of *Prunus* sp. charcoal were found within the possible hearth.

While the record of sloe at this date is not unusual the dimensions and shape of the fruit-stone specimens recovered require further comment. Two distinct types were present, a short, fat type and a much larger type with a somewhat flattened stone (Fig P6.1.1). While many of the stones were fragmentary it was possible to obtain the dimensions of some of the specimens. The largest specimen measured 10.5mm by 7mm (5mm breadth) which is slightly above the maximum length given in Clapham *et al* (1962; 1989) which specifies a range of 7.5–10mm in length and 6–8mm in width. The smallest specimen measured 6.5mm by 5.5mm (4mm breadth).

While such large stones might be taken as evidence for the presence of *Prunus domestica* ssp. *insititia* (bullace, wild plum, damson) it seems more likely that these stones are from *P. spinosa* var. *macrocarpa,* with var. *microcarpa* being represented by the smaller stones. According to Clapham *et al* (1962; 1989) *P. domestica* ssp. *insititia* is often con-sidered native, whereas Stace (1997, 365) regards all subspecies of P. *domestica* as introduced, remarking that as a result of hybridisation over many centuries the dif-ferent subspecies are hardly discernible. Stace also sees *P. spinosa* var. *macrocarpa* as a hybrid between *P. spinosa* and *P. domestica*.

Preston *et al* (2004) list *P. domestica* as an archaeophyte, though they do not distinguish between subspecies. There is a single Bronze Age record but many more dating from the Roman period, again suggesting Roman introduction. Interestingly Preston *et al* (2004) also record that the species has markedly increased its distribution in recent times perhaps reflecting the many types of ornamental plums that have been introduced into domestic gardens during the last century and from there hybridised with our native sloe.

Whatever the case regarding the genetic status of *P. spinosa* and *P. domestica* today, the results from Silbury show that both a large seeded sloe, most probably *P. spinosa* var. *macrocarpa,* and a small seeded sloe, most probably *P. spinosa* var. *microcarpa,* are present in a totally secure late Neolithic context. This suggests that *P. spinosa* var. *mac-rocarpa* did exist in the past and that Stace's (1997) suggestion that this variety should probably be regarded as a hybrid does not hold true.

Evidence that both small-fruited and large-fruited sloes have long been recognised by locals in Wiltshire is provided in Grose (1957, 219) who quotes Dartnell and Goddard's work (1891–9) referring to the local names for sloes with large fruits (hilps, sloes, slones or slues) and those with small fruits (hedge-specks, picks, slans, or snags).

Fig P6.1.1
*Remains of
Prunus spinosa.
(Gill Campbell,
© English Heritage)*

Fig 6.3
Wheat rachis from [4181].
It resembles a tetraploid
free-threshing rachis but is
very near to the base of the
ear and therefore could
come from a hulled or naked
wheat, though a naked
(free-threshing form)
seems more likely.
(Gill Campbell,
© English Heritage)

0   1 mm

fill including a number of charred plant remains: hazel nutshell, a seed fragment of *Mercurialis perennis* (dog's mercury), an *Arrhenatherum elatius* (onion couch) tuber and other remains of grasses. The plant remains preserved by anoxic conditions included a substantial woodland or scrub element with taxa such as yew, hazel, *Salix* sp. (willow), *Prunus spinosa* (sloe), *Crataegus* sp. (hawthorn), *Rubus* section *Glandulosus* (bramble), dog's mercury and elder all recorded. Some disturbed ground species were also recovered, although some of these plants could also have been growing along the woodland edge (Table 6.10).

Remains were sparser in the sample from the secondary fill. Woodland or scrub taxa like sloe and elder were still present, as were plants of disturbed ground/taller grassland such as stinging nettle. Also present were two species, *Rorippa nasturtium-aquatica* (watercress) and *Rhinanthus minor* (yellow rattle), that were not recorded from any of the other samples analysed as part of this project or as part of 1968–70 excavations. While yellow rattle can grow both on dry chalk grassland and in wet meadows, the presence of watercress would indicate wetter conditions.

The range of insect species was largely the same as from the Mini-mound itself (Table 6.11). The number of species of Carabidae was, however, greatly reduced and water beetles were absent. *Phyllopertha horticola* and *Agrypnus murinus* retained their presence amongst Species Group 11, while the scarabaeoid dung beetles of Species Group 2 formed a greater proportion of the assemblage as compared to the Mini-mound. However, the beetles of more general foul organic material, including *Megasternum obscurum* had declined in abundance to 5 per cent of the terrestrial Coleoptera. There was a single member of Species Group 4, the wood and tree-dependent Coleoptera, the wood-boring beetle *Grynobius planus* (Fig 6.1).

Biological remains from Phase 5 pits (Tables 6.15–6.18)

Pit [3067]

The main (secondary) fill [3066] of pit [3067] (Fig 2.12, and Foldout 1A) was the richest of assemblages obtained from the pit fills. Molluscan remains were abundant but there was a marked divide between fresh and worn elements. Some of the *Cochlicopa* cf. *lubrica*, *Vertigo pygmaea*, *Helicella itala itala*, many of the *Vallonia costata* and all of the *Aegopinella* were very fresh. In contrast most of the other species (such as *Pomatias elegans*, *Merdigera obscura* and *Clausilia bidentata*) were very worn (Table 6.18). Buttercup achenes were plentiful and some were well enough preserved to be tentatively identified as *R. bulbosus* (bulbous buttercup) and *R. acris* (meadow buttercup). Other remains included seeds of *Arenaria serpyllifolia* (thyme-leaved sandwort), *Cerastium* cf. *fontanum* (common mouse-ear), *Sanguisorba minor* ssp. *minor* (salad burnet), *Linum catharticum* (fairy flax), and grasses (Table 6.15).

The results for the Coleoptera fell into the pattern shown by the samples from the earlier phases (Table 6.16). The same species tended to predominate in the species groups, for example *Megasternum obscurum* in Species Group 7 and *Phyllopertha horticola* in Species Group 11. However, aquatic beetles and the tree and wood-dependent Coleoptera of Species Group 4 were absent (Fig 6.1). *Aphodius villosus* was also absent.

Pit [3074] (Fig 2.13, and Foldout 1C)

The remains from the fill of this pit were much less well preserved than those from pit [3067] and the mollusc assemblage was too small to merit analysis. The insect assemblage was of the same character as that from pit fill [3066]. The plant remains included seeds of buttercups, blinks, lesser stitchwort, elder and grasses. *Trifolium* type (clover etc type) flower fragments were also noted along with many moss fragments.

A few scraps of indeterminate bone, an anuran bone and a micro-mammal incisor were recovered from samples from these features (Worley 2011c). The results from both pits suggest that they were filled fairly rapidly with a mixture of turf and topsoil. There is no indication of rubbish dumping such as the deposition of hearth debris from the environmental remains, although the presence of small amounts of burnt flint in the fills indicates some activity involving fire.

Biological remains from the Upper Organic Mound Phase 6 (Tables 6.6, 6.19–6.25)

The remains recovered from Phase 6.1 of the Upper Organic Mound were similar to those recorded from the Lower Organic Mound and are generally indicative of grassland. *Cenococcum* sp. remains were particularly frequent probably reflecting a higher proportion of topsoil in the samples analysed for macroscopic plant remains (Table 6.19). The proportion of scarabaeoid dung beetles of Species Group 2 was, at 28.9 per cent, twice as high as from any of the other phases (Fig 6.1, Table 6.20) with some of the seeds recovered such as *Chenopodium* cf. *album* (fat hen), blinks, stinging nettle and common chickweed implying some disturbance. Pollen was generally very sparse and poorly preserved. One sample was analysed, but a count of only 300 total land pollen grains was achieved (against over 2000 *Lycopodium* spores used as a marker). SCPs were again present (Table 6.6).

A suid peripheral first phalanx was recovered from one of the samples. It was fully fused, but whether it came from a domestic pig or wild boar could not be established (Worley 2011c).

Only a single sample was analysed from the further dump layers as few remains were present in samples from this phase (6.2). This sample came from a dark grey band within layer [3084]

seen in the north face of the West Lateral which it was initially thought might represent a standstill episode (*see* Foldout 1C). Preservation of remains was very poor and concentration was low. Of the three mollusc shells recovered, two, *Punctum pygmaeum* and *Clausilia bidentata* are usually indicative of shaded conditions (Table 6.25). However the few insect and plant remains from the same sample suggest open grassland (Tables 6.19, 6.23, 6.24). Because this layer lies much further from the centre of the Hill and thus had been subject to some oxidation the remains recovered are fewer, but a mixture of turf, topsoil and some subsoil is suggested by the few remains recovered. It appears to represent a consolidation layer (*see* Chapter 5)

Animal bone from prehistoric contexts on the summit (Tables 6.26–6.27 – *see* end of this chapter)

A small assemblage of animal bone was recovered from Phase 16.2 (final mound construction) from the 2007 trench on the summit. Material was hand collected from six interwall deposits, a chalk rubble wall and a chalk layer, which was seen in the collapsed crater area (Table 6.26). Taxa represented include cattle, sheep/goat, probable pig, red deer (post-cranial bone; antler is reported separately, Worley Chapter 3), badger, mole and amphibian. The bones were mainly in good condition (75%), with some in moderate condition (19%) and a single bone in poor condition (6%). Root etching was recorded on four bones and carnivore gnawing on one.

Animal bones were also recovered from nine inter-wall deposit environmental samples assigned to Phase 16.2 (Table 6.27). The animal bone from these sample residues was predominantly anuran, but occasional pig, sheep or goat, badger, probable polecat and micro-mammal bones were also recovered. The badger and amphibian bones suggest a degree of disturbance on the Hill's summit (*see* Worley 2011c; and Chapter 9), meaning that the bones may not reflect activities in Phase 16.2, but rather may be intrusive from later phases.

There was no evidence for any butchery marks in the Phase 16.2 assemblage and only one bone exhibited pathology, a badger radius with exostoses in the form of lipping on the proximal and distal articulations. Given potential intrusive bones in this phase, the badger bones may be considered with the badger bone assemblage from later deposits within the summit trench (Worley, Chapter 9), all of which may represent a single individual.

Summit excavations in 1968–70 produced 129 identifiable fragments of animal bones (excluding antler) from Neolithic contexts. These were found to include cattle, pig, sheep, dog, red deer, fox, badger, beaver, hare and frog (Gardiner 1987, 46–52), a similar species list to that identified here. Re-analyses of the fragments identified as beaver suggest that they are badger bones. Like those from the 2007/8 excavations, it is possible that some of the 1968–70 bones were intrusive from later activity on the summit.

Understanding turves

Gill Campbell

Turves by their very nature attest to open environments. To produce a recognisable turf there has to be dense ground cover vegetation with a system of roots close to the surface such that the underlying soil remains attached. Such sods or turves can be cut and lifted as blocks and only form under open environments – grasslands, moorlands and heaths – so a paucity of evidence for woodland and wet habitats such as reed beds or stream sides from turves would be expected. In addition, for each turf three elements will be present when the turf is cut or scraped up:

1. living plants and invertebrates, including the flowers and seeds still attached to the plants
2. debris including seeds fallen from the living plants as well as dead and decaying invertebrates and vegetation
3. below ground parts of plants, including roots, rhizomes and tubers but also animal and plant material incorporated into the soil by various means including earthworm action and soil fauna (Hall 2003).

For each of these components some organisms will be present in greater numbers than others and some will survive better in the archaeological record. Preservation will particularly be influenced by the soil type of the turf. Thus for the material from Silbury, the pollen only survived reasonably well in the turf and topsoil originating from clay-with-flints material while molluscs only tended to be plentiful in rendzina type turf and topsoil.

Similarly, it is the woody parts and propagules, or seeds, of plants that are most likely to survive in a recognisable state. Where anoxic preservation conditions are very good, leaves, stems and flowering parts will also be preserved and can be identified to a greater or lesser extent (Hall 2003). Often stems and leaves can only be determined to family or genus level, however, and are thus of limited use in environmental reconstruction.

Invertebrates living both in the soil and on the surface of vegetation will form the major component of turf assemblages. At the same time some species such as ground beetles will tend only to be represented by a small number of individuals, while others, such as ants, will be present in large numbers. The numbers and types of different species present within the turf will also be influenced by the degree of disturbance to the vegetation cover, by the length of time that habitat has been in existence and by the proximity of different habitats such as woodland (Davies and Wolski 2001; Fenner and Thompson 2005; Davies 2008, chapter 4).

For example, within the below ground parts of the turf, plant species that have long-term persistent seed banks (plants whose seeds remain viable in the soil for at least five years) will predominate (Fenner and Thompson 2005, 76). These tend to be those species that produce seeds that are small and compact, and also annual plants that grow in environments that experience frequent, catastrophic and relatively unpredictable disturbances, in other words weeds typical of arable and waste ground (Fenner and Thompson 2005). It is also the case that soil seed banks contain species that are absent from the vegetation growing at the site (Fenner and Thompson 2005; Akinola *et al* 1998; Carruthers and Straker 1996). Therefore the plant remains found within archaeological turves will not only reflect the vegetation growing at the time of cutting but also to a certain extent the past environmental history of the turves. In addition, the amount of topsoil and subsoil within each sample will affect the relative contribution that the seed bank and seed flora (dead but undecayed seeds as adopted by Carruthers and Straker 1996) make to the archaeological assemblage (Hall 2003). Patchiness in terms of variation in the number of seeds present in the soil over small areas (Thompson 1986; Fenner and Thompson 2005) will also mean that some turves will be rich in seeds while others will contain very few.

Bearing these factors in mind, the first point that requires consideration is the source and longevity of the more robust remains recorded in the samples. This applies especially to elder seeds, which were recorded in nearly every sample and were sometimes the only uncharred plant remains present. Elder seeds consist mainly of ligno-cellulose. They are very resistant to decay and can survive over long periods in deposits. *Rubus* sp. (blackberry, raspberry) pips similarly have a high lignin content and are also resistant to decay (McCobb *et al* 2001; 2003; Carruthers and Straker 1996). Therefore, the presence of these decay resistant seeds is more likely to be a reflection of the amount of topsoil or subsoil present in a sample rather than the presence of elder trees. Dispersal by birds, however, may also account for the presence of the seeds in some of the deposits. This was suggested as a possible mechanism for the incorporation of seeds recovered in the turf stack and old ground surface of the experimental earthwork at Overton Down (Carruthers and Straker 1996, 135).

The presence of the resting bodies or sclerotia of the soil fungus of the genus *Cenococcum* can also be taken as a useful indication of the amount of topsoil in a given sample (cf Hall 2003). These remains were present in nearly all the samples from the organic mounds and were frequent in the pit fills. They were notably absent in some of the samples from the OLS and from the Gravel Mound despite being very resistant to decay. At the other extreme the remains of leaves and flower parts found in the samples, along with mosses, are more likely to reflect the vegetation growing on the turf when it was cut, although some material may have arrived in dung or been introduced by rodents, or have blown or washed in from nearby. Seeds of plants with transient seed banks, where the seeds persist in the soil for less than one year, and those species with short-term persistent seed banks, whose seeds remain viable in the soil for between one and five years (Fenner and Thompson 2005, 75), are also more likely to reflect the vegetation growing on the turf and its recent history.

Evidence for the environment

Gill Campbell, Mark Robinson, Allan Hall and Paul Davies

Given the constraints imposed by the nature of the evidence as discussed above, what can be said about the sources of the turf and topsoil used in the construction of the organic mounds? At a broad level the materials comprising the Lower and Upper Organic Mounds as well as that used to fill the two pits found during the excavations are very similar, attesting to very open environments, principally herb-rich pasture. It should be noted that the Lower Organic Mound, as observed in the tunnel sections, contained much more clay-with-flints type material than the Upper Organic Mound which was dominated by chalk rubble and rendzina type soils. Consequently this has influenced the type of remains recovered from these two phases.

The contents of the Mini-mound ([4181]) were, however, rather different, with the remains from trees and shrubs such as yew, oak, hazel, crab apple, sloe, hawthorn and bramble well represented alongside those of grassland. Some remains that could have formed part of the woodland ground flora were also recorded including *Stellaria* cf. *holostea* (greater stitchwort), dog's mercury, bugle, ground ivy and wavy hair grass. Woodland species of insect were also recorded from this context and the associated gully: the nut weevil *Curculio* cf. *nucum*, the wood-boring beetle *Grynobius planus,* and two ground beetles: *Pterostichus niger* and *Abax parallelepipedus*. Both these ground beetles are found in woods in southern England today although it has been argued that they more readily occurred in grassland during the Bronze Age (Robinson 1997, 43). Also, in sample <9809>, the few molluscs recovered included fresh specimens of *Clausilia bidentata* and *Cochlicopa* cf. *lubrica*. The former favours closed conditions including woodland, whilst the latter is found in a range of environments including woodland and is typical of damp conditions (Davies 2008; Kerney and Cameron 1979).

The presence of cereal remains and weeds of disturbed ground such as common chickweed, shepherd's purse, field pennycress, greater plantain and cleavers in this deposit suggests the presence of crop-processing waste. This waste probably arrived in the form of dung given the results of the insect analysis. The various Scarabaeoidea which feed on the droppings of the larger herbivores under pastureland, as opposed to manure heap conditions (Species Group 2), comprised 8.4 per cent of the terrestrial Coleoptera in this deposit. They included *Geotrupes* sp., *Aphodius* cf. *foetens, A.* cf. *sphacelatus* and *Onthophagus nutans*. In addition there were six individuals of *Aphodius villosus*. This is a beetle of sunny situations on sandy or chalky soils where it is regarded as being associated with decaying vegetable matter or dung (Jessop 1986, 19). Also the hydrophilid and staphylinid beetles of Species Group 7, which occur more generally in dung and also in other sorts of foul organic material, accounted for 9.7 per cent of the terrestrial Coleoptera. *Megasternum obscurum* predominated but there were also a few examples of *Cercyon* spp. and a single individual of *Anotylus sculpturatus* gp. (Fig 6.1).

Also of interest is the presence of heather pollen in this deposit. Clay-with-flints *sensu stricto* is mapped on upland areas further to the east of Silbury and in isolated pockets by the escarpment to the south of it, and these areas could have supported heathland vegetation in the Later Neolithic as is the case today at Kingley Vale, West Sussex. Two other sites in the area have also produced some evidence for heathland plants: *Ulex/Cytisus* sp. (gorse/broom) charcoal was recorded from the 1925–35 excavations at Windmill Hill (Dimbleby 1965) and from within the ditch of the Longstones enclosure (Gale 2008). It is interesting to note that gorse grows along the Beckhampton Road today (David Field, pers comm)

Overall the Mini-mound appears to have been formed by piling up material obtained from the woodland edge. Secondary woodland is suggested from the presence of yew, hazel and shrubby taxa while the evidence for dung and the likely proximity of stagnant pools from the few water beetles recovered might suggest that it was an area where animals sheltered, breaking up the ground and depositing their dung, their diet supplemented with crop processing waste (Fig 6.4).

Despite the similarities between the Lower Organic Mound, the Phase 5 pit fills and the Upper Organic Mound, there is considerable variation between samples and individual turves. The contents of sample <9200> from the Lower Organic Mound (from the east section of the Main Tunnel at Bay 74) suggest recently developed grassland, possibly on a south-facing slope given the presence of *Neckera complanata* (*see* Panel 6.2). Some past disturbance or bare ground is suggested by the numbers of nettle, knotgrass, parsley piert and ground ivy occurring together in the sample, although all have long-lived persistent seed banks. In addition, the very poorly preserved remains of *Rubus/Rosa* type (rose/bramble and similar) thorns along with fragments of seeds of dog's mercury imply the former presence or proximity of scrub/woodland.

In contrast, the contents of sample <9363> suggest a more species-rich grassland that may have had longer to develop. Seeds of all three species of buttercup which commonly occur in meadows and pastures were tentatively identified (meadow, creeping and bulbous buttercup) along with taxa typical of chalk grassland, such as fairy flax, eyebright (assuming this is more likely than red bartsia at this location) and, importantly, part of a calyx of horseshoe vetch and fragments of possible thyme leaves.

The main fill ([3066]) of pit [3067] contained a number of typical chalk grassland plants such as thyme-leaved sandwort, salad burnet and fairy flax. Thyme-leaved sandwort along with common mouse-ear have a particular affinity for ant hills so it is of interest that the main species responsible for these features, the yellow ant, was also recovered from this deposit (*see* Table P6.3.1 in Panel 6.3; Robinson 2011; Smith 1980, 284–5). The yellow ant is an indicator of older, established chalk grassland, implying that some of the material infilling the pit was harvested from well-established grassland. However, the presence of a very degraded sloe fruit stone fragment along with worn specimens of molluscs that prefer shaded conditions suggests the former presence of some scrub or woodland. Also, while occurrence of the moss *Rhytidiadelphus* cf. *triquetrus* (*see* Panel 6.2) suggests a north-facing slope, salad burnet might be regarded as more likely on southerly aspect. At Overton Down this plant was observed in the 1984 survey as having a marked preference for the south-west slope of the experimental earthwork 24 years after it was built (Hemsley 1996). One very fresh yew seed was also recovered from the pit. This could have been dispersed by a bird. Overall however, the evidence suggests multiple sources of turf and topsoil from the chalk for the contents of pit fill [3066].

Plant remains were much less well preserved in fill [3073] of the pit excavated in the West Lateral [3074]. Taxa such as greater plantain and blinks suggest disturbance. The presence of *Rhytidiadelphus* cf. *triquetrus* (*see* Panel 6.2) again might suggest a northerly aspect, while the occurrence of yellow ant suggests older grassland. There were very few molluscs retrieved from this context. Multiple sources for the material infilling the pit are likely but the paucity of the data make this difficult to prove.

Fig 6.4 (opposite) The Lower Organic Mound at Silbury is in place. This reconstruction drawing shows the Lower Organic Mound (LOM) with a flat top supported by a circle of wooden stakes. The Old Land Surface surrounding the LOM has been stripped of turf and sarsens moved to the side to create a clear space. In the foreground established chalk grassland with ant hills is shown as this is one of the areas from which the turves making up the Upper Organic Mound may have been sourced. Behind the LOM, secondary woodland and scrub is shown bordering the grassland with cattle being grazed along the woodland edge. The material comprising the Mini-mound at the end of the East Lateral could have come from this area. We have also included paths leading down to the valley. The dogs pictured in the foreground are of the maximum known height for dogs of this period (0.62m at the shoulder (Clarke 2006)). (Judith Dobie, © English Heritage)

The remains found within the Upper Organic Mound are similar to those obtained from the Lower Organic Mound indicating broadly the same range of habitats. Sample <9375> from a turf sampled in the back of the Main Tunnel contained some taxa associated with woodland or woodland edge. The single specimen of *Moehringia trinervia* (three-nerved sandwort) was very well preserved, the dog's mercury less so. The presence of some weeds of disturbed ground such as fat hen and common chickweed, which are generally absent from the other samples, suggests some disturbance. Worn, shade-loving molluscs were also recorded in this sample though the fresh specimens indicate short turf (Davies 2012). However, the yellow ant was also present (*see* Panel 6.3). As a whole this might suggest re-cutting of turf from an area that had already been stripped a few years previously with pioneer species thriving on what was once woodland edge. Three-nerved

sandwort can be a feature of chalk grassland that develops after clearance (Smith 1980, 232) and blinks might also favour such a situation (*see* Panel 6.4).

In contrast, sample <9335> produced a wider variety of remains including possible leaves of wild thyme, fairy flax and thyme-leaved sandwort. The occurrence of bulbous buttercup in association with these taxa along with the presence of yellow ant suggests a rather thin well-drained soil, although a north-facing slope might be suggested by *Rhytidiadelphus squarrosus*. On the other hand, in sample <9825> plants such as hardheads and docks suggest somewhat ranker or taller vegetation and might suggest that this turf was cut from an area where grazing pressure was reduced. This interpretation is somewhat supported by the few mollusc remains found in this sample which included *Cepaea* sp., *Trochulus hispidus* and *Cochlicopa* cf. *lubrica* (Davies 2012).

Panel 6.2 Mosses

Allan Hall and Gill Campbell

The remains of mosses from the 1968–70 excavations were analysed and reported on in some detail. Eleven different types were identified with *Neckera complanata, Pseudoscleropodium purum, Calliergon cuspidatum* and *Rhytidiadelphus squarrosus* the most frequent (Williams 1976; 1997; Hall 2012).

The 2007/8 excavations recovered remains of mosses from individual turves and from the general matrix of the organic mounds and associated features. Traces of moss were also found in samples from the OLS. The remains from the 2007/8 excavations are reported on in detail by Hall (2012). Nearly 20 different taxa were recognised (Table P6.2.1). All are generally consistent with an origin in chalk grassland. The species most frequently occurring (both in terms of numbers of samples and quantity within assemblage) – *Neckera complanata, Pseudoscleropodium purum* and the tentatively identified *Rhytidiadelphus triquetrus* – are all highly characteristic of such habitats.

To judge from Watson's (1960) survey of mosses on the chalklands of southern England (though with the *caveat* that his results relate to grassland of the mid-20th century on the South Downs and Chilterns), the two species of *Rhytidiadelphus* may be indicators of north-facing slopes, whilst the *Neckera* species may be more typical of south-facing ones, *P. purum* being indifferent with respect to aspect. The presence of these different mosses in individual turves can therefore be used to help suggest the areas from which the deposits may have been gleaned.

The only species identified from the 2007/8 excavations which is not, at first sight, consistent with an origin in chalk grassland is *Antitrichia curtipendula* (Fig P6.2.1), a species primarily of rocks and trees of northern and western distribution in Britain. This species was recovered from the organic Mini-mound at the end of the East Lateral where other woodland or scrub indicators were also found (amongst the other biological remains). There are very few records of this moss from southern England, probably because the species has fallen victim to loss of woodland

Table P6.2.1: Complete list of moss taxa from Silbury Hill 2007–8.
Nomenclature and taxonomic order follow Smith (1978). The number of contexts in which each taxon was recorded (% presence) is also given.
2+?2 indicates that there were both tentative and secure identifications.
* indicates that material of this taxon was present in more than just trace amounts in one or more assemblages.

1	*Fissidens* sp.
1	*Bryum* sp.
1	*Rhizomnium* sp.
1	cf. *Plagiomnium* sp.
1	*Antitrichia curtipendula* (Hedw.) Brid.
1	*Neckera crispa* Hedw.
7	*N. complanata* (Hedw.) Hüb.*
1	*Thamnobryum alopecurum* (Hedw.) Nieuwl.
1	cf. *Campylium* sp.
1	cf. *Amblystegium* sp.
1	*Isothecium myurum* Brid.
2+?2	*Brachythecium* sp(p).
5	*Pseudoscleropodium purum* (Hedw.) Fleisch.*
1	cf. *Eurhynchium striatum* (Hedw.) Schimp.
1	*Eurhynchium praelongum* (Hedw.) Br. Eur.
3	*Eurhynchium* sp(p).
3	*Hypnum* cf. *cupressiforme* Hedw.
8	*Rhytidiadelphus* cf. *triquetrus* (Hedw.) Warnst.
3	*R. squarrosus* (Hedw.) Warnst.

Fig P6.2.1
Remains of Antitrichia
curtipendula.
(Allan Hall,
© English Heritage)

and air pollution. However it was recorded at Heyshott Down, near Chichester, West Sussex in the latter half of the 20th century (Hill *et al* 1994). Heyshott Down is a Site of Special Scientific Interest comprising an area of former chalk pits abandoned in the 1930s. Quarrying, associated activities and the exclusion of sheep from the site for over 200 years means that the area is particularly rich in wildlife especially mosses and invertebrates (Fig. P6.2.2) (http://www.murraydown-landtrust.org.uk/).

Fig P6.2.2
Heyshott Down,
West Sussex.
(Gill Campbell,
© English Heritage)

Panel 6.3 Ants

Mark Robinson and Gill Campbell

The flying ants found during the 1969 excavations at Silbury Hill have achieved some notoriety. Their remains have been lost and all that survives in the Atkinson archive is a photograph of a number of sclerites and a set of wings of female ants, identified by Dr M Speight as *Myrmica sabuleti* (Fig P6.3.1 – notes accompanying this copy of the photograph allow more detail to be gleaned than was possible for the 1997 publication of the

1968–70 work; Robinson 1997, 41). The presence of queen ants at the winged stage has been taken as evidence that the turves were cut and that the monument was built in late July or August (*see* for example Malone 1994, 23). The remains could be present throughout most of the year however, because once the ants have landed in the turf following their mating flights they bite their wings off. These wings, and any dead ants, could become incorporated into the turf, and would be particularly abundant around any ant nests (Brian 1977, 14; Robinson 1997, 41 and 43).

Remains of *Myrmica rubra* (European fire ant), *Myrmica rubra* or *ruginodis*, *Myrmica scabrinodis* gp. and *Lasius flavus* gp (yellow ant), though notably no wings (Fig P6.3.2), were found in samples from the 1968–70 and the 2007/8 excavations in all the early phases of the mound. *Myrmica* ants are found in a number of habitats including grassland, gardens and woodland edges, building their nests in the soil, under stones or in old tree stumps. One sample (<9244> from pit fill [3066]) contained 22 *Myrmica scabrinodis* gp. worker ants, suggesting that an ant nest was included in the backfill of this pit (Robinson 2011; Leary and Field 2010, 102).

Lasius flavus gp ants, which construct mounds in old grassland and on the edge of woodland (Fig P6.3.3), were recovered in small numbers from the Phase 5 pit fills and from the Upper Organic Mound. Their colonies can reach very high numbers if they are not destroyed as a result of ploughing (Robinson 1997, 44; 2011; Wells *et al* 1976). They were not sufficiently abundant to imply many ant hills in the grassland from Phase 5 onwards but they possibly reflect the maturation of the grassland. The occurrence of at least three species of ant in the later phases illustrates the various microhabitats from which the turves and topsoil incorporated into the Upper Organic Mound and the pits were obtained. *Myrmica rubra* tends to favour sheltered habitats in pasture, whereas *Lasius flavus* prefers a warmer more open aspect (Brian 1977, 143–5; Bolton and Collingwood 1975, 17 and 26).

Panel 6.4 *Montia fontana* L. (blinks)

Gill Campbell

Montia fontana (blinks) is now generally associated with damp and wet places (Stace 1997, 156). However, during the Neolithic and early Bronze Age periods it seems to have been more typical of disturbed ground. This is probably because there were fewer disturbed ground and arable weed species present in England at this early date, meaning that blinks was able to compete successfully within this habitat. Our arable weed flora only became fully developed in the medieval period, though many weeds were introduced during the Iron Age and Roman periods (Preston *et al* 2004; Jones 1988). Interestingly, blinks is found in bulb fields on the Isles of Scilly. Here it is very wet in spring and the spacing between the bulbs is wide. This allows poorly competing weeds such as blinks a better chance of survival (Rodwell 2000, 338–9).

The occurrence of blinks seeds, in conjunction with a number of other species, can also be taken as indicative of the presence of turves in archaeological assemblages (Hall 2003, 29). Blinks, as well as being present in deposits at Silbury Hill, was recovered from turf layers at Newgrange (Groenman-van Waateringe and Pals 1982; Monk 1982). It colonised the long barrow at Irthlingborough, Northants and was found in some of the Bronze Age cremation deposits (Robinson forthcoming; Campbell forthcoming, cf http://www.english-heritage.org.uk/publications/neolithic-and-bronze-age-landscape/018-036chapter2final.pdf). It was also found in association with other plants of disturbed ground in a pit containing Mildenhall pottery in the interior of the causewayed enclosure at Etton (Nye and Scaife 1998, 292–3).

Fig P6.4.1
Remains of Montia
fontana.
(Gill Campbell,
© *English Heritage)*

Fig P6.4.2
Montia fontana
growing in
a stream bed.
(Sourced from Flickr –
© *C Whitehouse)*

While the interpretations given above regarding the possible sources or habitats from which each turf was cut are highly speculative, the remains recovered from these samples clearly show that a variety of habitats provided the turf and topsoil used in forming the organic mounds. These different habitats can all be found within a relatively small area and all could have existed within the valley and slopes immediately surrounding the construction site (*see* Fig 6.5). Cutting turves from the immediate vicinity would require the least effort but would have had a dramatic impact on the immediate surroundings of the monument.

Similar habitats, however, would also have been available within the wider area of the Marlborough Downs and the upper Kennet valley, so the harvesting and transport of materials from a wider area cannot be ruled out and the incorporation of different parts of the

N

Mini mound
Dog's mercury
beneath hazel scrub

9200
South facing slope
with cowslips

9825
Taller vegetation with
thistles and wild marjoram

9375
Ant hills on the
woodland edge

9335
Fairy flax in amongst
longer grass

9824
Moss with buttercups

9363
Chalk grassland
with wild thyme

0   500m
Scale 1:10,000

landscape into the mound could well have been important to the builders of the Hill (*see* Chapter 7).

Evidence for burning

The presence of SCPs within many of the samples and the burnt molluscs recovered from context [4166] may reflect past clearance episodes. However, these remains may also be the result of the firing of longer vegetation prior to the harvesting of turves (Ó Danachair 1957) or possibly the presence of nearby contemporary fires.

Evidence for wetland

A wetland environment is not really evident in the 2007/8 dataset; the only true aquatic plant species recovered was *Rorippa nasturtium-aquaticum* (watercress) which was found in sample <9813> from the secondary fill of the gully associated with the Mini-mound in the East Lateral and is likely to be derived from re-deposited material. A few water beetles were also recovered from this part of the monument.

Carex cf. *hirta* (hairy sedge), although it grows in damp places, would be likely to be fairly widespread in the lush grassland of the valley floor, as would rushes of the sub-genus *Genuini*. *Montia fontana* (blinks) seems to have been a weed of bare ground on acid to semi-neutral soils in the early prehistoric period rather than strongly associated with damp places (*see* Panel 6.4).

In contrast Williams (1997) identified four *Ranunculus* subgenus *Batrachium* (water crowfoot) and five *Stachys* cf. *palustris* (marsh woundwort) seeds in samples from the 1968–70 interventions. Water crowfoots grow in wet mud or water, including the dried up bed of the Winterbourne close to the Swallowhead Spring (Gill Campbell personal observation), whilst marsh woundwort generally favours wet places. Their presence in the samples suggests either that material from a wetland environment, such as a pond or stream edge, was incorporated into the monument in the early phases of construction or that the seeds were dispersed during one or more flooding episodes on to the grassland from which the turves and topsoil were harvested.

One possible explanation is that the water crowfoot and marsh woundwort recovered from the 1968–70 samples were retrieved from an area not sampled and investigated during the current research. A plausible candidate would

be the possible second Mini-mound recorded in section in the Main Tunnel between Bays 63 and 64 ([3095]). This section was not sampled during the current investigations because of the tunnel collapse in late July (*see* Chapter 10 and also methodology in Chapter 2).

Hydrology

Paul Whitehead, Mike Edmunds and Gill Campbell

One of the objectives of 2007/8 research was to further our understanding of the past hydrology of the area, since as Whittle stated in 1997 'the hydrological history of the Hill remains uncertain' (1997a, 7). To this end an assessment of the palaeohydrology of the Silbury Hill area in *c* 2500 cal BC was undertaken by Whitehead and Edmunds (2010; 2012). This used hydrogeological mapping and hydrological modelling techniques in conjunction with outputs from the historical runs of a Global Circulation Model (GCM) to recreate past flows and groundwater levels in the Upper Kennet.

As part of this work, information was obtained from the National Well record collection held at the British Geological Survey (BGS) which includes data on past water levels as well as the location of boreholes, wells and shafts. The BGS records on water levels in several parts of the Chalk aquifer were also consulted, as well as historical data on wells and boreholes published in Whitaker and Edmunds (1925). Recent information on ground and surface water management for the area was obtained from the Catchment Abstraction Management Strategy for the Kennet and Pang (EA 2006) and with reference to the Hydrogeological Map of the area (IGS 1978).

Information on the effect of water abstraction in recent decades was also obtained, including the views of local farmers as published on the Action for the River Kennet group website (www.riverkennet.org). One of the statements, by the owners of East Kennett Farm, about water flows in the past, is reproduced here as it serves to illustrate how conditions have changed since the 1950s.

Dr and Mrs B Cameron, of East Kennett Manor and Farm, East Kennett: have lived there and as a family farmed a riparian stretch since the 1940s. They say that there has been a steady lessening since the 1970s in the amount of water in the river and the length of time it flows each year. In the

Fig 6.5 (opposite) Locations in the vicinity of Silbury Hill from which individual turves may have been cut. (Gill Campbell and Eddie Lyons, © English Heritage, Aerial photography Licensed to English Heritage for PGA, through NextPerspectives™)

1950s, 1960s and 1970s it was a proper flowing river for 9 months of the year, usually drying up in October or November until its return around Christmas or New Year, but occasionally flowing all year. Often in winter and spring there was five feet depth of water at their footbridge – since the late 1970s it is never more than two feet there. During the 1980s, the river declined steadily overall (with some years better, then worse still). In 1990, the second drought year running, the river flowed at all only in January till late June in this stretch. In winter/spring 1991, the 3 springs in their water meadows (normally flowing January to April) remained dry for the first time in their more than 40 years there. The Kennet is no longer a fishing river in this stretch (which of course involves a financial loss on the value of their property), for no brown trout have been seen since the late 1970s. The Cameron's stable yard well dried up for the first time ever (to their knowledge) in 1985 or 1986, and has done on occasions since then – the well is 35ft deep and they have observed that the river flows when there is 20ft of water in the well.

Silbury Hill is sited where the Kennet valley bends from north–south to west–east (Whittle 1997a, 5; cf Whitehead and Edmunds 2012). The junction of the Middle and Lower Chalk passes beneath Silbury Hill and borehole logs show the main aquifer to be the Lower Chalk (Whitehead and Edmunds 2012). The change in direction of the valley marks the position of the Swallowhead Spring, just to the south of Silbury. Before the extraction of water from boreholes in recent times (Evans et al 1993, 142) the Kennet was a perennial stream down river from this point. Above the springs, the Kennet is called the Winterbourne and in keeping with its name, traditionally flowed only during the winter months.

The Chalk aquifer is recharged annually to a greater or lesser extent by rainfall which in this area has a long-term (modern) average of 800mm. The most complete record within 10 kilometres of Avebury is for the Rockley borehole

lying east of the area which provides information on fluctuations in water table from 1932 to the present day. In one year (1976) no recharge occurred at all, and there have been several periods in which a succession of below-average years have given rise to groundwater droughts (for example, 1995–7 and 2003–6). The extremes in fluctuation in water table at Rockley over the past 80-year period is 15.4m.

A full-time series plot of the levels at Rockley is shown in Figure 6.6 which indicates periods of low water levels every decade or so, such as in the mid-1930s, the 1950s and the 1976 drought. It is interesting to note that the mean level for the period 1932–60 was 134.27m and the mean level for 1970–2008 was 134.66m. In other words there was a slight increase in groundwater levels in recent years, despite water abstractions from the Kennet Chalk aquifer (Rushton et al 1989; Whitehead and Edmunds 2012).

There is considerable evidence from other palaeo-data and studies that the climate in 2500 cal BC was wetter and slightly warmer than the current climate (Newson and Hanwell 1982). An alternative and independent source of information is also available from Global Circulation Models (GCMs) of climate. These models simulate the world's weather patterns and provide grid squares of information across the world. They are generally used for future prediction, as in the UK Climate Impacts Project (UKCIP09, www.ukcip.org.uk). However, they have also been used to estimate past climates (Valdes et al 1999). The model used in the current study was developed at the Hadley Centre for Climate Prediction and Research, the details of which are described by Pope et al (2000). Historical model outputs for rainfall and temperature from these GCMs are available from the Bristol University web site (www.bridge.bristol.ac.uk). Such GCM model outputs have been used in a range of palaeoclimate studies by Haywood et al (2002) and by

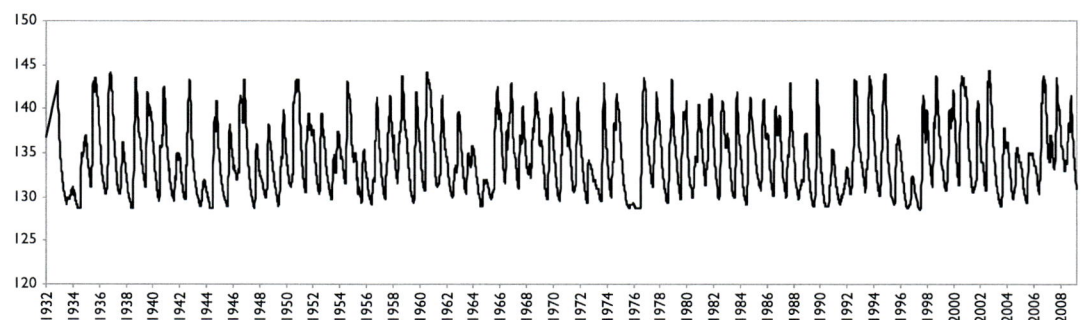

Fig 6.6
Monthly mean well levels
(metres above sea level
at Rockley
(1932–2008)
(Paul Whitehead
and Mike Edmunds,
© English Heritage)

Whitehead *et al* (2008) in a palaeohydrology study of the Bronze Age settlement of Jawa in Jordan.

Figure 6.7 shows the rainfall and runoff variations over the last 20,000 years generated using the HadCM3 version of the coupled atmosphere-ocean GCM for the Silbury Hill grid square. Both rainfall and runoff show significantly higher levels between 2500 and 2000 cal BC compared with the current values. The higher rainfall is equivalent to an 8 per cent increase compared to current levels whilst the runoff change is higher because of the effects of evapotranspiration and hydrological flowpaths moderating the runoff. While there is of course considerable uncertainty over Global Climate Models, they do provide a quantitative estimate of past conditions.

The hydrology of the Upper Kennet is complex as the flows are driven largely by groundwater from springs such as the Swallowhead Spring or springs further up the valley above Avebury. The flows at Marlborough are fed by a catchment area of 110 sq km whereas at Silbury the catchment area is only 25 sq km. The observed flows at Marlborough were used to estimate flows at Silbury from 1972 to 2008. This data was then compared to the GCM Bridge historical predictions for changes in runoff. Figure 6.8 shows a typical five-year set of data for the Silbury baseline flow and the estimated 2500 cal BC flow. The estimated 2500 cal BC flows were quite similar in summer but higher in winter as compared to the estimated baseline Silbury flow (Whitehead and Edmunds 2012).

The IHACRES modelling technique was also used to model well levels at the Rockley borehole using monthly rainfall and temperature for the area and this compared to the observed well levels (Jakeman *et al* 1990; Whitehead and Edmunds 2012). Good agreement was obtained, so the model for Rockley borehole was then converted into a simulation for the Avebury area using data from other boreholes and similar from the Avebury area to inform this simulation. The results were then compared with a simulation for 2500 cal BC based on the GCM Bridge model of climate change and also a simulation based on the UK Water Industry Research Group (UKWIR) climate change scenario for 2020. Figure 6.9 shows the effects of these two climate scenarios compared to the baseline estimated conditions for Silbury. The GCM Bridge scenario generates much higher well levels than the UKWIR scenario, but this

might be expected as the GCM Bridge scenario is considerably wetter and does not simulate the much dryer summers of the UKWIR scenario.

Overall, the results from this analysis indicated that groundwater levels at Silbury could have been about two to five metres higher on average in the past compared to current values. This would suggest that the Swallowhead Spring would most likely have been perennial at around 2500 cal BC and that the mean stream head would be located further upstream near the centre of Avebury (Whitehead and Edmunds 2012). Whilst a number of factors such as the extent of tree cover and the amount of permanent pasture versus arable would affect groundwater levels, the implication is that the environment in the vicinity of the Hill could have been wetter when construction began than it is

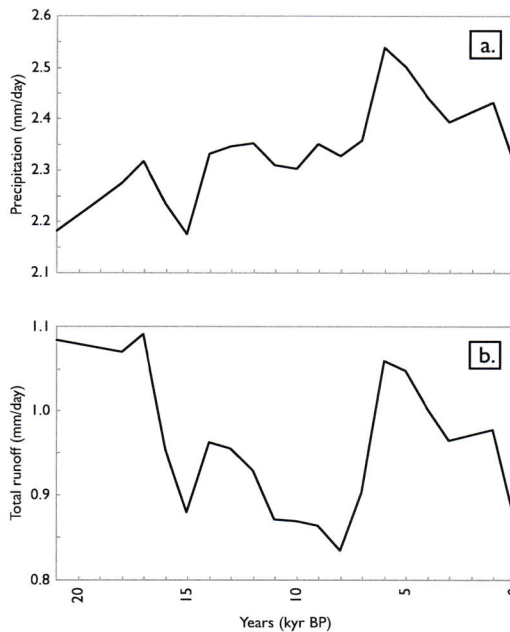

Fig 6.7
a) GCM Rainfall estimation for the Kennet area for the past 20,000 years;
b) GCM Runoff estimation for the Kennet area the past 20,000 years.
(Paul Whitehead and Mike Edmunds,
© English Heritage)

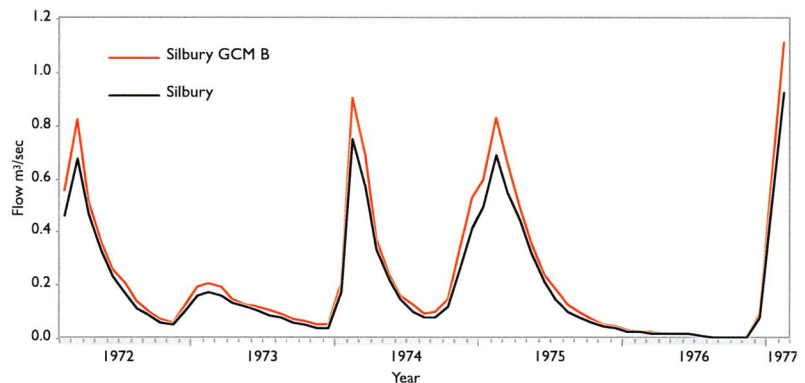

Fig 6.8 (below)
Estimated flow at Silbury together with a GCM climate change estimate of the Silbury flow over a typical five-year period.
(Paul Whitehead and Mike Edmunds,
© English Heritage)

at the present day, although during the summer months water supply may have been limited.

However, given that there is very limited evidence from the biological remains recovered from the early phases of the mound for wetland or marshy areas and assuming the turves were locally sourced (*see above*), it is likely that areas of water were very much confined, much as they are now. What we cannot be certain of is how the situation may have changed during the later phases of construction as the ditch and the ditch extension grew in size and depth. The construction of some kind of permanent water source such as a clay puddled pond may have been part of the monument complex essential either for ritual or as a water source for people and stock (*see* Chapter 8).

Alluviation

Gill Campbell and Peter Marshall

It has been argued that the building of Silbury Hill and other contemporaneous monuments in the area was associated with a renewed phase of clearance triggering alluviation (known as the West Overton Formation) (Evans *et al* 1993). While there is clear evidence for renewed clearance in the Later Neolithic (*see below*; Whittle 1993), the dating of the West Overton Formation at Avebury is in doubt. The charcoal from a cremation, cut from below or within the Avebury soil, and burnt flint found at the same

level were dated to 3020±70 BP (OxA-1348) and 3030±250 BP (TL date) respectively (Evans *et al* 1993, 146; Huxtable and Evans 1990) giving a calibrated date of 1440–1010 cal BC and 1580–570 cal BC respectively (there is some discrepancy concerning the TL date: Evans *et al* (1993, 167) state that the date was on burnt sarsen close to the cremation while the entry 35 in the TL date list (Huxtable and Evans 1990) states that the date was on burnt flint from the cremation hearth). A cattle skull from the surface of the soil (the onset of alluviation at this point) gave a date of 2980±100 BP (OxA-1045), 1440–910 cal BC (Evans *et al* 1993, 146, 163). Other dates from within the West Overton Formation (silt) give earlier dates but these could be on residual/re-deposited material (for example, the human femur from the Avebury cutting found low in the West Overton Formation (OxA–1221, 3800±60 BP) 2470–2030 cal BC. This would suggest a Middle Bronze Age date for the onset of alluviation rather than a Later Neolithic date (Fig 6.10, Table 6.28). This would fit far better with general agricultural expansion seen at this date including evidence for cultivation in the ditches of several long barrows (Whittle 1993; Gillings *et al* 2008).

Evidence for Neolithic cereal cultivation in the Avebury region

Gill Campbell

There is very little evidence for the cultivation of cereals within the vicinity of Avebury and Silbury Hill and this has implications for how the landscape in the vicinity of the monument may have been exploited. In the Early Neolithic, the most convincing evidence for the existence of cultivation plots in the area comes from underneath the South Street long barrow (Ashbee *et al* 1979). Two sets of grooves filled with humic material and crossing over each other at roughly right-angles were found scored into the subsoil surface beneath the barrow mound. These grooves have been interpreted as the remains of more than one episode of cross-ploughing, but could in fact represent the final stage of clearance activity needed to produce a level surface and suitable till for subsequent hoe cultivation (*see also* Kristiansen 1990; and Rowley Conwy 1987; Evans 2003, 58 for an alternative interpretation). Above the 'plough marks' was a poorly sorted horizon comprising

Fig 6.9 (below) Simulated Avebury baseline levels and the levels based on the GCM Bridge model and the UKWIR scenario. (Paul Whitehead and Mike Edmunds, © English Heritage)

Fig 6.10 (bottom) Calibrated dates for the West Overton Formation. (Pete Marshall, © English Heritage)

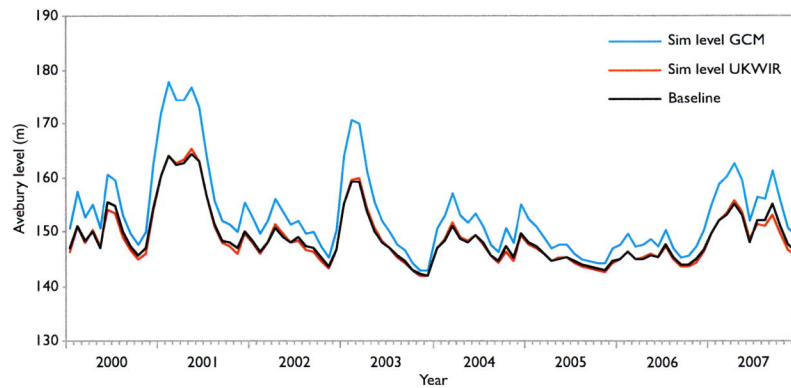

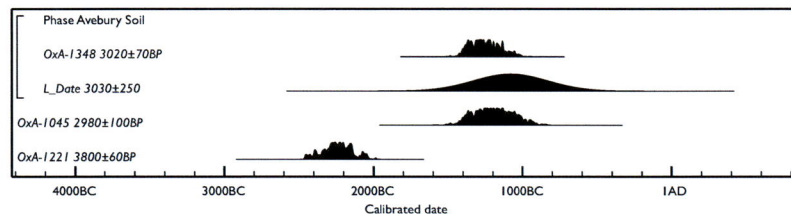

a dark chalk loam on which was developed a thin (30mm) stone-free horizon on which the barrow mound was constructed. The overall profile of this buried soil was undulating and in places there was a lower stone-free horizon underlying the poorly sorted layer. This sequence was interpreted as clearance followed by a period of stability after which hoe or spade cultivation took place resulting in the creation of the poorly sorted horizon and an uneven soil surface, following which the cultivation plot was converted to grassland before the barrow was built about 10–20 years later.

The lower stone-free horizon seen in some sections, rather than representing a period of stability, might show the depth of spade or hoe working. The association of burnt fern tracheids in the cultivation horizon along with a pollen profile showing a superabundance of bracken spores suggests that burnt bracken, and possibly unburnt bracken that had been used as animal bedding, was used to fertilise the plot. Some cereal type pollen was also recovered from this profile (Dimbleby 1979), while other possible evidence for burning and manuring is suggested by the animal bone, flint debris and calcined, unworked flint recovered from the same horizon.

The presence of bracken spores in the infill of the ditch associated with Beaker activity at Horslip long barrow may also suggest the use of bracken as a fertiliser, either in its own right or after use as animal bedding (Dimbleby 1979; Ashbee et al 1979). Burnt bracken is very high in potash and was used as a fertiliser in Scotland. While the green fronds can be used as a mulch affording protection against frost (Page 1988, 25–7), the old fronds once dried can be used as bedding for both humans and animals. It is this use as bedding which is most often referred to in archaeology (Page 1988, 25; Dimbleby and Evans 1974).

Bracken is unlikely to have grown on the rendzina soil underlying the South Street long barrow and was probably brought to site from elsewhere in the area. It would have grown on the more acidic soils developed on areas of clay-with-flints type material and could have been harvested from these areas as required.

Aside from this evidence for a cultivation plot underneath the South Street long barrow, much has been made of the occasional cereal type pollen grain recorded as part of soil pollen analysis of ditch fill sequences. The presence of a single cereal type pollen from underneath the Horslip long barrow was taken as evidence for

a cultivation episode sometime before barrow construction and led to the statement that the pre-barrow environment was open and that 'there were cereal crops on the site or in the vicinity' (Ashbee et al 1979, 211). This evidence, however, is not in line with that from the land snail analysis which suggested that the barrow was built on grassland. Furthermore there were cracks in the mound itself which meant that some of the snails in samples taken from the mound were derived from the modern plough soil (Ashbee et al 1979, 276). This suggests possible contamination of the pre-mound pollen assemblage with later material, especially given that this is pollen derived from a rendzina. Even if the cereal type pollen grain is accepted as ancient, it could derive from the processing of cereals at the site rather than cultivation (Robinson and Hubbard 1977), while cereal pollen may also have been present in the dung of animals fed on cereal chaff. None of these scenarios require cultivation on or adjacent to the monument, although they suggest it within the wider landscape.

Similar considerations pertain to instances of cereal type pollen recorded at other Early Neolithic monument contexts in the area. A single cereal type pollen grain was recovered from a spot sample taken from beneath the Beckhampton Road long barrow (Ashbee et al 1979) while cereal type pollen was recovered from underneath the bank at Windmill Hill (Dimbleby and Evans 1974, 128). Pre-barrow activity at Beckhampton Road may mean that the cereal pollen came from cereal processing and entered the deposits via the same route as the worked flint and dispersed animal bones and teeth (Ashbee et al 1979, 244). Similarly the pollen from Windmill Hill was retrieved from an occupation layer rather than a buried soil in the true sense (Dimbleby and Evans 1974, 128); contra Walker (1999), cereal type pollen was not recovered from Knap Hill (Dimbleby and Evans 1974, fig 2).

The other major source of evidence for cereal cultivation in the area comes from charred plant remains and also from impressions in ceramics. However, this evidence is largely confined to two sites: Windmill Hill (Dennell 1976; Helbaek 1952; Fairbairn 1999; 2000a) and the West Kennet Palisaded Enclosures (Fairbairn 1997), with a small amount of information from other locations: Easton Down (Fairbairn 1993), Dean Bottom and Burderop Down (Carruthers 1992), and the Longstones Enclosure (Young 2008).

SILBURY HILL

The scarcity of charred plant remains is partly down to the fact that many of the excavations took place before the 1980s, before taking flotation samples became the norm, but also because in many cases only very small volumes of material have been sampled from a given context, ten litres or less. Given that early prehistoric contexts tend only to produce charred plant remains in low concentrations, 40 to 60 litres of deposit would be required to obtain more meaningful numbers of plant remains (Campbell *et al* 2011). However, the small body of evidence, which mainly comprises assemblages of cereal grain and evidence for the later stages of crop processing relating to food preparation, may also reflect a genuine lack of activities involving crop processing pertaining to production at these non-domestic sites. As such it may be a true reflection of the extent of cereal cultivation taking place within the confines of what might be described as a ritual landscape (Fairbairn 1999, 156; Campbell and Straker 2003).

At Windmill Hill charred remains of emmer wheat, possible einkorn wheat, hulled and naked barley were recovered from Early Neolithic contexts (Fairbairn 1999; 2000a). These taxa were also found as impressions in pottery, with the addition of flax (Helbaek 1952). The only cereal chaff recovered from these contexts were a few possible emmer glume bases. This suggests that only semi-processed grain was brought to the site or was burnt at the site. The waste from the early stages of crop processing could have been disposed of elsewhere (at the location where processing took place such as cultivation plots) or fed to livestock rather than being burnt. The charred plant remains from two pits excavated as part of the 1992–3 excavations produced higher concentrations of charred plant remains than those excavated in 1988, just over 33 items per litre from one pit. This might suggest the deposition of accidentally burnt grain outside the enclosure or possibly deliberate burning of grain as an offering (Fairbairn 2000a).

Very few charred cereal remains were retrieved from Later Neolithic pits at Windmill Hill, suggesting a decline in agricultural activity at the site as compared to the earlier period (Fairbairn 1999; 2000a). Similarly, at the West Kennet Palisaded Enclosures charred cereal remains were only present in very small quantities. Probable emmer wheat and hulled six-row barley were retrieved from the ditches of Enclosure 1. In the structures of Enclosure 2 remains were more numerous and included some taxa not present in either of the enclosure ditches, amongst them some wheat chaff, possible bread wheat grain, two oat grains and a large legume, possibly a pea. However, given that large Saxon assemblages were recovered from the vicinity of these structures, these taxa could all be Saxon in date and intrusive in the prehistoric contexts (Fairbairn 1997).

This paucity of cereal remains in Later Neolithic contexts at Windmill Hill and the West Kennet Palisaded Enclosures suggests a decline in cereal cultivation in the Later Neolithic. This might represent a further movement away from cereal growing within the vicinity of the monuments or be indicative of a much wider phenomenon. One possibility is that there was a separation of female and male roles regarding food production whereby cultivation was the domain of women and separated from feasting and the visiting of sacred sites (Halstorf 1991). There is some evidence that men at this period were more mobile and physically active than women, which might indicate that hunting and herding of large ungulates was carried out by adult males with adult females undertaking a more domestic role (Pollard 2004, 61), although the strontium evidence suggests that women moved from their place of birth on marriage in early Neolithic Europe (Bentley *et al* 2012). Furthermore, strontium isotope analyses of pigs and cattle from Durrington Walls indicate that some animals were not raised on chalk downland, suggesting considerable movement of livestock (Madgwick *et al* 2012; Viner *et al* 2010).

Alternatively, cereal cultivation may have been much reduced over the region as a whole, with more reliance on wild foods and animal husbandry in the Middle and Later Neolithic as suggested by most recently by Stevens and Fuller (2012). They propose that this decline may be linked to climatic deterioration and that the building of monuments in the Late Neolithic took place during a period of reduced arable production. Regeneration of woodland might be linked to this and is attested both from the fossil beetle record and from pollen studies (Whitehouse and Smith 2010, cf Greig 1996). In a similar vein, Dark and Gent (2001) have suggested that cereal cultivation when first introduced would have enjoyed a honeymoon period relatively free from pests and diseases which were not able to survive under the new, rather different environmental conditions or were simply left behind when crops were taken to new regions. However, they point out that over time the pests and diseases would 'catch up' with the crop and that yields would subsequently fall. Such a scenario may have occurred in the Later Neolithic, although this may well have been followed by resurgence in cereal growing around 2300 cal BC (Stevens and Fuller 2012), around the time, or after, Silbury was built.

New batches of seed corn brought in from outside the region or from the continent may have led to renewed vigour in the wheat and barley population as a whole, but may also have been accompanied by new strains of diseases or even completely new organisms. Whatever the case the beginning of the second half of the 3rd millennium BC must have been a period of considerable change which would have surely brought with it the need for people to gain control and try to ensure prosperity or prevent disaster. This, as much as anything, could have provided the stimulus for building the mound (*see* Panel 8.2 for an analogy).

Land use and the management of the Silbury landscape

Gill Campbell and Mark Robinson

A wide range of different types of chalk grassland are suggested by the remains found within the Lower and Upper Organic Mounds and backfilled pits within Silbury Hill. However, residual remains, typical of woodland and scrub, in some of the samples suggest that the establishment of chalk grassland in the area, or areas, from which the turves were harvested, was relatively recent in some places. Evidence for older grassland is suggested by the presence of the yellow ant in samples from Phases 5 and 6 (*see* Panel 6.3; Robinson 2011), but this need not mean that the grassland is more than 50–100 years old.

The remains from the Mini-mound give a stronger indication of woodland, but the presence of yew, hazel and thorny shrubs such as sloe and hawthorn strongly suggest secondary rather than primary woodland (Thomas and Polwart 2003; Waller and Hamilton 2000). The presence of yew is of interest, because despite being poisonous this species is very susceptible to grazing and intolerant of fire. To become established it normally requires

another shrub, known as a nurse, to protect the young seedlings from grazing animals and will tend to expand when grazing pressure is reduced (Thomas and Polwart 2003). *Juniper communis* (juniper) is the preferred nurse for yew, though hawthorn can also play this role. Somewhat surprisingly, no macroscopic remains or pollen of juniper were found in any of the samples.

Juniper is very sensitive to fire and unlike yew has no effective seed bank. It is also extremely sensitive to winter grazing with the seeds needing bare ground to germinate (Thomas *et al* 2007). While it is difficult to argue from absence of evidence, it seems possible that the intensity of human activity in this area throughout the Neolithic may have effectively eliminated juniper from the environment, with the possibility that use of the land for winter grazing was the principal factor. Yew on the other hand was able to survive, with hawthorn potentially acting as a nurse shrub. Having a more effective seed bank, yew would be less susceptible to short-term disturbance than juniper and may be more able to withstand winter grazing pressure.

The evidence both for secondary woodland and for grassland less than a hundred years old might be taken as evidence for increased activity within the valley prior to the inception of Silbury. Pulses of activity preceding monument building or refurbishment have been recognised elsewhere (Harding and Healy 2007, 181) and are evident at South Street long barrow (Ashbee *et al* 1979), Easton Down long barrow (Whittle *et al* 1993) and Millbarrow Neolithic chambered tomb (Harris and Evans 1994).

At South Street long barrow the molluscan assemblage from the top part of the secondary ditch fill produced a rich woodland fauna and only 11 per cent open country species. The woodland taxa assemblage included species such as *Merdigera obscura* and *Acanthinula aculeata* which have rather narrow ecological requirements, although the extent and character of the woodland habitat these species require to flourish is not yet known (Davies and Wolksi 2001). Above this, and immediately below the rubble layer associated with cross-plough marks on the flanks of the ditch, some indicators of disturbance of the woodland environment were found: fresh examples of *Pomatias elegans* (which requires a loose substrate into which it can burrow) and increasing numbers of *Pupilla muscorum* and *Vallonia excentrica*. The rubble layer itself, which contained Beaker pottery and a large flint scraper, showed a dramatic increase in open country molluscs with very few woodland or shade-loving species. However, the clearance that produced this rubble layer and plough mark evidence does not appear to be followed by a change to an arable regime. The plough marks were not obliterated by continued ploughing and there were no plough soil accumulations above the rubble layer but rather soil development indicated by a relatively stone-free worm-sorted horizon. At the same time, although dominated by open country species, the overall numbers of molluscs recovered did not fall dramatically as would be expected from frequent disturbance as a result of cultivation (Ashbee *et al* 1979, 293, 298). This then suggests renewed activity at the monument or the area around it in the Beaker period with clearance involving ploughing but not necessarily cultivation, followed by the establishment of open grassland.

At Easton Down a long period of woodland cover at the site was followed by a similar clearance in the Later Neolithic/Early Bronze Age (Whittle *et al* 1993). The molluscan remains from the upper part of secondary fill of the south ditch of the long barrow, associated with a radiocarbon date on a *Bos* premolar (OxA-3761) of 3860±60 BP; 2480–2140 cal BC (Whittle *et al* 1993, 203), show an increase in open country species including a peak in *Pomatias elegans*. Immediately above this context there was some soil development. This soil layer produced numerous mollusc shells comprising a rich diversity of open country species, again suggesting the establishment of grassland rather than cultivation. The same context also produced banded shells of *Cepaea nemoralis* at the expense of unbanded forms. Species of this snail with banded shells have been found to be more common in grassland, where their coloration gives better camouflage, while unbanded forms are more prevalent in woodland where they less visible to predators in the leaf litter. Above this soil layer, cultivation is suggested by a poorly sorted tertiary infill which contained far fewer molluscan remains. Pottery from the soil layer suggests an Early Bronze Age date while the tertiary fill immediately above produced a crude flint assemblage of later Bronze Age character (Whittle *et al* 1993, 214–17).

Similarly, at Millbarrow chambered tomb, the molluscan analysis of the secondary fills of the outer ditches showed woodland regeneration followed by a return to open country conditions. Grassland rather than arable land use is suggested as there was a relatively high diversity of different molluscs with *Vertigo pygmaea*, a snail typical of grass swards, present (Harris and Evans 1994). Dating for woodland clearance and the re-establishment of a grassland setting for the monument at Millbarrow is unclear, although the recovery of a plano-convex knife from the outer ditch suggests a Later Neolithic date at the earliest (Harris and Evans 1994, 32; Whittle *et al* 1993).

It is worth emphasising at this point in our discussion that the undulating chalk downland surrounding Silbury, with gentle slopes leading down to a river valley of modest width, once deserted by humans and livestock, would eventually revert to woodland (Bennett 1989, 143; Whittle 1993), so this evidence for clearance followed by the establishment of grassland implies the presence of humans and their livestock. There are none of the very steep scarps present in parts of Hampshire and Sussex which might, as a result of erosion, support open vegetation consisting of a mixture of bare patches, grassland and scrub (Waller and Hamilton 2000). While there is evidence of open grassland in the area of Stonehenge and from Cranborne Chase at the beginning of the Neolithic where woodland development appears to have been slow in the early Holocene, in North Wiltshire substantial woodland cover is attested at the same period (Allen and Gardiner 2009; French 2009, 93; French *et al* 2007, 65).

The winterbournes, springs and small streams within the valley are of insufficient size to form braided channels or large gravel islands, even in times of flood. In the valley floor, the wetter areas could well have supported alder with lime and oak taking over in the drier areas on soils developed on clay-with-flints material (but *see below*). On the chalk slopes ash and hazel would be the main woodland trees, interspersed with some yew, field maple and elm (Bennett 1989).

While the existence of woodland clearings following tree fall and subsequent grazing of these areas by wild animals such as deer and aurochs would lead to some open areas, tree cover would tend to predominate where humans were absent. Indeed, grazing by wild animals as a mechanism by which closed woodland is converted into open grassland as put forward by Vera (2000) is now believed to be of minor importance in determining woodland cover, with use of fire and potentially woodland management by Mesolithic peoples being of far greater importance. In contrast the introduction of domestic livestock appears to have had a major impact (Mitchell 2005; Whitehouse and Smith 2010; *see also* Allen and Gardiner 2009).

Further evidence regarding the nature of the woodland resource around Silbury is provided from charcoal studies. Later Neolithic sites in the area generally produce a limited amount of oak and rather more ash than those in some other areas of the country like the Thames Valley (Smith 2002, table 9). It is also striking that often only small diameter round wood has been recovered from the Avebury region and that thorny and scrubby species tend to predominate (Smith 1984, 104). For example, charcoal remains associated with Beaker period clearance in the south ditch at Easton Down long barrow produced saplings and twigs of Pomoideae type (hawthorn, whitebeam and similar), ash and sloe contrasting somewhat with the evidence from the primary fill where oak and ash dominated the assemblage with some hazel and Pomoideae type also present. Even in the primary fill of this ditch, however, most of the fragments were from saplings and twigs (Cartwright 1993), suggesting use of underwood and scrub as fuel rather than the exploitation of larger timber. Similarly shrubby species: sloe, hazel, gorse or broom, birch and Pomoideae were recovered from the Later Neolithic contexts at the Longstones enclosure (Gale 2008).

Windmill Hill and the West Kennet Palisaded Enclosures are somewhat the exception. Charcoal recovered by hand from Alexander Keiller's excavations at Windmill Hill showed a predominance of hazel and sloe, accounting for over 50 per cent of the identifications. Oak and Pomoideae type were also fairly frequent with smaller amounts of ash, two fragments of elder, and single specimens of birch and broom or gorse (Dimbleby 1965). The charcoal assemblage from the later 1988 excavations, which was retrieved from flotation samples, provides a somewhat different picture. Oak was the most frequently recovered wood, although in many contexts this was round wood rather than trunk wood. Hazel was also frequent along with Pomoideae and smaller amounts of ash and *Prunus* spp., including sloe. Birch and yew were only recorded from the old ground surface (Cartwright 1999). The relative abundance of oak in these Early Neolithic contexts may reflect exploitation of primary woodland, where oak may have been more abundant but it could also

be that oak, with hazel, was locally abundant at this elevation with ash being more frequent in the valley sides. Alternatively oak could be frequent at the site because it was used more in construction, with the round wood potentially being waste which was burnt or used for building hurdles, roofing and so forth (Cartwright 1999).

Use of oak timber for construction purposes is clearly demonstrated at the West Kennet Palisaded Enclosures where the majority of the large (250–400mm in diameter) posts forming the palisades were found to be of oak (Cartwright 1997; Whittle 1997a, 152). This site also produced early evidence for beech and one of the few charcoal records of alder for the area. Beech was only recovered from Enclosure 2 and therefore might be intrusive and of medieval date, although, a single beech pollen grain was recorded in the 1968–70 samples from within Silbury Hill (Dimbleby in Whittle 1997a). Alder, with some willow or poplar, was retrieved from ditch contexts at West Kennet palisaded enclosures north of the river. This may represent exploitation of a very local patch of wet woodland.

The bones previously assigned to beaver from Silbury have been re-identified as badger (*see above* and Worley2011c). However, a single cervical vertebra of beaver was recovered from deep within the inner ditch of Enclosure 1 at the West Kennet Palisaded Enclosures (Edwards and Horne 1997, 123), while a single beaver incisor was also recovered from West Kennet long barrow where it was considered by Piggott (1962, 49, 54) to be a possible tool (miniature chisel). This part of the valley would not have contained sufficient permanent water bodies to support beaver, although further down the valley, possibly from Marlborough onwards, modification of watercourses by beaver would be expected.

The largely open habitats attested by biological remains from turves and topsoil from the early phases of Silbury as well as other Beaker and Neolithic sites in the area (*see,* for example, Gillings *et al* 2008, and above) reflect management by humans. It was a place bearing the mark of exploitation and manipulation over thousands of years and not a pristine wilderness into which people intruded from time to time.

While this may be stating the obvious it is an important point, for the lack of direct evidence for settlement and the idea that humans only visited the monuments at certain times of year can leave the impression that the area was deserted most of the time. The evidence for cereal cultivation in the immediate vicinity of the monuments is modest with good pollen evidence lacking and no real evidence for the early stages of crop processing which might suggest cultivation in the immediate area (*see above*). The macroscopic cereal remains from Silbury and other local sites could represent goods brought into the area from elsewhere: grain for consumption or exchange, while remains interpreted as being from dung could come from animals brought into the valley from elsewhere or fed on imported cereal chaff.

In contrast, the evidence for grazing by livestock is compelling. Open dry grassland is indicated by the material from the Lower and Upper Organic Mounds (Davies 2012; Evans 1997; Evans 1972, 265–7; Campbell 2011) with medium to light grazing by domestic livestock suggested by the Coleoptera (Robinson 2011). For the Early Neolithic, evidence from beneath the long barrows and from the base of their associated ditches in the vicinity of Silbury also provides consistent evidence that these monuments were set within a grazed landscape and built either within established grassland or at the ecotone between woodland and pasture (Whittle *et al* 1993; and *above*).

Some resurgence of activity in the valley prior to the beginning of construction at Silbury is suggested by the occurrence of decayed woodland taxa in the turves from the organic mounds and the absence of yellow ant from the Lower Organic Mound. This implies clearance, just as the presence of secondary woodland and scrub from the Mini-mound suggests the presence of regenerated woodland, a pattern mirrored at other sites in the area (*see above*).

Such an open landscape requires maintenance by humans. In other words it would need to be managed in order to maintain the interconnectivity of monuments and other special or sacred places. It is likely that this was achieved by keeping herds or flocks of animals permanently within the valley and surrounding area combined with judicious burning and clearing of scrub. One may imagine that the herds or flocks of animals were strictly controlled in where and when they could graze. They may have been part of a sacred herd, in permanent residence, and kept for specific purposes of sacrifice, feasting and the succour of pilgrims. Alternatively, it may be that the resident herds and flocks were continually in flux with new animals arriving all the time and others leaving or being killed as required, that is there was no resident livestock but rather a series of visiting herds/flocks and people.

Similar constraints may also have been applied to areas of woodland, with some areas managed as coppice, some as wood pasture and/or for the growth of large timber trees (cf Gale 2008; Cartwright 1997). This level of management implies a considerable level of control. While such control of movement and passage may not have existed everywhere it is suggested for Silbury and Avebury. It perhaps invokes the idea of individuals of power and influence who could direct people to do their bidding either through coercion or as a result of religious belief (*see* Panel 8.2).

Conclusion

The biological remains recovered from turves and topsoil within the centre of Silbury Hill provide overwhelming evidence for herb-rich chalk grassland, which results from management through grazing. There is limited evidence for other habitats. Some woodland is indicated but wetland indicators are rare, even though the head of the Kennet may have been further upstream in the Later Neolithic. This may be in part a product of the small area of the monument investigated coupled with the nature of the evidence, as it derives principally from turves and topsoil, but given the likely catchments of the different types of biological remains recovered, the results can probably be taken as indicative of the wider landscape.

In addition, very little in the way of charred plant remains, animal bone or material culture was retrieved from any of the phases sampled. This again may be a result of the small area excavated but seems also to suggest that construction was carried out separately from everyday living (*see* Bishop Chapter 3; and Chapter 7).

The paucity of evidence for cereal cultivation both from Silbury Hill itself and the wider Avebury area at this time may reflect a greater emphasis on stock rearing but could equally relate to the landscape management and land use with cereal cultivation occurring away from ceremonial sites. However, it may also be that this evidence is simply archaeologically invisible (*see* Chapter 8 regarding settlement sites).

Analysis of individual turves shows that they have varying histories and are indicative of a range of grassland habitats. While these habitats are all available with the area immediately around the site it is conceivable that they were brought from further afield. Their inclusion in the Hill could have been of considerable ritual importance (*see* Chapter 7).

The fact that some of the turves and samples are suggestive of former woodland may be linked to the other clearance episodes recorded within the ditches of a number of monuments in the area and point to renewed or increasing human influence in the valley, Whittle's phase E (Whittle 1997a, table 49). The inception and enlargement of Silbury may have as much to do with stress resulting from environmental pressures (disease, crop failure and disruption of food supplies) and the need to try to control these forces or produce better outcomes than from the desire to compete with others or provide proof of power.

Table 6.1: Details of the samples analysed for biological remains from Phases 2–6. SDD refers to site sub–division 5 = Main Tunnel, 8 = West Lateral, 9 = East Lateral, decimal refers to the bay and letter afterwards refers to the face (eg 8.06N refers to a sample taken from the north section of bay 6 in the West Lateral)

Sample no	Sub sample of	Sample size	Context no	SDD	Plant	Moss	Mollusc	Insect	Pollen	Phase	Context description
9834	9277	0.65 litres	3020	8.12	√					1	Natural
9832	9277	0.3 litres	3087/9	8.12	√					2	OLS
9833	9277	1 litres	3021	8.12	√					2	OLS
9238	N/A	2 litres	4041	5.80E	√		√	√		2	OLS
9815	9434	3 litres	4041	9.13	√			√		2	OLS
9821	9435	3.8 litres	4041	9.07S	√			√		2	OLS
9264/2	9264		3035	5.81W					√	2	Organic layer above OLS – preserved turf?
9814	9247	2 litres	3069	5.74W	√		√	√		3	Grey layer directly overlying the Gravel Mound
9819	9251	2 litres	4153	5.77E	√		√			3	Gravel Mound
9820	9252	2 litres	4166	5.77E	√	√	√	√		3	Dark silty layer on top Gravel Mound – poss soil horizon?
9439/2	9439		4181	9.13					(√)	4	Organic Mini-mound
9808	9425	2 litres	4181	9.13	√		√	√		4	Organic Mini-mound
9809	9425	3 litres	4181	9.13			√	√		4	Organic Mini-mound
9826	9425	8 litres	4181	9.13				√		4	Organic Mini-mound
9827	9425	2 litres	4181	9.13	√	√	√			4	Organic Mini-mound
9811	9338	2 litres	4170	9.12S	√	√		√		4	Primary fill of gully
9812	9338	3 litres	4170	9.12S				√		4	Primary fill of gully
9813	9339	2 litres	4173	9.12S	√	√		√		4	Secondary (main) fill of gully
9200	N/A	2 litres	4156	5.74E	√	√		√		4	Part of Lower Organic Mound
9264/4	9264		3046	5.81W					√	4	Part of Lower Organic Mound
9264/7	9264		3046	5.81W					(√)	4	Part of Lower Organic Mound
9264/8	9264		3046	5.81W					√	4	Part of Lower Organic Mound
9362	N/A	1.5 litres	3075	8.02S				√		4	Part of Lower Organic Mound
9363	N/A	0.5 litres	3075	8.02S	√					4	Part of Lower Organic Mound
9369/1	9369		3075	8.5N					√	4	Part of Lower Organic Mound
9824	9267	2 litres	3046	5.81W	√	√	√	√		4	Part of Lower Organic Mound.
9828	9267	2 litres	3046	5.81W	√	√	√			4	Part of Lower Organic Mound.
9236	N/A	2 litres	4156	5.80E			√			4	Part of Lower Organic Mound (this sample right at edge of Gravel Mound
9237	N/A	2 litres	4156	5.80E			√			4	Part of Lower Organic Mound (this sample right at edge of Gravel Mound
9379/1	9379		3046	5.80W					(√)	4	Part of Lower Organic Mound.
9810	9340	2 litres	3073	8.03N	√	√		√		5	Fill of pit [3074]
9816	9340	2 litres	3073	8.03N				√		5	Fill of pit [3074]
9817	9244	2 litres	3066	5.75/6W	√	√	√	√		5	Secondary fill of pit [3067]
9818	9244	3 litres	3066	5.75/6W				√		5	Secondary fill of pit [3067]
9823	9246	2 litres	3070	5.75/6W	√	√	√	√		5	Primary fill of pit [3067]
9353/2	9353		?3061	5.80W					(√)	6.1	Part of Upper Organic Mound

Table 6.1: Details of the samples analysed for biological remains from Phases 2–6. SDD refer to site sub–division 5 = Main Tunnel, 8 = West Lateral, 9 = East Lateral, decimal refers to the bay and letter afterwards refers to the face (eg 8.06N refers to a sample taken from the north section of bay 6 in the West Lateral)

Sample no	Sub sample of	Sample size	Context no	SDD	Plant	Moss	Mollusc	Insect	Pollen	Phase	Context description
9829	9277	0.3 litres	3083/4	8.12	√					6.1/2	Part of Upper Organic Mound
9830	9277	0.4 litres	3083/4	8.12	√					6.1/2	Part of Upper Organic Mound
9831	9277	0.55 litres	3083/4	8.12	√					6.1/2	Part of Upper Organic Mound
9335	N/A	2 litres	3078	8.06N	√	√	√	√		6.1	Part of Upper Organic Mound
9375	N/A	2 litres	3061	5.80W	√	√	√	√	(√)	6.1	Part of Upper Organic Mound
9407/1	9407		3083	8.12N					(√)	6.1	Part of Upper Organic Mound
9407/2	9407		3083	8.12N					(√)	6.1	Part of Upper Organic Mound
9407/3	9407		3083	8.12N					(√)	6.1	Part of Upper Organic Mound
9825	9276	2 litres	3083	8.12N	√	√	√	√		6.1	Part of Upper Organic Mound
9822	9320	2 litres	3084	8.13N	√	√	√	√		6.2	Further dump layers

Table 6.2: Coleoptera from Phase 2

	OLS			Habitat	Species group
Sample	9821	9815	9238		
Sub-sample of	9435	9434	N/A		
Context number	4041	4041	4041		
Sample weight (kg)	3.58	3.00	1.98		
Phase	2	2	2		
HYDROPHILIDAE					
Megasternum obscurum (Marsh.)	2	1	1	FVC	7
STAPHYLINIDAE					
Stenus spp.	2	1	1	TM	
Tachyporus sp.	–	1	–	T	
SCARABAEIDAE					
Aphodius spp. (not villosus)	1	1	2	mostly F	2
Phyllopertha horticola (L.)	1	1	–	larvae on roots in permanent grassland	11
ELATERIDAE					
Agrypnus murinus (L.)	1	–	–	G	11
Agriotes sp.	–	1	–	larvae mostly on roots of grassland plants	11
CHRYSOMELIDAE					
Longitarsus sp.	1	–	–	various herbs	
APIONIDAE					
Apion spp.	–	1	–	various herbs	3
CURCULIONIDAE					
Barynotus obscurus (F.)	1	–	2	various herbs	
Sitona sulcifrons (Thun.)	–	1	–	Fabaceae, mostly Trifolium spp.	
Liparus coronatus (Gz.)	–	–	1	Apiaceae	
Mecinus pyraster (Hbst.)	1	–	1	Plantago lanceolata L. and P. media L.	
Total	**10**	**8**	**8**		

Key for habitat information: B: bankside/water's edge; C: carrion; D: disturbed/bare ground; F: dung; G: grassland; M: marsh; T: terrestrial and occurring in several habitats; V: decaying plant remains; W: woodland or scrub. Less usual habitats are given in brackets

Table 6.3: Plant remains from Phases 2 and 3

		9815	9238	9821[1]	9814	9819	9820
Sample		9815	9238	9821[1]	9814	9819	9820
Sub-sample of		9434	N/A	9435	9247	9251	9252
Context number		4041	4041	4041	3069	4153	4166
Context		OLS	OLS	OLS	Grey layer over Gravel Mound	Gravel Mound	?pos soil
Volume in litres		3	2	3.8	3	2	2
Weight in kg		+/–3	1.984	3.579	2.187	1.916	1.916
Phase		2	2	2	3	3	3
Mesh size in microns		180	180	180	180	180	180

Taxon (element if not a seed)	Common name						
Ranunculus cf bulbosus L.	Bulbous buttercup	1					1
Ranunculus acris/ repens/ bulbosus	Buttercup						2
Ranunculus sp.	Buttercup, crowfoot	1	(4)	2			1
Urtica dioica L.	Stinging nettle						3
Corylus avellana (nutshell fragment)	Hazel	6c	3c		2c		
Montia fontana L.	Blinks						1
Stellaria graminea L.	Lesser stitchwort	1 (1)	(2)				3
Cerastium cf. fontanum Baumg.	Common mouse-ear						4 (1)
Caryophyllaceae indet.	Campion family		8	6			(10)
Plantago major L.	Greater plantain	2					
Euphrasia/ Odontites sp.	Eyebright/Red bartsia						2
Sambucus nigra L.	Elder	mni 2	mni 1	mni 1	mni 1	mni 1	4
Carduus/ Cirsium sp.	Thistle	(1)					
Carex sp.	Sedge						1
Festuca/ Lolium sp.	Fescue/ rye-grass						1
cf. Poa pratensis L.	Smooth meadow grass			1			
Arrhenatherum elatius var. bulbosum (tuber) (Willd.) St-Amans	Couch grass				1c		
Agrostis sp.	Bent						1
cf. Phleum pratense L.	Timothy						1
Poaceae indet.	Grass family	1		2 (1)	1		5
Poaceae indet. (culm node)	Grass family						3
Poaceae indet. (rhizome)	Grass family	1c				1c	
Monocot stem/leaves	Grass family	++		++			++
Indeterminate root/rhizome					2		+
Dicot node							1
IGNOTA				3	1		4
Bone						+	+
Burnt bone							+
Bud scales							1
Cenococcum sp.		(1)	4		2		3
Charcoal		++	+		++	++	+
Earthworm granules							*
Green plant					*		*
Molluscs							+++
Moss				++	+		+++
Insects +		+			+	+	+++
Wood					1		1

Key: *, present in additional Sub-sample; +, present; ++, frequent; +++.common; ++++, abundant. ( ) Indicate a tentative identification, c = charred
[1] Charcoal from this sample, which was from the possible hearth, was examined. The assemblage comprised: 29 fragments of hazel and two cf. hazel, 2 fragments of Prunus sp. (sloe, plum etc), 7 fragments of Maloidae and 2 of cf. Maloidae, 3 fragments of indeterminate root, and 6 indeterminate fragments.

Table 6.4: Other Insects from Phase 2 (for habitat key see Table 6.2)

		OLS			Habitat
Sample		**9821**	**9815**	**9238**	
Context number		4041	4041	4041	
Sub-sample of		9435	9434	N/A	
Sample weight (kg)		3.58	3.00	1.98	
Phase		2	2	2	
DIPTERA					
Diptera indet.	– puparium	I	I	I	T

Table 6.5: Shells recovered from the OLS (context 4041)

Sample	**9238**
Context number	4041
Species	
Trochulus hispidus gp.	4
Vertigo pygmaea Drap.	I
Vallonia costata Müller	3
Vallonia sp.	4

Table 6.6: Pollen counts from analysed samples

Sample		**9264/2**	**9264/8**	**9369/1**	**9264/4**	**9439/2**	**9407/2**
Context number		3035	3046	3075	3046	4181	3083
Taxa	**Common name**						
Pinus sylvestris L.	Scots pine	3.0	3.5	7.0	1.5	12.5	5.0
Taxus baccata L.	Yew			1.0	12.0	9.0	10.0
Ulmus sp.	Elm				5.0		
Quercus sp.	Oak			1.0	6.0	9.0	5.0
Betula sp.	Birch	4.0	1.0	0.0	1.0	4.0	4.0
Alnus glutinosa (L.) Gaertn.	Alder	22.0	12.0	8.0	11.0	15.0	13.0
Corylus avellana-type	Hazel, Sweet gale etc	102.0	84.0	36.0	273.0	118.0	69.0
Tilia undiff.	Lime	5.0	4.0	3.5	3.0	18.0	15.0
Salix sp.	Willow	2.0	1.0	1.0	6.0	3.0	5.0
Fraxinus excelsior L.	Ash			1.0			
Calluna vulgaris (L.) Hull	Heather					I	
Ericaceae undiff.	Heather family					I	
Ranunculus acris-type	Meadow buttercup type	5	2	5			I
Ranunculaceae undiff.	Buttercup family			I	4	I	5
Urtica dioica L.	Stinging nettle			3	9	2	
Chenopodiaceae undiff	Goosefoot family					I	I
Stellaria holostea L.	Greater stitchwort					2	
Caryophyllaceae undiff.	Campion family	10	2.5	2.5	2	20	
Rumex acetosella L.	Sheep's sorrel					I	
Filipendula sp.	Meadowsweet/Dropwort	8	I	2	I	I	I
Potentilla-type	Cinquefoil, wild Strawberry etc	3	0	I	I		
Rosaceae undiff.	Rose family	7	2	3	3	2	4
Fabaceae undiff.	Pea family			I			
Epilobium-type	Willowherb, rosebay Willowherb etc			I			
Apiaceae undiff.	Carrot family	2			I		2
Plantago lanceolata L.	Ribwort plantain	2			16.5	5	
Plantago media/major	Plantain						I
Rubiaceae undiff..	Bedstraw family	7			26	2	3
Valeriana dioica L.	Marsh valerian						I
Achillea-type	Yarrow, Mayweeds etc						I
Arctium-type	Burdock, Carline thistle etc					4	
Centaurea nigra L.	Hardheads			I			4
Solidago virgaurea-type	Thistles, Goldenrod etc		I				
Cichorium intybus-type	Hawkbit, Dandelion, Chicory etc	9	173	328	79	194	86

UNDERSTANDING THE ENVIRONMENT

Table 6.6: Pollen counts from analysed samples

		Sample	9264/2	9264/8	9369/1	9264/4	9439/2	9407/2
		Context number	3035	3046	3075	3046	4181	3083
Asteraceae undiff.	Daisy family		3	31	28	1	9	4
Poaceae undiff.	Grass family		313	182	69	46	87	36
Cyperaceae undiff.	Sedge family		8	5	3	2	10	13
Sparganium emersum-type	Bur-reed type						1	7
Nymphaea alba L.	White water-lily				1		1	5
Nuphar sp.	Yellow water-lily						1	1
Potamogeton natans-type	Pondweed type						3	4
Pteropsida (monolete) indet.	Fern family		62	66	31	11	43	24
Polypodium sp.	Polypody		23	18	22.5	29.5	61	77.5
Polypodiaceae undiff.	Polypody family						13	13
Pteridium aquilinum (L.) Kuhn	Bracken		5	2	2	2	17	17
Sphagnum sp.			2				1	1
Unid.degraded			231	56	32	70	50	47
Unid. broken			24	16	14	19	8	7
Unid. corroded			5	21	14	23	4	4
Unid. crushed			89	38	30	58	15	9
Unid. obscured			9	9	6	23	13	11
Lycopodium			189	193	612	243.5	2351	2070
Total land pollen			**497.0**	**508.5**	**503.0**	**508.5**	**500.5**	**299.0**
SCPs				17	15	21	11	18

Table 6.7: Coleoptera from Phase 3 (for habitat key see Table 6.2)

	Gravel	Mound	Habitat	Species group
Sample	9814	9820		
Sub-sample of	9247	9252		
Context number	3069	4166		
Sample weight (kg.)	2.19	1.92		
Phase	3	3		
CARABIDAE				
Calathus fuscipes (Gz.)	–	2	WDG – often in meadowland	
C. melanocephalus (L.)	–	1	GD(W)	
HYDROPHILIDAE				
Megasternum obscurum (Marsh.)	–	3	FVC	7
STAPHYLINIDAE				
Xantholinus glabratus (Grav.)	–	2	GDFV	
X. linearis (Ol.)	–	1	WGV(FC)	
Philonthus sp.	1	3	FVC(T)	
Aleocharinae indet.	–	1	TFVC	
GEOTRUPIDAE				
Geotrupes sp.	–	1	F	2
SCARABAEIDAE				
Aphodius cf. *sphacelatus* (Pz.)	–	1	FVC	2
A. villosus Gyl.	–	1	V(F)	
Aphodius spp. (not *villosus*)	–	1	mostly F	2
Onthophagus sp. (not *ovatus*)	–	1	F(C)	2
Phyllopertha horticola (L.)	1	1	larvae on roots in permanent grassland	11
ELATERIDAE				
Agrypnus murinus (L.)	1	1	G	11
Agriotes sp.	–	1	larvae mostly on roots of grassland plants	11
CHRYSOMELIDAE				
Longitarsus sp.	–	1	various herbs	

Table 6.7: Coleoptera from Phase 3 (for habitat key see Table 6.2)

	Gravel	Mound	Habitat	Species group
Sample	9814	9820		
Sub-sample of	9247	9252		
Context number	3069	4166		
Sample weight (kg.)	2.19	1.92		
Phase	3	3		
APIONIDAE				
Apion spp.	–	I	various herbs	3
CURCULIONIDAE				
Phyllobius or Polydrusus sp.	–	I	trees, shrubs and some herbs	
Barynotus obscurus (F.)	I	–	various herbs	
Sitona lepidus Gyll.	–	I	Leguminosae, mostly Trifolium spp.	3
Total	**4**	**25**		

Table 6.8: Other insects from Phase 3 (for habitat key see Table 6.3)

		Gravel	Mound	Habitat
Sample		9814	9820	
Sub-sample of		9247	9252	
Context number		3069	4166	
Sample weight (kg)		2.19	1.92	
HEMIPTERA	– HOMOPTERA			
Aphrodes bicinctus (Schr.)		–	I	grasses
Homoptera indet.		–	I	T
HYMENOPTERA	– FORMICIDAE			
Myrmica rubra (L.) or ruginodis Nyl.	– worker	I	–	T
M. scabrinodis gp.	– worker	–	4	T
Myrmica sp.	– worker	I	6	T
Myrmica sp.	– female	–	I	T
DIPTERA				
cf. Scathophaga stercorea (L.)	– puparium	–	I	fresh dung
Diptera indet.	– puparium	I	6	T

Table 6.9: Shells recovered from Phase 3

Sample	9819	9814	9820
Context number	4153	3069	4166
Species			
Cochlicopa cf. lubrica Müller	I	3	3
Vertigo pygmaea Drap.	II	5	24
Pupilla muscorum L.	–	4	–
Vallonia costata Müller	27	2	27
Vallonia excentrica Sterki	49	19	8
Vallonia sp.	60	18	100+
Vitrina pellucida Müller	I	–	–
Nesovitrea hammonis Ström	I	–	–
Aegopinella sp.	–	–	–
Punctum pygmaeum Drap.	–	–	I
Clausilia bidentata Ström	I	–	5
Helicella itala itala L.	5	6	13
Trochulus hispidus gp.	8	–	–
Cepaea sp.	–	–	2

Table 6.10: Plant remains from Phase 4 (for key see Table 6.3)

		9200	9363	9824	9828	9811	9813	9827¹	9808
	Sample	9200	9363	9824	9828	9811	9813	9827¹	9808
	Sub-sample of	N/A	N/A	9267	9267	9338	9339	9425	9425
	Context number	4156	3075	3046	3046	4170	4173	4181	4181
	Context	LOM	LOM	LOM	LOM	1st gully fill	2nd gully fill	Mini-mound	Mini-mound
	Volume in litres	2	0.5	2	2	2	2	2	2
	Weight in kg	2.089	0.665	1.966	1.894	2.078	2.141	2.125	2.236
	Phase	4	4	4	4	4	4	4	4
	Mesh size in microns	180	250	180	250	180	180	250	180
Taxon (element if not a seed)	**Common name**								
Taxus baccata L.	Yew					*		2	1
Ranunculus cf. *acris* L.	Meadow buttercup		6		8				
R. cf. *repens* L.	Creeping buttercup		5						
R. cf. *bulbosus* L.	Bulbous buttercup		7		5				
Ranunculus acris/ repens/ bulbosus	Buttercup	4 (5)	12	1	6	2		5	3
Ranunculus sect. *Ranunculus*	Buttercup		3						
Urtica dioica L.	Stinging nettle	28 (4)	9	1	6	*	3	5	1
cf. *Quercus petraea* (Matt.) Liebl. (acorn cupule fragment)	Sessile oak							2	
Quercus sp. (acorn fragment)	Oak							2	
Corylus avellana L. (nutshell fragment)	Hazel			1c		3/1c			1
Montia fontana L.	Blinks	1				1			1
Arenaria serpyllifolia L.	Thyme–leaved sandwort			1					
Stellaria media gp.	Common chickweed					*		8	1
S. cf. *holostea* L.	Greater stitchwort								1
S. graminea L.	Lesser stitchwort	11 (1)	15	3	3 (2)	3		3	1
Cerastium cf. *fontanum* Baumg.	Common mouse–ear	9	10	2	2		1	5	3
Caryophyllaceae indet.	Campion family	3	1	13	5				
Polygonum aviculare agg.	Knotgrass	6				(*)			
Rumex sp.	Dock	1			(1)	1			
Rumex sp. (perianth fragment)	Dock				2				
Polygonaceae indet.	Dock family					*			
Salix sp. (bud)	Willow					*			
Rorippa nasturtium –aquaticum L.	Watercress						1		
Capsella bursa–pastoris (L.) Medik.	Shepherd's purse							9	2
Thlaspi arvense L.	Field pennycress								1
Brassicaceae indet.	Cabbage family								2
Rubus section *Glandulosus*	Bramble					(1)		8	1
Rubus sp.	Bramble, raspberry etc			1				11	1
Rubus/ Rosa type (thorn)	Bramble/rose type	(20)						(1)	
Aphanes arvensis L.	Parsley-piert	13 (2)	2						
Prunus spinosa L.	Sloe					1	2	3	3
Prunus sp. (stone frags)	Sloe					2		26	11
Malus sylvestris L. (endocarp fragment)	Crab apple							2	1
1 *Crataegus* sp. (stone)	Hawthorn					2		7	4
Prunus/ Crataegus type (thorn)	Sloe/hawthorn type					*	1	9	2
Rosaceae indet (stone fragment)	Rose family							1	1
Rosaceae indet (bud scale)	Rose family					1	2		
Hippocrepis comosa L. (calyx)	Horseshoe vetch			1					
Trifolium type (flower)	Clover type	1		1	1	(1)/*	1	1	1
Trifolium type (calyx)	Clover type			1				1	
Mercurialis perennis L.	Dog's mercury	4 frgs mni 1			1frg	1+1c		1	1
cf. *Mercurialis perennis* L. (capsule frag)	Dog's mercury	1							
Linum catharticum L.	Fairy flax		4						
Geranium sp. (immature fruit)	Cranesbill							1(1)	
Apiaceae indet.	Carrot family							2	
Myosotis sp.	Forget-me-not							1	
Galeopsis sp.	Hemp-nettle								1
Ajuga reptans L..	Bugle							1	
Glechoma hederacea L.	Ground ivy	5 (2)						9	7(1)
Lamiaceae indet.	Thyme family	1				1		2	
Plantago major L.	Greater plantain					*		2	
P. media L.	Hoary plantain			1					
Scrophularia sp.	Figwort					*			
Veronica sp.	Speedwell	2			1				

Table 6.10: Plant remains from Phase 4 (for key see Table 6.3)

		9200	9363	9824	9828	9811	9813	9827¹	9808
Sample		9200	9363	9824	9828	9811	9813	9827¹	9808
Sub-sample of		N/A	N/A	9267	9267	9338	9339	9425	9425
Context number		4156	3075	3046	3046	4170	4173	4181	4181
Context		LOM	LOM	LOM	LOM	1st gully fill	2nd gully fill	Mini-mound	Mini-mound
Volume in litres		2	0.5	2	2	2	2	2	2
Weight in kg		2.089	0.665	1.966	1.894	2.078	2.141	2.125	2.236
Phase		4	4	4	4	4	4	4	4
Mesh size in microns		180	250	180	250	180	180	250	180
Taxon (element if not a seed)	**Common name**								
Euphrasia/ Odontites sp.	Eyebright/red bartsia			3	I				I
Rhinanthus minor L.	Yellow rattle						I		
Campanulaceae indet.	Bellflower family					*			
Galium cf. *aparine* L.	Cleavers							I	
Sambucus nigra L.	Elder	mni 6	mni I	mni I		5	I	35	I
Cirsium sp.	Thistle					*	26	2	
Carduus/ Cirsium sp.	Thistle			2		3		18	4
Leontodon cf. *saxatilis* Lam.	Lesser hawkbit	2							
Taraxacum sp.	Dandelions					I			I
Crepis cf. *biennis* L.	Rough hawk's beard							2	I
Asteraceae indet.	Daisy family			(I)				2	
Juncus subgen. *Genuini*	Soft rush					10			
Carex cf. *hirta* L.	Hairy sedge							2	3
Carex spp.	Sedges	2				I	2	4	6
Cyperaceae indet.	Sedge family							I	
Festuca/ Lolium sp.	Fescue/rye-grass						2	2	
cf. *Poa annua* type	Annual meadow-grass						I		
cf. *Poa pratensis* L.	Smooth meadow-grass			I				I	
Arrhenatherum elatius var. *bulbosum* (tuber) (Willd.) St–Amans	Couch grass						Ic	I	
cf. *A. elatius* (Willd.) St–Amans	Couch grass							I	
Deschampsia flexuosa (L.) Trin.	Wavy hair-grass							I	
cf. *Holcus lanatus* L.	Yorkshire-fog						I		
Agrostis sp.	Bent							I	
Alopecurus sp.	Foxtail						I		
cf. *Bromus* sp.	Brome							I	
Poaceae indet.	Grass family	13 (10) Ic		8	I (I)	20	3	35(3)	4
Poaceae indet.(floret)	Grass family							2	4
Poaceae indet. (chaff)	Grass family						I	3	2
Poaceae indet. (culm node)	Grass family	4		9	8	*(1)	*(2)	30	10
Poaceae indet. (culm base/ rhizome)	Grass family				Ic	6		7	
Monocot stem/leaves				++	++	++	++ /2c	6	
Dicot (stem node)				4				3	
Dicot stem				++	I		2		
Indeterminate seed				2		I	I	33	2
Indeterminate root/rhizome				++		Ic			
IGNOTA				6	4	2	2c		
Triticum sp.cf. free–threshing (rachis node)	Wheat								I
cf. *Hordeum* sp. (rachis)	Barley							I	
Cereales indet. (bran)	Cereal							+	
Bone							+		
Burnt bone						*			
Bud						I		2	I
Bud scales						3	+	9	2
Cenococcum sp.		43		5	4	6	I	3	6
Charcoal		+		++		+	+		
Charcoal <2mm				+		+	+		
Earthworm egg				*					
Green plant		++		++	++	+			
Molluscs				+++		+	+		
Chalk with lichen						2		6	
Wood						++	++		
Indet bract g		2			2			I	
Green leaf			*						*

¹ Pig tooth fragment in this sub-sample

Table 6.11: Coleoptera from Phase 4 (for habitat key see Table 6.2)

	Mini-mound		Gully	Lower Organic Mound			Habitat	Species Group
Sample/s	9808,9809,9826	9811,9812	9813	9824	9200	9362		
Sub-sample of	9425	9338	9339.	9267.	N/A	N/A		
Context number	4181	4170	4173	3046	4156	3075		
Sample weight (kg.)	13.56	5.49	2.14	1.97	2.10	1.23		
Phase	4	4	4	4	4	4		
CARABIDAE								
Cicindela campestris L.	1	–	–	–	–	–	T – light soil, open and sunny	
Carabus monilis F.	2	2	–	–	–	–	WGD	
C. problematicus Hbst.	1	–	–	–	–	–	T – open, dry	
Nebria brevicollis (F.)	1	–	–	–	–	–	WGD	
Loricera pilicornis (F.)	1	–	–	–	–	–	T – mostly moist	
Bembidion sp.	–	1	–	–	–	–	T	
Pterostichus cupreus (L.)	1	–	–	–	–	–	G (DW)	
P. diligens (Stürm.)	–	–	–	1	–	–	MG – wet	
P. niger (Sch.)	1	–	–	–	–	–	W(GD)	
P. strenuus (Pz.)	1	–	–	–	–	–	T – often near water	
P. cf. *strenuus* (Pz.)	1	–	–	–	–	–	as above	
P. cupreus (L.) or *versicolor* (Strm.)	1	2	–	–	–	–	G(DW)	
Abax parallelepipedus (P. & M.)	1	–	–	–	–	–	W(GDC)	
Calathus fuscipes (Gz.)	3	–	–	1	1	–	WDG – often in meadowland	
C. melanocephalus (L.)	2	–	–	1	–	–	GD(W)	
Agonum muelleri (Hbst.)	1	–	–	–	–	–	GD(W)	
Amara sp.	1	–	–	–	–	–	T	
Harpalus cf. *affinis* (Schr.)	1	–	–	–	–	–	DG(W)	
DYTISCIDAE								
Colymbetes fuscus (L.)	1	–	–	–	–	–	A – stagnant	1
HYDROPHILIDAE								
Helophorus cf. *brevipalpis* Bed.	1	–	–	–	–	–	A – but readily leaves water	1
Sphaeridium lunatum F. or *scarabaeoides* (L.)	1	1	–	–	–	–	F – esp cow dung (CV)	
Cercyon cf. *atomarius* (F.)	1	–	–	–	–	–	FVC	7
Cercyon sp.	1	–	–	1	–	1	FVC, some species on wet mud	7
Megasternum obscurum (Marsh.)	12	2	1	3	1	2	FVC	7
Hydrobius fuscipes (L.)	1	–	–	–	–	–	A – stagnant	1
HISTERIDAE								
Hister bissexstriatus F.	–	–	–	1	–	–	FV	
Histerinae indet.	1	–	–	–	–	–	FVC	
LEIODIDAE								
Choleva or *Catops* sp.	1	–	–	–	–	–	V – often leaf litter	
SILPHIDAE								
Nicrophorus sp.	1	–	–	–	–	–	C – burying small carcasses	
Silpha atrata L.	1	1	–	–	–	–	mostly under bark or in rotten wood (GDV)	
S. tristis Ill.	1	–	–	1	–	–	C(GDV)	
STAPHYLINIDAE								
Anotylus sculpturatus gp.	1	–	–	–	–	–	FVC	7
Stenus spp.	7	2	2	–	–	1	TM	
Lathrobium sp.	1	–	–	–	–	–	TV(C)	

Table 6.11: Coleoptera from Phase 4 (for habitat key see Table 6.2)

	Mini-mound	Gully		Lower Organic Mound			Habitat	Species Group
Sample/s	9808,9809,9826	9811,9812	9813	9824	9200	9362		
Sub-sample of	9425	9338	9339.	9267.	N/A	N/A		
Context number	4181	4170	4173	3046	4156	3075		
Sample weight (kg.)	13.56	5.49	2.14	1.97	2.10	1.23		
Phase	4	4	4	4	4	4		
Rugilus erichsoni (Fauv.) or *orbiculatus* (Pk.)	3	–	–	2	l	–	V(G)	
Xantholinus linearis (Ol.)	3	l	–	–	–	–	WGV(FC)	
X. longiventris Heer	–	–	–	l	–	–	WGV(FC)	
Philonthus sp.	4	l	–	–	l	–	FVC(T)	
Gabrius sp.	–	–	–	l	–	–	WGFVC	
Staphylinus caesareus Ced. or *dimidiaticornis* Gem.	l	–	–	–	–	–	T	
S. aeneocephalus Deg. or *fortunatarum* Woll.	l	l	l	–	–	–	WG	
S. olens Müll.	l	–	–	–	–	–	WG(D)	
Quedius sp.	3	–	–	–	–	–	T	
Philonthus or *Quedius* sp.	–	–	–	2	–	l	TFVC	
Tachyporus sp.	3	–	–	–	l	l	T	
Tachinus sp.	2	–	–	–	–	–	T	
Aleocharinae indet.	4	–	–	l	l	–	TFVC	
GEOTRUPIDAE								
Geotrupes sp.	3	2	l	–	–	–	F	2
SCARABAEIDAE								
Aphodius cf. *foetens* (F.)	l	–	–	–	–	–	F	2
A. cf. *sphacelatus* (Pz.)	3	l	–	l	l	–	FVC	2
A. villosus Gyl.	6	2	2	–	l	–	V(F)	
Aphodius spp. (not *villosus*)	4	2	l	–	l	l	mostly F	2
Onthophagus nutans (F.)	l	–	–	–	–	–	F	2
Onthophagus sp. (not *ovatus*)	l	l	–	–	–	l	F(C)	2
Hoplia philanthus (Fues.)	l	–	–	–	–	–	larvae on roots in permanent grassland	11
Phyllopertha horticola (L.)	7	2	l	–	l	l	larvae on roots in permanent grassland	11
DASCILLIDAE								
Dascillus cervinus (L.)	2	2	–	–	–	–	larvae on grass roots, adults on flowers and bushes	
ELATERIDAE								
Agrypnus murinus (L.)	3	2	–	–	l	l	G	11
Athous haemorrhoidalis (F.)	l	–	–	–	–	–	WG – esp. meadowland, larvae on roots esp. in grassland	11
A. hirtus (Hbst.)	l	–	l	–	–	–	WG – esp. meadowland, larvae on roots esp. in grassland	11
Actenicerus sjaelandicus (Müll.)	l	–	–	–	–	–	damp grassland	
Agriotes obscurus (L.)	2	l	–	–	–	–	larvae mostly on roots of grassland plants	11
A. sputator (L.)	l	l	–	–	–	–	as above	11
Agriotes sp.	l	l	–	l	–	–	as above	11
CANTHARIDAE								
Cantharis sp.	l	–	–	–	–	–	adults often on flowers	
ANOBIIDAE								
Grynobius planus (F.)	–	–	l	–	–	–	dead hardwood	4

Table 6.11: Coleoptera from Phase 4 (for habitat key see Table 6.2)

	Mini-mound	Gully		Lower Organic Mound			Habitat	Species Group
Sample/s	9808,9809,9826	9811,9812	9813	9824	9200	9362		
Sub-sample of	9425	9338	9339.	9267.	N/A	N/A		
Context number	4181	4170	4173	3046	4156	3075		
Sample weight (kg.)	13.56	5.49	2.14	1.97	2.10	1.23		
Phase	4	4	4	4	4	4		
NITIDULIDAE								
Omosita colon (L.)	–	1	–	–	–	–	C – dry	
CRYPTOPHAGIDAE								
Atomaria sp.	1	–	–	–	–	–	VT(F)	8
LATHRIDIIDAE								
Enicmus transversus (Ol.)	1	–	–	–	–	–	V(GW)	
CHRYSOMELIDAE								
Oulema sp.	1	–	–	–	–	–	grasses	
Chrysolina fastuosa (Scop.)	–	1	–	–	–	–	Lamiaceae	
C. haemoptera (L.)	–	1	–	–	–	–	*Plantago* spp.	
C. polita (L.)	1	–	–	–	–	–	Lamiaceae	
Gastrophysa viridula (Deg.)	1	–	–	–	–	–	*Rumex* and *Polygonum* spp.	
Hydrothassa glabra (Hbst.)	–	–	1	–	–	–	*Ranunculus* spp.	
Longitarsus sp.	2	1	–	–	–	–	various herbs	
Crepidodera ferruginea (Scop.)	1	–	–	–	–	–	mostly Poaceae	
Apteropeda orbiculata (Marsh.)	1	–	–	1	–	–	various herbs esp *Glechoma hederacea* L.	
Cassida sp.	1	–	–	–	–	–	various herbs	
APIONIDAE								
Apion spp.	3	–	1	1	1	1	various herbs	3
CURCULIONIDAE								
Phyllobius roboretanus Gred. or *viridiaeris* (Laich.)	1	–	–	–	–	1	trees, shrubs and some herbs	
Phyllobius or *Polydrusus* sp.	2	2	2	1	–	–	as above	
Sciaphilus asperatus (Bons.)	1	1	1	–	–	–	various herbs	
Barynotus obscurus (F.)	9	1	–	1	–	–	various herbs	
Sitona lepidus Gyll.	2	–	–	–	–	–	Falaceae, mostly *Trifolium* spp.	3
S. cf. *lineatus* (L.)	1	–	–	–	–	–	Falaceae	3
Sitona sp.	1	–	–	1	–	1	Falaceae	3
Cleonus piger (Scop.)	–	1	–	–	–	–	Asteraceae, usually *Carduus* and *Cirsium* spp.	
Hypera punctata (F.)	4	1	–	–	–	–	Falaceae esp. *Trifolium* spp.	
Hypera sp. (not *punctata*)	–	1	–	–	–	–	various herbs	
Liparus coronatus (Gz.)	1	–	–	–	–	–	Apiaceae	
Rhinoncus sp.	–	–	–	1	–	–	various herbs esp. Polygonaceae	
Ceuthorhynchinae indet.	–	1	–	–	1	–	various herbs	
Curculio cf. *nucum* L.	1	–	–	–	–	–	*Corylus avellana* L. – larvae in nuts	4
Mecinus pyraster (Hbst.)	4	1	–	1	2	–	*Plantago lanceolata* L. and *P. media* L.	
Gymnetron labile (Hbst.)	1	–	–	–	–	–	*Plantago lanceolata* L.	
Total	**158**	**44**	**16**	**25**	**15**	**13**		

Table 6.12: Other insects from Phase 4 (for habitat key see Table 6.2)

		Mini-mound	Gully		Lower Organic Mound			Habitat
Sample/s		9808,9809,9826	9811,9812	9813	9824	9200	9362	
Sub-sample of		9425	9338	9339.	9267.	N/A	N/A	
Context number		4181	4070	4173	3046	4156	3075	
Sub-samples		9808,9809,9826	9811,9812					
Sample weight (kg)		13.56	5.49	2.14	1.97	2.10	1.23	
Phase		4	4	4	4	4	4	
HEMIPTERA	– HOMOPTERA							
Aphrodes sp.		1	–	–	–	–	–	grasses
– HETEROPTERA								
Pentatoma rufipes (L.)		1	–	–	–	–	–	trees esp. *Quercus* sp.
HYMENOPTERA	– FORMICIDAE							
Myrmica rubra (L.)	– worker	–	–	–	–	2	–	T
M. rubra (L.) or *ruginodis* Nyl.	– worker	3	2	–	2	1	1	T
M. scabrinodis gp.	– worker	5	–	1	–	2	1	T
Myrmica sp.	– worker	1	–	–	–	–	–	T
Myrmica sp.	– male	4	–	1	–	–	–	T
OTHER HYMENOPTERA								
Hymenoptera indet. (not Formicidae)		–	1	–	–	–	–	T
DIPTERA								
cf. *Scathophaga stercorea* (L.)	– puparium	1	–	–	–	–	–	fresh dung
Diptera indet.	– puparium	21	7	–	5	6	3	T

Table 6.13: Shells recovered from organic Mini-mound (Phase 4)

Sample	9808	9809	9827
Context number	4181	4181	4181
Species			
Cochlicopa cf. *lubrica* Müller	–	1	–
Vallonia excentrica Sterki	1	3	–
Vallonia sp.	–	–	7
Clausilia bidentata Ström	–	1	–
Trochulus hispidus gp.	1	–	1

Table 6.14: Shells recovered from the Lower Organic Mound (Phase 4)

Sample	9824, 9828	9236	9237
Context number	3046	4156	4156
Species			
Pomatias elegans Müller	1	1	–
Cochlicopa cf. *lubrica* Müller	5	1	1
Vertigo pygmaea Drap.	27	–	2
Vallonia costata Müller	11	–	7
Vallonia excentrica Sterki	13	–	8
Vallonia sp.	30	4	–
Vitrina pellucida Müller	5	–	1
Punctum pygmaeum Drap.	–	–	2
Helicella itala itala L.	13	–	–
Trochulus hispidus gp	–	–	9
Cepaea sp.	1	–	–

Table 6.15: Plant remains from Phase 5 pits (for key see Table 6.3)

	Sample	9817	9823	9810
	Sub-sample of	9244	9246	9340
	Context number	3066	3070	3073
	Volume in litres	2	2	2
	Weight in kg	1926.4	2.444	2.135
	Phase	5	5	5
	Mesh size in microns	180	180	180
Taxon (element if not a seed)	**Common name**			
Taxus baccata L.	Yew	*		
Ranunculus cf. acris L.	Meadow buttercup	3		2
R. cf. bulbosus L.	Bulbous buttercup	4		
Ranunculus acris/ repens/ bulbosus	Buttercup	16		3
Urtica dioica L.	Stinging nettle	7		
cf. U. dioica L.	Stinging nettle			2
Montia fontana L.	Blinks			1
Arenaria serpyllifolia L.	Thyme-leaved sandwort	6		
Stellaria graminea L.	Lesser stitchwort			1
Cerastium cf. fontanum Baumg.	Common mouse-ear	11		1
Caryophyllaceae indet.	Campion family	1		
Sanguisorba minor ssp. minor Scop. (hypanthium)	Salad burnet	1		
cf. Prunus spinosa L. (fruitstone fragment)	Sloe	1		
cf. Malus sylvestris L.	Crab apple	1		
Trifolium type (flower)	Clover type			1
Mercurialis perennis L.	Dog's mercury		1	
Apiaceae indet.	Carrot family	3		
Linum catharticum L.	Fairy flax	4		
cf. L. catharticum L.	Fairy flax	1		1
cf. Lamiaceae indet.	Thyme family	1		1
cf. Plantago major L.	Greater plantain			1
cf. Veronica sp.	Speedwell	1		
Sambucus nigra L.	Elder	7	2	1
Cyperaceae indet.	Sedge family	1		
Cereal size (culm node)	Cereal size	1		
Poa pratensis L.	Smooth meadow-grass	2		
cf. Dactylis glomerata L.	Cock's-foot	1		
Agrostis sp.	Bent	1		
Poaceae indet.	Grass family	4	1	
Poaceae indet. (culm node)	Grass family	1		1
Monocot stem/leaves		12		1
Indeterminate fragments		16	1	2
Cenococcum sp.		++	+	++
Charcoal		+		
Earthworm egg		++		
Earthworm granules		*		
Green plant		*		*
Moss		+++	++	+++
Wood		+	+	+

Only tiny fragments of green plant in sample 9817
1 Charcoal frag >2mm in sample 9823 Prunus sp.

Table 6.16: Coleoptera from Phase 5 (for habitat key see Table 6.2)

	Pits			Habitat	Species Group
Sample/s	99823	9817, 9818	9810, 9816		
Sub-samples of	9246.	9244	9340		
Context number	3070	3066	3073		
Sample weight (kg)	2.44	5.02	4.14		
Phase	5	5	5		
CARABIDAE					
Carabus monilis F.	–	I	–	WGD	
Trechus obtusus Er. or *quadristriatus* (Schr.)	–	–	I	T	
Pterostichus cf. *strenuus* (Pz.)	–	I	–	T – often near water	
Calathus fuscipes (Gz.)	–	I	–	WDG – often in meadowland	
Amara sp.	–	–	I	T	
Badister bipustulatus (F.)	I	–	–	T – mostly damp	
HYDROPHILIDAE					
Cercyon cf. *haemorrhoidalis* (F.)	–	I	–	FV	7
Megasternum obscurum (Marsh.)	–	3	I	FVC	7
Cryptopleurum minutum (F.)	–	I	–	FVC	7
STAPHYLINIDAE					
Platystethus arenarius (Fouc.)	–	I	–	FV	7
Stenus spp.	–	I	2	TM	
Lathrobium sp.	–	I	–	TV(C)	
Rugilus erichsoni (Fauv.) or *orbiculatus* (Pk.)	–	I	–	V(G)	
Xantholinus glabratus (Grav.)	–	I	–	GDFV	
X. linearis (Ol.) or *longiventris* Heer	–	I	–	WGV(FC)	
Philonthus sp.	–	I	I	FVC(T)	
Staphylinus caesareus Ced. or *dimidiaticornis* Gem.	–	I	–	T	
Tachyporus sp.	–	I	I	T	
Aleocharinae indet.	–	2	–	TFVC	
GEOTRUPIDAE					
Geotrupes sp.	–	I	I	F	2
SCARABAEIDAE					
Aphodius porcus (F.)	–	I	–	F – in *Geotrupes* burrows	2
Aphodius spp. (not *villosus*)	–	I	–	mostly F	2
Onthophagus sp. (not *ovatus*)	I	I	–	F(C)	2
Phyllopertha horticola (L.)	–	2	I	larvae on roots in permanent grassland	II
ELATERIDAE					
Agrypnus murinus (L.)	–	I	–	G	II
Athous hirtus (Hbst.)	–	I	–	WG – esp. meadowland, larvae on roots esp. in grassland	II
Agriotes sp.	I	I	I	larvae mostly on roots of grassland plants	II
CRYPTOPHAGIDAE					
Atomaria sp.	–	I	–	VT(F)	8
CHRYSOMELIDAE					
Longitarsus sp.	–	2	–	various herbs	
APIONIDAE					
Apion spp.	–	I	–	various herbs	3
CURCULIONIDAE					
Barynotus obscurus (F.)	–	I	–	various herbs	
Sitona sp.	–	I	–	Leguminosae	3
Ceuthorhynchidius troglodytes (F.)	–	I	–	*Plantago lanceolata* L.	
Ceuthorhynchinae indet.	–	I	–	various herbs	
Mecinus pyraster (Hbst.)	–	I	–	*Plantago lanceolata* L. and *P. media* L.	
Total	**3**	**37**	**10**		

Table 6.17: Other insects from Phase 5 (for habitat key see Table 6.2)

			Pits		Habitat
Sample/s		99823	9817, 9818	9810, 9816	
Sub-samples of		9246.	9244	9340	
Context number		3070	3066	3073	
Sample weight (kg)		2.44	5.02	4.14	
Phase		5	5	5	
HEMIPTERA — HOMOPTERA					
Aphodes bifasciatus (L.)		–	I	–	grasses
HYMENOPTERA — FORMICIDAE					
Myrmica rubra (L.) or *ruginodis* Nyl.	– worker	I	–	–	T
M. scabrinodis gp.	– worker	–	22	3	T
Myrmica sp.	– worker	–	3	–	T
Lasius flavus gp.	– worker	I	I	I	mounds in old pasture and at edge of woodland
OTHER HYMENOPTERA					
Hymenoptera indet. (not Formicidae)		–	I	I	T
DIPTERA					
Diptera indet.	– puparium	I	4	3	T

Table 6.18: Shells recovered from primary and secondary fill of pit [3067]

	Sample	9823	9817
	Context number	3070	3066
Species			
Pomatias elegans Müller		3	26
Carychium tridentatum Risso.		–	6
Cochlicopa cf. *lubrica* Müller		–	17
Vertigo pygmaea Drap.		–	23
Pupilla muscorum L.		–	2
Vallonia costata Müller		4	183
V. excentrica Sterki		–	16
Vallonia sp.		8	93
Merdigera obscura Müller		–	3
Punctum pygmaeum Drap.		–	2
Nesovitrea hammonis Ström		–	2
Aegopinella nitidulai Drap.		–	I
A. pura Alder		–	I
Clausilia bidentata Ström		–	16
Helicella itala itala L.		2	61
Trochulus hispidus gp.		2	II
Cepaea sp.		–	14

Table 6.19: Plant remains from Phase 6.1 and 6.2 (for key see Table 6.3)

		9375	9335	9825	9822
	Sample	9375	9335	9825	9822
	Sub-sample of	N/A	N/A	9276	9320
	Context number	3061	3078	3083	3084
	Context	UOM	UOM	UOM	clay cap
	Volume in litres	2	2	2	2
	Weight in kg	2.313	1.91	2.206	2.093
	Phase	6.1	6.1	6.1	6.2
	Mesh size in microns	180	180	180	180
Taxon (element if not a seed)	**Common name**				
Ranunculus cf. *bulbosus* L.	Bulbous buttercup		1		1
R. acris/ repens/ bulbosus	Buttercup	3	1	3	
Ranunculus sp.	Buttercup, crowfoot	1		1	1
Urtica dioica L.	Stinging nettle		4	3	
Corylus avellana L. (nutshell fragment)	Hazel	1c			
Chenopodium cf. *album* L.	Fat hen	1			
Montia fontana L.	Blinks	2	1		
Arenaria serpyllifolia L.	Thyme-leaved sandwort		1		
Moehringia trinervia L. (Clairv.)	Three-nerved sandwort	1			
Stellaria media gp.	Common chickweed	1	(1)		
S. graminea L.	Lesser stitchwort	4	3	4	
Cerastium sp.	Mouse-ear	4	2		
Caryophyllaceae indet.	Campion family	2		1	
Polygonum aviculare agg.	Knotgrass			4	
Rumex sp. (perianth fragment)	Dock			(1)	
Prunus sp. (charred fruitstone frag.)	Sloe, plum etc				2
Viola section *Viola*	Violet		1		
Trifolium type (flower)	Clover type		1	1	
Trifolium type (calyx)	Clover type				1
Mercurialis perennis L.	Dog's mercury	1	1	1	
Linum catharticum L.	Fairy flax		(1)		(1)
Thymus cf. *polytrichus* A. Kern ex Borbás (leaf)	Wild thyme		1		
Lamiaceae (large) indet.	Thyme family	1			
Veronica sp.	Speedwell	1(1)	1	(1)	
Euphrasia/ Odontites sp.	Eyebright/Red bartsia	(1)			
Galium cf. *aparine* L.	Cleavers		1		
Sambucus nigra L.	Elder	mni 2	mni 2	4	mni 1
Centaurea nigra L. (phylary fragment)	Hardheads			1	
Carex sp.	Sedge		1(1)	1	
cf. *Poa annua* L.	Annual meadow-grass		1		
Poaceae indet.	Grass family	1(2)			1
Poaceae indet. (culm node)	Grass family		1	6	1
Poaceae indet. (culm base/rhizome	Grass family			5	
Monocot stem/leaves		+++	++	++	
Dicot stem		+		+	
Roots of herbaceous plants		++	+	+	+
Indeterminate seed		1	1		
Indeterminate bract			1	1	1
Cenococcum sp.		17	3	18	9
Charcoal		+		+	+
Earthworm egg		*	*	*	*
Earthworm granules				*	
Green plant		*	*	*	*
Molluscs		+		+	+
Moss		++	++	+	
Insects		++		++	
Wood				+	++

9375: 2 *Corylus* sp. charcoal frags, one indet and 1 vitrified indet – possible tar noted
9335 – tar and small pieces of charcoal also present.

Table 6.20: Coleoptera from Phase 6.1 (for habitat key see Table 6.2)

	Upper Organic Mound			Habitat	Species Group
Sample	9335	9825	9375		
Sub-sample of	N/A	9276	N/A		
Context number	3078	3083	3061		
Sample weight (kg.)	1.91	2.21	2.31		
Phase	6.1	6.1	6.1		
CARABIDAE					
Calathus fuscipes (Gz.)	–	1	–	WDG – often in meadowland	
Amara sp.	1	–	1	T	
HYDROPHILIDAE					
Sphaeridium lunatum F. or *scarabaeoides* (L.)	–	–	1	F – esp cow dung (CV)	
Megasternum obscurum (Marsh.)	1	1	–	FVC	7
STAPHYLINIDAE					
Platystethus arenarius (Fouc.)	–	–	1	FV	7
Stenus spp.	1	2	1	TM	
Rugilus erichsoni (Fauv.) or *orbiculatus* (Pk.)	–	1	–	V(G)	
Philonthus or *Quedius* sp.	–	–	1	TFVC	
Aleocharinae indet.	1	–	–	TFVC	
GEOTRUPIDAE					
Geotrupes sp.	1	–	–	F	2
SCARABAEIDAE					
Aphodius cf. *foetidus* (Hbst.)	–	1	–	FV	2
A. cf. *sphacelatus* (Pz.)	1	–	3	FVC	2
Aphodius spp. (not *villosus*)	1	1	3	mostly F	2
Phyllopertha horticola (L.)	–	–	1	larvae on roots in permanent grassland	11
DASCILLIDAE					
Dascillus cervinus (L.)	–	1	–	larvae on grass roots, adults on flowers and bushes	
ELATERIDAE					
Agrypnus murinus (L.)	–	1	1	G	11
APIONIDAE					
Apion spp.	–	2	1	various herbs	3
CURCULIONIDAE					3
Phyllobius roboretanus (Gred.) or *viridiaeris* (Laich.)	1	–	–	trees, shrubs and some herbs	
Barynotus obscurus (F.)	–	1	1	various herbs	
Sitona sulcifrons (Thun.)	–	1	–	Leguminosae, mostly *Trifolium* spp.	3
Liparus coronatus (Gz.)	–	2	–	Umbelliferae	
Total	**8**	**15**	**15**		

Table 6.21: Other insects from Phase 6.1 (for habitat key see Table 6.2)

		Upper Organic Mound			Habitat
Sample		**9335**	**9825**	**9375**	
Sub-sample of		N/A	9276	N/A	
Sample		9335	9825	9375	
Context number		3078	3083	3061	
Sample weight (kg)		1.91	2.21	2.31	
Phase		6. 1	6.1	6. 1	
HYMENOPTERA	– FORMICIDAE				
Myrmica rubra (L.) or *ruginodis* Nyl.	– worker	–	–	2	T
M. scabrinodis gp.	– worker	2	2	1	T
Lasius flavus gp.	– worker	2	–	1	mounds in old pasture and at edge of woodland
OTHER HYMENOPTERA					
Hymenoptera indet. (not Formicidae)		1	–	–	T
DIPTERA					
Diptera indet.	– puparium	1	5	12	T
Diptera indet.	– adult	–	–	1	T

Table 6.22: Shells recovered from the Upper Organic Mound (Phase 6.1)

Sample	9335	9375	9825
Context number	3078	3061	3083
Species			
Pomatias elegans Müller	3	1	–
Cochlicopa cf. *lubrica* Müller	1	–	1
Vertigo pygmaea Drap.	–	2	–
Pupilla muscorum L.	2	1	1
Vallonia costata Müller	4	–	–
Vallonia excentrica Sterki	1	–	–
Vallonia sp.	13	3	4
Discus rotundatus rotundatus Müller	2	–	–
Aegopinella nitidula Drap.	1	–	–
Clausilia bidentata Ström	2	1	–
Helicella *itala itala* L.	2	2	–
Trochulus hispidus gp.	–	1	1
Cepaea sp.	–	–	1

Table 6.23: Coleoptera from Phase 6.2 (for habitat key see Table 6.2)

	Clay Capping	Habitat	Species Group
Sample	9822		
Sub-sample of	9320		
Context number	3084		
Sample weight (kg)	2.09		
Phase	6.2		
CURCULIONIDAE			
Sciaphilus asperatus (Bons.)	1	various herbs	
Total	**1**		

Table 6.24: Other insects from Phase 6.2 (for habitat key see Table 6.2)

		Clay Capping	Habitat
Sample			**9822**
Sub-sample of			9320
Context number			3084
Sample weight (kg)			2.09
Phase			6.2
HYMENOPTERA	– FORMICIDAE		
Myrmica rubra (L.) or *ruginodis* Nyl.			
	– worker	I	T
DIPTERA			
Diptera indet.	– puparium	2	T

Table 6.25: Shells recovered from a sample from the further capping layer (Phase 6.2)

	Sample	9822
	Context number	3084
Species		
Punctum pygmaeum Drap.		I
Clausilia bidentata Ström		I
Cepaea sp.		I

Table 6.26: Phase 16.2 hand collected assemblage quantified by NISP (number of identified specimens). CW= chalk rubble wall, IW = inter–wall deposit, CL=chalk layer

Species	Context type	CW	IW	IW	IW	IW	IW	IW	CL	Total
	Context number	4808	4813	4835	4843	4844	4845	4848	4874	
Cattle		I	–	–	–	–	–	–	I	2
Red deer (not antler)		–	–	I	–	–	–	–	–	I
Cattle/Red deer		–	–	I	–	–	–	–	–	I
Cattle/Red deer?		–	–	–	–	–	–	I	–	I
Pig?		–	–	–	–	I	–	–	–	I
Sheep/Goat		–	I	–	I	I	–	–	–	3
Medium mammal (vertebra + ribs)		2	–	–	–	–	I	–	–	3
Badger		–	I	–	–	I	–	–	–	2
Mole		–	–	–	I	–	–	–	–	I
Amphibian		2	–	–	–	–	–	–	–	2
Grand total		**5**	**2**	**2**	**2**	**3**	**I**	**I**	**I**	**17**

Table 6.27: Phase 16.2 assemblage collected from sample residues

| | Context number | 4816 | 4817 | 4840 | 4843 | 4844 | 4845 | 4845 | 4846 | 4847 |
	Sample	9522	9523	9515	9517	9527	9526	9537	9525	9524
Micro–faunal from 2–4mm fraction										
Weight (g)		–	<0.0	5.3	0.2	3.8	23.2	21.8	<0.0	<0.0
Quantity (g/l processed)		–	<0.00	0.42	0.02	0.76	1.86	8.72	<0.00	<0.00
Micro–faunal from >4mm fraction										
Weight (g)		<0.0	–	3.9	0.2	1.0	3.4	4.6	–	<0.0
Quantity (g/l processed)		<0.00	–	0.08	0.01	0.05	0.07	0.46	–	0.00
Species identified (two largest samples only)										
Frog (MNI)		n/a	n/a	n/a	n/a	n/a	7	9	n/a	n/a
Common toad (MNI)		n/a	n/a	n/a	n/a	n/a	2	2	n/a	n/a
Vole sp.		n/a	n/a	n/a	n/a	n/a	✓	✓	n/a	n/a
Additional species identified (NISP, countable specimens only)										
Sheep/goat		–	–	–	–	1	–	–	–	–
Badger		–	–	1*	–	–	–	–	–	–
Cf. Polecat		–	–	–	–	–	–	2	–	–

Table 6.28: Radiocarbon measurements from work carried out by Evans et al (1993) at Avebury and West Overton

Laboratory number	Material and context	Luminescence age	Radiocarbon age	Calibrated age (68% confidence)	Calibrated age (95% confidence)
OxA–1348	Charcoal, *Quercus* and *Fraxinus* from cremation pit dug into palaeosoil		3020 ±70 BP	1390–1120 cal BC	1440–1010 cal BC
Ox88TLfg–727f	Burnt flint from the palaeosoil surface	3030 ± 250 BP		1330–820 cal BC	1580–570 cal BC
OxA–1045	Animal bone, *Bos taurus* skull, more or less complete, deliberately placed under boulder from lower part of alluvial silt (West Overton Formation) resting on palaeosoil.		2980 ± 100 BP	1390–1020 cal BC	1440–910 cal BC
OxA–1221	Human bone, femur, from near the base of alluvium (layer 6)		3800 ± 60 BP	2310–2140 cal BC	2470–2030 cal BC

7

Ways of Understanding Prehistoric Silbury Hill

JIM LEARY AND DAVID FIELD

This chapter focuses on interpretations of Silbury Hill. It is argued that previous interpretations have tended to take a top down approach to the Hill, concentrating on its final form and emphasising its large size. However, the archaeological evidence from the tunnel has given us a far more nuanced understanding of the construction; a sense of continuous developments and changing roles. This bottom up approach accentuates the process of construction as much as it does the form. Recording the variety of materials used as the mound developed has also led us to beg the question: 'Why these materials?' leading to a discussion of the materiality of stone, antler and soils used in the mound. The ditch, an important but rarely mentioned element of the monument, is then discussed. The chapter ends on an examination of the locality of Silbury, highlighting its low-lying position next to rivers and springs, and its position at the head of the River Kennet, a major tributary of the River Thames.

The deposits recorded in the tunnel suggest that Silbury Hill developed through a number of complex construction phases, hinted at by Atkinson but simplified in his much cited four-phase scheme. There is still a considerable degree of uncertainty about parts of the sequence, for example whether the internal ditch was present before the gravel mound, or whether the stake circle was free-standing. These caveats aside, the general sequence appears to be as follows (*see* Chapter 2 for a fuller description). Primary activity commenced with the ground being prepared (Phase 2) and a gravel mound piled on it (Phase 3), before a larger stake-defined mound attended by smaller mounds was constructed (Phase 4). During the next phase pits were dug into the top of the central mound (Phase 5) before the whole complex became rapidly covered by a larger

organic mound comprising interleaved dumps of topsoil, subsoil, turves, gravel, chalk and sarsen stone (Phase 6). The site then took on an entirely different character when a massive ditch was dug that probably formed an enclosing circuit 100m in diameter around this earlier activity and with an internal bank (Phase 7). The mound was subsequently enlarged with chalk, but not as a single construction; instead it happened incrementally with a series of concentric banks of chalk and clay being added to the outside of it (Phases 7–11). Further complex activity clearly occurred above these banks during these phases as evidenced by inter-leaved organic layers, possibly forming a mound, seen high up at the top of a void above the tunnel (Phase 11). Material was placed over the banks creating an ever higher mound. The enclosure ditch was backfilled, the unweathered sides showing that this had been a rapid process, and then it was re-cut at least four times (Phases 12–15), and probably many more since it may have advanced seamlessly, incrementally until it eventually manifested as the external ditch that is visible beyond the mound – and which itself may well be the result of several phases. The mound was further substantially added to. This construction phase, with its horizontal chalk dumps held in place by rough, steeply tilting, chalk revetment walls built in concentric rings was of a very different nature and style to the proceeding phases, and indeed far larger than anything that had gone before (Phase 16).

It is evident from this summary of the sequence that Silbury Hill was not a construction project formed of a single or even a few phases but the focus for an array of many disparate activities, and although for convenience it is separated out into phases in this monograph, the construction is likely to have been, to a greater or lesser extent, a continuous process; the mound developing, mutating and evolving through time – with the implication of changing roles. This is at variance with traditional interpretations of the site that largely focus on its final form. This point will now be elaborated upon, followed by a discussion of the materiality of the mound, the ditch phases and finally the location of Silbury.

The process and the form

In Western thought *form* is privileged over *process*. This is what anthropologist Tim Ingold calls the 'building perspective', which he contrasts with the 'dwelling perspective' (Ingold 2000, chapter 10). Ingold describes the essence of the 'building perspective' by the belief that 'worlds are made before they are lived in' (2000, 179), in other words a form is conceptualised before it is constructed. The 'building perspective' is how most prehistoric monuments have been described in the archaeological literature (and beyond); it is the hegemonic view and has led to a proliferation of interpretations that concern the monument's final form. In this way, monuments have been seen as requiring an ultimate purpose, as a symbol or an expression of dominance over the environment: the superiority of culture over nature – or other cultures. This approach is understandable from the fact that the final form of prehistoric monuments is often all archaeologists have available to base interpretations on, since most are Scheduled Ancient Monuments and have not been explored through excavation in any meaningful way. The various developmental phases that comprise many monuments, therefore, remain largely unknown and only the 'outer' shell – that is the monument in its last manifestation – is what is studied; the resultant interpretation is thus based on this. When landscape phenomenological archaeologists talk of 'experiencing' a site what they mean is the final form of the site. Silbury Hill is generally perceived as a finished artefact – complete spatially, rather than as a construct comprising generations (55–155 years in model B, Chapter 4) of additions, changes, demolitions and reconstructions, the processes of which are almost entirely ignored.

Privileging form over process is probably one of the reasons why so many people contend that Silbury Hill must have been raised over a burial or had a particular function. For example, in relation to the summit of the Hill, Paul Devereux uses its final form to produce sight-lines around the Avebury landscape, arguing that Silbury was very precisely constructed to be seen from various vantage points, its flat summit lining up with the skyline (Devereux 1991). Similarly, John Barrett declares that 'Perhaps the simplest thing to do is accept Silbury for what it is, an elevated platform. Not only is that platform, which seems to rise above the distant horizon when viewed from many places in the surrounding countryside, widely visible, but so are those who stand upon it' (1994, 31), suggesting that the summit formed an exclusive ceremonial arena for the elite. Plausibly this was the case once the mound had reached the later stages, but it cannot explain its development. As Barrett rightly states, monuments were 'not conceived as an entity, a plan in the mind of some autocratic chief' (1994, 13). More recently, anthropologist Lionel Sims (2009, 405) uses the final form to suggest that 'Silbury Hill in its landscape and monument context acts as a dynamic lunar facsimile in dark moon rituals at winter solstice. This structural property is designed, by aligning the Silbury summit in line with its back horizon, to rely on the agency of the participants to contrast the landscape as a journey into and out of the underworld.'

Elaborating on his 'dwelling perspective', Ingold draws directly from Heidegger's discussion of the origin of the word for the verb 'to build': *bauen*, which means in Old English and High German, interchangeably, to cultivate, to construct and to dwell (Ingold 2000, 185; Heidegger 1971). In other words to build is also to dwell, 'Building, then, cannot be understood as a simple process of transcription, of a pre-existing design of the final product onto a raw material substrate' (Ingold 2000, 186). As Ingold points out, this of course does not mean that people cannot envision a form prior to construction, but that that form cannot be disentangled from its surroundings, its materials and the conditions of its construction. In other words there is no dichotomy between the process of bringing a monument into being, and the monument itself. Rather than being a 'structurally coherent edifice, built to the specifications of an original design, and intended by its designers and builders to last in perpetuity as a memorial to their endeavour', Ingold argues that a round mound is 'a growth, that ... is not obedient to the dictates of any prior design, and that its form ... is not constant but ever evolving' (2010, 253). He relates the prevalent archaeological interpretation of round mounds to Aristotle's doctrine of hylomorphism, whereby a sculptor, for example, will start with the raw material (*hyle*) and an idea of the final form (*morphe*); thus the raw construction material is subservient to form (*see also* Deleuze and Guattari 1988, 407). Likewise, and again influenced by Heidegger (1971), architect Vittorio Gregotti highlights in his book *Architecture: Means and Ends* how the product (*poïesis*) has, in recent times, become disconnected from the means of production (*techné*), with the latter becoming ever more invisible. This has the effect of replacing meaning with the image (Gregotti 2010). *Techné* encompasses organisation (for Silbury Hill this might include the gathering of antlers and turning them into picks, the provision of meals and shelter, firewood for hearths and so on), the morphology (for example the form of the various phases), and 'the selection and treatment of materials and their method of assembly, and systems of joining and layering and their relative details' (Gregotti 2010, 3). In this way it can be seen that the means, the *techné*, are in fact as important as the ends, the latter of which 'can only be constituted through the combined presence of these different technics' (Gregotti 2010, 3).

Colin Richards has also discussed this point, arguing against the notion that a monument 'is built to provide a function only after completion' (2004, 72). Richards discusses the process of constructing monuments, in this case dolmens in Wales, in terms of 'the social practices that lie behind such forms. In particular, the acts of monumental construction where people in different places contributed in various ways to the building process and through their labour constructed both themselves and their relations with others' (2004, 72). Richards' focus is how the processes of construction reveal the networks of people involved in producing the work. This goes beyond discussions of the people concerned with the physical movement of stones, to include those involved in a variety of contexts, such as the preparation of tools, materials, offerings and food; he discusses the act of quarrying and the production of rope to move the stones, as well as the felling of trees to provide levers, rollers and sledges, and the dragging of stones across rough land (the *techné* in Gregotti's vocabulary). This 'created a web of relationships that enmeshed many people in many different places' (2004, 74). There are other, more nuanced, social relations taking place too: 'subtleties such as the sequence of food serving, when and to whom, which cuts of meat are offered and what ceramic vessels are used, and so on, a kind of social mapping is effected; an arena where identities and relationships are re-negotiated' (2004, 77). The monument, therefore, embodies these networks; it is a fusion of the social relations, the personal identities, the practices and the materials. The monument can not be simply reduced to its final form or indeed to over-simplistic discussions of labour forces.

Materials and form

Drawing our attention to material and form, several writers have indicated that materials should be given greater prominence in discussion of form (Boivin and Owoc 2004; Brittain 2004; Conneller 2011; Cummings 2002, 256; Deleuze and Guattari 1988, 401, 451; Thomas 2004a; Tilley 2004). Chantal Conneller, for example, and echoing Ingold (2007, 14), calls for materials to be taken more seriously, arguing that 'archaeologists have consistently privileged the study of forms over materials' (2011, 24). Arguing for an approach based on a more 'rhizomatic *châine opératoire*', Conneller argues that implicit in most archaeologists' approaches to materials is the view of them as a passive medium upon which mental representations are imposed; the form already existing in the head of the maker (*see* Thomas 2004a for the history of the distinction between form and matter). Conneller contends that matter is not necessarily inert or the form imposed – but that they both act together; form can be defined by the limits of the material. As Deleuze and Guattari propose, carpentry 'is a question of surrendering to the wood, then following where it leads by connecting operations to a materiality, instead of imposing a form upon a matter (1988, 451). These perspectives usefully place focus on the process of construction and the materials being used.

Architectural form

The contention here is that there was no pre-existing concept for the final form of Silbury Hill in the heads of the builders. This does not mean that the various phases did not have some degree of architectural form or coherence (*see* Field 2010). Indeed, the architectural form of the various phases may well have been important, but this form is only part of the story; one element of what we can call the mound-in-being – that is the mound in a continuous cycle of regeneration; the ongoing unfolding of the mound. As we have seen above, material and form are not separate but related, and this relationship emerges during the process of building.

There is a technical interaction with materials, and materials have different and varied properties: for example sarsen stones are heavy, chalk erodes and a pile of organic material retains form well, whereas loose gravel does not. The materials used constrain the form rather than the form being imposed on the material. This point is well illustrated by Ingold's description of weaving a basket (2000, chapter 18), whereby the basket-maker may have an idea of what the final form may look like prior to starting the basket although the actual form only 'comes into being through the gradual unfolding of that field of forces set up through the active and sensuous engagement of practitioner and material' (2000, 342). Similarly, discussing the construction of Gothic cathedrals in the 12th century, Deleuze and Guattari suggest that 'the static relation, form–matter, tends to fade into the background in favour of a dynamic relation, material–forces' (1988, 401).

In this way, the materials used in Silbury Hill will have suggested a certain form – such as a pile – and so if one phase was piled too high it would fall down; the angles of the slopes are dictated by the laws of physics and the incline at which various materials will settle. Additions to the pile could initially be made in an *ad hoc* way, like adding material to a compost heap, but as the mound developed and grew ever larger in size or more complex in structure there would come a point when decisions were needed to focus structure and form within the constraints of the materials and engineering principles. There is, at least in some stages of the structure, design which underpinned the emerging structural complexity of the Hill. This is perhaps why some of the later phases of Silbury Hill appear to involve a greater degree of planning.

We see this underlying design, for example, in the putative circular ditches: it is difficult to dig in a circle without an idea to drive the construction. It needs to be laid out, not precisely, but in the manner that one would lay out a new flower bed or vegetable patch. We also see it in the retaining walls in the later stages of the mound structure or the way the sides of the Gravel Mound appear to have been consolidated with soil. Whether or not this was a device deliberately to address problems of drainage and

stability is not clear but implicit is that there was some knowledge of construction needs that were evidently being addressed. There are other material technical interactions too, for example the gravel for the Gravel Mound was collected from a particular location and may have been processed, that is, sieved from its parent clay (*see* Canti, Chapter 5). No doubt capacity for design will have been present in the community through oral histories with its accrued experience of how other earthworks failed or succeeded – either as structures or in their purpose. This does not mean, however, that by the later stages of Silbury the materials – or the process of piling the materials up – was any less important, or that a 'final form' had cemented itself in the minds of the builders.

Just as those creating Silbury were operating within technical limitations imposed by the constraints implicit within their chosen materials, so too were they operating within a particular praxis: within the restraints of social mores. We can therefore perhaps see the various phases of Silbury as a merging of technical, political and aesthetic decisions. The rough revetment walls used in the later phases of the mound were not just an engineering solution to a construction problem, but the product of the processes and conditions that formed them. The use of blocks of sarsen stone within sections of the walls, which, given their heavy weight and the fact that they do not offer any structural advantage, seems to us illogical, should therefore be seen in this broader context (*see* the discussion on materiality below).

Social relations

The means of production also affect social relations. Richards (2004) has already drawn our attention to the numerous smaller, nuanced social relations that can occur at ceremonial sites. At Avebury Watson (2001) has discussed how social differences may have been expressed through people's spatial location relative to the Inner and Outer Circles. This is also apparent in the restricted number of individuals privileged to witness the midwinter sunrise within the chamber at Newgrange (Stout 2010) or at certain times of the year at Stonehenge. Similarly, at Silbury such social differences may have been expressed through the division of labour, gender or by restrictions on certain contributions to the endeavour.

A mound the size of Silbury Hill has engendered a huge amount of discussion about the size of the workforce (*see* Chapter 8 for current calculations), but as Whittle says 'The precise calculations do not matter' (1997a, 145); what is important is that it required a certain aggregation of people. Whereas Atkinson considered the time span for construction to be relatively short, analysis of the C14 determinations has provided a preferred model of a time span for construction probably between 55 and 155 years (Chapter 4). Whichever limit of that range we opt for, the workforce needed is much smaller than that supposed by Atkinson. Much of the monument consists of small-scale activities. Piling up of the gravel mound can only have taken a few people and earlier phases of the mound's development, such as the organic mounds and the banks, may have involved no more than the local community or a series of visitors. The later chalk phases, however, may have required far more people and perhaps we can envisage a number of communities being involved.

Similarly, gatherings for any ceremonial or ritual event may have been relatively small, at least until the mound attained proportions conducive to extra-regional celebrity and by which time its very *raison d'être* may have changed, been exhausted or played itself out. We can of course imagine that like fashion, the aims and function will have changed over time.

Silbury Hill can, then, perhaps be seen as a mediation between process, material, people, relations, events and form; that is the concept of the mound-in-being.

Rhythm and repetition

Through Ingold's example of basket weaving we also get a sense of movement in the creation of the form: 'the form of the basket emerges through a pattern of skilled movement, and it is the rhythmic repetition of that movement that gives rise to the regularity of form' (2000, 342). Alasdair Whittle has drawn attention to the archaeological applications of Wendy James's (2003) notion of a 'choreography' of movement: 'the flow or pattern of the affective sociality which constitutes their daily existence' (Whittle 2005, 65), and here we may imagine a choreography around Silbury Hill.

The presence of fresh snail shells in the Gravel Mound and the well-preserved plant remains and insects in the Lower and Upper Organic Mound at Silbury Hill suggest rapid burial. The various ditch re-cuts are also likely to have been hurriedly filled in, given the unweathered appearance of the sides. Some of the banks are remarkably consistent in their dimensions (and in some cases materials), despite being concealed by later phases, suggesting that a memory of the earlier banks remained. This perhaps has some bearing on the rate at which staged activity occurred and provides us with a sense of the rhythms that created the mound: the repeated bodily performances of bringing materials together and re-cutting ditches. Added to this we can imagine other movements, the routine, such as walking, and the less routine, such as dancing and whirling; all will have left a mark on the landscape, however ephemeral.

A social energy is implied by the construction of the mound. The community did not bite off more than it could chew but planned achievable objectives. It appeared to revel in construction, perhaps with one generation wishing to demonstrate that it could at least match the achievements of its predecessor, often in novel ways, such as the construction of the miniature satellite mounds. Or maybe the phases were bound closely with the rhythms of people, life cycles, or of the seasons, rather than competition between the generations. The local community had a long pedigree in such endeavours stretching back over a thousand years to the earthworks constructed on the summit of Windmill Hill (Chapter 8). At Avebury henge, scarcely a generation will have passed without some kind of communal monument construction, whether new build or re-cuts or additions to old sites. The phases of Silbury Hill were generated by the pattern of movements between people and the materials, the regular rhythmic motion producing the various forms and incarnations. These forms contain the gestures of the builders, their actions and their energy, and through repetition, 'habit is renovated and memory is refreshed' (Deleuze 1994, 118).

Thinking of Silbury in this way, through the rhythms, repetitions and embodied actions that created it (both large-scale public festivals and ceremonial performances, and small-scale daily routines), is a useful way of interpreting the mound, for it retains the focus on the process whilst attempting to understand the form and what may have underpinned the construction phases. And when huge constructions like Silbury seem to transcend normal parameters, it reminds us of the human dimension – the fact that *real* people lived, touched, experienced and constructed it.

Wrapping

Another useful way of looking at the phases of Silbury Hill, and again retaining attention on process, is the notion of 'wrapping' discussed by Colin Richards (forthcoming). In this way one phase encompasses or wraps earlier forms and all their meaning. Richards discusses five properties of wrapping: *concealment,* where something is deliberately hidden or obscured, is also a way of drawing attention to that being concealed; *protection,* either protecting the monument against external forces or the outside world from potent forces within the monument; *containment,* again if the earlier phases are powerful they may need to be controlled (*see*, for example, Panel 8.2 in Chapter 8); *unification,* that is the bringing together of different materials – the sum is greater than the parts; and *re-presentation* (Richards forthcoming). At Silbury Hill this last point may well have been important since later phases sheath earlier ones, allowing the monument to be liberated from prior forms and permitting it to take on fresh outward appearances, however capricious or unrecognisable.

In this way one could say that the organic mounds at Silbury wrap around earlier ones, which are themselves encircled by banks that form a ring, wrapping around the organic mounds, *unifying* the soils and *re-presenting* the form; the sarsen stone boulders may have been *concealed* within, and the antler picks *contained* or *protected*, and so on. In his discussion of wrapping, Richards also points out that this leads to the possibility of 'unwrapping', that is exposing the earlier phases. By the same token, at Silbury Hill we do not know how many times the soils were piled up only to be removed and returned to the ditch or used again elsewhere – a process of wrapping, unwrapping and re-wrapping that is now lost to us.

Incremental changes

We believe that there was no blueprint or mental template for the final form of Silbury Hill; no overarching structure to its sequence. Instead we see incremental changes; the mound protean and, we contend, largely unpredictable; a point that is also true of many buildings (*see* examples in Hollis 2009 and Turnbull 1993). Equally, this can be seen at many (perhaps most) Later Neolithic monuments. For example, the banks that surround Marden henge comprise a series of straight lengths of apparently uncoordinated

earthwork rather than a coherent monument, whilst Stonehenge is 'actually an amalgam of many different phases of construction and reconstruction' (Bradley 1998, 92). Similarly the numerous re-cut pits and postholes at the Sanctuary led Pitts (2000, 246) to remark: 'It was not a monument at all: it was a process'. This point is also true of the many re-cut postholes recorded at the Southern Circle in Durrington Walls (Parker Pearson *et al* 2006, 235), whilst Newgrange too is a multi-phased monument with numerous layers; it is 'more than a monument: Newgrange is also a process' (Eriksen 2008, 262). There appears to have been an obsessive need to alter, tweak and re-invent monuments throughout the Later Neolithic across Britain and Ireland.

Silbury was one such mutating monument, shape shifting from form to form, from generation to generation, in an inexorable cycle, only eventually becoming a spectacle. With each new phase the investment and embedded biographies were renewed, preserving tradition as much as changing and re-imagining it. This deliberate re-fashioning will have been a community restoring act – a form of social self-renovation, and was perhaps caught up in, even enactments of, stories and mythologies relating to the community, as Hall (1997, chapter 3) suggests for soils within some of the Hopewell mounds. And just as the monument did not start with a blue print, nor did it end with a finished product. The monument at any one time is on a continuum, one which persists up to the present day. As Ingold remarks '"ends" and "goals" are but landmarks on a journey' (2000, 172) – ends are endless and the mound continues to metamorphose.

There is another element to the mound too – expressive values were clearly attributed to the materials used with the mound. For this reason we will now discuss the materiality of three types of materials included in Silbury Hill: stone, antler and soil.

Materials and materiality

Stone

The materiality of stone has been widely discussed in the literature (for example, Scarre 2004; Tilley 2004; O'Conner *et al* 2010) and so we will use this to begin a discussion of Silbury materials and materialities. As O'Conner and Cooney point out in the introduction to

Materialitas. Working Stone, Carving Identity, stone is both enduring and yet capable of transformation, 'This enduring character means that stone is inextricably linked to notions of monumentality and remembrance, and formed an active medium in the creation of identities and memory life in a range of social contexts and practices' (O'Conner and Cooney 2010, xxii).

Sarsen stone boulders have been recorded from within Silbury Hill during the various investigations. In 2007 clusters of sarsen stone were recovered from excavations on the summit, and similar clusters were clearly exposed in the 1970 trench as evidenced by archive photographs (*see* for example Fig 7.1). Sarsen boulders were also recorded at various times between 2000 and 2008 within the shaft and in the collapsed area on the summit. Sarsen stone was also recorded within the Upper Organic Mound in 2007, and others are similarly evident in the plan prepared by John Taylor as part of the 1968–70 work (Fig 1.10), while sarsens were also noted in the centre of the Hill by both Merewether (1851a) and Tucker (1851). Sarsen stone, therefore, is likely to have been a widespread material throughout both the later stages of the mound as well as the Upper Organic Mound phase. Further, the 2007/8 work suggests that the sarsen fragments on the summit were different from those within the Upper Organic Mound: those from the summit were formed largely of fractured and reduced pieces, many with flake scars indicative of controlled direct percussion, compared to the natural, rounded stones recovered from inside the mound (*see* Pollard, Chapter 3).

As well as the sarsen boulders, numerous unworked flint nodules were recovered from the mound together with quantities of unworked burnt flint. As Bishop (Chapter 3) points out, these nodules would have been extracted from their parent chalk and brought to the site, but they were not knapped or used to produce flakes (*see* Cooney 2010 for a discussion of depositions of unworked stone in Neolithic sites). Although having different properties, the nodules might therefore be compared to the unworked sarsen boulders and used in similar ways. The seemingly deliberate inclusion of unworked flint nodules is in contrast to the worked flint, which appears to have been deliberately excluded. The lack of flint tools at Silbury is interesting, particularly given the relatively large quantities of micro-debitage. The micro-debitage indicates that flint may have been knapped during the construction,

but pieces large enough to see were collected up and disposed of elsewhere, leaving only the microscopic evidence. Combined with the evidence for the lack of ceramic or faunal remains, as well as the absence of charcoal remains from fires, this suggests that the whole area was deliberately kept relatively clean.

In an important and often cited article Parker Pearson and Ramilisonina (1998) suggest, based on ethnographic evidence from Madagascar, that the hardness and durability of stone in the Later Neolithic linked it to eternity and this was therefore reserved for the realm of the ancestors. This is used with explicit reference to Stonehenge and its surrounding monuments, suggesting that Stonehenge was built exclusively for the use of the ancestors, and that the relative lack of cultural debris within the monument is evidence that it was 'never the scene of feasting by the living' (1998, 316). This is contrasted with Durrington Walls, a site for the living, with timber circles rather than stone. Parker Pearson and Ramilisonina (1998) and Parker Pearson (2000) also apply this notion to the Avebury area, suggesting that Avebury henge with its large sarsen stone megaliths formed part of the domain of the dead, whilst the West Kennet palisade enclosures were within the land of the living; Silbury Hill, part way between the two, 'marks the transition point where death turns to life, a monument of renewal and rebirth' (1998, 319, fn15) (note that the 1998 scheme does not take into account chronological differences between the monuments – *see* Chapter 8).

Although the apparent cleanliness of Silbury Hill clearly shares similarities with Stonehenge, and noting that stone in some circumstances

Fig 7.1
1968–70 archive photograph showing the excavation trench on the summit. Clusters of grey sarsen stone boulders can clearly be seen.
(Courtesy Alexander Keiller Museum)

may be associated with the dead, there are, however, other ways of understanding the use of stone in prehistoric monuments. Associating stone only with the dead and timber with the living introduces a substantial dualism to the landscape. It conflates multiple phases across many generations into a single notion, and thus removes the *process* of constructing monuments, which themselves become inert representations inscribed into the landscape. Further, understanding stone only as a timeless representation of the ancestors privileges one quality of stone, its hardness and durability, over other qualities (*see also* Bishop's discussion in Chapter 3). As Conneller asserts, 'Material properties however emerge in particular types of engagement, and cannot be transposed across a modern category of material, which is itself in constant variation' (2011, 82). Although the durability of some types of stone might be obvious to us, this is just one perspective on one property out of many (Conneller 2011; Ingold 2007; Richards forthcoming). Stone can also be perceived as being alive or sacred or the embodiment of supernatural beings (*see* Brumm 2004, 146 and examples in Field 2005); it is highly variable and mutable, and a more nuanced approach is clearly needed.

Josh Pollard and Mark Gillings have drawn attention to the importance of sarsen stone in the Upper Kennet valley (2010), particularly the smaller sarsen boulders, which they term 'miniliths'. They discuss how sarsen quern stones often appear fragmented and 'distributed between people and locations in a process of enchainment'. They also consider the potential importance of polissoirs on sarsen stones in the landscape, such as the networks produced as people travelled to them, and their transformative properties to produce and regenerate stone axes (2010, 33). Although their discussion is based on Early Neolithic evidence, it also rings true for Silbury Hill, for sarsen boulders (miniliths) recorded on the summit had clearly been modified and transformed by splitting, flaking and in some cases burning. One even appears to have been worked into a quern roughout before being deposited in the mound without actually being turned into a quern or used as one. Another was roughly worked into a sub-oval shape, before being lightly pecked on one side and then ground, perhaps to turn it into a polissoir, before being deliberately split (or fragmented) by a single blow (*see* Pollard, Chapter 3). Two things are obvious: firstly, these

stone items are bound up in the world of the living; and secondly it is clear that a 'final form' was not intended here. Indeed, it could be argued that the process of production was what was important, in other words we have evidence here of process but not final form. The presence of both flint and sarsen transformed by burning is also interesting, and perhaps reflects the importance of the transformative qualities of fire and stone, or perhaps the process of direct transformation itself (*see* Conneller 2011 for a discussion on this). Chalk, the main component of the Hill, is also stone and highly mutable: it is sometimes hard in blocks, sometimes soft in heaps and can be mixed with water to form slurry or paint.

There is another side to the worked sarsen stone pieces. O'Conner (2010), in a discussion of redeposited grindstones and quern stones in Irish Bronze Age funerary monuments, has pointed out the symbolic nature of quern stones and their frequent inclusion within ritual monuments. 'These subtle connections suggest a broad resonance between acts of grinding, pecking, working and polishing stone in various forms, that somehow made these objects appropriate foci for special depositional acts' (O'Conner 2010, 158). O'Conner describes some of the sensory experiences of grinding stone: the rhythmic nature of it, the way the mind is allowed to wander and how this can often be a cathartic experience. Elsewhere, Maori practice suggests that grinding may have been accompanied by communal chanting and reciting of origin stories with the whole community present so that past and present are embedded in the stone (Field 2011b). Thus the fragmented sarsen may represent 'pieces of place', in this case a place associated with the beginnings of a great river and may be carried or passed to others carrying its biography. The presence of fragments of sarsen at Windmill Hill may have performed a similar function.

A process of knapping, cleaving, shaping, pecking, grinding and polishing would have been involved in the fragments of worked sarsen incorporated into the upper levels of Silbury Hill, and they would have carried all these actions with them; the multitude of behaviours, practices and customs that embodied the people. This would have created a network of relationships as presumably various people would have been involved in the different tasks. The sarsen stone and flint nodules incorporated within Silbury Hill, caught in the flows, processes and networks of life, were active agents in the production of the mound-in-being.

Antler

The worked sarsen stone from the summit largely came from a well-defined area within one of the revetment walls. Alongside the stones, and clearly associated with them, were three fragments of antler, two of which re-fitted. The association of sarsen and antler also seems to be confirmed from the earlier 1970 summit excavation where a photograph shows a large antler fragment alongside a sarsen boulder (Fig 7.2), whilst Merewether described an antler tine that was placed on top of a sarsen stone within the tunnel (Merewether 1851a, 80). There were, however, other fragments recovered from throughout the chalk phases of the mound.

It is tempting to see these small groups of antlers and stone as occasional ceremonial deposits within the broader process of construction, but the association of the two materials is interesting. Were they considered similar and therefore placed together or did they contrast so significantly that an association was drawn? We have discussed how stone can, at times, be interpreted as being associated with the dead. Perhaps, since antler once came from a living being, it was associated with life, and therefore the contradiction of life and death was brought together.

As described by Worley (Chapter 3), although the assemblage of antler from Silbury was fragmentary and therefore difficult to identify to a particular development stage, larger antlers seem to have been selected. For example, the fragments found alongside the sarsen on the summit are from antler crowns (normally interpreted as rakes) from a mature stag (stage D or above). This is the picture we get from most Neolithic antler pick assemblages; generally mature, but not post-prime, antlers were selected, and at some sites a preference for antlers from the left side of the deer is suggested (Worley and Serjeantson forthcoming). Within the literature this is frequently interpreted on technical grounds: larger antlers being stronger and more usable as a pick, with more tines, and the left side more convenient for right-handed users (Worley and Serjeantson forthcoming). In other words the antlers were selected because they were technically better suited for excavating chalk (also *see* Sharples 2000 for a critique of this approach). Such a view sees antlers as a natural resource to be exploited as

necessary. It says little, however, about the materiality of the antler or the relationship between people and deer, and there are other ways of looking at it.

Red deer antlers, in many ways, embody a certain machismo. Male red deer grow antlers which they then use during aggressive displays to compete with rival males for access to females during the annual rut in the autumn, the ruts being accompanied by loud, deep roars that can be heard across the landscape. The antlers selected are from stags at their most vigorous. Rather than understanding antler picks on technical grounds – as simply being passive tools manufactured out of an inert raw material – they may have harnessed this strength and energy, the picks embodying the essence of the stag. As Conneller describes in relation to red deer antler from the Mesolithic site of Star Carr, 'So harnessing deer affects would extend the human body and allow people to act in a "deerish" way' (2011, 62). This is an interesting point and perhaps we should understand the red deer antler as affecting people, perhaps by transforming them into a state of 'stagness'. We might then imagine that the thwack of antler pick into chalk was accompanied by a mighty stag-like roar – the antler shaping people as much as people shaped the antler. We should be careful here of privileging animal behaviour over other elements of the material, but through this discussion we can see that there are other ways of interpreting the selection of mature stag antlers for use as picks than simply its technical strength.

Another way of understanding the antler fragments deposited within Silbury Hill might

*Fig 7.2
Archive photograph showing a sarsen boulder and antler from the 1970 excavation trench.
(Courtesy Alexander Keiller Museum)*

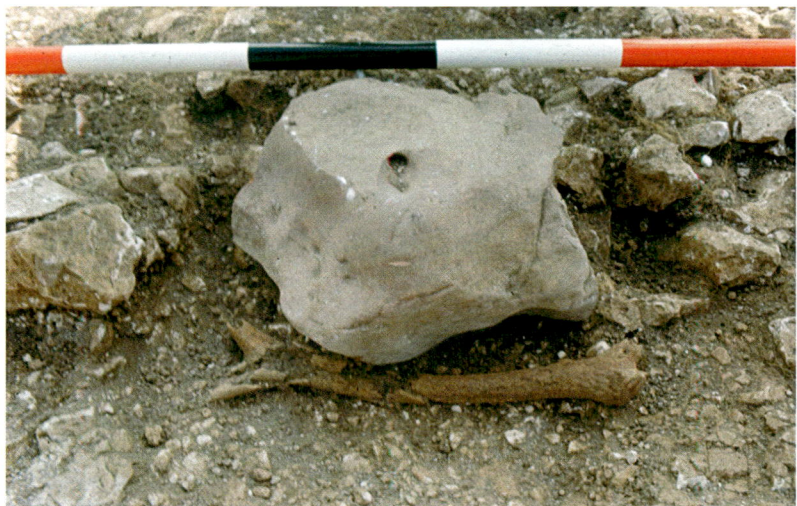

Panel 7.1 The Dolerite fragments

David Field and Jim Leary

There is a further conundrum to deal with when discussing stone at Silbury: that of the spotted dolerite from the summit (*see* Ixer, Chapter 3). Atkinson described finding from an 'undisturbed' context a fragment of rock 'apparently identical with one of the varieties of Stonehenge bluestone (volcanic ash)' (Atkinson 1970, 314). This, however, appears to have been in error, since although a fragment of spotted dolerite seems to have been recovered from the summit of Silbury in 1969 (now in the archive at the Alexander Keiller Museum), the label in the bag describes it as having come from the topsoil (Ros Cleal pers comm; *see* Ixer Chapter 3; Fig 3.5). A fragment of 'exotic' stone does appear to have come from an *in situ* Neolithic context – later described as 'small fragment found in clean chalk rubble on the top of Silbury Hill during excavations directed by Professor R J C Atkinson in 1970' (Clough and Cummins 1988, 162). However, when analysed, this was shown to be hornblende schist (Clough and Cummins 1988, 160). Atkinson may have conflated these two fragments, so that he had imagined the bluestone fragment came from the clean chalk rubble. To this one fragment

of 'bluestone' from the topsoil, we can now add three further small flakes from the subsoil of the 2007 summit excavations (Ixer, Chapter 3).

It is unfortunate that all these pieces come from uncertain contexts and cannot be related to prehistoric features. It is of course possible that it was brought to the site during the 18th or 19th century, or even during the 20th-century excavations. But the possibility of 'bluestone' being taken to the summit either as a boulder or fragments during the Neolithic cannot be ruled out, or perhaps we could even imagine that there was once a megalith or stone setting on the top, as at Pitnacree. If this had survived the Roman period it will have certainly been removed during the medieval remodelling of the summit. Silbury is of course closer to Preseli than Stonehenge and with Welsh material in the form of axes in earlier contexts at Windmill Hill (*see also* the rhyolite from near Silbury, Ixer Chapter 3); contact with that area would be of no surprise. The fragments could, however, be seen in the same light as that suggested here for the sarsen, and it is perhaps noteworthy that Darvill and Wainwright (2009) have recently suggested that there was deliberate Neolithic fragmentation and dispersal of 'bluestone' at Stonehenge.

Fig P7.1.1 Reconstructed profile of Silbury Hill, imagining what it would be like with a spotted dolerite monolith on top. (Eddie lyons, © English Heritage)

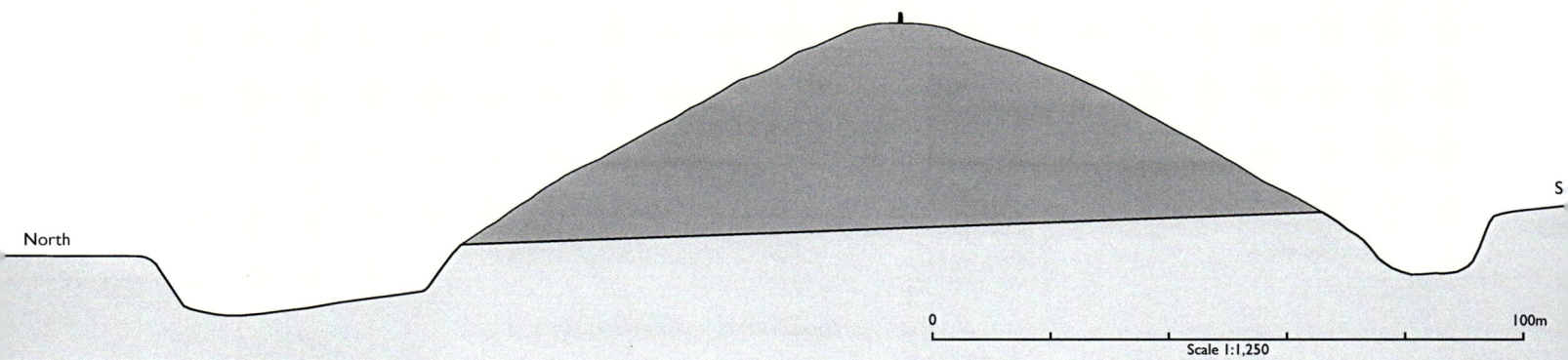

be to look at relations between people and deer. Worley and Serjeantson (forthcoming) suggest that there was a preference on Neolithic sites for shed antler rather than from hunted deer. This is despite the fact that antlers reach their optimal size and harden long before they are shed, and then when they are shed the antlers would

require a degree of foraging to find, and if left too long may become gnawed by scavengers or eaten by the deer themselves (Legge 1981, 100; Sharples 2000, 113; Worley and Serjeantson forthcoming). In other words, if needs were pressing it is easier to kill the deer for their antler than wait for the antler to be shed.

Whilst we could choose to frame this in purely economic terms – for example antler was needed year after year for monument construction and therefore the deer were a valuable resource to be preserved – we could also choose a more subtle and nuanced way of understanding it. Although we do not yet know whether deer were herded or allowed to move freely across the landscape, they would certainly need to be closely observed in order to collect the antler quickly. This close observance of deer will have led to an intimate relationship with people (Legge 1981, 100; Sharples 2000, 113). The deer had their own life history which would have become better known over time. As Conneller points out, in non-western groups, animals 'may be seen as persons, relatives or supernatural beings' (2011, 49; Ingold 2000), and the same may have been true of some deer in the Neolithic. These animals, with their fecund annual growth of antlers (Clark 1954, 171), may have been respected in ways that we little understand now.

Indeed, this predictable, cyclical shedding of antler (in spring) and the annual rut (in autumn) could have marked time in the annual cycle. To take this point further, although antlers are shed annually, they also develop over the lifetime of the stag and may similarly provide a metaphor for growth and the passing of time (Conneller 2011, 59). Of course, different stags may have been seen in very different ways and we should not simply assume that they were all viewed and treated in the same way. However, understanding human–deer relations in the Neolithic may be critical for a fuller under-standing of Neolithic monument construction.

Yet another way of understanding antler is through the process of modification to transform them into useable tools. This process was highly varied but involved collecting the antler, and for picks removing the crown and most of the tines, leaving (in most cases but not all) the brow tine, which was used as the blade of the pick. This process of transformation involved flint tools to cut off unwanted parts, but also, as is evident on one antler at Silbury, occasionally involved burning to assist removal. This *châine opératoire* was a physical, embodied experience that required an understanding of the properties of the material. Antler picks carried this *châine opératoire* with them. But more than this, as Worley and Serjeantson (forthcoming) point out, large-scale monuments such as Silbury Hill would have required a high level of organisation

to collect the quantities of antler required, and depending on the nature of this organisation this whole process could have involved many people, requiring networks of relationships, with groups of people gathering antlers at the appropriate time of year. The antlers were bound up in this 'process of enchainment' – the *techné* of the antlers – and embodied them.

Following use, quantities of antler picks, both broken and usable, were deposited within the mound, a process also true of many Neolithic monuments, including Avebury henge, Stonehenge, Durrington Walls, Marden henge and Grime's Graves flint mines. Indeed at the latter, as in other flint mines, antler was left in piles in the galleries rather than taken and re-used. There it was inferred that some kind of taboo related to taking the picks out of the mine (cf Flood 1983), while in some instances special dedicatory deposits were made (Topping 2004). Such fragments have in the past often been interpreted as representing broken picks thrown away and incorporated accidentally or 'tools thankfully thrown into the ditch when the exhausting work was done' (Burl 1979, 65). As discussed before (Leary 2010, 146; Leary and Field 2010, 121), it is difficult to see how these pieces of antler could have been incorporated through any other way than deliberate inclusion, and this is particularly so with Silbury Hill where an almost complete pick was recovered from the watching brief on the southern slope, while on the summit antler fragments were clearly associated with sarsen stone. We should see these antler fragments as deliberate inclusions, and at Silbury Hill, as noted above, the absence of animal bone and domestic debris generally suggests that the mound was kept clean; in this context the antler pick fragments are special.

Soil

Although soils have long been recognised by archaeologists as culturally meaningful, the materiality of soils has, compared to stone and antler at least, been under-discussed in the archaeological literature. However, as the papers in Boivin and Owoc (2004) show, in many instances non-western societies recognise particular types of soils as animate, powerful and/or the embodiment of a divine force. There can be strong symbolic and ritual associations with soils, and in a similar way to stones, these associations can be linked to colour and texture. People can travel great distances to acquire certain soils and stones from a particular source.

Boivin notes that 'In a wide variety of cultures, the value of a mineral is very often related as much to the journey that was made to acquire it as to the mineral itself' (2004, 10).

Although people may not have had to journey far to find the materials used for Silbury Hill, much of which could be found in the general locality, there does seem to have been a degree of deliberate selection of materials, suggesting that symbolic meanings underpinned that selection. The majority of soils that made up the Lower Organic Mound were derived from over the clay-with-flints geology, whereas the Upper Organic Mound (Fig 7.3) comprised soil largely derived from chalk; further, the soil used in one of the Mini-mounds seems to have come from a woodland edge setting, compared to the grassland setting from which the Lower and Upper Organic Mound material was derived (*see* Chapter 6). Indeed, there may well have been a subtle interplay between materials, colours and textures, with the dark organic mounds contrasting with the underlying yellow gravels used in the Gravel Mound, as well as the overlying white chalk phases.

The truncated OLS lay beneath all the early features at the centre of Silbury, and therefore, if the turf was used in the organic mounds it

Fig 7.3
A view of the end of the Main Tunnel showing a section through the basket loads of different material that forms the Upper Organic Mound.
(Duncan Stirk,
© English Heritage)

would first have to be stacked elsewhere. The source of the gravel in the Gravel Mound is unknown, but Canti (Chapter 5) suggests that it may have come from the underlying derived clay-with-flints. If this is the case, the gravel must have undergone technological processing to separate it from the clay, which may well have been a symbolically-laden process, and the gravels, thereafter, would have carried this *techné* with it.

This interplay of soils is ubiquitous in prehistoric monuments. Many Neolithic round mounds contain features of turf (Kinnes 1979) and often represent more than one phase of activity. At Duggleby Howe, Yorkshire, for example, a rectangular pit with five burials in and around it was subsequently covered with a primary mound of turf, some 23 metres in diameter, within which further burials were placed (Kinnes *et al* 1983; Gibson 2011; Gibson and Bayliss 2010). Similarly, Watson (2001) has discussed how particular riverine clay was used as packing material within the stone holes at the Avebury monument, despite the fact that other clay was more immediately available, and how similarly coloured soils were also used to fill clusters of pits. Watson suggests that the clay may have been selected because of 'its colour, as the dark brown riverine clay contrasts entirely against the pale bedrock clay' (2001, 301).

The use of turf is widespread in long barrows. At South Street long barrow turves were placed along the central spine of the monument, while at Beckhampton Road long barrow some of the bays were filled with turf (Ashbee *et al* 1979). Elsewhere, at for example Wor Barrow, Dorset (Pitt Rivers 1898) or Therfield Heath, Hertfordshire (Phillips 1935) turf formed round or oval mounds beneath the long mounds, or as at Thickthorn Down and Holdenhurst, Dorset, enclosures or revetments (Drew and Piggott 1936; Piggott 1937). The mound at Newgrange also has a component of soil and turves (Eriksen 2008).

To some extent this has also been observed in Bronze Age round barrows. Parker Pearson (2004; Parker Pearson *et al* 2006) has drawn attention to the importance of materiality of soil in the Stonehenge landscape, particularly the presence of ash, occupation debris, soil and turf in the construction of round barrows. This is particularly true of the massive mounds on King Barrows Ridge, which have turf cores (Cleal and Allen 1994, 57–60). The practice, however, was also widespread: in Sussex, excavation of a cemetery of round barrows at West Heath, Petersfield, revealed a component of turf (Drewett 1985; Drewett *et al* 1988). Combinations of soils were 'brought together in a meaningful dialogue' in Early Bronze Age burial mounds along the Welsh coast; these appeared 'to have been specifically selected and differentiated for deposition' (Brittain 2004, 229). Owoc also discusses the materials used in the construction of burial mounds and points out that as the burials are frequently given greater emphasis than the materials that they are formed out of: 'What is in fact far more compelling about the many Late Neolithic/Early Bronze Age "funerary" sites … is not their human remains at all, but the creation and composition of the sites themselves' (2004, 109), the round barrows having been formed out of different materials from a variety of locations in a careful, ordered and planned way (*see also* Nowakowski 2007; Pollard 2001b).

Kristiansen (1984, 94) suggested that this use of turf is closely related 'to the exploitation and control of land and ultimately to subsistence, by the repeated removal of the fertile upper layers for their construction', or as Bradley (2005, 23–8) put it 'the conspicuous consumption of pasture'. Turves do not appear to have been in short supply within the Silbury landscape, although their histories do vary (*see* Chapter 6), so it may be that the practice was related to a ritual recognition of the importance of the resource. Specimens of pasture, for example, are placed on a ritual table at ceremonies involving the branding of llamas in the Andes (Dransaart 2011, 126). As mentioned above, Hall (1997, chapter 3) has suggested that the use of sods in the construction of Hopewell mounds is related to the Earth Diver myth and which still figures in world renewal ceremonies performed by Plains Indians, the structure of the Hopewell mounds mirroring their conception of the universe and the process of construction a re-enactment of cosmological creation (*see also* Charles *et al* 2004, 58–60; Leary and Field 2010, 117–19).

Owoc also describes how at many round barrow sites the turf and subsoil were often stripped to reveal 'brighter subsoil components' (2004, 111). In a similar way, Parker Pearson suggests that if the turf for the burial mounds around Stonehenge came from the immediate vicinity it would have revealed the underlying chalk, laying 'bare a great swathe of land' (Parker Pearson 2004, 84; Parker Pearson *et al*

2006, 252). This can be compared to the stripping of much of the OLS at Silbury Hill, which would have exposed the underlying bright reddish-orange derived clay-with-flints material, contrasting markedly with the surrounding area. This is a process that would have needed to be continually renewed as the monument developed. Such a feature may have been intended as part of the display rather than seen as an accidental by-product (Field 2006; 2010).

Clearance of the ground surface is clearly not unusual; for example, the turf was stripped from the surface at the West Overton G6b barrow (Smith and Simpson 1966, 132) and from a much larger area at Duggleby Howe (Gibson 2011; Gibson and Bayliss 2010). A few hundred metres to the north-west of Silbury Hill, the ard marks recorded beneath South Street long barrow have been interpreted as ritual clearance in advance of mound construction (Rowley Conwy 1987; *contra* Kristiansen 1990). Many of the mounds at Cahokia, North America, for example, had the topsoil stripped and the ground surface levelled and sometimes light coloured sand spread over the ground prior to mound construction. There it is thought to be the result of dedication rituals (Iseminger 2010, 38, 93). While it has been assumed that such practices were to provide materials for building with, it is worth considering that the space thus cleared and manipulated was the desired objective in itself and the arena used in some ceremonial manner. Indeed, at Silbury vegetation may have been laid over the central area (*see* Chapters 2 and 6).

Perhaps the most provocative proponent of the materiality of soils was Evans (2003), who introduced the notion of 'texture' as a medium of social agency. For Evans soils were a way of manipulating social expression, and thus the stripping away or piling up of soil could be seen as a form of communication; as Evans says 'Textures help a person think' (2003, 45; also *see* Evans 2005 for a similar discussion with regard to tell mounds).

Encircling the mound

The materials are just one element of the mound-in-being; to understand Silbury fully we also need to understand its surrounding ditches. The enclosure phases of Silbury Hill are rarely considered (*also see* Leary 2010, 148; Leary and Field 2010, 106). However, an entirely different

Fig 7.4 (opposite)
*Plan of Silbury enclosure
(Ditch 1, with the Upper
Organic Mound in the
centre) compared alongside
a selection of other
enclosures.
(Eddie Lyons,
© English Heritage)*

monument is suggested by the enclosing aspect of a ditch and bank within which a varied set of activities may have taken place.

The first ditch (Ditch 1) recorded within the Silbury tunnel was the only one to have been excavated fully during the 2007/8 work. This showed that it is over 6.5m deep and almost 6m where seen in width, and had a bank on the inside. It clearly terminated in this area, which can be interpreted either as an entrance or the intersection of two ditch sections. Assuming it was circular in plan, Ditch 1 would have formed an enclosure around 100m in diameter. As a free-standing enclosure, the size and circular form of this Silbury ring ditch with its internal bank might be compared with that of the initial Stonehenge enclosure (Cleal *et al* 1995) or Flagstones, Dorset (Smith *et al* 1997, 30) both of which date earlier, to *c* 3000 cal BC. These have recently been termed 'Formative Henges' and compared with the Walton Gyrus, Ysceifiog, Llandegai A, Gwynedd, and the rather larger Priddy Circles, Somerset (Fig 7.4) (Burrow 2010b). A considerable berm would have been present between the ditch and the organic phases of the mound that recalls the enclosure and berm at Maes Howe, until it was covered in chalk when the encircling ditch may have enclosed a monument closer in size to Newgrange in Ireland or Le Hougie Bie in the Channel Islands.

Following the initial cut, Silbury Ditch 1 was rapidly (as indicated by the unweathered sides) and deliberately (as shown by the use of revetting walls) backfilled, the process of back-filling obviously requiring chalk from somewhere. Once backfilled, Ditch 1 was partially cut through by a second ditch (Ditch 2), which had the effect of pushing the encircling ditch slightly further out. This sequence occurred at least twice more (Ditches 3 and 4), each time the new profile cutting through the backfill of the previous cut, and each time the enclosure migrating further out – a process of cyclical backfilling and re-cutting. Ditch 4 was cut through by the external ditch and therefore we can envisage the backfilling and re-cutting as a continuous process that also includes the external ditch (that is, the ditch we can see today).

This external ditch, however, is also not a single phase but comprises a number of phases and re-cuts which creates a massive moat-like feature surrounding the mound. At least four phases can be speculated: the causeways in the

external ditch appear to preserve evidence for an earlier shallow ditch, which was widened and deepened. This was then extended to the west to form the huge rectangular area, which may also have then been re-cut (as indicated by a vegetation feature – *see* Chapter 1; Fig 1.18). The sequence is, however, only based on the evidence of the surface expression and is likely to be far more complex than this.

As at other monuments, the Silbury ditches have formerly been cast aside as mere quarries to provide material for a more meaningful mound; certainly Atkinson considered them in that manner. However, clearly the various phases of surrounding ditches were more than just quarries for raw material for the phases of the mound, and had greater significance than is usually ascribed. This continuous re-cutting emphasises, as with the mound sequence, process over form; the cutting of the ditch and the backfilling were important elements in the construction and reworking of the site.

Ditches, even large ones around henges or hillforts, need not be for defence or as simple quarries for material but, for example, might be barriers constructed to keep evil spirits out (Darling 1998), or as Gibson (2010, quoting Warner 2000) suggests to 'keep dangerous forces within' (*see also* Panel 8.2 in Chapter 8). Hopewell ring ditches and circular embanked enclosures in the Ohio Valley mark the Indian belief that the circle could confuse ghosts and malevolent spirits (Hall 1976) and this is not so far from the beliefs concerning confusing the devil in churches in historic Scotland (Peter Topping, pers comm; also *see* Gibson 2004 for further similar examples). However, even these examples favour explanations of final function over process and there is another way of interpreting these ditches. Discussing causewayed enclosures in particular, which frequently exhibit similar processes of re-cutting and back-filling, Paul Ashbee suggested that 'it is arguable the ditch silting, a patent product of weather and time, may have been thought of as access to, and contact with, a perceived past. The back-filling … could have been a ritual mimicry of the observed natural processes' (2004, 7). In this way we can interpret the deliberate backfilling of the Silbury ditches as a reference to the passage of time or perhaps the cyclical nature of time; an interpretation that satisfactorily emphasises process over form. Similarly, Nowakowski has discussed ditches around round barrows in Cornwall 'not as an

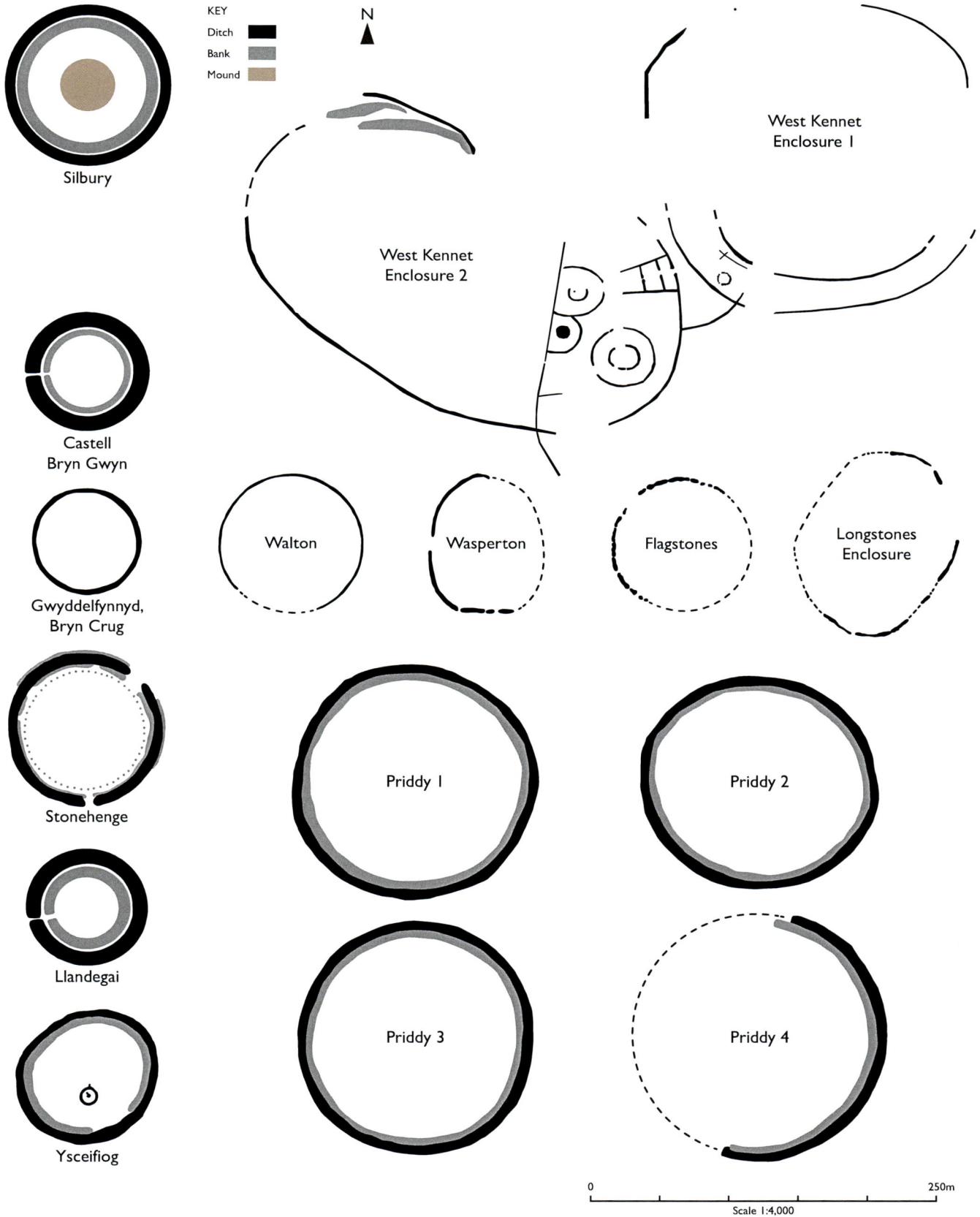

KEY

Ditch

Bank

Mound

N

Silbury

West Kennet
Enclosure 1

West Kennet
Enclosure 2

Castell
Bryn Gwyn

Gwyddelfynnyd,
Bryn Crug

Walton

Wasperton

Flagstones

Longstones
Enclosure

Stonehenge

Priddy 1

Priddy 2

Llandegai

Priddy 3

Priddy 4

Ysceifiog

0   250m

Scale 1:4,000

architectural feature or spatial attribute of a monument, but as a dynamic phenomenon which has the potential to forge a creative role central to the life story of a barrow' (2007, 92).

A place of water and stone

There is a further aspect to consider here alongside the mound and the ditch, and that is the location of Silbury Hill – the place. Human lives are enmeshed with place, and people, by nature, are embodied and located. Silbury Hill was set in a landscape saturated with the past, overlooked by the earlier Neolithic monuments of Windmill Hill and West Kennet long barrow, whilst also set within a complex of contemporary and near-contemporary monuments. Added to this, Silbury occupies a liminal zone; it sits on the toe of a chalk spur representing the edge of the dry chalk upland, which penetrates into the wetter lowland area. Further, the geology is unusual within the footprint of Silbury: overlying the chalk here is a mantle of clay-with-flints material, which is normally found on the top of upland areas (usually capping interfluves) but in this locality must have eroded down slope at some earlier point (see 'Topography and Geology' in Chapter 1). This unusual lowland setting for a displaced upland geology is unlikely to have gone unnoticed in the Neolithic period and may have added further significance to the place.

It is perhaps the lowland setting of Silbury and the fact that it is adjacent to streams and springs, however, that is of greater importance. Digital modelling of the surrounding valley floor highlights this lowland setting on the very edge of dry chalk, immediately adjacent to water. Like Pass, Petrie concluded that the low position of the mound, hidden from view by the local topography, could only reflect the importance of having a water-filled ditch about it. He suggested that the Avebury henge might also have been situated in order to utilise a flooded ditch (Petrie 1924, 217).

Whether water flowed perennially or inter-mittently during the period of construction remains uncertain (see Chapter 6). Work on the prehistoric environment of the valley floor (Evans *et al* 1993) initially indicated the presence of standing pools of water and this was taken as evidence for an almost dry stream bed. Recent empirical observations, however, a result of unusual weather conditions, have made it clear that such standing pools only develop on the porous chalk when the ground is already saturated and the stream bed full. The importance of the drainage system to the construction and meaning of Silbury is paramount and in this context it is perhaps surprising that there has been so little investigation of the ditch. Whether local springs fed the ditch is equally unclear. Pass (1887) indicated that even after a dry summer over two metres of water constantly stood in the bottom of his trenches.

The sub-rectangular plan of the basin to the west of the Hill appears designed to encase water and could have stored an important practical resource, both as a permanent water supply for people and livestock and as a supply for ritual bathing or related activities. Elsewhere cisterns are considered to have symbolic impli-cations as foci of ritual and ceremony (Ashmore and Knapp 1999, 137) and it is conceivable that the ditch extension was of similar importance here. The mirror-like quality of standing water may have had symbolic implications too and given recent archaeological fascination with shamanism it is not without interest that mirrors have been considered as symbols of shamanic ceremony and power (Ashmore and Knapp 1999).

To the south of Silbury Hill is the Swallowhead spring, and at this point the Winterbourne stream, which flows north to south just to the east of the Hill, changes direction and size to form the River Kennet. The location of the monument is such that it is difficult to imagine that in one way or another it was not associated with water, rivers and springs. Along with mountains, caves and lakes, springs invariably hold considerable spiritual significance to non-western societies and may be considered sacred (for example essays in Hirsch and O'Hanlon 1995). As potential interfaces with the spirit world they are increasingly recognised as having other than economic importance in archaeology (for example essays in Ashmore and Knapp 1999).

There is a recognition that many prehistoric artefacts have been recovered from rivers, bogs and springs (for example Bradley 1990; Needham and Burgess 1980; Field 1989; Field and Cotton 1987) and that many Neolithic and Bronze Age monuments focus on such places (Bradley 2000). The economic impact is of course implicit, but the sheer power of currents, tides and of life-giving properties must undoubtedly have had an enormous importance and influenced contemporary perceptions.

Interpretation, memory and tradition must have resulted in important ritual and ceremony adjacent to certain bodies of water.

Water represents a potent metaphor (Richards 1996a and 1996b) – a metaphor for movement and journeying, as well as carrying notions of purity; they create boundaries as well as links. In this sense, standing water in the ditch around the monument could be seen as a boundary or a transition, perhaps embodying aspects of purification (Fig 7.5). Furthermore, Silbury Hill is located at the head of the River Kennet, which together with the River Thames forms a substantial west to east flowing river, flowing out to the North Sea. Silbury Hill was located at the very point this river first emanates (a theme picked up again in Chapter 8).

While some henges have been noted previously as occupying low positions, bowls or dishes in the landscape often associated with springs or streams (Atkinson *et al* 1951; Harding and Lee 1987; Richards 1996a, 1996b; Harding 2003) and cursus monuments also have a riparian focus (for example RCHM 1960; Brophy 2000), it is less well remarked that Neolithic round mounds have a similar focus. The Hatfield Barrow, Beechingstoke, which lies within the Marden henge, is adjacent to the River Avon (Leary and Field 2012); Conquer Barrow, within the henge enclosure at Mount Pleasant, Dorset, to the Stour, while the Great Barrow at Knowlton, Dorset, 41m in diameter by 6.4m high, lies close to the River Allen. The Marlborough Mound (Leary *et al* forthcoming) (and potentially Hamstead Marshall – *see below*, Chapter 8) flanks the Kennet, while Duggleby Howe itself is situated close to the springhead of the Gypsey Race stream. Pitnacree is just one of a number of round mounds, some of great size, that closely hug the floodplain and alluvial gravels of the River Tay (Coles and Simpson 1965, 34) and Newgrange and other nearby mounds lie alongside the River Boyne. The same is true for many Bronze Age round barrows (Field 1998; McOmish *et al* 2002). Indeed, the well-known 'Golden' barrow at Upton Lovell is one of seven alongside the River Wylye that were levelled to make a system of floated water-meadows, while a cemetery of large round barrows, almost levelled, recorded from the air at Charlton near Marden are so close to the river that the ditches must have held water.

The broader area around Silbury Hill is also notable for sarsen stone boulders. Although only a few places now exhibit dense sarsen flows,

Fig 7.5
Silbury at night with a water-filled ditch.
(James O Davies, © English Heritage)

they would have once been much more extensive and Brentnall, quoting Sir Joseph Banks in 1767, suggested that there were numerous stones between Marlborough and Silbury Hill (1946, 423). The presence of sarsen boulders in this landscape has been discussed at length (for example Field 2005; Gillings and Pollard 1999; Pollard and Gillings 2010), and the materiality of sarsen stone is discussed above; however, such striking features as the presence of boulder 'streams' surrounded by rivers and springs, at the head of the Kennet/Thames, may well have led to the immediate area around Silbury becoming a special place, repeatedly visited. Perhaps the sarsen 'streams' appeared to flow towards the Swallowhead Spring where the river emerges. As Gillings and Pollard propose for the broader area 'Through repeated routine encounter and interaction, sarsen stones would have been an integral component of the experienced landscape of these communities' (1999, 183). Through such visits, memories, narratives and identities will have formed; relationships between people, stones, water and place developed, and the site, the stones and the water will have accrued meaning and been interlaced with myths and stories. Just as materials are active agents, so too is the landscape. And like the mound itself, place is continuously being re-imagined; a process rather than a finished product.

Conclusion: Mediating mound; symbolising soils

We can see from the above discussion that there are diverse ways of interpreting Silbury Hill. We should not, however, discuss it as passing on a single message or providing a simple metaphor; it did not have a single function, nor was it constructed out of inert materials on to passive land. Instead this discussion has emphasised the importance of the building process as much as the final or any intermediate form, it has discussed the importance of materials and the processes that involve the materials, and high-lighted the mound's active role in the creation of networks and social relationships. Monuments are more than symbolic and representational, for that suggests that they cannot change – nothing can be added and nothing removed. The materials used were animate, selected for their materiality, for the life histories and networks (or meshworks –

Ingold 2006; 2011) they embody, and were purposefully used, importance perhaps lying in the way they were manipulated, assembled and displayed.

All the materials could be found in the broader landscape, including the sarsens, and perhaps it is this that made them important. The mound did not simply reflect or reference the wider landscape – it physically embodied it and brought it together into one place, binding people to it. This is perhaps what Pollard and Gillings mean when they describe a 'social geology' (2010, 40). Such discussion of materiality needs to be set against the backdrop of contemporary and near-contemporary developments at Avebury and the West Kennet palisaded enclosures, where similarly massive monuments had been or were being constructed or modified and where materials, such as large stone megaliths or huge timber posts, were being worked and used. The landscape was fluid; it would have been marked by the evidence of extraction and construction, and the scoring of paths and accessways. The landscape, like the materials, grew out of the processes and flux of life; the ebb and flow of human interactions (*see* Chapter 8).

Julian Thomas describes monument building 'as a kind of *collage* or *montage* in which materials, substances, people, animals, plants and places, and their meanings, were bought together and new relationships between them were forged' (2004b, 175). This collage, or 'composition' in Watson's (2001) terms, is a useful way of thinking about Silbury; the materials used as a montage of the landscape – the mound becoming a colossal, perhaps at times chaotic, collage; and by incorporating the soils, sarsens, antlers, turves, buttercups, beetles and ants, the mound embodied their place, their precious world, in microcosm (Fig.7.6).

However, it was not just geology, flora and fauna that were incorporated, but social practices, beliefs, actions and events as well. The monument contained memories, emotions, embodied actions, personal histories and collective histories; it contained the ambiguous and the hidden. The place too will have carried with it memories and myths, some that may have gone back to the distant past, perhaps to a time when people built long mounds or dug concentric ring ditches. Communal memories such as these can provide a sense of cultural identity and a way of showing ancestral ties to an area, particularly at a time when new materials, ideas and indeed people were coming into the country (*see* Chapter 8). Identity is embedded in the world, with the surrounding environment, the distinctive 'texture' of the land. And the sherds of later Beaker pottery from the summit of Silbury remind us that place can also be used to appropriate or re-work the past just as much as represent it.

In this way, the mound, and the landscape it embodies, can perhaps best be seen as an accumulation of meanings used in a socially mediatory way, linking people, places and materials in a network of experience. Meaning built up through a continuous process of change, and this reinvention of the earlier forms kept the monument alive, allowing it to become

multi-coded with meanings preserved within later ones. Each alteration a retelling of its previous existence; the life of the monument perpetuated and transformed by the repeated acts of alteration and reuse. This mirrors the way stories and myths are passed from one generation to the next – and equally just as stories stop evolving when they are written down, so too do monuments when they are no longer reinvented. Indeed, perhaps people may choose to perceive Silbury Hill as a long narrative meditation; the materials used in the monument part of the narration, and the monument itself an evolving narrative experience (Leary and Field 2010). However, the materials used in the mound were not

Fig 7.6
A collage of Silbury Hill.
(Judith Dobie and
John Vallender,
© English Heritage)

*Fig 7.7
Reconstruction drawing
of the final phases of
prehistoric Silbury Hill.
(Judith Dobie,
© English Heritage)*

abstract symbols to those who built the Hill, but their meanings emerged through their properties and through people's active engagements with them. The mound and the materials that form the mound embodied the place, the experiences, memories, emotions, relationships, actions and spirituality of the people, and were active in shaping people, just as much as the mound was shaped and brought into being. This myriad of interacting networks and processes is the essence of the mound: the mound-in-being.

8

Neolithic Silbury in Context

DAVID FIELD, JIM LEARY AND PETER MARSHALL

This chapter outlines the possibilities of land-use on the North Wessex Downs and by using the evidence of monuments as a guide attempts to assess the extent and nature of occupation during the 4th and 3rd millennia cal BC. Local influence and development is emphasised although stimulus for excessive mound construction is sought in the social dynamics of the period with potential polities in the adjacent Avebury and Stonehenge areas providing an arena for competitiveness. The radiocarbon dates for mound construction place it within the period of transition from Grooved Ware to Beaker pottery use. But the former was in use much later here than has been modelled for the Boscombe area near Stonehenge, and it may be that expression in the form of earthwork construction, such as Silbury Hill, represented a reluctance to embrace new ideas. Neolithic round mounds elsewhere are compared and considered although only rarely do they reach great proportions, but the purpose behind the mound is seen in its location – the springs at the head of a river system.

Land use

Attention has already been drawn to the importance of the ditch surrounding Silbury Hill and its extension or basin with the possibilities of ritual or ceremonial use. In addition the location at the head of an important river system is considered to be highly relevant to its interpretation (Chapter 7). Whether water ran freely throughout the year in the upper reaches of the Kennet is therefore highly relevant to this, but also crucial to any understanding of the nature of local settlement along with associated subsistence activities on the chalk during the 3rd millennium cal BC, for the chalk soils are extremely porous and before the advent of piped water the construction of dew ponds was necessary in order to keep stock out on the hills. This lack of water retention along with the

unpredictability of winterbourne springs has influenced the location of historic and medieval settlement in the area which tends to focus on the more reliable reaches of the River Kennet. With a higher water table prior to extraction by water companies, this extended for a considerable distance further upstream along the present winterbourne, but today, flow is seasonal above the Swallowhead Spring and the 'winterbourne' only erupts during winter and spring or in periods of high rainfall. The fact that the flow may have been perennial further upstream during the 3rd millennium cal BC (*see* Chapter 6) is important, for it would allow cattle, which require 40–50 litres of water a day per animal (Reynolds 1987, 41), to be grazed on the downs throughout the year and additionally presents choices regarding location for permanent human occupancy.

Historically, the Higher Chalk (Gifford 1957) has been considered difficult for farming, almost marginal in terms of cultivation and generally not favoured for settlement (Barker and Webley 1978, 177). Early maps, for example that prepared by Thomas Alexander for Richard Holford in 1733 (WHC 1553/71), indicate that historic cultivation around Avebury was not extensive and for the most part focused closely around the village and the hamlet of Beckhampton. Beyond, the downland was used as sheep walk, a not untypical arrangement that applied right across the Higher Chalk of Wiltshire and much of Hampshire (Hoskins 1959; Scott 1959; Kerridge 1959; Molland 1959; Thompson 1959). Breakage of ploughshares is high on parts of the flint-laden Upper Chalk, particularly in areas of Clay-with-flints (as mapped by the BGS; *see also* Fig 1.20) (Cope 1976) and this latter area tended to be avoided even when the Higher Chalk was periodically set down to cultivation in response to economic need during, for example, the Napoleonic Wars, or by entrepreneurs when corn prices were high

(Jones 1960). The latter deposit at least retains water, but climate does not help, with the temperature being a degree colder than in the surrounding vales and it is not unknown for ground frost to be recorded at the weather station in Yatesbury during June (Field *et al* 2005, 18). The south-westerlies are strong and arrive directly from the Bristol Channel and as a result modern downland farm buildings are invariably sheltered by trees planted as windbreaks. It is unlikely that any of these difficulties were minimised during the 3rd millennium cal BC.

Ancient land

The most favoured areas for cultivation (and settlement) during historic times focused on the spring line of the Greensand bench at the western edge of the downs around Cherhill and to the south in the Vale of Pewsey (Barker and Webley 1978, 169; McOmish *et al* 2002; Brown *et al* 2005). Of course this need not inform us of activities several millennia earlier, but in contrast to much of the Higher Chalk, the soils at such locations are deemed most suitable for early agriculture, that is if cultivated with primitive ards or ploughs (Wooldridge and Linton 1933). Unfortunately they lie within Chris Taylor's 'zone of destruction' (1972), whereby successive populations have destroyed evidence of earlier activity. Elsewhere, the Greensand incorporates large numbers of Mesolithic and Neolithic flint scatters (*see*, for example, Rankine 1949) though here unfortunately, almost no archaeological investigation has taken place. It would be unwise to write off this lithology which within Wiltshire has only seen surface collection in the Vale of Wardour (Clay 1925; Gingell and Harding 1983) and where considerable quantities of flint material have been recovered (Field 2008). It is worth noting though, the Mesolithic and Neolithic occupation at Cherhill, the latter associated with stakeholes and boundary ditches (Evans and Smith 1983). Despite the poor response of Greensand soils to remote sensing, aerial survey of the Vale of Pewsey for the English Heritage National Mapping Programme (Carpenter and Winton 2011) has discovered what could be a long mortuary enclosure alongside a henge and other ring ditches not far from Marden and a long barrow in an area where numbers of ground axes have been recovered (Devizes Museum collections and

Paul Robinson, pers comm). Additionally, of course, the area harbours the considerably levelled Marden henge, one of the largest in the country along with the almost completely levelled Hatfield Barrow, once said to be only second to Silbury Hill (Leary and Field 2012). In the west, areas currently considered highly suitable for market gardening, such as Bromham, and covered with crop marks attributable to Iron Age and Roman activity (aerial photographs in NMR) have not been tested.

In contrast to these areas, the lack of intensive agricultural activity on the chalk downs during the historic period (that is, Taylor's zone of survival) has resulted in the preservation of earthworks from earlier periods, whose presence can usefully help provide an index of economic and social activity on that part of the landscape, but which has also attracted ever more archaeological investigation at the expense of other areas (Field 2008; 2011b). The Wessex chalk has thus been seen as one of the few receptacles of burial and ceremonial monuments – a ritual landscape. In recent decades other kinds of archaeological evidence, principally aerial photography, have redressed the balance, at least to a degree, by demonstrating the extent of monument distribution in other areas. Many river valleys contain large clusters of ring ditches and other levelled Neolithic and Bronze Age monuments (for example Deegan and Foard 2007; K Field 1975; Green 1975; Woodward 1978), the density of ring ditches in Thanet alone (RCHME 1989; Field 1998) almost matches that of Wessex. Fenner (1990) recorded 900 ring ditches along the Lower and Middle reaches of the Thames in areas accessible to aerial photography. Atkinson's excavation of a cursus, henge and ring ditch complex at Dorchester in the upper Thames valley (Atkinson *et al* 1951) was just the first of a number to turn up, for more recently the inventory accounted for 15 long barrows, 12 causewayed enclosures, 16 mortuary enclosures, 16 cursus monuments and four henges (Fenner 1990; also *see* Barclay and Hey 1999). Other complexes have been noted in river valleys elsewhere, for example in the Nene Valley (Deegan and Foard 2007; and *see* Harding and Healy 2007 for sites at Raunds); the Great Ouse at, for example, Eynesbury (Ellis 2004) and in Essex (Saunders 2011). While during the 1970s it was still possible to construct models largely based on Crawford's *Map of Neolithic Wessex* (Ordnance Survey 1932) it is no longer possible to do so. The National Mapping

Programme has changed everything and demonstrated that the terrain was very much more saturated with monuments and ceremonial sites than previously imagined. Perhaps Jacobi (1981, 23) was pointing to this when he indicated that the carrying capacity of natural resources in Hampshire had already been reached by the end of the 5th millennium cal BC.

Despite this and a number of programmes of excavation, the search for prehistoric settlement remains on the Wiltshire chalk has proved elusive. It may be that the soluble nature of the deposit has resulted in all but the deepest settlement features being eradicated (Atkinson 1957) or that later hillwash from, for example, Waden and Folly Hills and from the Beckhampton Downs accumulated on the valley and coombe floors and obscured traces of putative activity (Evans et al 1993; Allen 2005a and b). Groube and Bowden (1982, 17) concluded that truncation of the chalk is likely to have been accelerated by historic cultivation and around Avebury this may have been responsible for leaving remnants of the Horslip long barrow isolated on a plinth c 0.6m proud of the surrounding land (Ashbee et al 1979, 209–11). Under such circumstances it is extremely unlikely that more subtle ancient structures will have survived at all and the only determinant of activities will be by the careful recording of scatters of artefacts that remain in the ploughsoil.

Highlighting the shortage of evidence of domestic structures, Thomas (1991; 1999) emphasised the likely variable nature of subsistence during the Neolithic and with a critique of those who had considered that settlement may lie in the valleys, suggested that the lack of demonstrated housing encouraged a view of the population as highly mobile. However, as Milner (2005) acknowledged following evaluation of mobility by Rafferty (1985) such things need much greater definition, the modern workforce could after all be considered to be highly mobile and all things considered it seems much too simplistic an explanation of settlement and land use (Whittle 1997b; Field 2008, 98–101). To write off the valleys may be premature, not least given the discovery of buildings at Durrington Walls (Parker Pearson 2007) and Marden henge (Leary et al 2010). Allen (2005b, 223), for example, has demonstrated that much potential indeed lies beneath alluvium and colluvium including the presence of Beaker material at

Piggledene, West Overton, and he reiterated the view that archaeologists may have been 'looking in the wrong place'. Neolithic buildings are beginning to be recognised elsewhere in southern England, for example, Kingsmead Quarry, Horton, Berkshire (Chaffey and Brooks 2012); White Horse Stone in the Medway Valley (Garwood in Booth et al 2011) and for the Later Neolithic at Wyke Down, Dorset (French et al 2007); Durrington Walls (Parker Pearson 2007) and Marden, Wiltshire (Leary et al 2010). Whether any of these structures represent domestic houses, or whether they are ceremonial lodges, barns or sweat lodges is in this context rather beside the point and the matter can be pursued elsewhere, but they indicate a degree of habitation and stability beyond that of pitching a tent. The presence of flat-based pottery (Grooved Ware) at a number of sites even hints at furniture, or at least very flat floors, while the evidence for fixtures and fittings at Durrington Walls (Parker Pearson 2007, 46) supports that. Aside from Evans' excavations at Avebury and West Overton, no investigation has been made into deposits beneath Wessex water meadows and the continued focus on the chalkland plateau in some ways echoes Piggott's (1954, 18) view of the valleys as tangled, marshy, impenetrable morasses.

For the moment then, the best evidence for settlement or other occupation activities probably lies in the spreads of struck flint debris that have been recovered at various times across the downs, although such distribution is very uneven and unfortunately there has been no programme of fieldwalking of the Avebury area carried out to a common standard to match that at Stonehenge (Richards 1990). Evans et al (1993, 185) noted the presence of Mesolithic flint work within the valley at Avebury and West Overton, and Whittle (1993) thought of this as representing hunting camps. In fact, there is a small but increasing amount of evidence that indicates more widespread early activity. Whether the odd microlith found beneath monuments is really the residue of a Mesolithic presence or the result of the ceremonial scattering of ancestral material is for the moment unknown, but it is worth bearing in mind the presence of a microlith from the Avebury henge and the blade core recovered from the OLS at Silbury Hill in 1968–70 (Chapter 3), together with Mesolithic or Early Neolithic flintwork from the 2007/8 investigations (see Bishop, Chapter 3). A rod, a late form of microlith, was found in

Pit 2 during excavations at the site of round barrow Avebury G55 just 70 metres to the south-east of the Swallowhead Spring, while there are several rod-like (ie late) pieces from the trenches in the valley at Avebury (Evans *et al* 1993).

Whittle (1990, 106) suggested that the valley and downland 'was little used throughout the later Mesolithic period … It is most likely that use of the area was organised from camps or bases around or outside the area', the porous soil and lack of water being the greatest concern. He saw Neolithic exploitation of the area as 'a process of infill' 'gradual agricultural colonisation or intake' and 'not a primary zone for Neolithic beginnings' (Whittle 1990, 107–9). At the present time there is no need to adopt a different view, although as noted above investigation into the palaeo-hydrology suggests greater flow in the Kennet and tributaries than today (*see* Chapter 6) and provides other possibilities. Nevertheless, the radiocarbon dating of causewayed enclosures as part of the Gathering Time project appears to confirm the comparatively late interest in the Wiltshire Downs (Whittle *et al* 2011, 683–718).

Casual and random observation of cultivated surfaces in the area between Silbury Hill and Wansdyke indicates the widespread presence of struck flint, although test pits around the Easton Down long barrow revealed little of this (Whittle *et al* 1993). A small area of the Beckhampton–Devizes valley was sampled by Gillings *et al* (2008) but similarly produced little struck flint. To the north of the A4, Robin Holgate and Julian Thomas investigated some of the cultivated areas by fieldwalking in autumn 1983 and the results (Holgate 1987) did confirm the general pattern of flint scatters identified earlier in the 20th century by collectors (Kendall 1921). The densest scatters of Later Neolithic flintwork were found at a distance from Silbury Hill, on the northern slopes of Waden Hill and on Folly Hill, Beckhampton, 0.75km north-west and north-east respectively, and even further afield on the slopes of Windmill Hill where Whittle *et al* (1999) were able to refine the data. Fieldwalking on Folly Hill revealed a concentration of struck flints dating to the Mesolithic, Neolithic and Bronze Age periods, but very little on the south-eastern slopes facing Silbury Hill (Holgate 1987, 259–63; 1988, 91–6). Surface collection, however, has not taken place at the southern end of either Folly

Hill or Waden Hill. Chan (2011, 130–2) recently compared these data to the flint recovered from the Stonehenge environs (Richards 1990, 212–32) and found a much lower quantity of struck flint around Avebury, although this is not entirely surprising given that much of the surface collection around Avebury was from areas of Middle and Lower Chalk where raw material had to be brought in. It might be considered important that a programme of carefully planned and concentrated fieldwalking is established within the area to address this matter.

Taking an optimistic view of the evidence for domestic occupation, Smith (1984) considered there to be an unusual amount of pottery from non-burial contexts scattered around the valley slopes, much of which had been derived from beneath colluvium or other protected environments. A spread of material described as an occupation site lay to the north-west of the West Kennet long barrow, on the lower slopes of the down a little above the Swallowhead Spring and partially sealed beneath the remnants of a round barrow (Avebury G55). This comprised good quantities of Early Neolithic bowl, Peterborough Ware and Grooved Ware pottery and the deposit had been cut into by a series of pits of later Beaker affinities. The assemblage included several arrowheads of different types, a small, partly ground discoidal knife, over 50 scrapers, along with 100 cores and 1,000 waste flakes. It covered an area of some 45 metres diameter around the almost levelled mound and was so rich in other cultural debris – pottery and animal bone – that the excavator Isobel Smith (1965b) initially thought this the location of the offering house that Stuart Piggott speculated had held material prior to deposition in the West Kennet long barrow chambers (Piggott 1962, 75). Smith subsequently dismissed the idea on account of the lack of structural features although acknowledged that these could have been lost through modern ploughing.

This perhaps heightens the potential for settlement evidence surviving on the valley slopes, an area which has seen little archaeological investigation. A watching brief during the replacement of a main sewer pipe along the upper part of the Kennet valley in 1993 revealed no Neolithic structures (Powell *et al* 1996), but use of the re-entrant valleys to the south may well have been underway relatively early in the Neolithic, for the East and West Kennet long barrows are situated on the ridges between them.

For the moment, while the artefact coverage is not well resolved, perhaps the evidence of the distribution of monuments can be used to some advantage. The chronological span of these is, of course considerable, but in some ways this is helpful as it serves to emphasise the long-lived tradition in the area involving earth moving and construction projects.

Of the early monuments, the long barrows are the most numerous and it might be possible to deduce some indication of occupation from the pattern of distribution. Some 39 were reported by Barker (1985) from across the North Wessex Downs, of which 21 are located within the area chosen for environmental reconstruction drawings by Gillings *et al* (2008, 183–96 and figs 5.5 to 5.12), although pending the acquisition of further radiocarbon dates the contemporaneity of these cannot be demonstrated and it is unlikely that they were built at precisely the same time. Those with radiocarbon determinations cover a wide date range and additionally, dated samples derive from different parts of each structure so that it becomes difficult to compare events. Nevertheless, aside from West Kennet and possibly Horslip, there is an emphasis on the middle of the 4th millennium cal BC (Whittle *et al* 2011, 109). Each appears to represent communal activity over a period, in the case of the West Kennet long barrow, the best dated, the phase of burial deposition represents no more than 10 to 30 years of use (Bayliss *et al* 2007c) although other activities including construction, amendment and lengthening may have been carried out over very much longer periods.

It should be emphasised, however, that there is often also evidence of much earlier activity on site. Pre-monument evidence was not recorded at West Kennet, but pits and postholes may represent pre-barrow occupation at Millbarrow (Whittle 1994, 16–18). A line of 34 stakeholes set in a north-easterly axis and presumably representing a fence underlay the east-south-east axial stake alignment of the long barrow bays at South Street (Ashbee *et al* 1979, 265) and it is interesting that the criss-cross ard marks only appear to have been recorded to the west of this fence. Further, and it is difficult to be certain, the orientation of some of the ard marks is not far off that of the axis of the fence and it

is tempting to see the latter as bounding a cultivation plot. Any burial and associated barrow construction at these sites might only occur after a lengthy, perhaps intermittent, presence at the site. Construction and other activities might be much longer if sites were enlarged and modified. The second series of side ditches at Millbarrow suggests a further phase of construction, while it has been suggested that West Kennet and East Kennet, twice the length of most long barrows, may each comprise two confluent mounds (McOmish *et al* 2005, 14–15; Westlake 2005). It is evident that some at least of these sites were returned to before, during and after construction.

The spacing remains important. The long barrows focus on the rivers and re-entrant valleys, the highest upstream being Millbarrow at Winterbourne Monkton (and of course the Shelving Stones on the opposite slope may also be significant). There is (in landscape terms) reasonably regular spacing of these sites between Winterbourne Monkton and Marlborough, land that was sheep walk until the 20th century and therefore likely to retain extant prehistoric earthworks.

The density and spatial distribution of these monuments indicates that, while possible, it is perhaps unlikely that they were the constructions of a roving band of nomads who dispensed with one long barrow only to move two kilometres across the down to build another, or indeed that they represent many groups of travellers all periodically returning to their own pre-arranged plot – which, without co-ordination and agreement regarding pasture, surely creates a recipe for friction. The establishment of such closely set tenurial zones, if we can see them as marking such, is likely to have taken a considerable period of time to create, assuming of course, that it was not the hand of a higher social authority and it potentially hints at some process of emulation or even competition between communities. Thomas (1999, 26) suggested that the monuments represent 'fixed points within [a] seasonal round, places of sporadic or seasonal agglomeration for population and herds' and that seasonal occupation in these areas was responsible for bouts of intensive clearance and grazing. In this scenario considerable numbers of people were moving. In land-use terms such divisional arrangements could be considered to be 'ranching' (Ingold 1980, 5) and distinguished from open-ended nomadic 'pastoralism' where the grazed land was held in common. Although Ingold was referring to the herding of reindeer rather than cattle or pigs, the important point here is regarding tenure. There are other problems to explain. Were the latter situation to apply at Avebury, whose common land would it be? Nomads in search of scarce resources in, for example, Mongolia will move considerable distances within a radius of some 150km (Humphrey 1995), a home range over an area much bigger than Wiltshire. Most such analogies, however, take in areas where resources are scarce or where mobile groups dwell temporarily alongside often unmentioned sedentary populations (but *see* Clark 1972). In contrast, where resources are abundant there may be a greater tendency to stay put (Rowley-Conwy 1983; 1984).

Was this area the preserve of people either mobile or transhumant based off the chalk, or of the inhabitants of settlements along the Kennet and Winterbourne? In the case of transhumant groups based elsewhere, the underlying point is that pastoralism forms a minor component of the overall settlement pattern and that the greater part of the economy along with the population, ie those left at base, remain faceless.

That these are transhumance territory markers for settlements based elsewhere, while feasible, is difficult to explain for they are rather excessive structures to simply mark grazings. Historic transhumants needed no such markers, though in the case of northern England they would return to turf or drystone built huts or shielings (RCHM(E) 1970). In any case the effort involved in making such monuments seems to be far beyond the scope of the odd herdsman or shepherdess. Rather it is that of a considerable group and the construction and cultural complexities embodied within are more appropriate to the focal point of a domain than a distant pasture. In this context the continuing reference to these places coupled with albeit slight but persistent indications of cultivation (*see* Chapter 6) encourages the view of a degree of stability and the tie to monument construction along with traditions and rights concerning the use of local resources would appear deeply ingrained.

Whatever the purpose of cereal cultivation, for malting or animal feed (Dineley 2006) or spiritual purposes (Thomas 1999, 22–5; Fairbairn 2000b, 114–15; Fairbairn 1999, 150–4), there are indications from a number of widespread sites, beyond South Street long barrow (Ashbee *et al* 1979; *see* Rowley-Conwy 1984; *contra* Kristiansen 1990; Thomas 1999, 24) that cultivation was taking place to some extent during a lengthy chronological period on the chalk during the 4th millennium cal BC (Chapter 6). It is, of course, conceivable that cereals, the charred grains found beneath the bank or in the ditches at Windmill Hill or in pits to the south and similarly the potsherds with cereal grain impressions (Whittle *et al* 1999; Whittle *et al* 2011, 65; Macphail 1999; Helbaek 1952; also Fairbairn 2000a), were in each case brought in from, for example, the Greensand, but it does seem rather unnecessary to suggest so, particularly as there is more evidence on the chalk than off it. Querns were found at Windmill Hill (Smith 1965a, 121–3; Whittle *et al* 1999, 338–9) and West Kennet Avenue (Smith 1965a, 234) and off the chalk at Cherhill (Evans and Smith 1983) though, as with the cereal grains, it is again possible to consider these to be involved in special ceremonies and not related to everyday use. The point is important for, whatever use they are put to, it sets the baseline for discussion about what follows and notably whether we perceive the downs as an area inhabited by social groups and the extent of that occupancy, or whether the area was only intermittently visited, with those visitors bringing food and symbolic offerings with them. The former considers that the land whatever its qualities was actively utilised perhaps as part of a home range or series of such units; the latter sees it as a kind of economically unexploited sacred zone away from the core area of occupation activities a little as, say, the Lakota perceived the Black Hills of Dakota in North America (for example Price 1994; Kelley and Francis 1994).

In one way or another, the earlier monuments (long barrows and causewayed enclosures) make a statement concerning presence in the land and implicit in this is a right for the builders to be there. Notwithstanding likely belief systems that advocate that no one can own the land, at least in a western sense, these monuments appear to legitimise land rights and the spatial distribution encourages a view of tenurial relationships and home range. Assuming a broad contemporaneity between them, there is indeed some territorial imperative. Should these territories have persisted, perhaps through struggle or even amalgamation and re-inscribed through enclosure construction, it is evident that a strong sense of belonging and place but also land tenure existed here. Given the large number of such zones indicated by the long barrows, an equal number of dwelling locations perhaps with cultivation plots might be expected. Just how permanent these might be, either in the short or longer term, is open to interpretation but plots left untended during the seasonal round risk a very real possibility of crops being eaten by deer or other herbivores, and also indicate a remarkable degree of honesty that the need to mark pasture in such a way serves to contradict.

Hereditary rights

So why didn't this tenurial pattern persist? The early monuments, both causewayed enclosures and long barrows, suggest a degree of activity on the downs throughout the middle and latter half of the 4th millennium cal BC. While West Kennet and possibly Horslip date to the 37th century Cal BC and were in use at the same time as the Windmill Hill causewayed enclosure, the other four with dates, Millbarrow, Easton Down, South Street and Beckhampton Road, along with the causewayed enclosure at Knap Hill belong to sometime during the middle of the 4th millennium cal BC (Whittle *et al* 2011, 109). It may be that after several centuries of modification and refurbishment the long barrows became irrelevant and were left to decay. As Whittle suggested for the causewayed enclosures, some communities may have been slower than others at adopting, not wishing to be led by fashion and use of them may have dwindled in the same way (Whittle *et al* 2011, 903). While it is conceivable that some of the other long barrows may be of later date, linear cursus monuments became the norm. Again these make a statement about tenure although in a rather different way. Covering large areas, often several miles, they inhibit movement across the landscape and provide a serious barrier to both people and stock. They also provide a link to water; in the upper reaches of drainage patterns such as Cranborne Chase and Stonehenge, elsewhere literally butting up against rivers. No cursus monument is currently known from the North Wessex Downs or further east along the Kennet Valley, but they are frequently found on the terraces adjacent to the River Thames to the north (Fenner 1990; Barclay

and Hey 1999). Little investigation of the Kennet east of Marlborough has taken place, but where it has (for example Small 2002), a significant deposit of Clay-with-flints (as mapped by the BGS) encroaches on the valley leaving just a narrow strip of chalk and river gravel. Scattered ring ditches do occur, but modern development at Hungerford, Newbury and elsewhere also conspires against a productive response from aerial photography. In this respect the area has much in common with the North Hampshire Downs around Basingstoke where ring ditches and indeed other monuments avoid the Clay-with-flints and instead feature on the narrow bands of chalk edging the streams (Field 2008). The change in access to land conditioned by the cursus monuments is unlikely to have escaped communities on and around the North Wessex Downs. Whatever the reasons for change, the environmental evidence suggests that cultivation on the Downs did not persist or intensify, rather the opposite and the net result appears to be a reduction of agricultural activity (*see* Chapter 6; Gillings *et al* 2008, 187–90). Smith (1984) put this down to the spread of bracken choking cultivation plots and potentially poisoning stock, although as noted above (Chapter 6) the presence and use of bracken can be interpreted in other ways.

The reason may lie elsewhere; population decline as the result of epidemic or warfare, or alternatively disease amongst cattle will in turn affect the size of any cultivation plot that could be manured. It may be the lack of grazing that encouraged shrub growth, much as shrub growth has overtaken some of the farmsteads abandoned on the downs in the 19th century, or it may be other environmental factors. It may even be combinations of these. Whittle's Avebury Phase D (Whittle 1997a, 140), beginning towards *c* 3300 cal BC, marked the trend whereby the land was envisaged as potentially consisting of a kind of 'wood pasture' with scattered clearances (Whittle 1993, 41). This attribution, widely used in medieval archaeology is important, for the category signals a more open environment akin to historic 'parkland' (Rackham 1980, 173–201) and indicates the greater presence of grazing animals than would be the case if there were regeneration to closed woodland. However, it may be that it is the lack of monuments of this period and thereby appropriate excavation opportunities and environmental profiles that have left a view of inactivity, leading to an emphasis on regenerating landscape inferred from the ditches of old monuments peripheral to settlement. It may simply be a period of quiet contentment. As Steve Burrow (2012) points out in referring to the Welsh landscape, we can be sure that the resources were well known and understood and all corners of the landscape were named and appropriately utilised.

When monument construction re-occurs the earthworks are curvilinear and reflect the influences of the causewayed enclosure on Windmill Hill. The Longstones Enclosure situated at Beckhampton, 1.3km to the north-west of Silbury Hill just beyond Folly Hill, is considered to date to the first half of the 3rd millennium cal BC (Gillings *et al* 2008, 23–4). Suitable dating samples were confined to an articulated pig foot from the ditch floor in a terminal (Beta-140988). The remaining eight dates were measured on disarticulated bone and antler fragments and only provide *termini post quos*. Thus a single measurement provides the best estimate for a construction of 2840–2470 cal BC (95.4% confidence; Beta-140988, 4060±-50 BP) (Fig 8.1). Gillings *et al* depict both cleared pasture and cultivation expanding on their environmental reconstruction drawing. This is Whittle's Phase E, which is attributed to people depositing or creating larger lithic scatters and pit groups with episodes of renewed clearance around Millbarrow, South Street, Windmill Hill and Easton Down (Whittle 1993).

Whether or not used primarily in feasting and therefore unrepresentative of stock generally,

the predominance of pigs in animal bone assemblages at later 3rd-millennium sites (*see*, for example, Thomas 1999, 26; Albarella and Serjeantson 2002) indicates that a certain amount of activity was involved in their husbandry. At one level this might be paralleled by the situation in Papua New Guinea, where pigs lived among and with the household. The most readily grasped image, however, is of medieval pannage whereby pigs kept in the settlement would be sent out to the woods to feed on acorns during the autumn – something still enacted in the New Forest. But the pig population in the Later Neolithic would appear to have been relatively large and required more than acorns. A recent study by Albarella *et al* (2011) of pig herding in Sardinia noted that they were tended on common land in the hills allowing them to wander freely while avoiding any clash with the cultivated land close to the villages. In former days, in true transhumant style, they would be taken back to the harvested fields to feed on the stubble and returned to the hills in the spring.

As noted above (Chapter 6) environmental data for the Longstones Enclosure is extremely sparse and its construction is based on a single demonstrably non-residual radiocarbon date and needs to be treated with caution. Notwithstanding these caveats, open country appears to have been already present and increased in the second half of the millennium. Stock must have played a considerable part in this. An open country mollusc profile and an albeit short-lived episode of cultivation beneath the Avebury bank add to the general picture (Evans 1972, 272–4), while as noted above, the ditches at both Easton Down and Millbarrow provided evidence of increasing cultivation (Whittle 1997b, 142; Whittle 1997a, 140; Gillings *et al* 2008, 189–96; but *see* Chapter 6 for an alternative view) and at South Street cultivation marks lay across the barrow ditch. Even so there is no evidence of intense activity and no indication that the old plots, which must have been visible as earthworks and marked by different vegetation, were taboo. Cultivation simply appears to have taken place on the better sunlight and heat receiving locations, such as the valley side at Avebury (Evans *et al* 1993), which all implies that it was entrepreneurial rather than coordinated.

It is evident from this that the landscape appears to have been managed quite comprehensively, although insufficient evidence is

Fig 8.1
Probability distributions of dates of major archaeological events in the mid-3rd millennium cal BC. The estimates are based on the preferred chronological model for Silbury Hill (Chapter 4), Stonehenge (Darvill et al 2012), Durrington Walls (Marshall et al forthcoming), Beakers (Marshall in press). (Peter Marshall, © English Heritage)

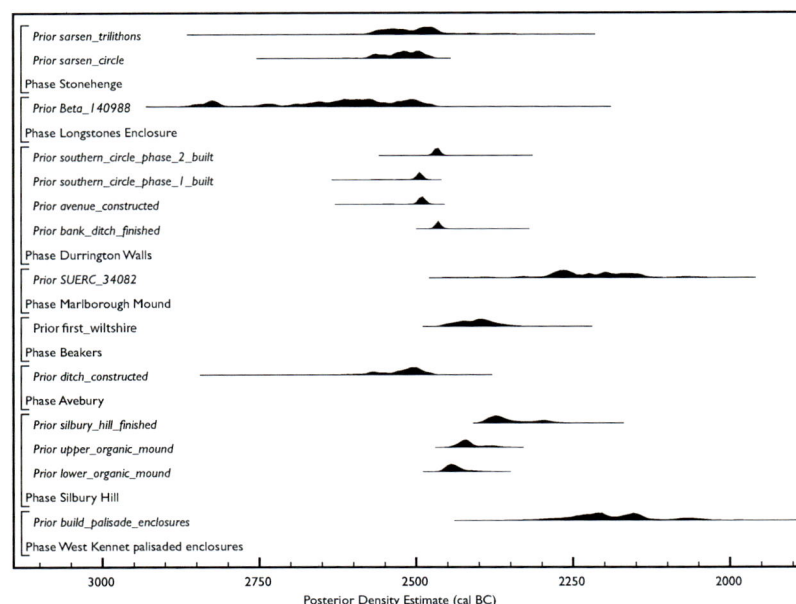

available to determine whether this was entirely down to wholly permanent occupation or to transhumance, but the cultivation does suggest at least a degree of sedentary activity. Of course, it may be that the evidence does not warrant this caution, for as noted above, the increasing numbers of monuments noted beyond the Avebury area indicate a well-populated countryside and even if at one time sparsely settled, there would have been increasing pressure on the chalk. However, while the 4th-millennium long barrows implied territoriality and the presence of a number of groups, this cannot be traced through into the 3rd millennium cal BC. Instead, a land with the residues of ancestral activity will have been largely visible and recognisable as denuded earthworks, while a patchwork of regenerating woodland would have marked the location of former occupation areas and old cultivation plots.

Social context

It is evident that grand monument construction had been under way for some time prior to the building of Silbury Hill. Many of the long barrows and causewayed enclosures were 500-year-old weathered and decayed earthworks when the Longstones Enclosure was constructed in the 3rd millennium BC, although as the excavators acknowledged, the latter site is hardly monumental in scale when compared to those in the vicinity that either preceded or followed it and it could have been constructed with relatively little effort (Gillings *et al* 2008, 54): that is to say in all probability by the local community. Available radiocarbon determinations from the base or primary ditch fills of the Avebury henge indicate that construction of the present earthwork can be estimated as *2600–2470 cal BC (95% probability; ditch_constructed)* and probably *2540–2485 cal BC (68% probability)* (Fig 8.1). A degree of contemporaneity with the Longstones Enclosure is possible with both being in use towards the end of the second quarter of the millennium, but backfilling and levelling of the Longstones Enclosure ditch is thought to have taken place no later than the middle of the millennium (Gillings *et al* 2008, 23–4). The backfilling is a curious event and the purpose unclear. Perhaps its function was subsumed by the new enclosure at Avebury, but the need to level it speaks of either a need to erase memory or perhaps to turn the land over to other uses. The undated Beckhampton Avenue

was later constructed across it and into the already existing Avebury henge (Gillings *et al* 2008, 119). Whether the West Kennet Avenue and indeed the stone circles within the henge were constructed at the same time is unclear for they also remain undated, but Whittle's (1997a) observation that prior to its sinuous swerve, the Avenue leads away from the henge entrance and may therefore pre-date at least its final phase bank, is important. In fact, the Avenue leads to a wide shallow depression outside the henge bank; although this is not the place to pursue discussion of that feature, it could be significant. The first phase bank at Avebury was a bigger undertaking than that of the Longstones Enclosure, but was nevertheless accomplishable by a committed local community. In contrast, the enormous second phase was another matter. Various authors have pointed to the amount of effort involved in this and in similar large henges (for example Startin 1982; Burl 2000, 324; Pitts 2000, 191; Gillings and Pollard 2004, 50) and it becomes questionable whether it was within the capacity of a small local community. It may of course mean that the local community was larger than we might anticipate. Indeed, it is easy to understand why many have considered that the size and complexity of the various structures around Avebury implied that the area was the focal point of a polity. It is the lack of local domestic settlement that discourages such a view and instead support for monument building is seen as coming from a larger area. Nevertheless it is evident that for several centuries preceding the events at Silbury Hill, communal earth moving and perhaps stone shifting had been taking place on a considerable scale.

The massive timber monuments known as the West Kennet Palisaded Enclosures (Whittle 1997a) are situated at less than one kilometre distant from Silbury Hill and are intervisible with it. They lie in such an integral part of the valley landscape that it is difficult to believe that there was not an intimate relationship between the two. Modelling of the dates from the enclosures, however, indicates that the two sites were not, in fact, contemporary with a cautious estimate of a construction date of the enclosures placing them at *2320–2115 cal BC (85% probability)* (Fig 8.1). Whittle (1997a, 164) preferred to see mound and enclosures as chronologically consecutive but certainly acknowledged that Silbury and the enclosures may have been 'inextricably linked' (*see* Whittle 1997a, 139–40).

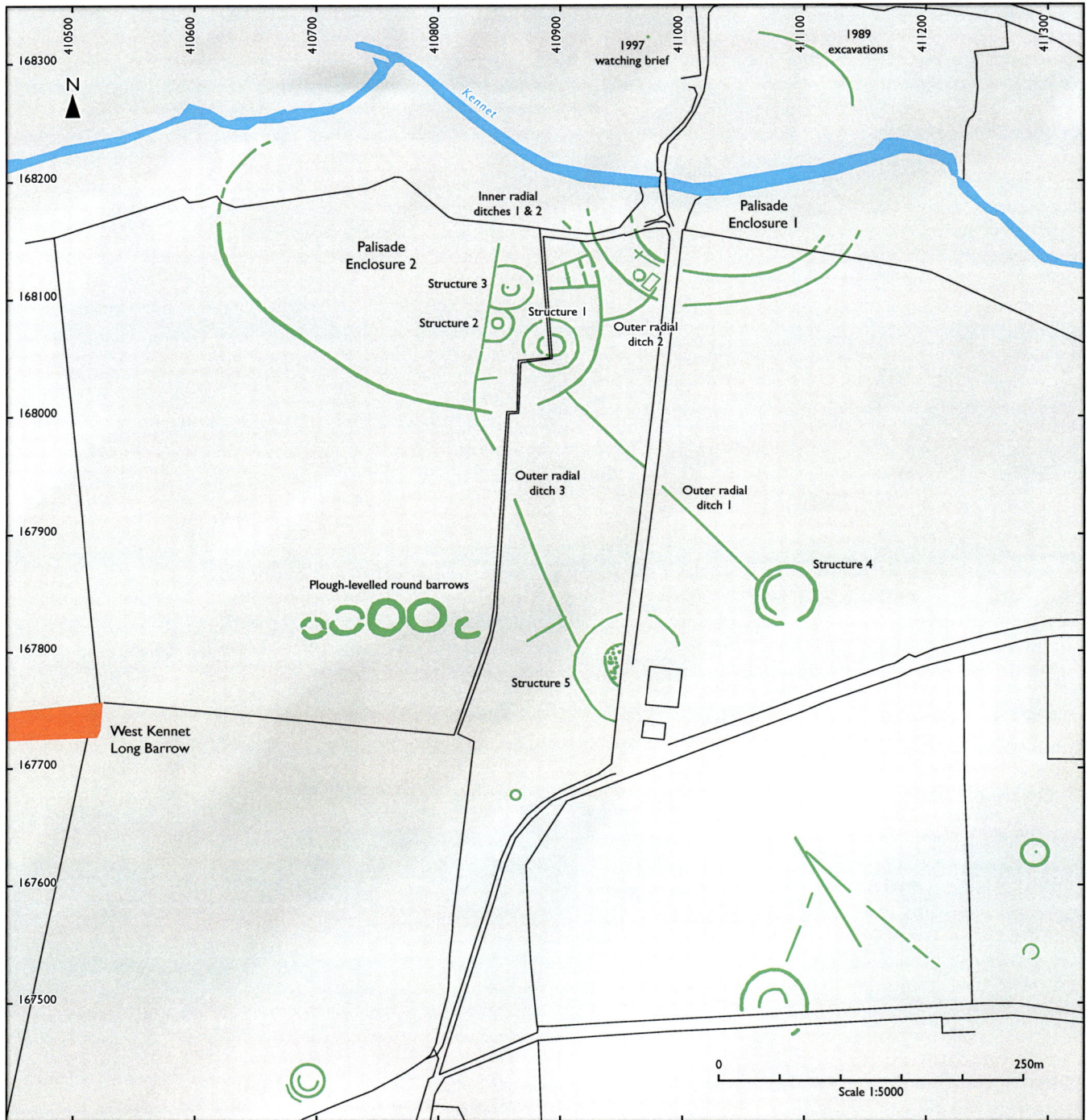

Enclosure 1 is situated on the valley floor and actually straddles the stream (Fig 8.2 and Panel 8.1). Along with Silbury, these sites if not linked by contemporaneity certainly display a physical link to the River Kennet. Following the work of Evans *et al* (1988; 1993), Whittle then acknowledged uncertainties concerning the degree of river flow in the Neolithic, but Mount (1991) has since suggested that the river ran throughout the Holocene, while as noted above (Chapter 6) the recent hydrological work suggests that the water table was higher than that of today. Enclosure 2 enters the flood plain and may have encompassed or perhaps abutted the stream, though unfortunately post-medieval water management associated with the creation of floated water meadows has ensured that the precise route of the Neolithic river is uncertain here. However, the course of the enclosure would pass close to the northern bluff of the valley floor (the southern end of Waden Hill) and to a spring, which, like its namesake to the west, was formerly known as the Swallowhead Spring (Hoare 1821, pl X fp70). Panel 8.1

If use of the two enclosures was successive rather than contemporary this would serve to lengthen the period of use of the site and provide a greater potential for contemporaneous use with Silbury. In contrast, Thomas (1999) pointed out that the configuration of fences form a linked and contemporary system of private or secure compartments and enclosed spaces. The duality might be explained in other ways, for example, gender, for it is not unknown, either in historic times or in ethnographic literature, for male and female activities to be separated (as discussed in Chapter 6).

The layout, with radial or antenna-like spines leading to further smaller enclosures, serves to support this view of segregated activity; at least it is difficult to view them as having any practical domestic purpose. The animal bone and other material found during excavation of the enclosures were interpreted as demarcating ritual or sacred space. If the evidence can be extrapolated across the rest of the site, it is representative of the consumption of thousands of young pigs (Edwards and Horne 1997, 124) that can only be interpreted as evidence of sacrificial activities, feasting, or both, and the pattern of deposition of pottery supports this interpretation. Most of this material was obtained from the foundation trenches for the palisades and little is known about the open spaces within, but if feasting continued after the palisades were constructed, then middens might be expected to develop and it could be from here that material for filling the West Kennet long barrow chambers originated.

Following Piggott's (1962, 27, 33, 68–71) discussion and explanation that the material found in the long barrow had been curated elsewhere, Case (1995) pointed to the widespread practice of depositing midden material in certain locations as a fertility rite, although it should be noted that recent dating does allow the possibility that the deposits accumulated through time and the mixing of deposits was due to animal disturbance (Bayliss et al 2007c, 97; Thomas and Whittle 1986). Deliberate deposition of 'midden' material or 'occupation

earth' is a long-standing practice that can indeed often be found in what might be taken to be ceremonial or burial sites (also see Chapter 7), for example, the long barrow at Skendleby, Lincolnshire (Phillips 1936), or causewayed enclosure ditches at Whitehawk, Sussex (Curwen 1934; 1936). Similarly at a round barrow at Tyning's Farm in Mendip, the excavator thought that deposits of animal bones, potsherds, flints and black ash had been curated and brought in from elsewhere (Taylor 1931–5, 68–71). Ashbee (1976) considered that such deposits found in chambered tombs on the Isles of Scilly indicated a relationship between domestic debris and plant growth and must have a symbolic value in terms of fecundity. Treatment of this kind of material is perhaps seen most dramatically at the East Chisenbury midden on Salisbury Plain (McOmish et al 2010). The latter is of Late Bronze Age–Early Iron Age date, but the interpretations of feasting debris curated as a social statement or fecund reservoir rather than being placed on the fields as manure is familiar. During historic times 'waste' was invariably put to use in other ways, bone for example recycled as glue, and the point has been made before that the modern concept of 'waste' only arrived with the provision of the corporation dustcart (McOmish et al 2010, 86).

The material from the West Kennet long barrow contained a certain amount of broken Grooved Ware mixed with other material and the Palisaded Enclosures would appear to be one of the closest activity areas from which it might have been derived, although Case (1995, 15) suggested that the material was likely to have originated from Peterborough Ware based middens subsequently added to by Grooved Ware and Beaker users. Thomas (1999, 210) pointed out that 'the context from which much of this material was recovered suggested that it was generated before or during the construction of the Palisaded Enclosures', but he also considered that the material from beneath barrows Avebury G55 and West Overton 6b, along with the debris from along the West Kennet Avenue, was midden material, its 'powerful location' being incorporated into later monuments. While the middens may represent curated material, it is not the middens themselves but the actions inherent in them that point to domestic activities here. The impression is obtained that, in this part of the valley at least, activities took place that involved the consumption of large quantities of food, perhaps

Fig 8.2 (opposite) Aerial survey plot of West Kennet Palisaded Enclosures. The palisaded enclosures and associated features as mapped from cropmarks visible on aerial photographs. This is based on Barber et al 2003, amended in the light of more recent reconnaissance photographs. Note that some more recent features, mostly medieval or later, have been removed for the sake of clarity. (Aerial Survey team and Eddie Lyons, © English Heritage)

Panel 8.1 West Kennet Late Neolithic Palisaded Enclosures

Martyn Barber

The complex at West Kennet (Fig 8.2) has been mapped from aerial photographs on four previous occasions, the most recent episode occurring in 2002 (Barber 2003; Barber *et al* 2003). Since then, further reconnaissance photography by Damian Grady of English Heritage in 2004 has led to revision of the 2002 mapping. Unusually, analysis of the 2005 aerial photographs has allowed not only for the addition of extra detail but also for the removal of features previously considered to be of possible archaeological origin, in the process raising questions about the sequence of construction of the various palisaded elements of the complex.

The mapping in 2002 occurred as a result of new cropmark detail being photographed from 2000 onwards during regular flights undertaken to monitor the condition of Silbury Hill from the air. These photographs also confirmed a number of cropmark features which had been mapped during the Avebury NMP as a result of the re-analysis of existing photographs (*see* Barber 2003 for a full discussion).

The two large enclosures were identified through a programme of exploratory excavations undertaken by Alasdair Whittle in three seasons between 1987 and 1992 (Whittle 1997a), although Enclosure 1, the eastern enclosure, had first been photographed as a cropmark in 1950, while part of Enclosure 2 is visible as a cropmark on an oblique in the NMR's Crawford Collection dating from the 1930s. Subsequent analysis of aerial photographs for the Avebury NMP and of those taken from 2000 onwards has both added to and refined existing knowledge of the complex.

The principal cropmark features of the West Kennet complex have been described in detail (in Barber 2003) and in a more summary fashion (in Barber *et al* 2003) as well as in Whittle's (1997a) excavation report. Here it is proposed to focus on the adjustments made to the existing mapping in the light of the 2004 reconnaissance photographs (NMR 23398/01, 23398/08–9, NMR 23398/12–13, all taken 17 May 2004) (*see* Fig 8.2). These mainly centre

on Outer Radial Ditch 3 and features directly associated with it. In 2003, it seemed possible that a linear feature extending north-west from the outer ditch of Structure 5, the circular enclosure towards the southern end of Gunsight Lane, and the two shorter lengths of linear ditch crossing the eastern side of Palisade Enclosure 2 in a NNE–SSW direction, actually comprised three sections of a single linear feature. The 2004 photographs make this far more likely. The section leading from Structure 5 can now be seen to continue further to the north-west, the cropmark fading from view only as it approaches the field boundary. Likewise, on the other side of the same field boundary, the linear feature reappears in the crop much closer to the edge of the field than on previous occasions, before changing direction and crossing the interior of the enclosure.

Inside Enclosure 2, what previously seemed to be two distinct sections of linear can now clearly be seen to comprise a single feature, and can be shown to continue a little further NNE than had been thought previously, again disappearing from view only as it approaches the edge of the crop. In 2002, it was suggested that within Enclosure 2, the linear seemed 'likely to be continuous, the cropmark only interrupted by vehicle tracks and cropmark damage' (Barber 2003, 30). However, while the 2004 photographs have confirmed this to be the case, there remains one small interruption in the course of the linear. Around 7m south of Structure 2 there is a definite gap *c* 1.8m wide.

Structures 2 and 3, circular timber structures examined by Whittle during his excavations do not continue west of Outer Radial Ditch 3. In the 2004 photographs, their cropmark traces clearly end against the latter, suggesting that they were built up against the timber palisade presumed to have stood within it. Meanwhile, features A1 and A2, mapped for the AWHSMP and again in 2002, but described at the time as not being 'wholly convincing as archaeological features' (Barber 2003, 24) have now been discounted as being of archaeological origin. They had been mapped as semi-circular arcs extending from the outer side of the palisade ditch of Enclosure 2, one either side of Outer Radial Ditch 1. Their complete absence from the 2004 photographs supports the doubts raised in 2002/3.

The problems over features such as A1 and A2 highlight a further difficulty with aerial photography at West Kennet. As noted previously:

> although the outlines of the major features are quite clear … the finer detail is more problematic. For all fields concerned, frequent darker patches of deeper soil either obscure archaeological cropmarks or prevent their formation …. The tendency of these darker patches to form circular or curvilinear shapes means that in some places it is extremely difficult to decide whether certain patches are of archaeological or natural origin (Barber 2003, 14)

At present, the bulk of the interior of Enclosure 2 seems devoid of archaeological features. It is not, however, devoid of cropmarks – the problem is that none of those cropmarks resemble anything that can be mapped with any certainty as being of archaeological origin.

It should be added at this point that none of the mapped features at West Kennet can be seen on the available lidar data.

The detail added and removed in the light of the 2004 reconnaissance photographs reinforces the suggestion made previously that 'all sorts of games can be played with the current plan and excavated evidence in order to try and tease out' a sequence of development for the complex (Barber 2003, 33). Certainly, this new plan further supports Pollard and Reynolds's (2002, 115) suggestion that 'the outer lines of palisade around Structures 2 and 3 look less like contemporary elements and more like secondary features that are subsequently enclosing' their respective inner settings. We can, of course, add that the outer palisades of Structures 2 and 3 seem likely to post-date Outer Radial Ditch 3, which in turn may well be later than the Enclosure 2's palisade. Beyond this, though, it is difficult to go further at present. For now, airborne remote sensing alone has probably taken us as far as we can go with this particular site.

intermittently but over a lengthy period of time. Of particular note is that the pottery from the enclosures is Grooved Ware, indicating that indigenous pot forms played an important role here.

Large mound

There is an assumption that an unusually large mound must relate in some way to a particularly complex society. This in part derives from models based on the analysis of prestigious burials or extravagant ritual monuments such as temples, along with the presence of some kind of supporting infrastructure. In Neolithic Wessex such an interpretation derives from modern explanations of social change whereby the control of labour is seen as a component of a ranked hierarchy – the well-known chiefdom model in which there was central control and co-ordination of economic resources and ceremonial activities (Renfrew 1973; 2008). Elaboration of the concept using examples from Minoan Crete, Egypt and Mayan America suggested that the energy spent on monument construction may represent expression by a society as it celebrates new ideas and aspirations

at a formative stage of its development (Cherry 1978, 428–31) or alternatively as it declines and struggles to encourage and channel energy into continuity of common direction. The implication was of a fragile or unstable hierarchy struggling to either assert or maintain itself. A different view was preferred by Whittle and others during the 1980s who considered that the 'chiefdom model does little justice to the complexity and change of the period' (Whittle 1981, 333) and he questioned the confidence of linking of assertions of central power and social ranking on the basis on monument construction (Whittle 1981, 320–1). Further analysis and discussion of these ideas suggested that it may have been ceremony and ritual that played a key role in political centralisation as much as any secular hierarchy or social ranking (Bradley 1984, 68–95) and consequently, when applied to Neolithic Wessex, the major henge enclosures along with Stonehenge and Silbury Hill – or rather the labour invested in them – could be seen as an indicator of the presence, or indeed the emergence, of an elite who manipulated communities via the spiritual aspects of life. The key in this respect is communal labour and the dichotomy between it and the rituals performed at such sites (Barrett 1994, 28–31, 73) although the two should not necessarily be seen as mutually exclusive. A 'ritual authority structure' was envisaged (Thorpe and Richards 1984) whereby control of ritual was expressed through an elite group shifting over time to one of concern with prestige goods, as ideas and materials, that is to say Beakers, were adopted from influential continental groups.

On a broader canvas, Trigger (1990, 119) defined monumental architecture by its sheer scale and elaboration that invariably exceeded the requirements of any practical function, whether that be burial, defence or ritual. In such cases the principles of least effort are discarded in favour of extravagance and in this respect the construction can be seen as a variation of conspicuous consumption on a massively explicit and physical scale. It was considered that such monuments expressed 'the ability of an authority to control the materials, specialised skills and labour required to create and maintain' them (Trigger 1990, 124–7). More recently, however, Whittle (1997a) has re-emphasised the nature and possibilities of harnessing religious fervour and motivation. Using examples such as Ngungdeng's mound in Sudan, he emphasised the 'sacred as well as the secular, the significance of the moral as well as the political order, and the ability of monuments and charismatic figures to mobilise people over long distances and thereby create new situations' (Whittle 1997a, 149; and see Panel 8.2). In this scenario the construction of the mound marks a transitory event that captures popular imagination but has little or no bearing on society at large.

Neither a burial nor a temple can be demonstrated to be present at Silbury, nor are there 'exotic' artefacts present, at least from the trenches excavated to date, from which we might postulate a high degree of social organisation or prestige artefact based economy. Instead we can only fall back on analysis of the mound material itself. Aspects of this have already been described in Chapter 7, but one further relationship that we might re-visit is the estimate of the amount of labour that might have been employed in order to build it. For good reason such an approach has been out of fashion in recent years. The recognition of phasing in the Avebury bank, for example, and the perceived complexity of construction over lengthy periods of time cast doubt on the value of earlier estimates of labour input and there was a danger that the approach would set

the agenda regarding analysis and discussion (Whittle 1981, 321; see also Gillings et al 2008, 173). Those figures (Atkinson 1978; Startin and Bradley 1981; Startin 1982; Parker Pearson 1993) did, nevertheless, help to emphasise the sheer scale of these endeavours even though they may have led to unrealistic expectations. The point here, however, is to seek to identify the scale of the project and whether construction may have been achieved by a small community or whether it was a much larger venture involving others from elsewhere. This is something of a challenging task for, as Whittle (1997a) has pointed out, there are so many variables. Nevertheless, as radiocarbon determinations have become more precise and chronological modelling allows archaeologically meaningful estimates to be calculated, there is a certain amount that can be added to the debate. There is now much greater certainty over one of those variables, that is the length of time that it took to build the mound. The earlier phases – the gravel and turf mounds – are well within the compass of a local community, as were some of the early stages of ditch cutting and chalk emplacement. It is possible that all of those accrued over several decades.

As we have seen, Bayesian modelling of the radiocarbon dates estimates that the mound may have been constructed in 55–155 years (68% probability; Model B), with the Lower Organic Mound/Mini-mound constructed in 2450–2410 cal BC (68% probability) and the mound as we see it today in 2335–2285 cal BC (68% probability). The freshly obtained dates, along with some 30 others taken from earlier material which have been reassessed (Bayliss et al 2007a; Chapter 4), hang together in a coherent fashion and provide some of the best chronological evidence for the 3rd millennium BC in the Avebury area. We can exercise some caution about the models, for they are exactly that, but bearing in mind that there are undoubtedly a number of phases of activity and there is little evidence for the development of soils (see Chapter 2) we can with reasonable confidence estimate that construction is likely to have taken place during the earlier part of that time span.

Startin's (1982) figures, based on careful assessment, observation and recording at the Overton Down experimental earthwork (Jewell 1963) tempered by the accounts of 18th- and 19th-century non-industrial engineering texts, resulted in a figure of four million man hours for the construction of the hill. The third major variable – the number of people involved – remains unknown, although with the crowded countryside that we now recognise much higher numbers than formerly imagined might be available. Startin's figure can now be broken down in several ways: four million/100 years gives 40,000 person hours per year and assuming a population of one hundred (the present population of Avebury is 486) this equates to 400 hours of work per year each, or put another way 33 hours per month. Taking the shorter option of 55 years to construct the mound, four million/55 years, equals 72,727 person hours per year which equates to one hundred people working for 727 hours per year or 60 hours per month each. It is very clear from this that even allowing for substantial errors, whichever of these options is used, with energy expended over a longer timespan the effort is greatly dissipated. In contrast to the received impression there is no need for huge numbers of people; construction of the monument could be accomplished by a local community.

Beakers

The major difficulty encountered in placing Silbury Hill within any social context is the almost entire lack of diagnostic cultural material available for study from any of the excavations. That is not to say that such material might not be present elsewhere in the monument, simply that it is not available to us. Cultural material of any description is in short supply. Of course only a small percentage of the enclosing re-cut ditches have been excavated, and when the large external ditch was excavated in 1970, finds attributable to the Roman period heavily out-weighed those from prehistory. A few flint flakes from the ditch extension (basin) were reported by Pass in 1887 (on inspection at Devizes Museum this amounted to three); similarly Petrie recovered a few flint flakes, reported by Passmore as 'very rough waste chippings with no secondary work' (Passmore in Petrie 1924). Flint flakes were recovered throughout the Silbury phases during the 2007/8 investigation, however, they were largely micro-debitage and undiagnostic flakes; larger and/or diagnostic pieces were hardly present at all (see Bishop, Chapter 3). In addition, the lack of in situ Neolithic pottery from such a major monument is particularly noticeable. In terms of material culture Silbury virtually sits in a cultural vacuum.

For the moment, perhaps the most useful piece of evidence is that of the radiocarbon dates. The robust, precise chronology for the monument provides an indication of the tempo of monumentalisation in the third quarter of the 3rd millennium cal BC. As noted above (Chapter 4) the preferred model (Model B) indicates construction in the late 25th or early 24th centuries cal BC. This places the construction of the mound after that of the erection of the sarsen settings at Stonehenge and several generations later than the major henges of Avebury and Durrington Walls (Fig 8.1). It is possible to envisage the kind of interplay between polities outlined by Whittle et al (2011, 903) with some areas keen to compete and others reluctantly joining in when it was all over. The earliest disarticulated burial in the Boscombe Bowmen 'collective' grave marginally precedes the start of Silbury (Barclay et al 2011). The start of use of English Beakers in graves has been modelled at *2475–2315 cal BC (95% probability)* (Bayliss et al 2007b, 50 fig 10) which corresponds quite neatly with the preferred date range of Silbury Hill. More informative is the date of the first Wiltshire beaker *2470–2360 cal BC (95% probability)* (see Fig 8.1) that pre-dates completion of Silbury; however, there is a 60% probability that the Upper Organic Mound was completed before the first dated Beaker in Wiltshire.

The construction of the mound at Silbury thus occurs at an interesting interface between the stone and metal ages: a time that saw not only the introduction of gold but also barbed and tanged arrowheads and a new type of pottery vessel, which along with the other accoutrements, formed part of a 'Beaker package'. Barbed and tanged arrowheads, one of which was found on the surface of the northern slopes of the mound (Fig 8.3), became the norm for the best part of perhaps a millennium while the new form of pottery eventually supplanted Grooved Ware. In the Boscombe area to the east of Stonehenge, the overlap has been modelled at lasting no more than 50–75 years spanning the turn of the 25th–24th centuries cal BC. However, modelling of the available radiocarbon dates from the West Kennet Palisaded Enclosures indicates that they were constructed after Silbury Hill (Fig 8.1) and consequently Grooved Ware must have been in use for longer here than further south.

This period presents a conundrum (unfortunately this volume went to press too

Panel 8.2 Ngundeng's Mound

Gill Campbell

Ngundeng Bong lived in Southern Sudan in the last quarter of the 19th century (d 1906). He was a prophet amongst the Nuer people, which is to say that he was the vessel of Deng, the most important of the Nuer divinities of the air. It is said that in his songs he predicted the second Sudanese war and its eventual outcome: 'We know that all these deaths are not meaningless because they were foreseen by Ngungdeng and will ultimately result in our Freedom', Eastern Gaajok fighter, 1990 (Hutchinson 1996, 338)

The importance of this charismatic figure in relation to Silbury Hill is that Ngundeng instigated and inspired the building of a large mound, over 18m high and over 30m in diameter at Weideang (Keij), the centre of eastern Nuer territory (Johnson 1994, 90; Whittle 1997a, 149; Fig P8.2.1). The mound was built as a response to twin epidemics of smallpox and rinderpest that occurred in 1888–9, these years also being drought years.

Ngundeng, who already had a considerable reputation as a prophet through military success and curing barrenness in women amongst other deeds, is said to have foreseen these diseases. By sacrificing dozens of cattle and leaving them to rot, he created a 'scorched earth' zone between the disease and the main body of cattle. At the same time the daily sacrificing of cattle in his own village, where the meat was eaten, helped keep the population healthy, and coupled with Ngundeng's instructions for people to leave their huts and sleep in the open and to not hold dances (congregate), the spread of smallpox was halted.

Deng, through Ngundeng, was seen as the vanquisher of these diseases (death and illness being generally attributed to the divinities of the earth), and the mound was built in Deng's honour to prevent a reoccurrence. Its construction was seen as a way of containing or burying evil thoughts and actions, diseases and epidemics, and all magic, as well as temporarily neutralising the particular earth divinities associated with them (Johnson 1994, 88; Hutchinson 1996, 307; Whittle 1997a, 149). The stimulus for construction was thus religious, springing from the need to control external forces that had had, or could have, devastating effects on the community.

The building process went through several phases. First supplies and lodging were procured for the workforce, followed by the laying of the foundations by local people. The mound was then added to by other groups. Coriat (1939, 224 quoted in Johnson 1994, 91) describes how:

Fig P8.2.1 Denkur/Ngundeng's Mound 1902. (Crispin; reproduced by kind permission of the Durham University Library)

word was passed far and wide summoning all tribesmen of the Nuer clans to a gathering at Keij on the full moon of the month of the saving [harvest] ... On the night of the full moon, in the light of a circle of fires Wundeng [Ngundeng] gave expression to the commands of the Spirit. Throughout the night he stood shouting exhortations to the assembled warriors. At dawn the following morning he carried the first load of earth to the site he had chosen for his *Luak Kwoth* (House of God) and thus began the building of the Pyramid itself. From that hour until it was completed he supervised and controlled the work of thousands of Nuer. Mud was dug from adjacent pools and khors [? cattle camps] and carried in baskets to the ground where it was slapped and pounded to the required dimensions. As the mound rose in height, tiers of workers handed up baskets to others above them. Bulls were brought from all over Nuer land and the meat was divided and eaten by the builders. When there was a shortage of bulls, corn was distributed from the granaries. Day after day the work continued. It is believed that four rain[y] seasons passed before the *Bie Dengkur* [mound of Dengkur] was finished.

However the builders did not necessarily stay for long as Evans-Pritchard's (1935, 62 quoted in Johnson 1994, 91) account states:

They would spend three or four nights in one of the temporary shelters, which others, since departed to their homes, had put up; and when the food they had brought with them was finished they would return to their homes also, and their places would be taken by other pilgrims.

The mound as finished by Ngundeng did not persist in this state for long. One of Ngundeng's youngest sons, Guek, was recognised as a prophet and following an outbreak of smallpox in 1920 he organised the repair and reconstruction of the mound, at least doubling it in size, and once again procuring help from a wide area (Johnson 1994, 175). Then, following the growing influence of Guek and the need of the British government to demonstrate its authority, the mound was blown up by the Royal Engineers on 20 February 1928 in front of 34 Lou chiefs. The blast only removed the top 40 feet of the mound, leaving the base intact, although this did not prevent the British from reporting that the mound had been completely destroyed (Johnson 1994, 195). Guek was killed by the British a year later. However the mound still survives, albeit in a reduced form, while Ngundeng's baton (staff/dang) has recently been returned to Sudan amid some controversy (*Sudan Tribune*, 19 May 2009).

early to benefit from the recent data and discussion relating to a Chalcolithic in Britain – see Allen *et al* 2012), for while copper was being obtained from Ireland and used in Wessex, the quintessentially Neolithic occupation of flint-mining was just getting underway at Grime's Graves (Ambers 1996; Varndell *et al* forthcoming). Authors have variously seen the period as one of invasion or immigration, with the introduction and use in burial of prestige high-status grave goods, either real or token warrior archer equipment (Case 2007, 249–50), or of the spread of materials and notions through acculturation: the diffusion and acceptance of a 'package of ideas' rather than migration of people (Burgess and Shennan 1976, 313). Burial practice, the apparently new procedure of inhumation burial was shown to have developed

Fig 8.3
Barbed and tanged arrowhead found in the topsoil on the northern slope of Silbury Hill during Atkinson's investigations. Along with two sherds of later Beaker ceramic found on the summit, this testifies to a Beaker presence at the site after construction had ceased.
(James O Davies,
© English Heritage, courtesy Alexander Keiller Museum)

through indigenous stages during the 3rd millennium cal BC (Kinnes 1979, 72–5; Gibson 2007) and Kinnes even then pointed out that given uncertainties in the interpretation of the evidence it was difficult to 'completely discount immigration'. Certainly some kind of movement from the continent is demonstrated by the isotope evidence from the Amesbury Archer (Chenery and Evans 2011), but how widespread this was and how significant an increase beyond long-established and traditional international connections remains to be seen. Traffic may have been two-way even though the momentum of the predominating cultural movement appears to have been in one direction (Needham 2007). While there is considerable evidence for Beaker-related activity within the Avebury area none of the associated skeletal material has so far been subjected to isotope analysis and in any case much of it can be considered relatively late in the sequence and consequently of little direct relevance to the Silbury Hill enquiry.

Within the region Needham (2005) listed Radley Barrow Hills F919, Boscombe Down West 1, Radley Hills Barrow 4a, the Boscombe Down 'collective grave' and the Chilbolton primary interment as belonging to his early Carinated Group category. These radiocarbon dated burials form part of a 'primary' Beaker package that was current during the third quarter of the 3rd millennium cal BC though still relatively rare at that time (Needham 2005, 207–10). In attempting to explain this introduction Needham suggested that the expansion in Beaker use may have been the result of Neolithic infatuation and requirement as much as Beaker exposure, increased demand leading to diversification of grave groups and the incorporation of new artefacts types, or what he described as a fission horizon between 2250 and 1950 cal BC when values incorporating Beaker use become very much the norm. The dates from Silbury Hill pre-date this horizon and, while there are a number of potentially early dated Beakers from elsewhere in Wiltshire, given the rarity of 'primary' Beakers from the North Wessex Downs it could be considered that there was little, if any, impact of Beaker users on any aspect of construction.

Silbury and identity

There appears to be no clear evidence either from the continent or within Britain to support a view that monumental architecture formed part of the Beaker package. Instead there was a move to utilise other, earlier monuments (Cunnington 1914, 390–1, 405–6, 412) or caves (Taylor 1921; 1923; 1924; 1925), or to bury individuals in flat graves (Cleal 2005, 118–19). The Beaker potsherds in the secondary filling of the chambers and forecourt at West Kennet long barrow may be of some relevance here. The long barrow stands directly opposite and in clear sight of Silbury Hill, little more than 0.9km distant and it has been suggested that the Beakers represent a style that may have been in use, or was not long out of use, in the fourth quarter of the 3rd millennium cal BC (Case 1995, 11–12). The Beakers from the north-west and north-east chambers respectively (Case 1995, fig 7) appear to be of Needham's Low Carinated category that he placed well within the 'primary package' with a start in the mid-25th century and general currency from 2400 to c 2200 cal BC. More recently chronological modelling has provided an estimated date for deposition of an articulated goat skeleton from Layer 3 in the north-west chamber at West Kennet (Bayliss et al 2007c, 97) of *2500–2335 cal BC (75% probability: OxA-13202) or 2570–2515 cal BC (20% probability)*, though the relevant Beaker here may have come from above the goat and may therefore be of later date. The nature of this secondary filling aside (Case 1995, 8–15; Thomas and Whittle 1986, 139–50; Bayliss et al 2007c, 97–8), the point here is that Beaker users may have been present at this location at a time when the radiocarbon dates indicate the commencement of activities at Silbury Hill. Some suggestion for an earlier use of Beaker comes from Stonehenge where sherds found in the stonehole for sarsen Stone 1 are thought to date to around 2500 cal BC (Parker Pearson et al 2007).

Elsewhere, Beaker burial in long barrows is normal, occurring at, for example, Wilsford G34, Winterbourne Stoke G35 and Figheldean G31 (Cunnington 1914; Field 2006, 153–6). These are not dated but equally there are no indications of a mound at the Boscombe Bowmen 'collective' grave, or at Chilbolton, in Hampshire, while flat and re-used graves are frequently encountered. A number of Beaker interments in the Avebury area were in flat graves and any mounds tend to be small, ephemeral and little more than upcast from the grave itself. As few as six sites might pre-date 2000 cal BC. Three of these were found adjacent to standing stones (Cleal 2005, 118) at

Longstones Cove (Cunnington 1913), West Kennet Avenue (Smith 1965a, 210) and the Sanctuary (Cunnington 1931, 313, 323), while two further flat grave burials, Beckhampton Grange (Fig 8.4; Young 1950, 311–26) and Lockeridge (Cleal 2005, 132), can be added to the list, and another containing mixed Beaker styles from the West Kennet Avenue (Cleal 2005, 118–19). The early grave at Chilbolton, Hampshire (Russel 1990) was left open to allow further insertion and while a shallow ring-ditch was present there is no evidence for a mound. Similar processes occurred at Wilsford cum Lake G52 where eight successive burials were made before any mound was constructed (Smith 1991, 19–22). A mound is presumed at Boscombe though there is no evidence for it. In view of the evidence for early Beaker activity found within the wider Avebury landscape (Fig 8.5), it is surprising that no contemporary Beaker material comes from Silbury Hill itself. Just two small fragments of later Beaker pottery were retrieved from the summit (see Cleal, Chapter 3).

Elsewhere on the Marlborough Downs, Beaker sherds from a pit in Dean Bottom (Gingell 1992, 159; Gillings and Pollard 2004, 125) were classified by Needham as Mid Carinated and associated with a radiocarbon date in the last half of the 3rd millennium cal BC (Kinnes et al 1991). This is a settlement situated on what might be considered to be marginal land in a gap in the Marlborough Downs (Fig 8.5) and the associated material indicates that users of this pottery were farming small niches on the downland by this date. Along with evidence for Beaker cultivation at South Street (though this might have been short-lived: see Chapter 6) and Cherhill, the view of Beaker users as farmers as suggested by Case (1977) has some resonance. Indeed it is not impossible that the 'meagre' evidence for cultivation noted above is attributable to pioneering Beaker agriculturalists. Case (1977, 74) and Whittle (1981, 307–10) both argued that there is little evidence for early Beaker settlement to set alongside the presence of pots in burial contexts and this has changed little. There appear to be more early Beakers in the Upper Thames Valley to the north and that area may be more of an early focus. But both the Thames and Kennet valleys would be natural routes for the infiltration of ideas emanating from the Lower Rhineland.

We might expect some of the unexcavated barrows in the vicinity to contain artefact assemblages similar to those recently excavated at Amesbury and Boscombe (Fitzpatrick 2011) and indeed some of those nearby that were plundered or levelled in the 19th and 20th centuries may have done so. One of the levelled barrows at the north-east end of West Kennet long barrow had a small-diameter segmented ditch (Barber et al 2003, 153, fig 5) that may have been of Beaker origin and it is tempting to link that site with the material in the secondary filling of the long barrow chambers. Few barrows in the vicinity have been excavated in modern times, and of those only West Overton G19 has a late Neolithic component, a burial with subsequent insertion potentially of Beaker date into the same grave (Swanton 1988, 181; Cleal 2005, 117) while two others, Winterbourne Monkton G9 (Merewether 1851a, 105) and Bishops Cannings 81 (Robertson Mackay 1980, 138) contained Beakers that may pre-date 2000 cal BC (Cleal 2005, 118).

None of the early Beaker burials either around Avebury or further afield provide evidence that supports an introduction of innovative monument design. Instead, the traditions

Fig 8.4
Beaker from Beckhampton Grange found with the skeleton of a child of about 5 years in a grave sealed by a sarsen stone. Height 140mm.
(James O Davies, © English Heritage, courtesy Alexander Keiller Museum)

Fig 8.5
Map of the locations of Beaker finds in the vicinity of Avebury mentioned in the text.
(Eddie Lyons, © English Heritage; height data licensed to English Heritage for PGA, through NextPerspectives™)

of earthmoving appear to be indigenous and come at the end of a sequence of constructions that employed successively greater amounts of energy. Nevertheless, it might be considered that the influences that led to the construction of such huge monuments might have been part of the same underlying processes of change that permitted such wholesale acceptance of the Beaker package. Gillings and Pollard (2004, 57–61) have argued that the influences for monument construction at Avebury came from a multitude of locations both local and further afield and indeed that Avebury should be seen as the 'culmination of many individual projects rather than a single planned vision'. The search for these influences and processes, however, may need to focus on indigenous society rather than seeking to account for them in response to invasions, immigrations or too many ideas from outside. Indeed, much as Thomas (2007) has indicated for changes during the Mesolithic–Neolithic transition, it may be a matter of identity. Long ago Case (1977, 74) suggested that the initial adoption of Beakers was simply fashion, much as the mods, rockers and hippies of the 1960s, the punks of the 70s, the yuppies of the 80s were defined by distinctive cultural factors that identified them as a sub-group with different ideas, technologies, art and dress code. Within a decade the latter had been adopted to some extent by society in general (though not, it must be said, in the case of Mohican hair style and safety pins). We may find that in the second half of the 3rd millennium cal BC the 'new way' simply expressed fresh meaning and enthusiasm for a different objective, perhaps as noted above, driven by agriculture along with a taste for whatever the pots contained (?beer). But there is a flamboyant element, new projectile points and flint daggers, the increasing use of copper knives and of course gold and as Parker Pearson (2008, 49) has suggested, flaunting such personal wealth may have led to new power structures.

Stimulus

It must be considered anything but a regular occurrence for a community (however defined) to develop the early phases of Silbury Hill into the later massive construction. Just 26 kilometres away, the final development of Stonehenge is also unique. The dating of it is on less certain ground than at Silbury: only one radiocarbon determination for the trilithons (OxA-4840; 3895±-45 BP; 2620–2340 cal BC) and one accepted for the sarsen arc (UB 3821: 4023+/-21 BP: 2620–2470 cal BC) and for the moment the preferred interpretation of these is that the sarsens were in position by about 2500 cal BC (Parker Pearson et al 2007). It would be surprising if construction using stone was not under way around Avebury soon after. Certainly earthmoving was taking place at around or soon after that time but the development of Silbury Hill had not yet begun (Fig 8.1). It has been suggested that the burials placed at Stonehenge throughout the first half of the 3rd millennium BC up to and during the period of sarsen erection may represent those of a single dynastic family with origins in North Wales: their powerful status being indicated by their incorporation in a monument that commanded great attention, not to mention influence over a significant workforce (Parker Pearson 2008, 36–7). Similar criteria could apply within the Avebury area and using long chronologies it is conceivable that

widespread contacts with distant parts demonstrated by the number of ground axeheads found on the North Wessex Downs, particularly from Windmill Hill (Pollard and Whittle 1999; Field 2011a) were maintained that led to similar arrangements. At Silbury itself, however, there is precious little hard evidence. The deposition of material possessions in any of the phases was evidently not important here. To some degree this might even support the suggestion proposed by Parker Pearson (2008, 44) that the period was one of austerity when free expression was repressed and that this might be evidence of a fundamentalist authority.

Whittle (1997a; Whittle et al 2011 898–903) has highlighted examples of such massive structures elsewhere and discussed the various social scenarios, including the possible role of 'big men', those with exceptional political control or prophet-like charisma who might command extraordinary communal enthusiasm. The example of the Nuer was referred to by Whittle (1997a, 149) and is elaborated on in Panel 8.2. None of these need necessarily relate to Silbury; and we should remember that the early phases of Silbury were somewhat diminutive and visually unstriking and it is difficult to see the origins at least as a development of intra-regional competition. The later phases, of course, were more impressive and could have had a different meaning, and it is not impossible that a charismatic individual re-invented the monument, exploiting whatever local appeal it may have had. We can probably dismiss the kind of social arrangements that supported the Mesopotamian ziggurats or Central American or Egyptian pyramids. It is unlikely too that the platform mounds of China and North America, both of which were at the centre of large well-structured townships with extensively organised hinterlands provide a model. For the moment we can also reject those large mounds that cover rich burials in Asia, the Balkans or of the Mississippian culture in the United States (see Panel 8.3). In historic times huge corporate monuments have been made in circumstances that commemorate major achievements or losses in warfare, or provided an overtly elaborate edifice to a meta-physical supreme being – God. There is perhaps a third category: expressions of confidence and ability amongst the body politic as for example occurred with the construction of communal buildings in towns during the Industrial Revolution or in the skyscrapers of Canary Wharf and 'gherkin' like buildings of modern London which impact upon the skyline. This would certainly fit with a view of the period as one of profound change in which the community was striving to be recognised by others.

It is possible to take a purely pragmatic approach to earthwork construction although we can find no practical planned purpose for continuing to build such a monumental mound as exemplified in the chalk stages of Silbury Hill and have outlined an alternative view (*see* Chapter 7). Since, at present, there is a lack of evidence for a burial, it is assumed that the mound does not commemorate an individual. Even at the shorter radiocarbon range the monument would not have been complete until long after an important individual's death and if planned in advance it would have had to have been from soon after birth. In any case there appear to be many separate phases of activity particularly in the earlier stages of construction that are likely to have had a completely different *raison d'être* to that of the chalk mound. Beyond the Upper Organic Mound which might be considered an appropriate-sized structure for the everyday British Neolithic, just what was it that provided the catalyst to resume construction on such a huge scale? The drive to continue building must have been occasioned by other concerns.

One object that fits the bill is Stonehenge. The major henges located in the respective areas, Avebury and Durrington Walls bespeak the presence of separate social organisations each based on a major drainage system. While in each case the purpose of the henges may relate to a contemporary belief system and in particular the role of water (Leary and Field 2011; 2012), some emulation is evident in the sheer size and drama of each. The Avebury henge, where monumental earthwork construction was based on the tradition of Windmill Hill causewayed enclosure and the Longstones Enclosure is presently considered to have been constructed first around *2620–2490 cal BC (at 95% probability)* and was not followed by Durrington Walls until *2480–2450 cal BC* (Fig 8.1). In terms of earthen monument construction the final form of Avebury was the greater achievement, but the final stages of Stonehenge broke the mould. While there was much sarsen available on the North Wessex Downs and it is conceivable that the stone settings at Avebury were contemporary with the henge, the massive sarsens at Stonehenge were shaped to impress in a totally different way. The shaping of stone is unknown from elsewhere in Britain at this time, except perhaps in the standing stone within the chamber at Byrn Celli Ddu (Burrow 2010a). The latter may reinforce a North Welsh connection as does the Stonehenge enclosure with Llandegai I (Burrow 2010b), but it is Brittany that may have provided the influence. Contact with Brittany in the form of ground and burnished jadeite axes was established in the Stonehenge area early in the 4th millennium cal BC (Sheridan *et al* 2010) and it would be of no surprise if this extended to ideas regarding structures as well. An 8.8m high standing stone, taller than the trilithons, one of a pair at Kergadiou was shaped into an axe-like form (for example Burl 1993, 183–4); a further 9.5m dressed example can be found at Kerloas (Burl 1985, 62–3) and another at Dol (Burl 1985, 83) and of course Le Grand Menhir Brisé (Burl 1985, 134–6), the largest of all, was dressed into an axe-like shape.

There is no reason to suppose that the Stonehenge sarsen came from the North Wessex Downs as is often suggested. True, sarsen boulders found on Salisbury Plain today reach nowhere near the size of the Stonehenge trilithons, but then neither do any on the Marlborough Downs. In greater likelihood it derived from a seam below ground, from swallow holes, being revealed in periglacial exposures where, incidentally, it would be more conducive to shaping, not having formed a hard weathered crust (Geddes 2000, 70) and the unexplained location of Stonehenge may be down to the unusual presence of a scatter of sarsen on the surface as much as any other factor (Petrie 1880, 16). There is thus no need to negotiate removal of sarsen from a different polity for what in an economic sense might be considered a rival and competitive purpose.

With plentiful sarsen at their disposal, the community around Avebury could have found employment in any innovative stone structure in corporate reaction, but the community was living in the past. Its response may have been based on its own traditions: earthmoving.

Round mounds in Britain

No other mound in Britain reached the enormous size of the final phases of Silbury Hill. Whether there were attempts by other communities to emulate it can, for the moment, only be speculated on. Archaeological investigations have shed light on the Hatfield Barrow at

Beechingstoke, Wiltshire, once said to be second only in size in the county to Silbury Hill (letter to *Salisbury Journal* Monday, 2 December 1776; Field *et al* 2009; Leary *et al* 2010; Leary and Field 2012; Leary and Marshall 2012). The Revd John Mayo had described this as 'about 70 or 80 yards diameter and about 30 feet high' (between 64 and 73 metres diameter by 9 metres high) (Gough 1806, 159), less than a third the size of Silbury, though it was evidently under the plough before 1789 (Withering 1822, 210–48: ref to Marden 236). By 1806 its height had decreased considerably as a result of it being in cultivation and Cunnington was able to report that in 1804 the wheat harvested from the barrow produced 'six Sacks' [of grain] (Cunnington MSS, Devizes Museum). By 1821 it had been reduced to 22.5 ft (7m) in height (Hoare 1821, 5–6) and little more than 20 years later the mound may have been almost level, for the map accompanying the deed and enfranchisement of 1845 (Hampshire Record Office 21M57T155) merely depicts a crescentic ditch, the portion closest to the highway having been filled in. The Revd Mayo's figures could have been an exaggeration, but the enormous ditch located by various surveys (Field *et al* 2009) and confirmed by excavation in 2010 (Leary *et al* 2010, 15; Leary and Field 2012) encloses an area of 70m diameter, not quite

the 100m enclosed by Ditch 1 at Silbury but substantial nevertheless.

Coring and radiocarbon dating at the 18m high Marlborough Mound (Fig 8.1 and Fig 8.6), long speculated to be of prehistoric date (for example Hoare 1821), has revealed that not only was it broadly contemporary with Silbury but that it reached at least 12.5m in height and probably more (Leary 2011; Leary *et al* forthcoming). When Whittle wrote in 1997, little was known of these mounds (1997a), but now it appears that in North Wiltshire, at least, such large round mounds were not as rare as once thought. Why they should be restricted to this part of central southern England is not clear, though perhaps the watershed is of some significance. The Hatfield Barrow and Silbury both mark the source of rivers, the Kennet and the Avon. Does this perhaps hint at the possibility of large mounds once marking similar spring sites elsewhere? The manner in which the Hatfield Barrow or that formerly recorded on Collingley Ridge, Chobham Heath, Surrey, recorded by Aubrey (Fowles 1980, 710–11) as 'larger than any he had seen in Wiltshire except Silbury Hill' but still levelled, points to the degree of deliberate destruction that can be achieved. Several enclosures and large ring ditches have been noted in Northamptonshire and perhaps of note is the 87m diameter ring

Fig 8.6
The Marlborough Mound, Wiltshire. Today the mound is closely surrounded by the buildings of Marlborough College, but the result of radiocarbon determinations taken from material in cores drilled from the summit by one of the authors (JL) and the Marlborough Mound Trust indicate that, although adapted during medieval and post medieval periods, it originated as a prehistoric structure.
(James O Davies
© English Heritage)

ditch at Shawell in Leicestershire (Deegan and Foard 2007, 39–40, 67), which contains a smaller 47m ring ditch offset within it potentially of earlier build. Consequently, the lack of obvious extant examples at the head of other rivers should not deter investigation of such locations.

The Marlborough Mound, however, now confirms the presence of an additional Neolithic site along this stretch of the Kennet (Leary *et al* forthcoming; Leary and Marshall 2012) so perhaps they do more than simply mark the backstop of rivers. There is little more than 8.3km separating Marlborough from Silbury Hill. So are there potentially others? A small case can be made for at least one of three mounds at Hamstead Marshall, West Berkshire, situated in a line just above the Kennet some 30 kilometres further downstream. Two lie side by side with just 50m separating them, the third some 800m away. They were marked on the early OS editions and recorded in the Victoria County History as tumuli (Peake 1906, 280) but subsequently, like Marlborough was, they have been interpreted as mottes (Myres 1932; Bonney and Dunn 1989).

All three, however, lie in the same parish, which is an extremely unusual circumstance for mottes and various unsatisfactory suggestions have been offered, proposing that they represent castle reorganisation, rebuilding or siegeworks. Two have baileys and nowhere do they reach anywhere near the scale and height of the examples mentioned above, but nevertheless they do fall within the scope of other large Neolithic mounds. They measure 62m in diameter by 6.8m high and 50m in diameter by 4.7m high respectively. A third, the largest, set in a near identical location to both Silbury Hill and the Marlborough Mound adjacent to a confluence of a small brook with the Kennet, is 62m in diameter and 7m in height. There was no bailey here; instead the mound is surrounded by a ditch with an external bank, the latter unusual at motte sites, and with a causeway through both bank and ditch in the north facing the river. Part of it is missing and consequently it has been suggested that it may have been either unfinished or part destroyed. No documentation exists of a castle in the parish but all are weak defensively and two are overlooked by higher ground at just 100m away.

While a broad date range of potential construction dates is possible, the likeliest motte construction period here is between AD 1135 and 1154 when King Stephen was on the throne,

the most probable protagonist being John Marshall after whom the manor was later named and who was involved in the conflict between Stephen and Matilda. Contemporary castles were built at Reading, Newbury, Marlborough and Devizes during this campaign and it was John who fortified both Marlborough and Ludgershall in AD 1138 (Addyman and Kightly 2000, 11–12). The former, as we now know, was not a new build but a modified pre-existing earthwork. The castle at Ludgershall is a ringwork with no evidence for a motte and it seems strange that a defensive feature, the motte, evidently so important at Marlborough, was not also required at Ludgershall. On reflection, however it was the pre-existing earthwork here also that was important for, like Marlborough, the medieval fortification utilised a former, probably Iron Age, earthwork (McOmish *et al* 2002, 131; Everson *et al* 2000).

In the hurry to fortify certain of his holdings, John evidently not only felt it more convenient to adapt and modify whatever existing features were to hand than to construct them from scratch, but by doing so was also claiming the legitimacy of ancient sites of power (Bowden 2005, 36–7). If this is so, it may be that the mounds at Hamstead Marshall were treated in the same way and one or more are in fact of prehistoric origin. Should this be so, with diameters in excess of 50 metres and heights in excess of four metres, it would be extremely unusual to imagine them in a Bronze Age context and they would be more comfortable in a Neolithic horizon. The henge-like outer bank and causeway at the easternmost site may even hint at an earlier monument.

Other mottes have been demonstrated to utilise prehistoric earthworks. Droughduil, the mound adjacent to the palisaded enclosure at Dunragit, Scotland, was formerly considered to be a motte (Thomas 2002) but its size, 50m diameter and 10m in height, coupled with the results of recent excavations that encountered a Bronze Age cairn on the summit, has encouraged comparisons with Silbury Hill (Brophy 2010, 13). Castle Hill, Catterick is a further motte site, in this case within sight of the palisaded enclosure at Marne Barracks that has been suggested as potentially Neolithic (Hale *et al* 2009, 286). There has long been a conviction among field archaeologists that in a number of cases motte construction simply involved adapting earlier monuments and in some cases this has been demonstrated (for example Higham and Barker 1992; Best 1997), but it would perhaps be easy to push these ideas too far and unwise to start to question the date of all supposed motte sites that occur in similar topographic locations.

A little further afield, Gop Mound in Flintshire, Wales is an oval mound composed of limestone blocks measuring 100m by 68m oriented north-west to south-east and 14m in height with a truncated summit as though there had been stone removal or a collapse from within. Boyd Dawkins dug a shaft 1.8m by 1.2m from the summit to the base and struck natural rock at a depth of eight metres indicating that the mound simply enhanced a natural eminence. A tunnel dug from the base of the shaft along the old rock surface 10.4m and a second at an angle to it encountered no central burial, but fragments of pig, sheep or goat, and ox or horse bone were recovered (Boyd Dawkins 1901). Below and in front of the mound a cave had been used during the Pleistocene but deposits were also encountered relating to the middle Neolithic and Bronze Age. A rectangular chamber had been constructed of limestone rubble and within it were more than fourteen skeletons. Associated was a sherd of a possible Mortlake Ware bowl, two jet belt sliders and a ground and possibly polished flint blade. All this appears to have been packed around with 'midden' material, broken animal bones, charcoal and a large quantity of human bones that appeared to be sealed by limestone slabs which were packed up to the cave roof. A fragment of Collared Urn was also found amongst this.

Round mounds are quite commonplace in the Neolithic of Britain (Kinnes 1979), appearing frequently as round cairns in the Highland zone and indeed it seems likely that a certain number presently categorised as Bronze Age may on investigation prove to be Neolithic. Of 48 Neolithic mounds listed by Kinnes (1979) that have measurements in two dimensions, most (63.2%) are quite small, between 10 and 20 metres in diameter, and 26.5% are just a little larger at between 20 and 30 metres. Beyond that there is a dramatic decrease in numbers as only 4%, two barrows, have greater diameters. In terms of height 48.9% are of one metre or less, 36.7% between one and two metres, 10.2% between two and three metres and just 4% between three and four metres. The tendency, therefore, is towards quite small round mounds and it is easy to see why most are overlooked particularly where they are subsequently

added to and become part of early Bronze Age cemeteries.

Whatever the purpose of such mounds, most communities felt no need to achieve great diameter or height. Set against the examples above certainly any structures beyond thirty metres in diameter and three metres in height might be deemed excessive and unusual and only occasional and well-known examples exceed 15 metres. Of the measurements noted by Kinnes (1979), only Tideslow at 40m diameter stands out from the others, while Duggleby Howe (Fig 8.7) at 23m by 3.4m and Wold Newton 284 at 25m by 3.7m, both flat-topped mounds mentioned by Mortimer, stand out in terms of height. At 2.7m in height, Pitnacree (Kinnes 1979, 11; Coles and Simpson 1965) hardly stands out against its neighbour at Courthill, Dalry, Ayrshire, which reached 4.5m in height (Coles and Simpson 1965,46), but the latter contained what was thought to be a secondary Beaker burial and could have been modified and enlarged to accept this. At 5–6m the Upper Organic Mound at Silbury is a little above the general pattern of Neolithic mound building but up to that point there is nothing in the construction to suggest that it was in any way exceptional.

Neolithic round mounds of lesser dimensions are certainly present across Wessex (Kinnes 1979), both as free-standing examples and components stratified beneath later Neolithic or Bronze Age monuments. On Salisbury Plain, mounds Amesbury 71, Mere 13d, and Warminster 10, together with Upton Lovell 2a, are known to be of Neolithic date (Kinnes 1979, 10, 21; McOmish et al 2002, 39–40), while excavation by William Cunnington at Silver Barrow, Tilshead, a large round mound with side ditches, revealed features similar to those found beneath local long barrows. Among these only Westbury 7, with a diameter of 60m and height of approximately 1.5m, stands out as larger than normal diameter. Attention is also drawn to Compton Barrow (Fig 8.8); undated but at 46m by 6m in height (McOmish et al 2002, 39–40) far exceeds most Bronze Age barrows and similar in size to the Silbury Upper Organic Mound. Most of these, however, occupy positions on the downs. Only Upton Lovell 2a occupies a valley location. Ultimately the origins of Silbury Hill lie in this circular mound building tradition, but other social drivers and the influence of monumentalised constructions were all around.

Fig 8.7
Duggleby Howe, Yorkshire. One of a number of Neolithic round mounds on the Yorkshire Wolds that were excavated during the 19th century, this one of considerable proportions. (© Alex Gibson)

Why?

Whether the final phase of construction at Silbury took place over 50 or 100 years, that is between two and four generations, it is not necessary to envisage enormous numbers of people being involved. That is not the same thing as saying that others did not participate and indeed it may have greased the wheels of social complexity and provided additional significance if people from disparate and far flung communities did indeed contribute. Construction of such an edifice at the source of the river system may have provided an ideal opportunity to consolidate and reinforce ties with related groups downstream. It may also have provided an opportunity for those living at a distance from the community as a result of marriage or alliance forming arrangements with other groups to revisit and reinforce relationships.

As Whittle (1997a) indicated long-distance interaction is important and it is evident that in Wessex patterns of contact with distant places were established from the beginning of the Neolithic if not before. The movement of jadeite axes into the region is one example (Sheridan *et al* 2010) and once established it is unlikely that links would have been entirely forgotten. Just how far such contact extended is difficult to know but Whittle outlined long-distance possibilities (whether directly or down the line) through the influence of exotic designs and site features and compared the mound with sites in Ireland, the Orkneys and Yorkshire, and even invoked the possible influence of Egypt. Again it is the size, the final figure, the overall achievement, that provides the comparison, for unlike Windmill Hill or Stonehenge, the ingredients here are all local and integral to the place.

Simply in practical terms, the area for hundreds of metres around the mound must have been one huge building site: the materials, chalk, gravel, sarsen, could all be obtained locally, but in addition the paraphernalia of extraction and construction, logistics of wood cutting and supply, arrangements for sustenance communal or private, would all have left their trace and resulted in the scoring of paths and access ways through the land. Assuming that Atkinson was right and the terraces were original levels that had simply been re-cut in later periods (Atkinson 1978, 170), it is conceivable that they marked episodes or standstills of construction, perhaps with chalk deposited on an annual basis. Bracing using retaining walls of chalk blocks as recorded on the summit may occur throughout the later phases of the mound and it is conceivable that the angularity marked in the contour survey also indicates some kind of internal buttress feature. All of this indicates a change of emphasis from the earlier phases. Certainly more organisation was needed: a little more planning, but even then there is no suggestion of a blueprint or plan with a final aim in mind. All of this activity also needs to be seen against the backdrop of contemporary (or near contemporary) developments at nearby Avebury, where similarly massive monuments had been or were being constructed or modified.

For the moment we do not know whether there was any intention to use the summit as a platform, or to construct a temple-like edifice or even sunken plaza-like feature as at Huaca Pieta (Dillehay *et al* 2012, 65–7), or whether as Atkinson suggested, the sides would be smoothed and perhaps the summit aesthetically domed like a piece of Neolithic artwork but if so, plans for any superstructure would be outdated by the time that the mound was finished. The construction appears to be some kind of communal display: perhaps corporate response in the face of Beaker innovations, the local population demonstrating that they can

still cut it. Or maybe in the face of changing environmental circumstances, particularly water-levels, as the climatic downturn of 2334–2345 cal BC approached, a period when Parker Pearson (2008, 51) has envisaged a collapse of a centralised authority. There is little evidence that there was any maintenance in the sense of keeping surfaces repaired and it may certainly be that the process of establishing a visible social structure was more important than any practical value of the monument (Cherry 1978, 429). Instead a process of backfilling and re-digging is evident in the deposits, and in this respect any direction from an authority speaks more of indecision than clear planning.

It is probably important to see the Avebury complex as part of a larger polity and given the geography of the region it is likely that any such social system was based on the

Fig 8.8
Aerial photograph of the Compton Barrow, Wiltshire (centre, bottom of photograph), set at the head of a now mostly dry winterbourne valley at its confluence with the River Avon. The trench in the summit was cut by an unknown individual with equally unknown results probably in the 18th century when it was mentioned in the Salisbury Journal. Larger than any Bronze Age mound in Wiltshire, the size of the barrow suggests that it may be Neolithic in date. The Iron Age hillfort of Casterley Camp can be seen in the distance (top right) (NMR 18255/06). (Roger Featherstone, © English Heritage)

drainage pattern (P D Jordan 2001; Field 2008) rather than cross cutting the topography. Consequently tribal relationship is likely to be with communities downstream and ultimately with those occupying the gravel terraces around London.

It is still possible to envisage the chalk as a 'special' or sacred area and that people travelled long distances from unnamed places to construct and attend ceremonies at monuments. If we do interpret the monument in this way, however, there is a problem to surmount in that the same line of reasoning should be applied to other ritual monuments across the region, Durrington Walls and Marden in particular, but similar principles must also apply to the complexes along the upper Thames valley and elsewhere, many of which are likely to be at least in part contemporary. The people from 'elsewhere' are considered as largely responsible for building the monument in each case and there is a danger of constructing a position in which people are constantly journeying from one location to another to construct monuments leaving little time or place in which to live.

However, the location of the mound at the source of a major river suggests that it may have been of more than local importance, and the juxtaposition with other major monuments serves to support that. Nevertheless, the location of other potentially broadly contemporary monuments, the Marlborough Mound and Hatfield Barrow at 8 and 10 kilometres distance respectively and the spacing of henges at Durrington and Marden suggest the presence of communities with separate statements to make. After all why should people come and help from elsewhere? Why not build one where they live? Indeed, the common thread that runs through the Avebury monuments across any boundaries of culture change is the location, in this case at the head of the Kennet.

Despite the innovative signal posted by Bradley (2000) in highlighting the importance of certain natural features in the landscape, until recently no spring has been targeted for excavation and little is known of their ritual use. David Jacques of the Open University has, however, undertaken excavation at a spring near Stonehenge and encountered the largest Mesolithic site in Wiltshire (Jacques pers comm). While the focus at Silbury has been on the monument, we have tried to emphasise the relationship with the water, the significance of the ditch and in particular the basin or cistern (Chapter 7).

Like Stonehenge, the mound could have been built anywhere, on Waden Hill to promote greater intervisibility, or within the henge at Avebury to add significance to an ancestral location. Rather it was constructed in the bottom of a valley surrounded by hills. A principal feature here is the water: the springs and brooks, the location being sacred as much as the mound.

Panel 8.3 Round Mounds Across the World

David Field

In terms of its size Silbury Hill is unique within Europe, where other large mounds barely attain half of its height. Whittle (1997a) has comprehensively provided comparisons with such structures elsewhere and the social structure that they represent. Suffice to say that there are larger examples even though poorly reported. Barrows, tumuli or kurgans, generally considered to be burial mounds built of earth or stone, can be found across the world. Similarly, in some places earthen mounds or cairns thought to have been built as a foundation for a temple or other structure occur. They can be distinguished from pyramids found in Egypt and parts of central and southern America where rock is extracted, shaped and set by masons and from ziggurats built in a similar way but of bricks.

Pyramids were of course foremost in the minds of early Silbury investigators, Stukeley, Drax, probably Petrie, and certainly Atkinson all mentioned them and in terms of size some are indeed comparable. There is, however, a further distinction to be drawn between pyramids and ziggurats in that one is essentially a burial monument, the other a temple. The distinction can be drawn within some earthen mounds. Some, such as the flat-topped mounds of pyramidal form in both China and the US appear to have supported structures; others such as the kurgans of Asia were for burial.

Within Europe monumental mounds settle at around half the size of Silbury. The cairn at Newgrange, Eire (Fig P8.3.1) measures some 85m by 78m with a maximum height of just over 13m (O'Kelly 1982). Le Hougue Bie at 50m diameter and 12m high (Burl 1985, 236) is the largest of the mounds on the Channel Islands. A little further afield, in Brittany, the Tumulus St-Michel at Carnac measures 125m by 60m and reaches 10m in height. Crucuny at Carnac is 55m by 23m and 13m in height, while Tumiac, Morbihan, is 50m diameter and 15m in height (Burl 1985, 125, 133, 165). Other substantial round mounds of later date occur in Europe. Probably chief among them in terms of dimensions is Krakus mound, Krakow, in Poland which at 16m is just half the height of Silbury. Excavations in the 1930s suggested that it dates to the 10th century AD, but intriguingly its construction was based around a central post from which seven fence lines separated nine different radially segmented deposits (Słupecki 2006, 127–8). A second mound near Krakow, the Wanda mound, at 14m in height is just a little smaller, but while documentary evidence indicates that it predates the 13th century AD it is of unknown date. Several burial mounds in Belgium achieve significant proportions: the Tumulus de Glimes, a Gallo-Roman mound at Incourt, has a basal diameter of 50m and height of 11m and another at Ramilies nearby, the Hottomont tumulus, is similar.

Fig P8.3.1
Newgrange, Ireland.
(© David Field)

Burial mounds appear for the first time in Greece during the Middle Neolithic (5800–5300 cal BC) (Gkioni 2006), but it is rather later that some become monumental. Situated among a cemetery of some 300 burial mounds at Vergina, in northern Greece, the Great Tumulus is the burial site of Philip II. Some 110m diameter and 13m high, it covered four royal tombs, two of which were found intact and contained rich grave goods. Some of the mounds in Turkey are said to be much larger, indeed amongst the largest in the world. One, 'the Great Tumulus' thought to be the burial place of King Alyattes II, is 355m diameter by 69m in height. On Mount Nemrut a mound 150m in diameter and 50m high is thought to be the burial place of King Antiochus. This too is a UNESCO World Heritage Site dating to the 1st century BC.

Further afield, many ancient mounds are known in parts of Asia (Davis-Kimball *et al* 2000). Most of these, often referred to as kurgans, are relatively small though some at least reach a considerable size. They were also made over a considerable, though perhaps intermittent, time span beginning in the 3rd millennium BC or earlier (Khokhlova *et al* 2006, 78); many were plundered during the 17th and 18th centuries. The Sargat kurgans of Western Siberia, dating from the 5th century BC to the 5th century AD, reflect a population largely based in permanent valley settlements, though the economy, based on cattle herding and sometimes metal extracting, appears to have involved an element of transhumance (Berseneva 2006, 12; Koryakova and Daire 2000). Here and elsewhere, environmental factors led to the displacement of Bronze Age mixed farming settlements and to the increasing use of the steppe for pasture (Bashilov and Yablonsky 2000; Vinogradov and Epimakhov 2000; Kuzmina 2000; Metzner-Nebelsick 2000, 163). Cemeteries of low kurgans, usually surrounded by one or more ditches cluster along river terraces and, like barrows in the UK, represent complex burial monuments with additions of secondary burials. The largest mounds covering elite burials reach 100m across and 6m in height (Berseneva 2006, 17). Among a cemetery of mounds at Ipatovo, 120km north-east of Stavropol, Kurgan 2 the largest in the area,

reached a height of seven metres (Belinskij *et al* 2000). Excavation in 1998–9 revealed twelve additions to the original mound covering a date range from the 4th millennium BC to the later 2nd millennium BC, and with an extremely rich 3rd-century BC burial with gold objects on the summit. Over 100 historic period burials were dug into the slopes of the mound and the excavators suggested that it was a focus of memory over successive cultural phases.

The enormous Solokha kurgan near Velikaya Znamenka in the Ukraine reached 100m diameter and height of 19m and contained two Scythian (4th century BC) tombs. One contained the burial of a king, five horses and an assistant. The main skeleton was covered in gold sheet. One of the earliest such sites reported in the UK was in the area of Tomsk in southern Siberia. In constructing a road to China, the desert between the Rivers Irtish and Obalet was found to contain many cemeteries of barrows. Disturbed at reports of the amount of rich grave goods being looted from them, the Russian court dispatched an officer and troop of soldiers to dig into any mound too large for the locals. Having surveyed many sites in the surrounding countryside the officer concluded that the largest must be the burial site of a prince or chief and dug into it and encountered three vaults: a male in one and female in another, both bedecked with jewels and lying between gold sheets and in the third a skeleton of a horse with saddle and other accoutrements (Demidoff 1773). It may be that other large mounds remain to be discovered (or site reports translated) in the former USSR. One mound on the crest of Mount Mithridates near Kertch in the Ukraine was said to be 30m high, while newspaper accounts of the removal of a cairn 76m in height at Ekatarinoslav, near Alexandropol (Gyumri), Ukraine (Smith 1862 163; Long 1857, 338) might be something of an exaggeration.

Large earthen mounds made their appearance in China during the Zhou, Bronze Age period between *c* 1000 and 221 cal BC, a time marked by the establishment of walled towns. Within these, large earthen platforms were sometimes constructed. At Han-tan 16 such platforms exist, the largest of which is 288m by 210m at the base and 13.5m in height.

Similarly, at Hsia-tu there are four platforms, the largest of which is 140m by 110m and 11m in height. At Lin-tzu, an oval mound known as the Mound of Duke Huan is 14m high. Most of the large earthen mounds in China have a square or rectangular base which makes for a pyramidal form. With flat summits to support a structure, some are of enormous proportions and are thought to have supported corporate structures of political or ceremonial importance (Chang 1978, 333–46). Mounds were also constructed over burials during this period, some of considerable size. The culmination of this period resulted in the unification of China under Shih Huang Ti and marked the beginning of the Han period. Undoubtedly the largest and internationally most famous mound covers his tomb, which lies beneath a huge pyramidal earthen mound. The site has lost its super-structure but with a base of 357m by 354m the mound survives to a height of 43m. Parts of the surrounding complex have been excavated revealing, amongst other startling discoveries, the well-known terracotta army.

A mound at Ma-wang-tui, near Ch'ang-sha, in the Yangtze valley, is some 100m diameter by 65m high. The name itself is said to mean 'mound of the horse king'. Excavation of two mounds on the summit revealed three tombs containing burials of the Han period (Buck 1975), although it is not clear whether the mound itself is natural. The Great White Pyramid, Sijiazi, Aohan, Inner Mongolia is 222m by 217m across the base.

Large numbers of mounds were built across parts of North America (Topping 2010), though very many were levelled by agriculture. More than 1,500 once existed in the Four Lakes area of Dane County, Wisconsin alone and one cemetery at Rice Lake once contained 51 mounds (Birmingham and Eisenberg 2000, 195). As in China, there was evidently a range of purposes: burials occur in some, others were evidently for ceremonial or ritual purposes, yet others provided platforms for buildings or temples. Equally the variety of forms and sizes, circular, conical or bowl-shaped mounds, are similar to those of the UK Bronze Age. Many accumulated in stages and represent several phases of activity. Clam Lake Mound, Wisconsin, is one such layered mound where the initial deposit reached just over one metre and was covered with red ochre. It was later

covered with beach sand while bundles of human bones brought from elsewhere were placed on the mound and covered with earth. A second layer of sand was added along with bones and the procedure repeated a third time leaving a 4 metre high mound (Birmingham and Eisenberg 2000, 137–9).

Simple conical or bowl-shaped mounds were constructed between about 1000 cal BC and 400 AD. Hedgepeth Mound A in Louisiana was first constructed to 0.40m in height and covered with a lens of orange soil. Alternating lenses of yellow-red and brown soils were added later (Saunders and Allen 1994, 479). Dating to 2888+/-100 cal BC, it was one of five mounds in Louisiana dating to the Archaic Period. Elsewhere, Adena culture mounds (1000 cal BC to AD 100) are the earliest and overlap with Hopewell (200 cal BC to AD 400). Hopewell mounds are often associated with enclosures and other earthworks and invariably occur in cemeteries (Snow 2006, 143).

Among the Adena mounds that at Miamisburg, some 20m in height, is remarkably Silbury-like and has suffered a similar history. A shaft was dug from the summit in 1869 and two horizontal tunnels from this at the base. At least two levels of inhumation were found in the upper half (Woodward and McDonald 2002, 205–6; Brine 1996, 56–9). The conical Grave Creek Mound, Marshall County, West Virginia originally stood to 21m on a 90m diameter base with an encircling ditch. In 1838 two tunnels were dug from the periphery to the centre, one at the base and the other about half way up the mound. Both encountered log tombs as did a shaft that was dug from the summit in to the old ground surface. The lower chamber was preserved and opened to the public and a museum building erected on the summit, though both closed before the Civil War. A second structure was built on the summit in 1915 (Woodward and McDonald 2002, 265–71; Brine 1996, 58–9). Others, the type-site Adena Mound and the Williamson Mound, Green County, Ohio each at around 8m high are a little less imposing (Woodward and McDonald 2002, 151–4, 217).

Long mounds occur as do animal and bird forms. The Seip Mound and Hopewell Mound 25 reach the proportions of some of those in Brittany, the former 73m by 48m by 9m high and the latter 152m by 54m by 10m (Woodward and McDonald 2002, 45, 226–8). The largest by far, however, in bulk not simply height are the rectangular platform mounds of the Mississippian culture. These are thought to have held important buildings or temples. Geophysics on the summit of the 19m high Mound A at Etowah revealed the presence of four buildings (King *et al* 2011, 311). There are numerous examples situated along the bluffs and terraces of the River Mississippi and other rivers in the USA (Fig P8.3.2), a point recognised by Whittle in considering comparanda (1997a, 147). Like the large mounds of China, many of the largest here are flat topped and of pyramidal form (Topping 2010). Despite a degree of quarrying, Mound A at Poverty Point, Louisiana, thought by some to represent a flying bird, measures 216m by 195m and reaches 21m in height (Gibson 1999, 11). Emerald Mound, Mississippi, covers

eight acres, and measures 234m by 132m and reaches 10m (Baca 1999), while Monks Mound, Cahokia, Illinois, the largest in North America is 30m high. Mounds in Central America also achieve considerable proportions; examples in Guatemala exceed 13.7m in height (Brine 1996, 190).

The location of effigy mounds, those constructed in the form of animals, is thought to reflect a belief system that recognised Upper and Lower worlds. Consequently bird effigies are often built on higher ground whereas water spirit mounds are situated on lower ground with mounds in the form of land animals, bears and so forth, located on land between them (Birmingham and Eisenberg 2000, 128–33). This need not concern us except insofar as the position of Silbury is just about as low as it was possible to get.

Fig P8.3.2
Ocmulgee mound, USA with swampland at the base immediately adjacent to the Ocmulgee River, Macon, Georgia.
(© David Field)

9

In the Shadow of the Hill: Silbury Hill in the Roman and the Medieval Periods

VICKY CROSBY, DAVID FIELD, NICOLA HEMBREY, JIM LEARY,
POLYDORA BAKER AND GILL CAMPBELL

*With contributions by Kayt Marter Brown, Amanda Chadburn, David A Hinton, Neil Linford,
Paul Linford, Louise Martin, Sam Moorhead, Quita Mould, Andy Payne, Jane Timby, and Fay Worley*

This chapter discusses how the results of various investigations undertaken as part of the Silbury Conservation Project have furthered our understanding of Silbury Hill from the later prehistoric period onwards, in particular the nature of Roman and medieval activity on and around the monument. The geophysical surveys carried out between 2005 and 2008 and recent airborne remote sensing investigations show the extent and nature of Romano-British settlement around the monument and formed the impetus for an archaeological evaluation south of the A4 in 2010, the results of which are briefly summarised. At the same time the re-examination of the Roman evidence recovered from the external ditch of Silbury Hill as part of the 1968–70 excavations has been integrated with the evidence available from previous discoveries allowing a re-consideration of Romano-British Silbury. The evidence obtained regarding medieval activity and remodelling of the monument is also presented along with a discussion on how the Hill may have been perceived and how settlement focus may have shifted.

Later prehistoric Silbury

There is little evidence for activity around the site in the millennium preceding the Roman invasion. A late Bronze Age/early Iron Age bracelet (*see* Panel 9.1) was retrieved from the external ditch of Silbury Hill during the 1968–70 excavations while a single pottery sherd of late Bronze Age/early Iron Age date was recovered from subsoil during the 2001 investigations on the summit (Fig 9.1; Marter Brown 2012).

In addition the 2007/8 work on the summit recovered a small amount of Late Iron Age pottery (*see* below).

Neither the Kennet Valley Pipeline excavations nor the 2010 evaluation produced any evidence for Iron Age occupation (Powell *et al* 1996, 83; *see* below). No concentrations of finds suggesting Iron Age domestic occupation have been identified, and although a few objects (including a La Tène 1 brooch, an urn and a few coins) may suggest that Silbury Hill could have acted as a focus, it is not one of the main concentrations of Iron Age metalwork identified in the Avebury WHS area. Indeed Chadburn and Corney (2001, 21–4) suggest that the area around Avebury and Silbury might have been avoided during the Iron Age, although geophysical data does indicate a possible late Iron Age temple (*see* Panel 9.2 and below).

Roman Silbury

It is likely that Silbury Hill dominated the experienced and perceived landscape in the Romano-British period (Leary and Field 2010). The Roman road was aligned on it and it would have been conspicuous from all parts of the settlement to its south and east. The Silbury settlement will have been experienced in different ways by those living in or near it and those passing through on the road to *Aquae Sulis* (Bath) or between the local small towns of *Verlucio* (Sandy Lane) and *Cunetio* (Mildenhall). This may explain why the settlement can be interpreted in many ways.

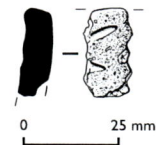

Fig 9.1
Rim sherd with slashed decoration, calcite-tempered fabric, late Bronze Age/early Iron Age context [2], sample <503> (2001). (Chris Evans, © English Heritage)

Panel 9.1 Copper alloy bracelet of possible late Bronze Age/ early Iron Age date

Nicola Hembrey, David Dungworth and Vicky Crosby

One particular artefact of interest came from the 1969 excavation of the external ditch. SF 353, a complete heavy copper-alloy penannular bracelet, was retrieved from directly below the Roman midden (*see* Table 9.1). Professor Atkinson's note on this find in his site diary entry of 22 July 1969 reads thus: 'In ditch, a well-preserved bronze bracelet with grooved T-shaped terminals found in layer 4 at base of RB midden.'

The bracelet is oval in section and in shape, with slight flattening and thickening mid-hoop, opposite the gap between the terminals. The hoop is plain, terminating in two short groove bands of incised decoration leading to expanded hammer-headed terminals with

Fig P9.1.1
Bracelet SF 353.
(Chris Evans,
© English Heritage)

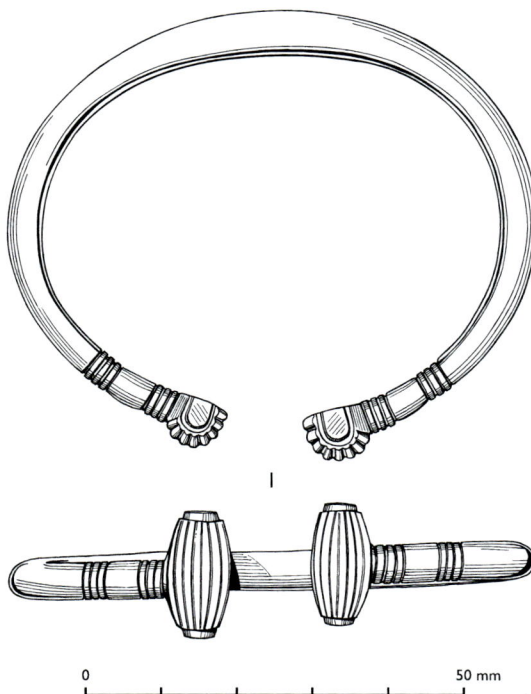

strong longitudinal ribbing. Side to side diameter external hoop 69mm, internal hoop 60mm; front to back diameter external hoop 58mm, internal hoop 47mm; terminals 17mm x max 7mm; weight 39g (Figs P9.1.1 and P9.1.2).

XRF analysis of the bracelet confirmed that the bracelet is made from a copper (Cu) alloy (Fig P9.1.3). The most significant alloying elements appear to be tin (Sn) and lead (Pb). It would be reasonable to assume that the bracelet is made from a leaded tin bronze; such alloys have been used extensively since the late Bronze Age. The virtual absence of zinc (Zn) is striking, as this element is routinely found in almost all copper alloys from the end of the Iron Age onwards (Dungworth 1996; 1997). The suite of trace elements, including arsenic (As), antimony (Sb), nickel (Ni), silver (Ag) and iron (Fe) revealed through XRF are likely to have derived from the original copper ore. These trace elements are most strongly associated with the exploitation of copper-arsenic-antimony ores of the fahlerz type (Ixer and Patrick 2003). The available data cannot, however, be used to determine which fahlerz type ore deposit was utilised. Such ores are known from England and Continental Europe.

The bracelet is not a full Bronze Age style. The composition of the metalwork is consistent with a late Bronze Age date, and this date may further be indicated by the hoop and penannular form, as well as by the incised decoration around the terminals. However, earlier Iron Age bracelets also display swelling mid-hoop and at the terminals. It has not been possible, despite extensive searching, to establish an exact parallel with a known class of Continental or British bracelet, although an unusual bronze bracelet (with circular bulbous terminals) from the Kilmurry, Co Kerry hoard displays similar banded transverse groove decoration, and has counterparts in Halstatt C contexts on the Continent, suggesting a date of deposition around 650 BC (Eogan 1983, 93, Cat 90, fig 46B). There also appear to be stylistic parallels for the terminals with a longitudinally-ribbed drum-headed pinhead recovered from the ploughsoil overlaying a late Bronze Age/earlier Iron Age midden at Whitchurch, Warwickshire (Waddington and Sharples 2011, 39, cat 180) which has been provisionally dated as *c* 800–600 BC, being similar to a cup-headed pin from a late Bronze Age/early Iron Age midden at Llanmaes in South Wales. Although it is tempting to speculate on the examples of this type of decoration from middens, one might best interpret this bracelet as an oddity of late Bronze Age (*c* 1150/1120–800 BC) or earlier Iron Age date (*c* 800–450/400 BC), and express a hope for a future parallel or further quantitative analysis.

When and how the bracelet was deposited is also open to speculation. No other material of this date range (apart from a single pot sherd found in 2001; Fig 9.1) has been recorded from the Hill, and the late Bronze/early Iron Age radiocarbon date from the east side of the mound reported on (and discounted) by Atkinson (1967, 262) is not reliable, as it mixed antler from two earlier excavations (Bayliss *et al* 2007a, 29). Layer 4 of the external ditch may have been present or accumulating during the late Bronze/early Iron Age, and the bracelet may have been deposited during this poorly defined phase; accidental loss is possible but seems unlikely, perhaps especially given the lack of other contemporary material.

Although layer 4 contained no Roman material it is clear from Atkinson's site diary that the bracelet was found just below the Roman midden. The bracelet could, then, alternatively have been deposited in the Iron Age or early in the Romano-British period, either as an 'ancestor artefact' (Caple 2010, 305–8), a 'venerable object' (*ibid*, 307–8), or a re-found object, discovered in the vicinity of Silbury and placed in the ditch in order to return it to its perceived owners. If it was deposited in the early Roman period, it might be considered together with a gold aureus of Nero reportedly found on the Hill in the 1880s (Moorhead 2011) as possibly indicative of early

Romano-British ritual deposition. (However, the aureus should be treated with some caution; Robinson (2003) has shown that several of the antiquities collected by Brooke have false provenances).

Regardless of the date of its manufacture or the nature of its deposition, this intriguing artefact represents a unique connection between those people who touched it and the place in which it was left, the story of which is likely to remain unknown.

Fig P9.1.2
Bracelet SF 353.
(James O Davies,
© English Heritage)

Fig P9.1.3
pXRF spectrum from
the bracelet (SF 353).
(David Dungworth,
© English Heritage)

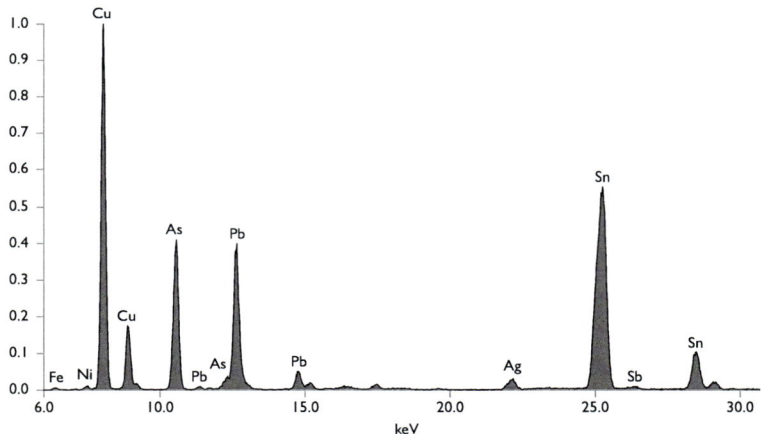

It has been described as a 'halting place for troops on the march from one station to another' (Brooke and Cunnington, 1897, 171), and as a small town, a local administrative centre whose facilities may have included a *mansio* (Corney 2001, 29) or perhaps a *mutatio* (Corney 1997a, 141; *see also* Leary and Field 2010). It might have been a *pagus* centre (Reynolds 2005, 171), or it might have been an agricultural village (Powell *et al* 1996, 57), perhaps including a villa (Fowler 2000b, 228). Evidence suggesting ritual activity can be interpreted as a wayside shrine in the Roman tradition or the veneration of an ancient monument (Robinson 2001, 162). But Roman Silbury is perhaps best approached as a significant focus for a range of people and activities, which need to be documented and explored both individually and collectively. The new evidence from survey and excavation allows us to begin this process.

Geophysical survey and the Romano-British settlement

Neil Linford, Paul Linford, Louise Martin, and Andy Payne

A series of surveys was conducted as part of the EH investigations at Silbury, using a range of techniques over a number of areas including the summit of the Hill following the initial collapse, along the floor of the re-excavated tunnel in 2008, examining the profile of the surrounding ditch and over the surrounding landscape to provide a context for the monument within its immediate environs. The initial impetus for the wider landscape survey came from a request to assist with the sighting of the compound and access route to the Hill to allow the remedial works to backfill the voids within the structure to go ahead (Harding 2005; McAvoy 2006, *see* Chapter 10). This phase of work proved highly successful, especially the results from high sensitivity caesium magnetometer coverage that revealed quite subtle anomalies over the areas of alluviated flood plain flanking the river Kennet (Linford *et al* 2007). The geophysical campaign was therefore extended, including an extensive area to the south of the A4, to produce a total area of 30.6ha of magnetic survey, augmented by additional earth resistance (5.5ha) and Ground Penetrating Radar (GPR) coverage (2.1ha). Technical details of all the geophysical surveys together with an in-depth analysis of the resulting data can be found in Linford *et al* (2009).

Despite the interference from the ferrous strategic pipeline buried to the south of the A4 the magnetic survey revealed a wealth of significant anomalies, particularly in areas where visibility through more conventional means, such as surface artefact recovery and aerial photography, has been compromised by the depth of alluvial overburden (*see* Foldout 3O(i) and O (ii). Perhaps the most significant revelation of this work has been the discovery of a sizeable, presumably Romano-British, settlement in the field immediately to the south of the A4. Whilst Roman activity has long been recognised in the vicinity of Silbury Hill and considerable evidence found to support speculation that such a settlement should indeed exist (for example Brooke and Cunnington 1897; Brooke 1910; Powell *et al* 1996; Corney 1997a; 2001; Robinson 2001; Leary and Field 2010), the geophysical survey convincingly unveils the extent of this occupation. In particular, the

geophysical survey results further indicate the presence of substantial masonry buildings, perhaps first recognised by the Rev Wilkinson (1867) and seen later as tantalising glimpses along the course of the foul sewer pipe trench to the north of the A4 (Powell *et al* 1996, Building I and Building II). However, the geophysical data provide details of buildings in the newly discovered settlement to the south and, to the north, in the immediate vicinity of the Roman buildings found along the pipe trench, a possible water mill – suggested by its apparent association with what appear to be stone-lined culverts.

The detail revealed by the GPR data demonstrates both the complexity of the masonry buildings, including internal room divisions, and evidence for surviving floors and associated thermoremanent magnetic anomalies that may well indicate the presence of a hypocaust heating system (Fig 9.2). Despite the possible threat from plough damage, the level of preservation appears to be relatively good with significant wall remains extending to at least one metre in depth from the current ground surface. It is possible that colluvial deposits washed downhill have contributed to the preservation of the building remains, whilst also obscuring their identification through cropmarks.

Powell *et al* (1996) described the extensive Roman activity revealed by the foul sewer excavations as the 'Winterbourne Romano-British settlement'. However, the much larger scale of this occupation, evident from cropmarks on the western slope of Waden Hill and the new geophysical survey data, suggests that acknowledging Silbury Hill itself as the focus of the Roman activity is perhaps more correct (Corney 1997a). The importance of the water course is still entirely valid, although it is now clear that the Roman settlement extends some distance to the south of the modern A4 encompassing the Swallowhead Spring. The practical need to cross the river at some point over the low-lying terrain immediately east of Silbury Hill could, to some extent, explain the development of a Roman settlement in the vicinity. Such a river crossing would be necessary not only for the major east–west Roman road from Mildenhall to Bath but also to join the extensive settlement now recognised to the north and south of the A4. The importance of a minor north–south route has, perhaps, been overlooked, although Corney (1997a) postulated from aerial photographic evidence

Fig 9.2 (opposite)
A possible hypocaust heating system as indicated by a) the magnetic survey, with the outline of the building shown in b) the GPR data. A combined graphical interpretation of the geophysical surveys is shown in c).
(Geophysics Team and Eddie Lyons, © English Heritage)

that this may well have run along the Winterbourne valley north to Avebury and the geophysical data now suggests a possible continuation to the south. Such a confluence of roadways at a defined river crossing certainly enhances the possibility that the Roman settlement at Silbury, in addition to any other agricultural role, may also have supported some function such as a *mutatio* or *mansio* (*see*, for example, Farley 1971; Burnham and Wacher 1990).

At Silbury one can never escape the significance of the ritual landscape, centred upon the manifestation of the Hill and surrounding ditch. This together with the river and the Swallowhead Spring must to some extent have influenced the development of Roman occupation at the site, perhaps even segregating the use of space within the settlement. Immediately east of the Hill there would certainly appear to be a contrast from the rectilinear, ladder-style pattern of settlement found to the north in the crop marks and to the south in the geophysical data. However, in the absence of any more direct evidence the function and indeed date of the enclosure activity adjacent to the Hill remains uncertain; very speculatively, though, it is tempting to suggest the presence of at least one sub-circular anomaly within a rectangular enclosure might reflect a continuing element of sanctity in this area (Panel 9.2). It is also, of course, possible that this lower-lying area was an active seasonal flood plain during the Roman period and the concentration of settlement would therefore be expected to be found on the higher ground.

Other, more enigmatic, anomalies have been found across the lower-lying water meadow, particularly in association with an area of raised ground to the south of the A4. Both the geophysical response and the topographic relief suggested a deliberate construction. The 2010 archaeological evaluation was able to show that these features pertain to management of the water meadows and probably date to the end of the 17th century (*see* Panel 9.3).

Evidence for Roman settlement from airborne remote sensing

Martyn Barber

The Avebury World Heritage Site Mapping Project (AWHSMP) considerably enhanced Corney's (1997a) interpretation of the

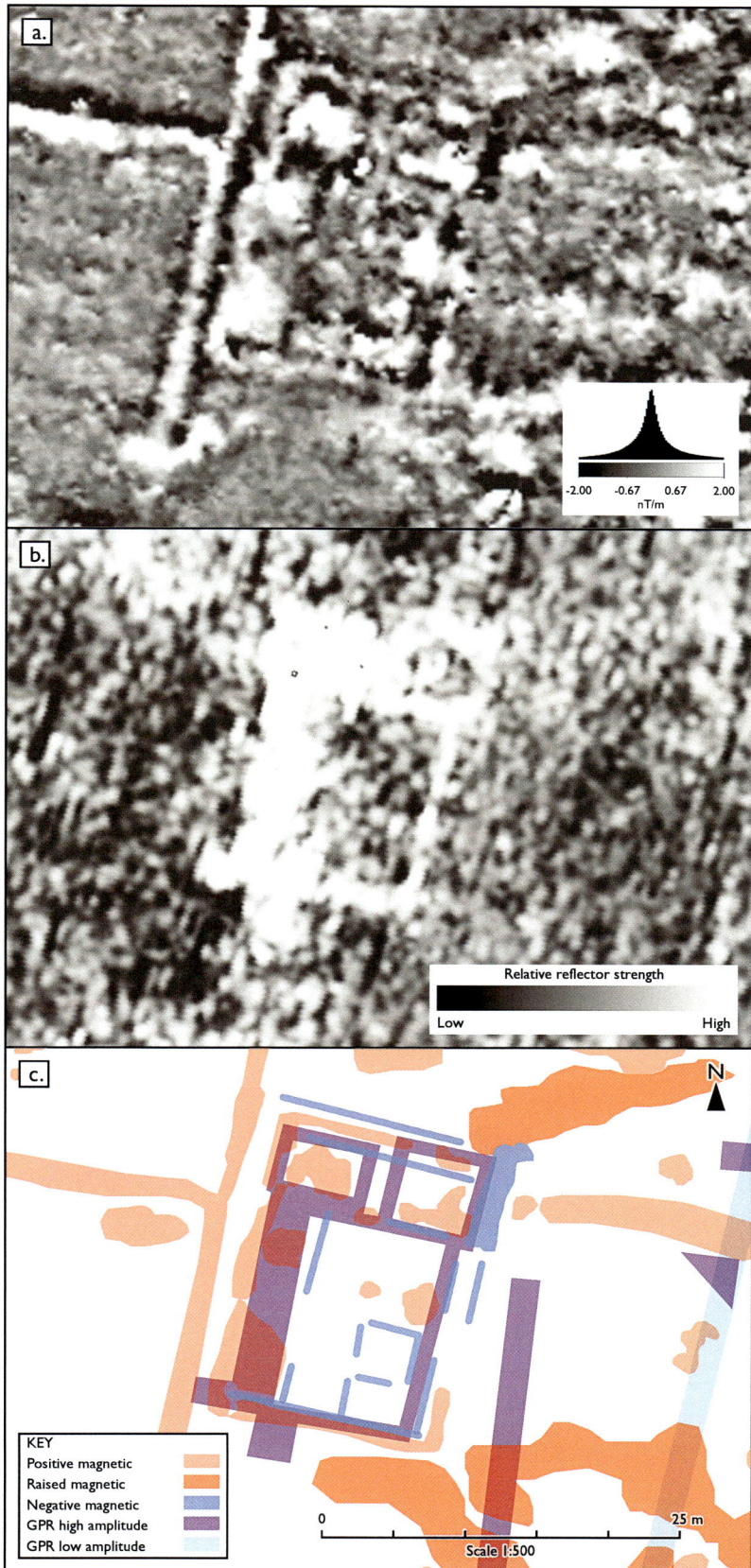

Panel 9.2 A possible Iron Age temple

Amanda Chadburn and Neil Linford

Geophysical data immediately to the east of Silbury Hill show remains which appear to be different in form to the ladder-style Roman pattern of settlement at Waden Hill, and other Roman settlement enclosures found south of the A4. The function and date of this activity remains uncertain, although it appears that a rectilinear enclosure encompassing a weakly-magnetised, incomplete circular anomaly (Fig P9.2.1) is distinct from the Roman activity.

The anomaly has a diameter of approximately 10m and appears to contain two, non-centrally located, pit-type features. A surrounding enclosure is approximately 40m by 40m, and may be associated with the circular remains. If they are of the same period, and the geophysical plot appears to suggest they are, then Iron Age sites appear to offer the most likely parallel. The anomalies could potentially represent a circular timber building surrounded by a square enclosing ditch, and there are two main possible interpretations: domestic or ritual. Domestic Iron Age round houses vary in diameter from approximately 5m to 15m, although the latter are exceptional in size. It is possible that these anomalies represent a domestic house within an enclosure. It is noteworthy that there are many domestic enclosures in Wessex and there are nine known enclosures in and around the Avebury World Heritage Site which are probably domestic and Iron Age (Chadburn and Corney 2001, 21). Alternatively, they could be the remains of an Iron Age round temple within a temple enclosure. Close proximity to the Hill and the form of the remains may suggest this is the more likely interpretation. Iron Age finds from the Silbury area include an Iron Age urn, a La Tène brooch and coins of the Durotriges (Chadburn and Corney 2001, 22–3), all of which could also relate to ritual activity. Iron Age coins are known from numerous Iron Age and Romano-British temple sites, including Harlow, Essex; Wanborough, Surrey; Caistor St Edmund, Norfolk; and Fison's Way, Thetford, Norfolk (Chadburn 2006, 97–100, 141–5, 342–6).

The ground plans of Iron Age temple sites are often difficult to detect as many underlie later Romano-British temples, such as at Wanborough, Surrey – but late Iron Age temples with similar plans to the Silbury remains are known from a number of sites including Hayling Island, Hampshire; Harlow, Essex (Cunliffe 1991, 515) and Fison's Way, Thetford, Norfolk (Gregory 1991). Hayling Island consists of a similar small ring ditch surrounded by a square enclosure of approximately 20m by 20m, with an entrance to the east. The complex of Iron Age ritual remains at Fison's Way, Thetford, is much larger, comprising a very large rectilinear enclosure with several circular buildings inside, the remains of an Iron Age mint, and an eastern entrance. The Iron Age temple at Silbury – if it is such – would fit comfortably into the known size range of such sites, and is not dissimilar to another possible Iron Age temple at Brown's Farm just south of Marlborough (Chadburn and Corney 2001, 23). The apparent entrance of the outer enclosure at Silbury faces south, as opposed to the more usual orientation of similar structures to the east or south-east, although some square 'shrines' at Danebury, Hampshire, and Westhampnett, Sussex (Fitzpatrick 1997, 223) have southern entrances. Perhaps this was influenced by the position of the Swallowhead Spring to the south and the course of the Winterbourne, which may well have provided a seasonally wet environment for the deposition of votive objects.

Examining the geophysical response of the circular anomaly reveals a much weaker level of magnetisation ($\sim$1nT) in comparison to the surrounding enclosure ditch ($>$5nT). This might suggest the two features are unrelated and were constructed under different site conditions, or if they are contemporary, some functional segregation of the sacred space surrounding the temple itself. At Hayling, the outer enclosure contained concentrations of burnt patches, and the remains of metal-working and minting were found at Thetford. Such a concentration of repeated burning could possibly explain the localised magnetic enhancement associated with the outer enclosure ditch and perhaps the apparent central strip of enhanced background magnetisation that runs through the centre of the enclosure.

Without invasive investigation it is difficult to speculate further over the precise nature of these geophysical anomalies. This is clearly a complex landscape where the use of space is dominated by a huge prehistoric ritual monument that influenced the development of later activities. In this respect, some continuity in the association with later ritual sites would not seem unusual and might suggest a relationship between Hill, the possible late Iron Age temple and possible Roman-British votive offerings or ritual activity.

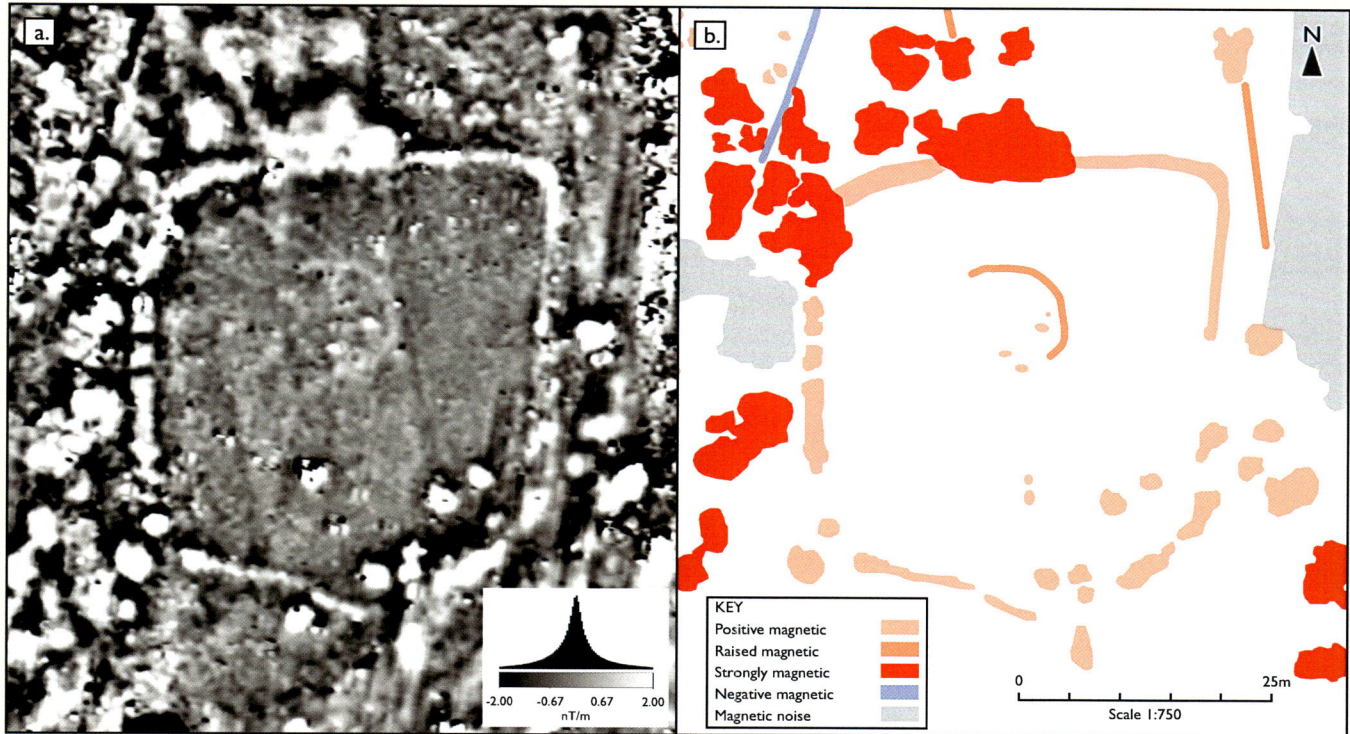

KEY
Positive magnetic
Raised magnetic
Strongly magnetic
Negative magnetic
Magnetic noise

0   25m
Scale 1:750

Fig P9.2.1

Extract from the caesium magnetometer survey, a) showing a possible late Iron Age temple, together with b), a graphical interpretation of the data, See Fig 9.7 for location. (Geophysics Team and Eddie Lyons, © English Heritage)

'Winterbourne Romano-British settlement' adding more detail and suggesting continuation south-east towards the A4 (Foldout 1E). In addition, a series of lynchets, running along the contours of the hill but overlying the Roman parchmarks, were also mapped. These clearly post-date the Roman settlement, possibly by some considerable time.

At the time of writing, analysis and mapping of the lidar data is ongoing, but it has added additional slight earthwork remains. These seem most likely to relate to the lynchets already noted rather than Roman settlement. They include a lengthy stretch of bank located a little further upslope than those mapped in AWHSMP, plus a probable plough headland running up the slope and across the Roman parchmarks. In addition, traces of plough ridges overlying the Roman settlement have also been identified though these may be of quite recent origin. Some traces of possible quarrying have also been mapped from the lidar, both on top of Waden Hill, and downslope, very close to the parchmarks.

The settlement south of Silbury Hill is largely a blank as far as aerial photographs are concerned. At its southernmost end some traces of tracks and lynchets connected to the field systems to the south are visible, but there is nothing within 800 metres of Silbury Hill itself. Slightly closer to Silbury, due west of the Swallowhead Spring, some probable lynchets were mapped. They lie outside the field containing the Roman settlement, and are aligned roughly north–south. They share the same broad alignment as both later prehistoric and medieval field systems mapped to the south and west. The area south-west of these does contain some cropmark features – there are, of course, the barrows, but also some ditched features which may represent traces of settlement within the later prehistoric field system.

Lidar has indicated further low banks probably associated with the field systems west of these lynchets. The unusual morphology of these banks immediately north and south of the barrows is noteworthy. Otherwise, the field south of the A4 containing the Roman settlement is as blank on lidar as it is on aerial photographs. In the case of the photographs, the area may just be too low-lying to suffer the sort of soil moisture deficit that would be sufficient to produce distinct cropmarks. The lidar suggests that there is little, if any, surface survival of any features associated with the Roman occupation.

Evidence for the Romano-British settlement from excavations

Vicky Crosby, Nicola Hembrey, Polydora Baker

Evidence from the external ditch of Silbury Hill

'the debris of what apparently was the staple pub lunch of the Roman world – oysters, probably from the South coast. And not just oyster shells, but the wherewithal to pay for them ... Two thousand years of bric-a-brac, the floor sweepings of the ages ... Out of the Silbury ditch came the fascinating and unlooked-for profile of twenty centuries of Wiltshire life.'

Magnus Magnusson narrating in the fourth *Chronicle* programme on 'The Silbury Dig' (Summer 1969, DVD in the Alexander Keiller Museum)

The excavation of the large external ditch around Silbury in 1969 yielded a moderate assemblage of finds but little interpretation, beyond the supposition that it represented rubbish taken from a small settlement (Atkinson 1978, 172). The focus of Whittle's (1997a) Silbury Hill monograph was the prehistoric evidence and the Roman finds were briefly summarised as: '"Roman midden". From this layer came Roman pottery, over 100 Roman coins, a bronze bracelet and much animal bone especially from the lower part of the layer'. Further work on the post-prehistoric finds by others was planned but in the event not carried out. Recent examination of this assemblage, though modest in size and dispersed in nature, has revealed interesting detail concerning the nature of Roman activity at Silbury Hill.

Nature of the evidence

A trench 5m wide (Cutting 1) was cut through the external ditch at a point south of the mound in 1969 (Whittle 1997a, fig 23; Foldout 2J). Atkinson's site diary for 1969 and the site drawing of the east section of Cutting 1 have been used to try to understand the stratigraphic context of the Romano-British material recovered, with additional information taken from letters in the project archive, labels on finds bags, and comments in the reports on the animal bone (Gardner 1987) and Romano-British pottery (Farley 1971). Atkinson's diary (22 July 1969) gives some indication of the problems encountered in recording the ditch, and we should acknowledge that we still have an incomplete picture of this intervention.

Finds context information is limited, and the site finds registers have not been located. For most artefacts the only context information available is what was written on the bags; for coins, a copy of the relevant parts of the finds register was made available to Moorhead (pers comm). Bulk finds 'were bagged up on site and each "bag" was allocated a number', but the 'terminology used by the excavators of the ditch ... was hard to match to the bag numbers' (letters from M Farley to N Gardner, 30 November 1986 and A Whittle, 12 March 1990). The animal bones have been individually numbered, but no concordance to relate them to context has been found (*see below*).

It is likely that some recent material was discarded – some modern artefacts are present, and the pottery record sheets note the presence of clay pipe and modern pottery in a few bags.

Stratigraphy
Vicky Crosby
The ditch fills were recorded as nine layers, and these numbers were marked on the original section drawing. Especially for the lower layers, they clearly oversimplify complex stratigraphy – Whittle's renumbering defined 44 separate contexts (1997a, 23–4). Layers 1 to 5 are described in Atkinson's diary (12 July 1969 and 14 July 1969). Layer 2 – the 'Roman midden' had three subdivisions: 2a, 2b (or 2L) and 2c. The stratigraphic information is summarised in Table 9.1, which provides a concordance of Atkinson's and Whittle's context numbers.

Roman material was recorded from layers 1, 2 and 3. The earliest of these, layer 3, the fine chalk silting described as 'rainwash' contained

Table 9.1: Summary of the stratigraphy of the external ditch section south of the mound. The layer numbers (1–9) are from Atkinson's original section drawing (AKM archive)

Layer	From diary	Comments
1	'Topsoil and top of R–B midden'	More than half the RB coins, most of the vessel glass and a few of the RB small finds from the ditch are recorded as coming from the topsoil. The 'turf and top 10cm of topsoil' also contained medieval pottery and 'other later materials to present day' (diary, 01/07/1969). The layer is up to 0.25m deep, and it is not noted if post–Roman material occurred throughout. Whittle context: 900 (1997a, 23–4 and fig 23).
2	'Dark earthy midden with sparse chalk'	Described on section as 'black soil' and 'Roman midden'. It was not present on the north side of the ditch (diary, 12/07/1969), but was up to 1m deep in the centre of the ditch. Most of the animal bone from the ditch was in this layer (but see layer 2b). Farley's analysis of the RB pottery of necessity treated all the material as if from a single stratigraphic unit, layer 2, but it was also present in 1, 2a–c and 3 (1971, 11–12). Whittle contexts: 901–902
2a	'Gravelly chalk, at E. end of side only'	Described on section as 'chalk gravel'. This is probably the layer described as 'chalk midden' on some of the finds bags. It contained RB pottery and coins, and several of the small finds. It is present only on the southern edge of the ditch. Not distinguished from 904 on Whittle's fig 23
2b (or 2L?)	[not mentioned]	Described on section as 'light grey black', and up to 0.4m deep. It may originally have been labelled 2L, and it may be the 'bottom of midden layer' which contained the concentration of animal bones noted in the diary (16/07/1969). Whittle context: 904
2c	[not mentioned]	Described on section as 'stone layer' and 'chalk and flint', and probably the 'flint rubble' layer referred to on some of the RB pot finds bags. Up to 0.2m deep. Whittle context: 905
3	'Chalk rain wash, fine grained, without chalk gravel, dropping to E. In the W. half this is mixed with lumps of black midden material.'	Described on section as 'buff silt', and up to 0.2m deep. The term 'rainwash' is used on the finds bags. It is unclear if the mixing with 'midden material' is post–depositional disturbance (such as badger activity) or reflects dumping of material while layer 3 was building up. There may have been a causeway across the ditch close to the west side of the section (diary 01/08/1969; Whittle 1997a, 22). Although some RB pottery is noted as from this layer, none of the late RB coins are. There were only 7 fragments of animal bone. Whittle context: 906
4	'Chalk silt, with high content of fine chalk gravel, of 5–8mm size'	This number appears to have been applied to many interleaved layers in the main body of the ditch fill, below layer 3 and above the chalk layers (8) overlying the revetment (9). No RB finds were noted from this layer, but the top of the layer produced a copper alloy bracelet (Panel 9.1), described in the diary for 22/07/2011: 'In ditch, a well–preserved bronze bracelet with grooved T–terminals found in layer 4 at base of R.B. midden.'' Whittle contexts: 907–921, 923–925
5	'At the S. end, on the w side below the first step, layer (5), a coarser and much whiter chalk gravel silt'	No finds or animal bones were recorded from this layer. Whittle contexts: 941–942
6	[not mentioned]	This number was used inconsistently on the section drawing: on the north side it is badger disturbance, and on the south side, an undescribed layer under 4 and above 5. Whittle contexts: 915–916 and un–numbered disturbance.
7	[not mentioned]	Layer, no description on section, shown on north side only and much cut by badger sett. Whittle context: 922
8	[not mentioned]	The chalk rubble over revetment 9, described variously as 'placed' or 'fallen' on the section. Whittle contexts: 936–939
9	[not mentioned]	The inserted revetment 'compact placed chalk' on the section. Whittle contexts: 926–935

some Romano-British pottery but none of the late Romano-British coins found throughout the upper ditch fills. It is hoped that additional work as part of the Later Silbury project may be able to establish if this pottery is earlier in date than that in layer 2. There may have been some dumping of material into the ditch from a putative adjacent causeway, but the 'lumps of black midden material' are as likely to be due to badger activity.

Layer 2c – the stone layer of chalk and flint rubble – may be more significant in terms of Romano-British activity. The flint may derive from construction of walls or surfaces (the road?) close to the ditch. Again, additional work may establish a date range for this layer (some of the pottery bags from 2c note that they contain 2nd- or 3rd-century AD pottery).

The 'Roman midden' layer 2 started to accumulate after this. It was described as dark and earthy, with a paler layer (2b or 2L) at its base. Low down in the midden, possibly in layer 2b/2L, were the 'many animal bones' referred to in the diary, which were noted by Gardner (1987, 46) as being in good condition, with very few signs of abrasion and lacking evidence for scavengers. Material evidently reached the midden from the south side, and the 'chalky midden' layer 2a was restricted to the south edge of the ditch. The extent of the midden is of course unknown, but it is worth noting that no similar deposits were recorded in pits excavated by Pass in the ditch west of the mound (Pass 1887, 248).

The interpretation of the 'Roman midden' layer remains uncertain. The high proportion of fine table wares is noted below, and a few finds may suggest a ritual aspect. But the number of small finds seems fairly low given the volume of material excavated, and nothing in the descriptions of the excavations suggests structured deposition (there are no whole vessels, smashed or intact, and no reference to articulated animal bones).

Given the nature of the excavation and recording, drawing inferences from a negative is of course risky, but on balance, it seems unlikely this is a primary ritual deposit. However, if the area east of the mound contained high-status buildings including a possible shrine or temple (see Panel 9.2), this could represent secondary disposal of material from ritual activities in that area. This was formalised in the use of favissae ('repositories into which cult material is deposited at the end of its working life') in classical and Roman provincial contexts (Haynes nd) but similar practices occur more widely. It may also account for some ritual deposits in wells and shafts in Roman Britain (Webster 1997, 139).

An extensive midden (about 1150 sq m) at Wayside Farm, Devizes has been similarly interpreted as redeposition of material from an unknown adjacent ritual site (Valentin and Robinson 2002, 207–9). Formed in a single episode of dumping, the midden deposit lay between (and in the fills of) two ditches (Valentin and Robinson 2002, 161 and fig 7). Taken as a group, the finds recovered from the midden and a pit, which it partly overlay, suggest a ritual or religious, rather than domestic, origin. Possible votive offerings included a deliberately folded copper alloy garment collar, a lead curse tablet and spoons, as well as other small personal items and coins. The pottery dated to c AD 370–420+, and Corney noted that the midden had a higher proportion of fine wares than the other contexts on the site (Corney 2002, 188–9 and table 9). The latest coins date to AD 388–402.

Layer 1 – 'topsoil and top of Romano-British midden' – could have formed in several ways. As well as gradual accumulation since the Romano-British period, Roman material could have entered the ditch as result of later events. For example, the lowering of the level of the turnpike road in the 18th century AD (referred to by Pass: 1887, 247) could have led to the destruction of archaeological deposits and the redeposition of material in the ditch. Given the evidence from other parts of the Silbury settlement, the scarcity of stone and ceramic building materials is interesting (but of course it is possible they were not retained). More than half the coins are recorded as coming from the topsoil (Table 9.2).

The role of badger disturbance in the formation of the ditch assemblages must also be taken into account. Although the section drawing shows disturbance only on the north (mound) side of the ditch and as cutting layers below the 'midden' deposits, it is likely that disturbance was present but less readily identifiable in the darker and earthier upper layers (Foldout 2J).

The artefacts

Pottery

Jane Timby
Substantial quantities of Roman pottery were recovered from the upper levels of the external

Table 9.2: Context information for coins from the external ditch. Taken from annotated copy of Moorhead 1999 held in AK Museum.

Coins from the external ditch

Context description	No	%	
Topsoil (45) or topsoil? (7) or midden topsoil (1)	53	55%	55% topsoil
Midden (14), chalk midden (12) or S2 (5)	31	32%	45% midden or ditch
Ditch (no further info)	12	12%	
Total	**96**		

ditch. Preliminary analysis of some of this material by Farley (1971) showed it to comprise wares typical of the later Roman period. Amongst these were vessels from Poole Harbour, Dorset (black-burnished ware) Overwey, Tilford (white wares) and the Oxfordshire and New Forest kilns (colour-coated wares, parchment ware and mortaria). Sherds of Midlands late Roman shelly ware indicate continued accumulation of material in the last quarter of the 4th century.

Roman pottery has been found at Silbury since the antiquarian excavations of the 19th century. Although the finds are now lost the descriptions are commensurate with a later Roman date. The unusually high preponderance of fine table wares from the external ditch and within this wider assemblage, along with various antiquarian architectural finds, might suggest a higher status structure adjacent to the Roman road.

Coins

Sam Moorhead

The 1968–70 excavations of at Silbury Hill produced 103 coins, one from the top step of the summit of the Hill and 102 from the external ditch (Whittle 1997a, 24; Moorhead 1997). Checking the site register, it can be ascertained that the coin from the summit of the Hill (SF 2329) and six from the ditch (SF nos 125, 153A, 165, 236, 277 (silver coin) and 282) have been lost and are no longer in the archive.

The author obtained the coins from Judith Atkinson, following the kind advice of John Casey, in the 1990s. The coins date from the late 3rd to the late 4th/early 5th centuries, with an overwhelming peak in the Valentinianic period, AD 364–78. A full catalogue is available in Moorhead 2011. The data are summarised in Tables 9.3 and 9.4.

The finds were interpreted as coming from a midden (Moorhead 1997; 1999), a view supported by John Casey (pers comm, letter 13/5/97). However, one should not rule out completely the possibility that these were votive deposits.

Other artefacts

Nicola Hembrey

Other than coins, most of the objects from the 1968–70 excavations are now at the Alexander Keiller Museum, Avebury. Most derive from layers 2 or 2a of the ditch, noted on the finds bags and in Atkinson's diary as 'midden' and 'chalky midden' respectively, and the majority are Roman or later pre-Roman in date. The exception is the heavy bronze bracelet from layer 4, below the midden; this has been tentatively identified as late Bronze Age or earlier Iron Age in date (*see above*, Panel 9.1). The few post-Roman finds are discussed with the other evidence of medieval activity later in this chapter.

Two copper alloy finds from the chalk midden (layer 2a) within the ditch may be slightly earlier than Roman in date. The first is a tin bronze rod, SF 237; probably an awl, it narrows to a point at one end and has a rounded flattened terminal at the other. Its material might suggest a late pre-Roman date. The second object, SF 251/301 is a straight cylindrical tube of tin bronze, broken into three pieces (and assigned two SF numbers, 301 and 251), with a short section of linear decoration at the slightly wider top end; its function is unclear – it may be a binding of some sort – and its material might also suggest a late pre-Roman date.

The Roman finds of greater interest are the three head fragments of bone hairpins. Typologically separated by perhaps a hundred years, this is not to say that the earlier one was not an heirloom or ancestor artefact (Caple 2010, 305) at the time of deposition. The one on the left of Figure 9.3 is a Crummy Type 2 pin dating to AD 50–200/50 (Crummy 1983, 21). It has one to four transverse grooves below a conical head; the tip of the head appears to be broken. The two remaining pins (Fig 9.3) are Crummy Type 4 pins which date to AD 250 (Crummy 1983, 240).

Table 9.3: Catalogue of the Roman coins from the Silbury excavations by Richard Atkinson in 1968–70 (Moorhead 1997 provides a more detailed catalogue of these coins).

No	Emperor	Dates	Reverse	References	Site find no
1	Barbarous Radiate – Victorinus	c 275–85	Unclear type	–	175
2	Barbarous Radiate – Tetricus I	c 275–85	- CV C C; Salus standing left at altar	cf Cunetio 2653; cf Normanby 1953	152
3	Barbarous Radiate – Gallic Empire	c. 275–85	?[INVICTVS], ?Sol	–	213
4	Carausius (possibly Barbarous)	c. 286–93	VIC-T-RIA; ?Pax standing left	cf RIC 1022	283

No	Reverse Type	Dates	Mint	Emperor	References	Site find no
5	Barbarous ?[CAESARVM NOSTRORVM], TOV/V	c 320	'Siscia'	House of Constantine	cf RIC 145/6; cf Boon pl. VII, 118	161
6	GLORIA EXERCITVS, 2 soldiers and 2 standards	?332–3	Trier	Constantius II (c)	cf RIC 546	141
7	As above	330–1	Lyons	Constantine I	RIC 243	219
8	As above	330–5	?	Constantius II (c)	–	145
9	GLORIA EXERCITVS, 2 soldiers and 1 standard	337–40	?Trier	?Constantius II (a)	cf RIC 82/83	254
10	As above	335–41	?Lyons or Arles	House of Constantine	cf RIC VIII Lyons 4ff; RIC VII Arles 381ff	153B
11	Victory on Prow left	?330	Trier	CONSTANTINOPOLIS	cf RIC 523	167
12	As above – probably barbarous	330–1	Arles	CONSTANTINOPOLIS	Type as RIC 532	131
13	As no 11	330–40	?Rome	CONSTANTINOPOLIS	cf RIC 355	181
14	As above – probably barbarous	330–40	?	CONSTANTINOPOLIS	–	134
15	As above – barbarous	330–40	?'Trier'	VEBS ROMA	cf Bancroft 64	127
16	As above – barbarous	330–40	?'Trier'	Constantine I	–	151
17	PAX PVBLICA; Pax standing left	337–41	?	Helena	–	249
18	PIETAS ROMANA; Pietas standing, holding infant	337–41	?	Theodora	–	174
19	VICTORIAE DD AVGGQ NN; Two Victories	347–8	Trier	Constantius II	RIC 85	203
20	As above	347–8	Trier	Constans	RIC 196	225
21	As above	347–8	Trier	Constans	RIC 210	154
22	As above – possibly barbarous	347–8	Trier	Constans	cf RIC pp 151–2	169
23	As no. 19	347–8	Lyons	Constantius II	RIC 49	179
24	As above	347–8	?	?Constans	–	289
25	As above – barbarous	347–8	'Trier'	Constans	RIC pp 151–2, cf 182ff	281
26	Barbarous: FEL TEMP REPARATIO; Emperor on galley, steered by Victory	c 348–53	?	House of Constantine	–	198
27	Barbarous: FELICITAS PVBLICE; Emperor standing	c 350–1	?'Trier'	Magnentius	cf Shipham 199	178
28	Barbarous: Illegible (12/13mm)	c 350–3	?	?Magnentius	cf Boon pl VIII, no 150; Colchester pl 12, nos 5, 9 & 11	155
29	FEL TEMP REPARATIO; Soldier spearing fallen horseman (c 17mm)	c. 351–5	?Heraclea	Constantius II	cf RIC 90	211
30	As above (c 15mm)	355–60	?	?Constantius II	–	129
31	As above – possibly barbarous (c 18mm)	355–60	?	Constantius II	–	159

Table 9.3: Catalogue of the Roman coins from the Silbury excavations by Richard Atkinson in 1968–70 (Moorhead 1997 provides a more detailed catalogue of these coins).

No	Reverse Type	Dates	Mint	Emperor	References	Site find no
32	Barbarous: FEL TEMP REPARATIO; Soldier spearing fallen horseman (c 16mm)	c 355–64	?'Trier'	Constantius II	cf RIC 350; cf Shipham 2010	157
33	As above (c 19mm)	c 355–64	'Lyons'	Constantius II	cf RIC 189; cf Shipham 236	218
34	As above (c 15mm)	c 355–64	?	Constantius II	–	199
35	As above (c 14mm)	c 355–64	?	Constantius II	–	162
36	As above (c 13mm)	c 355–64	?	Constantius II	–	200
37	As above (c 10mm)	c 355–60	?	Constantius II	–	229
38	Possibly of the above type (c 16mm)	?c 355–64	?	?Constantius II	–	139
39	Barbarous: silver siliqua: VOTIS / V / MVLTIS / X in wreath	360–3	Arles	Julian	Type as RIC 295; cf Bishops Cannings 195(S)	148
40	GLORIA ROMANORVM; Emperor advancing right, dragging captive and holding standard	?364–7	Lyons	Valentinian I	cf LRBC 286	202
41	As above	367–75	Lyons	Valentinan I	LRBC 307	149
42	As above	367–75	Lyons	Valentinian I	LRBC 307	184
43	As above	367–75	Lyons	?Valentinia I or Gratian	cf LRBC 307–8	250
44	As above	367–75	Lyons	House of Valentinian	cf LRBC 321	137
45	As above	367–75	Lyons	Valentinian I	LRBC 325/330	255
46	As above	367–75	Lyons	Gratian	LRBC 331/335	210
47	As above	375–8	Lyons	Gratian	LRBC 364	212
48	As above	364–75	Lyons	Valentinian I	LRBC 279ff	253
49	As above	364–75	Lyons	?Valens	cf LRBC 282ff	135
50	As above	364–75	Lyons	?Valens	cf LRBC 135	168
51	As above	364–75	Lyons	Valentinian I	cf LRBC 284ff	182
52	As above	364–75	Lyons	Valens	cf LRBC 288ff	133
53	As above – possibly barbarous	364–75	Lyons	Valens	cf LRBC 288ff	172
54	As no 40	?367–75	Lyons	House of Valentinian	–	279
55	As above	?367–75	Lyons	House of Valentinian	cf LRBC 302ff	256
56	As above	364–7	Arles	Valens	LRBC 489	224
57	As above	367–75	Arles	Valens	LRBC 520	191
58	As above	367–78	Arles	?Valens	LRBC 526/530	247
59	As above	367–78	Arles	Valens	LRBC 526/530	192
60	As above	364–75	?Arles	Valens	–	138
61	As above	364–75	?Arles	?Valentinian I	–	180
62	As above	364–7	Aquileia	Valentinian I	LRBC 965	215
63	As above	364–7	Aquileia	Valens	LRBC 966	197
64	As above	364–75	Aquileia	Valentinian I	LRBC 1017	244

Table 9.3: Catalogue of the Roman coins from the Silbury excavations by Richard Atkinson in 1968–70 (Moorhead 1997 provides a more detailed catalogue of these coins).

No	Reverse Type	Dates	Mint	Emperor	References	Site find no
65	As above	367–75	Siscia	Valentinian I	LRBC 1331	246
66	As above	367–75	Siscia	Valentinian I	LRBC 1308–11	185
67	As above	375–8	Siscia	?Valentinian II	cf LRBC 1494	140
68	SECVRITAS REI PVBLICAE; Victory advancing left	364–75	Lyons	Valens	RIC 12/21a	287
69	As above	364–7	Arles	?Valens	cf LRBC 489	220
70	As above	367–75	Arles	Valentinian I	LRBC 506	248
71	As above	367–75	Arles	Valentinian I	LRBC 514/515	243
72	As above – possibly barbarous	367–75	Arles	Valentinian I	cf LRBC 514/5	166
73	As above – possibly barbarous	?367–75	Arles	Valens	cf LRBC 516	128
74	As no. 68	?367–78	Arles	Valens	cf LRBC 528/532	183
75	As above	375–8	Arles	Gratian	LRBC 533	214
76	As above	364–75	?Arles	Valentinian I	LRBC 481ff	278
77	As above – possibly barbarous	364–75	?Arles	Valentinian I	cf LRBC 481ff	209
78	As above – possibly barbarous	364–75	?Arles	Valens	cf LRBC 483ff	170
79	As above – possibly barbarous	364–75	?Arles	?Valens	cf LRBC 483ff	130
80	As no. 68	364–75	?Arles	?Valens	cf LRBC 483ff	143
81	As above	364–75	?Arles	House of Valentinian	–	188
82	As above	367–75	Aquileia	Valentinian I	cf LRBC 1017	177
83	As above	364–75	??Arles	Valentinian I	–	201
84	As above	364–75	?Lyons or Arles	?Valens	–	142
85	As above	367–78	?	Gratian	–	223
86	GLORIA NOVI SAECVLI; Emperor standing with shield and a standard	367–75	Arles	Gratian	LRBC 511	171
87	As above	367–75	Arles	Gratian	LRBC 511	193
88	As above	367–75	Arles	Gratian	LRBC 523a	245
89	As above	367–75	Arles	Gratian	LRBC 529	176
90	As above	367–75	Arles	Gratian	LRBC 529	276
91	As above	367–75	Arles	Gratian	LRBC 517/523a	288
92	As above	367–75	Arles	Gratian	LRBC 505ff	136
93	VOT / XV / MVLT / XX in wreath	378–83	Lyons	Gratian	LRBC 378	222
94	VICTORIA AVGGG	388–95	?	House of Theodosius	–	221
95	Unclear type	4th cent	?	–	–	150
96	?Coin	?3rd / 4th cent	?	–	–	235

Note: 22. Mintmark B//TRP not published in RIC, so probably a contemporary copy
25. See also: Colchester, cf pl 11, 18ff and Coleshill cf 1885–6

Table 9.4: Major coin assemblages from the Silbury region, listed by Reece period (Reece 1972 and 1995)

Reece Period	Dates	Brooke Kennet	Brooke Wells	Atkinson 1968–70	EH 2010	Total	Per Mill
1	Pre–AD41	6	0	0	0	6	29.3
2	41–54	0	0	0	0	0	0
3	54–69	6	0	0	0	6	29.3
4	69–96	6	0	0	0	6	29.3
5	96–117	4	1	0	0	5	24.4
6	117–38	4	0	0	0	4	19.5
7	138–61	4	0	0	0	4	19.5
8	161–80	4	1?	0	0	5	24.4
9	180–92	0	0	0	0	0	0
10	193–222	3	0	0	0	3	14.6
11	222–35	2	0	0	0	2	9.75
12	235–60	6	0	0	0	6	29.3
13	260–75	2	1	3	0	6	29.3
14	275–96	2	1+1?	1	1	6	29.3
15	296–317	0	0	0	0	0	0
16	317–330	0	2+1?	1	0	4	19.5
17	330–348	0	9+1?	20	5	35	170.7
18	348–64	0	4	14	0	18	87.8
19	364–78	4	4	53	6	67	326.8
20	378–88	0	0	1	0	1	4.88
21	388–402	0	c. 16	1	4	21	102.4
Total		**53**	**42**	**94**	**16**	**205**	
Unc		1	7	2	1		

Brooke Kennet – coins recorded as being found at 'Kennet' in the 19th century by Joshua Brooke,
Brooke Wells – coins from the Silbury Wells excavations in 1896 (Well A) and 1908 (Well B),
Atkinson 1968–70 – coins from the external ditch and the summit, EH 2010 – coins from the 2010 Later Silbury excavations. (Further details can be found in Moorhead 2011)

They have a faceted cuboid head. All three pins were recovered from within layer 1 (topsoil/top of Roman midden) although it is not clear from exactly where they were retrieved.

The only other object that can be assigned to this context is SF 205, a probable sharpening stone of red sandstone, noted as coming from the south bank. Uneven and roughly L-shaped,

it has a deep groove running across its upper surface.

SF 231 is considered here as no context is given on the finds bag. It is a complete iron stylus with a triangular, flat-sectioned eraser above a square-sectioned tapering stem, which terminates in a sharp point. Found throughout the Roman period, it is of Manning type 3 (Manning 1985, 85) (Fig 9.4a).

The rest of the Roman assemblage comes from layer 2. SF 252 is a very simple brooch of copper alloy wire, bent into a U-shape and twisted to form a catch at both ends. Its simple, functional appearance may indicate either an early date or perhaps domestic manufacture. The only item of lead is a folded rectangular fragment, SF 286, likely to be a curse fragment. One iron snaffle (bridle) bit of mid-1st-century date (cf Manning 1985, H13) is also present, comprising an upper, oval ring of flat section, below which is a flat-sectioned link at right-angles, terminating in a simple loop (Fig 9.4b).

Also from this layer are SF 280, a large domed fragment of ironstone, a roughly-spherical pyrite (un-numbered) from sample 1174C, and an iron slag fragment (David Dungworth pers comm).

Fig 9.3
Fragments of bone hairpins from the external ditch at Silbury Hill. Left: Crummy Type 2 pin (L 44mm, pin head width 6mm); centre: Crummy Type 4 pin (L 27mm, pin head width 6mm); right: Crummy Type 4 pin (L 48mm, pin head width 6mm).
(James O Davies, © English Heritage)

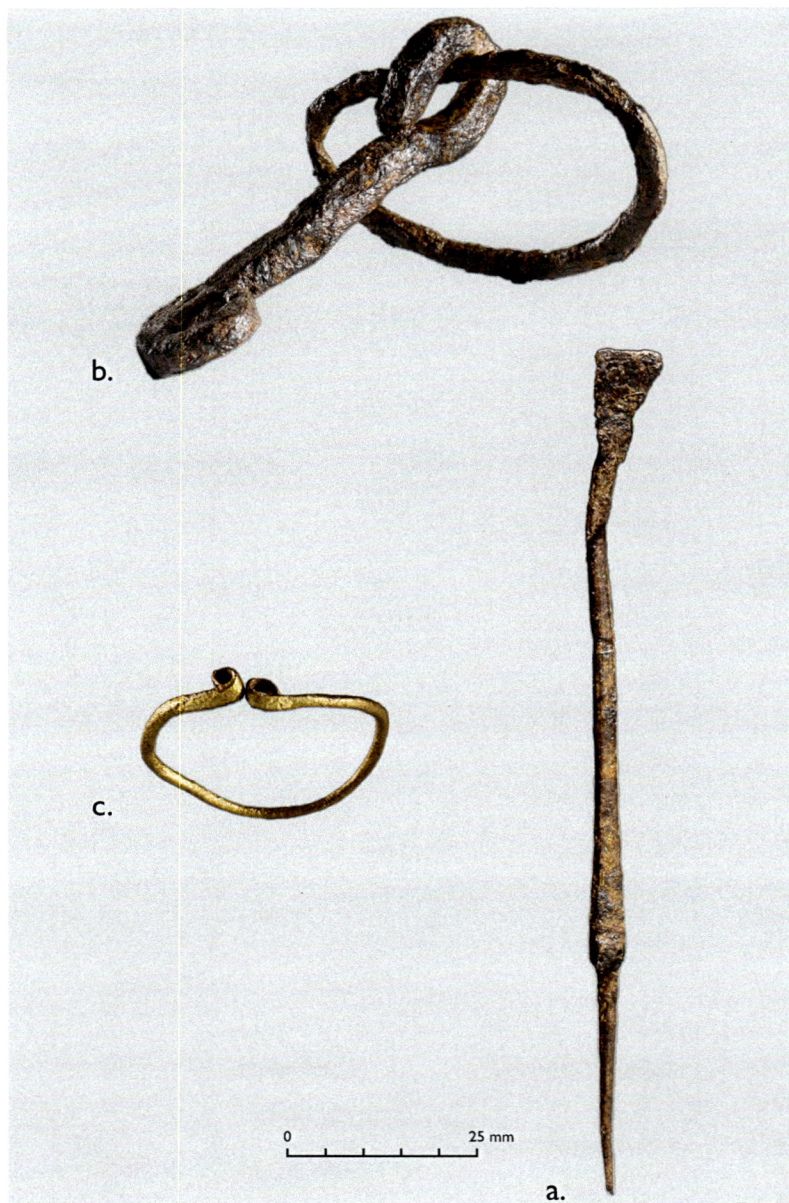

b.

c.

a.

0 ————————— 25 mm

Glass

Nicola Hembrey

Also contained within the ditch was a small assemblage of fine vessel glass, similar to the assemblage from the 2010 evaluation, and of probable Roman date. Eighteen fragments were collected: 15 clear light blue or light greenish-blue in colour and mostly with some surface weathering or decomposition, two fragments of clear yellowish-green and one (possibly residual) clear light pink with some surface decomposition. One light blue folded possible base fragment is the only piece from layer 2; the rest were recovered from topsoil.

The animal bone assemblage from the external ditch

Polydora Baker

The animal bone assemblage recovered from the Roman midden within the external ditch was studied by Neville Gardner (Gardner 1987) and summary data was subsequently published in Whittle (Gardner in Whittle 1997a; the latter also mentions an earlier study by Betty Westley). Unfortunately, due to the loss of contextual data, it is no longer possible to associate the bone finds with specific layers in the ditch though it may be possible to explore particular associations (for example groups of horse teeth or dog bones), though Gardner did not record evidence for articulation or associated bone groups.

In this overview, the data recorded and discussed by Gardner (1987) is reviewed briefly in the light of assemblages from local sites, and broader patterns of animal use, including ritual deposition, in the Romano-British period.

The majority of the assemblage was retrieved from layer 2. In addition layer 3 yielded one cattle, four pig, one sheep and one red deer bone (Gardner 1987, table 7.10). The bone from layer 2 was well preserved and was thought to derive from primary deposition, with little evidence for subsequent scavenging or disturbance (but *see above* regarding badger disturbance). Gardner identified *c* 750 bones and teeth (representing an estimated 118 animals), from cattle, horse, pig, sheep, dog, cat, red deer and roe deer (Gardner 1987, 55–8 and tables 4.4–4.8). No fragments were recorded as unidentified, so it is highly probable that recovery or analysis (with discard of unidentifiable fragments) was selective.

The most common species represented is sheep, followed by cattle, pig and horse. Gardner noted the predominance of cattle and sheep loose teeth and mandibles and distal limbs, suggesting deliberate discard of these elements and removal of the meatier or 'more useful portions' for consumption elsewhere and eventually disposal, possibly within an as yet unexcavated part of the ditch itself (Gardner 1987, 68). He noted also consistency in the butchery of cattle mandibles (smashing for removal from the skull) and cattle, sheep and pig limbs (butchery at shoulder and/or around the knee joint). The abundance of isolated teeth, proximal metapodia, distal humeri and tibiae may result in part from differential survival, as these are amongst the denser skeletal parts (Brain 1981;

Lyman 1994). This contrasts, however, with the good preservation attested by Gardner (1987). The scarcity of sheep and pig foot bones suggests a recovery bias against these and other smaller bones and fragments, though we might also expect far fewer teeth if this were the case. It is interesting to note the relatively large number of dogs (six) identified from only twelve fragments, which may indicate that many carcasses were present but became dispersed prior to or following disposal within the ditch. The age distribution of the main livestock including foetal, juvenile and old animals with a predominance of adults, suggests that some animals were raised locally and that cattle, horse and sheep were used for secondary products (eg wool and/or milk), traction and/or transport before being disposed of or consumed.

There are few contemporary assemblages from the surrounding area to which the Roman midden contents can be compared and the small size of these assemblages makes this problematic (see Hambleton 2008). The range and relative abundance of domestic mammals in the small assemblage from Longstones Field is similar to the midden data, with the predominance of

sheep/goat followed by cattle (Coward 2008; Gillings et al 2008). The Later Silbury excavations (Ayton in Crosby and Hembrey 2011), and earlier investigations of 'Winterbourne' Romano-British settlement (Powell et al 1996; Isles 1996) yielded hand-collected and sieved assemblages dominated by cattle, followed by sheep (Table 9.5).

In all three assemblages, pigs are markedly infrequent, a feature attributed by some to the possible lack of woodland (Isles 1996; Powell et al 1996, 57). Pannage is not strictly necessary for successful pig husbandry, however, and stall feeding is documented in Roman texts and evidenced in the zooarchaeological record elsewhere (Ward and Mainland 1999; Albarella 2006; Ervynck et al 2007). Bird remains were infrequent at all of these sites with the exception of the complete skeletons found at 'Winterbourne' (Isles 1996). The scarcity or absence of bird and fish bones may be due to recovery or preservation bias.

There is little in the midden assemblage to suggest convincingly that it originates from anything other than disposal of domestic food and butchery waste and unwanted animal

Fig 9.4 (opposite)
a) Complete Roman iron stylus found in the external ditch at Silbury Hill (L 129mm; width of eraser top 10mm; thickness 2mm; weight 4g);
b) 1st-century AD iron snaffle bit forming part of a bridle from layer 2 of the external ditch at Silbury Hill (total L 84mm; W 52mm; length of ring 32mm; width of loop 18mm; thickness 4mm; weight 23g);
c) Brass penannular brooch recovered from 'Steps cutting 2' as part of the 1968–70 excavations (L 34mm; W 26mm; T 1mm; weight 2g).
(James O Davies and Eddie Lyons, © English Heritage)

Table 9.5: Distribution of cattle, sheep, pig, horse and dog in Roman faunal assemblages from Silbury Hill and Avebury

I	SH midden (Layer 2)	SH 2010		Winterbourne**		Longstones Field***
	hc	hc	sv*	hc	sv	
NISP						
Cattle	166	70	14	35	2	10%
Sheep/goat	468	64	13	15	4	18%
Pig	53	21	3			<1%
Horse	42	8		4	0	2%
Dog	12	14	6	4	6	1%
Total	741	177	36	58	12	203
%						
Cattle	22.4	39.5	38.9	60.3	16.7	31.2
Sheep/goat	63.2	36.2	36.1	25.9	33.3	56.2
Pig	7.2	11.9	8.3			3.1
Horse	5.7	4.5		6.9		6.2
Dog	1.6	7.9	16.7	6.9	50.0	3.1

(Source of data: SH midden, Gardner 1987, text and figures 4.5–4.8; SH 2010, assessment data, Ayton in Crosby and Hembrey 2011, tables 7–8; Winterbourne, Isles 1996, table 10; Longstones Field, Coward 2008, table 7.). hc: hand–collected; sv: sieved; *>4; ** all data from ditches, pits, wall trenches; *** % data derived from %s and total fragment count provided in publication; recovery method not stated).

carcasses or carcass parts. Some aspects do merit further attention where possible. If deriving from 'tourist snacks', some uniformity in species, age or body parts might be expected (for example mutton chops and chicken joints at the legionary baths, Caerleon: O'Connor 1986). In this regard, the abundance of sheep mandibles, teeth and tibiae (Gardner 1987, fig 4.8) is of interest, as these could potentially represent meat packets (cheek and shank).

Feasting cannot be ruled out. The relative abundance of sheep and cattle mandibles, tibiae (at least half of which are distal ends) and metapodia, and consistency in butchery methods suggests that carcasses were butchered in a standard method and meat consumed elsewhere (Gardner 1987), though whether in a single event or over a longer period of time is not known. The presence of rainwashed silts in layer 3 suggests that the ditch was left exposed at least some of the time (Table 9.1). Gardner (1987) did not report any evidence of roasting (burning of exposed bone), though this is not strictly necessary for the preparation of large quantities of meat.

Votive offerings in temples or shrines are known from across Romano-British England and beyond (King 2005). The most striking deposits show a concentration on particular or uncommon species such as goat, restricted age groups with suggestions for seasonal slaughter, body parts and even sides of the body (Legge and Dorrington 1985; Legge *et al* 2000; Levitan 1993; Baxter 2011). However, in others, the deposits may not differ substantially from non-temple assemblages; in these cases it is often the context, associated structural evidence and/or artefacts which define them as offerings (King 2005). The predominance of sheep/goat in layer 2 is of interest, as it exceeds that in the wider settlement (Table 9.5). The relatively large number of newborn and juvenile animals may be indicative: one foetal, two newborn and 17 juvenile sheep make up *c* 37% of age groups represented (Gardner 1987, 70). The deposition of newborn and juvenile lambs, or part carcasses thereof, is a feature of temple/shrine deposits elsewhere in Southern England (King 2005; Hambleton 2008). High proportions of young animals may also derive from culling within dairy flocks; economic necessities and ritual motivations are not necessarily exclusive and may not always be disentangled.

The element distribution, including a high proportion of loose teeth (in particular from mandibles), distal tibiae and metapodia of sheep (and cattle) has been encountered in temple assemblages, often interpreted as waste from meat consumed elsewhere within or without the temple precincts. In our case whether such meat was destined for domestic consumption, feast or ritual offering is unknown. The relative abundance of horse and dog remains in the Silbury midden is not dissimilar to surrounding sites (Table 9.5), however the predominance of horse foot bones and teeth, and evidence for at least six dogs is of interest considering the known deposition of horse skulls and limbs and dogs elsewhere in pre-Roman and Roman England (Hambleton 2008; Maltby 2010).

The preponderance of sheep in the midden deposit is quite marked compared to the adjacent sites, though not dissimilar to Longstones Field (Table 9.5). This distribution contrasts with the cattle-dominated patterns for various Roman sites identified by King (1978), and by Maltby (1981) for Southern England, though there would have been local and regional variations (as recognised by Gardner 1987). The local chalkland environment would have provided good grazing for sheep and cattle and the presence, however limited, of woodland would have been favourable to both pig and cattle husbandry. The presence of roe and red deer bones suggests that these were available locally, and consequently that some woodland or tree cover must have been present. Nonetheless, the scarcity of wild animals (including wild fowl) indicates that hunting did not supplement the local diet to any great extent, or at least that their remains were not discarded in the ditch.

Iron Age and Roman activity on the mound

Nicola Hembrey and Vicky Crosby
Iron Age and Roman activity on the mound itself has proved elusive. This may be the result of Saxon and later activity causing the masking or destruction of evidence. Seven sherds of Late Iron Age pottery were recovered during the 2007/8 excavations on the summit; five sherds, all within the subsoil [4805], occur in a flint and grog-tempered fabric and derive from a single shouldered jar (Fig 9.5). The rim of this vessel is missing, however it is likely to be a bead-rim jar and consequently of mid-1st-century BC to mid–late 1st-century AD date. Two grog-tempered sherds are also likely to be pre-conquest in date.

A single flint and grog-tempered body sherd, with sooting deposits on the exterior, has been dated by fabric criteria alone to the late Iron Age/early Romano-British period (Marter Brown 2012; Table 9.6).

Some Roman objects and tile fragments have been found on the summit and close to the summit (*see below*), but it is possible that the tile was re-used in later periods. Re-use of Roman tile and brick in Saxon buildings may have had symbolic significance (Eaton 2000, 129–30). It is possible, however, that there was a Roman structure on the Hill. A Bronze Age round barrow (Barrow 5) at Irthlingborough, Northamptonshire, was used as a shrine with surrounding *temenos* throughout most of the Romano-British period, and there are several similar examples (Harding and Healy 2007, 196–8).

On the eastern slope of the Hill, Wilkinson (1867, 115) found 'a distinct semicircular space … hollowed out'. On a ledge inside this there was 'a deposit of wood ashes' and 'lying side by side … the blade of an iron clasp knife … and a small whetstone … having a hole, countersunk on both sides at the smaller end'. Although these objects have at times been described as Roman (*see* for example Leary and Field 2010, 155), they cannot be ascribed a secure Roman date. The knife blade fragment is non-diagnostic, and piercing of whetstones appears to be a post-Roman feature. No other finds were noted. This feature might be contemporary with the Saxon activity on the summit, but it could equally be later in date.

Only one artefact of a Roman date was found during the English Heritage watching brief on the summit of Silbury Hill in 2001; a coin of Constantine II, closely dated to AD 335–7, and identified by Sam Moorhead (British Museum)

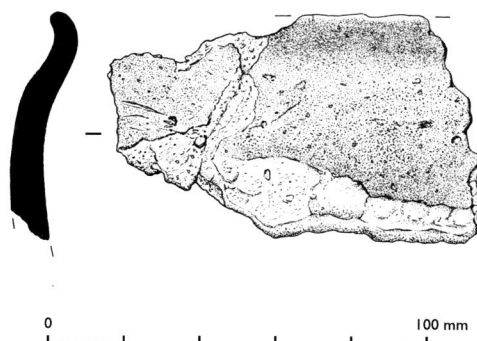

Fig 9.5
Shouldered jar, flint and grog-tempered fabric, late Iron Age, [4805], subsoil, SF numbers 8515, 8516, 8522 (2007).
(Chris Evans,
© English Heritage)

as a copper alloy *nummus* of Constantine II as Caesar (Fig 9.6). Stukeley also recorded the presence of Roman coins on the summit (Lukis 1887, 245; Leary and Field 2010, 155) and another coin was retrieved as part of the 1968–70 excavations (*see above*, and Moorhead 2011).

Several other Roman finds were recovered as part of the 1968–70 excavations on the Hill. A single brooch (SF 261) was recovered from Cutting 3 (Whittle 1997a, 21; *see* Fig 0.2), though the finds bag label reads 'steps cutting

Fig 9.6
Copper-alloy nummus of Constantine II dated to AD 335–7 (16/17mm; Die Axis 12) found on the summit of Silbury Hill in 2001.
(James O Davies,
© English Heritage)

Table 9.6: Pottery quantification by period/fabric

Period	Fabric	No of sherds	Weight
Prehistoric	Calcite-tempered	1	2
Late Iron Age/Early Romano–British	Flint/grog	6	89
Late Iron Age/Early Romano–British	Grog	2	7
Romano–British	Oxidised	3	7
Romano–British	Sandy	4	5
Romano–British	Shell-tempered	1	64
Medieval	Sandy	6	73
Medieval	Kennet Valley A	2	5
Medieval	Kennet Valley B	5	97
Medieval	Bath A	1	5
	Totals	**31**	**354**

Fig 9.7 (opposite)
Overall plan of Romano-
British activity around
Silbury Hill.
(Eddie Lyons, © English
Heritage; aerial
photography licensed to
English Heritage for PGA,
through NextPerspectives™).
Sources: magnetometer
survey interpretation,
Linford et al 2010, fig 25;
Powell et al 1996, fig 10;
wells and middens,
excavated before 1900,
Brooke and Cunnington,
1897; 1908 well,
Brooke 1910.

with 2 in a circle'. A brass penannular brooch of Hattat Type C (Hattat 1985), it is dated by its type and material to the 1st century AD or later. The brooch is formed of a single fragment of wire terminating in folded loops at either end, flattened at their base and its pin is missing (Alexander Keiller Museum records refer to it as a miniature bracelet) (Fig 9.4c).

Also found in the 'upper steps cut' layer 3 (cf Cutting 7) is a probable Roman floor tile fragment (bag number 1342), and SF 274, a Roman combed tile fragment from bag 1216 was found within 'upper steps cutting 2'. A further (un-numbered) small fragment of Roman flue tile was found within layer 2 of this cutting.

A tiny rim fragment of Roman greyware was recovered as SF 506 from topsoil around the entrance to the 1776 shaft as part of the 1968–70 excavations.

Evidence from the Later Silbury (2010) evaluation

Vicky Crosby and Nicola Hembrey
The extensive geophysical surveys offered the Later Silbury project a wide range of possibilities for evaluation. There were several constraints: the available resources meant we could not examine the stone buildings indicated by the ground-penetrating radar or fully excavate any wells found. In the field directly south of the Hill, there was a limited access period of three weeks. The section below presents a summary of the excavation results following assessment. Further details can be found in Crosby and Hembrey (2011 and 2013).

Three trenches excavated in the water meadow produced no Romano-British features, and surprisingly little Roman material of any kind. This may reflect changes made at the time the water meadows were established. The enclosure identified by Field (2002, 39–40) appears to be post-medieval (*see* Panel 9.3).

In the field directly south of the Hill, the geophysical surveys suggested a series of large sub-rectangular enclosure blocks lying either side of a trackway or minor road running south from the Roman road. Five evaluation trenches were sited to investigate one of the enclosure blocks and a smaller enclosure lying to its west, separated from it by another possible trackway (Fig 9.7). The archaeological deposits had been truncated by past ploughing, and features survived only where they cut into the chalk.

No surfaces remained and none of the features excavated produced evidence to indicate a prehistoric date (the small quantity of struck flint recovered was all from Roman or later contexts and suggests only low-key activity in the area). The Romano-British activity extended from the early/mid-2nd to at least the later 4th century AD.

An initial phase of land division dates to the early/mid-2nd century AD, with the establishment of the large enclosure (9003) and smaller enclosure (9004) to its west. The large enclosure was bounded by paired ditches except on the western side. The smaller of these did not show on the magnetic surveys (probably due to a lack of burnt material in its fills). It could represent an earlier phase of activity or a rapidly backfilled 'laying out feature'. Chalk was noted in part of the fill and may have been packing for a fence, later replaced by a line of postholes (structural group 9001) between the ditches. The smaller enclosure (9004) to the west had a single ditch. None of these ditches contained material later than the 2nd century AD, except for the larger ditch of 9003 facing the main trackway where the upper fills contained some possible 3rd-century pottery and a few 4th-century sherds.

The features identified within enclosure 9003 are not closely dated. Only the foundation trench of a building (9005) survived (represented on the magnetic survey by a staple-shaped positive anomaly). The building was probably of timber. The only possibly associated feature was a shallow irregular oval cut which contained two mid-4th-century coins. It might have been an internal feature, perhaps a truncated and disturbed posthole or post-pad cut, but it was not on the centre line of the building.

A large circular feature appears to have been a well (9006). Only its top fills were investigated, so the date of its construction and use are unknown. It is similar in size to the well excavated by Brooke (1910); comparing the description of the 1908 well's position with the survey suggests both were in similar locations within the enclosure and close to the trackway. An infant burial (9002) was found close to the well, and is undated. Both the building and the well are dated only by finds deposited after they were disused giving little information about their construction or period of use. The building contained late 4th-century pottery and coins in the backfill of its wall trench, while the upper fills of the well contained disturbed redeposited

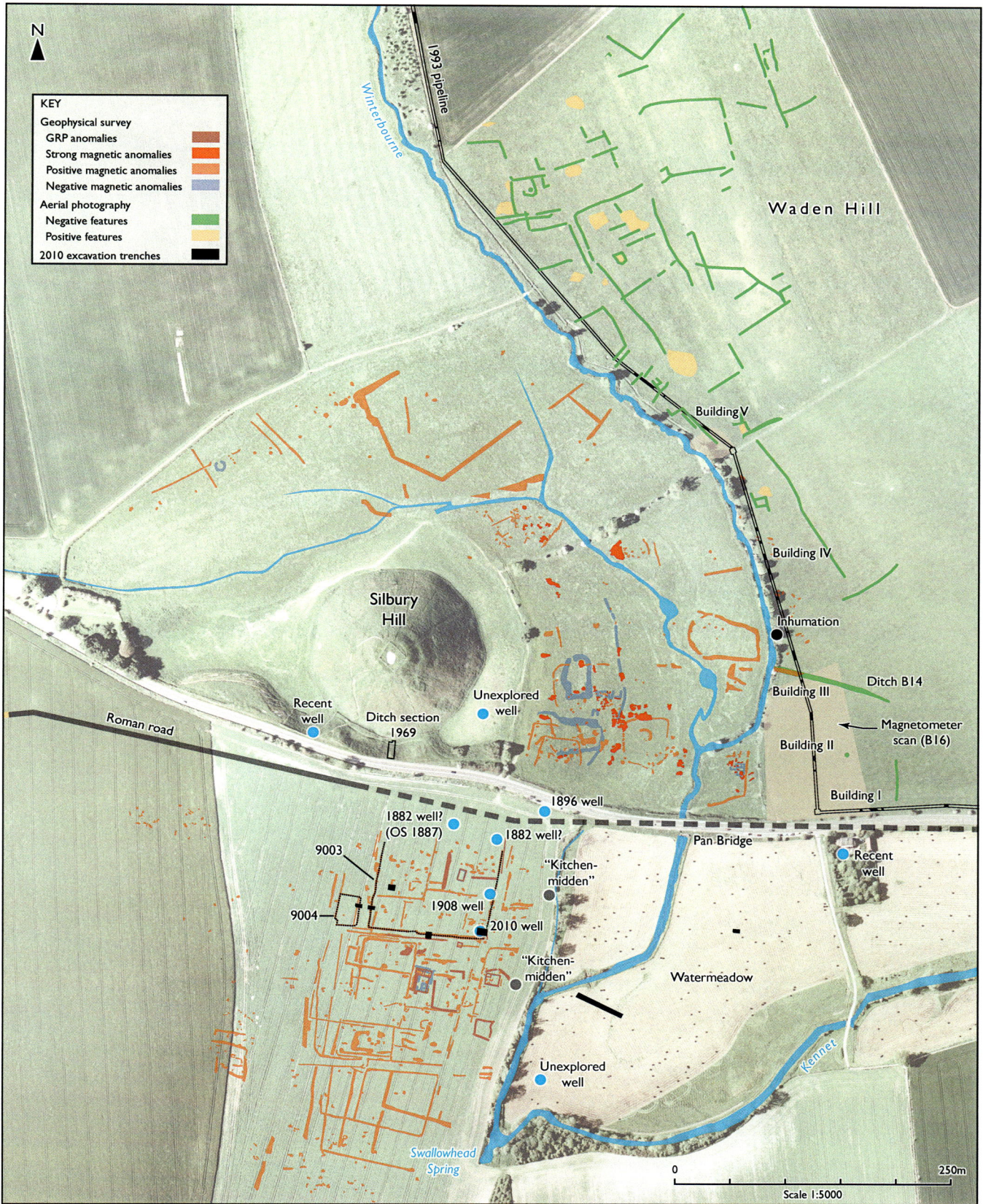

N

KEY

Geophysical survey
GRP anomalies
Strong magnetic anomalies
Positive magnetic anomalies
Negative magnetic anomalies
Aerial photography
Negative features
Positive features
2010 excavation trenches

Winterbourne

1993 pipeline

Waden Hill

Building V

Building IV

Silbury
Hill

Inhumation

Unexplored
well

Ditch B14

Building III

Recent
well

Ditch section
1969

Magnetometer
scan (B16)

Building II

Roman road

Building I

1896 well

1882 well?
(OS 1887)

1882 well?

Pan Bridge

Recent
well

9003

"Kitchen-
midden"

9004

1908 well

2010 well

"Kitchen-
midden"

Watermeadow

Kennet

Unexplored
well

Swallowhead
Spring

0   250m

Scale 1:5000

Panel 9.3 Water meadows around Silbury Hill

Martyn Barber, Vicky Crosby, David Field and Nicola Hembrey

The low-lying ground around the Silbury mound contains traces of a system of floated water meadows recorded as earthworks during survey. Unlike examples in the Kennet Valley further downstream, or further south along the River Avon (McOmish *et al* 2002), there is no uniformity or pattern to these. Rather they appear as a local response to the drainage problems of the immediate area, that is, the confluence of brooks and influence of the springs. Carriers both north and south of the road appear to fringe the higher ground, though no side carriers can be traced and it is conceivable that in part the system operated in a similar fashion to catchworks (Brown 2003). Both the ditch around Silbury Hill and the cistern were cut into by side drains as part of the system and this configuration may account, at least in part, for the atypical nature of the meadow system.

South of the A4 (Fig P9.3.1), a sub-rectangular enclosure (Field 2002) has been considerably plough-levelled but survives to a height of *c* 0.5m. Prior to excavation there was no evidence of date and while form and proximity to the Roman settlement allowed a possibility that it was of that period, a military pipeline appeared to cut across one corner. Proximity to the floated water meadow earthworks presented a further potential association, but excavations (*below*) did not produce clear evidence for a carrier, and it could instead be a stock enclosure of medieval or post medieval date.

Drainage and water meadow features around Silbury

The networks of drainage ditches and water meadows were also mapped from aerial photographs during the AWHSMP. Lidar has added a few additional ditches related to these networks, as well as some low earthwork banks most of which are presumably related to water management. Lidar has confirmed the presence of a sub-rectangular banked enclosure immediately north-west of Silbury. It appears to contain plough ridges. Lower, more spread banks to the north of the field boundary seem to be connected to this feature, which may owe its better definition to a changed alignment in the field boundary, which essentially removed this southernmost fragment from cultivation. Interestingly, some geophysical anomalies in this area may be related to this enclosure.

Excavation on the meadow to the southeast

Geophysical survey of two fields south of Silbury Hill at NGR SU101682 was undertaken in 2006 (Linford 2008; Linford *et al* 2010) and produced considerable detail of what was initially interpreted as part of the Roman settlement. A slightly raised plateau with a ditch around its base forms a 'tongue' of land between the Winterbourne and Kennet. The geophysical surveys produced a continuous high-resistance anomaly around the plateau, accompanied by a low-resistance ditch-type anomaly, and a line of regular-sized, discrete high resistance responses on the other side of the ditch towards the lower ground (Linford 2008, 13; Linford *et al* 2009, 12, fig 12). These appeared to relate to water management, but their interpretation and date remained unclear. Two trenches investigated the geophysics anomaly and the sub-rectangular enclosure referred to above as part of the 2010 evaluation. These are described in a further report (Crosby and Hembrey 2013). Trench 6 revealed the leat and bank of a catchwater system channelling water around the edge of the chalk plateau. The bank contained pot sherds dating to the period AD 1600–1800. The channel through the bank would have been blocked or opened as required to let water flow across the low ground adjacent to the river. A similar group of anomalies north of the road (Linford *et al* 2009, 11, figs 9 and 26) may relate to another part of this system.

In Trench 8, the boundary of the sub-rectangular earthwork enclosure consisted of a shallow ditch partly filled by the bank of light-coloured silty clay. Its purpose remains open to interpretation: it could be the slumped remains of a cob enclosure wall, or it may have supported a water meadow carrier, channelling water from the river via the bank seen running roughly NNE from the enclosure in the earthwork survey. The ditch does not seem to have been a water channel. The date is uncertain: 2nd-century AD sherds from the lower part of the bank may be residual material deriving from the subsoil cut by the ditch. Given the absence of Romano-British material from the ditch fill and topsoil, and the survival of the bank as a visible earthwork in a field which was probably considerably re-worked to create the water-meadow, a post-medieval date seems likely.

Origin and method of use of the system

The system appears to have been planned and implemented in conjunction with the Parliamentary Inclosure of the area that was announced in 1792 (WRO EA Avebury). A series of letters from Richard Hinckley, who was managing the estate, to Mrs Williamson, who was in Jamaica for an extended period, indicated that discussions regarding floating the meadows took place hand in hand with the

*Fig P9.3.1
Plan of the area of water meadows south of Silbury Hill.
(Eddie Lyons,
© English Heritage)*

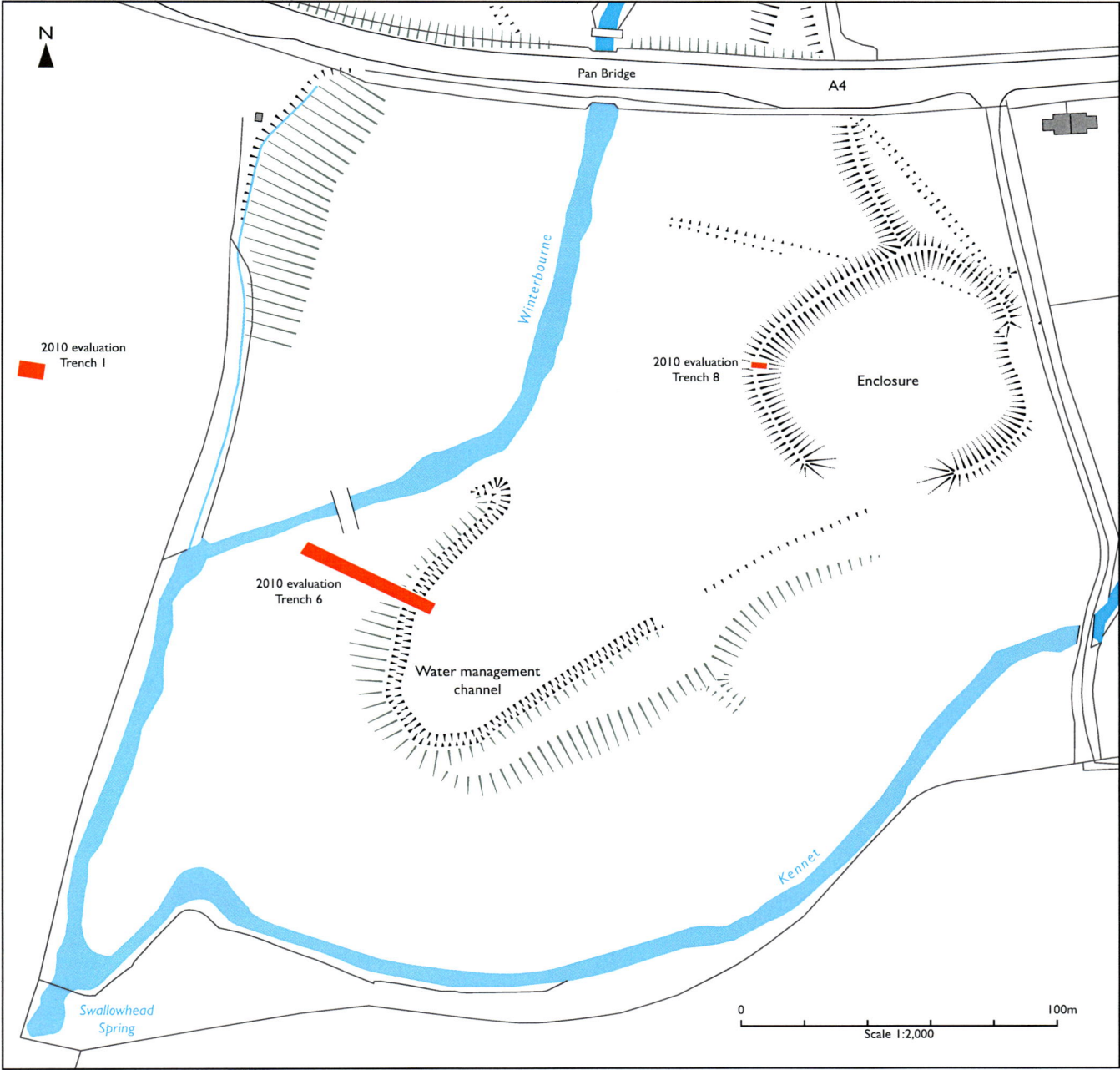

Inclosure Award process (WRO Estate Papers 184/6). The Commissioners instructed Hinckley to 'cleanse the river all down by South Meadow' and presumably the other land-owners were instructed likewise. The Award utilised a plan by B Haynes, surveyed in 1794, of the 'New Allotment and Exchanged lands in the Parish of Avebury …'. It depicts Silbury Hill bounded around the quarry ditch edge and labelled as owned by Adam Williamson. The water from the Beckhampton Brook was evidently channelled to flood the meadows during early spring, while the meadow to the north-west (Silbury Meadow) was divided between Peter Holford, James Sutton and the Duke of Marlborough, who shared

responsibility for repairing the hatches. The meadow to the east was retained by the Holford and Tanner families. The Commissioners instructed that the 'hatches and floodgates necessary to carry the above system of watering into effect shall be built and erected and for ever after kept in repair'. The respective owners were required to co-operate regarding use of the system and each should scour and clean the watercourses. Peter Holford could take the water for his exclusive use for three days from 1 November, after which he would close his hatches and the Duke of Marlborough would do likewise, followed in turn by the other owners, after which the procedure repeated itself.

late 4th-century pottery, a few fragments of hypocaust tile and the remains of another infant.

No structural evidence for craft activities or food processing was recovered. However, the upper fill of the enclosure ditch close to the well did indicate iron smithing nearby (Phelps in Crosby and Hembrey 2011). The assessment of the charred plant remains indicated spelt wheat and barley cultivation, but 'no evidence for exotics or unusual items which might reflect a ritual or high status aspect' (Pelling in Crosby and Hembrey 2011). The animal bone assemblage is dominated by cattle and sheep/goat, and contains smaller quantities of pig, dog, horse and fish bones, as well as micro-mammal and frog/toad bones (Table 9.5; Ayton in Crosby and Hembrey 2011).

Pottery makes up much of the artefact assemblage, with only a very small amount of ceramic building material present, as well as a larger amount of stone and worked flint. The assemblage of ceramic building material amounts to just 17 fragments of plain tile, box-flue tile and brick fragments, and there is one incomplete Forest of Dean Brownstone roof tile (Marter Brown in Crosby and Hembrey 2011).

The numbers of other artefacts recovered were also modest. Trench 1 yielded one iron buckle pin fragment, one iron probable hairpin, one possible and one probable copper alloy bracelet fragment, as well as one copper alloy cable-twisted bracelet fragment and a probable copper alloy toilet implement. One copper alloy T-shaped brooch was also found within Trench 1, and one copper alloy disc-shaped gold-leafed brooch was found within Trench 4. One copper

alloy probable finger-ring bezel was found within Trench 4.

A small assemblage of iron cleats was found, either from the soles or heels of boots, or used for fastening wood (Manning 1985, 131). 156 iron hobnails or parts thereof were also recovered, as were 79 iron nails or parts thereof, mostly Manning Type 1 (1985, 134–5), and 16 fragments of miscellaneous structural ironwork.

Single fragments of three different fine glass vessels (clear green, blue-green and colourless) of a type very similar to those found within the external ditch in 1969 were also recovered (see above). In addition, a saddle quern fragment (in quartz conglomerate sourced from the Forest of Dean) and fragments from two ferruginous sandstone whetstones were found within Trench 1.

There was a small assemblage of 17 coins, all of late Roman date within the date range AD 260–402, with all but two falling within AD 330–402. The profile of this assemblage is not dissimilar from the 96 coins recovered from the external ditch in 1969; in both groups the House of Constantine coins of 330–48 are the second largest group with the House of Valentinian coins of 364–78 providing the largest group. The high proportion of coins of the House of Theodosius 388–402 in Later Silbury is not matched by Silbury Ditch, but is by one of the Silbury wells excavated by Brooke. It is notable that almost 60 per cent are contemporary copies (Table 9.4; Moorhead in Crosby and Hembrey 2011; Moorhead 2011).

The pottery, very typical of a modest rural settlement, mainly comprises 'local' coarse wares and is dominated by jars. A few sherds of Samian and two pieces of Baetican olive oil amphora from southern Spain are the only foreign imports. Traded wares include further vessels from the same regional sources as those from the 1968–70 assemblage to which can be added South-West black burnished wares and Alice Holt grey ware. The local wares feature several large Savernake ware storage jars and various products of the North Wiltshire industries, including one glazed piece of early 2nd-century date (Timby in Crosby and Hembrey 2011).

The evidence obtained from the Later Silbury project 2010 evaluation is somewhat modest, due to the small scale of the evaluation undertaken and the excavation of features mostly associated with the periphery of enclosures, rather than the large buildings. It nonetheless provides an insight into the nature of the settlement, which is distinguished perhaps by its ordinariness, despite its proximity to Silbury Hill. As a small-scale investigation of an extensive settlement, interpretation is best made in the context of a summary of the Romano-British evidence for the area around Silbury Hill (*see below*). However, it is notable that nothing in these results indicates ritual or high-status activity. A fuller discussion of the evaluation and its context forms part of the publication of the Later Silbury project (Crosby and Hembrey 2013).

The Romano-British settlement at Silbury

Vicky Crosby, Polydora Baker and Nicola Hembrey

The existence of a Romano-British settlement near Silbury Hill (Fig 9.7) has been known since Wilkinson noted possible surface traces of a 'dwelling of some kind' and excavated a 'kitchen-midden' containing three small bronze coins, an iron stylus, part of a pair of shears, several large-headed nails and other pieces of iron, as well as much pottery, building material, whetstones, bone and oyster shell, and a fragment of human bone, while trying to trace the line of the Roman road east of the mound (1867, 117–18). Brooke and Cunnington excavated a well in 1896 and noted the presence of other wells and 'kitchen-middens' from which they inferred 'a halting place for troops' (1897, 171). Further small-scale discoveries and investigations followed,

including a second well (Brooke 1910) and an inhumation burial (Evans 1966). Excavation of the external ditch of Silbury Hill by Atkinson between 1968 and 1970 produced a further Roman midden deposit (*see above*).

A key increase in knowledge came with the excavations of the 'Winterbourne Romano-British settlement' on the line of the Kennet Valley Foul Sewer Pipeline in 1993 (Powell *et al* 1996) and Corney's discussion of their results in the context of aerial photographs taken in the dry summer of 1995 (Corney 1997a). The 'Winterbourne' section of the Silbury settlement lies on the west slope of Waden Hill, east and north-east of Silbury Hill. It has a rectilinear layout, with 'buildings set in rectangular ditched compounds laid out either side of the track or street' (Corney 1997a, 139, fig 1). The wall footings excavated suggested the stone buildings could have been substantial (Powell *et al* 1996, 31–4, 56). Corney suggested this was a linear 'small town', and raised the possibility that it was a religious focus, ideas developed in his 2002 paper (Corney 2002).

The geophysical surveys of 2005–8 and subsequent Later Silbury evaluation in 2010 indicate a similar rectilinear layout of ditched enclosures aligned on a trackway running south from the Roman road. The two stretches of trackway do not join the road in the same place, but together could have formed a significant local north–south route, sharing a river crossing with the road.

These two instances of extensive survey data, coupled with small-scale excavation which aids its interpretation, clearly increase our understanding of the settlement. Each also provides a context for some of the earlier finds; the possible building noted by Wilkinson (1867, 117) is probably 'Winterbourne' Building I (Powell *et al* 1996, 27), and the well excavated by Brooke in 1908 lies within the area of the geophysical surveys.

Both the structural evidence and the finds from the modern excavations are noticeably 'ordinary' – typical of a rural settlement with nothing to indicate either a ritual focus or a small town. This contrasts with the results of the earlier excavations nearer the road, reflecting variation within the settlement. Stone buildings were recorded in the 1996 excavations and the geophysical surveys in 2005–8 (*above*), but the occupation was not dense, although timber buildings may fill out the picture (one was found in 2010). There were no finds of painted wall plaster, though flue tile fragments were found in 2010 and the bricks found at 'Winterbourne' could have come from hypocaust *pilae*. There is evidence for iron smithing and crop processing.

However, both excavations were small-scale, and the 2010 evaluation deliberately avoided the stone buildings indicated in the geophysical surveys. Excavation of the larger and apparently more elaborate stone building (anomaly m 41 and gpr 5; Linford *et al* 2009, 8, 14, figs 25, 27) would doubtless indicate occupation of a significantly different nature and status.

It is important to acknowledge the gaps in the evidence. The Romano-British settlement at Silbury is accepted as a 'roadside settlement' but the information we have for the nature of the road frontage is limited to the geophysical surveys in the field east of the Hill (*see below*) and the 'Winterbourne' results further east, where stone and building materials from a ditch 55 metres to the east indicate buildings on the road frontage (Powell *et al* 1996, 56–7). Wilkinson failed to trace the course of the road 'as it passes over the infant Kennet, and up the next hill' (1867, 117), and it may lie under the present road (its line is known a short distance further the east, at West Kennett).

South and west of Silbury Hill, the line of the Roman road deviates from the A4, but the 'magnetic noise' from the pipelines in the magnetic survey has masked any roadside settlement which survives. The current road will also have destroyed evidence. If the settlement did extend along the road west of the mound, it will have suffered badly from past plough damage, as is clear from Wilkinson's account of locating the road and its ditches (1867). He noted no indications of buildings. However, it is possible the roadside settlement did lie mainly to the east of the mound. If, as Corney suggested, Silbury was the site of a roadside *mutatio* (1997a, 141), the evidence is only likely to survive if it lay in that area.

The 2010 evaluation trenches in the water meadow produced no Romano-British features and surprisingly little Romano-British material. Taken with the evidence for the catchwork water meadow system (which probably also extended north of the road near the Pan Bridge (Fig 9.7)), this suggests that much of the evidence here may have been removed. The drain at the bottom of the field south of the Hill and truncation of the slope also suggests that changes to ground surfaces have occurred.

The Roman road must have crossed the Winterbourne/Kennet (*see above*), but no evidence for the crossing survives. The course of the river in the Romano-British period is not known, and it may have moved within the low-lying area between the hill slopes and the tongue of chalk in the water meadow. East of the Hill, the river has truncated a Roman burial (Evans 1966, 97). Possible palaeochannels can be seen on the geophysical surveys (Linford *et al* 2009, 8 and fig 25: anomalies m42 and m44). It is not certain exactly where the Swallowhead Spring would have emerged in the Roman period. There may have been significant changes due to post-medieval water management (*see* Panel 9.3).

The area north of the Roman road, east of the mound and west of the Winterbourne seems to be different in nature from the other two areas. The geophysical surveys indicate a group of enclosures rather than a rectilinear layout, though some of the enclosures are on the same alignment as the trackway south of the road. It is possible that this area formed a ritual focus (*see* Panel 9.2). The material from the midden (layer 2) of the external ditch of Silbury Hill probably derived from this area, though the upper layers could have come from destruction of roadside deposits during the lowering of the turnpike road in the 18th century as referred to by Pass (1887, 247). The excavators believed that the well excavated in 1896 lay within this area, between the Roman and the 19th-century roads (Brooke and Cunnington 1897, 166).

This well produced a large assemblage of objects including a quern stone, a large iron double hook, three massive Romano-British pitcher handles, one blade from a set of shears, a small iron stylus, part of a pillar, an iron cleat, a simple bronze finger ring or earring, a bronze beam, a tiny notched fragment of a small pair of scales, broken tiles and several large sarsens and flints. It also contained two bronze coins (Arcadius, AD 383–95 and Theodosius, AD 408–50) as well as animal bone, oyster and snail shells. The report lists the following species: deer (including an antler pick), fox, pig, horse etc (Brooke and Cunnington 1897, 167–9).

There has been an increasing recognition of Romano-British ritual use of prehistoric monuments, especially following Williams' important assessment of the evidence (1998b). A ritual focus east of Silbury Hill would fit this pattern. Within the World Heritage Site, the Romano-British features from the small-scale excavation at Stonehenge suggested that reconsideration of the material from earlier interventions is needed (Darvill and Wainwright 2009, 14–15); the Roman coins from the West Kennet long barrow (Piggott 1962, 55–6; Moorhead 2011) are another example.

In contrast, the new evidence south of the road provides a different setting for the well excavated by Brooke in 1908 and the kitchen-middens, placing them within a settlement context. From the measurements given, the well lies just west of the trackway within an enclosure which also contained a stone building (anomaly m39/gpr7, Linford *et al* 2009, 8, 14, figs 25, 27; Fig 9.7). With the exception of a substantial number of Roman coins (Moorhead 2011), this well produced a less impressive finds assemblage than the well excavated in 1896: various bronze relics, beads, stone building material including the base of a column, iron nails, an iron bucket-handle clip, pottery, glass and oyster shell. The vertebrate remains listed are deer (including antler picks), dog, sheep, ox, pig and rat (Brooke 1910). The stone building could have been the source of the building stones (moulded corbel, column base, roof tiles) and other finds from this well. The well found in 2010 was in a similar location, within the enclosure and close to the trackway, and about 30m south of the 1908 well. The location of these wells suggests their primary purpose was water supply.

It is worth reconsidering, at this point, the suggestion that the Silbury wells represent a ring of ritual shafts around the mound (Corney 2001, 29; Leary and Field 2010). Only two of the wells shown in Brooke and Cunnington's figure (1897) had been excavated and dated, and Brooke (1910) believed that the well excavated in 1908 was one of these. The other wells shown are 'unexplored' or used 'within living memory' (Brooke 1910, 166), and further wells are shown on the 19th-century OS 1:2500 maps in the gardens of houses along the road to the east. The suggestion by Pollard and Reynolds (2002, 178) that the wells around Silbury Hill are unlikely to

be domestic due to the proximity of the Kennet, Winterbourne and the Swallowhead Spring probably underestimates the importance of wells for regular water supply, particularly in the drier summer months, as well as the need for uncontaminated water in a settlement set within an agrarian landscape. The climate at this time was slighter warmer than the present day with relatively drier summers (Dark and Dark 1997, 18–19). Hydrological conditions were probably broadly similar to the present day, with the Winterbourne dry for part of the year (*see also* Chapter 6).

There are numerous examples of ritual use of wells and shafts in the Romano-British period. Good examples include Folly Lane, Verulamium (Niblett 1999, 82–90, 412–15), Swan Street, Southwark (Beasley 2006), Jordon Hill, Weymouth (Lewis 1966, 44–5; Manning 1972, 247) and Baldock (Stead and Rigby 1986, 44–7). However, where ritual deposits can be recognised, there are still several possible interpretations (*see* Table 9.7). Closing deposits of 'ritual' nature are commonplace in wells and pits evidently dug for practical purposes throughout Roman Britain (for example Fulford 2001, 215). It is also necessary to be cautious about the suggestion that ritual use of wells and shafts was a tradition during the Iron Age. Webster's re-evaluation of the evidence presented by Ross (1968) and Wait (1985) found little securely dated later Iron Age evidence for this, and she suggested it was a new and specifically Romano-British practice (Webster 1997, 136–7, 140–1). The deep pits from the 'Winterbourne settlement' are interesting in this context, but there is little except for an almost complete chicken skeleton from one pit to suggest any ritual activity (Powell *et al* 1996, 34–5, 53).

This raises the issue of what we imply by 'ritual' – there is a danger that recognition of ritual permeating the domestic leads to the term itself becoming almost meaningless. As Fulford has shown, ritual behaviour in secular contexts

Table 9.7: Models for considering ritual deposition in wells and shafts

	Primary purpose of well/shaft ritual	*Primary purpose of well practical*
Primary ritual deposition of material	Shaft or well specifically dug for ritual activity	Well with ritual 'closing deposits'
Secondary ritual deposition of material	Shaft specifically dug to receive redeposited ritual material (the favissa concept)	Well used to receive redeposited ritual material – note that other cut features such as ditches and pits were also used in this way.

(as demonstrated by structured deposits) was both prevalent and varied throughout the Romano-British period, in cities and small towns as much as in the countryside (2001, 213–16). To investigate the ritual significance of Silbury Hill in the Romano-British period, we need to look for something distinct from the normal ritual of a rural settlement or small town. One approach is to try to distinguish ritual integrated into domestic life from ritual separated from it in some way – ritual with a separate location or involving a differently composed group of people. The area east of the mound may provide this evidence. It can be suggested that at Silbury there was both a ritual focus in the area east of the mound, and a wider area where ritual was of the mundane and 'everyday' variety embedded in the domestic and agricultural cycle.

The only adult burial known from the settlement was observed in exposed deposits in the bank of the Winterbourne; the head had been removed by the stream (Evans 1966). The burial was of a male and finds from the grave included later Romano-British pottery and 30 hobnails at the feet. The sherds, while small, were noticeably fresher than the numerous abraded sherds from the overlying layers.

While there are exceptions, the siting of burials in Roman Britain does show some consistent patterns for different types of site (Esmonde Cleary 2000). For towns and some larger small towns, cemeteries were typically sited outside the town and alongside the roads, while other small towns often had burials in groups in the 'backlands' of settlement enclosures, away from the road and close to boundary ditches (Esmonde Cleary 2000, 129). The association with boundary ditches is also seen at villas and other rural settlements. The 'Winterbourne' burial lay close to the Kennet Valley pipeline excavation, in particular to ditch 164 (anomaly B14). This was a substantial boundary, 9.5m wide and identified from air photographs as at least 100m long; the ditch was open until at least the mid-3rd century AD (Powell *et al* 1996, 27–30, 37–8, figs 10 and 13). The burial may have been part of a cemetery lying away from the road and north of the boundary (whose line may have persisted long after the ditch had silted up). Cemeteries are rarely associated closely with temples (Esmonde Cleary 2000, 133–4), and if Silbury Hill was venerated in the Roman period, it is probably unlikely to have been used for burial. Robinson (2001, 147) made mention of 'a miniature vessel and group of metal rings' from the south of Silbury Hill, although these objects have not been located by the authors, and are not in the Devizes Museum.

Silbury has yet to produce any high-status or unusual burials such as the three drum-shaped tombs on Overton Down. These contained cremations dated to the early 2nd century AD and accompanied by copper alloy objects, which although heat affected had clearly been of fine quality (Smith and Simpson 1964). Fowler has suggested the tombs may have been associated with the probable villa at Headlands, from which they could have been visible (2000b, 59). If this is the case, it may be significant that high-status burials were associated with a villa rather than situated in the outskirts of the settlement at Silbury.

The two recent excavations were limited in scope – a watching brief and a small-scale evaluation which avoided the areas where large masonry buildings were known. The area immediately east of the Hill where a ritual focus is suspected has not had any modern excavation, and the area alongside the Roman road has suffered from ploughing, later road building and the insertion of government oil pipelines, which also affected the magnetic surveys. Interpretations therefore must be tentative.

The settlement has no known Iron Age antecedent. Pottery from both excavations indicates a start date early in the Romano-British period (late 1st century or early 2nd century) and occupation continuing into the later 4th or early 5th century AD. The earlier features dated in the 'Winterbourne settlement' are close to the road, so it is possible the settlement expanded to the north, but the dating evidence is limited (Powell *et al* 1996, 48, 56). The uniform appearance of the enclosure blocks south of the road might suggest they were set out together in the early 2nd century AD.

The Roman occupation at Silbury continued until the end of the 4th century AD and probably into the 5th. The latest pottery from both recent excavations dates to the later 4th century or beyond (Timby, in Crosby and Hembrey 2011, 31; and 2013; Powell *et al* 1996, 48, 57). Moorhead (2011) lists coins of Reece's Issue Period 21 (AD 388–402) from the wells excavated in 1897 and 1908 and the Silbury Hill external ditch, as well as from the 2010 evaluation. No organic-tempered pottery or distinctively 5th century finds have been recorded from the excavations. This contrasts with the evidence from the Fyfield and Overton Down project. At settlement ODXII, late Roman coins and 5th-century glass bottles and tableware 'present a convincing picture of activity ... and relative wealth into the 5th century' (Fowler 2000b, 229). Fowler suggests the Headlands complex also continued in use, based on three or four possible 'timber buildings of post-Roman form' identified from air photographs and the 5th- and 6th-century AD material which accompanied the secondary burials at the Overton Down Roman tombs (Fowler 2000b, 230).

It seems clear that Silbury can be regarded as a 'small town', but as Burnham notes, this has become rather a 'catch-all category' (1995, 10). His review illustrates the need to consider the evidence for different classes of activity at individual sites. Using his classification based on structural and functional indicators, the present evidence suggests Silbury lies at the lower end of the 'middle order settlements'. It is likely to have comprised linear settlement along the road and the trackways running north and south from it, possibly with a specialist religious function and a considerable emphasis on agriculture. The regular enclosures south of the road and either side of the trackway seem unlikely to indicate a street grid plan layout. The rural settlements on Overton Down also developed in a 'rectilinear grid plan perpetuated over some four centuries' (Fowler 2000b, discussion). Burnham and Wacher (1990, 17) note the frequent occurrence of buildings, usually domestic, set in large plots and often with a range of agricultural features.

Strip buildings along the road frontage can be important, indicating shops, workshops and specialised activities (Burnham 1995, 10), but evidence for the road frontage is largely lacking from Silbury (see above). The 'Winterbourne' settlement Building 1, close to a possible roadside ditch (115), may be of this type, but only one stretch of wall was investigated (Powell et al 1996, 31, 37). The magnetometer scan suggested there remains potential for recovering evidence for roadside activity in that area (B16; Powell et al 1996, 30 and fig 9).

Burnham notes that small towns often have a 'surprisingly restricted range' of building types, and that 'most of the Romanised buildings developed away from the central area of the sites, reflecting their secondary importance to the plan and the settlement's function' (1995, 9). At Silbury the picture is clearly incomplete,

but the substantial buildings identified on the air photographs by Corney (1997a, fig 1) and the two more complex buildings (gpr anomalies 5 and 7) shown by the ground penetrating radar survey (Linford et al, 2009 14 and fig 27) are set well back from the road. These buildings (and the simpler rectilinear structure gpr anomaly 6) and their enclosures could be agricultural complexes. Only excavation would resolve the question of function. Burnham has noted the increasing evidence for the importance of agriculture at most small towns (1995, 10), and Fowler (2000a, 228) has suggested there is likely to be a villa at Silbury.

The lack of defences or a defended strongpoint at Silbury contrasts with the enclosed small towns of *Verlucio* (Corney 2001, 29–30) and *Cunetio* (Corney 1997b), and it seems more likely that local administrative functions, were based there. Silbury could have had a *mutatio* – but identifying it would be difficult due to 'an almost complete ignorance of what we are looking for' (Burnham and Wacher 1990, 38). The term *mutatio* may in any case imply the obligation of a settlement to provide for the needs of official travellers rather than the presence of any purpose-built accommodation (Black 1995, 12–13 and 89–90).

For the ritual aspect, there are possible parallels with the earlier phases at Nettleton, where a circular temple built in the later 1st century AD was interpreted as a roadside shrine on the Fosse Way to Bath (Wedlake 1982). This temple was also close to a river crossing and springs. There was evidence for late Iron Age activity and Wedlake (1982, 99) suggested that the springs may already have had ritual significance by then. Robinson has queried why Silbury Hill should have been singled out in this way. He suggested that its location adjacent to a major road provides the answer: the possible temple was built 'as much as a wayside shrine as a temple to the veneration of a prehistoric monument' (2001, 162). Despite some well-known examples, ritual reuse of prehistoric monuments as shrines or temples is not common in Roman Britain, and where evident generally follows a lengthy period where there is no evidence for ritual activity (Williams 1998b, 72–3, 76). Perhaps surprisingly, it seems to be more unusual in Britain than in other areas of the Western Roman Empire. A wide range of possible explanations can and has been postulated, but Williams suggests that 'over the long term, ancient structures may have held an important place in the construction of local and regional identities in Roman Britain' (Williams 1998b, 77). The instances of re-use as discussed by Williams may have different roots and motivations to the cases where a Roman ritual site develops from a later Iron Age religious focus. This points to the difference between Silbury and sites such as Nettleton, and again raises the question of whether there was an Iron Age ritual focus associated with Silbury Hill or the Swallowhead Spring.

Saxon Silbury

David Field, Jim Leary, Nicola Hembrey with Vicky Crosby

There are two known foci of early Saxon activity close to Silbury. The settlement at Avebury lay outside the henge to its south-west towards the Winterbourne, and Gillings and Pollard suggest it may have started as an off-shoot from the Silbury settlement (2004, 104 and fig 9.12). The site is mostly unpublished, but is described by Pollard and Reynolds (2002, 192–8). The settlement, which may have included four sunken-featured buildings and a pit with two phases of hearths (but *see* Last 2002, 10, 14). Two of the buildings were dated by 6th-century glass beads. Another nearby settlement is suggested by early or mid-Saxon organic-tempered pottery from the upper fills of features in enclosure 2 at the West Kennet Palisaded Enclosures (Draper 2006, 144; Pollard and Reynolds 2002, 216–18). The Saxon material from Whittle's excavations at West Kennet remains unpublished, but over 200 sherds were recovered (Whittle 1997a, tables 26–7). A natural channel produced grass-tempered sherds of 5th- or 6th-century AD date, and a few post-Roman or later ditches were noted in the area of palisade enclosure 1 (Whittle 1997a, 86), though mid to late Saxon and medieval activity has been demonstrated by subsequent excavations in this area.

There has been no investigation at Beck-hampton, which by Domesday was a reasonably substantial settlement with four villagers, seven smallholders and five cottages eligible for tax (Thorn and Thorn 1979). The presence of slight earthworks coupled with regressive map analysis indicates that Beckhampton village may once have reached closer to Silbury Hill than it does today. Ogilby's map of the London to Bristol road (Ogilby 1675) depicted Silbury Hill as a steep conical mound, unfortunately without further detail, with the road curving around it,

but two local side roads form junctions almost opposite the monument (the line of one of these still visible on the ground as a soil mark) one of which is marked 'to ye Devizes'. Buildings are depicted on either side of the road between the mound and the site of the present Beckhampton roundabout.

There is some indication that Saxon set-tlement occurs on the fringes of existing estates (Swanton and Fowler 2001, 27–8, 50) and these examples might fit that pattern. In the case of the Roman settlement at Silbury this makes some sense in terms of a potential shift to Beckhampton or to East/West Kennett.

The precise role that the Hill played in these developments is unclear. Traces of early medieval activity on the summit are limited but significant. Although disturbance of early medieval archaeological deposits by a series of historically attested events, including that of archaeological excavation (*see* Chapters 1 and 10), obscures earlier traces and has made the identification of them difficult. This is equally true of the visible features on the summit as much as those excavated.

Excavations on the summit: the medieval and later evidence

Jim Leary

Two small trenches were excavated on the summit in 2001 (measuring 3m x 1.5m and 4m x 1.5m) and a larger one in 2007 (measuring 5m x 3m). These were excavated to evaluate material being eroded into the crater and to answer questions about the prehistoric phases of the mound (*see* Chapter 2). However, a series of later features were also recorded cutting the prehistoric deposits, some of which undoubtedly represent postholes, whilst others had an amorphous appearance, suggesting disturbance caused by burrowing animals, and the digging of tree pits and associated root action. These features are described below.

Medieval activity from the mound (Phase 17)

Three possible postholes were recorded on a north-north-west to south-south-east alignment in the north-west corner of the 2007 excavation trench. Cut [4842], which measured 0.43m wide and 0.4m deep, was only seen in section (and therefore not shown in Fig 9.8). The irregular nature of its sides suggests that it could also be interpreted as animal activity, although it aligns with other putative postholes.

Alongside this was cut [4870], a much more convincing posthole, which had both a diameter and depth of 0.65m although it extended beyond the limit of excavation to the west and therefore was not fully excavated (Fig 9.8). Just to the south-east of this was another possible posthole [4831], which measured 0.65m in diameter and 0.56m deep.

These three possible postholes were all replaced by similar postholes. Feature [4842] was cut by [4825], a sub-square feature in the north-west corner of the trench, extending beyond the excavated area (Fig 9.8). This feature measured 0.5m wide as seen, and 0.3m deep, and had chalk blocks at the base possibly representing post-packing. Posthole [4870] was cut by feature [4833], an oval-shaped feature with steeply sloping regular sides and measuring 0.86m long, 0.65m wide and 0.51m deep (Fig 9.8). Although damaged by animal disturbance (cut [4827], which contained badger and fox bones; one of the badger bones showed evidence for butchery – Worley this chapter), posthole [4831] was cut by feature [4823], another possible posthole, which measured 0.48m in diameter and only 0.16m deep (Fig 9.8). As with the earlier features, these three postholes ([4825], [4833] and [4823]) are aligned north-north-west to south-south-east, and their close association with one another, and the fact that all three seem to have replaced earlier similar features, supports the interpretation that they represent the fragmentary remains of postholes.

Recorded on the eastern side of the trench, and also on a north-north-west to south-south-east alignment, were three further possible postholes, all of which had been truncated on the eastern side by Atkinson's Cutting 3. Feature [4850] (fill [4849]) was irregular in plan measuring 0.42m by 0.29m and 0.36m deep; feature [4852] (fill [4851]) was more regular, and on the whole, a lot more convincing as a posthole, measuring 0.52m in diameter and 0.38m deep; possible posthole [4854] (fill [4853]) had a diameter of 0.42m and a depth of 0.37m and was circular in plan (Fig 9.8).

A further possible posthole or post-pit was recorded in the central area of the trench. This was recorded as [4858], a large oval feature which measured 0.9m long, 0.69m wide and 0.36m deep and contained a chalk block and fragment of sarsen on the bottom, possibly used as post-packing (Fig 9.8). This pit seemed to cut a patch of disturbed ground possibly caused by animal activity (cut [4872]).

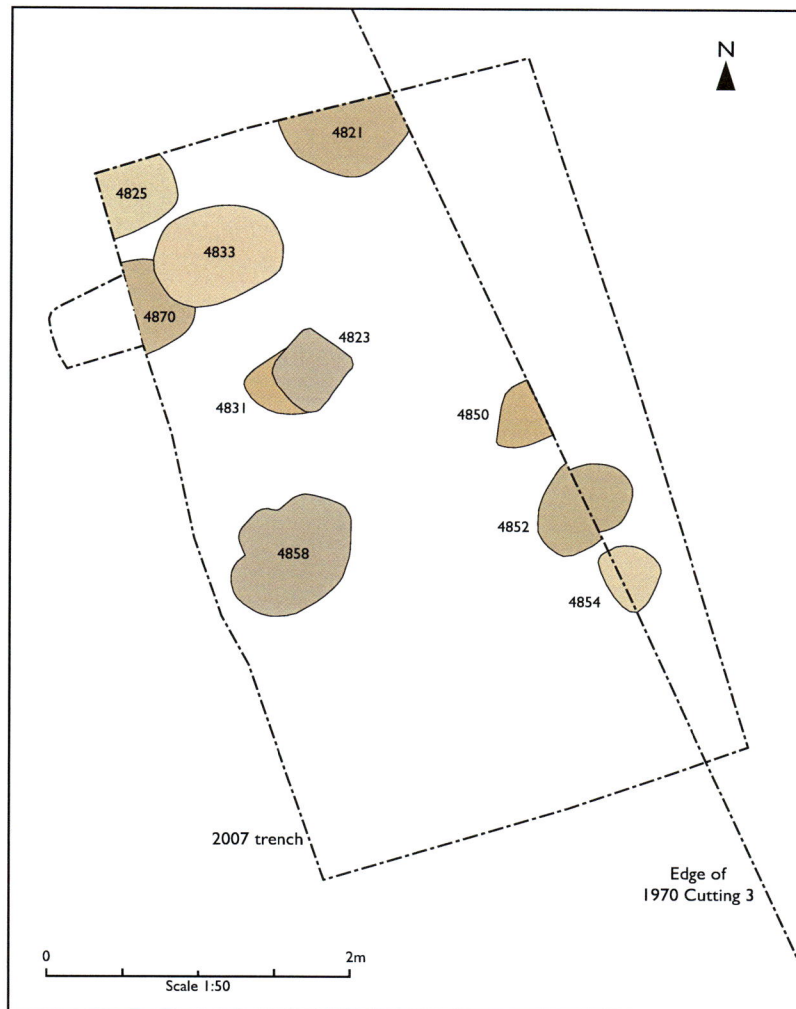

The most substantial feature recorded from this phase on the summit, however, was posthole [4821] (Figs 9.8, 9.9 and 9.10); this was 0.98m deep and had a diameter of 0.87m as seen, although it continued beyond the limit of excavation to the north and was cut by Atkinson's Cutting 3 (cut [4803]) to the east (indeed it would have been clearly visible to the 1968–70 team in their western section – see Fig 9.10). Had the full extent of this posthole been seen in plan, it is estimated that the diameter would have been at least 1m. It was filled with light greyish-brown silty clay ([4820]) and packed at the base with pieces of broken sarsen stone – presumably pieces re-used from the prehistoric deposits. Two small and residual late Iron Age grog-tempered pottery sherds were recovered from this fill (SF 8518 and SF 8519) (Marter Brown 2012), as well as residual flint flakes (Bishop Chapter 3) and fragments of animal

Fig 9.8
Plan of possible medieval features in the 2007 trench on the summit.
(Eddie Lyons,
© English Heritage)

Fig 9.9
Posthole [4821] after
excavation.
(Duncan Stirk,
© English Heritage)

from the large posthole (*see* Marshall *et al* Chapter 4).

Two large features were recorded opposite one another on the northern and southern side of the collapsed area on the summit in 2008. These were both only recorded in section and therefore their full extent was not seen. On the northern side was feature [4878], which measured 3.02m east west and 1.11m deep, and next to this was a small posthole [4880]. On the southern side another pit was visible in the facing section. This was recorded as [4876] and measured 5.25m wide (although possibly incorporating an adjacent feature) and 1.39m deep. The secondary fill of this feature contained medieval ceramics indicating a date of 11th to 13th century (Marter Brown this chapter; 2012), as well as residual struck flint. Both putative pits had a distinctive V-shaped profile, far more like a ditch profile than a pit, and it is not inconceivable, since they lie opposite one another, that they form part of a ditch across the top of the mound.

All the above features were heavily disturbed and many of the artefacts and ecofacts may be either residual or intrusive, as indicated by badger bones, which are distributed across Phases 16, 17 and 20.1 (Worley, this chapter). Other than the three radiocarbon dates (one from posthole [4821] and two from pit [15]) and pottery from pit [4876], little datable material was recovered from the fills of the features and therefore the placing of them within the medieval period is speculative. However, general medieval activity is indicated by the number of finds of this date recovered from the topsoil and subsoil on the summit (*see* Hembrey, this chapter).

During a watching brief in 2001, when fence posts were inserted on the summit, a few fragments of late 12th- or early 13th-century pottery were recovered (from [16], [17] and [18]) (Marter Brown, this chapter; 2012),

bones, including a butchered pig tarsal (Worley, this chapter). A pig pre-maxilla was also recorded from this fill and was submitted for radiocarbon dating. This provides a *terminus post quem* for the infilling of the posthole of cal AD 890–1030 (Marshall *et al*, Chapter 4). This posthole was recorded cutting a long sinuous feature, representing either an animal burrow or a root hole (cut [4829]), the fill of which contained a single prehistoric trimming flake as well as 16 animal bones, the majority of which were frog and toad and presumed intrusive (Worley, this chapter; Bishop Chapter 3).

Pit [15] (fill [9]) in Trench B (2001, see Fig 2.1 for trench location – pit outline not shown) contained a residual Romano-British coarseware sherd (Marter Brown 2012). The fill also contained a wheat grain and a fragment of Pomoideae charcoal, which were submitted for radiocarbon dating. Both gave consistent radiocarbon dates with the latest date OxA-20809 (cal AD 895–1025) providing the best estimate for the infilling (and consistent with the date

Fig 9.10
Section through the 2007
trench on the summit – the
medieval postholes can be
seen cutting the prehistoric
deposits.
(Eddie Lyons,
© English Heritage)

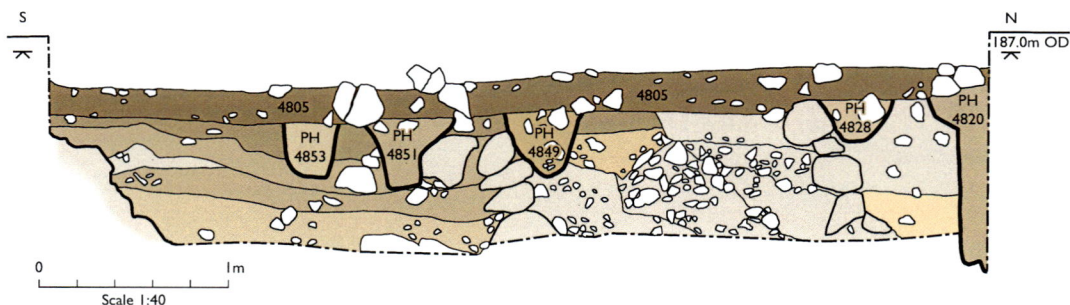

Table 9.8 Medieval (Phase 17) contexts

5	Disturbed interwall deposit	Summit (2001 Trench A)
9	Fill of pit [15]	Summit (2001 Trench B)
11	Interwall deposit	Summit (2001 Trench B)
15	Pit or posthole	Summit (2001 Trench B)
4820	Fill of posthole [4821]	Summit (2007 excavation)
4821	Large posthole	Summit (2007 excavation)
4822	Fill of poss posthole [4823]	Summit (2007 excavation)
4823	Poss shallow posthole	Summit (2007 excavation)
4824	Fill of posthole [4825]	Summit (2007 excavation)
4825	Posthole	Summit (2007 excavation)
4826	Fill of pit/ animal disturbance [4827]	Summit (2007 excavation)
4827	Pit or poss animal disturbance	Summit (2007 excavation)
4828	Fill of poss animal disturbance [4829]	Summit (2007 excavation)
4829	Poss animal disturbance or root action	Summit (2007 excavation)
4830	Fill of posthole [4831]	Summit (2007 excavation)
4831	Posthole – poss part of sequence incl [4825] and [4833]	Summit (2007 excavation)
4832	Fill of posthole [4833]	Summit (2007 excavation)
4833	Poss posthole or natural feature	Summit (2007 excavation)
4834	Fill of pit/animal disturbance [4827]	Summit (2007 excavation)
4841	Fill of poss posthole [4842]	Summit (2007 excavation)
4842	Poss posthole	Summit (2007 excavation)
4849	Fill of feature [4850]	Summit (2007 excavation)
4850	Root action, animal disturbance or poss posthole	Summit (2007 excavation)
4851	Fill of poss posthole [4852]	Summit (2007 excavation)
4852	Posthole	Summit (2007 excavation)
4853	Fill of feature [4854]	Summit (2007 excavation)
4854	Root action, animal disturbance or poss posthole	Summit (2007 excavation)
4857	Fill of pit [4858]	Summit (2007 excavation)
4858	Pit cut	Summit (2007 excavation)
4869	Fill of posthole [4870]	Summit (2007 excavation)
4870	Poss large posthole	Summit (2007 excavation)
4871	Fill of animal disturbance [4872]	Summit (2007 excavation)
4872	Animal disturbance	Summit (2007 excavation)
4875	Primary fill of poss pit [4876]	Summit (2007 excavation)
4876	Poss pit seen in collapsed crater area	Summit (2007 excavation)
4877	Fill of poss pit [4878]	Summit (2007 excavation)
4878	Poss pit seen in collapsed crater area	Summit (2007 excavation)
4879	Fill of poss pit/posthole [4880]	Summit (2007 excavation)
4880	Poss pit/posthole seen in collapsed crater area	Summit (2007 excavation)
4886	Secondary fill of poss pit [4876]	Summit (2007 excavation)

although it is worth noting that [17] also contained fragments of modern wire and is therefore likely to be a disturbed layer. Other finds recovered from subsoil on the summit date from the mid-9th to early 10th century and from the late medieval to mid-16th century (Hembrey, this chapter).

Eighteenth-century and later activity from the mound (Phase 18)

Although undated archaeologically, a series of features appears to be associated with the episode of tree planting that Stukeley recorded on the summit of Silbury in 1723 (*see* Chapter 1), and the associated damage the roots caused

(Fig. 9.11) (recorded as Phase 18). In the 2007 excavation trench this included a possible tree pit [4864], which was irregular in plan and had a maximum diameter of 0.85m and a depth of 0.26m, and there were various patches of disturbance attributed to root action. These features were all highly irregular in shape and the fills comprised loose, mid to light greyish-brown silty loam. A further possible tree pit was recorded in the collapsed area in 2001 ([28]), as was the 1776 shaft (cut [25]). It should be noted though that nothing further is known of these trees, either the size of them when planted or what became of them and there is no mention of them in any of the accounts of the 1776 excavations.

Fig 9.11
Plan of summit showing earthworks and excavation trenches with a post-medieval/modern feature highlighted.
(Eddie Lyons,
© English Heritage)

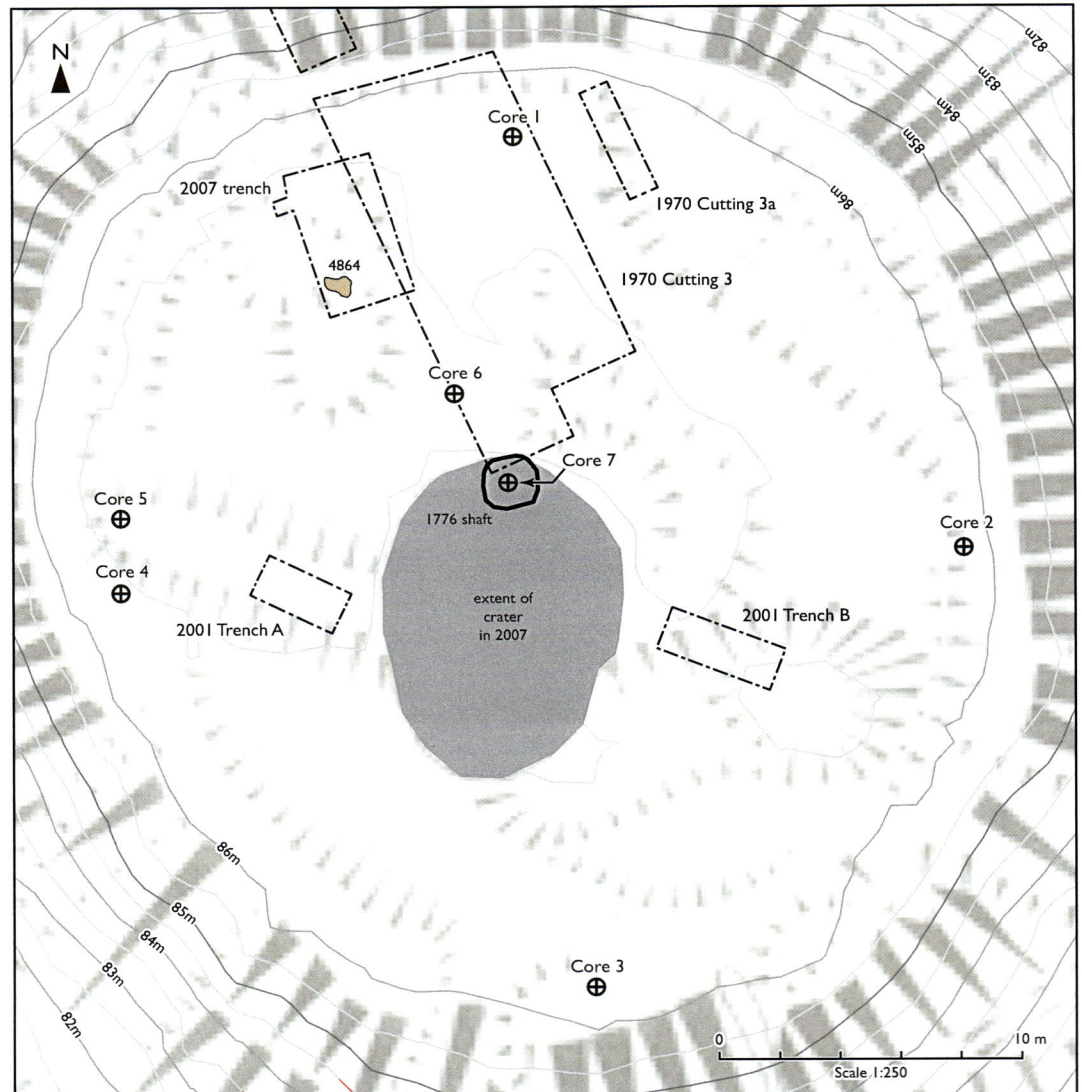

Evidence for later activity is indicated by finds of coins ranging from an 1881 half-penny to a 1979 ten pence piece recovered from the topsoil and subsoil (*see* Table 9.9). Evidence for a butchered badger was recovered from a number of contexts across the above phases, as well as numerous frog and toad bones (Worley, this Chapter). A quantity of crystals and semi-precious stones were buried into topsoil on the summit, and lay testament to the continued spiritual importance of the monument, whilst modern coins, tent pegs, bottle tops and ring pulls provide further indication that people still visit. The most enigmatic of these was a small plastic pyramid filled with plaster that had been buried into the top of the 2001 polystyrene blocks (Fig 9.12).

The medieval pottery

Kayt Marter Brown

A small medieval pottery assemblage was recovered from the 2001 and 2007 investigations on the summit comprising 14 sherds dating from the 11th to the 13th centuries (*see* Table 9.6; and Marter Brown 2012 for further detail). The assemblage includes both flint-tempered and chalk/flint-tempered Kennet Valley-type wares, a single Laverstock coarse sandy ware, local (unsourced) sandy wares and a single rim sherd of Bath fabric A from a pit fill [4886] within the collapsed area (Fig 9.13). The Kennet Valley-type wares were first defined as 'Newbury wares' (groups A and B; Vince 1997) and 'early to late medieval east Wiltshire wares' (Mellor 1994,

100–6), but the distribution of these wares has resulted in the encompassing and appropriate term 'Kennet Valley wares' (Mepham 2000, 63), which has been used in this report. The flint-tempered wares (Kennet Valley A) first appear during the early 11th century at Newbury, supplemented by the chalk/flint-tempered wares (type B) from the late 11th century, but the latter do not appear in any great quantity until the early 12th century (Mepham 2000, 53). Laverstock coarsewares also originate in the 11th century but are more common from the 12th century onwards, a date which also applies to the local sandy coarsewares.

With the exception of the single Bath A rim sherd from pit [4876], the remainder of the assemblage comprises residual material, occurring either in the upper layers and fills, which had suffered disturbance from later activity on the summit or comprised unstratified finds recovered from the crater collapse area. The wares represented are typical for the area and the quantities too small for any but the most general of comments.

The medieval and post-medieval finds other than pottery

Nicola Hembrey and Quita Mould

Despite the intensive sampling strategy adopted during the 2001 and 2007/8 interventions on the summit (*see* methodology section Chapter 2; and Hembrey and Mould 2012), very few artefacts were recovered and these came principally from subsoil and the topsoil. Eight of the objects are diagnostic of a particular period; of those four can be broadly dated to the Saxo-Norman period, as can the bridle bit obtained by Stukeley and supposedly recovered during

Fig 9.12
Recent placed deposit on the summit. A plastic pyramid filled with plaster of Paris. Scale 0.5m. (Duncan Stirk, © English Heritage)

preparations for tree planting in 1723 (*see* Chapter 1; Reynolds and Brookes 2013, fig 15). These early medieval artefacts are SF 862 from [2] (subsoil), a near-complete iron dress pin dated mid to late 9th to early 10th century (Fig 9.14a); SF 851 from [14] (subsoil), a near-complete iron prick spur typologically dated to the second half of the 11th century (Fig 9.14b); and two projectile points. The first, SF 8514 from [4805] (subsoil), is a long, slender socketed iron arrowhead, of the type thought to have been specifically designed to counter the increased use of defensive armour, and often, although not exclusively, associated with military use, with examples seeming to occur from the late Anglo-Scandinavian through into the medieval period, though mostly 11th to 12th century (Fig 9.14c). The second, SF 8501, retrieved from [4804] (topsoil), is an iron socketed arrowhead with some of the wooden haft remaining, which was identified as ash (*Fraxinus* sp.) from a mature tree. This type of wood ensures a greater control over the flight of the arrow (J Watson, pers comm, Fig 9.14d). A common type of arrowhead, it consists of a small, flat-sectioned leaf-shaped

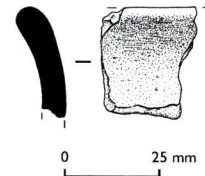

Fig 9.13
Bath A fabric rim sherd, 11th–13th century from [4886], fill of pit [4876], SF 8766. (Chris Evans, © English Heritage)

Table 9.9 Modern finds retrieved from the summit

Intervention	Small find	Context number	Description
2007/8	SF 8505	4804	(broken) glass and metal pendant (modern)
2007/8	SF 8504	4804	1979 ten-pence piece
2007/8	SF 8506	4804	1971 one-pence piece
2007/8	SF 8521	4804	19th- or 20th-century brass and iron anchor button
2007/8	SF 8528	4801	1969 ten-pence piece
2001	Not registered	1	1881 half-penny
2001	Not registered	1	1954 three-penny bit
2001	Not registered	1	1956 six-penny bit
2001	Not registered	3	1915 penny
2001	Not registered	3	1948 penny
2001	Not registered	8	1942 three-penny bit
2001	Not registered	16	1929 half-penny

1969–70: two pennies, one modern clear glass fragment, and a modern 20in gold chain, a green metal toy car, a small bone fragment and a George V penny.

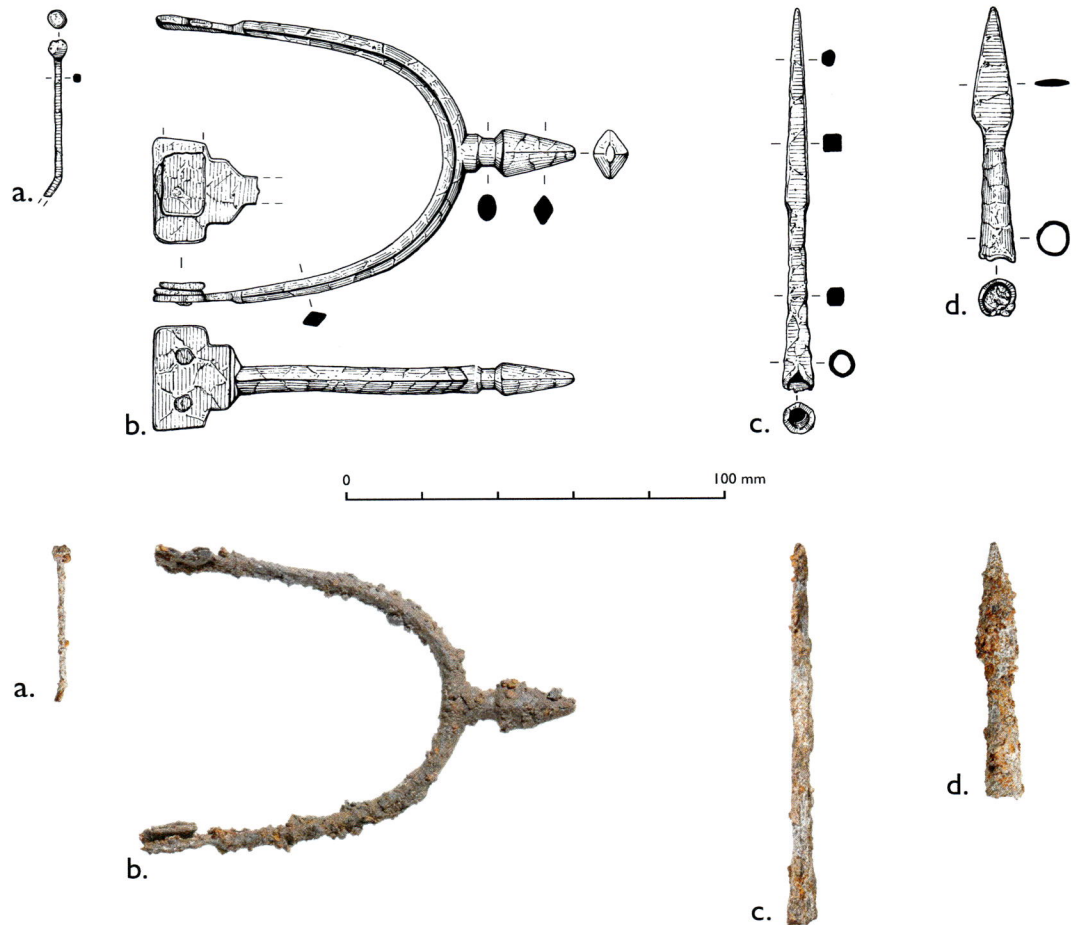

Fig 9.14
Early medieval and later
metal artefacts.
a) Anglo-Saxon pin SF 862
(L 42mm; W of head 3mm;
th of shaft 1mm);
b) prick spur SF 851
(Overall L 119mm; L of neck
and goad 29mm; max W
at terminal 80mm; max W
of terminal 30mm);
c) arrowhead SF 8514
(L 104mm; D of socket
8mm; max W of blade 6mm;
W at tip 2mm);
d) arrowhead SF 8501
(L 70mm; max W of blade
11mm; D of socket 8mm).
(Chris Evans, Ian Leonard
and Eddie Lyons,
© English Heritage)

blade with rounded shoulders and a round-sectioned socket; dated to the mid to late 13th century, these arrowheads are believed to be a multi-purpose projectile used either for hunting or in a military capacity.

Also of interest is an iron arrowhead (DM 2885) found 'in a shaft' during Pass' excavations in 1887, and now in Devizes Museum (Pass 1887, Chapter 1). A four-sided, socketed arrowhead, it is thought to be of 15th-century date (Jessop 1996, 195, type U2).

Finally, Atkinson notes a 'metal spearhead', found just next to the tunnel entrance; this has long been missing, but it appears briefly in one of the BBC *Chronicle* programmes, seemingly of iron, complete, leaf-shaped, with an intact socket with a brief glimpse of the wooden haft remaining inside. A search of the archive at the Alexander Keiller Museum has yielded an illustration of a spearhead with a pronounced mid-rib that would appear to be of the same leaf-shaped blade type and, although it appears to be larger in the illustration (which has no

annotation, scale or caption) than it does in the *Chronicle* footage, it is presumed to be the one referred to, but even with this information it is not possible to assign a date to this object (Figs 9.15 and 9.16).

In addition to these finds a possible chalk lamp was recovered from Atkinson's 'Cutting 5' on the slope of the Hill. This is reported on by Hinton (*below*).

The few objects within this Saxo-Norman assemblage cannot cast a great deal of light on what activities were taking place on top of the Hill, other than to attribute them to casual loss from visitors. The projectiles may be the result of target practice either at or from the Hill (although this would mark extreme carelessness over armatures); these two (and possible others if we include the Pass and Atkinson examples above) are not sufficient to indicate military activity, although a general medieval presence can be inferred.

As would be expected, objects of a post-medieval date are also present. From the

1968–70 excavations on the summit came one fragment of post-medieval green glass; from the 'summit top steps cutting layer 3' (? Cutting 7; Fig 0.2) came a brick fragment, SF 364. SF 505, a post-medieval fragment of dark green glass, and SF 508. Two more fragments of dark green post-medieval glass came from around the 1776 shaft.

A further three fine brass dress pins (SF 8530, 8531, 8532, from [4806], fill of tree pit [4807]) and a box-lid handle SF 852 (from [14], subsoil) date from the later medieval period to the mid-16th century. With the exception of the Roman coin (see above), none of the other objects can be closely dated. They comprise two iron buckle pins, an iron tanged awl or reamer, three iron nails, an iron strip fragment and an iron strap-arm, as well as a single fragment of post-medieval tile from [3], and four tiny scraps of post-medieval brick from [10]/[11], a small fragment of ceramic building material from [9], too small to be diagnostic, and presumed to be post-medieval in date, and stem fragments from four clay pipes from the summit [2], [14] and [4828], and slope [4889].

The strength of this assemblage, however, particularly when considered along with the casual losses or intentional offerings from modern-day visitors (see above and Table 9.9), lies in the confirmation of the continuation of interest and usage of the site through time.

The chalk lamp

David A Hinton (with David Field)

A carved chalk lamp was recovered by the 1968–70 team from a lower terrace on the northern slope (Cutting 5) (Figs 0.2, 9.17 and 9.18). Measuring 115mm across (100mm across the base) and reaching a maximum of 65mm high (40mm deep internally), the material is quite dense and very hard. Given the proximity of the Melbourne Rock (a hard band forming part of the Middle Chalk), it is suggested that this is the likely source. No fossils are visible with a hand lens. The object appears to have been carved by fluting and graving, there are tool marks – a narrow gouge and smoothing tool – on most surfaces. The internal surface is, however, very irregular and the internal base is uneven, but there are no obvious deliberate depressions or holes. In one corner there are three very small depressions at the base of a groove down the wall but these appear to be the result of the gouge over-hitting rather than anything more deliberate. One side of the upper edge has been

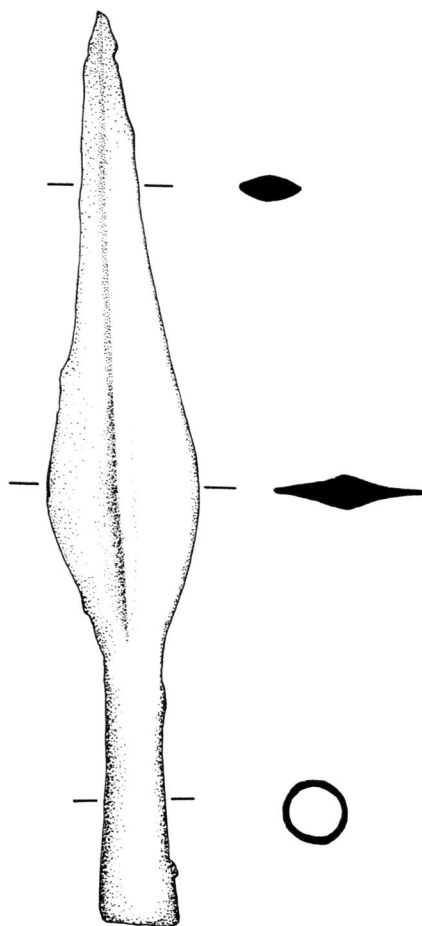

Scale 1:2
0   100 mm

Fig 9.15
Illustration of presumed 1968–70 spearhead from Atkinson Archive. This is believed to be the spearhead that was found close to the tunnel entrance and was featured in the Chronicle programme. Copy of drawing held in the Alexander Keiller Museum (location of the original is unknown and the scale is conjectural).

Fig 9.16 (below)
Screen grab showing the spearhead as shown on 'Chronicle'.
(Courtesy of the BBC)

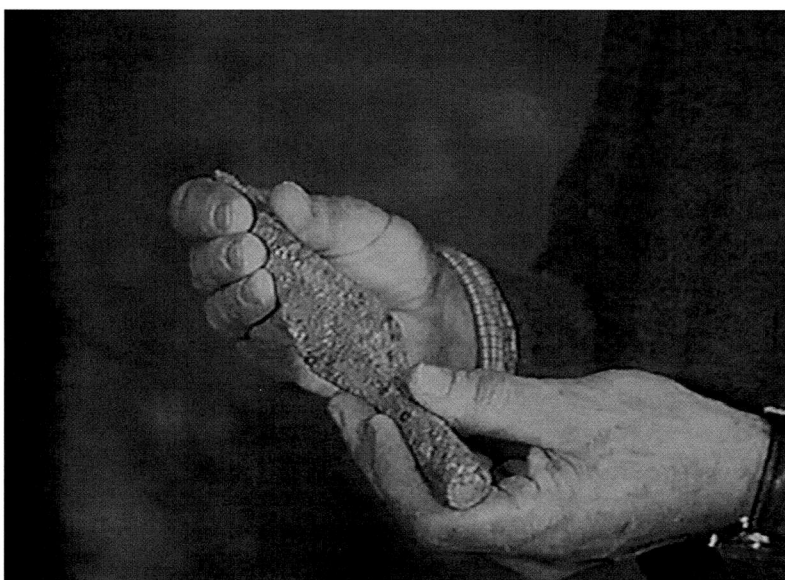

Fig 9.17
Chalk lamp.
(James O Davies,
© English Heritage)

damaged, at least it is lower than the rest of the rim, but it could be that this was a deliberate feature. The upper part of the inner face is blackened, potentially with soot. This forms an encrustation in some places and appears to be more than superficial. A clear division exists that contrasts with the unstained lower part of the inner face and base.

Stone bowls like this one are thought to have been used as lamps; often encrusted on their sides are residues left by burning, as on this one, caused by a wick floating in oil or tallow. One possibility is that they were used as holders for spiked pottery lamps (Barclay and Biddle 1990, 985), though the amount of burning on this one and others indicates that many were themselves the reservoirs. Also like this one, they were often roughly hewn and are therefore unlikely to have been the work of a specialist carver. They are surprisingly diagnostic of a late Saxon or Norman date. Their introduction seems not to have been until the 10th century to judge from the negative evidence that can be adduced from the growing body of settlement data. Their end-date is more problematic, as although they may get broken they are ultimately indestructible. A few have been found in later medieval contexts, as in Winchester (Barclay and Biddle 1990, 991–3) where their presence may be residual. Egan made the point that stone bowls are amongst the artefacts published in the volume on late Saxon and Norman London (Pritchard 1991, 160–1), but not in his work on artefacts of 1150 and after (Egan 1998, 126–7).

A similar case can be cited nearer to Silbury, as some were found in Old Sarum but not in New Salisbury except for one multi-celled example (Drinkwater 1991, 173); multi-celled lamps required more skill to carve.

The medieval environmental evidence

Gill Campbell

Analysis of the molluscs from the later deposits on the summit was not undertaken because of the degree of animal disturbance and the loose nature of the much of the matrix. A sample taken from within one of the interwall deposits during the 2007/8 investigations where no disturbance was evident was assessed for molluscs, however none were present (Davies 2012).

The flotation samples from the summit almost all contained large numbers of molluscs and anuran bone as well as small quantities of rodent and other animal bone (*see* Worley this chapter). Charred remains including charcoal were only present in some samples, and then only in very small quantities.

It is probable that the small numbers of cereal grain, comprising several naked wheat-type grains (probably bread wheat) and a single *Avena* sp. (oat) grain, which could come from either a wild or cultivated oat, relate to the 11th-century occupation of the site (Campbell 2011; Smith and Campbell 2001). The wheat grain from pit fill [9] and a fragment of Pomoideae charcoal were subject to radiocarbon dating (*see above* and Marshall *et al*, Chapter 4).

The utilisation of free-threshing wheat, and potentially oat, on the site at this period is consistent with the national picture where threshing wheat, principally *Triticum aestivum* (bread wheat) but also *Triticum turgidum* (rivet wheat), replaces *Triticum spelta* (spelt wheat) and *Triticum dicoccum* (emmer wheat) as the major wheat crop in the early medieval period. Oat also becomes a major crop in this period, probably because of the need for good quality fodder for horses and its importance in the brewing of ale (Campbell *et al* forthcoming; Greig 1988).

There is very little evidence from other sites regarding crops grown in this area of Wiltshire in the early medieval period. A bread wheat grain and two indeterminate wheat grains recovered from a buried soil in two separate cuttings close to the Winterbourne stream at Avebury gave calibrated radiocarbon dates of cal AD 1020–1290 (OxA-1051; 850±80 BP, cal AD 1050–1400 (OxA-1053; 760± 80 BP),

Fig 9.18
Chalk lamp.
(Chris Evans,
© English Heritage)

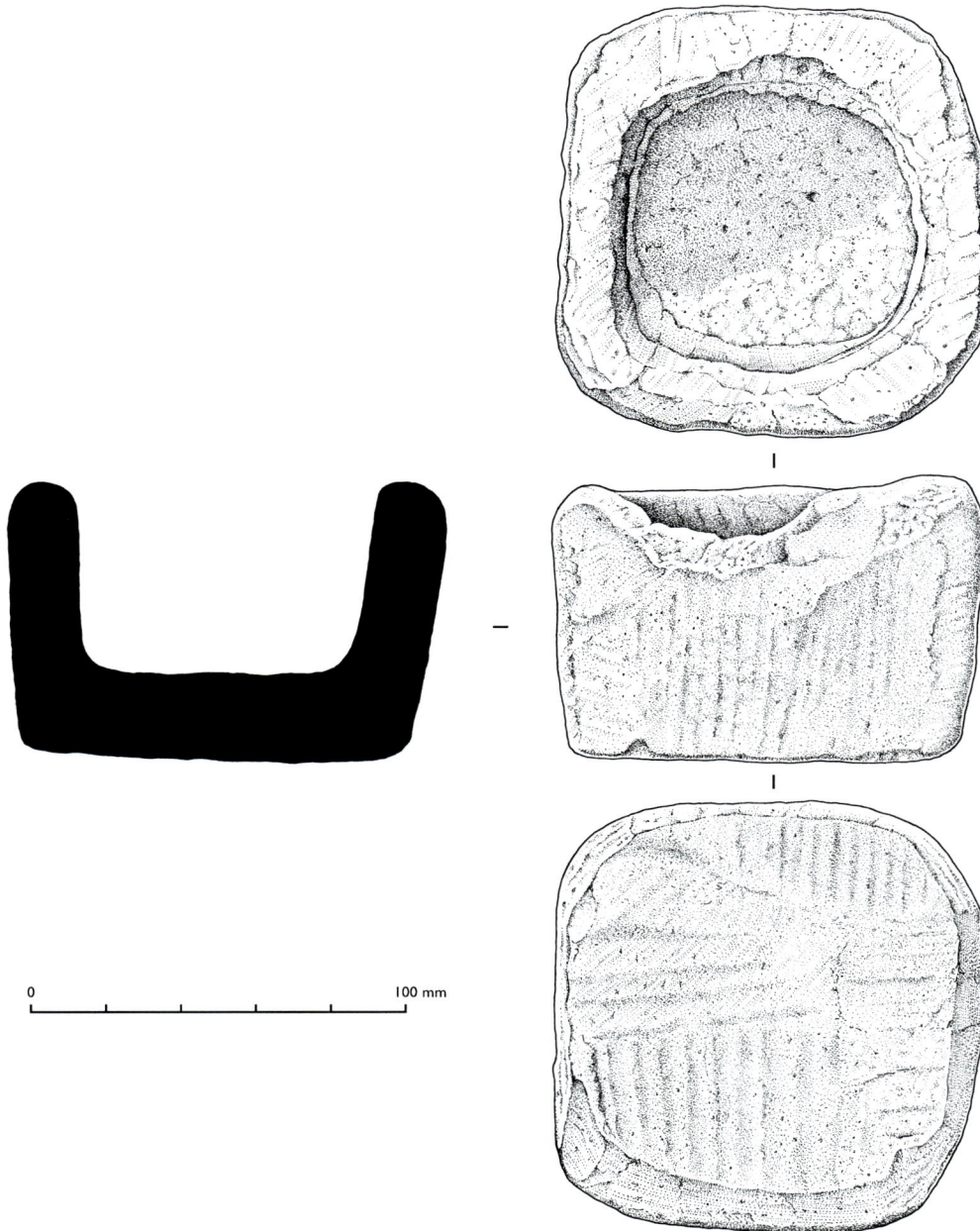

0   100 mm

and cal AD 1190–1400 (OxA-1052; 720± 70 BP) respectively (Evans *et al* 1993, 146). It is also a distinct possibility that the bread wheat grain found in prehistoric contexts during excavations at the West Kennet Palisaded Enclosures is medieval in date given the Saxon remains from the site (the plant remains from Saxon contexts recovered from this intervention have not been published) (Fairbairn 1997).

Further afield, excavations at Salisbury Street, Amesbury (Stevens 2009; Stevens unpublished), and in Malmesbury (Jones 2006) have produced much better evidence for the range of crops grown. At both sites bread wheat was the most commonly occurring cereal, while *Hordeum vulgare* (hulled barley) was present in small quantities in most contexts. Several contexts at Salisbury Street produced reasonable quantities of *Secale cereale* (rye), while one pit fill contained well-preserved remains of *Pisum sativum* (pea), *Vicia faba* (broad bean) as well as a possible *Lens culinaris* (lentil). Rye was absent in the late Saxon plant assemblages from Malmesbury and pulses were only represented by a single broad bean recovered from post-Conquest pit fill. However, oat was a frequent find at this site, though again only grain was found so the remains could be from a crop, a weed, or both.

The animal bone from the medieval and later phases

Fay Worley
The animal bone recovered from medieval and modern contexts excavated on the summit produced the majority of animal bone (98% recordable bones) recovered from the 2007/8 intervention. However, a total of only 148 recordable hand-collected fragments were recovered representing a variety of wild and domestic species. For a full report of all animal bones recovered from the 2007/8 excavations *see* Worley (2011c). The antler assemblage from the summit is presented in Chapter 3; these remains are all believed to be Later Neolithic in date.

Methods

Animal bones recovered by hand and those from floated environmental samples were analysed separately. Hand-collected bones were washed prior to analysis. All countable hand-collected animal bones were identified as precisely as possible to element and species and recorded. Details are included in the research archive. Corvid species' bones were distinguished using Tomek and Bocheński (2000) and select anuran (frog or toad) bones were identified to species using Bailon (1999) when possible. Fish bones were analysed by Rebecca Nicholson, whose identifications are included here. A total of three fully fused and suitably complete bones were measureable following standard published sources (von den Driesch 1976; Tomek and Bocheński 2000).

The high frequency of micro-faunal (predominantly anuran) remains in many sample residues precluded individually recording each bone, rather the sample fractions were weighed and the average weight per litre volume processed was calculated to provide an estimate of relative prevalence between samples. Within the two largest samples for each phase, the number of anuran ilia were counted to provide an estimate of the minimum number of individuals (MNI) represented and species identifications, micro-faunal dental elements and micro-mammal post-cranial elements were also identified to taxon. Further details on methodology and the osteometric data is presented in Worley (2011c).

Results and discussion

Hand-collected bones, and those retrieved from samples, were recovered from Phase 17 (medieval), 18 (18th century), 20.1 and 20.2 (20th/21st century) deposits (Tables 9.10 and 9.11), although a number of badger and amphibian bones found throughout the phases suggest that there may be a significant amount of contamination between deposits. The majority of the hand-collected assemblage was recovered from modern (52% identified bones) or medieval (30% identified bones) contexts.

The assemblage holds little economic information for husbandry or hunting during each phase and there are too few bones to consider the relative proportions of species in any meaningful way. Conclusions are therefore largely limited to the occurrence of species within phases.

Both domestic and wild taxa were recovered from all phases containing animal bones. Domestic species represented at least 39 per cent of all hand-collected remains; cattle bones were recovered from all phases, sheep or goat and pig from all phases except Phase 18, cat from Phase 17, horse from Phase 20.1 and chicken or galliform bones from Phases 17 and 20.1. Pig and domestic boar bones can be difficult to distinguish, however, a measurable pig astragalus from Phase 17 had a GLl of 37.1mm (following von den Driesch 1976, 91), smaller than those of all wild boar recorded in Magnell (2006) and therefore more likely to represent a pig than wild boar.

Wild taxa were well represented in the assemblage: red deer bones were recovered from Phases 20.1, 20.2, and possible red deer bones from Phase 18; red fox bones were recovered from Phases 17 and 18; hare and lagomorph bones from Phases 17, 20.1 and 20.2; and badger bones from all phases except 18. A few bones of smaller taxa (mole, possible black rat, water vole, small rodent, corvid and amphibian) were also hand-collected from deposits of all phases, while sample residues often contained large numbers of anuran bones. Fish remains were

Table 9.10: Recordable hand collected animal bones recovered from the summit excavation quantified by NISP and presented by phase

Species	Phase					Total
	17	18	20.1	20.2	unstrat	–
Cattle	2	1	9	1	–	13
Sheep/Goat	5	–	10	1	4	20
Pig	7	–	8	3	1	19
Horse	–	–	2	–	–	2
Cat	2	–	–	–	–	2
Red deer	–	–	1	1	–	2
Cattle/Red deer	–	1	–	–	–	1
Cattle/Red deer?	–	–	1	–	–	1
Red fox	1	–	–	–	–	1
Red fox?	1	1	–	–	2	4
Large mammal (vertebra + ribs)	2	1	4	–	–	7
Medium mammal (vertebra + ribs)	1	1	12	3	1	18
Hare	–	–	–	1	–	1
Lagomorph	2	–	1	–	–	3
Badger	4	–	5	1	2	12
Badger?	4	–	6	–	–	10
Mole	–	–	–	1	–	1
Black rat?	–	–	–	1	–	1
Water vole	1	–	–	–	–	1
Small rodent?	1	–	–	–	–	1
Chicken	1	–	–	–	–	1
Chicken/Guinea fowl/Pheasant	–	–	–	–	1	1
Chicken/Guinea fowl/Pheasant?	–	–	1	–	–	1
Corvid	–	–	–	1	1	2
Toad	–	1	–	–	–	1
Amphibian	11	5	2	–	3	21
Perch	–	–	–	1	–	1
Totals	**45**	**11**	**62**	**15**	**15**	**148**

Table 9.11: Animal taxa collected from sample residues, presented by phase. Taxa are quantified by number of recordable specimens (NISP) for medium/large mammals and fish, minimum number of individuals (MNI) for anura, and presence (P) or absence for other micro–mammals

	Phase 17	Phase 18	Phase 20.1
Number of samples	15	2	2
Anura (MNI)			
Frog	32*	15	5
Common toad	11*	2	3
Micro-mammals			
Mole	P	–	–
Common shrew	–	P	–
Vole sp.	P	P	P
Micro–mammal (post-cranial)	P	P	P
Additional Species (recordable elements)			
Sheep/goat (NISP)	5	–	–
Pig (NISP)	2	–	1
Badger (NISP)	11**	–	6**
Cervid/bovid (NISP)	1	–	–
Lagomorph (NISP)	–	1	–
Eel (NISP)	3	–	–

* Anuran MNI only calculated for the two largest samples in phase 17,

** includes probable identifications.

recovered from Phase 17 and 20.2. These were identified as eel and perch respectively, the perch bone indicating a 200–250mm individual (Nicholson in Worley 2011c).

The Phase 20.1 assemblage was hand collected from topsoil, subsoil and the fill of a tree hollow. Similarly the Phase 20.2 assemblage was recovered from topsoil and trench backfill. Whilst ordinarily animal bone from these contexts would be considered to be of probable mixed and recent origin, in this instance the presence of elements of a badger skeleton, which was also recovered from earlier deposits, together with large and medium domestic mammal bones, and the location of the deposits on the summit of Silbury Hill, suggests that the bones may partially result from archaeological activity on the Hilltop rather than casual discard or manuring. They were therefore fully identified and are reported here.

The surface condition of hand-collected bones was generally good or moderate (Table 9.12). There were no discernable differences between the phases, although, as might be expected, those closer to the turf line displayed more ubiquitous root etching. Traces of carnivore and rodent gnawing were seen on a minority of bone fragments. Only one fragment displayed any signs of burning.

Evidence of carcass processing was not commonly identified, however 12 bones from Phases 17, 20.1, 20.2 and unstratified locations did bear butchery marks. The Phase 17 butchered bones comprised a pig tarsal from [4820], which indicated that the foot had been disarticulated at this point, and a badger sacrum from [4826], which is discussed further below.

The Phase 20.1 butchered bones comprised two medium mammal lumbar vertebrae, a pig skull fragment and a sheep tibia and scapula. The butchery marks primarily represent division of the carcass through portioning the spine, removing loin cuts, axially splitting the scapula, and removal of the mandible. A medium mammal rib from Phase 20.2 backfill [4802] has been disarticulated and its meat filleted. The four unstratified butchered bones were a large and a medium mammal lumbar vertebra, a sheep or goat sacrum and a sheep or goat scapula. The vertebrae exhibited chops from the division of the spine and the butchered sacrum indicated that the sheep (or goat) was portioned into left and right flanks. The scapula exhibited three puncture wounds to the blade, although whether these are a result of carcass processing or post-depositional damage is not clear.

The badger bones

Twenty-two badger, or probable badger, elements were hand collected, and a further 17 fragments were recovered from samples. The bones represent a minimum of one individual, based on minimum number of elements and taking into account bone development. Fused rib heads, distal scapula, proximal and distal humerus and radius, proximal ulna, and metapodials (with the exception of one unfused distal metapodial) indicate that the animal was skeletally mature, approximately 24–28 months old (following Ahnlund 1976). The badger bones were found in 12 different contexts covering three phases of activity within the small excavation trench, although with concentrations in subsoil (Phase 20.1, and seven elements in

Table 9.12: Condition of hand-collected bones (excluding teeth) from the summit, presented by phase

Data	17	18	20.1	20.1	Unstrat
Surface condition					
Good	70%	82%	60%	80%	87%
Moderate	16%	18%	31%	10%	7%
Poor	14%	0%	10%	10%	7%
Root etching					
Present	55%	36%	87%	70%	67%
Gnawing					
Carnivore	2%	0%	2%	0%	7%
Rodent	0%	9%	2%	0%	0%
Burning					
Present	0%	0%	2%	0%	0%
NISP	44	11	62	10	15

Phase 17 possible pit fill [4826]). In addition, three further badger bones were recovered from Phase 16.2 (Neolithic) contexts in the same trench (Worley, Chapter 6). The badger bones were originally thought to be indicative of animal disturbance to the archaeological layers, and Gardner (1987, 52) noted the proximity of 20th-century badger setts to the Hill. However, on closer examination it was noted that the sacrum from [4826] had been butchered – its caudal segment has been chopped off transversely. This indicates that at least some of the badger bones do not represent a natural death assemblage. Butchered badger bones are not commonly recorded in archaeological assemblages, although there are occasional popular and scientific references to badger meat being eaten (for example, *see* the badger recipes in Cameron 1977; and Smith nd, 36–7). One can speculate that the butchery of the sacrum might relate to discarding the badger's anal scent glands (*see* Corbet and Southern 1977, 359, 363) prior to further carcass processing, whether that be for the procurement of meat or the animal's skin and hair. It seems unlikely that the activity was Neolithic, with a medieval or later source seeming more probable.

The anuran bones

Anuran bones were recovered from nearly every sample that contained animal bone. While both frog and toad bones were identified, the majority were frog, often representing many individuals in each sample (*see* Table 9.11; and Worley 2011c). The large numbers of anuran remains probably represent natural casualties of animals either hibernating on, or inhabiting, the Hill. Their behaviour together with the small size of their bones means that they may travel within small voids in the Hill and are therefore likely to be intrusive in archaeological layers. Indeed, a live frog was seen hiding within a void in the chalk during the 2007/8 excavations, and a toad entered the tunnel.

Animal remains from 1969–70 excavations on the summit

Previous summit excavations also produced an assemblage of animal bone identified as late Saxon (Gardner 1987). This assemblage of 41 identifiable fragments included a range of domestic and wild species (pig, sheep, dog, red deer, roe deer and fox). Additionally, an assemblage of small mammal, amphibian and rabbit bones were recovered, but considered intrusive.

Conclusions

The animal bone assemblage from excavations on the summit of Silbury is poorly stratified and therefore also poorly understood. Some of the animal bones may represent a naturally accumulated death assemblage, but the presence of domestic animal bones and those of larger wild taxa suggests human activity on the hilltop, although its nature cannot be known. The presence of horse and a butchered badger, suggests that the assemblage most likely reflects various mixed activities, rather than simply food debris from occupation of the summit.

The nature of medieval occupation on the summit

David Field and Jim Leary

The certain and possible postholes excavated on the summit in 2007/8 show occupation on the summit probably related to fortification. The large posthole [4821], is likely to have formed part of a defensive structure, such as a palisade around the edge of the summit, although it could also relate to the corner post of a large building, such as a hall. While William Stukeley (1743, 41) believed the name Silbury to be of Saxon origin and interpreted it as 'the great or marvellous Hill …', it is worth noting that more recent workers (Gover *et al* 1939, 295) suggest that it may derive from Old English 'Sele' meaning 'hall'; Silbury is referred to as Seleburgh in an Assize Roll (No 1005m.117) dating to 1281. Whatever the nature of the building on the summit, the cereal grain and butchered animal attest to food preparation while the butchered badger could indicate carcass processing for the procurement of fur. The results of the radio-carbon dating programme show this activity to have taken place in the 10th or 11th centuries cal AD (*see* Marshall *et al* Chapter 4).

Atkinson was emphatic that trenching on the summit revealed no post-Neolithic structures, but having noted the medieval revetting on the terraces (*see below*) suggested that the site may have been fortified against the Danes (Atkinson 1970, 314; 1978, 170). The terraces themselves he considered to be original Neolithic features but with the inner angle of each re-cut and revetted by timber posts secured with iron nails. The association with Saxo-Norman pottery and the discovery of a clipped silver penny of Ethelred II on the second terrace suggested a date of between AD 1009 and 1016 (Atkinson

1970, 314; 1978, 170) for this activity and is thereby consistent with the 2007/8 evidence for occupation of the summit.

The early years of the 11th century were fraught with concern about Viking raids and could well have encouraged local inhabitants to look to defensible positions (*see* Reynolds and Brookes 2013). In 1006 a battle nearby at East Kennett was fought and lost whereby the Danes plundered the area (Garmonsway 1972, 137). It could be that Silbury was in fact the location of this event although there is no indication of any burning in the archaeological record. The decorated Late Saxon copper alloy mount, probably from a stirrup (Robinson 1992, 64; Reynolds and Brookes 2013, fig 20) found in the bed of the Kennet near the mound could have been lost at this time. Whether by then, the old *herepath* through Avebury and the defended enclosures along it were brought into play is uncertain, but it is worth noting that a re-used barrow within the enclosure at Yatesbury is inter-visible with Silbury Hill but not Avebury (Pollard and Reynolds 2002, 228, fig 103). Furthermore, Reynolds and Brookes (2013) have suggested that the summit of Silbury Hill was the site of a beacon forming part of a beacon system linking Yatesbury with the proposed late Saxon *burh* to the west of the henge at Avebury, and also with Marlborough (Reynolds 2001; 2005; Reynolds and Brookes 2013).

In 1010 attacks were made locally on All Cannings and Bishops Cannings and both settlements were destroyed by fire (Garmonsway 1972, 141). Some of the iron points found on the summit and slopes of Silbury Hill could result from encounters at this time. Curiously there is no evidence of fortification at the time of Stephen and Matilda, either documentary or in the archaeological record, contrasting with both Marlborough and Hamstead Marshal which were fortified at this time. It should be noted though, that further defensive measures could have been taken at the base of the Hill, including restricting access across the 'causeways'.

Terracing as revealed by the 1968–70 excavations and recent survey

Atkinson placed two trenches (Cuttings 7 and 4; Fig 0.2) across the uppermost ledge of the Hill. Cutting 4 revealed what was described as 'near vertical rough chalk walling' (Whittle 1997a, 21) situated on the inside of the ledge. As this chalk feature appeared to extend inwards under the

topmost level of the mound Atkinson believed that both terrace and wall were Neolithic, the surface of the terrace being 'trampled smooth by workers' (Atkinson 1968b, 170). No dating material is recorded and although cautious, Whittle considered that there was no evidence to suggest that the feature was not part of the original construction. Cutting 7, however, did not locate the feature and Whittle surmised that it may have been because the trench was not taken as far back into the mound as Cutting 4. However, small postholes were recorded in this cutting along with iron nails and sherds of Saxo-Norman fabric (Whittle 1997a, 22). Atkinson finally concluded that both upper and second terraces had been 'later cut back to a vertical face and revetted by timber secured with nails' (Atkinson 1968b, 170). These were not revealed in Cutting 4, indicating that any revetment or other wooden feature need not be considered as continuous.

The remains of the second terrace were investigated in Cutting 4; its almost vertical walling (Whittle 1997a, fig 20) consisted of small sarsen boulders and blocks of chalk surmounted by rubble and silt (Whittle 1997a, 22). Hard against and partly within this terrace were a series of six postholes placed a few centimetres apart from each other. The postholes were thus considered to be chronologically inseparable from the rough walling (Whittle 1997a, 22). Finds, evidently from this level included crucially the silver coin of Ethelred II, along with iron nails, and early medieval potsherds (*see above*). The position of these postholes located on the inside of the terrace step, hard against the mound implies revetment, perhaps to ensure the stability of the slopes, rather than fortification. Leaving the ledges themselves exposed, with the shelter of a revetment on the inner edge would have presented a perfect access route for attackers (and a blind spot for defenders).

There is less certainty about the location of Cutting 5 designed to investigate terracing lower down the slope of the Hill. Excavation of this is only described in general terms as 'downslope' from that across the second ledge (Whittle 1997a, 22). Here no wall was described but the mound was said to be composed of compacted chalk rubble and silt, evidently with a chalk step cut into it (Whittle 1997a, 22). A search of the 1968–70 archive revealed a section drawing of what is believed to be this cutting (Fig 9.19). Early medieval potsherds were again apparently found associated. A 35mm slide in the archive depicts the late Saxo-Norman chalk lamp *in situ* and suggests that it may have sat within a small niche cut into the chalk, but, as found, it lay on its side. David Hinton (*above*) suggests that is it of late Saxon or Norman date and therefore contemporary with the re-cutting and revetting of the terraces. Location of the lamp is curious for, if used, it would indicate that the ledge was marked at night. It is possible that the ledge could have served as a lookout post with the lamp hidden behind screening or alternatively the ledge with its light could have acted as a staging point in a ritual, ceremonial or memorial context.

Atkinson was evidently intrigued by features at this level, so much so that he planned to extend the trench in 1970. Writing in support of his application he described how in 1969

> Halfway down the north side of the mound … last summer we made a small cutting, 6ft by 12ft long to investigate a slight step or terrace which breaks the smooth profile of the mound at this point. This appeared to have been formed, like other similar terraces higher up the mound, in late Saxon times, possibly for defensive purposes; but below it the cutting revealed what may have been an associated ditch, of which it was possible to excavate only the inner edge. I am anxious to extend this cutting downhill for a limited distance (probably not more than another 12ft) in order to establish more reliably the character and date of this feature …'

(letter, 22 April 1970 M Walker to Messrs Golding Hargrove WRO 3293/1)

The location of the Cutting 5 (Fig 0.2) suggests that Atkinson had in fact encountered the platform revealed in the earthwork survey as being in this position. It is also perhaps this platform that was noted by seismic tomographic surveys and dubbed 'the northern anomaly' (*see* Chapter 10).

Whether or not re-cut, the stepped arrangement, of concentric circles or some kind of spiral, is essentially of early medieval date. It is conceivable, as Atkinson believed, that the form reflects an earlier construction feature, though while making sense in terms of both construction and accessibility there is very little evidence to support such an assertion, and Atkinson himself relied on the polished surface of the first terrace as an indicator of antiquity (*see above*). All of this has some implication for the stability of the mound. For revetment to be necessary early medieval users must have

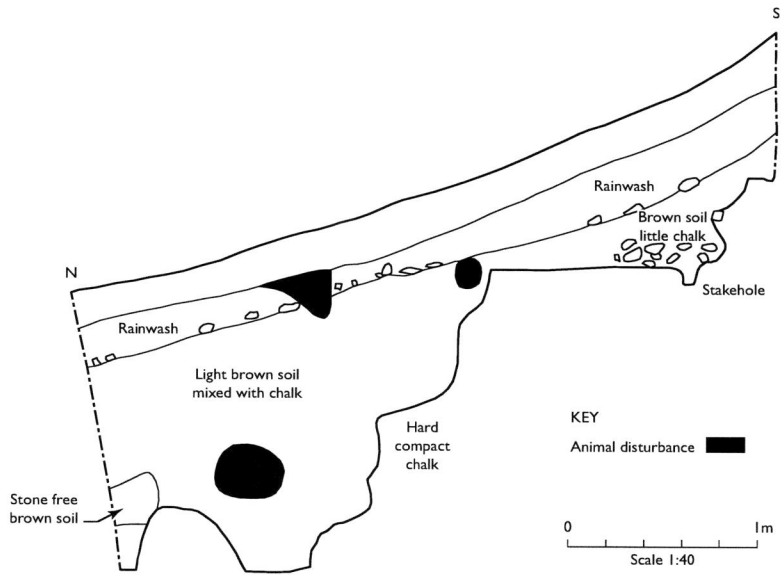

considered the mound to be in an insecure state and it could have been crumbling quite significantly before the cutting (or revetting) of the terraces. Secondly, the smoothed surface that exists today is not the product of good Neolithic building, for the infill of the steps must have developed around early medieval posts, and indeed occurred as they rotted. Assuming a fresh, clean cut revetted appearance in the early medieval period, the terrace fill is entirely a product of historic times.

Saxon perceptions of Silbury

It is difficult to know exactly what Saxon invaders encountered and how they may have perceived the mound. Use of barrows for burial was widespread in the early Anglo-Saxon period, perhaps as Williams (1998a, 95, 102) has suggested to construct relationships with the past and the supernatural, in a process that involved 'the exercise of display and power by new leaders through appeal to a mythical past'. None can have been more important than Silbury Hill. A number of Anglo-Saxon insertions in earlier barrows occurred on Overton Hill just north of the Sanctuary (Eagles 1986) and another on the top of a Bronze Age barrow in Ogbourne St Andrew churchyard (Swanton and Fowler 2001, 50), whilst further afield ostentatious burials were being inserted in prehistoric mounds during the 6th century (Eagles and Field 2004, 65). It may be, however, that Silbury Hill was perceived in a rather

*Fig 9.19
Section drawing from the 1969/70 cutting on the north slope (after Atkinson). This appears to depict the 'associated ditch' described by Atkinson. (Eddie Lyons, © English Heritage)*

different way and obtained a mythology that encouraged taboo concerning burial.

Locally the struggle to emphasise Christianity appears to have been quite important. The presence of a Saxon cross, followed by the establishment of Christian church, possibly a Minster (Reynolds 1999, 94), at Avebury both within sight of Silbury, emphasises the enormous Christian interest in the area. Avebury subsequently attracted a Benedictine monastic cell, and suffered attempts to destroy the standing stones. Given this concern to Christianise pagan monuments it would be no surprise if Silbury Hill saw some form of Christian usurpation and modification.

Conclusion

To date there is very little evidence for later prehistoric activity on and around Silbury Hill, although the late Bronze Age/early Iron Age bracelet and the possible late Iron Age temple may indicate that the Hill, the Winterbourne

and/or the Swallowhead Spring were of religious significance. There is little trace of Roman activity on the Hill itself. The Romano-British settlement around Silbury appears, on present evidence, to have been established in the late 1st or early 2nd century, continuing into the later 4th or early 5th century AD. While the area east of the Hill may have formed a ritual zone, the settlement to the south of the A4 and on the side of Waden Hill seems to have been a commonplace roadside rural settlement, with some substantial stone buildings set away from the roadside.

The small town did not survive far into the 5th century AD. In the early Saxon period, there was occupation at West Kennett and Avebury, and by Domesday a more substantial settlement at Beckhampton. The terracing of the Hill probably dates to the early medieval period and there is evidence for the fortification and occupation of the summit in the 10th or 11th century AD. This probably represents a response to Danish raids in the early 11th century.

Fig 9.20
One interpretation of Silbury Hill in the Roman period. Here the Hill is depicted as being already terraced to some extent and supporting small shrines or mausolea (but it should be stressed that this is only one possibility – there is no archaeological evidence that the Hill was used in this way at this time and the terracing would appear to be of early medieval date). The external ditch extension is pictured as a large body of water, with the ditch immediately surrounding the Hill not especially singled out as a place for ritual activity. Possible shops and other buildings forming part of the Romano-British settlement are shown set back a little from the metalled road with individual plots behind them. To the north of the road a simple Romano-British temple stands on the site of the possible Iron Age temple, while the surrounding hills are seen as agricultural estates. In the foreground a young girl carries a chicken, while sheep graze the chalk pasture.
(Judith Dobie, © English Heritage)

Fig 9.21
Early medieval Silbury.
This reconstruction shows
Silbury Hill in the 10th to
11th century with the
summit of the Hill removed
to provide a flat large
platform for construction
purposes. A watchtower is
conjectured as a possible
building related to the large
posthole found within the
2007 trench and forming
part of the fortification of
the summit at this time.
The summit is depicted as
inhabited, with horses
within the compound and
the early medieval terracing
of the monument is shown in
high relief suggesting
possibly remodelling or fresh
cutting. The landscape
surrounding the Hill is
pictured as fairly intensively
farmed with a bread wheat
crop being harvested and
gleaned in the foreground.
Vestiges of the Romano-
British settlement are
depicted as surviving
towards West Kennett
alongside the road.
(Judith Dobie,
© English Heritage)

Today it is the Hill itself that imposes its presence on the visitor. Its shadow looms large in our consciousness and we interpret and respond to it in differing ways. This may have been true in these earlier periods – the mound may have been important as a landmark for travellers and as a focus of local identity and at times defence. Perhaps it was seen as a place of great power and as a consequence either attracting people or repelling them. At times the Hill may have been of less significance than the waters surrounding it – the wide ditch, the reliable Swallowhead Spring, the vanishing and reappearing Winterbourne – or than the great monument and Christian focus at Avebury. For the moment we can explore these questions, but we cannot answer them with any certainty.

Desposition of bronze bracelet.

Deposition of bronze bracelet in Roman times.

Fig 9.22
Depositing the late Bronze
Age/earlier Iron Age bronze
bracelet. a) Here we imagine
the ditch surrounding
Silbury Hill as a depository
for objects including the
copper alloy bracelet.
The Hill is depicted in the
late Bronze Age as a place
for public spectacle; b) here
we imagine the bracelet
being returned to the
ancestors or deity of the Hill
(Judith Dobie,
© English Heritage)

Fig 9.23
Contextualising the
chalk lamp.
a) Here the chalk lamp
provides light for
a soldier acting as lookout
on the side of the Hill.
b) Here the chalk lamp is
seen lighting a path to the
summit and embedded in
ritual, the flowers and fruits
deposited as an offering.
(However, it should be
stressed that no evidence for
fruit or flowers associated
with the lamp has
been found).
(Judith Dobie,
© English Heritage)

10

The Conservation of Silbury Hill

ROB HARDING, AMANDA CHADBURN, GILL CAMPBELL, AND JIM LEARY

With Matt Canti, David Field, Nicola Hembrey, Neil Linford and Paul Linford

The surveys and other investigations that were undertaken in order to arrive at a better understanding of the state of the Hill following the discovery of the hole on the summit on 29 May 2000 are detailed here. How the decision to re-enter, and directly backfill the tunnels, shaft and all known and predicted voids was reached is outlined. The planned programme for these remedial works is laid out, followed by a description of how works proceeded. Descriptions of the 1968–70 and 1849 tunnels and their remains are included, as is an account of how the engineering solution to the conservation the Hill was modified as the true state of the interior became apparent. The chapter ends with a discussion of what could have caused the collapse.

Investigations into the cause of the collapse and the condition of the monument

Rob Harding and Amanda Chadburn

The discovery of the hole and the initial responses

Since 1994, English Heritage, which is responsible to the government for the upkeep of Silbury Hill, had devolved its day-to-day management responsibilities to the National Trust under a legal agreement. The latter controlled burrowing animals and scrub, undertook litter picking in the car park, maintained fences and signage, and discouraged visitors from climbing the Hill. In early 2000, Silbury Hill was considered to be a monument in good condition. Indeed, the Avebury WHS Condition Survey – published ironically in May 2000 (Oxford Archaeological Unit/EPDM Consultancy) – had indicated that the problems

with the Hill were of a relatively minor nature, with concerns relating to erosion caused by unauthorised visitors, including a fire scar on the summit (*see* Fig 10.1b), burrowing animals and a lack of grazing.

There was no evidence of any movement at the summit or elsewhere and efforts to backfill slumping above the entrance to the 1849 Archaeological Institute tunnel had been discontinued as the scar appeared to have stabilised. Memories that the 1776 shaft had opened up and been capped in the 1930s had long since faded.

On Monday, 29 May 2000 – a Bank Holiday – the National Trust Property Manager Chris Gingell was contacted by a visitor who had made an unauthorised visit to the summit, and who reported a hole in the Hill. English Heritage was informed the next working day on 30 May, and one of the authors, the then regional Inspector of Ancient Monuments, Amanda Chadburn, went out to visit. It was immediately apparent that there was a serious problem, and National Trust and English Heritage engineers were called, and arrived later that day to make an assessment, while Damian Grady of the English Heritage aerial survey section monitored the site from the air (Fig 10.1a). The hole (Fig 10.1b) – by this point identified as likely to be the remains of the Drax shaft – was roped off and danger signs erected, and the engineers designed a secure sloping, corrugated steel cover, which was erected on 31 May. The primary concern was to protect the safety of the public for, despite there being no public access to the Hill, visitors frequently climbed to the summit. However, there were also concerns about the conservation of the monument and it was hoped that the cover would prevent weathering of the sides of the collapse and stop rainwater collecting and causing further instability.

Fig 10.1
a) Aerial photograph of the
top of the Hill 30 May 2000,
showing the summit roped
off and the fencing in place;
b) close up of hole taken
on the same day.
The fire scar is visible in
the foreground.
(Damian Grady
and Arthur McCallum,
© English Heritage)

Fig 10.2 (opposite)
a) Photograph of
cover gantry;
b) shaft seen from below;
c) View of cavity at bottom
of shaft.
(© English Heritage)

had been capped close to the surface (as we know it has been because of the air photographic evidence – *see* Chapter 1). They recorded locating the top of collapsed material within the shaft at approximately ten metres below the surface of the summit (Figs 10.2c and 10.3). It was here that part of the shaft wall had sheared away to create a cavity recorded on the digital camera survey, leading away from the main 1776 shaft. The cavity itself was considered to have resulted either from works associated with the 1776 shaft, such as the construction of intermediate adits or laterals (Fig 10.3), or from the various tunnelling operations to the centre of the mound carried out close to the original ground level which had collapsed and were starting to migrate upwards, possibly as the result of water ingress.

A series of further collapses occurred over the winter expanding and enlarging the hole into a small crater which by March 2001 was 7.2m by 5.5m wide and 3.8m deep. The temporary cover was evidently not protecting the sides of the shaft and there were concerns that, by concentrating rainwater around its perimeter, it could be weakening the surrounding ground. It was therefore decided to remove it and replace it with a fence to protect unauthorised visitors to the summit (Fig 10.4). These works were accompanied by further archaeological investigations as outlined in Chapter 1.

Seismic tomographic survey and related investigations

The further collapses around the sides of the 1776 shaft and a growing concern regarding the best conservation strategy for the Hill, led English Heritage to establish a Project Board in May 2001, to provide a focus for decision-making that would identify and execute appropriate remedial works and ensure that the necessary resources were made available to carry them out. It was quite possible that unknown cavities existed within the mound and the Board realised that the initial idea of simply backfilling the collapse at the top of the shaft could, through adding a considerable weight of material above possible hidden voids, lead to further collapses and damage to archaeological stratigraphy. Overall, greater knowledge of the composition of the Hill was badly needed alongside a better understanding of the history of past interventions. Based on this, a clear idea of the

A hatch within the corrugated steel cover allowed access to archaeologists and engineers to begin the work of recording and investigating the cause of the collapse (Fig 10.2). A digital video camera was lowered into the hole revealing the clean cut sides of the shaft sunk by Edward Drax in 1776, which was recorded in historical literature, but about which very little was known (Fig 10.2b). Also thought to be visible were at least two, and possibly up to four, lateral openings leading off from the central shaft (McAvoy 2000, 1). Prior to 2000 it had been assumed that the 1776 shaft had been backfilled, although this was now questioned.

An evaluation was carried out on 8 August 2000 by Graham Daws Associates, specialists in rock mechanics. In their report (Daws 2000) they described no actual evidence that the shaft options available for remedial work could then be formulated.

Whilst previous geophysical surveys of the summit had pointed to the location of anomalies (Linford and Martin 2001; Linford 2001), these methods were unable to provide information about voids deep within the Hill because of the limited penetration depth of the equipment. In an attempt to remedy this an advisor, Professor Michael Worthington, then Professor of Geophysics at the London School of Mines, Imperial College, was engaged, and with his assistance a brief for the further geophysical investigation of the Hill was put out to tender. The objective of this was to locate any voids and zones or planes of weakness within the mound. It was hoped to determine the present position of the 1849 and 1968–70 tunnels as well as to locate and map any structural features contemporary with the construction of the mound and to get a general idea of its make up.

Skanska, a company with considerable geotechnical experience, were awarded the contract for these investigations on the basis of their proposal for the execution of a seismic tomography survey. The theory behind this technique is that seismic energy travels through different materials at different velocities. This enables the nature of the interior of an object to be reconstructed by interrogating different areas of the object with an energy source and examining the transmitted and scattered wavefields. This technique had not been used before to look deep within a structure such as Silbury Hill to help determine stability and reveal archaeological history. It was recognised, however, as the only technique which might potentially reveal the nature of the mound at depth.

The method for executing the survey was to drill four vertical boreholes from the summit of the Hill to its base (Fig 0.2). Cross-hole data would then be collected utilising an airgun source and in-hole hydrophones. The in-hole to Hill slope surface source data would be collected using hammer strikes on the surface to send seismic waves to in-hole hydrophones, although this method was changed, following trials, to the use of an airgun source at the bottom of the boreholes and surface receiving hydrophones (Skanska 2001a).

In order to stabilise the crater to prevent the loss of further archaeological deposits and to allow drilling operations to take place, the hole

Fig 10.3
Plan and profile of shaft
as recorded.
(G Daws and Eddie Lyons,
© English Heritage)

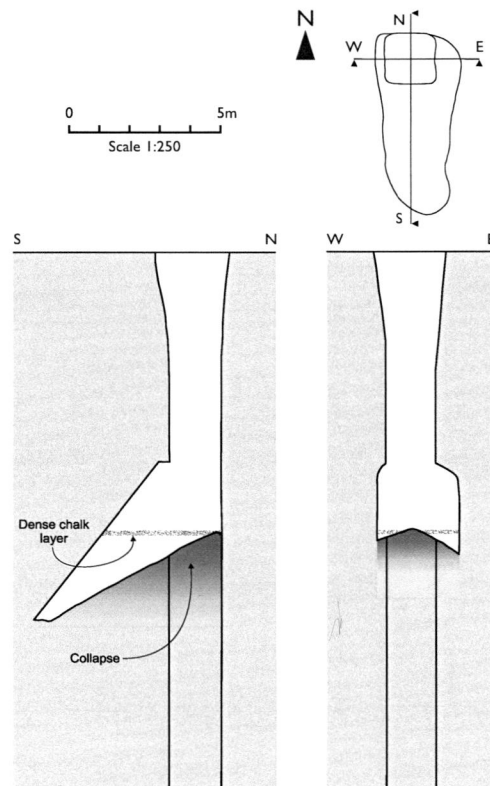

0   5m
Scale 1:250

N
W   E
S

Dense chalk layer

Collapse

was temporarily filled by lining the crater with a geo-membrane and covering this with polystyrene blocks with a topping of chalk. Twenty-four polystyrene (2.44m x 1.22m x 0.3m) blocks and 31 (2.44m x 1.22m x 0.61m) blocks were laid in layers with a few cut down to fill around the edges (Fig 10.5).

Borehole 4 penetrated the Western Lateral of the 1968–70 tunnel. Drilling was stopped and a CCTV camera lowered down the hole into the lateral. This critically revealed, for the first time, that the 1968–70 tunnels had not been fully backfilled as was then thought. The roof of the lateral had collapsed and partially filled the tunnel (McAvoy 2005b; Fig 10.6 left). This information, along with subsequent confirmation from investigations to the 1776 shaft, was to have an important influence on the final decision to re-enter the 1968–70 tunnels and thoroughly backfill them. As this particular borehole could not be used to complete the seismic survey, a fifth borehole (Borehole 5) had to be sunk nearby to complete the seismic survey. Geotechnical logging and archaeological examination of the boreholes were carried out by English Heritage (see Canti 2011; and Chapter 5). Skanska presented their tomographic survey report, which included the geological logs,

seismic data record sheets and seismic images in November 2001 (Skanska 2001b).

The principal findings were that significant anomalies were located at some, but not all, of the areas of earlier intervention, the 1776 shaft and the 1849 tunnel and 1968–70 re-use of it. They also drew attention to a number of 'significant low velocity anomalies', in particular one in the central 'core' of the Hill, corresponding with the surroundings of the 1776 shaft and the 1968–70 tunnel excavations, and another rising up the northern slope whose location corresponded with earthworks noted on the surface (above Chapter 9) and which was henceforth referred to as the 'northern anomaly' (Skanska 2001b figs H2–H5, H15–H19 and H21–H24). They suggested that others could correspond to the position of known interventions by Wilkinson and Petrie (Fig 0.2) and that these should be investigated further. Laboratory testing showed that the mound material had typical strength and angle of friction values for reconsolidated chalk. There appeared to be no significant risk of severe slope instability, but Skanska highlighted the risk of continued upward migration of voids, potentially resulting in further surface collapse.

Following Skanska's on-site investigations, there was intensive debate between Michael Worthington and Skanska regarding the method and detail of processing the collected data and the conclusions that could be drawn. In studying the results, Worthington concentrated on two recorded anomalies, those to the north slope (northern anomaly) and the central 'core' (Worthington 2002a). With regard to the northern anomaly, he felt that the tomography ray coverage was good and that the interpretation of the travel times was consistent with the presence of an anomaly. He felt, however, that further investigation was necessary to confirm its existence and identify its precise nature. With regard to the central 'core', he considered the ray coverage inadequate and the travel times unreliable. As such, he concluded that, from the investigations carried out thus far, there was no evidence for the existence of a low velocity zone at the base of the central 'core' of the mound between the boreholes and recommended that another cross-hole survey should be conducted to investigate this region.

In order to test the northern anomaly the Project Board decided to carry out further investigations in this area. Skanska was asked to undertake a surface-based refraction survey on the Hill adjacent to the northern anomaly (Skanska 2002a) and English Heritage undertook a coring transect across the anomaly using Eijkelkamp system to investigate the buried deposits (*see* McAvoy 2002, fig 3; and Fig 0.2: Cores 8–11; the Eijkelkamp system is fully described in Canti and Meddens 1998).

The results of the refraction survey confirmed, in Skanska's opinion, their earlier findings (Skanska 2002a). The coring transect revealed marked contrasts in the nature of the deposits on this part of the Hill, with 'soil' being found to a greater depth in the area of the possible platform. Chalk and subsoil 'mound' deposits comparable to those in earlier Skanska cores (Fig 0.2: Cores 1–5) were, however, seen in all four cores (Cores 8–11) (McAvoy 2002; Field 2002).

As Skanska's data relating to the core of the mound, collected during the seismic tomographic survey in 2001 (Skanska 2001b), were considered inconclusive the area was resurveyed in April 2002 using additional equipment (Skanska 2002b). This work also concluded that that there were a number of low velocity anomalies, the most significant of which were located below the stabilised crater, to the northern slope and to the 1968–70 tunnel portal. Other significant anomalies were situated in the central lower 'core' and between this and the overlying crater zone. The results of Skanska's three reports from November 2001, April 2002 and June 2002 were combined in their final report published in August 2002 (Skanska 2002c).

Having dealt with the borehole to surface images in his earlier report (Worthington 2002a), Michael Worthington considered the degree of confidence that could be placed in the seismic velocity images within the central 'core' of the mound between the four boreholes (Fig 0.2: Cores 1, 2, 3 and 5) and identified two relevant possible causes of error (Worthington 2002b). The first was travel-time picking error and in this case he considered the error estimates to be over-optimistic for source and receiver depths of less than 20 metres. He therefore argued that a low level of confidence should be attached to the smaller, anomalous, low velocity features. The second possible cause of error was uneven ray coverage. As a result of the paucity of ray paths in certain areas there was doubt as to the existence of the vertical elongated low velocity anomalies which appeared to run parallel to the shaft. Worthington did, however,

consider that the anomaly at a high level associated with uncompacted material at the top of the shaft and the anomaly in the region of the chalk bedrock and the bottom of the mound material were well resolved. He concluded, 'My overall impression of what can be deduced from this survey is that the mound is essentially rather homogeneous' (Worthington 2002b, 13).

In October 2002 the Silbury Hill Project Board considered the results of geophysical investigations up to that date. They were assisted by Professor Worthington and also by Professor Richard Chandler, Professor of Geotechnical Engineering at Imperial College London and a chartered civil engineer who was employed by the Board to advise on the interpretation of the geophysical investigations and the design of any possible remedial work.

It was concluded that geotechnical survey

Fig 10.4
a) Aerial photograph showing the enlarged hole following further collapse and the parch mark from the removal of the protective cover (SU1068/250 NMR21097/06 3 January 2001);
b) Aerial photograph showing further collapse. The inner fence is no longer present (SU1068/335 NMR 21034/24 14 February 2001). (Damian Grady, © English Heritage)

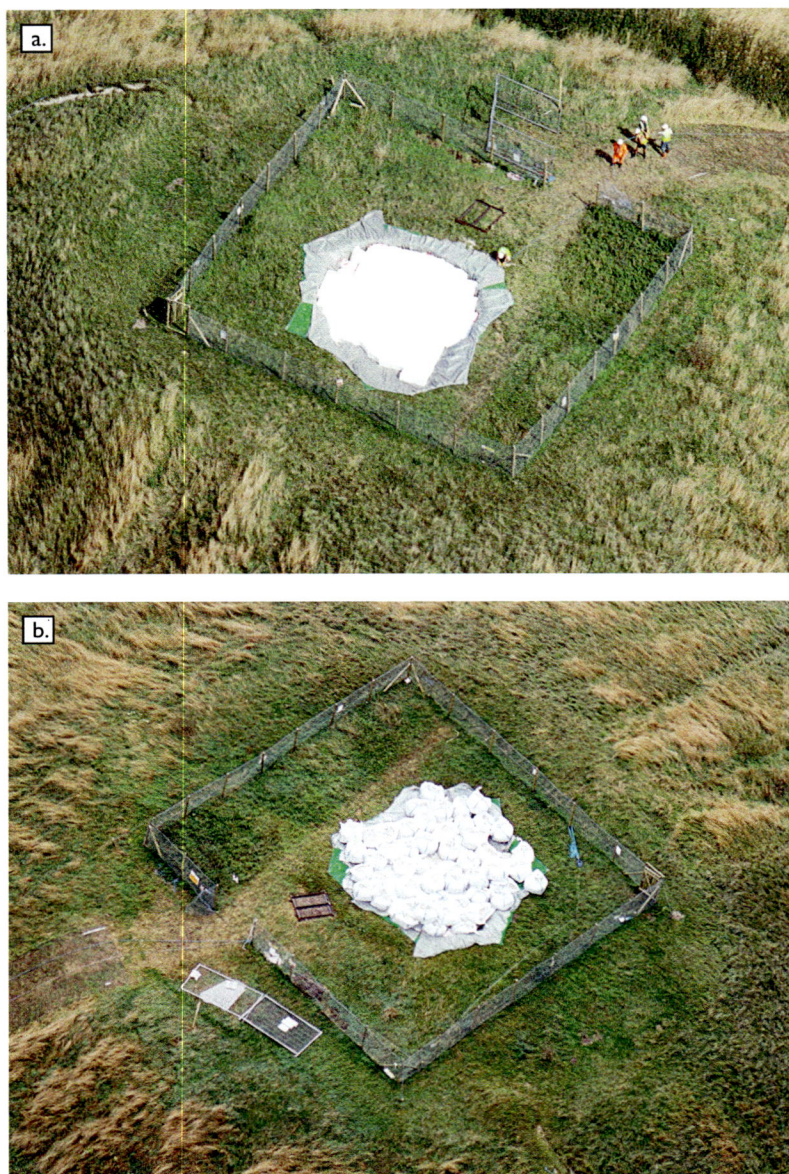

necessary in two areas to ascertain the extent and compactness of the fill to the 1776 shaft, and to investigate the 'chimney' anomaly which ran parallel to the shaft and which appeared to run within an area of poor or zero ray coverage (Worthington 2002b; Skanska 2002c, fig 1 anomaly A2; Fig 10.7).

The brief required the drilling of two vertical boreholes in the areas concerned (Fig 0.2: Cores 6 and 7), the recovery of columns of continuous, undamaged material for archaeological study and the execution of geotechnical testing of the boreholes to determine water content and bulk density.

Skanska responded with a proposed methodology (Skanska 2002d) and work commenced on site in March 2003. Borehole 7 (Fig 0.2: Core 7) to the shaft encountered, at its base, the steel support to the 1968–70 tunnel and a significant cavity below it. A CCTV borehole inspection camera was lowered and the cavity inspected. At this point the 1968–70 tunnel was found to be in reasonable condition with little sign of disturbance or collapse since excavation (Fig 10.6 right; Skanska 2003, 12–13; McAvoy 2005a, fig 13). The borehole (Core 6), through the chimney-type anomaly, showed reasonably consistent barrel penetration and recovery rates with material similar to that recovered in the first five boreholes (Fig 0.2: Cores 1–5). No voids were encountered (Skanska 2003, fig 1b).

By contrast Core 7, down the centre-line of the 1776 shaft, encountered significantly different material including some very soft layers, although again no voids, and a particularly poorly compacted zone above the steel arch of the 1968–70 tunnel (Skanska 2003, fig 1b). These were thought to be related to a series of discrete sequences of collapses or infilling events which could correlate with archaeological evidence from the sides of the collapse. Significantly higher moisture content was also recorded in this borehole, raising concerns that the poorly filled shaft was acting as a conduit for water passing through the mound (Skanska 2003, 22).

The final phase of these investigations was carried out in 2004 when the 1968–70 tunnel entrance was located and re-opened. It was found that, unlike the centre of the Hill, the outer four metres at least of the 1968–70 tunnel had been backfilled with road stone (McAvoy 2005a, 8). By this stage a reasonable understanding of the extent of the voids and the nature of the collapses had been gained (Fig 10.7).

Fig 10.5
a) Aerial photograph showing the geo-membrane and first layer of polystyrene blocks in place (SU 1068/402 NMR 21391/01 15 August 2001);
b) With the polystyrene infill completed (SU 1068/417 NMR 21393/09 16 August 2001).
(Damian Grady,
© English Heritage)

had been taken as far as the limits of the technology would allow. It had indicated that there were voids in the 1968–70 tunnels and there was confidence in the results regarding poorly filled areas at the top and bottom of the 1776 shaft. Separately, earthwork survey had established that there was evidence for the construction of a 'platform' on the surface of the northern slope, although aside from a greater depth of soil, below it the composition of the Hill was similar to that found elsewhere (see Chapter 1, Chapter 9). Discrepancies between Skanska's results were noted (McAvoy 2002) which cast further doubt on the evidence of a subterranean anomaly. Further investigations were still felt to be

Conservation risk assessment

Five options for remedial works were considered (Skanska 2003). They were:
1. No further works to the Hill, ie leave as is.
2. Directional drilling and grouting.
3. Re-excavating the existing tunnels and either supporting them or backfilling.
4. Re-excavating the 1776 shaft and backfilling.
5. Installing a temporary cap over the collapsed shaft fill.

A report to the Project Board by Richard Chandler (2003) dealt with these in turn. In his view, the Hill had probably deteriorated more since the first intervention in 1776 than in all the years previously and every collapse would represent a further weakening of its structure. He advised against leaving the Hill for more than a few years without some repair work. He also cautioned against grouting, highlighting the problem that it would be difficult to control grout penetration and ensure that it filled all the voids. He was also concerned about the possible interaction between the chemical composition of standard grout mixes and the materials making up the Hill.

Material from the drilling of borehole 5 had shown that Silbury I, and in particularly the capping layers (*see* Chapter 1 for a summary of Atkinson's phases) contained better than expected biological evidence (Canti *et al* 2004).

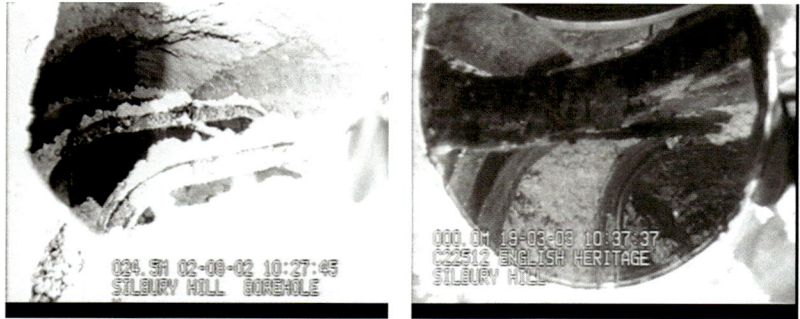

This biological evidence could be jeopardised by increased levels of oxygen reaching the deposits and compromising the anaerobic conditions (Project Board Minutes 12/11/2003NMR; Canti *et al* 2004). The problem of exposure and gaseous exchange militated against re-excavating the tunnels and supporting them. Backfilling them with chalk, however, had the attraction of having confidence that all known voids would be comprehensively filled thus preventing further collapses. It would also return the Hill to its pre-1776 state as far as practicable. Concerns were raised by Professor Chandler as to whether excavating the shaft might without destabilising the adjacent ground prove difficult. Putting a temporary cap on the shaft and monitoring the progressive settlement of the fill within it, on the other hand, appeared to risk further loss of irreplaceable archaeology.

These issues were explored further in an

Fig 10.6
West lateral photographed from the bottom of Borehole 4 (left); Void beneath the 1776 shaft photographed from Borehole 7 (right). (Courtesy Skanska)

Fig 10.7
Section showing the voids and position of the tunnels as understood before the remedial works began. (Eddie Lyons, © English Heritage)

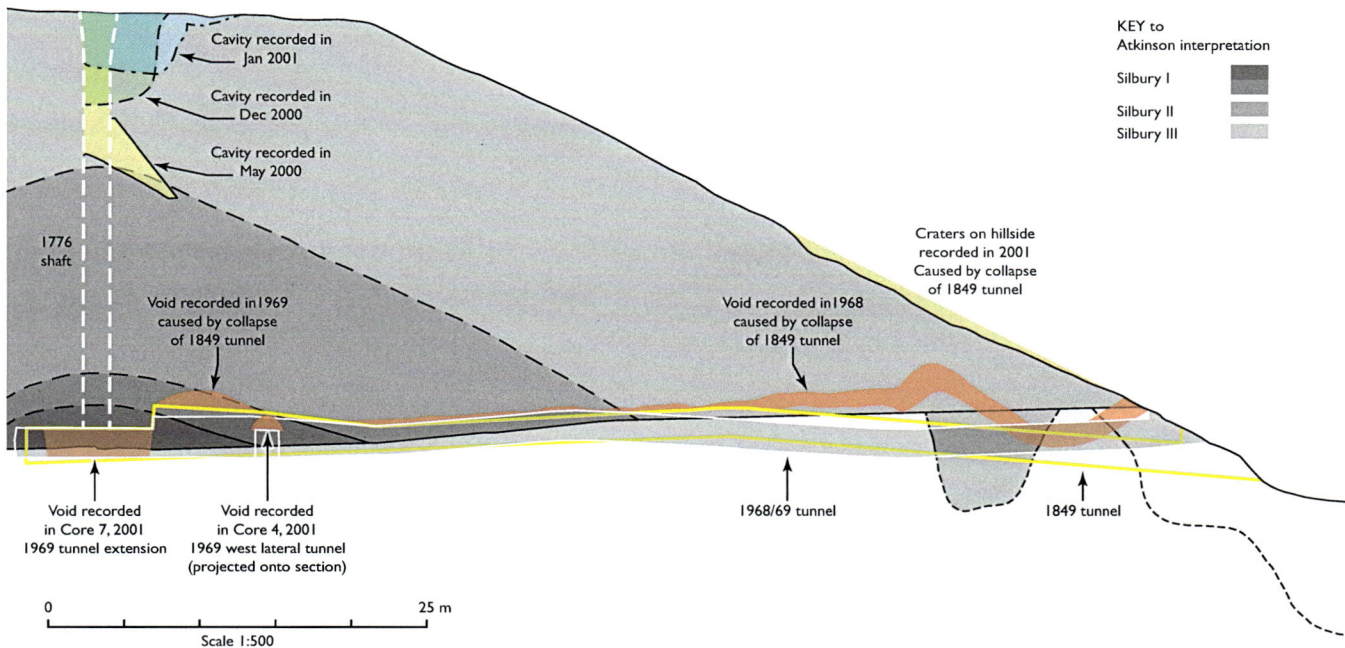

assessment of the conservation risks (McAvoy 2005a). This assessed the likely extent of further damage to the Hill's unique archaeology from known or predicted voids, by quantifying the likely existing voids from previous mining operations and by identifying the predicted pattern of future subsidence. Two modes of collapse were identified: those leaving shallow voids close to the surface, which were likely to migrate upwards in a widening cone pattern, and deeper cavities where material collapsed and the void migrated upwards stopping at or sometime before the loose debris filled the void. The example given was that of the 1849 Archaeological Institute tunnel which, at points less than 3.5m below the Hill's surface, had migrated upwards to form a wide surface depression. Further into the interior, voids had migrated by between 0.4m and 1.3m over the period prior to the tunnel's partial reopening during the 1968–70 excavations.

The damage assessment was set out in relation to the varied components of the Hill using Atkinson's phasing (*see* Chapter 1). It was established that relatively large parts of the primary mound and its capping (Silbury I) would be directly affected by a 'do nothing' scenario as further collapses inevitably occurred, this phase being where delicate biological remains were known to be present (Canti *et al* 2004). Such remains that are directly associated with archaeological sites are extremely rare for the early prehistoric period in England. By contrast the percentage disruption to Silbury II and III would be far lower (McAvoy 2005a, 14).

The report then went on to look at the risks and benefits to the Hill's archaeology arising from the possible interventions discussed by Skanska (2003) and Chandler (2003) and weighted them against the conservation principles set out in the 'Brief for Project to Stabilise the Monument' (English Heritage 2001) adopted by the Project Board. As expected, there were varying degrees of risk and benefits associated with each option. Drilling and remotely filling the voids was considered to cause the least level of mechanical damage but also gave a lower degree of confidence regarding the filling of voids compared to re-entering the tunnels and backfilling, although this option might cause more mechanical damage. Although all predictions contained a degree of uncertainty, the exercise clearly demonstrated that all options for interventions would result in less damage to the Hill's archaeology than the option

of taking no action, because of the real risk of further collapse.

This assessment was presented before a seminar in Devizes on 28 September 2004 for peer review by invited members of the archaeological community, local stakeholders and other interested parties. A range of views were expressed as to how English Heritage should proceed. Three key conclusions were reached. Firstly, there was little support for remotely filling the voids; secondly, there was considerable support for re-excavating the tunnels and backfilling them directly; thirdly, if such an intervention took place it should be accompanied by the highest level of archaeological recording and investigation.

The Project Board considered this feedback and agreed that in order to effectively meet the project's original objective of filling all known and predicted voids, the tunnels, 1776 shaft and all workings would need to be thoroughly backfilled directly and made safe. Alongside this there should be a programme of archaeological watching briefs and appropriate levels of recording. This approach was subsequently endorsed by the English Heritage Advisory Committee and Commissioners.

Contractors were subsequently invited to submit details of proposed schemes to fill all known and predicted voids whilst working within the constraints of causing the least possible damage to the Hill and permitting full archaeological access for observation and recording. Skanska won the tender process ('Silbury Hill Remedial Works Proposal 2005/2006'), and undertook the works alongside the English Heritage archaeological team.

The remedial works

Permissions

Amanda Chadburn and Rob Harding
As noted in Chapter 1, Silbury Hill is a designated Scheduled Monument and as such is statutorily protected under the 1979 Ancient Monuments and Archaeological Areas Act. Under this Act all works to scheduled monuments such as the Hill require Scheduled Monument Consent from the DCMS. In the case of works undertaken by English Heritage, the Government's statutory advisor, there is a special procedure whereby a Class VI consent

is sought and obtained before works can be carried out. Class VI consents were obtained for all investigations that involved a physical intervention in the Hill.

In the case of the remedial works to the Hill, Class VI consent was obtained following submission of detailed method statements for the works and the development of the necessary accompanying archaeological recording procedures. Although the consent application was dealt with in the Region by the Casework Team Leader, one of the authors (AC), it was reviewed by Andrew Brown from English Heritage's South-East Region to ensure transparency and objectivity in the consent application process. When tunnelling conditions were found to vary from those predicted and the backfilling methodology needed to be changed, a further Class VI consent application was submitted and granted.

As a SSSI, Silbury Hill also has statutory protection under Section 28 of the Wildlife and Countryside Act of 1981. Assent was sought and obtained from English Nature, as it was then known, for the works and for remedial measures to restore disturbed ground. A further assent was obtained from English Nature (now Natural England) for remedial works to make good the slumping of the shaft infilling at the end of the works contract's 12 months defects liability period. In both cases appropriate species seed mixes were to be used for re-seeding disturbed areas.

The planned programme for the remedial works

Rob Harding and Amanda Chadburn

The remedial works were planned to take place over four months at a cost of £600,000. The work was scheduled to take place over the driest months of the year (May to August) and included an outreach and education programme. The method for re-excavating the tunnels included both manual and mechanical removal of collapsed material and fill. The 1968–70 tunnels would be re-excavated in order to reach the centre of the Hill and minimise the loss of undisturbed archaeological deposits. Skanska proposed utilising the existing steel arches left from the Atkinson excavations supplemented by the insertion of timber boards and steel tunnel sheeting overhead to support the tunnel roof (Skanska 2007c), with archaeological recording of the tunnel roof deposits effected by using

a camera mounted on a ROVVER (Bryan *et al* 2007). As the opening up of the tunnel progressed, services to provide ventilation, lighting, power, compressed air, communications and an alarm system were to be installed.

Between each day's work activities there would be periods when the contractor's workers would be stood down to allow archaeological recording. A particular challenge during the emptying of the Main Tunnel was the archaeological investigation of a buried ditch (thought at the time to form part of Atkinson's phase Silbury II, *see* Chapter 1). This ditch had not been bottomed as part of the 1968–70 excavations and the remedial works provided an ideal opportunity to establish the form of this feature and recover material for environmental study and scientific dating (McAvoy 2005b; 2006; Cleal 2001, 63). This required the installation of sheeting and temporary protection to the ditch sides along with a winch to provide a safe working environment for the excavations which were to take place within a very confined space (Skanksa 2007d).

Backfilling of the tunnel would commence once the excavation of the Main Tunnel and laterals had been completed, archaeological recording and sampling carried out, and monitoring and survey equipment installed. Skanska were proposing to test their backfilling methodology by filling a steel transport container of similar width and height to the tunnel and checking the fill for adequate compaction (Skanksa 2007e). Their proposed method relied on the mechanical compaction of chalk fill to the bulk of the tunnel, the process being completed by blown chalk and compaction with hand tools to the final void under the crown of the tunnel and to other small voids (Skanksa 2007c).

For the summit of the Hill, remedial work would be carried out to the boreholes with one being left open above the turf mound for future survey work and an extensometer installed in another to monitor future settlement to the shaft (Skanksa 2007f). With regard to the crater at the top of the shaft, the temporary chalk capping and polystyrene fill would be removed. The crater would then be backfilled using chalk brought to the summit by a temporarily installed monorail. This chalk would then be compacted by hand tools and trampling (Skanksa 2007g).

Finally work would be carried out in sequence to the three depressions to the hillside over the outer sections of the collapsed 1849 tunnel. Here the turf would be stripped and then bagged

chalk winched up the Hill and spread using a mini-digger. The set-aside turves would then be replaced (Skanksa 2007h).

In order to backfill the Hill with as compatible a material as possible and return it close to its original state, English Heritage decided to try to obtain the chalk required from a geologically identical source to that quarried by Silbury's original builders from the ditch around the Hill. Analysis of the chalk at Silbury was carried out by Skanska Technology (Skanska 2007i) and found to be from the Holywell Nodular Chalk Member of the Middle Chalk Formation and probably the Zig Zag Chalk Member of the underlying Lower Chalk Formation. Chalk from the same members was sourced first from the Lafarge Beggar's Knoll Quarry, Westbury, and secondly from the Sonborne Quarry, Basingstoke, to supplement that salvaged from the excavations.

Implementation

Rob Harding, Amanda Chadburn, Gill Campbell, Jim Leary and Nicola Hembrey

Prior to establishing the site compound in the field directly to the east of the Hill (Skanska 2007a) geophysical survey had been undertaken to establish the nature of the below ground archaeology and determine where best to place temporary site offices, tool stores and so forth. Protective measures were taken both in the area covered by the site compound and as part of providing a temporary road for access to the Hill.

Preparations for re-entering the Hill to start the remedial works began with the exposure of the portal to the 1968–70 tunnels in October 2006. The fill on the outside of the portal area was removed, to expose the tunnel entrance (Fig 10.8) and the ground was scraped around the portal using the machine in order to reduce the floor level and facilitate access (this material probably represents primarily trample from 1968–70). The door to the 1968–70 tunnel was opened on the 11 May 2007 and the tunnel was found, as expected, to have been filled with type 1 road stone (formed of 50–100mm angular limestone) on the top of which sat collapsed chalk material from the tunnel roof with some voiding above (Fig 10.9). The road stone backfill had been poorly compacted and, in some places, only took up 75 per cent of the internal dimensions within the steel arch supports. The void above the road stone had allowed the chalk from the roof and upper walls to unravel (fall in) as predicted by Professor Chandler (and detailed in McAvoy 2005b). Generally this ravelling had not extended more than 5 metres above the tunnel arches. Chalk was found to have been packed between the tunnel sides and the archwork especially to the west side of the tunnel.

Both the road stone backfill and the collapsed chalk were removed with a machine under watching brief conditions. The collapsed chalk was recorded as a series of context numbers according to which bay (or groups of bays, depending on which was possible given the confines of the tunnel) it had been recovered from. The chalk was then loaded onto a conveyor belt and visually scanned for finds, which, when recovered, could then be related by their context number back to the bay or a group of bays from which they originated (*see* methodology in Chapter 2). Since these finds were recovered from post-1970 collapsed material (recorded as Phase 20) they were not *in situ*, however, they are unlikely to have moved far and clearly originated from the body of the mound and thus could potentially be used for dating the different phases of the Hill.

The road stone and collapsed chalk infilling continued until Bay 57. Significant and unpredicted voiding was encountered close to the meeting of the 1968–70 and 1849 tunnels (between Bays 18 and 22, Fig 10.10). Mark Kirkbride, the Skanska engineering manager, in 'Summary of Construction Works' (2008) estimated that this void had a volume of approximately 18 cubic metres, was about 14 metres wide and extended as a narrow slot at an angle of approximately 30 degrees up into the Hill. A second void was encountered at Bays 39 to 43 extending back towards the first void. Smaller than the first, it was estimated that it had a total volume of about 12 cubic metres. Both voids were large enough for at least one person to get up into and were recorded as far as possible with the Total Station Theodolite. However, for health and safety reasons it was not possible to climb up the full length of the voids and therefore they were not fully surveyed.

It is known that John Taylor, the 1968–70 director of engineering, mapped the open sections of the 1849 tunnel in advance of the 1968–70 works (*see* Fig 1.10) and that no attempt was made to backfill the voids recorded. These voids along with the poor quality of the backfilling to the 1968–70 tunnels had led to a column of chalk progressively collapsing above each void and reconsolidating. A volumetric comparison and their geographical relationship linked them to the depressions seen on the south slope of the Hill (Figs 10.7, 10.11).

Also related to this voiding was a large crater ([4903], Phase 20) recorded on the surface of the Hill overlying the area where the 1968–70 Main Tunnel merged with the 1849 tunnel. The primary fill was a thin lens of washed-in topsoil, whilst the secondary fill appeared to be backfill, comprising spoil from the tunnelling works, including some fragments of organic material

and a residual retouched flint flake. Also recovered from this context was a drinks can (Coca-Cola) and some bottle glass, suggesting that this material was deposited at the time of the 1968–70 excavation; the crater was probably the result of a collapse into the tunnel during the work at this time.

The voids were in a state of equilibrium at the time when the Main Tunnel backfill was first removed and did not significantly hinder tunnelling operations, although they did necessitate some additional clearance of debris. However, their deteriorating condition as excavations progressed and winter closed in, along with the irregular shape of the voids, did pose a significant challenge to the effectiveness and efficiency of the backfilling operations (*see below*).

After Bay 57 where the road stone fill stopped abruptly, the tunnel was found to be filled with clay mixed with chalk. At first it was thought that this might be a 'plug' of heavy material deliberately placed to act as a backstop to the road stone fill. If so, it was expected, based on

Fig 10.10
Photomosaic of the void over bays 18–22, seen from bay 19 [3810].
(Eddie Lyons, © English Heritage)

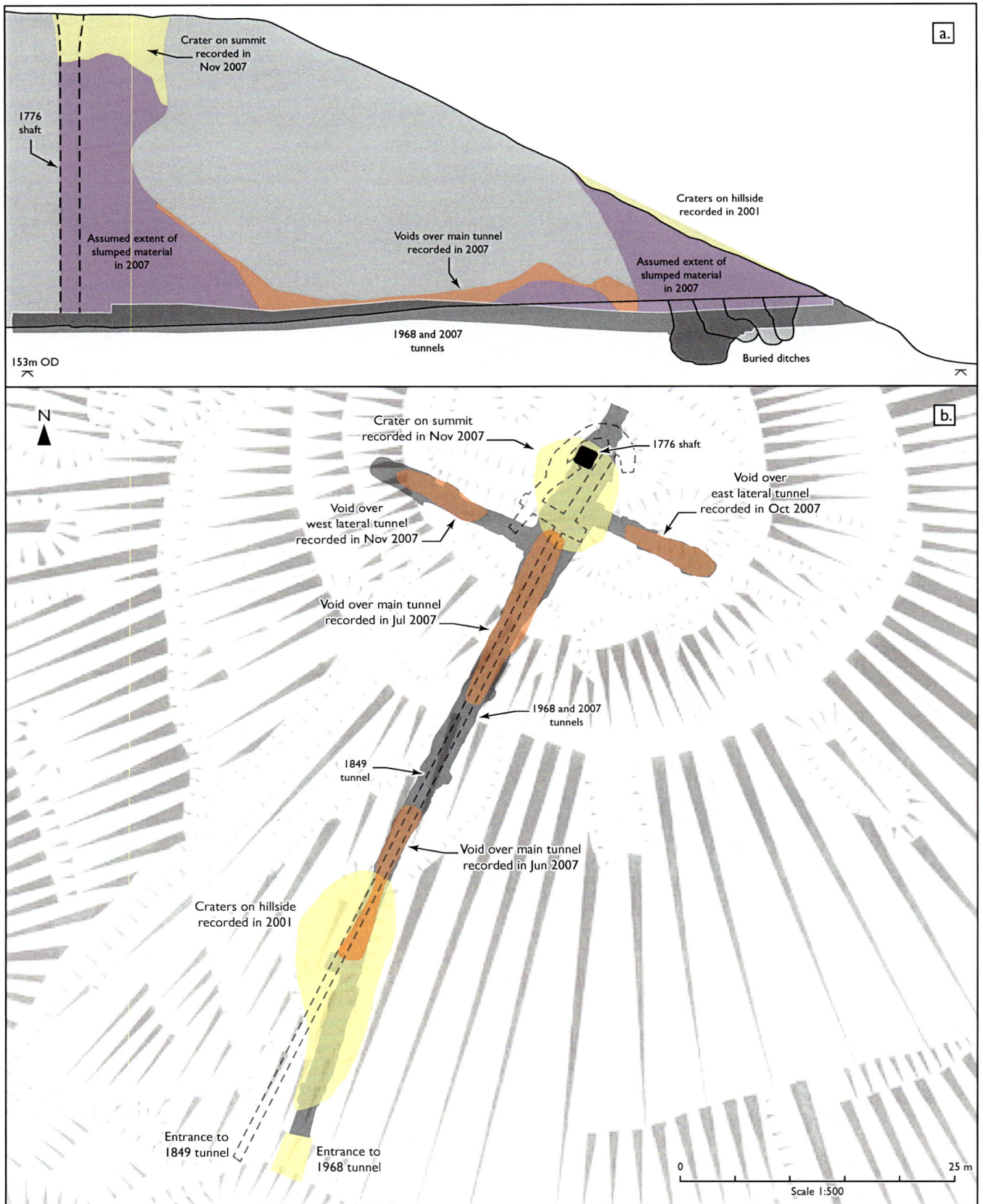

what was seen through the borehole cameras, that after a short distance the excavations would reach the widest part of the 1968–70 tunnel, termed the central chamber, which was known to continue until Bay 73 (Whittle 1997a, 13) and here find a voided area partially filled with debris from the roof.

However this infill (recorded as [3834], Phase 20) was eventually found to continue until nearly the end of the Main Tunnel (Bay 82). Varying in composition, it was a light to mid-yellowish-brown sticky clay and chalk mix, which contained frequent small to medium angular pieces of chalk and moderate medium sub-angular flint as well as some organic material. It also produced 14 pieces of sarsen stone, which had clearly derived from earlier phases of the mound (see Pollard, Chapter 3), as well as a modern nail. In places, it was highly stratified with thin bands of very fine chalk between clay layers, suggesting that it had washed into the tunnel (Fig 10.12).

The project engineers put forward the hypothesis that the infill was the result of the material used to backfill the 1776 shaft becoming saturated and flowing as clay slurry into the Merewether workings, which Atkinson had noted as extending above his central chamber (Fig 10.13). From the 1849 tunnel workings this slurry had then entered the Main Tunnel and filled the approach and parts of the 1968–70 central chamber including the entrance to the West Lateral.

At Bay 68 of the Main Tunnel, where it widened and the roof began to rise as the tunnel entered the central chamber, the excavated face above the clay infill changed composition to that of a mass of chalk fragments. This loose chalk debris proceeded to collapse into the tunnel as clearing operations continued. It became apparent that the debris was running down from a steeply piled bank of chalk which had eroded from the roof of the central chamber as it unravelled upwards. This, it was argued, was the result of a continuous loosening and collapse of the chalk roof above the central chamber, exacerbated by voids left by the 1849 investigations. During the 1968–70 excavations it had been recorded that chalk could be heard falling on the temporary roof to the central chamber.

The void remaining above the central chamber was inspected by project engineers and was found to run for a linear distance of 10 metres at an angle of 45 degrees towards the 1776 shaft. It had a maximum width of 3 metres

and was estimated to be 125 cubic metres in volume (Fig 10.7). No further collapsed or weakened zone carrying on into the roof and no apparent column of failed or structurally disturbed material above was recorded. If left undisturbed the roof of this void would have continued to unravel and eventually the void would have expressed itself at the surface of the Hill. However, engineers were confident that if filled, further damage to the in situ archaeology of the Hill could be prevented.

The looseness of the chalk was thought to be exacerbated by the wet weather which affects suction conditions within chalk and its performance (when saturated the chalk particles tend to be held less tightly because capillary action is reduced). The weight of the loose chalk and the pressure from the mobilised clay/chalk slurry had twisted and deformed the 1968–70 steel mining rings.

Geophysical investigations prior to re-entering the Hill (see above) had not indicated the presence of this void above the washed-in infill of the central chamber. Boreholes sunk during the tomographic survey had located voided areas to the West Lateral and central chamber (Fig 10.6). From camera surveys down these boreholes it was assumed that the central chamber and laterals of the 1968–70 tunnel had not been backfilled and that generally they would be found to be largely empty.

Shortly after the central chamber of the 1968–70 main tunnel had been reached, the combination of the mass of chalk rubble above the tunnel, the unusually wet conditions and the

Fig 10.11 (opposite)
a) schematic part section showing slumping and voids in the Hill above the tunnels; b) plan showing voids at the surface, and presence of voids within the body of the hill. This shows the situation as understood following the completion of the remedial works.
(Eddie Lyons,
© English Heritage)

Fig 10.12
The clay infill of the unbackfilled sections of the tunnel at Bay 69 showing the laminated clay and chalk layers.
(Duncan Stirk,
© English Heritage)

Fig 10.13
The central chamber with
Magnus Magnusson
(centre), Richard Atkinson
(left), John Taylor (third
from left) and others.
(Courtesy of the BBC)

removal of the clay infill resulted in the arches becoming unstable. Following a series of collapses of material and further distortion of the archwork culminating in a major collapse in the tunnel on 23 July 2007 (Fig 10.14), the whole project team were forced to withdraw as working conditions became unsafe and work was suspended until a new method of supporting the tunnel and stabilising the loose chalk could be established. Cameras were again lowered down the boreholes and they established that, beside some further collapse in the West Lateral, conditions had not significantly changed in these particular areas.

Having revised mining techniques which involved the construction of a new tunnel within the collapsed 1968–70 main tunnel (the 2007 tunnel, *see below*), and with improving weather

Fig 10.14 (above)
The Main Tunnel following
the major collapse from Bay
48 onwards.
(Ellie Leary,
© English Heritage)

conditions, progress resumed and the miners broke through into the void adjacent to the 1776 shaft. Here again the 1968–70 steel mining arches had come under considerable pressure from the loading above. From the images returned from the camera in the borehole it was thought that the void within the steel mining rings had been partially filled by debris from above. However, in fact, considerably less of the void had been filled by debris with the shortening of the tunnel height being mainly due to the pressure on the steel mining rings forcing them down virtually one metre into the floor of the tunnel. The 1849 side tunnels were located, containing the remains of timber packing but completely filled with material from the organic mounds which had been squeezed under pressure into the voids. The base of the shaft above the chamber was found to be filled with chalk rubble and there was evidence for the continuous washing down of chalk and other material into the central chamber.

The entrance to the West Lateral was found to be completely filled with washed-in clayey material (*see above*). There was also evidence of chalk washed down from above. Again the steel mining arches were severely distorted for the first few metres into this lateral but after 12 metres the excavations broke through to the void seen in the down borehole camera. The condition of this tunnel was then much as expected except for some irregular voiding to the roof.

The East Lateral was initially completely filled with material from the organic mounds which had been squeezed under pressure into the excavation and distorted the steel mining arches. Once past this material the last six mining rings of this tunnel were found to be clear but a void could be seen running back from above the East Lateral over the central chamber.

Concurrent with the tunnelling operations and, later, while recording and sampling work was carried out within the central chamber, the condition of the temporary capping to the shaft was checked and made ready for backfilling. In late July 2007, after excavations had to be suspended due to conditions within the tunnel, the top of the collapsed material within the shaft was checked but not found to have settled significantly. In late August, however, it was discovered that there had been some settlement to the southern edge of the temporary polystyrene infill and on further inspection it was found that an area of failed chalk which had been left *in situ* in 2000 had subsequently collapsed creating a void of 78 cubic metres. There was no evidence that it had been destabilised by the tunnel excavations and Professor Chandler put forward the hypothesis that the area beneath the 2000 crater might have been in a semi-static condition and that the collapse might be associated with one or more of the voids within the 1776 shaft which had remained open or loosely filled. The collapse could also be linked to the voiding created over the unfilled 1849 and 1968–70 workings (Fig 10.15).

As the Hill was backfilled, further collapses were expressed over the voids above the 1968–70 tunnels and directly over the 2007 tunnel. These followed prolonged heavy rainfall and appeared as depressions in the already scarred hillside. Those collapsing directly into the Main Tunnel led to further delays in the works programme as the debris was cleared, additional support provided and access maintained to the backfilling operations deep in the Hill.

The 1968–70 arches (mining rings) were present throughout the tunnel in varying stated of repair. However, all timber supports between and above them had either been removed or rotted away and there was much evidence of fungal hyphae within any remaining timber. Fungal hyphae were also observed over the surface of the tunnel sides and penetrating into cracks in the deposits as seen in the tunnel sides, especially around the junction of the laterals with the Main Tunnel and within the area of the 1776 shaft. Live earthworms were also recovered from deep within the Hill both from the tunnel sides and within the infilled tunnels. The sides of the tunnels were also very unstable meaning that the sampling methodology had to be adapted from that originally planned (see Chapter 2; Chapter 5; Campbell 2011; Campbell et al 2007).

As well as the mining arches, a number of objects relating to the 1968–70 intervention were recovered and retained. These included two time capsules (see Panel 10.1), metal braces used in the construction of the tunnel, an iron pick end (although this possibly dates to the earlier 1849 tunnelling works), a large spanner and a plumb bob compete with plastic string. Three tobacco tins were recorded outside the portal area, and anecdotal evidence suggests that these belonged to the 1968–70 miners, who left them at the entrance whilst working in the tunnel. A red foil milk bottle top, glass bottle fragments, as well as foil and plastic MAGGI

Fig 10.15
Mining arches and void as seen in 1968 above the tunnel, caused by the collapse of the 1849 tunnel. (Photomosaic of multiple screengrabs, courtesy of the BBC. Eddie Lyons, © English Heritage)

soup powder packets (one mushroom and one spring vegetable) were also noted but not retained.

The 1848 tunnel

Jim Leary

At various places within the 1968 tunnel evidence for the 1849 tunnel was encountered and recorded as Phase 19. This was first visible in the western section between Bays 16 and 19, where the 1968 tunnel merged with it (cut [3017]). The 1849 tunnel was subsequently subsumed within the 1968–70 tunnel and was only visible again in the tunnel sections towards the centre where it had been excavated in a series of diverse directions. It was recorded in Bay 69 (cut [3051]), between Bays 73 and 74 (cut [3060]), and between Bays 76 and 78 (cut [3065]) on the west side of the Main Tunnel. It was also recorded between Bays 78 and 79 on the east side of the Main Tunnel (cut [4159]), as well as in Bay 2 on the northern side of the West Lateral (cut [3080]). Where seen, the 1849 tunnel was filled with collapsed material, confirming that it had been left open after the work had finished and that the surrounding material had squeezed into it over time.

How the engineering solution developed

Rob Harding, Gill Campbell, and Amanda Chadburn

Soon after work began on 30 April 2007 very wet weather occurred with significantly higher than average rainfall. This continued throughout much of the summer, which produced some of the wettest weather on record, meaning that the project faced a number of additional challenges. Not only was access across the east ditch intermittently blocked by flooding but tunnelling conditions were made significantly worse by water percolating down through the Hill, and particularly by water ingress in the centre of the Hill down the 1776 shaft.

Additional ground protection to the compound area was necessary, sited as it was in an area known to contain the below-ground remains of the Romano-British settlement. Further work was also required to protect the archaeology of the external ditch beneath the roadway from the compound to the tunnel portal. The excavated road stone from the backfilling of the Main Tunnel was used for this purpose.

Initially, tunnelling conditions were found to be very much as expected. The 1968–70 arches were in good condition although they had sunk into the floor, necessitating shallow excavation into the natural chalk ground below to give adequate headroom. The works to excavate the buried ditch proceeded as planned and the locating of voids above the tunnel at Bays 18 to 22 and Bays 39 to 43 was easily dealt with through the provision of additional propping.

Major problems were encountered when the tunnel entered clay infill which slowed progress to two bays a day. Even more serious was the finding of a significant amount of chalk rubble at the entrance to the 1968–70 central chamber of the Main Tunnel, which blocked the way to the voided area which had been seen from the down borehole camera. As emptying of the tunnel proceeded, this chalk rubble would fall into the cleared tunnel sometimes necessitating the removal of up to three times as much rubble as would be needed to fill the original tunnel profile. Following the major collapse on the 23 July 2007, work had to be suspended on health and safety grounds. This event necessitated a review of options for continuing the project and achieving the aims of the brief.

The down borehole cameras had indicated that significant voids existed at least to the central chamber and West Lateral (Fig 10.6) but possibly to other areas as well. Consideration was given to stopping tunnelling and trying to remotely fill these voids via the use of boreholes and a chalk based slurry. It was realised, however, that it would be difficult to ensure the slurry flowed into all the voids and it would not be known if all the voids had been comprehensively filled. Another possibility was to construct an entirely new tunnel alongside the 1968–70 one to access the centre of the Hill but this would have caused a substantial amount of damage to *in situ* archaeology.

The solution which was adopted was to remove the overloaded and twisted 1968–70 mining arches and insert new steel arches, rigidly inter-connected with steel struts and back sheeted with corrugated steel sheets (Fig 10.16). The new tunnel arches, which were slightly larger than the earlier ones, could still be inserted without 'trimming' the tunnel walls and further loss of undisturbed Neolithic deposits. The new tunnel rings, together comprising the 2007 tunnel, were inserted from Bay 47 through to where the central chamber was open. Within the central chamber, where it passed through clay fill or collapsed material, the new tunnel did not extend to the full width of the chamber, so only a partial archaeological record could be made of the chamber walls, and environmental sampling from the cleaned tunnel section sides between Bays 47 to 68 was not possible following the July tunnel collapse. Sampling for Optically Stimulated Luminescence dating was completed for this part of the tunnel, however, as this took place just prior to withdrawal on health and safety grounds.

Fig 10.16
The 2007 tunnel showing the method of construction.
(Duncan Stirk,
© English Heritage)

THE CONSERVATION OF SILBURY HILL

Panel 10.1 Time capsules

Jim Leary

Two 1968–70 'time capsules' were left within the Silbury tunnel, one at the beginning and the other at the end of the investigations, and both were recovered as part of the 2007/8 work. The first of these was incorporated within the 1968 concrete lintel at the entrance to the tunnel. A glass bottle, which had clearly been pushed into the concrete whilst it was still wet, contained a rolled up letter with the following typed on it:

From Professor R. J. C Atkinson,
The Old Rectory, Wenvoe, Glamorgan.
National Grid Reference: ST 122726
Telephone: Wenvoe 340
Please add to the above address postal code
CF5 6AN
19th April, 1968.

This tunnel was started on April 7th, and in the next two weeks advanced 18 yards, before a manhole was made to join the new tunnel with that made in 1849. The B.B.C. sponsored this operation, the N.C.B. loaned much of the equipment.

Those taking part were Dr. John Taylor, who was in charge of the tunnel, Mr. Bill Curtis, tunnelling expert, Collis James, Keith Smith, Ted Blackmore, miners; Professor Atkinson, Major Lance Vatcher, David Clarke, Stephen Green archaeologists; Commander J.D.R.Davies, Information Officer; Gillian Lancaster, David Fairhurst, Caterers; Hester Atkinson secretary.

In attendance were Sir Henry de Baskerville, dog; Ambrose, cat. Many others helped in various ways.

On the reverse of this typed letter a rather hasty-looking handwritten note read:

The BBC contribution was chiefly made by Paul Johnstone, David Collison, Elea Birdell, Jimmy Dewar, Peter Bale, Buck Buckinger.
The great British (including Scottish) was represented by Magnus Magnusson.
Photographs by John Wright.

The other time capsule took the form of a green metal box with a wooden inner lining and bearing the BBC insignia. It was recovered from the back of the Main Tunnel ([3834], SF 8033, Fig P10.1.1). The box contained three reels of film in two metal film canisters, a series of paper publications (publicity pamphlets, BBC newsletter), the minutes of a meeting held in Devizes, two little lapel badges with the stylised Silbury 'S' and a 1969 50p coin. The 50p coin was first minted in October 1969 so must have been almost brand new when deposited. All the items had been wrapped in plastic sheeting inside the container; however, water had leaked in over the intervening 40 years and preservation was variable. A badly damaged handwritten note read:

[missing] box was deposited at 15.00 hours on Tuesday 28th October, 1969 by Paul Johnstone and Ray Kite at the furthest end of the tunnel dug into Silbury Hill by Professor Richard [missing] in the course of [missing].

Fig P10.1.1
The BBC time capsule.
(Karla Graham,
© English Heritage)

Another problem which had to be overcome in order to reach the centre of the Hill was the chalk rubble from the collapsed roof of the voids over the 1968–70 central chamber spilling into the 2007 tunnel. A number of options were considered to stabilise the ground above the tunnel including sprayed concrete, additional temporary props and mesh and rock pins. In the end a specialist foaming resin was used which was mixed on site and injected into the area of rubble immediately above the roof. It set within four minutes and once it had done so, set the rubble so it would be sufficiently solid and competent enough to allow tunnelling to resume below and new supports to be inserted. The resin selected was inert with no chemical inter-reaction with the chalk host material. As the tunnel was driven forward, steel sheets and fibreglass dowels were also used to restrain the chalk rubble from flowing into the new tunnel workings.

Skanska's tendered proposals for backfilling the tunnels were based on the assumption that they would be backfilling relatively stable, roughly horizontal tunnels. Their method envisaged the backfilling of the larger part of the height of a tunnel by mechanical means, with the final void beneath the roof being filled either by hand or with hand-blown chalk. However, the method was based on the prediction that the tunnel roofs would ravel in a fairly uniform way to create voids of a much more regular shape than those actually encountered.

The extent and size of the voids encountered running up into the Hill along with unstable ground conditions meant that most of them could not, either practically or safely, be filled mechanically. Rick Pollard Associates were employed by Skanska to come up with revised proposals (Rick Pollard Associates 2007). They considered a range of options for the emplacement of chalk backfill including manual and mechanical stowing, pneumatic conveyance and hydraulic transport. Only hydraulic transport was considered suitable for filling the voids outlined above. Rick Pollard Associates went on to consider the use of a chalk paste or slurry, with the key advantage of a paste being that the drainage and disposal of surplus water used to transport the chalk mix would not be required. To improve the flow it was suggested that a small quantity of super-plasticiser, a water-soluble organic compound, be added to the mix. Also, to improve the set of the paste, it was suggested that hydraulic lime be added.

The addition of hydraulic lime raised concerns as to the mix's permeability and the pH of the paste, especially the placing of a highly alkaline paste next to the organic mounds and the delicate biological remains contained within these deposits, not to mention any features associated with them on the OLS in the centre of the Hill. Tests were carried out on a range of mixes using variable quantities of lime and the results considered. Concerns as to the effect on the delicate biological remains preserved within the organic mounds remained and it was decided that all areas adjacent, either horizontally or vertically, to the organic mounds and associated deposits, including the OLS, would be backfilled with pure chalk. Walls consisting of pure quarried chalk packed polypropylene bags would be stacked against the tunnel sides in the central part of the Hill (Phases 4 to 6.1), supplemented with loose quarried chalk to protect these vulnerable deposits. Polypropylene sacks would be used as opposed to hessian or another natural material in order to minimise the inclusion of new organic matter into the monument and thus reduce further fungal growth. Away from these deposits, that is Phases 6.2 and above, including the crater to the summit, chalk paste with the addition of hydraulic lime and a super-plasticiser would be used as required.

Backfilling the tunnels

On 20 November 2007, backfilling of the central section of the mound commenced. All areas of the central chamber abutting the remains of the organic mounds and Gravel Mound were backfilled using bagged chalk with remaining minor voids filled with hand or mechanically impacted chalk. Approximately 3,500 bags of chalk were used in the central chamber alone. No organic materials or additives were present in this backfilling.

The end of the East Lateral was also filled with bagged chalk (Fig 10.17) and then the remainder of the East Lateral and the void above it were filled with chalk paste without the addition of lime. The method for filling the voids which rose up into the Hill was to build a bagged chalk retaining wall to seal off the base of the void having first installed a pipe to deliver the paste to the highest point of the void. An air return pipe would ensure that trapped air did not prevent the complete filling of the void and, when air ceased to return, would indicate when the paste had reached the top of the void. Once full, all pipework would be withdrawn.

Where possible the remaining 1968–70 arches and the 2007 tunnel arches were removed but in places health and safety concerns prevented this. Side sheeting was also removed to allow the chalk paste to flow round any remaining support and fill all voids. The end of the West Lateral was filled with bagged chalk and then pumped full with the chalk paste without the additional of hydraulic lime. It had been estimated that 12 cubic metres of paste would be needed to complete the filling of the West Lateral. In fact 50 cubic metres were used and it is thought that the paste found its way into the remaining voids from 1849 workings and at least partially filled these as well.

With the central chamber of the Main Tunnel and laterals filled, attention turned to backfilling the rest of the Main Tunnel. The 2007 tunnel which was driven through clay slurry and chalk rubble to reach the central chamber did not touch on the organic mounds. Again, it was dammed with chalk bags, and chalk paste (here with the addition of hydraulic lime) was used to completely fill the tunnel (Fig 10.18). A similar method was used for the remaining Main Tunnel with roof voids being filled with the same technique as described for the central voids which rose up into the Hill. Between Bays 21 and 47, the stretch of Main Tunnel found to have major voids above, it had been estimated that 150 tonnes of chalk paste would be required. In the event, 229 tonnes were used and it is believed that the additional paste flowed into unfilled sections of the 1849 tunnel. Finally, with the portal frame and door having been removed to the Alexander Keiller Museum at Avebury, a berm built of layers of compacted chalk was constructed across the entrance of the tunnel and the remaining section filled with chalk paste. The ground above the tunnel entrance was then restored to the Hill's original profile as part of the Hillside works. In total, some 885 tonnes of chalk were used in backfilling the tunnels of which 678 tonnes were in the form of chalk paste.

Infilling the hillside scar and crater

Once the tunnels and known voids observable from within the tunnels had been backfilled, attention turned to filling the crater at the top of the 1776 shaft. The temporary chalk capping and polystyrene blocks from the crater had been removed during final days of archaeological recording and sampling. As the sides of the

crater were in a fragile state, mesh and rock pins were used to stabilise them temporarily.

Originally, the plan was to tip natural crushed chalk, brought to the hilltop using a winch and monorail, into the crater. It would then be spread by hand-raking and compacted by trampling and under its own weight. However, as Professor Chandler noted, the shape and dimensions of the crater and the risk of further collapse either to the sides or to the deposits beneath now made this too risky. Alternative proposals were therefore developed to fill the crater with chalk paste prepared and pumped up from a station at the base of the Hill. This proceeded in stages, to allow time for the excess water to seep through the Hill. The last one metre or so of the crater was then finished with a crushed chalk capping.

In all, 497 tonnes of chalk paste were used to fill the crater. It had been estimated that the capacity of the crater was 240 tonnes. This suggests that infilling led to a considerable

Fig 10.17
The East Lateral showing the bagged chalk being put in place.
(Duncan Stirk,
© English Heritage)

Fig 10.18
Chalk paste being used to infill the 2007 tunnel.
(Arthur McCallum,
© English Heritage)

Fig 10.19
Completion of the
hillside works.
(Duncan Stirk,
© English Heritage)

Fig 10.20 (below)
Reseeding the summit with
unimproved chalk downland
seed mix (from the left,
Mark Kirkbride, Skanska;
Rob Harding, EH and
Amanda Chadburn, EH.
(Matt Faber)

amount of consolidation of the previously poorly backfilled shaft and, possibly, associated voids. Thirty tonnes of chalk were used for the capping.

Work was also carried out to the boreholes used for the geophysical survey and for accessing the voids deep in the Hill with the down borehole cameras. The steel covers to the tops of the casings to five of the boreholes were removed and the boreholes were filled with graded chalk. One borehole was left covered, but open below, to allow future geophysical monitoring and another borehole was used for the installation of an extensometer to measure any movement in the shaft fill.

Following on from this, work started on infilling the Hillside depressions above the back-filled tunnels. In the planning stages of the project it had been decided that the three interconnected depressions would be filled in sequence from the bottom up with crushed chalk. However, due to the extent of further collapses to the Hillside during the remedial works, the whole area was dealt with as a continuous strip with the ground first consolidated, then spread with crushed chalk and any salvaged turf from the surface replaced (Fig 10.19). Both the hilltop and hillside works were re-seeded using an English Nature (as it was then) approved unimproved chalk downland seed mix (Fig 10.20). As part of the backfilling process provision was made for the monitoring of the condition of the Hill in future years details of which are given in Panel 10.2.

On inspection of the works in April 2009 the infill to the crater was found to have suffered from a small amount of shrinkage. This was expected, given that the bulk of the infill material had been pumped to the surface as a water-borne paste. The shrinkage ranged from 200mm at the north/north-west edge to virtually 0mm closer to the centre. A small quantity of chalk and subsoil, the latter providing a capping to help vegetation re-establish, was air-lifted to the summit of the Hill and spread over the site of the former crater.

The extent of disruption to the monument and what caused the collapses at Silbury Hill

Archival research and archaeological recording carried out after the 2000 collapse has shown that the shaft, at the summit at least, has opened up and been backfilled at various times during the last 235 years (see Chapter 1). We have already noted that William Lukis's drawing (Fig 1.5; Merewether 1851a, 74) and Flinders Petrie's drawing (1924) might indicate that the 1776 shaft was open in 1849 and 1922 respectively, as well as Merewether's remarks concerning the spoil heaps on the summit in 1849 (Merewether 1851b, 10). The evidence from the air photographs has also been presented, showing that the shaft opened up in the mid-1920s and possibly remained so until some time between 1934 and 1936 (see Chapter 1). Written accounts in the Ministry of Works files (for example a document dated 1 April

1925) also talk about the 'hole on the top of the Hill'.

We also know that despite his complaints about the spoil left by the 1776 excavations, no attempt was made by Merewether to backfill the 1849 tunnel to the centre of the Hill, though apparently some of the propping was withdrawn and a wall of bricks constructed to block the entrance (Tucker 1851, 302). In addition, on 24 March 1915, the Deputy Constable of Wiltshire wrote to the Secretary of the Ministry of Works 'Sir, I have the honour to inform you that the chalk has fallen in on the side of Silbury Hill'. This was almost certainly the result of the progressive upward collapse and migration of the 1849 tunnel until the outer section broke through the surface of the Hill. For some years thereafter locals record being able to access the tunnel and crawl to the central chamber of Merewether's excavations (Fig 10.21), with the earliest written record being that of 1910, when Bill Deacon recalls discovering the tunnel when he was out hunting rabbits at the age of 16 (Edwards 2010a, footnote 63). In time, however, the tunnel entrance was blocked by a door and then finally covered over in May 1923 (Passmore unpublished). The tunnel itself was still substantially open when Atkinson came to drive his tunnel to the centre of the Hill in 1968. However, roof collapses led to the tunnel migrating up through the Hill causing the ground to subside to the outer section. For a number of years, workers from the Ministry of Works valiantly laboured up the Hill carrying sacks of chalk to top up the sinking ground but this practice had long been discontinued by the time of the 2000 collapse to the shaft, and a scar tracing the line of the Merewether tunnel could be clearly seen on the south-west side of the Hill.

What we now know about the extent of voiding and the migration of the tunnels up through the Hill following the completion of the remedial works is graphically illustrated in Figure 10.11. There is an oval-shaped slot of redeposited chalk and 2008 chalk backfill centred around the conjunction of the 1849 and 1968–70 tunnels estimated to be between 20 and 25 metres in length and with a maximum width at the surface of approximately 10 metres (though full volumetric analysis remains to be done). The area of disruption is wider at the top than the bottom, because of the extent of slumping on the surface but indubitably extends somewhat beyond the footprint of the tunnels, although still representing only a tiny proportion of the monument. This is largely the result of the incomplete fill of the 1849 tunnel and the meeting up of the voids recorded between Bays 18 and 22 and Bays 39 and 42 and the gradual migration of the unbackfilled 1849 tunnel up through the Hill.

Similarly, the central area of slumped and re-deposited material is centred on the central chamber of the 1968–70 tunnel, the 1776 shaft and to a lesser extent the East and West Laterals, where considerable voids were recorded. This area of disruption appears to have resulted from a combination of the partially or loosely filled 1776 shaft acting as a conduit for rainwater ingress coupled with the fact that the central chamber and laterals of the 1968–70 tunnels were not backfilled. The hole that opened up on the summit of the Hill was in some ways the tip of the iceberg and indicative of a much wider problem of voiding and migration of material deep within the Hill.

Conclusions

In the end the remedial works undertaken as part of the Silbury Conservation Project took over a year, finishing on the 16 May 2008, cost in the order of £1.8 million and involved the deployment of just under 1500 tonnes of chalk. However, the objectives of the project, to fill directly all known and predicted voids and to restore the Hill as far as possible to its original condition, were met despite the enterprise proving far from the expected challenge. We cannot be certain that the delicate biological remains within the centre of the monument will continue to be preserved in such an excellent state but we have done what we can to insure that degradation is reduced.

Fig 10.21
Mr Charles Perry at Silbury Hill, 1922, showing the open entrance to the 1849 tunnel. (Courtesy of the Estates of Charles Perry and Josephine Ovens)

Panel 10.2 Monitoring

Monitoring the infill of the shaft

In order to assess geophysical and environmental conditions within the Hill, provision was made for future monitoring. In relation to the stability of the backfilling of the shaft, a rod-type, multi-point extensometer was installed down Borehole 7 (the one sunk down the 1776 shaft). The aim of this installation was to monitor differential settlement between the shaft sides and the new fill over the full depth of the shaft. The extensometer was provided with eight monitoring locations, one at the underside of the crater capping, one mid-way in the fill and six evenly placed in the shaft below the fill. The extensometer was installed as planned with the head hidden beneath the surface; however unfortunately, it was later located by someone on the summit, possibly with the aid of a metal detector, and the head vandalised, rendering it inoperable.

Fig P10.2.1
Installing the permanent electrode imaging cable into a trench dug into the floor of the tunnel. (Geophysics Team, © English Heritage)

Monitoring conditions within the tunnel

Neil Linford, Paul Linford, Matt Canti and Rob Harding

A shallow trench was dug along the floor of the Main Tunnel (through the natural chalk beneath the Hill and not within the monument itself) to install a permanent electrode imaging cable (Fig P10.2.1). The aim of this array was to both monitor the re-instatement works and provide a means for future geophysical imaging of the interior of the Hill. Whilst a number of proposals for the monitoring equipment were considered, including a small diameter instrument access conduit, the electrical imaging cable was chosen on the grounds of cost and the importance of preserving environmental conditions once the backfilling was complete. The imaging cable consists of a multi-core cable with 128 electrode take-outs, spaced at 0.5m intervals, from the centre of the Hill. The full spatial position of each electrode take-out was recorded and then set in highly conductive bentonite clay to lower the contact resistance with the surrounding chalk. The terminal of the cable has been sheathed to protect it from rodent damage and can be accessed from a discrete junction box buried close to the tunnel portal where it ends in four multicore connectors, each addressing 32 separate electrodes in the imaging cable, compatible with the Allied Associates Tigre earth resistance meter system.

Figure P10.2.2 shows model resistivity data calculated from two sets of measurements made from the imaging cable shortly after its installation in November 2007 and a repeat survey conducted in September 2008. These initial representations of the data do not account for the cylindrical ambiguity associated with the geometry of a buried electrode cable and simply depict the data with topographic corrections as if it were collected from a surface mounted array. The array begins from the portal entrance at 0m crossing an anomaly at 12m, in the vicinity of the earlier buried ditch, continuing towards the centre of the Hill where a more extensive area of low resistance is found from 44m, possibly related to the chalk slurry used to backfill the inaccessible void spaces. Longer term monitoring will, hopefully, establish whether variations in the background resistance and in the readings close to the electrode array can be related to short-term wetting events and the settling of the back-fill into the cable trench. Further experiments, perhaps utilising both the buried imaging cable and electrodes placed on the flanks of the hill, may improve the imaging and allow unexcavated areas to either side of the tunnel to be investigated.

An Aquaflex TDR (Time domain reflectometry) system, supplied by Streat Instruments of Christchurch, New Zealand (www.streatsahead.com) was used to monitor the temperature and moisture inside the Hill. It was placed around the edge of the central chamber and then buried into the trench dug in the Main Tunnel floor, alongside the permanent electrode imaging cable. Temperature and moisture content were recorded for 21 months between June 2008 and March 2010 when some of the equipment failed. Both parameters remained almost constant throughout the period, with temperature at 10–11°C and volumetric moisture in the range 28–29 per cent.

Fig P10.2.2
Resistivity data from the tunnel
a) 19 November 2007;
b) 16 September 2008.
(Geophysics Team and Eddie Lyons,
© English Heritage)

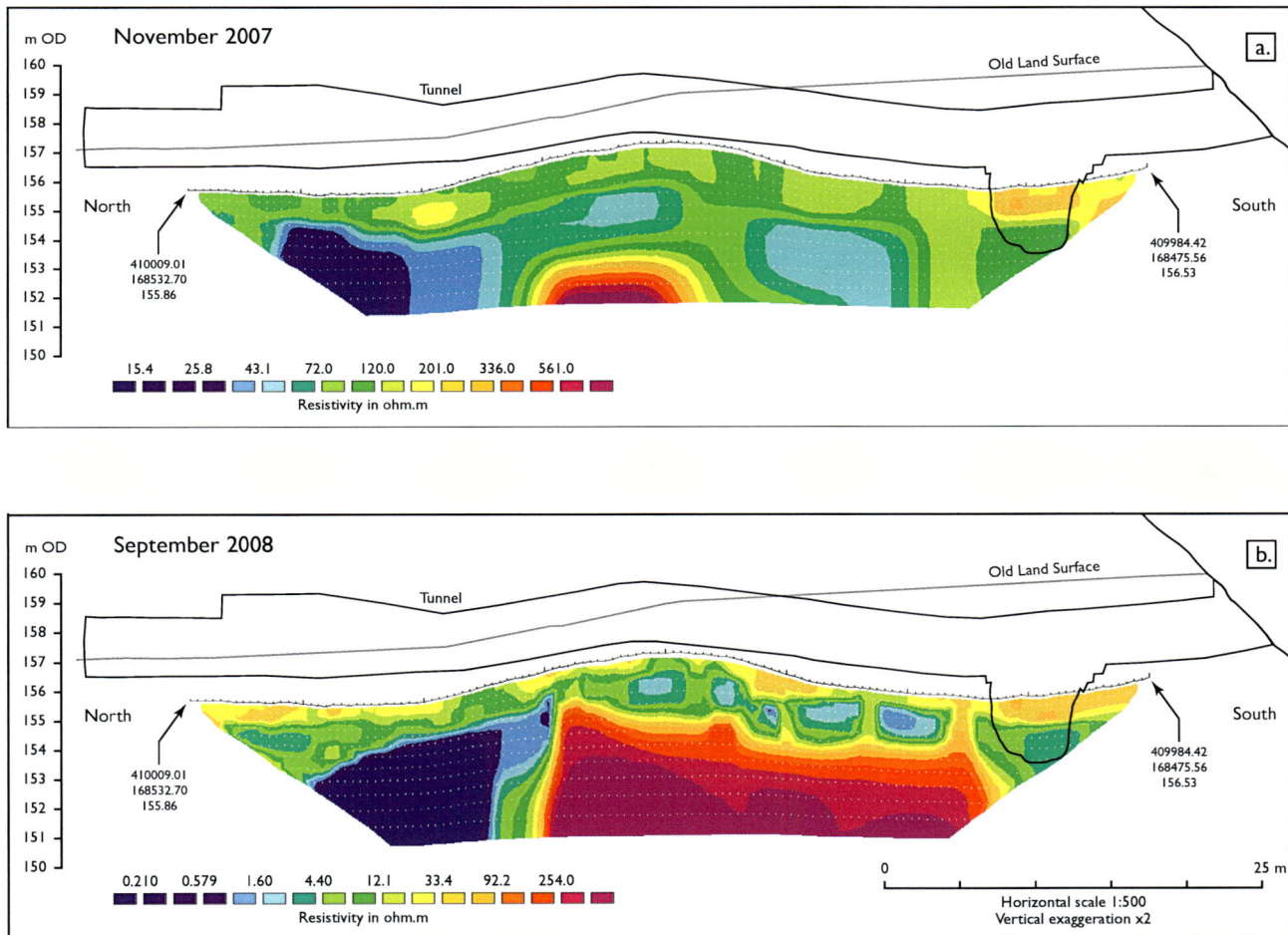

11

Coda

JIM LEARY, DAVID FIELD AND GILL CAMPBELL

In the form that we see it today, the Silbury monument is the product of four millennia of weathering, erosion and modification. This attrition was caused in part by the elements, but also by intermittent episodes of more intense human and animal activity that have left their marks across the surface. That the mound has remained so intact, and evidently stable, has been put down to its superb construction (Atkinson 1968b, 169–70), Passmore (in Petrie 1924, 218) being led to comment that the Hill must have been 'turfed over as made' in order to ensure that no slippage of rubble occurred. The question of whether turves would stay in place on such a slope was not addressed. However, as Atkinson's excavations demonstrated, in all probability few of the features that we see clearly today are those left by the original builders. Even the well-known steps or terraces are the product of early medieval use, although whether they respected or reflected earlier construction details, as Atkinson believed, requires further investigation. It is important to recognise the validity of the many phases of activity. Teasing out details that mark any one stage of Later Neolithic construction is, of course, an important factor, but it is a transitory phase in the monument's varied history and evidence of other phases is perhaps of equal value and importance to the story of Silbury Hill.

The interventions of the first decade of the 21st century were a response to unforeseen events caused by unstable elements within the structure, themselves the product of earlier excavations. They were not designed to answer pressing research questions about the nature of the mound. That must wait for the future. Nevertheless, the opportunity was taken of elucidating the detail of the deposits encountered during 1968–70 excavation and looking at them with a modern eye. The records of that occasion are essentially sound and not so different from those presented here. Atkinson of course presented his four-stage model as a simplification but was well aware of the true complexity of the deposits (*see* for example Atkinson 1969b). That complexity is interpreted here in a different way.

The Conservation Project has also provided an opportunity for detailed sampling of the anoxic deposits within the centre of the Hill. They preserve a whole range of delicate biological remains that are rarely preserved on archaeological sites of this date. The investigations have involved applying new techniques and have helped revolutionise our understanding of the length of time over which construction of the Hill took place. In addition, the geophysical and other surveys have allowed us to the place the mound within a greater chronological and spatial context.

Work does not stop here – samples and materials retrieved as part of the Silbury Conservation Project and preserved *ex situ* at English Heritage (Fort Cumberland, Portsmouth), the British Ocean Sediment Core Research Facility (Southampton) and the Alexander Keiller Museum (Avebury), means that the investigation of Silbury can continue. Silbury now enters a new phase for which this publication we hope provides the springboard.

Our knowledge of Silbury Hill has been considerably enhanced and in turn the work will no doubt make an important contribution to allied studies. During the lifespan of the project enormous strides have been made in Neolithic research: the Gathering Time Project (Whittle *et al* 2011), the Stonehenge Riverside Project (Parker Pearson 2007), Avebury (Gillings *et al* 2008) and excavations at Beaker sites at Amesbury and Boscombe by Wessex Archaeology (Fitzpatrick 2011) have all had a considerable impact and their influence can easily be detected in the chapters above. It would appear that modern analysis of the great monuments at the heart of British Neolithic archaeology has resulted in our knowledge of these sites approaching a threshold. Radiocarbon dating is at the core of this providing ever tighter chronologies and comparisons between sites, but aerial photography is also playing a part in providing unexpected wider spatial contrasts. The potential struggle for pre-eminence and the dynamics between the Stonehenge and Avebury sites has become really intriguing and there are other sites with fresh information to dial into the mix, monuments in the Vale of Pewsey such as Marden and the Hatfield Barrow (Leary and Field 2012), for example, as well as the Marlborough Mound (Leary *et al* forthcoming). We are surely about to enter a new phase, where dating of events allows us to build up local and regional histories and assign social context on the basis of greater certainty. For Neolithic archaeology the prospects are really exciting. We can plan new research with this in mind.

REFERENCES

AAHRG, Avebury Archaeological and Historical Research Group 2001 *Archaeological Research Agenda for the Avebury World Heritage Site*. Salisbury: Wessex Archaeology for English Heritage and AAHRG

Addyman, P and Kightly, C 2000 'The historical and documentary background', *in* Ellis, P (ed) *Ludgershall Castle, Wiltshire: A Report on the Excavations by Peter Addyman 1964–1972*. Devizes: WANHS Monograph **2**, 11–18

Ahlén, I, 1965 'Studies of the red deer, *Cervus elaphus* L., in Scandinavia'. *Viltrevy* **3**, 1–3

Ahnlund, H 1976 'Age determination in the European badger, *Meles meles* L'. *Zeitschrift für Säugetierkunde* **41**, 119–25

Akinola, M O, Thompson, K and Hillier, S H 1988 'Development of soil seed banks beneath synthesized meadow communities after seven years of climate and management manipulations'. *Seed Science Research* **8**, 493–500

Albarella, U, 2006 'Pig husbandry and pork consumption in Medieval England', *in* Woolgar, C M, Serjeantson, D and Waldron, T (eds) *Food in Medieval England*. Oxford: Oxford University Press, 201–14

Albarella, U and Serjeantson, D 2002 'A passion for pork: Butchery and cooking at the British Neolithic site of Durrington Walls', *in* Milner, N and Miracle P (eds) *Consuming Passions and Patterns of Consumption*. Cambridge: MacDonald Institute, 33–49

Albarella, U, Manconi, F, and Trentacoste 2011 'A week on the plateau: Pig husbandry, mobility and resource exploitation in central Sardinia', *in* Albarella, U and Trentacoste, A (eds) *Ethnozooarchaeology: The Present and Past of Human–Animal Relationships*. Oxford: Oxbow, 142–59

Allen, M J 2005a 'Considering prehistoric environmental change on the Marlborough Downs', *in* Brown, G, Field, D and McOmish, D (eds) *The Avebury Landscape: Aspects of Field Archaeology on the Marlborough Downs*. Oxford: Oxbow, 77–86

Allen, M 2005b 'Beaker settlement and environment on the chalk downs of southern England'. *Proc Prehist Soc* **71**, 219–46

Allen, M and Gardiner J 2009 'If you go down to the woods today; a re-evaluation of the chalkland postglacial woodland: implications for prehistoric communities', *in* Allen, M J, Sharples, N and O'Connor, T (eds) *Land and People: Papers in Memory of John G Evans*, Oxford: Oxbow Books (Prehistoric Society Research Paper **2**), 49–66

Allen, M J, Gardiner, J and Sheridan, A 2012 *Is there a British Chalcolithic? People, Place and Polity in the Late 3rd Millennium*. Oxford: Oxbow Books (Prehistoric Society Research Paper 4)

Ambers, J 1996 'Radiocarbon analyses from the Grime's Graves mines', *in* Longworth, I and Varndell, G (eds) *Excavations at Grime's Graves, Norfolk 1972–1976. Fascicule 5: Mining in the Deeper Mines*. London: British Museum, 000–000

Anderson, R. 2005 'Annotated list of the non-marine Mollusca of Britain and Ireland'. *Journal of Conchology* **38**, 607–37

Anon 2006 'Sensational new discoveries at Bryn Celli Ddu'. *Brit Archaeol* **89**, 6

Ashbee, P 1976 'Bant's Carn St Mary's, Isles of Scilly'. *Cornish Archaeol* **15**, 11–26

Ashbee, P 2004 'Early ditches: Their forms and infills', *in* Cleal, R and Pollard, J (eds) *Monuments and Material Culture. Papers in Honour of Avebury Archaeologists: Isobel Smith*. Salisbury: Hobnob Press, 1–14

Ashbee, P, Smith, I F and Evans, J G 1979 'Excavation of three long barrows near Avebury, Wiltshire'. *Proc Prehist Soc* **45**, 207–300

Ashmore, P 1999 'Radiocarbon dating: avoiding errors by avoiding mixed samples'. *Antiquity* **73**, 124–30

Ashmore, W, and Knapp, B A 1999 *Archaeologies of Landscape: Contemporary Perspectives*. Oxford: Blackwell

Atkinson, R J C 1957 'Worms and weathering'. *Antiquity* **31**, 219–33

Atkinson, R J C 1967 'Silbury Hill'. *Antiquity* **41**, 259–62

Atkinson, R J C 1968a 'Silbury Hill, 1968'. *Antiquity* **42**, 299

Atkinson, R J C 1968b *Silbury Hill*. London: British Broadcasting Corporation

Atkinson, R J C 1969a 'The date of Silbury Hill'. *Antiquity* **43**, 216

Atkinson, R J C 1969b 'A season at Silbury'. *The Listener*, 16 January

Atkinson, R J C 1970 'Silbury Hill, 1969–70'. *Antiquity* **44**, 313–14

Atkinson, R J C 1978 'Silbury Hill', *in* Sutcliffe, R (ed) *Chronicle: Essays from Ten Years of Television Archaeology*. London: British Broadcasting Corporation, 159–73

Atkinson, R J C and Sorrell, A 1959 *Stonehenge and Avebury*. London: Her Majesty's Stationery Office

Atkinson, R J C, Piggott, C M and Sandars, N K 1951 *Excavations at Dorchester, Oxon: First Report. Sites I, II, IV, V and VI, With a Chapter on Henge Monuments*. Oxford: Ashmolean Museum

Attenborough, D 2010 'Foreword', *in* Leary, J and Field, D 2010 *The Story of Silbury Hill*. Swindon: English Heritage Publishing, x–xi

Baca, K A 1999 *Indian Mounds of Mississippi: A Visitor's Guide*. Jackson, Mississippi: Department of Archives and History

Bailon, S 1999 *No 1: Différenciation Ostéologique des Anoures (Amphibia, Anura) de France*. Fiches D'Osteologie Animale Pour L'Archéologie Série C: Varia. APDCA Antibes: Centre de Recherches Archéologiques du CNRS

Baker, P 2001a 'A note on the antler tine from Silbury Hill'. Unpublished report. Portsmouth, English Heritage

Baker, P 2001b 'A second antler fragment from Silbury Hill (661)'. Unpublished report. Portsmouth, English Heritage

Barber, M 2003 *Late Neolithic Palisade Enclosures at West Kennet: Report on the Aerial Photographic Transcription and Analysis*. English Heritage Aerial Survey Report Series AER/1/2003. Swindon: English Heritage

Barber, M, Field, D and Topping, P 1999 *The Neolithic Flint Mines of England*. Swindon: RCHME

Barber, M, Grady, D and Winton, H 2003 'From pit circles to propellers: recent results from air survey in Wiltshire'. *Wiltshire Archaeol Natur Hist Soc Mag* **96**, 148–60

Barclay, K, and Biddle, M 1990 'Stone and pottery lamps', *in* Biddle, M. (ed) *Objects and Economy in Medieval Winchester. Winchester Studies, 7.ii, Artefacts from Medieval Winchester*. Oxford: Clarendon Press, 983–1000

Barclay, A and Hey, G 1999 'Cattle, cursus monuments and the river: the development of ritual and domestic landscapes in the Upper Thames Valley', *in* Barclay, A and Harding, J (eds) *Pathways and Ceremonies: The Cursus Monuments of Britain and Ireland*, Oxford: Oxbow, 67–76

Barclay, A, Marshal P, and Fitzpatrick A 2011 'Radiocarbon dates and chronology', *in* Fitpatrick, A P (ed) *The Amesbury Archer and the Boscombe Bowmen: Early Bell Beaker Burials at Boscombe Down, Amesbury, Wiltshire, Great Britain: Excavations at Boscombe Down, Volume 1*. Oxford: Oxbow, 000–000

Barker, C 1985 'The long mounds of the Avebury region'. *Wiltshire Archaeol Natur Hist Mag* **79**, 7–38

Barker, G and Webley, D 1978 'Causewayed camps and Early Neolithic economies in central southern England'. *Proc Prehist Soc* **44**, 161–86

Barrett, J 1994 *Fragments from Antiquity. An Archaeology of Social Life in Britain, 2900–1200 BC*. Oxford: Blackwell Publishers

Bartoš, L and Hyánek, J 1983 'Social position in the red deer stag. I. The effect on developing antlers', *in* Brown, R D (ed) *Antler Development in Cervidae*. Kingsville: Caesar Kleberg Wildlife Research Institute, 451–61

Bashilov, V A and Yablonsky, L T 2000 'Some current problems concerning the history of Early Iron Age Eurasian Steppe nomadic societies', *in* Davis-Kimball, J, Murphy, E M, Koryakova, L and Yablonsky, L T (eds) *Kurgans, Ritual Sites, and Settlements: Eurasian Bronze and Iron Age*, Oxford: Archaeopress BAR International Series **890**, 9–12

Baxter, I L 2011 'Faunal remains, Temple Precinct', *in* Medlycott, M, 'The Roman Town of Great Chesterford'. *East Anglian Archaeol* **137**, 320–44 and appendix 5.1 (CD)

Bayliss, A 2009 'Rolling out revolution: using radiocarbon dating in archaeology'. *Radiocarbon* **51**, 123–47

Bayliss, A, McAvoy, F, and Whittle, A, 2007a 'The world recreated: redating Silbury Hill in its monumental landscape'. *Antiquity* **81**, 26–53

Bayliss, A, Bronk Ramsey, C, van der Plicht, J, and Whittle, A 2007b 'Bradshaw and Bayes: towards a timetable for the Neolithic', *in* Bayliss A and Whittle A (eds) *Histories of the Dead: Building Chronologies for Five Southern British Long Barrows*. Cambridge: *Cambridge Archaeol J* **17** Supplement S1, 1–28

Bayliss, A, Whittle, A and Mysocki, M 2007c 'Talking about my generation: The date of the West Kennet long barrow', *in* Bayliss A and Whittle A (eds) *Histories of the Dead: Building Chronologies for Five Southern British Long Barrows*. Cambridge: *Cambridge Archaeol J* **17** Supplement S1, 85–101

Beasley, M 2006 'Roman boundaries, roads and ritual: Excavations at the Old Sorting Office, Swan Street, Southwark'. *Trans London Middlesex Archaeol Soc* **57**, 23–68

Belinskij, A B, Kalmykov, A A, Korenevskij, S N and Harke, H 2000 'The Ipatovo kurgan on the North Caucasian Steppe'. *Antiquity* **74**, 773–4

Bender, B 1998 *Stonehenge: Making space*. Berg: London

Bennett, K D 1989 'A provisional map of forest types for the British Isles 5000 years ago'. *Journal of Quaternary Science* **4**(2), 141–4

Bentley, R A, Bickle, P, Fibiger, L, Nowell, G M, Dale, C W, Hedges, R E M, Hamilton, J, Wahl, J, Francken, M, Grupe, G, Lenneis, E, Teschler-Nicola, M, Arborgast R-M, Hofmann, D, and Whittle, A 2012 'Community differentiation and kinship among Europe's first farmers' *Proc National Academy Sciences* **109**, 9326-30

Berseneva, N 2006 'Spatial organisation of the Sargat funeral sites', *in* Šmejda L (ed) *Archaeology of Burial Mounds*. Plze : University of West Bohemia, 12–21

Best, J 1997 'Appendix: The Marlborough Mound', *in* Whittle, A *Sacred Mound: Holy Rings: Silbury Hill and the West Kennet Palisade Enclosure: A Later Neolithic Complex in North Wiltshire*. Oxford: Oxbow Books (Monograph **74**) 169–70

Bevins, R E, Lees, G J and Roach R A 1989 'Ordovician intrusions of the Strumble Head-Mynydd Preseli region, Wales: lateral extension of the Fishguard Volcanic Complex'. *J Geol Soc London* **146**, 113–23

Bewley, R H, Crutchley, S P and Shell, C A 2005 'New light on an ancient landscape: lidar survey in the Stonehenge World Heritage Site'. *Antiquity* **79**, 636–47

BGS, 1974 *Marlborough (Sheet 266)*. Keyworth: British Geological Survey

Biddle, M 1990 *Objects and Economy in Medieval Winchester. Winchester Studies 7.ii, Artefacts from Medieval Winchester*. Oxford: Clarendon Press

Birmingham, R A and Eisenberg, L E 2000 *Indian Mounds of Wisconsin*. Madison: University of Wisconsin Press

Black, E W 1995 *Cursus Publicus: The Infrastructure of Government in Roman Britain*. Oxford: Brit Archaeol Rep, Brit Ser **241**

Boase, W N 1918 'Flax and fibre cultivation'. *Scottish J Agriculture* **1**, 140–7

Boivin, N 2004 'From veneration to exploitation. Human engagement with the mineral world', *in* Boivin, N and Owoc, M A (eds) *Soils, Stones and Symbols: Cultural Perceptions of the Mineral World*. London: UCL Press, 1–29

Boivin, N and Owoc, M A (eds) 2004 *Soils, Stones and Symbols: Cultural Perceptions of the Mineral World*. London: UCL Press

Bolton, B and Collingwood, C 1975 *Hymenoptera: Formicidae* (Handbook for the Identification of British Insects **6**, pt 3c,). London: Royal Entomological Society of London

Bonney, D J and Dunn, C J 1989 'Earthwork castles and settlement at Hamstead Marshall, Berkshire', *in* Bowden, M, Mackay D and Topping P (eds) *From Cornwall to Caithness: Some Aspects of British Field Archaeology*. Oxford: Brit Archaeol Rep, Brit Ser **209**, 173–82

Booth, P, Champion, T, Foreman, S, Garwood, P, Glass, H, Munby, J, and Reynolds, A 2011 *On Track: The Archaeology of High Speed 1 Section 1 in Kent*. Oxford: Wessex Archaeology

Bowden, M 2005 *The Malvern Hills: An Ancient Landscape*. Swindon: English Heritage

Bowen, H C and Smith, I F 1977 'Sarsen stones in Wessex: The society's first investigation in the evolution of the landscape project'. *Antiq J* **57**, 185–96

Boyd Dawkins, W 1901 'The cairn and sepulchral cave at Gop, near Prestatyn'. *Archaeol J* **58**, 322–41

Bradley, R 1984 *The Social Foundations of Prehistoric Britain*.Harlow: Longman

Bradley, R 1990 *The Passage of Arms. An Archaeological Analysis of Prehistoric Hoards and Votive Deposits*. Cambridge: Cambridge University Press

Bradley, R 1998 *The Significance of Monuments. On the Shaping of Human Experience in Neolithic and Bronze Age Europe*. London: Routledge

Bradley, R 2000 *An Archaeology of Natural Places*. London: Routledge

Bradley, R 2005 *Ritual and Domestic Life in Prehistoric Europe*. London: Routledge

Brain, C K, 1981 *The Hunters or the Hunted?* Chicago and London: The University of Chicago Press

Brentnall, H C 1946 'Sarsens'. *Wiltshire Archaeol Natur Hist Mag* **51**, 419–39

Breuning-Madsen, H, Holst, M K, and Rasmussen, M, 2002 'Iron pan formation in burial mounds, Denmark', *in 17th WCSS, Thailand*, Paper 202

Brian, M V 1977 *Ants*. New Naturalist **59**. London: Collins

Brine, L 1996 *The Ancient Earthworks and Temples of the American Indians*. Royston: Oracle

Brittain, M 2004 'Layers of life and death: Aspects of monumentality in the early Bronze Age of Wales', *in* Cummings V and Fowler C *The Neolithic of the Irish Sea. Materiality and Traditions of Practice*. Oxford: Oxbow Books, 224–32

Brock, F, Higham, T, Ditchfield, P, and Bronk Ramsey, C 2010 'Current pretreatment methods for AMS radiocarbon dating at the Oxford Radiocarbon Accelerator Unit (ORAU)'. *Radiocarbon* **52**, 103–12

Bronk Ramsey, C 1995 'Radiocarbon calibration and analysis of stratigraphy: the OxCal program'. *Radiocarbon*, **37**, 425–30

Bronk Ramsey, C 1998 'Probability and dating'. *Radiocarbon* **40**, 461–74

Bronk Ramsey, C 2001 'Development of the radiocarbon calibration program OxCal'. *Radiocarbon* **43**, 355–63

Bronk Ramsey, C 2009 'Bayesian analysis of radiocarbon dates'. *Radiocarbon* **51**, 337–60

Bronk Ramsey, C, Higham, T F G, Bowles, A, and Hedges, R E M 2004a 'Improvements to the pretreatment of bone at Oxford'. *Radiocarbon* **46**, 155–63

Bronk Ramsey, C, Ditchfield, P, and Humm, M 2004b 'Using a gas ion source for radiocarbon AMS and GC-AMS'. *Radiocarbon*, **46**, 25–32

Brooke, J W 1910 'The excavation of a Roman well near Silbury Hill, October, 1908'. *Wiltshire Archaeol Natur Hist Mag* **36**, 373–5

Brooke, J W and Cunnington, B H 1897 'Excavation of a Roman well near Silbury Hill, July and October 1896'. *Wiltshire Archaeol Natur Hist Mag* **29** (1896–7), 166–71

Brophy, K 2000 'Water Coincidence? Cursus Monuments and Rivers', *in* Ritchie A (ed) *Neolithic Orkney in its European Context*. Cambridge: MacDonald Institute for Archaeological Research, 59–60

Brophy, K 2010 '"… a place where they tried their criminals": Neolithic round mounds in Perth and Kinross', *in* Leary, J, Darvill, T and Field, D (eds) *Round Mounds and Monumentality in the British Neolithic and Beyond*. Oxford: Oxbow (Neolithic Studies Group Seminar Papers **10**), 10–27

Brown, G 2003 'Irrigation of water meadows in England', *in* Ruralia V *Water Management in Medieval Rural Economy*. Prague: Institute of Archaeology, Academy of Sciences of the Czech Republic, 84–92

Brown, G, Field, D and McOmish, D (eds) 2005 *The Avebury Landscape: Aspects of the Field Archaeology of the Marlborough Downs*. Oxford: Oxbow Books

Brück, J 1999 'What's in a settlement? Domestic residential practice and residential mobility in Early Bronze Age southern England', *in* Brück, J and Goodman, M (eds) *Making Places in the Prehistoric World: Themes in Settlement Archaeology*. London: UCL Press, 52–75

Brumm, A 2004 'An axe to grind: Symbolic considerations of stone axe use in ancient Australia', *in* Boivin, N and Owoc, M A (eds) *Soils, Stones and Symbols: Cultural Perceptions of the Mineral World*. London: UCL Press, 143–63

Bryan, P, Cromwell, T, McAvoy, F, and McCallum, A 2007 'Silbury Hill: Archaeological evidence; specific procedures for recording in the tunnel MS06.15.01'. Unpublished report, Skanksa/English Heritage

Bryan, P and Cromwell T 2008 'Tunnel vision – the challenges faced in recording Atkinson's tunnel'. *Research News* **10**, 21–3

Bubenik, A B 1983 'The behavioral aspects of antlerogenesis', *in* Brown R D (ed) *Antler Development in Cervidae*. Kingsville: Caesar Kleberg Wildlife Research Institute, 389–449

Buck, C E, Litton, C D, and Smith, A F M 1992 'Calibration of radiocarbon results pertaining to related archaeological events'. *J Archaeol Sci* **19**, 497–512

Buck, C E, Cavanagh, W G, and Litton, C D 1996 *Bayesian Approach to Interpreting Archaeological Data*. Chichester: Wiley-Blackwell

Buck, D D 1975 'Three Han Dynasty tombs at Ma-wang-tui'. *World Archaeol* **7**, 30–45

Burgess, C and Shennan, S 1976 'The Beaker Phenomenon, some suggestions', *in* Burgess C and Miket R (eds) *Settlement and Economy in the Third Millennium BC*. Oxford: Brit Archaeol Rep, Brit Ser **33**, 309–31

Burl, A 1979 *Prehistoric Avebury*. London: Yale University Press

Burl, A, 1985 *Megalithic Brittany*. London: Thames and Hudson

Burl, A 1993 *From Carnac to Callanish: The Prehistoric Stone Rows and Avenues of Britain, Ireland and Brittany*. New Haven and London: Yale University Press

Burl, A 2000 *The Stone Circles of Britain, Ireland, and Brittany*. New Haven: Yale University Press

Burnham, B C 1995 'Small towns: the British perspective', *in* Brown, A E (ed) *Roman Small Towns in Eastern England and Beyond*. Oxford: Oxbow Monograph **52**, 7–17

Burnham, B and Wacher, J 1990 *The Small Towns of Roman Britain*. London: Batsford

Burrow, S 2010a 'Bryn Celli Ddu passage tomb, Anglesey: alignment, construction, date and ritual'. *Proc Prehist Soc* **76**, 249–70

Burrow, S 2010b 'The Formative Henge: speculations drawn from the circular traditions of Wales and adjacent counties', *in* Leary, J, Darvill, T and Field, D (eds) *Round Mounds and Monumentality in the British Neolithic and Beyond*. Oxford: Oxbow Books, 182–96

Burrow, S 2012 *Shadowlands*. Cardiff: National Museum of Wales

Burton, J 1984 'Axe makers of the Wahgi: Pre-colonial industrialists of the Papua New Guinea highlands'. Unpublished PhD Thesis, Australian National University

Cameron, L 1977 *The Wild Foods of Great Britain*. Dorchester: Prism Press

Campbell, G 2011 *Analysis of macroscopic remains from Silbury Hill excavations 2007/8*. Portsmouth: English Heritage (Research Department Report Series **67**/2011)

Campbell, G, forthcoming 'SS4.5 Charred plant remains and charcoal', *in* Harding, J and Healy, F (eds) *The Raunds Area Project. A Neolithic and Bronze Age Landscape in Northamptonshire*, Vol 2, *Supplementary Studies*. Swindon: English Heritage

Campbell, G and Straker, V 2003 'Prehistoric crop husbandry and plant use in southern England: Development and regionality', *in* Robson Brown, K A (ed) *Archaeological Sciences 1999*. Oxford: Archaeopress, Brit Archaeol Rep Int Ser **111**, 14–30

Campbell, G, Hembrey, N, and McAvoy, F 2007 'Silbury Hill: Archaeological evidence; Procedures for on-site recovery, processing, recording, archive & appraisal, MS06.14.07'. Unpublished report Skanska/English Heritage

Campbell, G, Moffett, L and Straker V 2011 *Environmental Archaeology. A Guide to the Theory and Practice of Methods, from Sampling and Recovery to Post-excavation*. Swindon: English Heritage

Campbell, G, Pelling, R and Straker, V forthcoming *A Review of Macroscopic Plant Remains Studies in Southern England*. Portsmouth: English Heritage (Research Report Series)

Cannon, J 2005 'New myths at Swallowhead: the past and the present in the landscape of the Marlborough Downs', *in* Brown, G, Field, D and McOmish, D (eds) *The Avebury Landscape: Aspects of the Field Archaeology of the Marlborough Downs*. Oxford: Oxbow, 202–11

Cannon, J and Constantine, M-A 2004 'A Welsh Bard in Wiltshire: Iolo Morganwg, Silbury and the sarsens'. *Wiltshire Archaeol Natur Hist Mag* **97**, 78–88

Canti, M G 2003 'Earthworm activity and archaeological stratigraphy: a review of products and processes'. *J Archaeol Sci* **30**, 135–48

Canti, M G 2009 'Geoarchaeological studies associated with remedial measures at Silbury Hill, Wiltshire, UK'. *Catena* **78**, 301–9

Canti, M G 2011 *Geoarchaeological Analysis from Silbury Hill Excavations 2007/2008*. Portsmouth: English Heritage (Research Department Report Series **58**/2011)

Canti, M G and Meddens F M 1998 'Mechanical coring as an aid to archaeological projects'. *J Field Archaeol* **25**, 97–105

Canti, M G, Campbell, G, Robinson, D and Robinson, M 2004 *Site Formation, Preservation and Remedial Measures at Silbury Hill*. Portsmouth: English Heritage (Centre for Archaeology Report **61**/2004)

Caple, C 2010 'Ancestor artefacts – ancestor materials'. *Oxford J Archaeol* **29(3)**, 305–18

Carpenter E and Winton H 2011 *Marden Henge and Environs, Vale of Pewsey, Wiltshire: A Report for the National Mapping Programme*. Portsmouth: English Heritage (Research Department Report Series **76**/2011)

Carruthers, W 1992 'The carbonised plant remains', *in* Gingell, C *The Marlborough Downs: A Later Bronze Age Landscape and Its Origins*. Wiltshire Archaeol Natur Hist Soc Monograph **1**, 143–4

Carruthers, W and Straker, V 1996 'Seed flora studies of the buried soil bank, ditch fills, and modern soil pits', *in* Bell, M, Fowler, P, J, and Hillson, S W (eds) *The Experimental Earthwork Project 1962–1992*. York: CBA Res Rep **100**, 134–8

Cartwright, C 1993 'Wood charcoal', *in* Whittle A, Rouse A J and Evans J G 'A Neolithic downland monument in its environment: excavations at the Easton Down Long Barrow, Bishops Cannings, North Wiltshire'. *Proc Prehist Soc* **59**, 221–2

Cartwright, C 1997 'The wood charcoal', *in* Whittle, A *Sacred Mound, Holy Rings. Silbury Hill and the West Kennet Palisade Enclosures: A Later Neolithic Complex in North Wiltshire*. Oxford: Oxbow Books (Monograph **74**), 129–34

Cartwright, C 1999 'The charcoal assemblages', *in* Whittle, A Pollard, J, and Grigson, C *The Harmony of Symbols: The Windmill Hill Causewayed Enclosure*. Oxford: Oxbow Books, 157–61

Case, H 1977 'The Beaker Culture in Britain and Ireland', *in* Mercer R (ed) *Beakers in Britain and Europe: Four Studies*. Oxford: Brit Archaeol Rep S**26**, 71–101

Case, H 1995 'Some Wiltshire Beakers and their contexts'. *Wiltshire Archaeol Natur Hist Soc Mag* **88**, 1–17

Case, H 2007 'Beakers and the Beaker Culture', *in* Burgess, C, Topping, P and Lynch, F (eds) *Beyond Stonehenge: Essays on the Bronze Age in Honour of Colin Burgess*. Oxford: Oxbow Books, 237–54

Catt J A 1986 'The nature, origin, geomorphological significance of Clay-with-flints', *in* Sieveking G and Hart M B (eds) *The Scientific Study of Flint and Chert*. Cambridge: Cambridge University Press, 151–9

Chadburn, A 2001 'Progress at Silbury Hill'. *PAST* **39**, 7–8

Chadburn A 2006 'Aspects of the Iron Age coinages of northern East Anglia with especial reference to hoards'. Unpublished PhD thesis, University of Nottingham. http://etheses.nottingham.ac.uk/1946/ [Accessed November 2011]

Chadburn, A 2008 'The conservation project at Silbury Hill 2000–2008'. *Research News* **10**, 8–9

Chadburn, A and Corney, M 2001 'The Iron Age', *in* AAHRG *Archaeological Research Agenda for the Avebury World Heritage Site*. Salisbury: Wessex Archaeology for English Heritage and AAHRG, 19–24

Chadburn, A, McAvoy, F, and Campbell, G 2005 *Inside the Hill*. British Archaeology **80**, 12–15

Chaffey, G and Brooks, E, with Pelling, R Barclay, A and Marshall P 2012 'Domesticity in the Neolithic: excavations at Kingsmead quarry, Horton, Berkshire', *in* Lamdin-Wymark, H and Thomas, J (eds) *Beyond the Mundane: Regional Perspectives on Neolithic Pit Deposition*. Oxford: Oxbow (Neolithic Studies Group Seminar Series), 200–15

Chan, B 2009 'Life amongst the rubbish: Middening and conspicuous consumption at Durrington Walls', *internet Archaeology*, **26**. http://intarch.ac.uk/journal/issue26/chan_index.html

Chan, B T 2011 'Stonehenge, looking from the inside out: a comparative analysis of landscape surveys in southern Britain', *in* Saville A (ed) *Flint and Stone in the Neolithic Period*. Oxford: Oxbow Books (Neolithic Seminar Papers **11**), 116–38

Chandler, R J 2003 'Report on geotechnical aspects of the stabilisation of Silbury Hill'. Unpublished report for English Heritage

Chang, Kwang-Chih 1978 *The Archaeology of Ancient China*. Massachusetts: Murray Printing (third edition)

Charles, D K, Van Nest, J and Buikstra, J E 2004 'From the earth. Minerals and meaning in the Hopewellian world', *in* Boivin, N and Owoc, M A (eds) *Soils, Stones and Symbols. Cultural Perceptions of the Mineral World*. London: University College London Press, 43–70

Chenery and Evans 2011 'The oxygen isotope evidence', *in* Fitpatrick A P (ed) *The Amesbury Archer and the Boscombe Bowmen: Early Bell Beaker Burials at Boscombe Down, Amesbury, Wiltshire, Great Britain: Excavations at Boscombe Down, Volume 1*. Oxford: Oxbow

Cherry, J F 1978 'Generalisation and the archaeology of the state', *in* Green, D, Haslegrove, C and Spriggs, M (eds) *Social Organisation and Settlement*. Oxford: Brit Archaeol Rep Int Ser **47**, 411–37

Clapham, A R, Tutin, T G, and Warburg, E F 1962 *Flora of the British Isles*. Cambridge: Cambridge University Press (2nd edition)

Clapham, A J, Tutin, T G and Moore, D M, 1989 *Flora of the British Isles*. Cambridge: Cambridge University Press (1st paperback edition, with corrections)

Clark, G 1940 *Prehistoric England*. London: Batsford

Clark, J D 1972 'Mobility and settlement patterns in sub-Saharan Africa: a comparison of late prehistoric hunter-gatherers and early agricultural occupation units', *in* Ucko, P J, Tringham, R and Dimbleby, G W (eds) *Man, Settlement and Urbanism*. Cambridge, Massachusetts: Schenkman Publishing Co, 127–48

Clark, J G D 1954 *Excavations at Star Carr*. Cambridge: Cambridge University Press.

Clarke, D L 1970 *Beaker Pottery of Great Britain and Ireland*. Cambridge: University Press

Clarke, K 2006 'Dogs and wolves in the Neolithic of Britain', *in* Serjeantson, D and Field, D (eds) *Animals in the Neolithic of Britain and Europe*. Oxford: Oxbow, 32–41

Clarke, W G 1914 'The antler-picks', *in* Clarke, W G (ed) *Report on the Excavations at Grime's Graves, Weeting, Norfolk, March–May, 1914*. London: Prehistoric Society of East Anglia, 142–6

Clay, R CC 1925 'Flint implements from the Nadder Valley, South Wilts', *Wiltshire Archaeol Natur Hist Soc Mag* **43**, 156–62

Cleal, R M J 1992 'The pottery', *in* Gingell, C *The Marlborough Downs: A Later Bronze Age Landscape and its Origins*. Devizes: Wiltshire Archaeological and Natural History Society Monograph **1**, 61–71

Cleal, R M J 1995a 'Pottery fabrics in Wessex in the fourth to second millennia BC', *in* Kinnes, I and Varndell, G (eds) *Unbaked Urns of Rudely Shape: Essays on British and Irish Pottery for Ian Longworth*. Oxford: Oxbow Monograph **55**, 185–94

Cleal, R M J 1995b 'The stone settings, phase 3', in Cleal, R M J, Walker, K E and Montague, R (eds) *Stonehenge in its Landscape: Twentieth-Century Excavations*. London: English Heritage Archaeology Report **10**, 168–331

Cleal, R M J 2001 'Neolithic and Bronze Age (Research Strategy)', *in* AAHRG *Archaeological Research Agenda for the Avebury World Heritage*, Salisbury: Wessex Archaeology for English Heritage and AAHRG, 63–4

Cleal, R M J 2005 '"The small compass of a grave": Early Bronze Age burial in and around Avebury and the Marlborough Downs', *in* Brown, G, Field, D and McOmish, D (eds) *The Avebury Landscape: Aspects of the Field Archaeology of the Marlborough Downs*. Oxford: Oxbow Books, 115–32

Cleal, R M J and Allen M J 1994 'Investigation of tree-damaged barrows on King Barrow Ridge, Amesbury'. *Wiltshire Archaeol Natur Hist Soc Mag* **87**, 54–84

Cleal, R M J, Walker, K E and Montague, R 1995 *Stonehenge in its Landscape: Twentieth-Century Excavations*. London: English Heritage Archaeology Report **10**

Clough, T H McK and Cummins, W A 1988 *Stone Axe Studies 2*. London:. CBA Research Report **67**

Clutton-Brock, J 1984 *Excavations at Grimes Graves, Norfolk 1972–1976. Fascicule 1: Neolithic Antler Picks from Grimes Graves, Norfolk, and Durrington Walls, Wiltshire: A Biometrical Analysis*. London: British Museum Publications

Clutton-Brock, J, Guinness, F E and Albon, S D (eds) 1982 *Red Deer: Behaviour and Ecology of Two Sexes*. Chicago: University of Chicago Press

Coles, B 2006 *Beavers in Britain's Past*. Oxford: Oxbow Books

Coles, J M and Simpson, D D A 1965 'The excavation of a Neolithic round barrow at Pitnacree, Perthshire, Scotland', *Proc Preh Soc* **31**, 34–57

Collinson, M E 2011 'Molecular taphonomy of plant organic skeletons', in Allison, P A and Bottjer, D J (eds) *Taphonomy: Process and Bias Through Time*. Dordrecht: Springer, 2 edn, (Topics in Geobiology **32**), 223–47

Collinson, M E, Mösle, B, Finch, P, Scott, AC, and Wilson, R 1998 'The preservation of plant cuticle in the fossil record: a chemical and microscopical investigation'. *Ancient Biomolecules* **2**, 251–65

Collinson, M E, Brain, A P R. and Campbell, G V 2011a *Cellular and Ultrastructural Preservation of Organic Material Within Organic Mound Deposits Recovered from Silbury Hill 2007/8 Excavations*. Portsmouth: English Heritage (Research Department Report Series **60/2011**)

Collinson, M E, Brain, T, and Campbell, G 2011b *Green Plant Material Recovered From the Early Phases of Silbury Hill (2007/08 Excavations): An Explanation for the Unusual Preservation?* Portsmouth: English Heritage (Research Department Report Series **61/2011**)

Conneller, C 2008 'Lithic technology and the *châine opératoire*', *in* Pollard J (ed) *Prehistoric Britain*. Oxford: Blackwell, 160–76

Conneller, C 2011 *An Archaeology of Materials. Substantial Transformations in Early Prehistoric Europe*. New York and Abingdon: Routledge

Cooney, G. 1998 'Breaking stones, making places: The social landscape of axe production sites', *in* Gibson, A and Simpson, D (eds) *Prehistoric Ritual and Religion: Essays in Honour of Aubrey Burl*. Stroud: Sutton, 108–18

Cooney, G 2010 'Mundane stone and its meaning in the Neolithic', *in* O' Conner, Cooney, G and Chapman, J (eds) *Materialitas. Working Stone, Carving Identity*. Oxford: Oxbow Books (Prehistoric Society Research Paper **3**), 64–74

Cope, D W 1976 *Soils in Wiltshire I*. Harpenden: Soil Survey

Corbet, G B and Southern H N (eds) 1977 *The Handbook of British Mammals*. Oxford: Blackwell Scientific Publications (2nd edn)

Coriat, P 1939 'Gwek the witch doctor and the pyramid of Dengkur'. *Sudan Notes and News* **22/2**, 224

Corney, M 1997a 'New evidence for the Romano-British settlement by Silbury Hill'. *Wiltshire Archaeol Natur Hist Mag* **90**, 139–41

Corney, M 1997b 'The origins and development of the 'small town' of *Cunetio*, Mildenhall, Wiltshire'. *Britannia* **28**, 337–50

Corney, M 2001 'The Romano-British nucleated settlements of Wiltshire', in Ellis, P (ed) *Roman Wiltshire and After: Papers in Honour of Ken Annable*. Devizes: Wiltshire Archaeological and Natural History Society, 5–38

Corney, M 2002 'The late Iron Age and Romano-British pottery', in Valentin, J and Robinson, S 2002 'Excavations in 1999 on land adjacent to Wayside Farm, Nursteed Road, Devizes'. *Wiltshire Archaeol Natur Hist Mag* **95**, 147–213, 181–93

Cornwall, I, Dimbleby, G W, and Evans, J G 1997 'Soils', in Whittle, A *Sacred Mound, Holy Rings. Silbury Hill and the West Kennet Palisade Enclosures: A Later Neolithic Complex in North Wiltshire*. Oxford: Oxbow Books (Monograph **74**), 26–29

Coward, F, 2008 'Faunal remains', in Gillings, M. Pollard, J, Wheatley, D and Peterson, R (eds) *Landscape of the Megaliths. Excavation and Fieldwork on the Avebury Monuments, 1997–2003*.Oxford: Oxbow Books, 30–9, 234–5

Crosby, V and Hembrey, N 2011 *Assessment report: Evaluation of the Roman-British settlement in the fields south of Silbury Hill (NGR SU101682)*. Portsmouth: English Heritage (Research Department Report Series **101**/2011)

Crosby, V and Hembrey N 2013 'An evaluation in the fields south of Silbury Hill in 2010: Romano-British settlement, later alteration and water meadows'. *Wiltshire Archaeol Natur Hist Soc Mag* **106**, 101–66

Crummy, N 1983 *The Roman Small Finds from Excavations in Colchester 1971–9*. Colchester: Colchester Archaeological Trust (Colchester Archaeology Report **2**)

Crutchley, S 2005 'Recent aerial survey work in the Marlborough Downs region', in Brown, G, Field, D and McOmish, D (eds) *The Avebury Landscape: Aspects of Field Archaeology on the Marlborough Downs*. Oxford: Oxbow

Cummings, V 2002 'Experiencing texture and transformation in the British Neolithic'. *Oxford J Archaeol* **21**(3), 249–61

Cunliffe, B 1991 *Iron Age Communities in Britain*. Abingdon: Routledge (3rd edn)

Cunnington, M E 1913 'The re-erection of two fallen stones and the discovery of an interment with drinking cup at Avebury'. *Wiltshire Archaeol Natur Hist Soc Mag* **38**(119), 1–7

Cunnington, M E 1914 'List of the long barrows of Wiltshire'. *Wiltshire Archaeol Natur Hist Soc Mag* **38**, 379–414

Cunnington, M E 1927 *The Pottery from the Long Barrow at West Kennet, Wilts*. Devizes: Geo. Simpson

Cunnington, M E 1931 'The 'Sanctuary' on Overton Hill, near Avebury'. *Wiltshire Archaeol Natur Hist Mag* **45**, 300–35

Curwen, E C 1934 'Excavations at Whitehawk Neolithic Camp, Brighton 1932–33'. *Antiq J* **14**, 99–133

Curwen, E C 1936 'Excavations in Whitehawk Camp, Brighton. Third Season 1935'. *Sussex Archaeol Coll* **77**, 60–92

Cutshall, A 1943 'Hemp, wartime crop in the corn belt'. *Geographical Rev* **33**:3, 498–9

Darling, P 1998 'Aerial archaeology in Africa: The challenge of a continent'. *AARGnews: The Newsletter of the Aerial Archaeological Research Group* **17**, 9–18

Dark, K and Dark, P 1997 *The Landscape of Roman Britain*. Frome: Sutton

Dark, P and Gent, H 2001 'Pests and diseases of prehistoric crops: a yield 'honeymoon' for early grain crops in Europe?'. *Oxford J Archaeol* **201**(1), 59–78

Dartnell, G E and Goddard, E H 1891–9 'Contributions towards a Wiltshire glossary'. *Wiltshire Archaeol Natur Hist Mag* **30**, 233

Darvill, T, and Wainwright, G 2009 'Stonehenge Excavations 2008'. *Antiq J* **89**, 1–19

Darvill, T, Wainwright, G, Armstrong, K and Ixer, R A 2008 'Strumble–Preseli ancient communities and environment study (SPACES): Sixth Report 2007–08'. *Archaeology in Wales* **48**, 47–55

Darvill, T, Marshall, P, Parker Pearson, M and Wainwright, G 2012 'Stonehenge remodelled'. *Antiquity* **86**(334), 1021–40

David, A and Williams, G 1995 'Stone axe-head manufacture: New evidence from the Preseli Hills, West Wales'. *Proc Prehist Soc* **61**, 433–60

Davies, P 2008 *Snails: Archaeology and Landscape Change*. Oxford: Oxbow Books

Davies, P 2012 *Land snail analyses carried out on samples recovered from the 2007/8 excavations at Silbury Hill*. Portsmouth: English Heritage (Research Department Report Series **47**/2012

Davies, P and Wolski, C 2001 'Later Neolithic woodland regeneration in the long barrow ditch fills of the Avebury area: the molluscan evidence'. *Oxford J Archaeol* **20**, 311–17

Davis-Kimball, J, Murphy, E M, Koryakova, L and Yablonsky, L T (eds) 2000 *Kurgans, Ritual Sites, and Settlements: Eurasian Bronze and Iron Age*. Oxford: Brit Archaeol Rep Int Ser **S890**

Daws G 2000 'Note on visit of 8th August'. Unpublished report for English Heritage

Deegan, A and Foard, G 2007 *Mapping Ancient Landscapes in Northamptonshire*. Swindon: English Heritage

Deleuze, G 1994 (Trans) *Difference and Repetition*. London: Athlone Press

Deleuze, G and Guattari, F 1988 (Trans) *A Thousand Plateaus. Capitalism and Schizophrenia*. London: Athlone Press

Demidoff, P, 1773 'Some account of certain Tartarian Antiquities, in a letter from Paul Demidoff, Esquire, at Petersburg, to Mr Peter Collinson, dated September 17, 1764'. *Archaeologia* **2**, 222–6

Dennell, R W 1976 'Prehistoric crop cultivation in southern England: A reconsideration'. *Antiq J* **56** 11–23

Devereux, P 1991 'Three-dimensional aspects of apparent relationships between selected natural and artificial features within the topography of the Avebury complex'. *Antiquity* **65**, 894–8

Dillehay, T D, Bonavia, D, Goodbred, S, Pino, M, Vasquez, V, Rosales Tham, T, Conklin, W, Splitstazer, J, Pierno, D, Iriarte, J, Grobman, A, Levi-Lazzaris, G, Moreira, D, Lopez, M, Tung, T, Titelbaum, A, Verano, J, Adovasio, J, Scott Cummings, L, Bearez, P, Dufour, E, Tombret, D, Ramirez, M, Beavins, R, DeSantis, L, Rey, I, Mink, P, Maggard, G, and Franco, T 2012 'Chronology, mound building and environment at Huaca Prieta, coastal Peru, from 13,700 to 4000 years ago'. *Antiquity* **86**, 48–70

Dimbleby, G W 1965 'Charcoal identifications', in Smith, I F *Windmill Hill and Avebury: excavations by Alexander Keiller 1925–1939*. Oxford: Clarendon Press, 38

Dimbleby, G W 1979 'Pollen analysis', in Ashbee, P, Smith, I F, and Evans, J G 'Excavations of three long barrows near Avebury, Wiltshire'. *Proc Prehist Soc* **45**, 284–8

Dimbleby, G W and Evans, J G 1974 'Pollen and land snail analysis of calcareous soils'. *J Archaeol Sci* **1**, 117–33

Dineley, M 2006 'The use of spent grain as animal feed during the Neolithic', *in* Serjeantson, D and Field, D (eds) *Animals in the Neolithic of Britain and Europe*. Oxford: Oxbow (Neolithic Studies Group Seminars Paper 7), 56–62

Douglas, Rev J 1793 *Nenia Britannica: Or a Sepulchral History of Britain*. London: Benjamin and John White

Douterelo-Soler, I 2007 'A multi-disciplinary approach to the characterisation of waterlogged burial environments: Assessing the potential for the in situ preservation of organic archaeological remains'. Unpublished PhD thesis University of Hull

Dransart, P 2011 'Social principles of Andean camelid pastoralism and archaeological interpretation', in Albarella, U and Trentacoste A (eds) *Ethnozooarchaeology: The Present and Past of Human–Animal Relationships*. Oxford: Oxbow Books, 124–30

Draper, S 2006 *Landscape, Settlement and Society in Roman and Early Medieval Wiltshire*. Oxford: Brit Archaeol Rep Brit Ser **419**

Drew, C D and Piggott, S 1936 'The excavation of long barrow 163 on Thickthorn Down, Dorset'. *Proc Prehist Soc* **2**, 77–96

Drewett, P 1985 'The excavation of barrows V–IX at West Heath, Harting, 1980'. *Sussex Archaeol Coll* **123**, 35–60

Drewett, P, Rudling, D, and Gardiner, M 1988 *The South-east to AD 1000*. London: Longman

Drinkwater, N 1991 'Domestic stonework', *in* Saunders, P and E (eds) *Salisbury Museum Medieval Catalogue. Part I*. Salisbury: Salisbury and South Wiltshire Museum, 169–83

Dungworth, D 1997 'Roman copper metallurgy: results from the analysis of artefacts'. *J Archaeol Sc* **24**, 901–10

Dungworth, D 1996 'The production of bronzes in Iron Age Britain'. *Proc Prehist Soc* **26**, 1–23

EA (Environment Agency) 2006 *Kennet and Pang CAMS Document* http://www.environment-agency.gov.uk/research/ planning/33436.aspx [Accessed July 2011]

Eagles, B N 1986 'Pagan Anglo-Saxon burials at West Overton'. *Wiltshire Archaeol Natur Hist Soc Mag* **79**, 103–19

Eagles, B and Field, D 2004 'William Cunnington and the long barrows of the River Wylye', *in* Cleal, R and Pollard, J (eds.) *Monuments and Material Culture*. Salisbury: Hobnob Press, 47–69

Eaton, T 2000 *Plundering the Past: Roman Stonework in Medieval Britain*. Stroud: Tempus

Edmonds, J 2000 *The History of Woad and the Medieval Woad Vat*. Chalfont: John Edmonds

Edmonds, M 1995 *Stone Tools and Society*. London: Batsford

Edmonds, M 1997 'Taskscape, technology and tradition'. *Analecta Praehistorica Leidensia* 29, 99–110

Edmonds, M 1998 'Sermons in stone: identity, value and stone tools in Later Neolithic Britain', *in* Edmonds M and Richards C (eds) *Understanding the Neolithic of North-Western Europe*. Glasgow: Cruithne Press, 250–76

Edwards, A and Horne, M 1997 'Animal bone', *in* Whittle, A *Sacred Mound, Holy Rings. Silbury Hill and the West Kennet Palisade Enclosures: A Later Neolithic Complex in North Wiltshire*. Oxford: Oxbow Books (Monograph **74**), 117–29

Edwards, B 2001 'A missing drawing and an overlooked text: Silbury Hill archive finds'. *Wiltshire Archaeol Natur Hist Mag* **95**, 89–92

Edwards, B 2010a 'Silbury Hill: Edward Drax and the excavations of 1776'. *Wiltshire Archaeol Natur Hist Mag* **103**, 257–68

Edwards, B 2010b 'Silbury Hill: Stukeley's bridle and other finds: Some reports from 1771 and 1850'. *Wiltshire Archaeol Natur Hist Mag* **103**, 323–5

Edwards, B 2013 'Imagining "Silbury and Parnassus the same": Edward Drax and the Batheaston Vase adventure'.

Reginal Historian **26**, 21–6

Egan, G 1998 *Medieval Finds from Excavations in London: 6. The Medieval Household. Daily Living* c *1150–*c *1450*. London: HMSO

Eogan, G 1983 *The Hoards of the Irish Later Bronze Age*. Dublin: University College, Dublin

Ellis, C J 2004 *A Prehistoric Ritual Complex at Eynesbury, Cambridgeshire: Excavation of a Multi Period Site in the Great Ouse Valley 2000–2001*. Salisbury: Wessex Archaeology (East Anglian Archaeology **17**)

English Heritage 2001 'Silbury Hill – brief for project to stabilise the monument'. Unpublished report, English Heritage

Eriksen, P 2008 'The great mound of Newgrange. An Irish multi-period mound spanning from the megalithic tomb period to the Early Bronze Age'. *Acta Archaeologica* **79**, 250–73

Ervynck, A, Lentacker, A, Müldner, Richards, M, Dobney, K 2007 'An investigation into the transition from forest dwelling pigs to farm animals in medieval Flanders, Belgium', in Albarella, U, Dobney, K, Ervynck, A and Rowley-Conwy, P (eds) *Pigs and Humans: 10000 Years of Interaction*. Oxford: Oxford University Press, 171–93

Esmonde Cleary, S 2000 'Putting the dead in their place: burial location in Roman Britain', in Pearce, J, Millett, M and Struck, M (eds) *Burial, Society and Context in the Roman World*. Oxford: Oxbow Books, 127–42

Evans, J G, 1966 'A Romano-British interment in the bank of the Winterbourne, near Avebury'. *Wiltshire Archaeol Natur Hist Mag* **61**, 97–8

Evans, J G 1968 'Periglacial deposits on the Chalk of Wiltshire'. *Wiltshire Archaeol Natur Hist Mag* **63**, 12–26

Evans, J G 1972 *Land Snails in Archaeology*. London: Seminar Press

Evans, J G 1997 'Mollusca ', *in* Whittle, A *Sacred Mound, Holy Rings. Silbury Hill and the West Kennet Palisade Enclosures: A Later Neolithic Complex in North Wiltshire*. Oxford: Oxbow Books (Monograph **74**), 47

Evans, J G 2003 *Environmental Archaeology and the Social Order*. London: Routledge

Evans, J G 2005 'Memory and ordination: Environmental archaeology in tells', *in* Bailey, D, Whittle, A and Cummings, V (eds) *(Un)settling the Neolithic*. Oxford: Oxbow Books, 112–25

Evans, J G and Smith, I F 1983 'Excavations at Cherhill, North Wiltshire 1967'. *Proc Prehist Soc* **49**, 43–117

Evans, J G, Limbrey, S, Máté, I, Mount, R, 1993 'An environmental history of the Upper Kennet valley, Wiltshire, for the last 10,000 years'. *Proc Prehist Soc* **59**, 139–95

Evans, J G, Limbrey, S, Máté, I and Mount, R 1988 'Environmental change and land-use history in a Wiltshire river valley in the last 14,000 years', *in* Barrett, J C and Kinnes, I (eds) *The Archaeology of Context in the Neolithic and Bronze Age: Recent Trends*, 97–103. Sheffield: J R Collis

Evans-Pritchard, E E 1935 'The Nuer: tribe and clan'. *Sudan Notes and News* **18/1**, 62–3

Everson, P, Brown, G and Stocker, D 2000 'The castle earthworks and landscape context', *in* Ellis P (ed) *Ludgershall Castle, Wiltshire: A Report on the Excavations by Peter Addyman 1964–1972*. Devizes: WANHS (Monograph **2**), 97–114

Fairbairn, A 1993 'Charred plant remains', *in* Whittle A, Rouse A J and Evans J G 'A Neolithic downland monument in its environment: excavations at the Easton Down Long Barrow, Bishops Cannings, North Wiltshire'. *Proc Prehist Soc* **59**, 221

Fairbairn, A 1997 'Charred plant remains', *in* Whittle, A *Sacred Mound, Holy Rings. Silbury Hill and the West Kennet Palisade Enclosures: A Later Neolithic Complex in North Wiltshire*. Oxford: Oxbow Books (Monograph **74**), 134–8

Fairbairn, A 1999 'Charred plant remains', *in* Whittle, A, Pollard, J, and Grigson, C *The Harmony of Symbols: The Windmill Hill Causewayed Enclosure*. Oxford: Oxbow Books, 139–56

Fairbairn, A 2000a 'Charred seeds, fruits and tubers', *in* Whittle A, Davies J J, Dennis I, Fairbairn A S and Hamilton M A 'Neolithic activity and occupation outside Windmill Hill causewayed enclosure, Wiltshire: survey and excavation 1992–3'. *Wiltshire Archaeol Natur Hist Mag* **93**, 168–75

Fairbairn, A 2000b 'On the spread of plants crops across Neolithic Britain with special reference to southern England', *in* Fairbairn A (ed) *Plants in Neolithic Britain and Beyond*. Oxford: Oxbow (Neolithic Studies Group Seminars Papers **5**), 107–22

Farley, M E 1971 'The Roman Evidence from Silbury Hill, Wiltshire'. Unpublished BSc Thesis, Cardiff University

Fenner, V E P 1990 *The Thames Valley Project: A Report for the National Mapping Programme*. Swindon: RCHME

Fenner, M and Thompson, K 2005 *The Ecology of Seeds*. Cambridge: Cambridge University Press

Field, D 1989 'Tranchet axes and Thames picks: Mesolithic core-tools from the West London Thames'. *Trans London Middlesex Archaeol Soc* **40**, 1–46

Field, D 1998 'Round barrows and the harmonious landscape: placing early Bronze Age burial monuments in south-east England'. *Oxford J Archaeol* **17(3)**, 309–26

Field, D 2002 *The Investigation and Analytical Survey of Silbury Hill*. English Heritage Archaeological Investigation Report Series AI/22/2002

Field, D 2005 'Some observations on perception, consolidation and change in a land of stones', *in* Brown, G, Field, D and McOmish, D (eds) *The Avebury Landscape: Aspects of the Field Archaeology of the Marlborough Downs*. Oxford: Oxbow Books, 87–94

Field, D 2006 *Earthen Long Barrows*. Stroud: Tempus

Field, D 2008 *Use of Land in Central Southern England During the Neolithic and Early Bronze Age*. Oxford: Brit Archaeol Rep Brit Ser **458**

Field, D 2009 'Neolithic ground axe-heads and monuments in Wessex', *Internet Archaeology* **26**. http://intarch.ac.uk/journal/issue26/13/1.html

Field, D 2010 'Design, geometry and the metamorphosis of monuments', *in* Leary, J, Darvill, T and Field, D (eds) *Round Mounds and Monumentality in the British Neolithic and Beyond*. Oxford: Oxbow Books, 1–9

Field, D 2011a 'Moving on in landscape studies: Goodbye Wessex. Hello German Bight', *in* Jones, A M and Kirkham, G (eds) *Beyond the Core: Reflections on Regionality in Prehistory*. Oxford: Oxbow

Field, D 2011b 'Neolithic ground axe-heads and monuments in Wessex', *in* Davis, V and Edmonds, M (eds) *Stone Axe Studies III*. Oxford: Oxbow, 325–32

Field, D, and Cotton, J, 1987 'Neolithic Surrey: a survey of the evidence', *in* Bird, J and Bird, D G (eds) *The Archaeology of Surrey to 1540*. Guildford: Surrey Archaeological Society, 71–96

Field, D, Brown, G, and Crockett, A 2001 'The Marlborough Mound revisited'. *Wiltshire Archaeol Natur Hist Mag* **94**, 195–204

Field, D, Brown, G and McOmish, D 2005 'Some observations on change, consolidation, and perception in a chalk landscape', *in* Brown, G, Field, D and McOmish, D (eds) *The Avebury Landscape: Aspects of the Field Archaeology of the Marlborough Downs*. Oxford: Oxbow, 1–11

Field, D, Martin, L and Winton, H 2009 *The Hatfield Earthworks, Marden, Wiltshire*. Swindon: English Heritage (Research Department Report Series **96/2009**)

Field, K 1975 'Ring ditches of the upper and middle Great Ouse Valley'. *Archaeol J* **131**, 58–74

Fielden, K 2013 *Archive Research on Silbury Hill*. Portsmouth: English Heritage (Research Department Report Series **43/2012**)

Fitzpatrick, A 2011 *The Amesbury Archer and the Beaker Bowmen: Bell Beaker Burials at Boscombe Down, Amesbury, Wiltshire*. Salisbury: Wessex Archaeology

Fitzpatrick, A 1997 *Archaeological Excavations on the Route of the A27 Westhampnett Bypass, West Sussex, 1992*. Salisbury: Wessex Archaeology (Wessex Archaeology Report **12**)

Flood, J 1983 *The Archaeology of the Dreamtime*. London: Collins

Forrest, A J, 1983 *Masters of Flint*. Lavenham: Terence Dalton Ltd

Forster, E, Robinson, D E and Campbell G 2012 *Pollen Studies Undertaken as Part of the 2007/08 Intervention at Silbury Hill, Wiltshire*. Portsmouth: English Heritage (Research Department Report Series **48/2012**)

Fowler, P J 2000a *Landscape Plotted and Pieced: Landscape History and Local Archaeology in Fyfield and Overton, Wiltshire*. London: Society of Antiquaries of London Research Report **64**

Fowler, P J 2000b *The Excavation of a Settlement of the Fourth and Fifth Centuries AD on Overton Down, West Overton, Wiltshire*. Fyfod Working Paper FWP 64. Part of Archaeology Data Service Archive for the 'Fyfield and Overton Project, 1959–1998'. ADS Collection: 302. doi:10.5284/1000336

Fowles, J (ed) 1980 *Monumenta Brtiannica: John Aubrey (1626–97)*. Annotated by R Legg. Sherborne: DPC Publishing

French, C 2009 'A landscape tale of two soil horizons in lowland zones of England: the fen-edge of Cambridgeshire and the downland of Cranborne Chase', *in* Allen, M J, Sharples, N and O'Connor, T (eds) *Land and People: Papers in Memory of John G Evans*, Oxford: Oxbow Books (Prehistoric Society Research Paper **2**), 89–104

French, C, Lewis, H, Allen, M J, Green, M, Scaife, R and Gardiner, J 2007 *Prehistoric Landscape Development and Human Impact in the Upper Allen Valley, Cranborne Chase, Dorset*. Cambridge: McDonald Institute Monographs

Fulford, M 2001 'Links with the past: pervasive 'ritual' behaviour in Roman Britain'. *Britannia* **32**, 199–218

Gale, R 1996 'Charcoal from the Pound Field barrow', *in* Powell, A B, Allen, M J, Allen, Barnes, I *Archaeology in the Amesbury Area, Wiltshire: Recent Discoveries Along the Line of the Kennet Valley Foul Sewer Pipeline, 1993*. Salisbury: Trust for Wessex Archaeology (Wessex Archaeological Report **8**), 19

Gale, R 2008 'Charcoal', *in* Gillings, M, Pollard, J, Wheatley, D and Peterson, R *Landscape of the Megaliths: Excavation and Fieldwork on the Avebury Monuments, 1997–2003*. Oxford: Oxbow Books, 42–4

Gale, R and Cutler, D F 2000 *Plants and Archaeology: Identification Manual of Vegetative Plant Materials Used in Europe and the Mediterranean to c 1500*. Otley: Westbury Academic and Scientific Publishing and the Royal Botanic Gardens, Kew

Gardner, N P 1987 *The Animal Bones from Excavations at Wayland's Smithy, Berkshire (1962–63) and Silbury Hill, Wiltshire (1968–70)*. Unpublished undergraduate dissertation, University College, Cardiff.

Gardner, N, 1997 'Vertebrates and small vertebrates', *in* Whittle, A *Sacred Mound, Holy Rings. Silbury Hill and the West Kennet Palisade Enclosures: A Later Neolithic Complex in North Wiltshire*. Oxford: Oxbow Books (Monograph **74**), 47–9

Garmonsway, G N (trans) 1972 *The Anglo-Saxon Chronicle*. London: Dent

Garrard, L S 1984 'Some Manx plant-lore', *in* Vickery, R (ed) *Plant-Lore Studies* (BSBI Conference Report **18**/The Folklore Society Mistletoe Series **18**). London: The Folklore Society, 75–83

Geddes, I 2000 *Hidden Depths: Wiltshire's Geology and Landscapes*. Salisbury: Ex Libris Press

Geddes, I and H Walkington 2005 'The geological history of the Marlborough Downs', *in* Brown, G, Field, D and McOmish, D (eds) *The Avebury Landscape: Aspects of Field Archaeology in the Marlborough Downs*. Oxford: Oxbow Books, 58–65

Gibson, A 2004 'Round in circles. Timber circles, henges and stone circles: Some possible relationships and transformations', *in* Cleal, R and Pollard, J (eds) *Monuments and Material Culture. Papers in Honour of Avebury Archaeologists: Isobel Smith*. Salisbury: Hobnob Press, 70–82

Gibson, A 2007 'A Beaker veneer? Some evidence for the burial record', *in* M Larsson and M Parker Pearson (eds) *From the Baltic to Stonehenge: Living With Cultural Diversity in the 3rd Millennium BC*. Oxford: Brit Archaeol Rep Int Ser **1692**, 47–64

Gibson, A 2010 'Excavation and survey at the Dyffryn Lane henge complex, Powys, and a reconsideration of the dating of henges'. *Proc Prehist Soc* **76**, 213–48

Gibson, A 2011 'Report on the excavation at the Duggleby Howe causewayed enclosure – May–July 2009'. Unpublished report, University of Bradford

Gibson A and Bayliss A 2010 'Recent research at Duggleby Howe, North Yorkshire'. *Archaeol J* **166** (2009), 39–78

Gibson, J L, 1999 *Poverty Point: A Terminal Archaic Culture of the Lower Mississippi Valley*. Baton Rouge, Louisiana: Dept of Culture (2nd edn)

Gifford, J 1957 'The Physique of Wiltshire', *in* Pugh, R B and Crittall E (eds) VCH, *A History of Wiltshire*, Vol 1 part 1, 1–20

Gillings, M and Pollard, J 1999 'Non-portable stone artefacts and contexts of meaning: the tale of Grey Wether' (www.museum.ncl.ac.uk/Avebury/stone4.htm). *World Archaeology* **31**, 179–93

Gillings, M and Pollard, J 2004 *Avebury*. London: Duckworth

Gillings, M, Pollard, J, Wheatley, D and Peterson, R 2008 *Landscape of the Megaliths: Excavation and Fieldwork on the Avebury Monuments, 1997–2003*. Oxford: Oxbow Books

Gingell, C 1992 *The Marlborough Downs: A Later Bronze Age Landscape and Its Origins*. Devizes: Wiltshire Archaeological and Natural History Society/Trust for Wessex Archaeology

Gingell, C and Harding, P 1983 'A fieldwalking survey in the Vale of Wardour'. *Wiltshire Archaeol Natur Hist Mag* **77**, 11–25

Gkioni, L K 2006 'Burial practices in Neolithic Greece: the case of tumuli', *in* Šmejda L (ed) *Archaeology of Burial Mounds*. Plze : University of West Bohemia

Goodman, C H, Frost, M, Curwen, E and Curwen, E C 1924 'Blackpatch flint-mine excavation, 1922. Report prepared on behalf of the Worthing Archaeological Society'. *Sussex Archaeol Collect* **65**, 69–111

Gough, W and R, 1806 (Trans) (originally published 1610) *William Camden's Britannia*. London: John Stockdale

Gover, J, Maer, A, and Stenton, F 1939 *The Place-Names of Wiltshire* (English Place-Name Society **16**). Cambridge: Cambridge University Press

Gray, H St G 1935 'The Avebury excavations'. *Archaeologia* **84**, 99–162

Green, H S 1975 'Early Bronze Age burial, territory, and population in Milton Keynes, Buckinghamshire, and the Great Ouse Valley'. *Archaeol J* **131** (for 1974), 75–139

Gregory, T 1991 *Excavations in Thetford 1980–1982, Fison Way. Vol 1*. Dereham: Norfolk Museum Service (East Anglian Archaeology Monograph **53**)

Gregotti, V 2010 (Trans) *Architecture: Means and Ends*. Chicago: University of Chicago Press

Greig, J 1988 'Plant resources', *in* Astill, G, and Grant A (eds) *The Countryside of Medieval England*. Oxford: Blackwell, 108–27

Greig, J 1996 'Great Britain-England', *in* Berglund, B E, Birks, H J B, and Ralska-Jasiewiczowa, M, Wright, H E (eds) *Palaeoecological Events During the Last 15000 years*. Chichester: Wiley and Sons, 15–76

Griffin, A R 1971 *Coalmining*. London: Longman

Grigson, C 1965 '3. Measurements of bones, horncores, antler, and teeth', *in* Smith, I F (ed) *Windmill Hill and Avebury. Excavations by Alexander Keiller 1925–1939*. Oxford: Oxford University Press

Groenman-van Waateringe, W, and Pals, J P 1982 'Appendix D: Pollen and seed analysis', *in* O'Kelly, M J *Newgrange: Archaeology, Art and Legend*. London: Thames and Hudson, 219–23

Groube, L and Bowden, M 1982 *The Archaeology of Rural Dorset*. Dorchester: Dorset Natural History and Archaeological Society Monograph **4**

Grose, D 1957 *The Flora of Wiltshire*. Devizes: Wiltshire Archaeological and Natural History Society

Gupta, N S and Briggs, D E G 2011 'Taphonomy of animal organic skeletons through time', *in* Allison, P A and Bottjer, D J (eds) *Taphonomy: Process and Bias Through Time*. Dordrecht: Springer, 2 edn (Topics in Geobiology **32**), 199–221

Gupta, N S, Briggs, D E G, Collinson, M E, Evershed, R P, Michels, R. and Pancost, R D 2007a 'Molecular preservation of plant and insect cuticles from the Oligocene Enspel Formation, Germany: evidence against derivation of aliphatic polymer from sediment'. *Organic Geochemistry* **38**, 404–18

Gupta, N S, Briggs, D E G, Collinson, M E, Evershed, R P, Michels, R., Jack, K S and Pancost, R D 2007b 'Evidence for in situ polymerisation of labile aliphatic organic compounds during preservation of fossil leaves : implications for organic matter preservation'. *Organic Geochemistry* **38**, 499–522

Gupta, N S, Yang, H, Leng, Q, Briggs, D E G, Cody, G D and Summons, R E 2009 'Diagenesis of plant biopolymers: decay and macromolecular preservation of Metasequoia'. *Organic Geochemistry* **40**, 802–9

Hale, D, Platell, A and Millard, A 2009 'A Late Neolithic palisaded enclosure at Marne Barracks, Catterick, North Yorkshire'. *Proc Prehist Soc* **75**, 265–304

Hall, A 2003 *Recognition and Characterisation of Turves in Archaeological Occupation Deposits by means of Macrofossil Plant Remains.* Portsmouth: English Heritage (Centre for Archaeology Report **16**/2003)

Hall, A 2012 *Mosses from Silbury Hill: 2007 Excavations.* Portsmouth: English Heritage (Research Department Report Series **49**/2012)

Hall, R 1976 'Ghosts, water barriers, Corn, and sacred enclosures in the Eastern Woodlands'. *American Antiquity* 41, 360–4

Hall, R L 1997 *An Archaeology of the Soul. North American Indian Belief and Ritual.* Illinois: the University of Illinois Press

Halstorf, C A 1991 'Gender, space and food in prehistory', *in* Gero, J M, and Conkey, M W *Engendering Archaeology: Women and Prehistory.* Oxford: Blackwell, 132–59

Haltenorth, T and Trense, W 1956 *Das Großwild der Erde und seine Trophäen.* Bonn: Bayerischer Landwirtschaftsverlag

Hambleton, E 2008 *Review of Middle Bronze Age/Late Iron Age Faunal Assemblages from Southern Britain.* Portsmouth: English Heritage (Research Department Report Series **71**/2008)

Hamilton, M 1999 'Late Neolithic and Bronze Age [pottery]', *in* Whittle, A, Pollard, J and Grigson, C, *The Harmony of Symbols. The Windmill Hill Causewayed Enclosure.* Oxford: Oxbow Books, 292–310

Harding, A and Lee, G E 1987 *Henge Monuments and Related Sites of Great Britain: Air Photographic Evidence and Catalogue.* Oxford: Brit Archaeol Rep Brit Ser **175**

Harding, J 2003 *Henge Monuments of the British Isles.* London: Tempus

Harding J and Healy, F 2007 *The Raunds Area Project: A Neolithic and Bronze Age Landscape in Northamptonshire.* Swindon: English Heritage

Harding, R 2005 'Silbury Hill, Wiltshire: English Heritage's investigations into the collapse at the top of the shaft and the stability of Silbury Hill'. Unpublished report, English Heritage

Harding, R, Chadburn, A, McAvoy, F, and Campbell, G 2005 'The future'. *British Archaeol* **80**, 18–19

Harris, J and Evans, J G 1994 'Molluscan analysis', *in* Whittle, A 'Excavations at Millbarrow Neolithic chambered tomb, Winterbourne Monkton, North Wiltshire'. *Wiltshire Archaeol Natur Hist Mag* **87**, 26–32

Hattat, R 1985 *Iron Age and Roman Brooches.* Oxford: Oxbow Books

Hattat, R 1987 *Brooches of Antiquity.* Oxford: Oxbow Books

Haynes, I nd '*The Favissae Project homepage*'. http://www.bbk.ac.uk/hca/staff/haynes/favissae.htm, updated 02/12/2009. [Accessed 03/06/2011]

Haywood, A M, Valdes, P J, Sellwood, B W, Kaplan, J O 2002 'Antarctic climate during the middle Pliocene: Model sensitivity to ice sheet variation'. *Palaeogeography, Palaeoclimatology, Palaeoecology* **182**, 93–115

Heidegger, M 1971 (Trans) *Poetry, Language, Thought.* New York: Harper and Row

Helbaek, H 1952 'Early crops in southern England'. *Proc Prehist Soc* **12**, 194–233

Hembrey, N and Mould, Q 2012 *Silbury Hill, Wiltshire (Project 661) Artefacts from the 2007/8 excavations.* Portsmouth: English Heritage (Research Department Report Series **46**/2012)

Hemsley, J H 1996 'The vegetation of the Overton site 1969–92', *in* Bell M, Fowler, P, J, and Hillson, S W (eds) *The Experimental Earthwork Project 1962–1992.* York: Council for British Archaeology (Research Report **100**), 13–26

Hendry, G A F, Bland, S R, and Thompson, K 1996 'Seed persistence and plant decomposition after soil burial for 32 years', *in* Bell, M, Fowler, P J and Hillson S W (eds) *The Experimental Earthwork Project, 1960–1992.* York: CBA (Research Rep **100**), 138–40

Henriksson, G, Akin, D E, Hanlin, R T, Rodriguez, C, Archibald, D D, Rigsby, L L, and Eriksson, K-LE L, 1997 'Identification and retting efficiencies of fungi isolated from dew-retted flax in the United States and Europe. *Applied and Environmental Microbiology* **63**/10, 3950–6

Higham, R A and Barker, P 1992 *Timber Castles.* London: Batsford

Hill, M O, Preston, C D and Smith, A J E 1994 *Atlas of Bryophytes of Britain and Ireland. 3 Mosses (Diplolepideae).* Colchester: Harley Books

Hillson, S 1992 *Mammal Bones and Teeth: An Introductory Guide to Methods of Identification.* Dorchester: Dorset Press

Hirsh, E and O'Hanlon, M (eds) 1995 *The Anthropology of Landscape.* Oxford: Clarendon Press

Hoare, R C 1821 *A History of Ancient Wiltshire 2.* London: Lackington, Hughes, Harding, Maver and Lepard

Hodgson J M, Catt J A, Weir A H 1967 'The origin and development of Clay-with-flints and associated soil horizons on the South Downs'. *J Soil Sci* **18**, 85–102

Hole, C 1978 *A Dictionary of British Folk Customs.* London: Paladin

Holgate, R 1987 'Neolithic settlement patterns at Avebury, Wiltshire'. *Antiquity* **61** (232), 259–63

Holgate, R 1988 *Neolithic of the Thames Basin.* Oxford: Brit Archaeol Rep Brit Ser **194**

Hollis, E 2009 *The Secret Lives of Buildings.* London: Portabello Books Ltd

Holst, M K, Breuning-Madsen, H, and Rasmussen, M 2001 'The south Scandinavian barrows with well-preserved oak-log coffins.' *Antiquity* **75**, 126–36

Hoskins, W G 1959 'Economic history', *in* Crittal E (ed) VCH *A History of Wiltshire Vol 4.* London: Oxford University Press, 1–7

Hutchinson, S E 1996 *Nuer Dilemmas: Coping With Money, War, and the State.* Berkeley: University of California Press

Humphrey, C 1995 'Chiefly and shamanist landscapes in Mongolia', *in* Hirsh E and O'Hanlon M (eds) *The Anthropology of Landscape.* Oxford: Clarendon Press, 135–62

Huxtable, J and Evans, J, 1990 'Ancient TL, supplement date list I, entry 2'. *Ancient TL* **5**(3)

IGS 1978 *Hydrogeological Map of the South West Chilterns and the Berkshire and Marlborough Downs*. London: HMSO, Institute of Geological Sciences and Thames Water Authority

Ingold, T 1980 *Hunters, Pastoralists and Ranchers*. Cambridge: Cambridge University Press

Ingold, T 2000 *The Perception of the Environment. Essays in Livelihood, Dwelling and Skill*. Oxford: Routledge

Ingold, T 2006 'Rethinking the animate, re-animating the thought'. *Ethnos* **71**(1), 9–20

Ingold, T 2007 'Materials against materiality'. *Archaeological Dialogues* **14**(1), 1–16

Ingold, T 2010 'The round mound is not a monument', *in* Leary, J, Darvill, T and Field, D (eds) *Round Mounds and Monumentality in the British Neolithic and beyond*. Oxford: Oxbow Books, 253–60

Ingold, T 2011 *Being Alive. Essays on Movement, Knowledge and Description*. Abingdon: Routledge

Iseminger, W R 2010 *Cahokia Mounds: America's First City*. Charleston, SC and London: The History Press

Isles, M 1996 'Animal bones from the Winterbourne Romano-British settlement', *in* Powell, A B, Allen, M J, and Barnes, I 1996 *Archaeology in the Amesbury Area, Wiltshire: Recent Discoveries Along the Line of the Kennet Valley Foul Sewer Pipeline, 1993*. Salisbury: Wessex Archaeology (Wessex Archaeology Report **8**), 52–3

Ixer, R A 1996 'Ore petrography and archaeological provenance'. *Feature Mineralogical Society Bulletin* **113**, 17–19

Ixer, R A 1997 'Detailed provenancing of the Stonehenge Dolerites using reflected light petrography – a return to the light', *in* Sinclair, A, Slater, E and Gowlett, J, (eds) *Archaeological Sciences 1995*. Oxbow Monograph **64**, 11–17

Ixer, R A and Bevins, R E 2010 'The petrography, affinity and provenance of lithics from the Cursus Field, Stonehenge'. *Wiltshire Archaeol Natur Hist Mag* **103**, 1–15

Ixer, R A and Bevins, R E 2011a 'The detailed petrography of six orthostats from the bluestone circle, Stonehenge'. *Wiltshire Archaeol Natur Hist Mag* **104**, 1–14

Ixer, R A and Bevins, R E 2011b 'Craig Rhos-y-felin, Pont Saeson is the dominant source of the Stonehenge rhyolitic "debitage"'. *Archaeology in Wales* **50**, 21–31

Ixer R A and Patrick R A D 2003, 'Copper-arsenic ores and Bronze Age mining and metallurgy with special reference to the British Isles', *in* Craddock, P T and Lang, J (eds), *Mining and Metal Production Through the Ages*. London: British Museum, 9–20

Jackson, J E (ed) 1862 *Wiltshire: The Topographical Collections of John Aubrey FRS Corrected and Enlarged by John Edward Jackson*. Devizes: Wiltshire Archaeological and Natural History Society

Jacobi, R M 1981 'The last hunters in Hampshire', *in* Shennan, S J and Shadla Hall, R T (eds) *The Archaeology of Hampshire from the Palaeolithic to the Industrial Revolution*. Winchester: Hampshire Field Club and Archaeological Society (Hampshire Field Club Monograph **1**), 10–25

Jakeman, A J, Littlewood, I G and Whitehead, P G 1990 'Computation of the instantaneous unit hydrograph and identifiable component flows with application to two small upland catchments'. *J Hydrology* **117**, 275–300

James, W 2003 *The Ceremonial Animal. A New Portrait of Anthropology*. Oxford: Oxford University Press

Jessop, L 1986 *Dung Beetles and Chafers, Coleoptera: Scarabaeoidea*. London: Royal Entomological Society (Royal Entomological Society Handbook for the Identification of British Insects **5**, pt 11)

Jessop, O 1996 'A new artefact typology for the study of medieval arrowheads'. *Medieval Archaeol* **40**, 192–205

Jewell, P A 1963 *The Experimental Earthwork on Overton Down, Wiltshire 1960*. London: British Association Advancement Science

Jin, J J H and Shipman, P 2010 'Documenting natural wear on antlers: A first step in identifying use-wear on purported antler tools'. *Quaternary International* **211**, 91–102

Johnson, D H 1994 *Nuer Prophets: A History of Prophecy from the Upper Nile in the Nineteenth and Twentieth Centuries*. Oxford: Clarendon Press

Jones, E 1960 'Eighteenth century changes in Hampshire chalkland farming'. *Agricultural Hist Rev* **8**, 5–19

Jones, J 2006 'Charred plant remains', *in* Longman, T 'Iron Age and later defences at Malmesbury: Excavations 1998–2000'. *Wiltshire Archaeol Natur Hist Mag* **99**, 105–64, 151–8

Jones, M 1988 'The arable field: a botanical battleground', *in* Jones M (ed) *Archaeology and the Flora of the British Isles*. Oxford: Oxbow Books (Oxford University Committee for Archaeology Monograph **14**), 86–92

Jones, M C and Williams-Thorpe, O 2001 'An illustration of the use of an atypicality index in provenancing British stone axes'. *Archaeometry* **43**, 1–18

Jordan, B A 2001 'Site characteristics impacting the survival of historic waterlogged wood: A review', *International Biodeterioration and Biodegradation* **47**, 47–54

Jordan, P D 2001 'Cultural landscapes in Colonial Siberia: Khanty settlements of the sacred, the living and the dead'. *Landscapes* **2**/2, 83–105

Keiller, A 1939 'Avebury. Summary of excavations, 1937 and 1938'. *Antiquity* **13**(50), 223–33

Keiller, A, Piggott, S and Wallis, F S 1941 'First report of the sub-committee of the south-western group of museums and art galleries on the petrological determination of stone axes'. *Proc Prehist Soc* **7**, 50–72

Kelley, K B and Francis, H 1994 *Navaho Sacred Places*. Bloomington & Indianapolis: Indiana University Press

Kendall, H G O 1921 'Scraper-care industries in north Wiltshire'. *Proc Prehist Soc East Anglia* **3**, 515–41

Kerney, M P, and Cameron, A D 1979 *A Field Guide to the Land Snails of Britain and North-West Europe*. London: Collins

Kerridge, E 1959 'Agriculture 1500–1793', *in* Crittal E (ed) VCH *A History of Wiltshire Vol 4*. London: Oxford University Press, 43–64

Khokhlova, O S, Khokhlov, A A and Morgunova, N L 2006 'Paleopedological study of the Pit-Grave culture Kurgans on the Southern Pre-Ural steppe of Russia', *in* Šmejda L (ed) *Archaeology of Burial Mounds*. Plze : University of West Bohemia, 78–82

Kim, Y S and Singh, A P 2000 'Micromorphological characterisation of wood biodegradation in wet environments: a review', *Int Assoc Wood Anatomists J* **21**, 135–55

King, A C, 1978 *A Comparative Survey of Bone Assemblages from Roman Sites in Britain*. London: Institute of Archaeology (Bulletin of the Institute of Archaeology, University of London **15**), 207–32

King, A C, 2005 'Animal remains from temple sites in Roman Britain'. *Britannia* **36**, 329–69

King, A, Walker, C P, Sharp, R V, Kent Reilly, F and McKinnon, D P 2011 'Remote sensing data from Etowah's Mound A: Architecture and the re-creation of Mississippian tradition'. *American Antiq* **76**, 355–71

King, N E 1968 'The Kennet Valley sarsen industry'. *Wiltshire Archaeol Natur Hist Mag* **63**, 83–93

Kinnes, I 1978 'The Beaker grave group from East Kennet'. *Wiltshire Archaeol Natur Hist Mag* **73**, 167–70

Kinnes, I 1979 *Round Barrows and Ring-Ditches in the British Neolithic*. London: British Museum (Occasional Paper **7**)

Kinnes, I, Gibson, A, Ambers, J, Bowman, S Leese, M and Boast, R 1991 'Radiocarbon dating and British Beakers: The British Museum programme'. *Scot Archaeol Rev* **8**, 35–68

Kinnes, I A Schadla-Hall, T, Chadwick, P and Dean, P 1983 'Duggleby Howe reconsidered'. *Archaeol J* **140**, 83-108

Kirkbride, M 2008 'Summary of construction works: Completion report'. Unpublished Skanska report for English Heritage

Kloet, G S and Hincks, W D 1977 *A Check List of British Insects: Coleoptera and Strepsiptera*. London: Royal Entomological Society of London, Handbook for the Identification of British Insects **11**:3 (2nd edn, rev)

Koller, B, Schmitt, J M and Tishendorf, G 2005 'Cellular fine structures and histochemical reactions in the tissue of a cypress twig preserved in Baltic amber'. *Proc Roy Soc* B: **272**, 121–6

Koryakova, L and Daire, M Y 2000 'Burials and settlements at the Eurasian crossroads: Joint Franco-Russian project', *in* J Davis-Kimball, E M Murphy, L Koryakova and L T Yablonsky (eds) *Kurgans, Ritual Sites, and Settlements: Eurasian Bronze and Iron Age*. Oxford: Archaeopress (Brit Archaeol Rep Int Ser **890**), 63–74

Kristiansen, K 1984 'Ideology and material culture: An archaeological perspective', *in* Spriggs, M (ed) *Marxist Perspectives in Archaeology*. Cambridge: Cambridge University Press, 72–100

Kristiansen, K 1990 'Ard marks under barrows: A response to Peter Rowley Conwy'. *Antiquity* **64**, 322–7

Kuzmina, E 2000 'The Eurasian Steppes: The transition from early urbanism to nomadism', *in* Davis-Kimball, J, Murphy, E M, Koryakova, L and Yablonksy, L T (eds) *Kurgans, Ritual Sites, and Settlements: Eurasian Bronze and Iron Age,*. Oxford: Archaeopress (Brit Archaeol Rep Int Ser **890**), 118–25

Last, J 2002 *Avebury Southern Car Park (Glebe Field): a desk-based assessment*. Unpublished rep, English Heritage Centre for Archaeology Report **29/2002**

Leary, J 2009 'Silbury Hill Conservation Project 2007/2008 Archaeological Assessment Report'. Unpublished report, English Heritage

Leary, J 2010 'Silbury Hill: A monument in motion', *in* Leary, J, Darvill, T and Field, D (eds) *Round Mounds and Monumentality in the British Neolithic and Beyond*. Oxford: Oxbow Books, 139–52

Leary J and Field D 2010 *The Story of Silbury Hill*. Swindon: English Heritage Publishing

Leary, J 2011 'It's official – the Marlborough mound is prehistoric'. *PAST* **68**, 4–5

Leary, J and Field, D 2011 'Great monuments, great rivers'. *Brit Archaeol* **120**

Leary, J and Field, D 2012 'Journeys and juxtapositions. Marden henge and the view from the Vale', *in* Gibson, A (ed) *Enclosing the Neolithic: Recent Studies in Britain and Europe*, Oxford: Archaeopress (British Archaeological Reports International Series 2440), 55–65

Leary, J and Marshall, P 2012 'The Giants of Wessex: The chronology of the three largest mounds in Wiltshire, UK'. *Antiquity* **86**(334), Project Gallery

Leary, J, Field, D and Russell, M 2010 'Marvels at Marden Henge'. *PAST* **66**, 14–16

Leary, J, Canti, M, Field, D, Fowler, P, Marshall, P and Campbell, G forthcoming, 'The Marlborough Mound, Wiltshire: A further Neolithic monumental mound by the River Kennet' *Proc Prehist Soc* **79**

Lefebvre, H 2004 (Trans.). *Rhythmanalysis. Space, Time and Everyday Life*. London: Continuum

Legge A J 1981 'The agricultural economy', *in* Mercer R J (ed) *Grimes Graves, Norfolk: Excavations 1971–72, vol I*. London: HMSO, 79–103

Legge, A J 2008 'Livestock and Neolithic society at Hambledon Hill', *in* Mercer, R M and Healy, F (eds) *Hambledon Hill, Dorset, England. Excavation and Survey of a Neolithic Monument Complex and its Surrounding Landscape*. Swindon: English Heritage, 356–86

Legge, A and Dorrington, E J 1985 'The animal bones', *in* France, N B and Gobel, B M *The Romano-British Temple at Harlow, Essex*. Gloucester: West Essex Archaeological Group, 122–33

Legge, A, Williams, J and Williams, P, 2000 'Lambs to the slaughter: Sacrifice at two Roman temples in southern England', *in* Rowley-Conwy, P (ed) *Animal Bones, Human Societies*. Oxford: Oxbow Books, 152–7

Levitan, B, 1993 'Vertebrate remains', *in* Woodward, A and Leach, P (eds) *The Uley Shrines Excavation of a Ritual Complex on West Hill, Uley, Gloucestershire, 1977–79*. London: Historic Buildings and Monuments Commission (Archaeological Report **17**), 257–301

Lewis, M J T 1966 *Temples in Roman Britain*. Cambridge: Cambridge University Press

Lillie, M C, Smith, R J and Douterelo-Soler, I forthcoming *Microbiological Assessment of Cores <9444> and <9447> From Excavations at Silbury Hill 2007/8: Phase 1*. Portsmouth: English Heritage (Research Report Series **50/2012**)

Lillie, M C and Smith, R J 2008 'Understanding waterlogged burial environments: The impacts of aggregates extraction and de-watering on the buried archaeological resource'. Unpublished report, University of Hull Wetland Archaeology and Environments Research Centre

Linford, N 2008 *Geophysical Survey in the Shadow of the Hill*. English Heritage: Research News **10**, 10–13

Linford, N and Martin, L 2001 'Silbury Hill, Wiltshire: report on geophysical survey'. Unpublished report, English Heritage, Centre for Archaeology Reports **21/2001**

Linford, N, Linford, P, Martin, L and Payne, A 2007 'Recent results from the English Heritage caesium magnetometer system in comparison to recent fluxgate gradiometers'. *Archaeol Prospection* **14**(3), 151–66

Linford, N, Linford, P, Martin, L and Payne, A 2009 *Silbury Hill Environs, Avebury, Wiltshire: Report on Geophysical Surveys, 2005–2008*. Portsmouth: English Heritage (Research Department Report series **105/2009**)

Linford P 2001 'Silbury Hill, Wiltshire: Report on Geophysical Survey, June 2001'. Unpublished report, Centre for Archaeology Report 65/2001

Long, W 1858 *Abury Illustrated*. Devizes: Bull

Long, W 1857 'Abury'. *Wiltshire Archaeol Natur Hist Mag* 4, 309–42

Longin, R 1971 'New method of collagen extraction for radiocarbon dating'. *Nature* 230, 241–2

Loveday J 1962 'Plateau deposits of the southern Chiltern Hills'. *Proc Geol Assoc* 73, 83–102

Lukis, W C (ed) 1887 *The Family Memoirs of the Rev William Stukeley MD vol 3*. Durham: The Publications of the Surtees Society 80

Lyman, L 1994 *Vertebrate Taphonomy*. Cambridge: Cambridge University Press

Macphail, R I 1999 'Micromorphological analysis of soils and sediments', *in* Whittle A 'Excavations at Millbarrow chambered tomb, Winterbourne Monkton, North Wiltshire'. *Wiltshire Archaeol Natur Hist Mag* 87, 32–4

Madgwick, R, Mulville, J and Evans, J 2012 'Investigating diagenesis and the suitability of porcine enamel for strontium (^{87}Sr/^{86}Sr) isotope analysis'. *J Analytical Atomic Spectrometry* 27, 733–42

Magnell, O 2006 *Tracking Wild Boar and Hunters: Osteology of Wild Boar in Mesolithic South Scandinavia*. Lund: Acta Archaeologica Lundensia Series in 8o, No 51. Studies in Osteology 1

Malone, C 1994 *The Prehistoric Monuments of Avebury*. London: English Heritage (2nd edn)

Maltby, M 1981 'Iron Age, Romano-British and Anglo-Saxon animal husbandry – a review of the faunal evidence', *in* Jones, M and Dimblebey, G (eds) *The Environment of Man: Iron Age to the Anglo-Saxon Period*. Oxford: Brit Archaeol Rep Brit Ser 87, 155–203

Maltby, M, 2010 'Zooarchaeology and the interpretation of deposition in shafts', *in* Morris, J and Maltby, M (ed) *Integrating Social and Environmental Archaeologies: Reconsidering Deposition*. Oxford: Archaeopress (Brit Archaeol Rep Int Ser 2077), 24–32

Manning, W 1972 'Ironworks hoards in Iron Age and Roman Britain'. *Britannia* 3, 224–50

Manning, W 1985 *Catalogue of Romano-British Iron Tools, Fittings and Weapons in the British Museum*. London: British Museum Press

Marshall, P in press 'Bayesian modelling of dates', *in* Parker Pearson, M, Richards, M, Chamberlain, A and Jay, M (eds) *The Beaker People: Isotopes, Mobility and Diet in Prehistoric Britain*. Oxford, Oxbow (Prehistoric Society Monograph)

Marshall, P, Bronk Ramsey, C, Cook, G, Parker Pearson, M, Pollard, J, Thomas, J, Richards, C and Welham, K forthcoming 'Radiocarbon dating', *in* Parker Pearson, M, Pollard, J, Thomas, J, Richards, C and Welham, K *Durrington Walls and Woodhenge: A Place for the Living. The Stonehenge Riverside Project Volume 2*. Oxford: Oxbow (Prehistoric Society Monograph)

Marter Brown 2012 *The Pottery: Silbury Hill*. Portsmouth: English Heritage (Research Department Report Series 45/2012)

McAvoy, F 2000 'Silbury Hill shaft: A desk-based assessment of the potential for archaeological recording and investigation'. Unpublished report Portsmouth: English Heritage

McAvoy, F 2002 'Silbury Hill, Wiltshire: Report on the evaluation through coring of physical and geophysical anomalies on the northern aspect of the mound'. Unpublished report, Portsmouth: English Heritage

McAvoy, F 2005a 'Silbury Hill: An assessment of the conservation risks and possible response arising from antiquarian and archaeological investigations deep into the Hill'. Unpublished report, Portsmouth: English Heritage

McAvoy, F 2005b 'Silbury Hill: Archive and assessment report with proposals for further work'. Unpublished report, Portsmouth: English Heritage

McAvoy, F 2006 'Silbury Hill Project Design'. Portsmouth: English Heritage, unpublished project design

McBryde, I 1984 'Kulin Greenstone quarries: The social contexts of production and distribution for the Mt William site'. *World Archaeol* 16/2, 267–85

McBryde, I 1997 'The landscape is a series of stories. Grindstones, quarries and exchange in Aboriginal Australia: a Lake Eyre case study', *in* Ramos-Millan, A and Bustillo, M A (eds) *Siliceous Rocks and Culture*. Grenada: University of Grenada

McCobb, L M E, Briggs, D E G, Evershed, R P, Hall, A R and Hall, R A 2001 'Preservation of fossil seeds from a tenth century AD cess pit at Coppergate, York'. *J Archaeol Sci* 29(9), 929–40

McCobb, L M E, Briggs, D E G, Carruthers, W J, Evershed, R P 2003 'Phosphatisation of seeds and roots in a late Bronze Age deposit at Potterne, Wiltshire, UK'. *J Archaeol Sci* 30, 1269–81

McFadyen, L 2008 'Temporary spaces in the Mesolithic and Neolithic: Understanding landscapes', *in* Pollard, J (ed) *Prehistoric Britain*. Oxford: Blackwell, 121–34

McKim, F R 1959 'An attempt to locate a burial chamber in Silbury Hill'. *Wiltshire Archaeol Natur Hist Mag* 57, 176–8

McOmish, D Field, D and Brown, G 2002 *The Field Archaeology of Salisbury Plain Training Area*. Swindon: English Heritage

McOmish, D, Riley, H, Lewis, C and Field, D 2005 'Field work in the Avebury Area', *in* Brown, G, Field, D and McOmish, D (eds.) *The Avebury Landscape: Aspects of Field Archaeology on the Marlborough Down*. Oxford: Oxbow, 12–33

McOmish, D, Field, D and Brown, G 2010 'The Late Bronze Age and Early Iron Age midden site at East Chisenbury, Wiltshire'. *Wiltshire Archaeol Natur Hist Mag* 103, 35–101

Mellor, M 1994 'A synthesis of middle and late Saxon, medieval and early post-medieval pottery in the Oxford region'. *Oxoniensia* 49, 17–217

Mepham, L., 2000, 'Enborne Street and Wheatlands Lane: medieval pottery', *in* Allen, M J, Andrews, P, Bellamy, P S, Cooke, N, Ede, J, Rowena Gale, R, James, S E, Loader, E, Macphail, R I, Mepham, L, Frances Raymond, F, Seager Smith, R and Wyles, S F *Archaeological Investigations on the A34 Newbury Bypass, Berkshire/Hampshire, 1991–7*. Salisbury: Wessex Archaeology Technical reports, 52–66

Merewether, J, Very Rev 1851a 'The examination of Silbury Hill, *in* 'Memoirs illustrative of the history and antiquities of Wiltshire and the City of Salisbury'. *Proceedings of the Meeting of the Archaeological Institute at Salisbury 1849*, 73–82. London: Archaeological Institute of Great Britain and Ireland

Merewether, J 1851b *Diary of a Dean: being an account of the examination of Silbury Hill and or various barrows and other earthworks on the Downs of north Wilts, opened and investigated in the months of July and August 1849*'. London: George Bell

Metzner-Nebelsick, C 2000 'Early Iron Age pastoral nomadism in the Great Hungarian Plains: Migration or assimilation? The Thraco-Cimmerian problem revisited', *in* Davis-Kimball, J, Murphy, E M, Koryakova, L and Yablonksy, L T (eds.) *Kurgans, Ritual Sites, and Settlements: Eurasian Bronze and Iron Age*, Oxford: Archaeopress (Brit Archaeol Rep Int Ser **890**), 160–84

Meyers, P A, Leenheer, M and Bourbonniere, R A 1995 'Diagenesis of vascular plant organic matter components during burial in lake sediments'. *Aquatic Geochemistry* **1**, 35–52

Milner, N 2005 'Can seasonality studies be used to identify sedentism in the past?', *in* Bailey, D, Whittle, A and Cummings, V (eds) *(Un)settling the Neolithic*. Oxford: Oxbow, 32–7

Mitchell, F J G 2005 'How open were the European forests? Hypothesis testing using palaeoecological data'. *J Ecol* **93**, 168–77

Molland, R 1959 'Agriculture 1793–1870', *in* Crittal E (ed) VCH *A History of Wiltshir) Vol 4*. London: Oxford University Press, 65–91

Monk, M A 1982 'Appendix E: Macroscopic plant remains', *in* O'Kelly, M J *Newgrange: Archaeology, Art and Legend*. London: Thames and Hudson, 223–5

Mook, W G 1986 'Business Meeting: recommendations/resolutions adopted by the twelfth international radiocarbon conference'. *Radiocarbon* **28**, 799

Moore, A W 1891 *Folklore of the Isle of Man*. Amazon kindle edition

Moorhead, S 1997 'Roman coins found in Richard Atkinson's Excavation at Silbury Hill, 1969–70'. Unpublished archive report held in the Alexander Keiller Museum

Moorhead S 1999 'Roman coins found in Richard Atkinson's excavation at Silbury Hill, 1969–70, and other Roman Coin finds made by Joshua Brooke in the area'. Unpublished archive report held in Alexander Keiller Museum, Avebury

Moorhead, S 2011 *Roman Coins from the Silbury region*. Portsmouth: English Heritage (Research Department Report Series **102/2011**)

Morphy, H 1989 'On representing ancestral beings', *in* Morphy H (ed) *Animals Into Art*. London: Unwin Hyman, 144–60

Mount, R 1991 'An environmental history of the Upper Kennet river valley and some implications for human communities'. Unpublished PhD thesis, University of Cardiff

Myres, J N L 1932 'Three unrecognised mounds at Hamstead Marshall'. *Trans Newbury Dist Fld Club* **6**, 114–26

Needham, S 2005 'Transforming Beaker culture in north-west Europe; processes of fusion and fission'. *Proc Prehist Soc* **71**, 171–218

Needham, S 2007 'Isotope aliens: Beaker movement and cultural transmissions', *in* Larssen, M and Parker Pearson, M (eds) *From the Baltic to Stonehenge: Living with Cultural Diversity in the 3rd Millennium BC*, Oxford: Brit Archaeol Rep Int Ser **1692**, 41–6

Needham, S P and Burgess, C B, 1980. 'The later Bronze Age in the lower Thames valley: the metalwork evidence', *in* Barrett, J C and Bradley, R J (eds), *The British Later Bronze Age*. Oxford: Brit Archaeol Rep Brit Ser **83**, 437–69

Newson, M D, and Hanwell, J D 1982 *Systematic Physical Geography*. Houndsmills: Macmillan

Niblett, R 1999 *Excavation of a Ceremonial Site at Folly Lane, Verulamium*. London: Society for the Promotion of Roman Studies (Britannia Monograph Ser **14**)

Niklas, K J and Brown, R M 1981 'Ultrastructural and palaeobiological correlations among fossil leaf tissues from the St Maries river (Clarkia) area, northern Idaho, USA'. *American J Botany* **68**, 332–41

Nowakowski, J A 2007 'Digging deeper into barrow ditches: Investigating the making of early Bronze Age memories in Cornwall', *in* Last J (ed) *Beyond the Grave: New Perspectives on Barrows*. Oxford: Oxbow Books, 92–113

Nye, S and Scaife, R 1998 'Plant macrofossil remains', *in* Pryor, F *Excavations at a Neolithic Causewayed Enclosure near Maxey Cambridgeshire*. Swindon: English Heritage, Archaeological Report **18**, 289–300

O' Conner, B 2010 'Re-collected objects: Carved, worked and unworked stone in Bronze Age funerary monuments', *in* O' Conner, Cooney, G and Chapman, J (eds) *Materialitas. Working Stone, Carving Identity*. Oxford: Oxbow Books (Prehistoric Society Research Paper **3**), 147–60

O' Conner, B, and Cooney, G 2010 'Introduction: *Materialitas* and the significance of stone', *in* O' Conner, Cooney, G and Chapman, J (eds) *Materialitas. Working Stone Carving Identity*. Oxford: Oxbow Books (Prehistoric Society Research Paper 3), xxi–xxv

O' Conner, B, Cooney, G and Chapman, J (eds) 2010 *Materialitas. Working Stone, Carving Identity*. Oxford: Oxbow Books (Prehistoric Society Research Paper **3**)

O'Connor, T 1986 'The animal bones', *in* Zienkiewicz, D (ed) *The Legionary Fortress Baths at Caerleon*. Cardiff: National Museum of Wales, 225–48

Ó Danachair, C 1957 'Materials and methods in Irish traditional building'. *J Roy Soc Antiq Ireland* **7**, 61–74

O'Kelly, M J 1982 *Newgrange: Archaeology, Art and Legend*. London: Thames and Hudson

Ogilby, J 1675 *Britannia, Volume the first: or an illustration of the Kingdom of England and Dominion of Wales*. London: printed by the author

Olsen, S L 1989 'On distinguishing natural from cultural damage on archaeological antler'. *J Archaeol Sci* **16**, 125–35

Ordnance Survey 1932 *Map of Neolithic Wessex: Showing the Distribution of Long Barrows, Circles, Habitations Sites, Flint Mines*. Southampton: Ordnance Survey

Owoc, M A 2004 'A phenomenology of the buried landscape. Soil as material culture in the Bronze Age of south-west Britain', *in* Boivin, N and Owoc, M A (eds) *Soils, Stones and Symbols: Cultural Perceptions of the Mineral World*. London: UCL Press, 107–21

Page, C N, 1988 *Ferns*. London: Collins

Parker Pearson, M 1993 *Bronze Age Britain*. London, Batsford

Parker Pearson, M 2000 'Ancestors, bones and stones in Neolithic and Early Bronze Age Britain and Ireland', *in* Ritchie, A (ed) *Neolithic Orkney in its European Context*. Cambridge: McDonald Institute for Archaeological Research, 203–14

Parker Pearson, M 2004 'Earth, wood and fire. Materiality and Stonehenge', *in* Boivin, N and Owoc, M A (eds) *Soils, Stones and Symbols: Cultural Perceptions of the Mineral World*. London: UCL Press, 71–89

Parker Pearson, M 2007 'The Stonehenge Riverside Project: excavations in the eastern entrance of Durrington Walls', *in* Larsson, M and Parker Pearson, M (eds) *From Stonehenge to the Baltic*. Oxford: Brit Archaeol Rep Int Ser **1692**, 125–44

Parker Pearson, M 2008 'Chieftains and pastoralists in Neolithic and Bronze Age Wessex', *in* Rainbird P (ed) *Monuments and Landscape.* Stroud: Tempus, 34–53

Parker Pearson, M and Ramilisonina 1998 'Stonehenge for the ancestors: the stones pass on the message'. *Antiquity* **72**, 308–26

Parker Pearson, M, Pollard, J, Richards, C, Thomas, J, Tilley, C, Welham, K, Albarella, U 2006 'Materializing Stonehenge. The Stonehenge Riverside Project and new discoveries'. *J Material Culture* **11**, 227–61

Parker Pearson, M, Cleal, R, Marshall, P, Needham, S, Pollard, J, Richards, C, Ruggles, C, Sheridan, A, Thomas, J, Tilley, C, Welham, K, Chamberlain, A, Chenery, C, Evans, J, Knusel, C, Linford, N, Martin, L, Montgomery, J, Payne, A, Richards, M 2007 'The Age of Stonehenge'. *Antiquity* **81** (313), 617–39

Parker Pearson, M, Chamberlain, A, Jay, M, Marshall, P, Pollard, J, Richards, C, Thomas, J, Tilley, C and Welham, K 2009 'Who was buried at Stonehenge?'. *Antiquity* **83**, 23–39

Pass, A C, 1887 'Recent explorations at Silbury Hill'. *Wiltshire Archaeol Natur Hist Mag* **23**, 245–54

Passmore, A D 1940 'A disc barrow containing curious flints near Stonehenge'. *Wiltshire Archaeol Natur Hist Mag* **49**, 238

Passmore, A D, unpublished manuscript in the Wiltshire Archaeological and Natural History Society Museum, Devizes

Peake, H T E 1906 'Ancient Earthworks', *in* Page W (ed) *The Victoria History of Berkshire vol 1.* London: St Catherines Press, 251–84

Petrie, W M Flinders 1880 *Stonehenge: Plans, Description, and Theories.* London (facsimile 1989 c/w Stonehenge Astronomy – an update by Gerald Hawkins London: Histories & Mysteries of Man Ltd)

Petrie, W F 1924 'Report of diggings in Silbury Hill, August 1922'. *Wiltshire Archaeol Natur Hist Mag* **42**, 215–18

Philips, C W 1935 'A re-examination of the Therfield Heath long barrow, Royston, Hertfordshire'. *Proc Prehist Soc* **1**, 101–7

Phillips, C W 1936 'The excavation of the Giants Hills Long barrow, Skendleby, Lincolnshire'. *Archaeologia* **85**, 37–106

Piggott, S 1937 'Excavation of a long barrow at Holdenhurst'. *Proc Prehist Soc* **3**, 1–14

Piggott, S 1954 *Neolithic Cultures of the British Isles.* Cambridge: Cambridge University Press

Piggott, S 1962 *The West Kennet Long Barrow: Excavations 1955–56.* London: HMSO (Ministry of Works Archaeological Reports No **4**)

Pitt Rivers, A H L 1898 *Excavations in Cranborne Chase 4.* Printed privately

Pitts, M 1978 'Towards an understanding of flint industries in post-glacial England'. *Bull Inst Archaeol* **15**, 179–97

Pitts, M 2000 *Hengeworld.* London: Arrow Books

Pollard, J 1992 'The Sanctuary, Overton Hill, Wiltshire: a re-examination'. *Proc Prehist Soc* **58**, 213–26

Pollard, J 1999 '"These places have their moments": Thoughts on settlement practices in the British Neolithic', *in* Brück J and Goodman M (eds) *Making Places in the Prehistoric World: Themes in Settlement Archaeology.* London: University College of London Press, 76–93

Pollard, J 2001a 'Lithics', *in* Pitts M 'Excavating the Sanctuary: New investigations on Overton Hill, Avebury'. *Wiltshire Archaeol Natur Hist Mag* **94**, 1–23

Pollard, J 2001b 'The aesthetics of depositional practice'. *World Archaeol* **33**(2), 315–33

Pollard, J 2004 'A "movement of becoming": Realms of existence in the early Neolithic of southern Britain', *in* Chadwick, A (ed) *Stories from the Landscape: Archaeologies of Inhabitation.* Oxford: Archaeopress Brit Archaeol Rep Int Ser **1238**, 55–69

Pollard, J and Whittle, A 1999 'Other finds', *in* Whittle, A, Pollards, J and Grigson C (eds) *Harmony of Symbols: The Windmill Hill Causewayed Enclosure, Wiltshire.* Oxford: Oxbow, 338–43

Pollard, J and Reynolds, A 2002 *Avebury: The Biography of a Landscape.* Stroud: Tempus

Pollard, J and Gillings, M 2010 'The world of Grey Wethers', *in* O' Conner, B, Cooney, G and Chapman, J (eds) *Materialitas. Working Stone, Carving Identity.* Oxford: Oxbow Books (Prehistoric Society Research Paper **3**), 29–41

Pope, V D, Gallani, M L, Rowntree, P R, Stratton, R A 2000 'The impact of new physical parametrizations in the Hadley Centre climate model: HadAM3'. *Climate Dynamics* **16**, 123–46

Powell, A B, Allen, M J and Barnes, I 1996 *Archaeology in the Amesbury Area, Wiltshire: Recent Discoveries along the Line of the Kennet Valley Foul Sewer Pipeline, 1993.* Salisbury: Trust for Wessex Archaeology (Wessex Archaeological Report **8**)

Preston, C D, Pearman, D A, and Hall, A R, 2004 'Archaeophytes in Britain'. *Botanical J Linnaean Soc* **145**, 257–94

Price, N 1994 'Tourism and the Bighorn Medicine Wheel', *in* Carmichael, D, Hubert, J, Reeves, B and Schanche, A (eds) *Sacred Sites, Sacred Places.* London & New York: Routledge, 259–64

Pritchard, F 1991 'The small finds', *in* Vince, A (ed) *Aspects of Saxo-Norman London: 2. Finds and Environmental Evidence.* London: London and Middlesex Archaeological Society Special Paper **12**, 120–278

Quesnel, F, Catt, J, Laignel, B, Bourdillon, C and Meyer, R 2003 'The Neogene and Quaternary Clay-with-flints north and south of the English Channel: comparisons of distribution, age, genetic processes and geodynamics'. *J Quaternary Sci* **18**, 283–94

Rackham, O 1980 *Ancient Woodland: Its History, Vegetation and Uses in England.* London: Edward Arnold

Rafferty, J E 1985 'The archaeological record on sedentariness: recognition, development and implications'. *Advances in Archaeological Method and Theory* **8**, 113–56

Rankine, W F R 1949 *A Mesolithic Survey of the West Surrey Greensand.* Guildford: Surrey Archaeological Society (Research Paper **2**)

RCHM 1960 *A Matter of Time: An Archaeological Survey of the River Gravels of England.* London: HMSO

RCHM(E) 1970 *Shielings and Bastles.* London: HMSO

RCHME 1989 *The Classification of Cropmarks in Kent: A Report for the National Monuments Protection Programme.* London: RCHME

Reece, R. 1972 'A short survey of the Roman coins found on fourteen sites in Britain'. *Britannia* **3**, 269–76

Reece, R. 1995 'Site-finds in Roman Britain'. *Britannia* **26**, 179–206

Reimer, P J, Baillie, M G L, Bard, E, Bayliss, A, Beck, J W, Blackwell, P G, Bronk Ramsey, C, Buck, C E, Burr, G, Edwards, R L, Friedrich, M, Grootes, P M, Guilderson, T P, Hajdas, I, Heaton, T J, Hogg, A G, Hughen, K A, Kaiser, K F, Kromer, B, McCormac, F G, Manning, S W, Reimer, R W, Richards, D A, Southon, J R, Talamo, S, Turney, C S M, van der Plicht, J, and Weyhenmeyer, C E, 2009 'IntCal09 and Marine09 radiocarbon age calibration curves, 0–50,000 years cal BP'. *Radiocarbon* **51**, 1111–50

Renfrew C 1973 'Monuments, mobilisation and social organisation in Neolithic Wessex', *in* Renfrew C (ed) *The Explanation of Culture Change: Models in Prehistory*. London: Duckworth, 539–58

Renfrew, C 2008 *Archaeology: Theories, Method and Practice*. London: Thames & Hudson (5th edn)

Reynolds, A 1999 *Later Anglo-Saxon England*. Stroud: Tempus

Reynolds, A 2001 'Avebury: a Late Anglo-Saxan *burh*?'. *Antiquity* **75**, 29–30

Reynolds, A 2005 'From *pagus* to parish: Territory and settlement in the Avebury region from the Late Roman period to the Domesday survey', *in* Brown, G, Field, D and McOmish, D (eds) *The Avebury Landscape: Aspects of the Field Archaeology of the Marlborough Downs*. Oxford: Oxbow Books, 164–80

Reynolds, A and Brookes, S 2013 'Anglo-Saxon civil defence in the Viking Age: a case-study of the Avebury region', *in* Reynolds, A and Webster, L (eds) *Early Medieval Art and Archaeology in the Northern World*. Boston: Brill, 561–606

Reynolds, P J, 1987 *Ancient Farming*. Oxford: Shire

Richards C 1996a 'Monuments as landscape: Creating the centre of the world in Late Neolithic Orkney'. *World Archaeology* **28**(2), 190–208

Richards C 1996b 'Henges and water: towards an elemental understanding of monumentality and landscape in late Neolithic Britain'. *J Material Culture* **1**(3), 313–36

Richards C 2004 'Labouring with monuments: Constructing the dolmen at Carreg Samson, south-west Wales', *in* Cummings V and Fowler C *The Neolithic of the Irish Sea. Materiality and Traditions of Practice*. Oxford: Oxbow Books, 72–80

Richards, C forthcoming *Monuments in the Making: Building the Great Stone Circles of the North*. Oxford: Windgather Press

Richards, J 1990 *The Stonehenge Environs Project*. London: HBMC

Richter, S L, Johnson, A H, Dranoff, M M LePage, B A and Williams, C J 2008 'Oxygen isotope ratios in fossil wood cellulose: Isotopic composition of Eocene to Holocene-aged cellulose'. *Geochimica et Cosmochimica Acta* **72**, 2744–53

Rick Pollard Associates 2007 'Silbury Hill: The Conservation of Silbury Hill – Proposals for Backfilling'. Unpublished report for English Heritage

Rickman, J, 1840 'On the Antiquity of Abury and Stonehenge'. *Archaeologia* **28**, 399–415

Rimmer, M B 2007 'The geoarchaeology of Silbury Hill Wiltshire: An analysis of buried soil materials and organic preservation'. Unpublished MSc thesis, University of Reading,

Robertson Mackay, M E 1980 'A 'head and hoofs' burial beneath a round barrow, with other Neolithic and Bronze Age sites, on Hemp Knoll, near Avebury, Wiltshire'. *Proc Prehist Soc* **46**, 123–76

Robinson, M 1991 'The Neolithic and late Bronze Age insect assemblages', *in* Needham, S P *Excavation and Salvage at Runnymede Bridge, 1978: The Late Bronze Age Waterfront Site*. London: British Museum Press, 277–326

Robinson, M, 1997 'The insects from Silbury Hill', *in* Whittle, A *Sacred Mound, Holy Rings. Silbury Hill and the West Kennet Palisade Enclosures: A Later Neolithic Complex in North Wiltshire*. Oxford: Oxbow Books (Monograph **74)**, 36–47

Robinson, M 2004 'Evaluation of the macroscopic biological remains from the turf stack'. Unpublished report, English Heritage

Robinson, M 2011 *Silbury Hill, Wiltshire: Insect Remains from the 2007/8 Tunnelling*. Portsmouth: English Heritage (Research Department Report Series 5/2011

Robinson, M forthcoming 'SS4.3.1 Environmental remains from waterlogged deposits in the Long Barrow ditches', *in* Harding, J and Healy, F (eds) *The Raunds Area Project. A Neolithic and Bronze Age Landscape in Northamptonshire*. Vol 2. *Supplementary Studies*. Swindon: English Heritage

Robinson, M and Hubbard, R N L B 1977 'The transport of pollen in the bracts of hulled cereals. *J Archaeol Sc* **4**(2), 197–9

Robinson, P 1992 'Some late Saxon Mounts from Wiltshire'. *Wiltshire Archaeol Natur Hist Mag* **85**, 63–9

Robinson, P 2001 'Religion in Roman Wiltshire', *in* Ellis, P (ed) *Roman Wiltshire and After: Papers in Honour of Ken Annable*. Devizes: Wiltshire Archaeological and Natural History Society, 147–64

Robinson, P 2003 'Etruscan and other figurines from Avebury and nearby'. *Wiltshire Archaeol Natur Hist Mag* **96**, 33–9

Rodwell, J S 2000 *British Plant Communities*, Vol 5, *Maritime Communities and Vegetation of Open Habitats*. Cambridge: Cambridge University Press

Ross, A 1968 'Shafts, pits, wells – sanctuaries of the Belgic Britons?', *in* Coles, J M and Simpson, D D A (eds) *Studies in Ancient Europe*. Leicester: Leicester University Press, 255–85

Rowley-Conwy, P 1983 'Sedentary hunters: the Ertobolle example', in Bailley, G (ed) *Hunter-Gatherer Economy in Prehistory: A European Perspective*. Cambridge: Cambridge University Press

Rowley-Conwy, P 1984 'The laziness of the short-distance hunter: The origins of agriculture in Western Denmark'. *J Anthropol Archaeol* **3**, 300–24

Rowley-Conwy, P 1987 'The interpretation of ard marks'. *Antiquity* **61**, 263–6

Rushton K B, Connorton, B J and Tomlinson, L M 1989 'Estimation of the groundwater resources of the Berkshire Downs supported by mathematical modelling'. *Quarterly J Engineering Geol* **22**, 329–41

Russel, A D 1990 'Two Beaker burials from Chilbolton, Hampshire'. *Proc Prehist Soc* **56**, 153–72

Sanders, H W 1910 'On the use of the deer-horn pick in the mining operations of the ancients'. *Archaeologia* **62**, 101–24

Saunders, H 2011 'Prehistoric landscapes', *in* Ingle, C and Saunders, H (eds) *Aerial Archaeology in Essex: The Role of the National Mapping Programme in Interpreting the Landscape*, 15–54. Essex County Council: Historic Environment (East Anglian Archaeology Report **136**)

Saunders, J W and Allen, T 1994 'Hedgepeth Mounds: An Archaic mound complex in north-central Louisiana'. *American Antiquity* **59**(3), 471–89

Saunders, N J 2004 'The cosmic earth: Materiality and mineralogy in the Americas', *in* Boivin, N and Owoc, M.A (eds) *Soils, Stones and Symbols: Cultural Perceptions of the Mineral World*. London, UCL Press, 123–41

Scarre, C 2004 'Displaying the stones: The materiality of 'megalithic' monuments', *in* DeMarrais, Gosden, C and Renfrew, C (eds) *Rethinking Materiality: The Engagement of Mind with the Material World*. Cambridge: McDonald Institute Monographs, 141–52

Schmid, E 1972 *Atlas of Animal Bones for Prehistorians, Archaeologists and Quaternary Geologists*. Amsterdam: Elsevier

Schoenhut, K, Vann, D R and LePage, B A 2004 'Cytological and ultrastructural preservation in Eocene Metasequoia leaves from the Canadian high arctic'. *American J Botany* **91**, 816–24

Scott, E M 2003 'The third international radiocarbon intercomparison (TIRI) and the fourth international radiocarbon intercomparison (FIRI) 1990–2002: Results, analyses, and conclusions'. *Radiocarbon* **45**, 135–408

Scott, R 1959 'Medieval agriculture', *in* Crittal, E (ed) VCH *A History of Wiltshire Vol 4*. London: Oxford University Press, 8–24

Scott-Jackson, J E 2005 'The Palaeolithic of the Marlborough Downs and Avebury area', *in* Brown, G, Field D and McOmish D (eds) *The Avebury Landscape: Aspects of Field Archaeology in the Marlborough Downs*. Oxford: Oxbow Books, 66–76

Scott-Jackson, J E and Walkington, H 2005 'Methodological issues raised by laser particle size analysis of deposits mapped as Clay-with-flints from the Palaeolithic site of Dickett's Field, Yarnhams Farm, Hampshire, UK'. *J Archaeol Sci* **32**(7), 969–80

Sebire, H 2008–9 'Early recording at Silbury Hill'. *Research News* 10, 6–7

Serjeantson, D and Gardiner, J 1995 'Red deer antler implements and ox scapula shovels', *in* Cleal, R M J, Walker, K E and Montague, R (eds) *Stonehenge in Its Landscape: Twentieth-Century Excavations*. London: English Heritage, 414–30

Sharples, N 2000 'Antlers and Orcadian rituals: Ambiguous role for red deer in the Neolithic', *in* Ritchie A (ed) *Neolithic Orkney in its European Context*. Cambridge: McDonald Institute Monographs, 107–16

Sheridan, A, Field, D, Pailler, Y, Petrequin, P, Errera, M and Cassen, S 2010 'The Breamore jadeite axehead and other Neolithic axeheads of jadeite rock from central southern England'. *Wiltshire Archaeol Natur Hist Mag* **103**, 16–34

Sidell, J 2009 'Diatoms', *in* Leary, J 'Silbury Hill conservation project 2007/8: Archaeological assessment report'. Unpublished report for English Heritage, 127

Sims, L 2009 'Entering, and returning from, the underworld: Reconstituting Silbury Hill by combining a quantified landscape phenomenology with archaeoastronomy'. *J Royal Anthropol Inst* **15**, 386–408

Skanska 2001a 'English Heritage: Geophysical investigation on Silbury Hill, Avebury, Wiltshire (tender prepared by 3D Tomographics, Cementation Skanska)'. Unpublished report for English Heritage

Skanska 2001b 'Silbury Hill, Wiltshire: Report of tomographic survey'. Unpublished report for English Heritage (November 2001)

Skanska 2002a 'Silbury Hill, Wilshire: Report of surface tomographic survey'. Unpublished report for English Heritage (April 2002)

Skanska 2002b 'Silbury Hill, Wiltshire: Report of central core tomographic survey'. Unpublished report for English Heritage (June 2002)

Skanska 2002c 'Silbury Hill, Wiltshire: Final report of geophysical investigation'. Unpublished report for English Heritage (August 2002)

Skanska 2002d 'English Heritage Stage III geotechnical investigation of Silbury Hill, Avebury, Wiltshire (tender prepared by Cementation Skanska)'. Unpublished report for English Heritage

Skanska 2003 'English Heritage geotechnical investigation of Silbury Hill, Avebury, Wiltshire'. Unpublished report for English Heritage. Report No R/03/C2001 (April 2003)

Skanska 2007a 'Site establishment. Report MS06.02.05'. Unpublished report for English Heritage

Skanska 2007b 'Portal temporary re-exposure works. Report MS06.0001.02'. Unpublished report for English Heritage

Skanska 2007c 'Tunnel works. Report MS06.04.05'. Unpublished report for English Heritage

Skanska 2007d 'Tunnel buried quarry works. Report MS06.05.02'. Unpublished report for English Heritage

Skanska 2007e 'Pre-works testing. Report MS06.01.04'. Unpublished report for English Heritage

Skanska 2007f 'Hill top borehole works. Report MS06.09.04'. Unpublished report for English Heritage

Skanska 2007g 'Hill top works. Report MS06.08.04'. Unpublished report for English Heritage

Skanska 2007h 'Hillside works. Report MS06.13.04'. Unpublished report for English Heritage

Skanska 2007i 'Silbury Hill conservation works: Geological desk study and report of field visits'. Unpublished report for English Heritage

Slota, Jr P J, Jull, A J T, Linick, T W, and Toolin, L J 1987 'Preparation of small samples for 14C accelerator targets by catalytic reduction of CO'. *Radiocarbon* **29**, 303–6

Słupecki, L P 2006 'Large burial mounds of Cracow', *in* Smejda L (ed) *Archaeology of Burial Mounds*. Plze : University of West Bohemia, 119–42

Small, F 2002 *The Lamborne Downs: A Report for the National Mapping Programme*. English Heritage Aerial Survey Report Series AER/13/2002 Swindon: English Heritage

Smith, A C 1862 'Silbury'. *Wiltshire Archaeol Natur Hist Mag* **7**, 145–91

Smith A C 1884 *Guide to the British and Roman Antiquities of the North Wiltshire Downs*. Devizes: Wiltshire Archaeological and Natural History Society

Smith, A C 1885 *A Guide to the British and Roman Antiquities of the North Wiltshire Downs*. Devizes: Wiltshire Archaeological and Natural History Society

Smith, A J E 1978 *The Moss Flora of Britain and Ireland*. Cambridge: Cambridge University Press

Smith, C J 1980 *Ecology of the English Chalk*. London: Academic Press

Smith, H. (nd). *The Master Book of Poultry and Game*. London: Spring Books

Smith, I F 1965a *Windmill Hill and Avebury: Excavations by Alexander Keiller, 1925–1939*. Oxford: Clarendon Press

Smith, I F 1965b 'Excavation of a Bell Barrow, Avebury G55'. *Wiltshire Archaeol Natur Hist Mag* **60**, 24–46

Smith, I F 1991 'Round barrows Wilsford cum Lake G51-G54. Excavations by Earnest Greenfield in 1958'. *Wiltshire Archaeol Natur Hist Mag* **84**, 11–39

Smith, I F and Simpson, D D A 1964 'Excavation of three Roman tombs and a prehistoric pit on Overton Down'. *Wiltshire Archaeol Natur Hist Mag* **59**, 68–85

Smith, I F and Simpson, D D A 1966 'Excavation of a round barrow on Overton Hill, north Wilts'. *Proc Prehist Soc* **32**, 122–55

Smith, R J 2005 'The degradation and preservation of oak wood under different burial environments'. Unpublished PhD thesis, University of Hull

Smith, R J forthcoming *Microbiological Assessment of Cores <9444> and <9447> From Excavations at Silbury Hill 2007/8: Phase 2.* Portsmouth: English Heritage (Research Report Series **51**/2012)

Smith, R J and Lille, M C 2007 'Using a lysimeter study to assess the parameters responsible for oak wood decay from waterlogged burial environments and their implication for the in situ preservation of archaeological remains'. *International J Biodeterioration Biodegradation* **60**, 40–9

Smith, R G C, Healy, F, Allen, M J, Morris, E L, Barnes, I and Woodward, P J, 1997 *Excavations Along the Route of the Dorchester By Pass, Dorset 1986–8.* Salisbury: Wessex Archaeology

Smith, R W 1984 'The ecology of Neolithic farming systems as exemplified by the Avebury region of Wiltshire'. *Proc Prehist Soc* **50**, 99–120

Smith, W 2002 *A Review of Wood Analyses in Southern England.* Swindon: English Heritage (Centre for Archaeology Report **75**/2002)

Smith, W and Campbell, G 2001 'Evaluation of the charred plant remains and charcoal from CfA Excavations at Silbury Hill, Wiltshire'. Unpublished report English Heritage

Snashall, N 2008 'Worked flint from the Longstones Cove and Beckhampton Avenue', *in* Gillings, M, Pollard, J, Wheatley, D and Peterson, R *Landscape of the Megaliths: Excavation and Fieldwork on the Avebury Monuments, 1997–2003.* Oxford: Oxbow, 90–102

Snow, D R 2006 'The dynamics of burial mound building: An American perspective', *in* Šmejda L (ed) *Archaeology of Burial Mounds.* Plze : University of West Bohemia, 143–9

Stace, C, 1997 *Flora of the British Isles.* Cambridge: Cambridge University Press (second edition)

Startin, D W A 1982 'Prehistoric earthmoving', *in* Case, H J and Whittle, A W R (eds) *Settlement Patterns in the Oxford Region: Excavations at the Abingdon Causewayed Enclosure and Other Sites.* Oxford: Council for British Archaeology and Ashmolean Museum, 153–6

Startin, W and Bradley, R J 1981 'Some notes on work organisation and society in prehistoric Wessex', *in* Ruggles, C and Whittle, A (eds) *Astronomy and Society During the Period 4000–1500BC.* Oxford: Brit Archaeol Rep Brit Ser **88**, 289–96

Stead, I M and Rigby, V 1986 *Baldock: The Excavation of a Roman and Pre-Roman Settlement 1968–72.* London: Society for the Promotion of Roman Studies (Britannia Monograph Series **7**)

Stenhouse, M J, and Baxter, M S 1983 '14C dating reproducibility: evidence from routine dating of archaeological samples'. *PACT* **8**, 147–61

Stevens, C 2009 'Plant remains', *in* Powell, A B, Chandler, J, and Godden, D, 'Late Saxon and medieval occupation near Salisbury Street, Amesbury'. *Wiltshire Archaeol Natur Hist Mag* **102**, 197–8

Stevens, C unpublished *Plant remains from Salisbury Street, Amesbury.* Salisbury: Wessex Archaeology, WA project 600033

Stevens, C J and Fuller D Q 2012 'Did Neolithic farming fail? The case for a Bronze Age Agricultural Revolution in the British Isles'. *Antiquity* **86**, 707–22

Stone, J F S and Wallis, F S 1951 'Third report of the sub-committee of the south-western group of museums and art galleries on the petrological determination of stone axes'. *Proc Prehist Soc* **17**, 99–158.

Stout, G 2010 'Monumentality and inclusion in the Boyne Valley, County Meath, Ireland', *in* Leary, J, Darvill, T and Field, D (eds) *Round Mounds and Monumentality in the British Neolithic and Beyond.* Oxford: Oxbow Books, 197–210

Stuiver, M, and Kra, R S 1986 'Editorial comment'. *Radiocarbon* **28**(2B), ii

Stuiver, M, and Polach, H A 1977 'Reporting of 14C data'. *Radiocarbon* **19**, 355–63

Stuiver, M, and Reimer, P J 1986 'A computer program for radiocarbon age calculation'. *Radiocarbon* **28**, 1022–30

Stuiver, M, and Reimer, P J 1993 'Extended 14C data base and revised CALIB 3.0 14C age calibration program'. *Radiocarbon* **35**, 215–30

Stukeley, W 1743 *Abury, a temple of the British Druids with some others, described wherein is a more particular account of the first and patriarchal religion; and of the peopling of the British Islands. Volume the second.* London: printed for the author

Suttie, J M and Kay, R N B 1983 'The influence of nutrition and photoperiod on the growth of antlers of young red deer', *in* Brown, R D (ed) *Antler Development in Cervidae.* Kingsville: Caesar Kleberg Wildlife Research Institute, 61–71

Swanton, G 1988 'West Overton', *in* 'Excavation and fieldwork in Wiltshire 1987'. *Wiltshire Archaeol Natur Hist Mag* **82**, 181–2

Swanton, G and Fowler, P 2001 'Post-Roman and early Saxon', in AAHRG *Archaeological Research Agenda for the Avebury World Heritage Site.* Salisbury: Wessex Archaeology for English Heritage and AAHRG, 27–8, 50

Taçon, P S C 1991 'The power of stone: Symbolic aspects of stone use and tool development in western Arnham Land, Australia'. *Antiquity* **65**, 192–207

Taçon, P S C and Ouzman, S 2004 'Worlds within stone: The inner and outer rock-art landscapes of northern Australia and southern Africa', *in* Chippendale, C and Nash G (eds) *The Figured Landscapes of Rock-Art: Looking at Pictures in Places.* Cambridge: Cambridge University Press, 39–68

Taylor, C 1972 'The study of settlement patterns in pre-Saxon Britain', *in* Ucko, P, Tringham, R and Dimbleby, G (eds) *Man, Settlement and Urbanism.* Cambridge, Massachusetts: Schenkman Publishing, 109–13

Taylor, H 1921 'Rowberrow Cavern'. *Univ Bristol Speleol Soc Proc* **1**(2) 83–6

Taylor, H 1923 'Second report on Rowberrow Cavern'. *Univ Bristol Speleol Soc Proc* **1**(3), 130–4

Taylor, H 1924 'Third report on Rowberrow Cavern'. *Univ Bristol Speleol Soc Proc* **2**(1), 40–50

Taylor, H 1925 'Fourth report on Rowberrow Cavern'. *Univ Bristol Speleol Soc Proc* **2**(2), 122–4

Taylor, H 1931–5 'The Tyning's Barrow Group-Second Report'. *Proc Bristol Speleol Soc* **4**, 67–119

Thomas, H H 1923 'The source of the stones of Stonehenge'. *Antiq J* **3** 239–60

Thomas, J 1991 *Rethinking the Neolithic.* Cambridge: Cambridge University Press

Thomas, J 1999 *Understanding the Neolithic.* London: Routledge

Thomas, J 2002 'Excavations at Dunragit 2002'. Unpublished interim report (*see* http://orgs.man.ac.uk/research/dunragit)

Thomas J 2004a *Archaeology and Modernity*. London: Routledge

Thomas J 2004b 'Materiality and traditions of practice in Neolithic south-west Scotland', *in* Cummings, V and Fowler, C *The Neolithic of the Irish Sea. Materiality and Traditions of Practice*. Oxford: Oxbow Books, 174–84

Thomas, J 2007 'Mesolithic–Neolithic transitions in Britain: from essence to inhabitation'. *Proc Brit Acad* **144**, 423–40

Thomas J and Whittle, A 1986 'Anatomy of a tomb – West Kennet revisited'. *Oxford J Archaeol* **5**, 129–56

Thomas, P A, and Polwart, A 2003 'Biological flora of the British Isles: *Taxus baccata* L.'. *J Ecol* **91**, 489–524

Thomas, P A, El-Barghathi, M, and Powart, A 2007 'Biological flora of the British Isles: *Juniper communis* L.'. *J Ecol* **95**, 1404–40

Thompson, F M L 1959 'Agriculture since 1870', *in* Crittal E (ed) VCH *A History of Wiltshire Vol 4*. London: Oxford University Press, 92–114

Thompson, K 1986 'Small-scale heterogeneity in the seed bank of an acidic grassland'. *J Ecol* **74**, 733–8

Thorn, C and Thorn F (eds) 1979 *Domesday Book 6 Wiltshire*. Chichester: Phillimore

Thorpe, I J and Richards, C 1984 'The decline of ritual authority and the introduction of Beakers into Britain', *in* Bradley, R and Gardiner, J (eds) *Neolithic Studies*. Oxford: Brit Archaeol Rep Brit Ser **133**, 64–84

Thorpe, R S, Williams-Thorpe, O, Jenkins, D G and Watson J S with contributions by Ixer, R A and Thomas R G 1991 'The geological sources and transport of the bluestones of Stonehenge, Wiltshire, UK'. *Proc Prehist Soc* **57**, 103–57

Tilley, C 1994 *A Phenomenology of Landscape*. London: Berg

Tilley, C 2004 *The Materiality of Stone: Explorations in Landscape Phenomenology*. Oxford: Berg

Tomek, T and Bocheński, Z M 2000 *The Comparative Osteology of European Corvids (Aves: Corvidae), With a Key Top the Identification of their Skeletal Elements*. Kraków: Wydawnictwa Instytutu Systematyki I Ewolucji Zwierz t PAN

Topping, P 2004 'The South Downs flint mines: Towards an ethnography of prehistoric flint extraction', *in* Cotton, J and Field, D (eds) *Towards a New Stone Age: Aspects of the Neolithic in South-East England*. York: Council for British Archaeology (Research Report **137**), 177–90

Topping, P 2005 'Shaft 27 revisited: An ethnography of Neolithic flint extraction', *in* Topping, P and Lynott, M (eds) *The Cultural Landscape of Prehistoric Mines*. Oxford: Oxbow, 63–93

Topping, P 2010 'Native American mound building traditions', *in* Leary, J, Darvill, T and Field, D (eds) *Round Mounds and Monumentality in the British Neolithic and Beyond*. Oxford: Oxbow Books, 219–52

Toulmin Smith, L (ed) 1964 *The Itinery of John Leland, vol 5*. London: Centaur Press

Trigger, B 1990 'Monumental architecture: A thermodynamic explanation of symbolic behaviour'. *World Archaeol* **22**, 119–32

Tucker, C 1851 'Report of the examination of Silbury Hill Memoirs illustrative of the history and antiquities of Wiltshire and the City of Salisbury'. *Proceedings of the Meeting of the Archaeological Institute at Salisbury 1849*. Archaeological Institute of Great Britain and Ireland

Turnbull, D 1993 'The ad hoc collective work of building Gothic cathedrals with templates, string and geometry'. *Science, Technology and Human Values* **18**(3), 315–40

Valdes, P J, Spicer, R A, Sellwood, B W, Palmer, D C 1999 *Understanding Past Climates: Modelling Ancient Weather*. New York: Routledge (CD-ROM)

Valentin, J and Robinson, S 2002 'Excavations in 1999 on land adjacent to Wayside Farm, Nursteed Road, Devizes'. *Wiltshire Archaeol Natur Hist Mag* **95**, 147–213

van Bergen, P F, Collinson, M E, Hatcher, P G and de Leeuw, J W 1994 'Lithological control on the state of preservation of fossil seed coats of water plants'. *Organic Geochemistry* **22**, 683–702

van Bergen, P F, Poole, I, Ogilvie, T M A, Caple, C and Evershed, R P 2000 'Evidence for demethylation of syringl moieties in archaeological wood using pyrolysis-gas chromatography/mass spectrometry'. *Rapid Communications in Mass Spectrometry* **14**, 71–9

van Bergen, P F, Blokker, P, Collinson, M E, Sinninghe Damsté, J S and de Leeuw, J W 2004 'Structural biomacromolecules in plants: What can be learned from the fossil record?', *in* Hemsley, A R and Poole, I (eds) *The Evolution of Plant Physiology*. London: Elsevier (Linnean Society Symposium Series **21**), 133–54

Vandeputte, K, Moens, L, Dams, R 1996 'Improved sealed-tube combustion of organic samples to CO_2 for stable isotopic analysis, radiocarbon dating and percent carbon determinations'. *Analytical Letters* **29**, 2761–74

van Nest, J, Charles, D K, Buidtra, J E, Asch, D L 2001 'Sod blocks in Illinois Hopewell Mounds'. *American Antiquity* **66**, 633–50

van Strydonck, M, Nelson, D E, Crombé, P, Bronk Ramsey, C, Scott, E M, van der Plicht, J, and Hedges, R E M 1999 'What's in a [1] [4]C date?', *in* Evin, J, Oberlin, C, Daugas, J P and Salles, J F (eds) *Actes du 3eme congres international 'Archaeologie et 14C', Lyon, 6–10 Avril 1998*. Revue d'Archeometrie Supplément 1999 et Société Préhistorique Française Memoire **26**, 433–48

Varndell, G, Topping, P and Healy, F forthcoming, 'Grime's Graves', *in* J L Lech and A Saville (eds) *Prehistoric Flint Mines in Europe*. Warsaw: UISPP Commission on Flint Mining in Pre- and Protohistoric Times and Institute of Archaeology and Ethnology, Polish Academy of Sciences

Vera, F W M 2000 *Grazing Ecology and Forest History*. Wallingford: CABI

Vince, A G 1997 'Excavations at Nos 143–5 Bartholomew Street, 1979', *in* Vince, A G, Lobb, S J, Richards, J C and Mepham, L *Excavations in Newbury 1979–1990*. Salisbury: Wessex Archaeological Monographs **13**, 7–85

Viner, S, Evans, J, Albarella, U and Parker Pearson M 2010 'Cattle mobility in prehistoric Britain: Strontium isotope analysis of cattle teeth from Durrington Walls (Wiltshire, Britain)'. *J Archaeol Sci* **37**, 2812–20

Vinogradov, N B and Epimakhov, V 2000 'Variants in models of transition: The Cimmerian traditions of the Gordion Tumuli (Phrygia): Found in the Altai barrows (Bashadar, Pazyryk)', *in* Davis-Kimball, J, Murphy, E M, Koryakova, L and Yablonksy, L T (eds) *Kurgans, Ritual Sites, and Settlements: Eurasian Bronze and Iron Age*. Oxford: Archaeopress (Brit Archaeol Rep Int Ser **890**), 247–58

von den Driesch, A 1976 *A Guide to the Measurement of Animal Bones from Archaeological Sites*. Harvard: Peabody Museum of Archaeology and Ethnology (Peabody Museum Bulletin **1**)

Waddington, K and Sharples, N 2011 *The Excavations at Whitchurch 2006–9: An Interim Report.* Cardiff: Cardiff University (Cardiff Studies in Archaeology Specialist Report **31**)

Wainwright, G J 1971 'The excavation of a Late Neolithic enclosure at Marden, Wiltshire. *Antiq J* **51**, 177–239

Wainwright, G J 1979 *Mount Pleasant, Dorset: Excavations 1970–1971, Incorporating an Account of Excavations Undertaken at Woodhenge in 1970.* London: Society of Antiquaries of London (Research Report **37**)

Wait, G A 1985 *Ritual and Religion in Iron Age Britain.* Oxford: Brit Archaeol Rep Brit Ser **149**

Walker, M 1999 'Pollen analysis', *in* Whittle, A, Pollard, J, and Grigson, C *The Harmony of Symbols: The Windmill Hill Causewayed Enclosure.* Oxford: Oxbow Books, 162–3

Waller, M P, and Hamilton, S 2000 'Vegetation history of the English chalklands: A mid-Holocene pollen sequence from Cadburn, East Sussex'. *J Quaternary Sci* **15**, 253–72

Ward, G K, and Wilson, S R 1978 'Procedures for comparing and combining radiocarbon age determinations: a critique'. *Archaeometry* **20**, 19–31

Ward, J and Mainland, I L 1999 'Microwear in modern rooting and stall-fed pigs: The potential of dental microwear analysis for exploring pig diet and management in the past'. *Environmental Archaeol* **4**, 25–32

Warner, R 2000 'Keeping out the Otherworld: the internal ditch at Navan and other Iron Age 'hengiform' enclosures'. *Emania* **18**, 39–44

Waterbolk, H T 1971 'Working with radiocarbon dates'. *Proc Prehist Soc* **37**, 15–33

Watson, A 2001 'Composing Avebury'. *World Archaeology* **33**, 296–314

Watson, E V 1960 'A quantitative study of the bryophytes of chalk grassland. *J Ecol* **48**, 397–414

Webster, J 1997 'Text expectations: the archaeology of "Celtic" ritual wells and shafts', *in* Gwilt, A and Haselgrove, C (eds) *Reconstructing Iron Age Societies.* Oxford: Oxbow Books (Monograph **71**), 134–44

Wedlake, W J 1982 *The Excavation of the Shrine of Apollo at Nettleton, Wiltshire, 1956–1971.* London: Society of Antiquaries of London (Research Report **40**)

Wells, T C E, Sheail, J, Ball, D F and Ward, L K 1976 'Ecological studies on the Porton Ranges: Relationship between, vegetation, soils, and land use history'. *J Ecol* **64**, 589–626

Westlake, S 2005 *East Kennet Long Barrow, Wiltshire.* Swindon: English Heritage (Archaeological Investigation Report Series AI/10/2005)

Whitaker W and Edmunds, F H 1925. *The Water Supply of Wiltshire from Underground Sources.* London: HMSO

White, H and Canti, M 2011 *Comparison of clay with flints from Silbury and local Neolithic pottery fabrics.* English Heritage Research Department Rep Ser **122/2011**

Whitehead, P and Edmunds, M 2010 'Palaeo-hydrology and hydrogeology of the Upper Kennet at Silbury Hill in 4200 BP'. *BHS Third International Symposium, Managing Consequences of a Changing Global Environment, Newcastle. British Hydrological Society*

Whitehead, P and Edmunds, M 2012 *The Palaeohydrology of the Kennet, Swallowhead Springs and the Siting of Silbury Hill.* Portsmouth: English Heritage (Research Department Report Series **12**/2012)

Whitehead, P, Smith, S J, Wade, A J, Mithen, S.J, Finlayson, B L, Sellwood, B, and Valdes, P J 2008 'Modelling of hydrology and potential population levels at Bronze Age Jawa, Northern Jordan: A Monte Carlo approach to cope with uncertainty'. *J Archaeol Sci* **35**, 517–29

Whitehouse, N J, and Smith, D 2010 'How fragmented was the British Holocene wildwood? Perspectives on the "Vera" grazing debate from the fossil beetle record'. *Quaternary Sci Rev* **29**, 539–53

Whittle, A 1981 'Later Neolithic Society in Britain: A realignment', *in* Ruggles C L N and Whittle A W R (eds) *Astronomy and Society in Britain during the period 4000–1500BC.* Oxford: Brit Archaeol Rep Brit Ser **88**, 297–342

Whittle, A 1990 'A model for the Mesolithic–Neolithic transition in the Upper Kennet Valley, North Wiltshire'. *Proc Prehist Soc* **56**, 101–10

Whittle, A 1993 'The Neolithic of the Avebury area: Sequence, environment, settlement and monuments'. *Oxford J Archaeol* **12(1)**, 29–53

Whittle, A 1994 'Excavations at Millbarrow Neolithic chambered tomb, Winterbourne Monkton, North Wiltshire'. *Wiltshire Archaeol Natur Hist Mag* **87**, 1–53

Whittle, A 1997a *Sacred Mound, Holy Rings. Silbury Hill and the West Kennet Palisade Enclosures: A Later Neolithic Complex in North Wiltshire.* Oxford: Oxbow Books (Monograph **74**)

Whittle, A 1997b 'Moving on and moving around: Neolithic settlement and mobility', *in* Topping, P (ed) *Neolithic Landscapes.* Oxford: Oxbow Books, 15–31

Whittle, A 2005 'Lived experience in the Early Neolithic of the Great Hungarian Plain', *in* Bailey, D, Whittle, A and Cummings, V (eds) *(Un)settling the Neolithic.* Oxford: Oxbow Books, 64–70

Whittle, A, Rouse A J and Evans, J G 1993 'A Neolithic downland monument in its environment: Excavations at the Easton Down long barrow, Bishops Cannings, North Wiltshire'. *Proc Prehist Soc* **59**, 197–239

Whittle, A, Pollard, J, Grigson, C 1999 *The Harmony of Symbols: The Windmill Hill Causewayed Enclosure.* Oxford: Oxbow

Whittle, A, Davies, J J, Dennis, I, Fairbairn, A S and Hamilton, M A 2000 'Neolithic activity and occupation outside Windmill Hill causewayed enclosure, Wiltshire: Survey and excavation 1992–93'. *Wiltshire Archaeol Natur Hist Mag* **93**, 131–80

Whittle, A, Healy, F and Bayliss, A 2011 *Gathering Time: Dating the Early Neolithic Enclosures of Southern Britain and Ireland.* Oxford: Oxbow Books

Wilkinson, Rev Prebendary 1867 'A report of diggings made in Silbury Hill and in the ground adjoining'. *Wiltshire Archaeological and Natural History Society* **11**, 113–18

Williams D, 1976 'A Neolithic moss flora from Silbury Hill, Wiltshire'. *J Archaeol Sc* **3**, 267–70

Williams, D, 1997 'Macroscopic plant remains', *in* Whittle, A, *Sacred Mound, Holy Rings. Silbury Hill and the West Kennet Palisade Enclosures: A Later Neolithic Complex in North Wiltshire.* Oxford: Oxbow Books (Monograph **74**), 32–6

Williams, H 1998a 'Mounds and the past in early Anglo-Saxon England'. *World Archaeol* **30**, 90–108

Williams, H 1998b 'The ancient monument in Romano-British ritual practices', *in* Forcey, C, Hawthorne, J and Witcher, R (eds) *TRAC 97: Proceedings of the Seventh Annual Theoretical Roman Archaeology Conference.* Oxford: Oxbow Books, 71–86

Withering, W (Junior) 1822 *The Miscellaneous Tracts of the Late William Withering Vol 1*. London: Longman, Hurst, Rees, Orme and Brown

Woodward, P 1978 'Flint distribution, ring ditches and Bronze Age settlement patterns in the Great Ouse Valley' *Archaeol J* **135**, 32–57

Woodward, S L and McDonald, J N 2002 *Indian Mounds of the Middle Ohio Valley: A Guide to Mounds and Earthworks of the Adena, Hopewell, Cole, and Fort Ancient People*. Virginia, Blacksburg: The McDonald and Woodward Publishing Company

Wooldridge, S W and Linton, D L 1933 'The loam terrains of south-east England and their relation to its early history'. *Antiquity* **7**, 297–310

Worley, F 2011a *The Antler Assemblage Excavated from Silbury Hill in 2007/8*. Portsmouth: English Heritage (Research Department Report Series **17**/2011)

Worley, F, 2011b *Reanalysis of the Antler Assemblage Excavated from Silbury Hill in 1969–70*. Portsmouth: English Heritage (Research Department Report Series **18**/2011)

Worley, F, 2011c *The animal bone assemblage excavated from Silbury Hill in 2007/8*. Portsmouth: English Heritage (Research Department Report **16**/2011)

Worley, F in preparation *A Reanalysis of the Red Deer antlers Excavated from Marden Henge in 1969*. Portsmouth: English Heritage (Research Department Report Series **20**/2011)

Worley, F and Serjeantson, D forthcoming 'The importance of red deer (*Cervus elaphus*) antlers for the creation of Neolithic monuments in Britain'. ICAZ

Worthington, M H 2002a 'Assessment of the results of a seismic tomographic survey at Silbury Hill, Wiltshire'. Unpublished report for English Heritage

Worthington, M H 2002b 'Assessment of the results within Cementation Skanska Report no C100975/CR4: Silbury Hill, Wiltshire. Final report of geophysical investigation, August 2002'. Unpublished report for English Heritage

Xu, S, Anderson, R, Bryant, C, Cook, G T, Dougans, A, Freeman, S, Naysmith, P, Schnabel, C, and Scott, E M 2004 'Capabilities of the new SUERC 5MV AMS facility for (super 14) C dating'. *Radiocarbon* **46**, 59–64

Yang, H, Huang, Y, Huang, Y, Leng, Q, LePage, B A and Williams, C J 2005 'Biomolecular preservation of Tertiary Metasequoia fossil Lagerstätten revealed by comparative pyrolysis analysis'. *Review of Palaeobotany and Palynology* **134**, 237–56

Young, R 2008 'Archaeobotanical material', *in* Gillings, M, Pollard, J, Wheatley, D and Peterson, R *Landscape of the Megaliths: Excavation and Fieldwork on the Avebury Monuments, 1997–2003*. Oxford: Oxbow Books, 44–5

Young, W E V 1950 'A Beaker interment at Beckhampton'. *Wiltshire Archaeol Natur Hist Mag* **53**, 311–27

Zohary, D and Hopf, M 1994 *Domestication of Plants in the Old World*. Oxford: Clarendon Press (2nd edn)

INDEX

I

J

K

L

M

coins 11, 264, 265, *265*, *266–9*, 273, **273**, 278, 279, 280, 281, 282
cropmarks 258, 261
cylindrical tube, bronze 265
enclosures 274
glass 270, 278
hairpins 265, 269
hypocaust heating system 258, **259**
ironstone fragment 269
Later Silbury (2010) evaluation 274, 278–9
lynchets 261
midden 262, 264, 279
mound activity 272–4, **273**, *273*, **299**
pottery 264–5, *273*, 274, 278, 278–9, 282, 286
quarrying 261
quern stones 278
ritual activity 257, 281–2
ritual use of prehistoric monuments 280–1, 283–4
ritual use of wells 281–2, *281*
settlement xx, 255, 257
sewer excavations 258
SF 205 269
snaffle bit 269, **270**
stylus 269, **270**
tile fragments 274
well 63, 82, 274, 278, 279, 280–2
Roman road 9, 10, 20, 255, 258–9, 279, 280, **299**
Romano-British settlement 279–80, 299, **299**; *see also* Roman and Romano-British Silbury
administrative function 283
aerial photographic survey 279
airborne remote sensing 259, 261–2
animal bone 262, 271, *271*, 280
buildings 279–80, 283
coins 264, 265, *265*, *266–9*, 279, 280, 282
context information 262
early activity 279
enclosures 280
excavation evidence 262, *263*, 264–5, *265*, *266–9*, 269–72, **269**, **270**, *271*
excavations 279–80, 282
gaps in evidence 280
geophysical survey 258–9, **259**, 279, 280
layout 283
lidar data 261–2
magnetometer scan 283

occupation 282–3
pottery 262, 264, 264–5, *273*, 282–3
ritual site 264, 283–4
river crossing 280
roadside activity 283
Romano-British ritual use of monument 280–1
size 279, 283
strip buildings 283
votive offerings 264, 265
wall footings 279
well 278, 279, 280–2
well assemblage 280
rootlets **119**, **124**, 125, 126, 129
Rorippa nasturtium-aquatica (watercress) 162
Ross, A 281
round houses 260
round mounds 244–7, **245**, **248**
dimensions 247, 251
worldwide 251–4, **251**, **254**
Royal Commission on the Historical Monuments of England (RCHME) 24
Royal Society 6
Ryder, Jenny **xv**

S

sacred herd 182
Salisbury Plain 247
Salisbury Street, Amesbury 293
sample numbers 34
samples, preservation 326
Sanctuary, the
burials 241
flint assemblage 73
Sanders, H W 95
sarsen stones 9, 11, 12, **12**, 18, 21, 56–7, 63, 74, 220, 315
antler associations 211, **211**
and architectural form 206
archive notes 76–7, 79
association with water 219–20
Atkinson's topsoil 75, 76, 76–7, *76*
Beckhampton Avenue 80
boulders 25, 61, 209, **211**, 219–20
burnt 76, 176, 210
capping 79
chalk walls 77, 79
crater 76

cultural and symbolic properties 75
depositional acts 80
description 75–6
discussion 79–80
distribution 75
excavation 75
first recorded 75
fractured 77, 79, 209
fragmentary 76, 77, 79
importance 210
materiality 220
miniliths 210
modification 75, 210
original size 79
power 80
qualitative differences 79
Stonehenge 244
streams 219–20
summit 76, 79, 79–80, 209, **209**, 210
tunnel fill 76
Upper Organic Mound 42–3, 79, 209
use 80
Wall 2 79
West Kennet Avenue 80
West Kennet Palisaded Enclosures 80
Windmill Hill 210
worked **77**, **78**
Saxon period 284, 297–8, 299
coins 107
crescentic platforms 20
insertions 299
perceptions of Silbury 299–300
plant remains 293
pottery 14, 107, 298
Scheduled Monument Consent 310–11
Scottish Universities Environmental Research Centre (SUERC) 99
scrapers 226
scrub 99, 162, **167**
sediments, valley 155, **156**
seeds 36, 159, 163, 166
dating 98
decomposition 98
survival 98
turf and turves 164–5
seismic topographic survey 5, 12, 138, 140–1, **140**, 305–6, 307
setting 2, 218–20, **219**, 223
settlement 181–2
Beaker 241
Neolithic 224–6, 228
Roman xx, 255, 257

Romano-British, *see* Romano-British settlement
Saxon period 284
transhumant 228
shaft, 1776 xx, 2, 6–7, **7**, 26, **58**, **288**, 304, 306, **309**, 322, 323
anomalies 5
antler 89–90
backfilling 6–7, 26–7, 308
capping 7
collapse xvii, 7
condition 308
the Drax letters 28–30
depth 28
infill monitoring 324
spoil heap 19
shamanism 218
shark teeth 159
Shawell 246
sheep/goat bones 163, 164, *201*, *202*, 270, 271, *271*, 272, 294, *295*, 296
shells, *see* mollusc samples
Shelving Stones 227
sight-lines 204
Sil, King 2, 6
Silbury Conservation Project xvii, 2, 5, 15, 323, 326
Silbury Hill
collage **221**
from the south-east **1**
Silbury Hill Project Board 304, 307–8, 309–10
'Silbury Hill Remedial Works Proposal 2005/2006' (Skanska) 310
Silbury I 13–14, 37, 43, 44, 103, 309, 310
Silbury II 14, 46, 103, 310
Silbury III 14, 46, 103, 310
Silbury IV 14
Silbury spur 134
Silver Barrow 247
Sims, Lionel 204
Site of Special Scientific Interest 2
Skanska
engineering solution 320–2
planned programme for remedial works 311–12
remedial works, tunnel, 1968–70 312–13, **313**, **314**, 315–17, **315**, **316**, **317**
surveys 305–8
tender 310
Skanska Technology 312
Skendleby **3(map)**
Skendleby long barrow 233
sloe 36, 161, **161**, 181
slug faeces 149, **150**, 151